MANAGERIAL COST ACCOUNTING

Second Edition

Macmillan Publishing Co., Inc.
New York

Collier Macmillan Publishers
London

Selected questions and problems in this book have been taken from Chapters 21, 22, 23, 24, 25, 28, and 29 of H. Bierman, *Financial and Managerial Accounting,* Macmillan Publishing Co., Inc., 1963, by permission.

Macmillan Publishing Co., Inc.
866 Third Avenue, New York, New York 10022

Collier Macmillan Canada, Ltd.

Library of Congress Cataloging in Publication Data

Bierman, Harold.
  Managerial cost accounting.

Includes bibliographies and index.
  1. Cost accounting. 2. Industrial management.
I. Dyckman, Thomas R., joint author. II. Title.
HF5686.C8B47   1976   658.1'552   75-5532
ISBN 0-02-309720-5

Printing: 3 4 5 6 7 8   Year: 7 8 9 0 1 2

Preface

The general orientation of this book is toward decision-making situations that involve the use of accounting data and that practicing accountants (or other business managers) are frequently called on to resolve or assist in resolving. It will therefore be helpful to the person whose job requires an understanding of the analysis and use of accounting data.

This book is designed to be used in a flexible manner, but it does assume a working knowledge of financial accounting. It can be used immediately after financial accounting to introduce managerial cost accounting or after an introductory managerial accounting course. There are more chapters in the book than can be comfortably used in a one-semester course. The professor can choose those chapters that fit the students' preparation. For example, if the students have had an introductory managerial accounting course, the first five chapters can be used as a review of the material already covered, and there are enough advanced topics to fill a semester. If the book is used immediately after introductory financial accounting, the introductory cost accounting chapters can be used as well as selected advanced topics. We consider the material contained in Chapter 13 to be essential for many of the chapters that follow it, but aside from that one chapter, the user has complete flexibility.

Some knowledge of elementary economic theory, introductory statistical decision theory, and organizational theory and behavior is required to complete the material successfully. However, a student need not know the calculus to profit from this volume (there is some calculus used in footnotes and appendixes). The reader will also find that occasionally a knowledge of linear programming and basic regression analysis will prove to be useful.

Several topics (such as capital budgeting) have received particularly detailed treatment, since these topics are especially relevant to practicing accountants and managers. The report of the Committee on Education and Experience Requirements for CPA's (AICPA,

v

March 1969) that describes the cost accounting requirement states ". . . it is believed important that he know how cost accounting can contribute to decision making and planning. Typical problems might involve make-or-buy decisions, product mix, capital budgeting, and inventory planning. The methodologies might include present value analysis, models, and incremental analysis."

The report of the American Accounting Association's Committee to Compile a Revised Statement of Educational Policy (*Committee Reports*, American Accounting Association, 1968) reaches a similar conclusion. "In recent years management has come to recognize that accountants are in a strategic position to make significant contributions in the area of resource planning." The committee then presents a long list of relevant topics and includes such items as lease-or-buy decisions, capital budgeting, investment decisions, and return on investment.

There is no question that any of the items cited and found in this book might be covered elsewhere in a curriculum. We have included only items for which no other functional area in business or basic skill courses has obvious first claim and which we think are highly relevant to the job of the management accountant.

The questions and problems are an integral part of each chapter. In answering them it will often be necessary to refer to the text. Indeed, problem solving is a necessary step toward understanding the main ideas in each chapter. The reader should not expect to have full command of the material after a first reading. Problem solving followed by additional readings is recommended.

In many ways the present volume serves only as an introduction to the topics covered. In order that the reader may pursue an interest in one or more of the subject areas, selected bibliographies are provided.

We owe debts to many individuals for the ideas contained in this volume; occasionally their names appear in the footnotes. Perhaps foremost among our debts, however, is that owed to our teachers at the University of Michigan, who started us on our present path; our colleagues at Cornell, who refined many of our ideas; our students, who challenged us; and our families, who sustained our efforts and tolerated our venture. We also wish to thank Professor Myron Uretsky of Columbia University for his particularly helpful comments on an early draft of the manuscript. Many of his suggestions were incorporated in the final version. We would also like to thank Mr. Robert Magee for help with problems and many authors of cost accounting textbooks whose ideas we have used in our own problems.

H. B.

T. R. D.

Contents

Part II
Special Topics in Cost Accounting and Control

Part III
Capital Budgeting and Related Topics

Part IV
Measuring Performance

Part V
Advanced Models and Techniques Useful in Managerial Cost Accounting

Part I

An Introduction to Cost Classification, Accumulation, and Control

Chapter 1

The Accountant's Role

Consider any large organization, say a major chemical company, bank, medical care facility, or governmental agency. Imagine for the moment that all of its accounting records (payroll records, ledgers, performance reports, tax records, and so on) have been destroyed by fire. What problems do you see created? Do you think the organization would experience serious operating problems? Now suppose that the firm were forbidden both to replace these records and to produce new ones. How much more difficult would it be to operate profitably?

Would you expect a much smaller organization, say a Mom and Pop grocery store, to experience similar problems if its records were destroyed and were irreplaceable? Perhaps, but we would expect these problems to be less serious to the continued operation of the smaller activity. The manager of a relatively small activity has a large degree of familiarity with the total operation. In a very large organization the same degree of familiarity is impossible. In both situations some financial record system (accounting) is required to maintain a history of relevant events, and the accounting function's importance grows in direct relationship with the size of the organization.

The accounting function we have stressed in the above two paragraphs is that of record keeping. Record keeping is an essential task that facilitates several additional functions that a managerial accountant should render to his organization.

These additional functions are suggested by several questions constantly asked at all managerial levels. First, what problems do I have and what data can I obtain that will help me understand my problems better? Second, of the alternative solutions that should be considered, which is best given my objectives? Third, how have we done in terms of our established goals over the past period and how can we do better? These questions and their answers are not independent of one another. Improving on past performance, for example, often follows the recognition and resolution of a difficult problem.

1.1 Objectives of the Accounting Activity

The questions posed in the preceding paragraph suggest several functions of an accounting department. They include:

1. The determination of income and financial position.
2. Assisting in cost control.
3. Motivating employees toward organizational goals.
4. Provision of data for decision making and planning.

These four items are not listed in order of importance nor are they all inclusive or mutually exclusive.

1.1.1 Determination of Income and Financial Position

This function is one you have probably already studied in your work in financial accounting. In part, the internal accounting function is designed to meet financial accounting objectives. This requires the recording and allocation of many costs, including, for example, those associated with labor, materials, and overhead. But this is just one reason and, in our opinion, not the most important justification for an elaborate cost-accounting system.

The determination of income and financial position is important, but any determination is going to be inexact and subject to numerous assumptions. For example, are fixed costs period costs, or are they costs which should be attached to product? Although a certain amount of cost accounting is necessary to accomplish the objectives of income determination, the necessary system could be much simpler than the cost-accounting systems commonly used in most manufacturing companies. Much of the detail could be eliminated with little loss of accuracy. For example, if a department manufactures automobile generators, the total cost incurred in the department must be known before the unit cost can be determined, but it is not necessary to know the cost of each step in the manufacture of each part and the exact nature of each cost. The importance of the problem of common costs (costs of a single resource used in more than one cost center or incurred in the production of more than one product) would be reduced because interest would center on the broad measures needed for financial accounting purposes and not on the more exact measures needed for cost control and decision making.

It is interesting to note that no matter how elaborate the cost-accounting system, there would still exist problems of income and financial position determination. One such problem is whether fixed costs should be considered costs of product. If so, should all the fixed costs be considered as costs of the product, or should some of the fixed costs be considered as costs of idleness when less than normal activity is attained? The problems of joint and common costs also prevent exact financial measures of financial activity, especially where there are inventory changes that involve one or more of the joint products.

It is very important to distinguish between product costing and the other uses of cost data. Many of the problems in cost accounting arise because data derived for one purpose are inappropriately used for another.

1.1.2 Assisting in Cost Control

Control or reduction of costs requires a detailed cost-accounting system. It is necessary to know when and where the costs were incurred (the accounting period and the department or cost center where they were incurred), as well as the nature of the costs. Equally important, the actual amount of the cost and the amount that the cost should have been (the budgeted or standard amount) must be known. Unless all this information is available, the cost-accounting system cannot be effective in the control of costs.

The control procedure is built around a comparison of the budgeted amounts with the actual amounts. The type of comparison is suggested in Exhibit 1-1 for a particular department. These comparisons are made for particular periods of time and over all managerial levels. Managers can then concentrate their attention on those items that are out of line. This represents an application of management by exception.

Exhibit 1–1   Budgeted and Actual Activity Comparison: Operating Department A

Item	Budget	Actual	Variance or Difference	Explanation
A1	xxx	xxx	xx	—
A2	xxx	xx	x	—
A3	xxx	xxx	xx	—
Totals	xxxx	xxx	xx	—

Of course, setting the budget and measuring actual activity levels present problems. Just how these determinations are made, how comparisons are formulated, and how conclusions are arrived at and reported in performance reports is a subject that we shall return to often in this book.

1.1.3 Motivation of Employees Toward Organizational Goals

Budgets and performance reports have an impact on motivation. Furthermore, an organization will find that the reporting procedures in use have motivational effects not only on cost control, but also on risk-taking behavior and creativity. In some organizations, an unfavorable report requires the responsible manager to write a detailed explanation, including a description of the remedial actions to be undertaken. Favorable reports, on the other hand, may be overlooked or ignored. Such behavior is bound to have a motivational impact on the manager reporting.

The use by many organizations of participatory budgeting techniques is, in part, a recognition of the importance of motivational factors. The subject of motivation is important enough to justify a separate chapter (see Chapter 6).

1.1.4 Decision Making and Planning

Cost information for managerial decision making and planning is the most important justification of a detailed cost-accounting system. A schematic diagram of the accounting cycle as it relates to this broad interpretation of decision making is useful at this point. Figure 1.1 suggests the accounting cycle by which

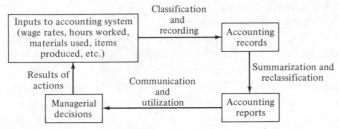

Figure 1.1   The accounting cycle.

information reaches the decision maker. But we need a second diagram to suggest just how the various types of information are selected and used in conjunction with a decision model to yield choices. This is provided in Figure 1.2.[1]

It would be easy to conclude that only future and not historical costs are relevant to managerial decisions. This position is common since it is generally agreed that the manager must use the relevant future costs to make decisions. However, historical cost data are relevant to the estimation of relevant future costs as well as the control of present costs. Figure 1.2 shows how historical costs feed into the model which generates relevant costs for decision making.

The environment influences internal and external data as well as the need for

---

[1] This figure is based on a report presented by the American Accounting Association Committee on Managerial Decision Models, *Supplement to the Accounting Review*, 1969, p. 48.

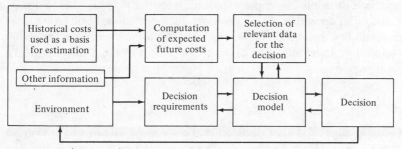

Figure 1.2 A generalized decision model. *Source*: Based on a report presented by the American Accounting Association Committee on Managerial Decision Models, *Supplement to the Accounting Review*, 1969, p. 48.

decisions. The decision requirements are used, in turn, to define a model for the decision. The choice of the decision model influences the data selection, and the model, together with the data, leads to a decision. This decision, in turn, affects the environment and hence the data for future decisions. The environment and the data may, for a given decision, be internal, external, or both. The arrow from the decision to the decision model represents the feedback mechanism by which the results of a decision are retained for evaluation purposes and possible revision of the model itself. There is also a path from the decision model to the relevant data that permits the model and the data to respond iteratively to the decision requirements.

After a decision model is selected, five additional elements must be specified.

1. The set of variables under the manager's control.
2. The set of variables not under the manager's control.
3. The goals or more formally, the objective function.
4. The constraints under which the manager must operate.
5. The estimates of the parameter values that facilitate interrelating the goals and the constraint requirements.

The information requirements of the decision model are dictated by the need to determine the relevant variables, the constraint formulations, the objective function, and the proper parameter values needed to predict the optimal values of the controllable variables. Similarly, information is required to detect significant variations in these factors and to implement the resultant solution.

Most problems are ill-structured and require solution in a subjective setting. When this is the case, many aspects of the decision process are heuristic. The result is that in these situations the determination of the precise information requirements of an organization is impossible. One alternative is to make available an extensive data bank from which data can be obtained easily by the manager for application to the problem at hand.

The generalized decision model presented in Figure 1.2 is applicable to a wide range of managerial decisions. These decisions include: capital budgeting, cost control, performance evaluation, pricing, cost estimation, decisions involving inventory levels, and many others. Cost data are central to the decision model's informational requirements.

1.1.5 Goals of a Firm

It is frequently suggested that decision makers should attempt to maximize the profits of the firm. Each decision, then, should take into consideration the effect of that decision on the other sections of the firm so that the firm's profits are maximized in a global sense. There are, however, two major difficulties with global profit maximization from an operational point of view. First, rather than maximize profits, the firm may reasonably prefer to maximize something else (which we will call utility here). The use of profit maximization (even when profits are correctly defined) has several disadvantages as a goal for the firm. For example, it generally does not adequately take into account nonmonetary factors (such as growth, market size, and prestige), indirect contributions to society (such as the creation of jobs), or costs to society (such as pollution). In addition, expressing the consequences of decisions in monetary terms may not adequately reflect the impact of these events on the firm.

For example, suppose it is believed that if it occurs, event A, a loss of $1 million, will lead to certain bankruptcy, whereas event B, a loss of $500,000 will not lead to bankruptcy. Under these conditions, the first loss may in some very real sense be more than twice as serious as the second. The fact that a firm takes out insurance to protect itself against large losses, even when the premium is greater than the mathematical expectation of the loss, provides evidence of the incompleteness of monetary values as the sole guide to decisions. Thus, in the previous example the firm may be unwilling to pay more than $500 for insurance against event B (a loss of $500,000 with a probability of occurrence of 0.001), and yet be willing to pay more than $1,000, say $1,200, for insurance against event A (a loss of $1 million with the same probability of occurrence, 0.001). Furthermore, another equally likely event C (a loss of $2 million with a probability of occurrence of 0.001) may not lead to a willingness on the part of management to pay a much higher insurance premium than $1,200, since any loss greater than $1 million also leads to bankruptcy and nothing more serious can occur.

A similar situation often exists for positive monetary values as well. Thus, a $1 million increase in profits may not be considered twice as desirable as a $500,000 increase. Utility theory can be used to take into consideration the psychological reactions to gains and losses that the profit measure alone ignores.

The second difficulty with global profit maximization is that the decision maker's ability to cope with global optimization may be limited. In a dynamic economy many things are changing continuously. These changes may prevent the decision maker from reacting optimally on several fronts at once. Furthermore, he may be unable to digest all the information available to him resulting from the ripple effects of a decision, and even the simplest decision may become impossible to make if the decision maker insists on analyzing all its implications. Despite these difficulties, global maximization should be the goal. Frequently, however, only suboptimal decision-making procedures may be feasible.

An alternative approach is to view the manager as maximizing profits, or some alternative factor, subject to a set of constraints.[2] For example, the manager of a division may wish to maximize net cash flows, market values, or something else subject to restrictions on liquidity and total capital expenditures. The manager of a cost center may desire to minimize costs subject to output requirements and the likelihood of a cost investigation analysis of his activity. To make the approaches feasible, only the most critical variables would be considered.

Both of the major difficulties (choosing what to maximize and the limited ability to cope) may combine in specific situations. Consider the optimization problem of the cost-center manager again, but this time from a utility viewpoint. Suppose this manager is concerned about a cost that seems to be excessively high, although the organization's operating procedures do not require a report or an investigation. If he investigates and finds a correctable cause, he may save the firm several thousand dollars. On the other hand, perhaps he should spend his time and resources on other activities that, although likely to benefit the company less, are more visible to his superiors. There is the further problem associated with the reporting techniques used. How will the discovery and report of an out-of-control cost look on his record? Finally, the utilization of resources to investigate the suspected activity should theoretically be considered as only one among several uses to which these resources might be put. Opportunities available throughout the organization should be considered as alternatives to undertaking the proposed cost investigation.

For the above reasons, this book deals with decisions on a suboptimization basis. Suboptimization should, however, include the more relevant effects that each decision may have on the overall well-being of the organization. For example, an optimal advertising policy may lead to losses if productive capacity is not simultaneously taken into consideration.

This book deals with cost control as if accounting could make a significant contribution toward effective decisions in the control of costs. It might be argued that a nonaccounting method (such as making all workers part owners of the plant) would be more effective. But even in this situation some workers would tend to avoid work and others would excel; thus, some means of measuring efficiency is still desirable. Therefore, the implicit assumption is made that quantitative measures of efficiency are useful, and the task remaining is to seek the best available measures.

[2] See A. Charnes and W. W. Cooper, "Some Network Characteristics for Mathematical Programming and Accounting Approaches to Planning and Control," *The Accounting Review*, January 1967, pp. 24–52.

1.2   Accounting : A Staff Function

Understanding the organization of a large corporation helps us to understand managerial cost accounting and what the accountant's function is. At the very top of the organization are the owners or shareholders. The shareholders exercise control by electing the board of directors, who in turn choose the executives responsible for administering the general policies decided on by the board of directors.

The amount of control that the individual shareholder possesses is limited by the relative size of his holdings, but as a group, the stockholders are powerful. The "proxy" battles which are frequently publicized in the newspapers are actually fights for the votes of the stockholders so that one or another group may control the board of directors, and thus control the corporation. The threat of a potential takeover is a real consideration to a board of directors and hence influences their actions relative to investments, dividends, managerial compensation, and so on.

Liaison between the board of directors and operating management is frequently implemented by the president of the firm. In other firms the connecting link is maintained by the use of committees such as the "Executive Committee" and the "Finance Committee." These committees frequently include members of management who are also on the board of directors. In some situations the chairman of the board of directors is also the chief executive officer of the corporation. Thus, the same man who is directly responsible to the stockholders may also be in charge of the everyday operation of the corporation.

Working under the president (the chief executive officer) are various vice-presidents. If the corporation is organized along decentralized divisional lines, the list of vice-presidents would include those men in charge of operating groups or divisions as well as those in charge of staff or functional operations.

Among the "Vice-Presidents" is one or more vice-presidents who may be *accountants* (these include the Financial Vice-President, the Controller, and the Treasurer). These executives are staff officers, since they are only indirectly associated with the production of the end product or service. They are more concerned with supplying information to the operating personnel. This is illustrated in Figure 1.3, which can be generalized to any organization. Note that the custodianship and record keeping functions relative to the company's cash are separated. This division of responsibilities is part of the company's internal control. *Internal control* refers to the various procedures set up to help prevent waste, fraud, and theft of the company's assets. The exact duties of the treasurer and the controller vary from company to company, but this division between the custodian and recorder of cash transactions is likely to exist at all levels of operations.

We shall generally assume a complex organizational structure in which subsidiary or decentralized operating units, such as divisions and plants, are

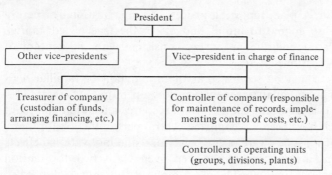

Figure 1.3   Top management structure.

present. In such cases the division or plant controller supplies information to the plant manager, but he is directly responsible to the divisional controller. If the plant controller is placed under the authority of the plant manager (as he often is), the person whose efficiency is being measured, the plant manager, would be in a position to influence the methods used to measure that efficiency.

1.3   Summary

In contrast to line managers, who are responsible for the production, sale, and delivery of the product or service, the accountant occupies a staff position, in which he is responsible for providing information and advice to operating managers. In this regard, the accountant has been compared to the navigator of a ship. He advises the captain on course, speed, position, and deviations between the present course and the desired one, but he does not command. The accountant also plays a major role in the budgeting process, in cost-control efforts, and in performance evaluation. These duties create problems for him, as we shall see later.

The accountant, then, is involved in organizational planning, the purpose of which is to determine what goals are desired and how they are to be achieved. He is also involved in the control process by which progress toward attainment of goals is evaluated and communicated. The process is circular, with the evaluation phase, it is hoped, leading to better plans and decisions. This feedback loop is essential if improved planning is to result. On the other hand, complete conformance is fruitless if the plan itself is faulty.

The planning–control process uses budgets and performance reports as means by which deviations from plans are brought to light. The manager learns to concentrate on the substantive deviations that he can influence to improve his performance and thereby increase conformity of actual results to organizational goals. This is the principle of management by exception. We also note that well-conceived plans must provide sufficient flexibility to allow the manager to pursue opportunities that arise. A plan, reporting process, or organizational structure that causes managers to adhere to initial budgets in the face of substantive changes in their operating environment is *not* consistent with the concept of planning and control envisioned here.

The areas of decision making require that the accountant be familiar with the new decision models and analytical tools used by operating managers. This is in addition to a knowledge of the economics of resource allocation and plant fiscal operations, which have been a recognized central part of the job for many years. Furthermore, he must be aware of the behavioral and motivational effects of his activities. This last area of concern has been given relatively little attention by many practicing cost accountants. The accountant of the future will need to be generally knowledgeable in all the areas of management if he is going to provide a useful service to operating managers and simultaneously assist the organization in attaining its objectives.

This will require a total management information system. In fact, one finds it difficult to imagine a large and complex organization without a comprehensive management information system. But agreeing that such a system is essential is the easy part. The important questions that we have to resolve have to do with the components of the system. What types of information should be supplied, and how should that information be incorporated into plans and decisions?

The successful managerial accountant of the year 2000 will be a person who fully understands the sources of information required in his organization, as well as how that information should be used to arrive at decisions that will maximize the well-being of the stockholders and the other parties vitally interested in the activities of the firm. He should prepare himself to accomplish these objectives.

QUESTIONS AND PROBLEMS

1-1 The New York Oil Company owns one tanker that has a value of $10 million. A careful study indicates there is a 0.005 probability of the ship being a total loss in the coming year as a result of a nautical disaster. The company has contracted to pay $60,000 insurance for the year against this event. The company has an opportunity to acquire a small oil wildcating firm at a cost of $10 million. The present value of the expected benefits from owning the firm are $11 million gross and $1 million net. The probability distribution of outcomes has a large variance. The opportunity is rejected despite its favorable expectation. The New York Oil Company has an annual income of $1 million and assets of $100 million.

Required: Explain the thinking that may have led to the two decisions. Are the decisions consistent?

1-2 A credit manager of The Chase Manhattan Bank has to decide whether to offer credit to a small manufacturer. There is a significant risk of the firm failing, but the expected value of the loan is positive.

Required: Discuss the considerations that might affect the credit manager's decision.

1–3 The manager of the grinding department of a manufacturing plant has recommended the acquisition of a new machine that is fully automatic and that is fed information from a central computer station. The computer is currently being used for a variety of purposes within the company. The analysis used to justify the acquisition compared the direct economic savings (essentially savings in labor) with the explicit cost of the equipment (assume the basic investment analysis was done in a reasonable manner).

Required: If the analysis were to be made on a global basis, what other factors might be considered?

1–4 Accounting reports indicate what has happened in the past; what we want is information relating to the future. The past is gone and not relevant.

Required: Discuss this statement.

1–5 The president of the ABC Company has suggested to his controller that costs be classified and recorded according to whether or not they are relevant. What should be the controller's response?

1–6 The XYZ Company has listed on one of its financial reports (statement of operating income), "Depreciation, $50,000." A note explains that depreciation expense measures the cost of using the long-lived assets during the accounting period. State whether you would accept the $50,000 as a significant figure. Explain.

1–7 Accounting is one type of information system. Name several other systems supplying information to business managers.

1–8 A firm with $100,000,000 of assets is currently earning $10,000,000. The president of the firm wants to retain the $10,000,000 of earnings to increase the firm's earnings to $10,100,000. He argues that this action is consistent with profit maximization, since earnings are increased. Comment on this position.

1–9 What "ripple" effects does a decision to increase advertising expenditures have?

1–10 Consider a plant manager of a plant designed to supply covers for convertible automobiles. In recent years the profits of the plant have been decreasing.

Required: To what extent do you hold the plant manager responsible for the profit decrease?

1–11 The early role of accounting was described as a "judiciary" one in which accountants kept records to verify the honesty of those in control of valuable resources. How well does this role describe the present functioning of the managerial accountant?

1–12 How might an accountant determine the information needs of an operating department or manager? Do you see any problems in the methods you specify?

1–13 It is often argued that the responsibility of management is to maximize the wealth of owners of the firm. Discuss some general factors that make this a difficult responsibility to define and attain.

1–14 Is accounting in a better position to suggest alternative courses of action or to assist in the evaluation of alternatives, once proposed?

1–15 If accounting is defined to be an information processing operation with the ultimate objective of assisting internal decision making, establish a list of decisions that must be made by the accountant in the design of such a system.

1–16 Budgeting and performance evaluation are important functions in managing a firm. With respect to these activities, why might the study of human behavior be useful to an accountant?

1–17 Does the form of the organization determine the appropriate accounting information system or does the information system determine the best organizational form?

1–18 An elaborate, detailed cost-accounting system is a necessary part of the financial reporting function. Moreover, this system may often be integrated into the management planning and control function. Comment.

1–19 Firms are beginning to use more complex approaches to problem solving, including, for example, operations research techniques. How does this alter the function of the managerial accountant?

1–20 In a not-for-profit organization where the goal is, by definition, not profit maximization, what role does the accountant play?

Chapter 2

Cost Classification

The type of cost data a manager needs as well as the most effective means of organizing and reporting the data depends on the nature of his job and the decisions he must make. For example, assume that a worker earns a week's wages and is paid by his organization. The accountant has to record the payment. A naive financial accountant might recognize an increase in an expense (wages) and a decrease in the organization's bank account.

    Dr: Wage Expense $xx
          Cr: Bank $xx
          To record wages paid to employee

A managerial accountant would have no objection to starting with the above transaction (although he might record the debit item as a cost factor or asset rather than as an expense). However, he would also recognize that much more information would have to be recorded. For example, it is useful to identify the division, the plant, the department, the shift, and the operation(s) of the worker, as well as the product or products that benefited from the labor, and the type of labor performed.

Frequently, it is long after the labor is performed that some manager requests all or part of this information. Unless it has been stored in a file (computer or other) that is readily accessible, the preparation of routine reports or special reports for particular decisions will be very costly. The storing and retrieval function is facilitated by locating like costs together. This, in turn, necessitates a cost classification system. Cost classification is also useful in preparing readable reports. Hence, cost classification is an essential feature of a total cost system.

2.1   Classification of Costs

Managerial accountants find it necessary and useful to classify costs in many different ways. One of the more fundamental classifications involves the distinction between a cost and an expense.

A *cost* is an asset value. Although it may have been processed within the company and changed form, it may still be traced within the company. Thus, the labor of a man on the production line may be traced to the product on which he is working, and the same is true of factory depreciation.

An *expense* is a *cost* or *asset* that has been used up in gaining revenues. It has left the company. Thus, when the manufactured goods are shipped to the customers, all the costs that went into the production of those goods, and which up to this point have been considered assets, become expenses, if revenues are recognized at the time of sale. If revenues are recognized on a different basis, an attempt is made to match the revenues and expenses of earning the revenues.

The accounting profession does not universally recognize this distinction between cost and expense in its terminology. Thus "cost of goods sold" is used to describe an expense rather than the more exact "expense of goods sold" or "cost of goods sold expense."

Other bases of cost classification often found in practice include:

1. Reaction to changes in activity (fixed or variable).
2. Responsibility (plant, department, process, or cost center where it was incurred).
3. Degree to which the cost can be traced to the end product (direct, indirect).
4. Natural characteristics (labor, material, supplies, etc.).
5. Function (manufacturing, administrative, selling).
6. Reference to a particular decision; and by miscellaneous economic characteristics (joint, common, out-of-pocket, opportunity, avoidable, etc.).

The accountant does not set up accounts for every one of the above classifications; in fact, it would not be desirable to do this. A good accounting system is both flexible and a ready source of cost information. However, generally analysis and rearrangement of the costs are necessary for specific decisions. In some cases it is evident that certain types of useful data for decision purposes are not currently being gathered and processed by the firm's information system. When this is the case, a study of the costs and benefits of obtaining and processing the desired data should be made. A corollary to this recommendation is that costs and benefits of current data collection processes also be periodically reviewed.

2.1.1 Changes in Activity and Costs

The terms *fixed* and *variable* are generally used to describe how a cost reacts to changes in activity. A variable cost is a cost which is proportional to the level of activity (total cost increases as activity increases), and a fixed cost is constant in total over the relevant range of expected activity under consideration. Sometimes the terms *avoidable* and *unavoidable* are used in place of the words *variable* and *fixed*, respectively. These terms are better used, however, to describe costs associated with particular decisions. For example, the salary of a particular foreman would be avoidable if he has not yet been hired, but once hired, his salary is fixed regardless of the level of activity (assuming he cannot, or will not, be fired because of a decrease in activity).

If there is a decrease in activity, there is the option of not replacing the next foreman that leaves the company. Although this type of long-run change cannot be relied on in the short run to adjust the firm's costs, supervisory costs may still behave as a step function if it is recognized that the adjustment of cost to volume changes may lag. It is best not to use the terminology variable cost interchangeably with avoidable costs, since a fixed cost may also be avoidable (although perhaps with a lag).

The terms variable and fixed may be made more useful by the addition of prefixes. The modified terms are: *semivariable*, *semifixed*, and *avoidable-fixed* (see Figure 2.1). *Semivariable* can be used to refer to a cost that is basically variable but whose slope may change abruptly when a certain activity level is reached. For example, hours of work in excess of the normal 40-hour week give rise to overtime or shift premiums and result in direct labor increasing more rapidly as activity increases than if additional overtime premiums were not incurred at that point.

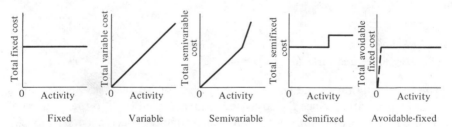

Figure 2.1   Cost characteristics.

Semifixed refers to a cost which is essentially fixed over the relevant activity range but which may have to be increased substantially at several activity levels if production is increased. Thus, quality-control costs may be fixed over wide ranges, but an additional man may be required if production is above a given activity level. The result of adding identical machines at discrete intervals, as output requirements increase, provides another example of a *semifixed* cost.

Avoidable-fixed refers to costs that may not be incurred under certain circumstances. For example, if the firm is shut down (or its activities scaled down), many of the costs associated with running staff functions, such as accounting, are avoidable. Accounting supplies and the salaries of personnel who could be laid off provide specific illustration of fixed costs that can be avoided.

Figure 2.1 shows some cost-characteristic alternatives but does not include all the possibilities. For example, a cost such as maintenance may have an avoidable-fixed component at very low levels of activity but may vary directly with increases in activity at higher levels. This type of cost is sometimes said to be a variable cost with a fixed-cost component. (Compare Figures 2.1 and 2.2.)

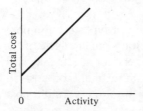

Figure 2.2   Variable cost with a fixed-cost component (or a semivariable cost).

Instead of showing the total cost, it is frequently useful to show (or compute) costs on a unit basis. Figure 2.3a shows the cost per unit for a fixed cost, and Figure 2.3b illustrates the cost per unit for a variable cost (under constant efficiency).

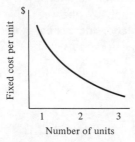   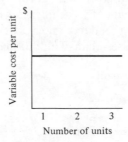

Figure 2.3   Fixed and variable costs per unit.

The interpretation of the cost per unit curve for a fixed-cost item requires careful interpretation, since the cost itself is invariant in total to the number of units produced. For example, we cannot determine the marginal cost (the cost of one more unit) using Figure 2.3a. If a cost is truly fixed, we know that the marginal cost is zero. The first graph in Figure 2.1 does suggest this conclusion. On the other hand, using Figure 2.3b we can determine that the unit variable cost is equal to the marginal cost since the cost per unit is a constant. The second graph from the left in Figure 2.1 indicates the same result, since the slope is constant and nonzero. The reader is cautioned to pick the type of graph based on the visual impression desired. The wrong graph can add confusion rather than bring clarification.

2.1.2 Responsibility

Classification of costs by responsibility is important because it provides the basis of cost control. The first step in the control of costs is knowledge of where the cost was incurred and who was responsible.

The allocation of service department costs (building, power, heat, cafeteria, accounting, etc.) to operating departments for purposes of computing unit costs or profits by product line often thwarts the cost-control function. These allocations are not essential to the control of costs, since costs must be controlled where they are incurred. Allocations of service department costs to operating departments are generally not useful for cost-control purposes. An exception to this rule is illustrated by some repair department costs which are controllable both by the repair department (to ensure that repairs are implemented efficiently) and by the operating department (to ensure that preventive maintenance and proper operation reduces the need for repairs).

Cost-control reports should be prepared so that only costs for which the manager has responsibility are reported as being controllable. Although someone can be held responsible for the ultimate decision for any cost, even the leasing or buying of equipment that took place many years ago, the inclusion of costs that a manager cannot control merely acts as a detraction and may have a negative effect on morale. This does not prevent other allocated costs, about which the firm's officers believe the manager should be aware, from being reported to him. It does imply that the latter costs should be separately listed and appropriately described as not (currently) controllable by the manager in question. Also, decisions made in one cost center can affect costs incurred in another center. These interdependencies are important to cost-control procedures.

2.1.3 Product Line; Tracing Costs to End Product

The classification of costs by product line is essential in determining the profitability of various activities of the firm. The total contribution margin earned (as well as the profitability per dollar of sales) in the various activities is often relevant to decisions involving expanding or contracting the activity, product promotion, product research, improving the productive process, and developing better cost-control techniques. Cost identifiable with a product line are called *direct costs*.

The main problem in classifying costs by product line is that many costs cannot be directly identified with any one product because they are associated with several products. A cost of this nature is called an *indirect cost*. The term *indirect* is used with a cost which cannot be directly identified with a product line, job, process, department, etc. It is necessary, then, to know for what purpose a cost is being identified and, thus, whether it is being associated with a product line, sales area, department, or some other activity before a classification of direct or indirect can be made. For example, if a salesman simultaneously handles several product lines, his salary is an indirect cost for each product line but a direct cost to his sales area.

If there are indirect costs, then reports by product line must be carefully prepared. Instead of showing one income figure, it is desirable to show a series of subtotals. The report in Exhibit 2-1 highlights those costs directly associated with the product line and subordinates those costs indirectly associated with the product line. Additionally, it distinguishes between variable and fixed costs.

Exhibit 2–1   Income Statement for Product A

Sales	$5,000
Less: Direct variable costs (materials, etc.)	2,000
	$3,000
Direct-fixed costs (managers' salaries etc.)	800
Excess of revenues over direct costs	$2,200
Less: Indirect-variable costs (repairs, etc.)	1,000
	$1,200
Indirect-fixed costs (rent, etc.)	400
Net income—product A	$ 800

Instead of first subtracting the costs directly identified with the product line, the variable costs can be subtracted first and the fixed costs second, as in Exhibit 2–2. This report highlights the *contribution* of the product to the total fixed costs and profit of the firm.

Exhibit 2–2   Income Statement for Product A

Sales		$5,000
Less: Direct-variable costs	$2,000	
Indirect-variable costs	1,000	3,000
Excess of sales over variable costs (the contribution)		$2,000
Less: Direct-fixed costs	$ 800	
Indirect-fixed costs	400	1,200
Net income—product A		$ 800

Indirect fixed and variable costs are usually determined using what are called *overhead rates*. The total fixed cost for the period may be divided by the normal level of output to obtain a rate per unit of activity. One procedure is to relate this cost to the number of direct-labor hours at the normal output level. The fixed cost per labor hour is then multiplied by the number of direct-labor hours used to obtain the related fixed overhead cost. The same is done for indirect variable costs. (This subject is discussed in more detail in Chapter 3.)

The choice as to which report (Exhibit 2–1 or Exhibit 2–2) is better depends upon the purpose for which the data are required. If a decision is being made to expand or contract a product line, a decision maker would want to know the change in the total contribution margin that would result from such a decision. If some indirect- or direct-fixed costs are avoidable, then neither statement is ideal for a decision to contract operations. It is worth adding that other considerations, including future market expectations, complementarity to other product lines, other opportunities, the time value of money, and so on, would also be relevant to and perhaps controlling in a given decision situation. The analysis of accounting information is only a first step, albeit a necessary one. Furthermore, a decision maker is well advised to question closely the origin, nature, relevance, and validity of the data supplied to him by the accounting information system. For example, one of the direct costs associated with product A is depreciation on machinery used in its production, based on the original cost and calculated using either the straight-line or an accelerated depreciation method. If a decision is to be made on whether to retain product A or cease production, the conventionally determined depreciation cost is not the relevant cost measure.

2.1.4 Natural and Functional Classifications

The term *natural classification* refers to the basic physical aspects of the cost (labor, material, supplies, etc.). *Functional* refers to how the cost was used (manufacturing, administration, or selling). A need for both natural and functional classifications exists. The prime conflict between the two classifications is in the preparation of income statements, that is, for product-costing purposes rather than for decision purposes. Should the expenses be classified according to natural or functional classifications? The answer must depend on the use of the report, but no matter which classification is used additional information should be supplied. For example in financial reports, if the functional classification is used, the depreciation expense and labor expense of the period should also be shown, perhaps in a footnote.

2.2 Economic Characteristics of Costs

The accountant can classify costs in many ways, but he cannot record a cost as *relevant* or *irrelevant* to decisions, this will depend on the particular decision being made. In like manner the principle of opportunity costs is of great importance to decision making, but the accountant does not record opportunity costs because these generally depend on the alternative uses of the resources at the time of the decision. Hence, the opportunity cost cannot be known in advance but only at the time the decision is made. The opportunity cost depends on the alternatives available when the decision is made. Opportunities foregone at the time a decision is made should be noted and the *ex post* payoffs estimated and recorded, if possible, for feedback, decision evaluation, and control purposes.

Yet, even if an alternative decision would have been best in an *ex post* sense, the decision actually made may still have been the best given the information available at the time the decision had to be made. *Ex ante* estimates of the payoffs for different alternatives and under different future states may be made, but if an alternative is not selected, the *ex post* payoff, and therefore the *ex post* opportunity cost, is likely to be unknown. We do not know what the costs would have been using new equipment if we do not acquire the equipment.

2.2.1 Sunk Costs

A cost that has been incurred is "sunk," thus not relevant to a decision. The term *sunk cost* is frequently used to refer to a cost such as the historic cost of a machine. The historic cost, once incurred, is not relevant for decisions (taxes aside). The accountant must be careful to recognize that the relevant measure of both the machine's worth and the periodic decline therein depend upon the potential usefulness of the machine through time.

The accountant does allocate indirect costs to different products, but for decision making these allocations should be examined to determine their relevance. This is not to say that the accountant is wrong to make the allocations for purposes of income and inventory determination, but it would be incorrect to use these same allocations for purposes for which they were not intended and for which they are not correct.

A transaction may have important economic characteristics that do not enter the accounting records. When there is occasion to make decisions, the relevant costs must be extracted from the accounting records and properly arrayed. It is not possible for the accounting system automatically to record and report costs in all relevant ways, for all possible decisions. However, the availability of high-speed computers has increased the amount of information which can be stored and obtained quickly.

Previously, we discussed the term unavoidable costs. It is important to observe that an unavoidable cost may not be a sunk cost. The president's salary is generally unavoidable, but it is also out-of-pocket. A useful generalization is that unavoidable costs are fixed.

2.2.2 Relevant and Irrelevant Costs

The purpose of this classification is to point up the fact that not all costs are relevant for specific decisions. The relevant cost concept cannot help determine how to compute costs, but it is a useful reminder that the cost measured should be a function of how the measure is to be used.

Except for tax considerations, the book depreciation or book value of a machine currently being used is not relevant in making the decision of whether or not to replace that machine. In measuring an organization's ability to survive short-run adversity, only the out-of-pocket costs are relevant. In pricing a bid for a government contract, only the opportunity cost of the factors of production (based on alternative uses), variable and certain semivariable costs are relevant. Thus, for each decision, the manager must determine which costs are relevant.

How many executives, when faced with the decision of whether or not to replace a long-lived asset, first check with the accounting department to find out if the asset being replaced is fully depreciated? The purchase cost of the asset being replaced is a "sunk cost," and the depreciation charged or not charged does not affect the replacement decision, except for tax considerations. Something akin to depreciation can affect the decision, namely, the future expected decrease in salvage or resale value. This is a relevant cost and should be considered.

The following example attempts to illustrate why the extent of accounting depreciation is not relevant in making a replacement decision. The fact that money has value over time has been left out of the illustration to avoid an unnecessary complication, but it obviously should be included in an actual decision-making situation. The tax implications have also been ignored for now. We shall take up these issues later.

Assume that management is considering the replacement of an asset that cost $40,000 and which is 75% depreciated (the net book value is $10,000) with a new piece of equipment which costs $50,000. The new asset will result in a total saving of labor and material over a five-year period of $56,000. The resale value of the old equipment is equal to the removal cost (no net salvage).

Should the asset be replaced? Two possible solutions are offered here. One includes the depreciated cost of the old asset, the other ignores this cost. The data are given in Exhibit 2–3.

Exhibit 2–3   Replacement Example

	Correct Procedure (excludes depreciated cost)	Incorrect Procedure (includes depreciated cost)
Indicated gross savings	$56,000	$56,000
Less: Cost of new asset	50,000	50,000
Depreciated cost of old asset		10,000
Net saving (dissaving)	$ 6,000	($ 4,000)

One procedure (correct) suggests replacement; the other (incorrect) suggest retention of the old asset. Let us see what happens following the decision. Assume that revenues for the five-year period total $100,000. This figure is net of all expenses except those factors being considered in this example. The results are given in Exhibit 2–4. Costs common to both procedures are omitted.

Exhibit 2–4   Future Results

	Results of Operations	
	Correct Decision	Incorrect Decision
Net revenues	$100,000	$100,000
Less: Write-off of old asset	10,000	10,000
Depreciation of new asset	50,000	
Additional cost incurred (because new machine was not purchased		56,000
Total deductions	$ 60,000	$ 66,000
Net income	$ 40,000	$ 34,000

The financial position of the firm following the correct procedure of ignoring the depreciated cost on the old asset is $6,000 better than the position if the firm followed the incorrect procedure of including the depreciated cost in the replacement calculations. To make a proper replacement decision, it is necessary to compare the value of the savings with the cost of the new asset. The accounting book value of the asset being replaced should not affect the decision. (Recall that taxes were omitted from the example.)

2.2.3 Opportunity Costs

The principle of opportunity costs is very important to the analysis of accounting data and to business decision making. It defines the cost of one course of action in terms of the opportunities which are given up to carry out that course of action. If an asset can be used to perform only one function, and it cannot be used in other ways or sold as scrap, the opportunity costs of that asset are zero. Thus, the opportunity costs of using the underground gas pipe of a gas company in the city of Chicago are zero, because the pipe is going to carry gas and nothing but gas in Chicago. As long as the revenues from carrying the gas are greater than the incremental costs connected with delivering the gas, it will be desirable for the company to continue to deliver the gas. The costs of using the gas pipe are zero, because there are no alternative opportunities. In a theoretical as well as a physical sense, the costs of the gas pipe are sunk; the pipe has zero opportunity cost.

A machine used to make product A will have an opportunity cost if the machine can be sold or if it can also make product B. For example, assume that a period's production of B can be sold for $10,000 and that the costs which vary directly with production are $8,000. The period's opportunity cost of not producing product B is $2,000. The proceeds that are forsaken by producing A instead of B are actually a cost of producing A. The opportunity cost principle is extremely useful in deciding on alternative uses of productive facilities.

2.2.4 Controllable and Noncontrollable Costs

The concept of controllable costs is important because, if properly applied, it helps avoid much confusion in the area of cost control. It is generally accepted that a person should be held responsible for only those costs which he can control. A corollary of this position is that reports to junior managers should contain only those costs which they control. Thus, the foreman of an operating department should not receive a report comparing actual building depreciation with budgeted depreciation, since the foreman can neither control the rate of building depreciation nor the decision to acquire the building in the first place.

2.2.5 Marginal and Incremental (or Differential) Costs

The *marginal cost* is the cost added by producing one more unit. The *incremental cost* (or differential cost) is the cost added by producing more than one unit. Both definitions are extremely important, since many decisions are based on marginal or incremental costs.

The accountant often takes a practical shortcut and assumes that the incremental cost is equal to the variable cost multiplied by the number of additional units to be produced. Any fixed (or semivariable) costs related to the production of the additional units must, of course, be added. This procedure ignores changes in efficiency, but otherwise it is a useful approximation. Incremental costs (and revenues) provide the basic costs needed for good managerial decision making.

2.3   Marginal and Differential Cost Analysis

Two of the most important decisions that managers must make are the pricing decision and the decision as to level of activity (or output). How are these decisions made? This question has never been answered in a completely satisfactory way. Economists have evolved a theory of the firm which is based on marginal analysis and which shows how the managers should make these decisions. The method should be understood in its basic form by all students of management. The basic principles are valid, whether or not they are actually applied in their pure theoretical form. Instead of marginal analysis, the manager frequently thinks in terms of differential revenues and costs, since this often is the closest that the accounting records can come to marginal costs.

2.3.1 Marginal Analysis: The Economic Approach

The managerial economist states that to maximize profits production should be at a level where marginal costs equal marginal revenues. At this point profits are maximized. As long as the revenue from the next unit (the marginal revenue)

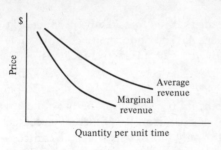

Figure 2.4   **Marginal and average revenue.**

is greater than the costs of producing that unit (the marginal costs), the unit should be produced. The logic of this line of argument is reinforced by a graphic presentation. See Figures 2.4, 2.5 and 2.6.

It is assumed that the lower price of the product, the more units of the product which will be sold. The average-revenue curve slopes downward to the right (this is also the price curve). The marginal-revenue curve slopes downward to the right also and is below the average-revenue curve. The revenue added by the sale of an additional unit is less than the price, since the price of all units must be lowered to make the additional sale.

The average variable-cost curve in Figure 2.5 first slopes downward to the right, reflecting increasing efficiency. It then curves upward when the quantity produced exceeds the point of maximum efficiency. The marginal-cost curve passes through the average variable-cost curve at its minimum point. When marginal cost exceeds average variable cost, the average variable cost must rise.

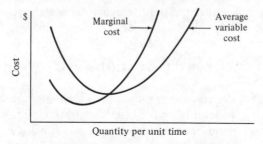

Figure 2.5   **Marginal and average variable cost.**

The next step is to combine the two graphs. This is done in Figure 2.6. The optimum level of production for a profit-maximizing firm is where marginal costs equal marginal revenues.[1] The price to be charged for the product, P, is obtained by finding the average revenue (price) necessary to sell A units. It is important to recognize that the price charged is *not* the marginal revenue, M. The intersection of the marginal-revenue and marginal-cost curves determines the optimal output, but the price is determined by the intersection of a vertical line from the optimal output level to the average-revenue curve.

[1] The firm will not produce in excess of A units, since the costs of each additional unit are in excess of the revenues of those units.

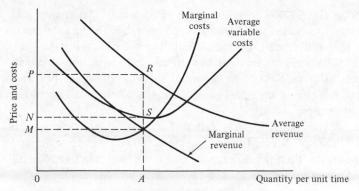

Figure 2.6 Determining optimal output and price.

In Figure 2.6, the average revenues are greater than average variable costs at the optimum level of output. Thus, it is possible that there is a profit. To know for certain, it is necessary also to consider the fixed costs of operation.[2]

If average revenues exceed average total cost at the optimal output, there is a profit. Total revenues for the case illustrated in Figure 2.6 are given by price times output, $P \times A$. Total revenues are represented by the area $OPRA$. Total variable costs are given by the product of average variable cost by input, $N \times A$. Total variable costs are represented by the area $ONSA$. The difference, $NPRS$, represents the contribution margin available to cover fixed costs and, if anything is left over, to provide a profit.

This is not the complete story of marginal analysis. Among the questions ignored is the question of the degree of competition. Is the average revenue line for the firm a horizontal straight line? If not, what is its slope? What is the shape of the average-variable cost curve? What conditions are necessary for a condition of equilibrium? Most important, does the individual businessman know the shape of all or any of these curves closely enough to use this analysis?

The marginal cost curve is not readily available from the accounting records. This is not merely an oversight on the part of the accountant. The informed accountant appreciates the importance of marginal costs, but also recognizes the expense of accumulating this information when the change in costs is caused by adding or dropping a *single unit* in production at each step. Instead, the accountant compromises and substitutes a technique that uses *differential costs* instead.

2.3.2 Differential Costs: The Accounting Approach

The economic approach concerned itself with the increase in revenues and expenses arising from the additional production and sale of one unit. The accounting approach concerns itself with the increase in revenues and expenses arising from the additional sale of a block or group of units. For instance, what

---

[2] One way to do this is to draw in the average-total-cost curve. This curve is always above the average-variable cost curve and approaches it as output increases.

will be the effect of a sale of 1,000 units at a price of $5 a unit? To answer this question, the total costs without the sale must be compared with the total costs if the sale is made. The difference is the "differential cost" of making the sale. If the revenues ($5,000) are greater than the differential costs, the sale will increase total profits. *Differential costs* also equal the variable costs per unit times the number of additional units *plus* any "fixed costs" that will be added because of the additional production.

Differential cost analysis is particularly valuable in making a decision as to the desirability of "bidding" for additional business. If the revenues obtained from these sales are greater than the differential costs, the firm is better off with the new business.[3] Opportunity costs should be included where relevant.

Example

The ABC Company has an opportunity to bid for the right to sell 1,000 containers to the government. A study reveals the following information:

Direct-material costs per container $2.50
Direct-labor costs per container   1.25 (per hour of direct labor)

The company has the following overhead rates[4]:

Fixed costs $2.25 per direct-labor hour
Variable costs   1.50 per direct-labor hour

In addition, the company will have to buy special equipment costing $500. This equipment has no foreseeable use or value after this contract.

Let us compute the minimum revenue the company must obtain for it to be no worse off than if it did not get the order. Assume that the company has the excess capacity required to take on this business and that the facilities have no alternative use.

Solution:

Direct material	$2.50 × 1,000 = $2,500
Direct labor	1.25 × 1,000 = 1,250
Variable overhead	1.50 × 1,000 = 1,500
Cost of additional equipment	0.50 × 1,000 = 500
Differential costs per unit (not the marginal cost)[5]	$5.75
Differential costs of the sale of 1,000 units	$5,750

---

[3] Other factors such as long-run effects on quality and the ability to continue to serve large and profitable customers, for example, should also be considered.

[4] The overhead rates are designed to allocate fixed and indirect-variable costs to units produced.

[5] The marginal cost of the first unit is $505.25. This strange answer arises because of the discontinuity of the costs. The first unit bears the total cost of the equipment. Fixed overhead costs are not relevant.

If revenues of $5,750 can be obtained for the 1,000 containers, the firm will be no worse off than if it did not have the order, since the differential costs are equal to the additional revenues. Actually the firm would bid something higher than $5.75 per unit to better its position by the transaction. However, the maximum price bid is tempered by the fear of losing the bid and possibly by noneconomic motives (such as patriotism) as well. Note that fixed overhead is not relevant. The assumption is that these are sunk costs with no alternative use.

2.4 Accounting Data and Decision Making

The problems and reading material in accounting textbooks generally imply that decisions can be made by using only accounting data. Accounting information can help in making decisions, but it does not replace judgment. The manager must look beyond the accounting analysis to be able to choose the best course of action.

Information for decisions generally incorporates estimates and forecasts. This is especially true in pricing decisions. The costs for different levels of production must be predicted, as well as the levels of sale at different unit prices. This means that uncertainty is typically present, and we shall show by examples later how uncertainty can be incorporated into the analysis. Regardless of whether forecasts and estimates are subject to uncertainty, other considerations must be reviewed. What will be the effect of a price rise on customer goodwill? What will be the long-run impact of a price change? How will a price change affect the company's labor relations? Are there any legal implications? These factors and others must always be considered before an intelligent decision can be made.

2.5 Summary

Several important ways to define and classify costs have been discussed in this chapter. The easiest way to specify the correct cost is to say that the "relevant" cost is required. Unfortunately, this is essentially a tautological statement. It is not very helpful, since different costs are usually needed for different purposes. For example, the relevant cost for a contractor selling to the federal government may be different than the relevant cost when the contractor is attempting to decide whether or not to expand his plant or to measure his work in process inventory. One of the most useful and practical means of isolating the relevant costs in a specific situation is to use the differential (incremental) cost approach.

Decisions throughout this book will focus on the measure of how costs change when a decision is undertaken. The relevant cost for a decision is very rarely the amount originally paid (the purchase cost). Rather, the opportunity cost concept will be the basis of decision making. Nevertheless, for cost control and cost-determination purposes, we must be able to assign and trace costs through the accounts in a reasonable manner. This topic is developed in the next two chapters.

QUESTIONS AND PROBLEMS

2–1 Assume a situation where you can hire workers when you need them but you cannot fire them when they are not needed except at a very large cost. How would this information affect decision making?

2–2 It is difficult for a firm separately to classify its costs as fixed or variable, but it can be done. As an illustration, take the costs of owning and operating an automobile and divide the costs into fixed and variable classifications.

2–3 Consider education as a product. What are the direct and the indirect costs to a university of educating a student?

2–4 The concept of *opportunity cost* is extremely important to decision making. Discuss the following:
   a. Deciding how space in a department store is to be used.
   b. Deciding how much salary to offer a college graduate being considered for employment.
   c. The importance of the reserve clause to professional baseball (a ballplayer plays only for the team he has signed with or does not play).
   d. The decision of a student to obtain an MBA degree.

2–5 The demand for a product can be 0, 1, or 2, with equal probability. The payoffs in dollars for three alternative order decisions are:

Alternatives: (Order)	States: (Demand is) 0	1	2
0	0	0	0
1	−5	8	8
2	−10	3	16

Required:
   a. Assuming that one unit is ordered, what is the opportunity cost for the three possible states that might occur?
   b. What is the expected opportunity cost of ordering one unit?
   c. If two units are ordered and the event "demand is two" occurs, what is the opportunity cost?
   d. What additional information might be desired to make an order decision?

2–6 The New York Oil Company has just bought 1 million barrels of oil. A consultant has argued that the cost of the oil is a sunk cost and thus not relevant to any decision the company faces. The president of the firm realized that the cost of his pipelines was a sunk cost but found it difficult to consider his inventory to be sunk.

Required: Discuss whether or not the cost of the inventory is a sunk cost.

2–7 The salary of the president of the firm is usually considered a fixed cost. Is it a relevant cost when pricing the product for sale to the government? Is it a relevant cost in a decision to sell the organization? Explain.

2 8 Certain costs are controllable and others are noncontrollable. This is a meaningless statement unless we define the segment of the organization that is being discussed. Explain.

2–9 The ABC Manufacturing Company is considering expanding by acquiring a plant currently being operated by the XYZ Company. The XYZ Company has submitted the following list of costs for a normal level of operations:

Direct labor	$100,000
Direct material	200,000
Indirect manufacturing costs, fixed	
Plant and equipment depreciation	150,000
Salaries of personnel (includes allocation of central office salaries, $100,000)	200,000
Indirect manufacturing costs, variable	40,000
	$690,000

The plant is so designed that it can produce only widgets. Widgets sell for a price of $1 per unit. The widget industry is very competitive, and a price change is very unlikely. At a normal level of operations, the plant produces 500,000 widgets.

The XYZ Company has operated the plant efficiently, and it is unlikely that the ABC Company could introduce additional efficiencies. Selling costs are nominal. The ABC Company would not have to add to its central office staff.

Required:
a. In computing the maximum price that the ABC Company should offer for the plant, what "income" figure should be used? (Assume normal sales.)
b. If the XYZ Company cannot sell the plant, should they close it? Explain.

2–10 The president of the ABC Company in an effort to find out why profits were down, closely inspected the variable costs incurred and compared the actual costs with the costs which should have been incurred at the actual level of operations. He ignored the fixed-cost classification, since fixed costs are "fixed." Discuss.

2–11 The Miner Company is considering the elimination of an outlying plant. The elimination would result in increased efficiency because of savings in transportation of material and parts. The present plant, which is 40 miles from the main plant, would be replaced by a plant adjacent to the main plant. In preparing an analysis of the pros and cons of the elimination, one of the researchers suggested that a portion of the salaries of the executives of the plant and head-quarters should be considered, i.e., the portion reflecting the amount of time spent traveling during company hours between the plants. Another researcher said: "The salaries should not be considered, because they are a fixed cost. The executives would be paid the same amount whether they traveled or not; thus the cost is not relevant."

Required:
a. Should the time the executives spent traveling be considered in making the decision whether or not to replace the present plant?
b. What other information would you want if you were going to make the decision?

2–12 The Miller Company is considering the sale of the physical assets of a subsidiary company. The president of the Miller Company has requested an analysis of the costs of the subsidiary and has been given a breakdown of costs (assuming normal operations) into fixed and variable classifications.

Required:
a. Name some "fixed" costs that would be avoidable if the subsidiary were sold.
b. Name some "fixed" costs that would be avoidable if the subsidiary were retained but not operated.
c. Name some costs that would continue even if the subsidiary were not operated (assuming that it were not sold).

2–13 A President of a company described his situation as follows: "My problem is having too low a volume of sales. I have fixed costs of $100,000 and variable costs of $1 per unit of product. With my present volume of 10,000 units, the average cost of product is $11 per unit. If I could sell 100,000 units, the average cost would be $2 per unit. My selling price is $11 per unit."

Required:
a. Compute the income presently being earned by the firm.
b. Assume that the firm could increase its volume to 200,000 units by decreasing its price to $1,80 per unit. Would this price reduction be desirable, assuming that the present plant capacity is adequate?
c. The generalization is often made that "with high fixed costs, the only answer is to increase production and sales." Discuss the validity of this statement.

2–14 The Marshall Company is about to bid for a government contract. The president of the firm desires to know the minimum bid which the company can make in order for the firm to be no worse off than if the firm did not get the order. Assume that the firm has adequate capacity to produce the product for the government without adding to plant. The contract will be for 10,000 units.

The analyst prepared the following report:

	Per Unit	Total
Direct-material costs	$ 1.30	$ 13,000
Direct-labor costs	4.60	46,000
Overtime incurred because of contract	0.10	1,000
Overhead		
Variable overhead	1.00	10,000
Fixed overhead	2.00	20,000
Special equipment (to be purchased)	4.00	40,000
Allocation of selling and administrative expenses		
(fixed costs)	3.00	30,000
Safety factor (100% of the overhead rate)	3.00	30,000
Minimum price	$19.00	$190,000

Required: Prepare a supplemental report for the president.

2–15 The Make-or-Buy Company uses machine tools which it has been manufacturing. The company currently has excess capacity, and the tools are being manufactured in a part of the plant that would otherwise lie idle.

A salesman of machine tools, who has been attempting to sell to The Make-or-Buy Company, has prepared the following analysis in cooperation with company personnel:

	Cost of Manufacturing the Next Year's Supply of Tools	Cost of Buying the Next Year's Supply of Tools
Cost of purchasing tools		$210,000
Cost of parts and material	$100,000	
Labor (especially hired for this type of work)	40,000	
Labor (distribution of labor costs of regular hourly workers based on hours of actual labor)	30,000	
Labor (allocation of labor costs of salaried employees)	20,000	
Variable overhead	10,000	
Fixed overhead (includes $20,000 of depreciation of equipment especially purchased for this purpose in the past)	40,000	
	$240,000	$210,000

The purchased machine tools will have no operating advantage over the tools made by the plant itself.

Required: Prepare an analysis showing whether The Make-or-Buy Company should purchase or make its machine tools to fill its needs.

2–16 The production manager of a pulp and paper mill wanted to know if it would be better if the pulp mill ran only one kind of pulp. At that time, the pulp mill manufactured 75% hi-bright pulp and 25% regular to meet the demands of the various grades of paper produced in the paper mill. The production manager felt that if the pulp mill would make only hi-bright, savings could be realized in decreased cost of chemicals, improved uniformity, decreased loss in time because of changeovers, and decreased cost of titanium to hold or increase brightness. In order to obtain the necessary regular pulp needed in the manufacture of certain grades, he felt that the hi-bright pulp could be "dyed back" to a regular brightness. He realized that an all hi-bright production meant increased steam cost (as the pulp would have to be cooked longer) as well as an increase in certain other chemical costs.

The following memo is the answer the financial analyst department submitted to him in reply to the request.

Memo
To: Mr. X
From: Mr Y
Subject: Analysis of cost of manufacturing all hi-bright pulp vs. our present
method of running two blends.
Assumptions:
1. We currently make about 75% hi-bright pulp and 25% regular brightness. At a production of 3,600 tons per month, this would mean bringing our present 900 regular tons to high brightness.
2. The only way we can jusitfy changing to all hi-bright pulp is by assuming that we will be able to cook enough pine separately to replace *all* the outside pulp that we now use (average of 150 tons per month).

Increased Costs of Making 900 Tons More Hi-Bright per Month

	Monthly Total
1. Increased cost of bleaching—$2.63/ton	$ 2,367
2. Increased steam cost $\frac{1}{10}$ meg/ton @ $0.528/meg	50
3. Assume 20% more TiO_2 in coating to increase opacity	1,800
4. Assume double present amount of dye on coated grades to reduce brightness	500
Total increased costs	$ 4,717

Savings to Accrue from Making 900 Tons More Hi-Bright per Month (Using 300 tons of pine pulp)

	Monthly Total
1. Assume making 300 tons pine pulp (enough to replace 150 tons purchased pulp and 150 tons regular pulp). Present incremental cost of 150 tons of present blend hi-bright	$ 9,600
Present cost of 150 tons of purchased pulp	24,000
	33,600
Anticipated incremental cost of 300 tons of pine pulp	20,250
Savings	$13,350
2. Decreased rejections for low brightness and paper lost in changing from regular to hi-bright on paper machine—30 tons	1,500
Total savings	$14,850
Total increased costs	4,717
Total net savings per month	$10,133

Should the mill make only hi-bright pulp?

2-17 The Spring Manufacturing Company is considering accepting a special order for 50,000 mattresses which it received from a large chain of department stores. The order specified a price of $30 per unit. This compared unfavorably to the company's regular price of $33 per unit. The accounting department prepared the following analysis in an attempt to show that there would be cost saving resulting from the additional sales:

	Cost per Unit Without the Additional Sales (100,000 units)	Cost per Unit With the Additional Sales (150,000 units)
Variable costs	$20	$20
Fixed costs	9	6
	$29	$26

No additional fixed costs would be incurred since there was excess capacity. Since the average cost per unit will be reduced from $29 to $26, the president of the firm believes he would be justified in reducing the price by $3 to sell to the department store chain.

Required: Should the order for the 50,000 units at a price of $30 be accepted? Explain.

2–18 A star professional football player has asked you for advice. His club has offered him a contract paying $200,000 for a season. He wants to know whether he should sign. His club has a viable backup player. What do you advise him?

2–19 A professor charges $1,500 per day for consulting. If he charged $200 per day, he would obtain many more days of consulting and thereby substantively increase his total take-home pay (while still performing his teaching responsibilities). Why may his current pricing policy be reasonable?

2–20 A student graduating from engineering college is thinking of entering a graduate school of business. She has been offered a job as an engineer at a salary of $12,000 per year. If she returns to school, tuition will be $4,000 per year (it is a 2-year program) and living costs $3,000 per year (to live on a comparable style will cost $7,500 if she takes the job). What is the cost of continuing her education? Ignore income taxes.

2–21 The following statement was taken from a managerial report.

> During the year a Merchandise Control Section was established whose function has been to hold a tight rein on inventory position and to plan for the maximum turnover of merchandise. The success of this function has been apparent in the approximately four-time turnover of inventories during the year. In addition, short-term seasonal borrowings have been held to a minimum, since funds were not unnecessarily tied up in inventory.

Required: Comment on the statement.

2–22 Comment on the following:
  a. Despite the fact that direct labor is commonly thought of as a variable cost and depreciation is commonly thought of as a fixed cost, circumstances may call for a completely opposite treatment in budgeting. Can you give an example?
  b. Why do many companies refrain from reporting fixed costs in performance reports?
  c. Graph the behavior of the following costs vs. volume per period:
     (1) Depreciation computed on a sum-of-the-years digits method.
     (2) Variable cost per unit of output.
     (3) Power cost where a minimum amount is supplied at a specified total charge. Additional usage is at a constant rate per K.W.H. until a given number of K.W.H.'s after which time the hourly rate is cut in half.
  d. Is the pricing policy of c(3) desirable?

Chapter 3

Accounting for
Overhead Costs

All operating costs other than direct labor and direct material are usually classified as *overhead* by the accountant. This view differs somewhat from the economist's definition of overhead, which includes only fixed costs. The difference in the two definitions is not important as long as we recognize which is being used. In this chapter, manufacturing overhead refers to all fixed and variable costs that cannot be readily identified with a specific product, service, process, or job.

Overhead includes a wide range of costs. They may be fixed or variable, sunk or out-of-pocket, avoidable or unavoidable, and so on. Some examples of overhead costs include:

1. Building depreciation cost
2. Heating cost
3. Repair cost
4. Indirect labor: cleaners, electricians, shippers, etc.
5. Supplies: cleaning supplies, small tools, gloves, etc.
6. Taxes: payroll taxes (the payroll taxes on direct labor are often treated as overhead for practical reasons)
7. Cafeteria cost
8. Foreman's salary
9. Cost Accounting Department cost.

Overhead costs must be both controlled and applied to product. To accomplish control and also to obtain a sensible allocation of the costs, overhead (or burden) centers are established. Each department (operating or service) has at least one such overhead center. Overhead costs are first recorded here. The *distribution* of costs is accomplished by identifying which manager or department is responsible for them. This is a matter of identification and not one of arbitrary allocation. For example, repair costs would first be accumulated in an account called *Repair Department*.

The next step is to assign each overhead cost to an operating (or producing) department. Some of the costs may be directly identified with an operating department by the original cost-distribution procedure. An example would be the use of repairmen by an operating department. However, many overhead costs will have been distributed directly to service departments rather than to operating departments. These costs have to be *allocated* to the operating departments for product-costing purposes. This allocation of the costs is often made using arbitrary bases, and therefore the allocated costs may not be useful for purposes of cost control.

After the allocation of service department costs to the operating departments, the last step in product costing is to *absorb* or *apply* the overhead costs to product.

It should be noted that there are actually three steps in recording overhead:

1. *Distributing* overhead cost to department overhead (or burden) centers. This is called *cost distribution*.
2. *Allocating* the costs of service departments to operating departments.
3. *Absorbing* or *applying* the overhead to product.

The overhead is first charged to (distributed to) the burden centers where these costs are incurred. It is during this step that the responsibility for the cost is established. Only if the responsibility for cost incurrence is clearly defined can costs be effectively controlled. For example, the costs of maintaining the factory building should first be classified as a building department cost for cost-control purposes. They should then be allocated to the various operating departments so that the products being produced may be charged with a pro rata share of the costs of maintaining the building. This allocation should be based on the benefits received by the operating departments.

The methods of *allocating* the overhead to operating departments and *absorbing* the overhead to product vary from company to company and even within different plants of the same company. The purpose of this chapter is twofold. One is to suggest possible accounting systems for recording overhead. The second is to clarify the theory of accounting for overhead by explaining the relation of overhead application to income measurement and the determination of financial position.

The initial distribution of overhead costs to those departments responsible for their incurrence represents the key step in cost control. Responsibility for the costs must be clearly established before the distribution is made. This control is facilitated by the recording process described in the next section.

3.1 Recording Overhead

The first step in accounting for overhead is recording the amounts by basic function or by their natural classification. This is accomplished using the general and subsidiary ledgers of the organization.

3.1.1 General Ledger Accounts

Theoretically only one organization account is needed to record overhead in the general ledger. This overhead account can be used to record all indirect costs. Subsidiary accounts can be used to record detailed information such as the natural classification of the cost and the department where it was incurred. A refinement of this procedure would be to use two accounts: one to record the overhead costs as they are incurred, *overhead incurred*, and a second, *overhead applied*, to record the application of the costs to product. This would be done by a debit to work in process and a credit to overhead applied. This procedure has the advantage of retaining in one account the total costs incurred. The overhead incurred account also acts as a control account for the overhead incurred accounts in the departmental subsidiary ledgers.[1]

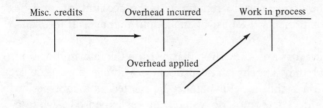

Example

The company has incurred $120,000 of overhead costs during the month of January. It has applied to product $105,000 of this overhead. The $105,000 is determined by the use of predetermined overhead rates. (The means by which these rates are established are discussed later.) Recording this information in the appropriate general ledger accounts is accomplished as follows:

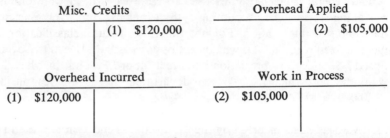

[1] It would also be possible to use separate overhead accounts (or pairs of accounts) for each major overhead classification.

Explanation of Entries

1. Records the incurrence of the overhead costs.
2. Records the application (absorption) of the overhead to product. (The $105,000 could have been credited directly to the overhead incurred account.)

What is the disposition of the balance of $15,000 (the $120,000 cost incurred, less the $105,000 applied to product)? One possibility is to carry this balance forward from month to month and then close the final balance to a loss (or a gain if a credit balance) account at the end of the year. An alternative treatment is to close the "Overhead Incurred and Applied" accounts each month to a loss (or gain) account or prorate it to inventory and cost of goods sold accounts. The latter solution would mean that the $15,000 would be debited to one or perhaps several accounts, including work in process and cost of sales.

Is it better to close the overhead accounts or to carry the balances forward to the end of the year? For a company whose operations are irregular, say for seasonal reasons, there is much merit in carrying forward the accounts and not attempting to close the balance until the end of the year. Where operations are uniform over the year, the choice should remain with the accountant, and he should use the system that presents the best financial and managerial information.

If the balances are carried forward, they should appear on the interim position statements. Where should they appear? The proper location is a subject of controversy. One suggestion is that a debit balance be treated as a subtraction from retained earnings (a cost factor of no value, not yet expensed), while a credit balance should be treated as an addition to retained earnings (the cost of product has been overstated; the cost of goods sold has been overstated and income understated). This is not a perfect solution to the dilemma of where to put this item, but it is one possibility. In practice they are typically carried near or with the inventory values.

3.1.2 Subsidiary Ledger Accounts

The general ledger accounts used to record overhead were discussed in the preceding section. An accounting system that used only these accounts would have omitted information. For one thing, the natural classification of the cost has not been recorded. Of what types of costs is the $120,000 of overhead composed? Supplies? Depreciation? Indirect labor? Second, in what departments were the costs incurred? Which department heads are responsible for the $120,000?

The first of these questions can be answered relatively simply by first recording the overhead costs incurred by their natural classification and then transferring the balances in these accounts to the department (say, for example, manufacturing) overhead account. But the second question remains unanswered. What department is responsible for the overhead costs? The costs as they are incurred should be assigned to departments, so that the person responsible for each department can be held accountable for the costs incurred in the department.

One solution is to set up subsidiary records for overhead costs. These records commonly take the form of departmental cost ledgers, for example, one set of accounting cards for each department or a cost distribution sheet for each department. These departmental cost ledgers record by department the natural classification of each cost incurred. For example, assume that supplies costing $1,000 were used as follows:

Building Department	$200
Operating Department 1	300
Operating Department 2	500

The following entry would be made in the *general ledger*:

Supplies Inventory		Overhead Incurred	
$50,000	(1) $1,000	(1) $1,000	

The debit of the same transaction would also be recorded in detail in the appropriate departmental subsidiary cost ledgers.

Building Department, Cost Ledger

Indirect Labor	Allocation from Service Depts.	Supplies Used	(Other columns)
		$200	

Operating Department 1, Cost Ledger

Indirect Labor	Allocation from Service Depts.	Supplies Used	(Other columns)
		$300	

Operating Department 2, Cost Ledger

Indirect Labor	Allocation from Service Depts.	Supplies Used	(Other columns)
		$500	

For greater usefulness, the natural classifications may be broken down into even finer divisions. Types of supplies may be identified as cleaning supplies, office supplies, first aid supplies, small tools, and so on. When subsidiary ledgers are used, no entry can be made to the overhead incurred account without there being an equal amount recorded in the departmental subsidiary ledgers. The total debit balance in the overhead incurred account must equal the total costs recorded in the departmental subsidiary cost ledgers. In this way the overhead incurred account acts as a control account.

The use of electronic computers has tended to replace the "cost ledgers," but although the form has changed, the necessity of recording costs in total and in detail remains.

3.2 Allocating Overhead Costs

The necessity, for cost-control purposes, of assigning overhead costs to the departments in which they are incurred has been explained. It is also necessary to allocate these costs in computing the total cost of product. Overhead is generally applied to a firm's products using overhead rates. These rates should reflect the level of activity in the department that is most closely associated with the benefits derived from the particular overhead item.

3.2.1 Departmental Overhead Rates

A common overhead-rate base is the direct-labor hours[2] worked in a department. It is often felt that overhead cost incurrence is closely related to this measure of activity. If so, the overhead rate is determined by dividing the budgeted overhead cost by the budgeted direct-labor hours to obtain the overhead rate. Of course, other bases may be used instead of or in addition to direct-labor hours. Common examples include direct-labor cost and machine hours. Different overhead rates may be necessary for each operating department, and several rates may be needed in the same department for different overhead items. In computing reasonable rates, the costs of the service departments should first be allocated to the operating departments based on the benefits actually received or expected to be received.

The importance of absorbing overhead to product using different overhead rates will be shown by an example.

Example
Two operating departments have the following characteristics:

	Operating Department 1	Operating Department 2
Direct-labor hours (at normal activity)	10,000	10,000
Machinery and equipment (cost)	None	$5,000,000
Floor space	1,000 ft²	29,000 ft²
Power cost	$100 (lighting only)	$5,000

[2] We shall sometimes refer to these as DLH.

If only one overhead rate is used for the entire plant and both departments are worked at normal activity, the product of the two departments will receive the same amount of overhead. With an overhead rate of $4.255 per direct-labor hour (determined from data given below), $42,550 would be applied to product in each department. Is this reasonable? We believe not. Department 2 should bear a larger share of the overhead than Department 1, because it uses more floor space, more equipment, and more power. If overhead were first allocated to departments and separate overhead rates were computed for the two departments, Department 2 would have a higher overhead rate, and the product being produced in Department 2 would then bear a more equitable overhead cost.

Assume that the following costs are budgeted for the year and are the basis for the one company-wide overhead rate:

Depreciation of machinery and equipment	$50,000
Building costs	30,000
Power costs	5,100
	$85,100

The overhead rate is $85,100 divided by 20,000, or $4.255 per direct-labor hour. Assume that each unit of product produced in Department 1 and Department 2 requires 1 hour of direct labor, and $5.00 of costs other than overhead. According to the figures developed, each unit of product, whether produced in Department 1 or 2, will be allocated $9.255 ($5 of direct costs, $4.255 of overhead) of cost. Instead of using one overhead rate, let us now compute departmental rates.

	Allocation of Costs	
	Dept. 1	Dept. 2
Depreciation of machinery and equipment	$——	$50,000
Building costs (allocation based on floor space)	1,000	29,000
Power	100	5,000
	$1,100	$84,000
Overhead rates (based on 10,000 direct-labor hours in each department)	$0.11	$8.40

The cost of the product made in Department 1 is now $5.11 (the direct costs of $5.00 plus the overhead of $0.11). The cost of the product made in Department 2 is $13.40 (the direct costs of $5.00 plus the overhead of $8.40).

3.2.2 Allocation of Overhead to Operating Departments

Assume that all costs connected with maintaining and running the factory building are first accumulated in an overhead center called "Building Overhead." It is next necessary for costing purposes to allocate this overhead cost to the various operating departments. What would be a reasonable basis? Floor space occupied by each operating department is one likely choice. Cubic volume occupied might also be reasonable. Consider the following example.

Example

The following items have been debited to the account "Building Overhead":

Factory Building:
Depreciation	$10,000
Repairs	150
Cleaning supplies	100
Labor	2,750
	$13,000

There are four operating departments, and they use the following floor space:

Operating Departments:
1	3,000 ft²
2	2,000 ft²
3	4,000 ft²
4	1,000 ft²
	10,000 ft²

Computation of the allocation of building overhead to the operating departments is shown in Exhibit 3–1.

Exhibit 3–1   Allocation of Building Overhead

Department	Floor Space (ft²)	Basis of Allocation (%)	Building Costs	Allocation of Building Costs
1	3,000	30	$13,000	$ 3,900
2	2,000	20	13,000	2,600
3	4,000	40	13,000	5,200
4	1,000	10	13,000	1,300
	10,000	100		$13,000

The allocation of building overhead cost is based on the floor space used (an assumed valid measure of the benefit received). If a department was shut down, it might still be reasonable to assign it the same amount of costs, since the building costs were incurred with the expectation of servicing that department. The department was expected to benefit from the cost.

The journal entry to record the allocation of overhead would be:

Operating Department 1 Overhead		$3,900	
,, ,, 2 ,,		2,600	
,, ,, 3 ,,		5,200	
,, ,, 4 ,,		1,300	
Building overhead applied			$13,000
(to allocate overhead of factory building to operating departments)			

(If there is only one overhead account in the general ledger, no formal journal entry is required; the transfer would take place in the subsidiary records.)

There are no exact rules for choosing the basis of allocation. The overhead of the service departments is generally allocated on some basis which is considered reasonable. The following list indicates some of the more likely choices:

Overhead Costs to Be Allocated	Basis of Allocation
Power	Rated horsepower of equipment
Heat	Cubic volume of space used
Water	Engineering study of usage
Repair Shop	Actual costs incurred by each department
Personnel Department	Number of personnel
Cafeteria	Number of personnel
Payroll Department	Number of personnel
Purchasing Department	Cost of material used

Service department costs must be allocated to determine product costs. These costs should be allocated to the departments based on estimated benefits actually received by the departments. Predetermined assignments are often used for the allocation of fixed costs, since the amount of cost is not a function of activity but rather of the capacity which is made available.

However, the allocation of service department costs may not be useful from a cost-control standpoint unless the operating manager has responsibility for the incurrence of the cost or efficient use of the service. The key question from a control viewpoint is who is responsible for the various costs. The answer can be different depending on the particular cost involved. Thus an operating department manager may or may not be responsible for the efficient use and repair of that portion of the building he uses. If he is responsible, it is reasonable to allocate these costs to him for control purposes as well as for product-costing purposes.

3.3   Absorption of Overhead to Product

To this point we have been concerned with the recording and the allocation of overhead costs to the various operating departments. The next task is to apply the costs to work in process. This is accomplished by the use of an overhead rate. The overhead rate is applied to some measure of activity. Among the possible choices for the measure of activity are:

Direct-labor dollars
Direct-labor hours
Units of product
Hours of machine operation
Dollars of material used.

These items are listed in approximate frequency of use. Any of the above can be appropriate in a given setting, but the ultimate choice depends on the facts. For example, machine hours is not a good measure of activity where machines play only a small part in the manufacturing process. The same can be true of direct labor where heavy automation is present. In some cases the information needed to compute the best measure, such as direct-labor hours, is not readily available. In this case an alternative, such as direct-labor dollars, is used instead. Indeed, this is one reason for the extensive use of labor dollars as a measure of activity.

One or more of the above measures of activity are used to obtain an overhead rate, which is used in turn to accomplish the absorption of overhead to product. The general formula for calculating this rate is:

$$\text{overhead rate} = \frac{\text{budgeted overhead for some level of activity}}{\text{level of activity}}$$

Example
For the Manufacturing Department the budgeted fixed costs are $50,000 and the budgeted variable overhead for a level of activity of 100,000 direct-labor hours is $150,000. A possible computation of the overhead rate is:

$$\text{manufacturing department overhead rate} = \frac{\$50,000 + \$150,000}{100,000}$$

$$= \$2/\text{direct-labor hour.}$$

Note that the costs used in the numerator of the formula are budgeted overhead costs and not the actual costs. Overhead rates are generally computed before we know what the actual costs of the period are going to be. The above rate can be broken down, if desired, into its fixed and variable components of $0.50 and $1.50, respectively.

3.3.1 Capacity Considerations

It would be possible to compute the overhead absorbed by product using an overhead rate based on the actual fixed cost divided by the actual level of activity. Thus, if the overhead were $10,000 (all fixed costs) and there were only one unit produced, the overhead per unit would be $10,000. If 1,000 units were produced instead of one unit, the overhead per unit using this method would be $10 per unit. This wide change in the overhead per unit is caused by fluctuations in production. To avoid the possibility that unit costs would be affected merely by changes in the level of production, accountants have elected to compute the overhead rate based on capacity operations. If actual operations are less than capacity, the unabsorbed overhead is considered a cost of idle capacity. This, however, leads to additional problems. One is the definition of capacity. Another is the fact that many accountants believe that all the overhead ought to be absorbed by product, if not at capacity then at a normal level of operations. Other accountants believe that overhead should be entirely absorbed at the expected level of operations.

As a result of the complications, many different methods of choosing the level of activity for computing overhead rates are found in practice. Among the more common are:

Practical (or attainable) capacity:	That activity or output level where long-run and short-run costs are equal. If the firm wants to produce more than practical capacity, it should obtain more fixed factors of production.
Normal (or average) activity:	That level of output necessary to satisfy average consumer demand. Typically, this concept represents a long-run notion covering cyclical as well as trend and seasonal influences. It may represent an average over several years.
Expected activity:	That level of output anticipated for the period in question.
Actual activity:	That level of output experienced over the period in question.

There is no general agreement as to which of these bases is the best one to use. Actual and expected activity are probably the least desirable. Practical capacity is the procedure with the best theoretical justification, but it is difficult to operationalize. Normal activity is a reasonable compromise. In a period of normal activity, all overhead would be absorbed. The result of using this concept is a more nearly constant overhead rate over time. But even if we were to agree to use the concept of a normal-activity-based rate, some troublesome definitional problems remain. For example, over how many months or years should the average output requirement be estimated? How should the estimate be made? How often should it be changed? These and other questions must be given reasonable answers before this definition can be operationalized.

Should the normal activity be based on an 8-hour day, a 16-hour day, or a 24-hour day? (The choice is important in the absorption of fixed overhead costs.) This question asks directly how many shifts are required. To answer, we need to estimate future demand. Hence, the solutions to operationalizing the capacity measure elected are both important and difficult. The accountant is advised to consider in advance the effects of his choice on product costs, the decisions based on product costs, and the effect on the interpretation of overhead cost variances (see Chapter 6) in selecting and defining capacity.

Once the overhead rate has been computed, it is applied to the *actual* level of activity to find the amount of overhead transferred from the operating department overhead account to the work in process account.

Example

Assume that the following information is available for the month of January and that overhead is to be absorbed using direct-labor hours:

	Direct-Labor Hours at Given Activity Level	Total Budgeted Overhead at Given Activity Level
Practical capacity	100,000	$340,000
Normal (or average) activity	60,000	300,000
Expected activity	50,000	290,000
Actual activity	40,000	280,000

The different overhead rates possible are computed by dividing the second column by the first column:

	Overhead Rate
Practical capacity	$3.40/direct-labor hour
Normal (or average) activity	5.00/direct-labor hour
Expected activity	5.80/direct-labor hour
Actual activity	7.00/direct-labor hour

The overhead absorbed by work in process in January, based on actual activity of 40,000, is:

Using practical capacity	$3.40 × 40,000 = $136,000
Using normal (or average) activity	5.00 × 40,000 = 200,000
Using expected activity	5.80 × 40,000 = 232,000
Using actual activity	7.00 × 40,000 = 280,000

The wide differences in overhead costs transferred to work in process affect the income for the period and the valuation of inventories. This points up the importance of the choice of activity level for the computation of the overhead rates. The use of any level of operations other than practical capacity results in a portion of the cost of idle capacity being transferred to product and being lodged in inventory. The analysis for cost-control purposes of the difference between actual overhead incurred (not given here) and the amount transferred to work in process is treated in Chapter 5.

3.3.2 Fixed- and Variable-Overhead Rates

For many business decisions, it is necessary to have the total costs separated into the fixed and variable components. Thus, the accountant commonly computes two overhead rates, a fixed-overhead rate and a variable-overhead rate.

Example
The budgeted fixed costs are $240,000 and the budgeted variable costs are $100,000 at practical capacity. The variable- and fixed-overhead rates, using a practical capacity of 100,000 direct-labor hours are:

$$\text{fixed-overhead rate} = \frac{\$240,000}{100,000} = \$2.40/\text{direct-labor hour}$$

$$\text{variable-overhead rate} = \frac{\$100,000}{100,000} = \$1.00/\text{direct-labor hour}$$

$$\text{total overhead rate} = \frac{\$340,000}{100,000} = \underline{\$3.40}/\text{direct-labor hour}$$

If, instead of practical capacity, an expected activity of 50,000 direct-labor hours were used, the two overhead rates based on the budget of $290,000 would be:

$$\text{fixed-overhead rate} = \frac{\$240,000}{50,000} = \$4.80/\text{direct-labor hour}$$

$$\text{variable-overhead rate} = \frac{\$50,000}{50,000} = \$1.00/\text{direct-labor hour}$$

$$\text{total overhead rate} = \frac{\$290,000}{50,000} = \underline{\$5.80}/\text{direct-labor hour}$$

The variable-overhead rate is unchanged, but the fixed-overhead rate has changed radically. The choice of the activity level always affects the fixed-overhead rate (and by affecting the fixed-overhead rate, it affects the total overhead rate). The absorption of fixed-overhead costs is a troublesome item, since it is so dependent on the choice of the activity level at which the fixed overhead rate is computed. For certain purposes, better information is obtained if fixed costs are not absorbed by product but are treated as period costs. This possibility is covered more completely in Chapter 11, where we discuss the concept of variable costing.

3.4 Summary

The reader should keep in mind the objectives connected with the accounting for manufacturing overhead. The accountant wants to:

1. Control costs.
2. Determine costs of product for purposes of measuring income, determining financial position, and decision making.

The objectives are not always compatible, and the accountant may have to make special computations to accomplish the specific objectives at hand.

The control of costs is facilitated by the recording of overhead costs by cost centers and by the identifying of costs in as much detail as is possible. Periodically the actual costs are compared with the budgeted costs to determine whether the specified level of efficiency has been attained. This is a subject that is given further consideration in Chapter 6.

The cost of products is determined by the use of predetermined overhead costing rates. These costing rates should be broken up into their fixed and variable components, so that costs for different purposes may be computed. The costing rates should be computed not for the company or plant as a whole but for each operating department (or cost center). The use of departmental overhead rates gives more realistic unit-cost figures, since the cost of the product includes those costs which are identified with the product either through direct identification or through reasonable bases for the allocation of indirect costs not directly identified with an operating department. The activity level used in constructing these bases should reflect the association of the cost being allocated with the benefit received.

Since the cost of product as computed by a cost-accounting system is greatly affected by the method used to absorb fixed costs to product, the unit cost of a product should be accepted only after due consideration is paid to the method used to absorb fixed-overhead cost to each unit of product.

It should be noted that the allocation of overhead to operating departments and the absorption of overhead by product are not useful for the control of costs. Costs should be controlled at the point of incurrence by the person who is responsible for the area where they are incurred. For example, costs in the accounting department are controlled by the controller, not by the operating department foreman, who may have some of the accounting department costs allocated to his department for purposes of determining product costs.

Why, then, should costs of an indirect nature be allocated to operating departments and absorbed by product? There are several valid purposes. They include:

1. Determining income of a product or division, department, etc.
2. Determining cost of the goods remaining in inventory.
3. Determining cost for government "cost-plus" contracts.
4. Determining cost of product sold to discover how well unit price recovers total unit cost.

Knowing how the allocations of overhead costs cannot be used is just as important as knowing how they can be used. A great deal of effort is wasted in trying to use overhead allocations for purposes for which they are inappropriate. It should be noted that the above list does not include "determining costs for decisions." The allocation of costs as illustrated in this chapter is not generally relevant for decisions. Chapter 20 discusses linear programming as a method of determining decision-relevant costs for factors of production for which there are no current outlays but which act as constraints on production.

QUESTIONS AND PROBLEMS

3–1 The Absorption Corporation is in the process of changing its cost-accounting system. It has decided on the use of direct-labor dollars as the basis for absorbing overhead into work in process.

Required:

a. Given the following information, compute the different variable and fixed overhead rates which might be used.

Budget Information for Coming Year

	Budgeted Direct-Labor Dollars	Budgeted Fixed Overhead	Budgeted Variable Overhead
Practical capacity	$200,000	$450,000	$400,000
Normal (average) activity	90,000	450,000	180,000
Expected activity	100,000	450,000	200,000

b. Compute the overhead absorbed by product in January if $10,000 direct-labor dollars of cost were incurred. Fixed overhead incurred was $38,000, and variable overhead was $22,000. Give four different answers based on four different assumptions. State the assumptions.

c. Explain the difficulties connected with determining the "actual" cost of product.

d. In this problem, overhead is absorbed, using direct-labor dollars. What other measures of activity could be used?

3–2 Part I. The Allocation Company has two operating departments and three service departments. The costs of the service departments are assumed to be *fixed*.

Service Department	Basis of Allocation	Budgeted Cost for Year
Cafeteria	Personnel budgeted	$ 45,000
Building	Floor space	120,000
Repair Shop	Past experience (the previous year's assignment of costs)	31,200

Operating Department	Personnel Budgeted	Floor Space (ft²)	Repair Shop Jobs: Past Year
1	50	4,000	$10,000
2	100	6,000	20,000

In addition to the above indirect costs, the only other overhead costs are manufacturing supplies and indirect labor. These are budgeted as follows:

Operating Department	A Year's Normal Activity (DLH)	Manufacturing Supplies, Fixed	Year's Budgeted Costs for Normal Activity		
			Manufacturing Supplies, Variable	Indirect Labor, Variable	Indirect Labor, Fixed
1	100,000	$ 9,000	$20,000	$75,000	$50,000
2	200,000	15,000	30,000	80,000	60,000

Required:

a. Prepare a schedule that allocates the service department budgeted cost to the operating departments.

b. Compute one overhead rate for the Allocation Company as a whole.

c. Compute separate overhead rates for the two operating departments.

d. Comment briefly on the relative usefulness of the various overhead rates computed above.

Part II. During the month of January the following costs were incurred:

	Cafeteria Dept.	Building Dept.	Repair Shop	Operating Dept. 1	Operating Dept. 2
Direct labor (the hourly rate is $2.00)				$20,000	$32,000
Direct material				40,000	70,000
Indirect labor	$2,000	$1,000	$3,000	14,000	15,000
Manufacturing supplies	200	100	1,000	1,500	1,900
Fuel + power	600	1,200		1,000	4,000

Required:

a. Record the incurrence of the costs in the appropriate cost (burden) centers. (Use both factory ledger and departmental subsidiary records.)

b. Record the allocation of the service department costs to the operating departments (also prepare a schedule of the allocation).

c. Record the debits made to the work in process account during the month. Show the entries using "T" accounts. Use the overhead rates computed in Part Ic.

d. From the point of view of controlling costs, is the allocation of costs in parts b and c useful?

3–3 The following is taken from the *Progress Report to the Congress 1973* (Cost Accounting Standards Board):

HIERARCHY FOR ALLOCATING COST POOLS

Costs not directly identified with final cost objectives should be grouped into logical and homogeneous expense pools and should be allocated in accordance with a hierarchy of preferable techniques. The costs of like functions have a direct and definitive relationship to the cost objectives for which the functions are performed, and the grouping of such costs in homogeneous pools for allocation to benefiting cost objectives results in better identification of cost with cost objectives.

The Board believes there is a hierarchy of preferable allocation techniques for distributing homogeneous pools of cost. The preferred representation of the relationship between the pooled cost and the benefiting cost objectives is a measure of the activity of the function represented by the pool of cost. Measures of the activities of such functions ordinarily can be expressed in such terms as labor hours, machine hours, or square footage. Accordingly, costs of these functions can be allocated by use of a rate, such as a rate per labor hour, rate per machine hour, or cost per square foot, unless such measures are unavailable or impractical to ascertain. In the latter cases, the basis for allocation can be a measurement of the output of the supporting function. Output is measured in terms of units of end product produced by the supporting functions, as for example, number of printed pages for a print shop, number of purchase orders processed by a purchasing department, number of hires by an employment office.

Where neither activity nor output of the supporting function can be measured practically, a surrogate for the beneficial or causal relationship should be selected. Surrogates used to represent the relationship are generally measures of the activity of the cost objectives receiving the service. Any surrogate used should be a reasonable measure of the services received and should vary in proportion to the services received.

Pooled costs which cannot readily be allocated on measures of specific beneficial or causal relationship generally represent the cost of overall management activities. These costs should be grouped in relation to the activities managed and the base selected to measure the allocation of these indirect costs to cost objectives should be a base representative of the entire activity being managed. For example, the total cost of plant activities managed might be a reasonable base for allocation of general plant indirect costs. The use of a portion of a total activity, such as direct labor costs or direct material costs only, as a substitute for a total activity base, is acceptable only if the base is a good representative of the total activity being managed.

Required: Evaluate the suggested procedures.

3-4 The Williams Manufacturing Company's production activities involve three producing departments and a factory office. All materials are added at the start of process 1. Processed material moves from process 1 through process 2, then through process 3, where the product is completed.

The following account balances reflect costs of the Williams Company for the month of January:

Materials used	$ 8,200
Direct labor	11,600
Indirect labor	1,700
Sales salaries	4,200
Taxes, properties	2,100
Depreciation of factory building	714
Depreciation of equipment	550
Advertising	1,455
Factory office labor	900

Direct-labor costs were as follows:

Process 1	$ 4,900
Process 2	2,700
Process 3	4,000

Indirect labor is primarily janitorial in nature, and distribution is made to the three producing departments and the factory office, giving double weight to the producing departments. Floor space is as follows:

Process 1	2,500 ft^2
Process 2	3,500
Process 3	2,000
Factory office	1,000

Property tax valuations are as follows:

Process 1	$13,000
Process 2	16,000
Process 3	10,000
Factory office	3,000

Depreciation is charged at a uniform rate on all equipment. The cost of equipment in each department is as follows:

Process 1	$ 7,500
Process 2	5,500
Process 3	13,000
Factory office	1,500

Since the factory office is maintained primarily for timekeeping and employee services, the cost of operating the office is distributed to the producing departments on the basis of the number of workers in each department. They are as follows:

Process 1	10 workers
Process 2	4
Process 3	6
Factory office	2

Required: Prepare a schedule allocating production costs to the three producing departments. Set up overhead accounts for each of the four departments. Make entries to these accounts, showing the results of the allocation.

3–5 The Webster Corporation uses normal activity for determining overhead rates. Overhead is applied to product, using direct-labor hours.

Part I. Determining Overhead Rates:

	Dept. 1 Normal Activity	Dept. 2 Normal Activity
Budgeted direct-labor dollars	$200,000	$400,000
Budgeted direct-labor hours	100,000	200,000
Budgeted fixed overhead	50,000	40,000
Budgeted variable overhead	150,000	180,000

Required:
a. Compute the fixed and variable overhead rates for the two departments.
b. Explain briefly how the amounts of fixed overhead were obtained for the two departments.
c. Explain how the above computations would be changed by the use of practical capacity instead of normal activity.

Part II. Recording Overhead in Burden Centers
During the month of January the following overhead costs were incurred:

	Building Dept.	Dept. 1	Dept. 2
Indirect labor (fixed)	$200	$ 4,000	$ 2,000
Indirect supplies (fixed)	$100	1,000	1,200
Indirect labor (variable)		10,000	11,000
Indirect supplies (variable)		2,000	3,000

Required:
a. Record the given information in general ledger accounts.
b. Record the given information in departmental subsidiary ledgers.
c. If the direct-labor hours actually worked during the month were 9,000 in Department 1 and 18,500 in Department 2, are the variable overhead costs under or over the budgeted amounts? Prepare a schedule.

Part III. Allocation of Overhead to Operating Departments
The Building Department costs are allocated to the two operating departments, based on the floor space used.

Department	Floor Space Used (ft²)
1	30,000
2	10,000

Required:

a. Record the allocation of the Building Department overhead to the two operating departments in the departmental subsidiary ledgers.

b. Would the allocation of Building Department costs be relevant for controlling the costs of the Building Department or the operating departments? Explain.

Part IV. Absorption of Overhead by Product

During the month of January there were 9,000 direct-labor hours worked in Department 1 and 18,500 worked in Department 2.

Required:

a. Record the absorption of overhead by product in the general ledger.

b. What are the factors that caused the amount of overhead absorbed by product to be different from the amount incurred?

c. What disposition do you suggest for the overhead variances?

3–6 The Ithaca Oil Company prepares income statements by product line and by customers for each product. It sells directly to gasoline stations, to wholesalers, and to jobbers. The following report was prepared for the sale of gasoline to gasoline stations.

The Ithaca Oil Company

Income Statement
for month ending March 31

Sales (400,000 gallons)		$200,000
Expenses:		
Cost of product sold*	$120,000	
Local delivery	8,000	
Storage and handling	2,000	
Selling costs	1,000	
Accounting and credit	800	
Administrative	1,200	
Advertising and sales promotion	4,000	
Headquarters	10,000	
Total expenses		147,000
Net income		$ 53,000

* Transfer price from the manufacturing division times 400,000 gallons.

Required:

a. For each expense discuss the nature of the assignment of the cost. Was it a direct cost or an allocation? What is the nature and basis of the allocations?

b. Assume that you are attempting to measure the performance of the manager in charge of sales of gasoline to gasoline stations. Would you use the figure of $53,000? Explain.

c. Assume that you are considering the construction of an additional gasoline station. What quantitative factors would you take into consideration? Which costs would be relevant? Explain any assumption which you may make in answering the question.

d. Assume that the cost of product sold was $190,000 instead of $120,000. Should the sale of the product to gasoline stations be dropped? Assume that the present prices of the product sold and purchased are expected to continue in the foreseeable future.

3-7 The City Steel Company sells five different product lines. The costs which are regularly incurred include the following:

Cost of sales
Purchasing
Order processing
Materials handling
Delivery (including shipping)
Storage
Advertising
Selling
Credit and collection
Bad debts
General administrative
Public relations
Auditing (fee to public accounting firm)

Required:

a. For each expense discuss how (if at all) each cost should be assigned to the five product lines.

b. Assume that you are considering dropping one of the product lines. Which of the above costs would be relevant to the decision? Explain.

3-8 The following cost information applies to a product:

Units	Total Cost for a Week
100	$10,000
200	25,000
300	50,000

The fixed-cost component of cost is $5,000 per week, and this would not increase if additional units are produced. Additional equipment can be obtained. The unit cost (excluding fixed costs, which should be incurred in any event) would be $150 per unit for the additional units if the new equipment is obtained.

What is the practical capacity of the present long-lived assets?

3–9 The following is taken from the *Progress Report to the Congress 1973* (Cost Accounting Standards Board):

COST-ALLOCATION CONCEPTS

The Board's primary goal is increased uniformity and consistency in treatment of costs as they are related to negotiated defense contracts. Set forth herein are discussions of a number of important concepts which the Board will use in developing cost-accounting standards.

Cost accounting for negotiated government contracts has long been on the basis of full allocation of costs, including general and administrative expenses and all other indirect costs. The allocation of all period costs to the products and services of the period is not a common practice either for public reporting or for internal management purposes; yet this has long been the established cost principle for costing defense procurement. The Board will adhere to the concept to full costing wherever appropriate.

A cost objective is "a function, organizational subdivision, contract, or other work unit for which cost data are desired and for which provision is made to accumulate and measure the cost of processes, products, jobs, capitalized projects, etc." This definition has been promulgated by the Board.

Cost-accounting systems are developed to provide a means for assigning all costs to appropriate cost objectives. Under the full costing concept, all costs initially allocated to intermediate cost objectives are reallocated to final cost objectives. Costs which are identified for special treatment (unreasonable costs, or costs unallowable for other reasons) may be assigned to final cost objectives established for that purpose.

Even with the foregoing concept, there are occasional difficult questions as to whether specified units of an organization or its work should be allocated cost on a full costing basis. The Board will attempt to identify and dispose of such questions in individual cost-accounting standards.

Required: Evaluate the cost-allocation concepts.

3–10 "The labor cost of material handlers is generally treated as indirect labor."
   a. How are such costs generally applied to product for costing purposes?
   b. Suggest an alternative solution and explain why one might be useful.
   c. What is the major reason such costs are treated as indirect labor?

3–11 The Pokerface Playing Card Company uses an overhead rate of $3.00 per direct labor hour, based on expected variable overhead of $100,000 per year, and expected fixed overhead of $200,000 per year. Data for the year's operations are as follows

	D.L.H. Used	Overhead Costs Incurred*
First 6 months	60,000	$168,000
Last 6 months	36,000	136,000

* Fixed costs equaled budgeted fixed costs throughout the year, and were incurred uniformly over the year.

a. What is the under (over) applied overhead for each 6-month period in total and broken down by fixed and variable components.

b. Give plausible reasons for the amounts or any subamounts of the figures determined in part a.

3–12 It is a time of severe business depression throughout the capital goods industries. A division manager for a large corporation in a heavy-machine company is confused and unhappy. He is distressed with the controller, whose cost department keeps feeding the manager costs that are of little use because they are higher than ever before. At the same time, the manager has to quote lower prices than before in order to get any business

a. What activity base is probably being used for the application of overhead?

b. How might overhead be applied in order to make the cost data more useful in making price quotations?

c. Would the product costs furnished by the cost department be satisfactory for costing the annual inventory?

3–13 Pashaw and Co. produces a single product in a single department under a standard cost system. Standard costs per finished unit include $16.00 for direct material and $9 for direct labor. Four units of direct material are required per finished unit. The standard direct labor rate is $3.00 per hour. Condensed monthly flexible budget data follows:

	Operating Levels		
Direct Labor Standard Hours Per Month	60,000	80,000	100,000
Supplies	$ 9,000	$ 12,000	$ 15,000
Indirect labor	33,000	44,000	55,000
Other variable overhead	6,000	8,000	10,000
	$ 48,000	$ 64,000	$ 80,000
Depreciation	$ 60,000	$ 60,000	$ 60,000
Supervision	50,000	50,000	50,000
Other fixed overhead	17,500	17,500	17,500
	$127,500	$127,500	$127,500

The company uses a combined overhead rate of 6.90 per finished unit for product-costing. Data for the month of June follow:

Units produced 31,000.

Units sold 26,000.

Inventory June 1 (at standard) 50,000 units (raw material).

Direct material purchased 100,000 units @ $4.20.
Direct materials used 126,000 units.
Direct labor: 96,000 actual hours, $281,280.
Total overhead incurred, $203,000.

Required:
a. The cost of sales for June (at standard).
b. Normal monthly capacity in standard direct labor hours.

3–14 Respond to the following questions concerning the quotations from a cost accounting text.

a. "The practical problems of applying various elements of overhead to physical units are fraught with trouble spots. An understanding of the limitations of overhead application should accompany an understanding of the technique." What is *the* primary reason for these problems?

b. "Overhead is applied to product because of the managerial need for a close approximation of costs of different products prior to the end of the fiscal period." Why (for what purposes) does this need exist? (Give two.)

c. "Accountants have chosen an averaging process for attaching overhead to product." What is this process and in what way is it an averaging process?

d. "The total forecasted overhead is related to some common denominator or base. . . ." Name three such bases and give, in one sentence, the reason for the existence of more than one basis.

e. "Overhead costs are also accumulated weekly or monthly on departmental cost sheets without regard to their application to specific jobs." What is the purpose of such cost accumulation and what additional steps or precautions are necessary to effect this purpose? (List 3 major items.)

3–15 What factors must be considered in deciding upon bases for allocating service department costs to producing departments?

3–16 A large dairy company relies heavily upon competitive bidding for securing contracts for the production of private-label dairy products. Small errors in calculating costs can be extremely disastrous since competition for contracts is keen.

Included in the calculation of its bid, the company uses an overhead application rate which last year was:

$$\frac{\text{Overhead}}{\text{Direct labor cost}} = \frac{\$150,000}{\$\ 75,000} = \$2.00$$

Of the $150,000 overhead, $50,000 is variable overhead. Since this application rate was developed, direct laborers earned a 5% increase in wages and related benefits. In submitting a recent bid, the plant manager failed to consider this wage increase. What effect will this have upon his bid?

3–17 Fine Products, Inc., wants to develop departmental overhead rates for product costing. The company has prepared the following budgeted overhead for next year based upon normal capacity:

Department	Budgeted Overhead
Building and Grounds	$ 50,000
Cafeteria	25,000
Personnel	10,000
Power	100,000
Material Stores	45,000
Producing: 1	50,000
Producing: 2	75,000
Total	$335,000

In order to determine departmental overhead application rates, service department overhead must be allocated to the two producing departments.

The following data are available for choosing allocation bases:

	Producing: 1	Producing 2:
Direct labor hours—Normal capacity	10,500	15,000
Number of employees	50	75
Square feet of space	25,000	10,000
Metered power—Last year	5,500	3,200
Number of material requisitions—		
Last year	500	250

Required:
a. Allocate the service department budgeted costs to the producing departments.
b. Compute departmental overhead allocation rates based upon direct labor hours.

3–18 Able Body Products, Ltd., produces 2 models of exercising machines. Each model begins processing in the Assembly Department and then is transferred to the Finishing Department where the final touches are added. Model 1 requires the assembly of several small components, but it requires little in the way of finishing. Thus each unit requires 3 hours of direct labor in the Assembly Department but only 1 hour in the Finishing Department. Model 2 requires little in the way of assembly, but the machine is given a high polish in the Finishing Department which requires about 5 hours of direct labor. Model 2 requires about 2 hours of direct labor in the Assembly Department.

For the year just ended, Able Body had used a company-wide overhead application rate based on direct labor hours for determining product costs. The company developed the rate from the following budget information:

	Budgeted Overhead	Normal Capacity*
Assembly Department	$ 50,000	10,000
Finishing Department	200,000	20,000

* Direct labor hours.

The budgeted level of activity was met exactly and the only ending inventories for the year were 100 units of model 1 and 800 units of model 2 in finished goods.

Required:
a. Find the overhead application rate used by the company.
b. Find departmental overhead rates.
c. How would the company's net income have changed if it had used departmental overhead application rates?

3-19 The Overhead Company has five departments, two of which are producing departments. Overhead costs are first identified with the department responsible for the costs, and then all costs are allocated to the two producing departments. Producing Department 1 has a normal capacity of 50,000 direct labor hours, and Producing Department 2 has a normal capacity of 100,000 direct labor hours. Factory office costs are all fixed costs and are budgeted at $110,500. Costs for the materials handling department are all fixed and are budgeted at $75,000. Costs for the machinery repairs department are budgeted as follows:

Fixed Costs	$14,000.00
Variable Costs per hour	2.20

Producing Department 1 is scheduled for 1200 hours of machinery repairs while Producing Department 2 is scheduled for 3,000 hours. Budgeted overhead costs for the two producing departments are as follows:

	Variable* Costs	Fixed Costs
Producing Department 1	0.52	$125,000
Producing Department 2	0.65	198,000

* Per direct labor hour.

Factory office costs are allocated on the basis of direct labor hours. Producing Department 1 is budgeted to requisition 5,000 units of material while Producing Department 2 is budgeted to requisition 10,000 units of material.

Required: Compute overhead application rates for each of the two producing departments.

SUPPLEMENTARY READING

GREEN, D., "Towards a Theory of Interim Reports," *Journal of Accounting Research*, Spring 1964, pp. 35–49.

RAPPAPORT, A., "Towards a Theory of Interim Reports: A Modification and an Extension," *Journal of Accounting Research*, Spring 1966, pp. 121–126.

Chapter 4

Cost-Accounting Systems

The purpose of this chapter is to discuss systems by which cost data are accumulated, classified, and communicated for the purpose of product costing. This accumulation is also an essential first step in cost control. Product costing and control are, however, separable activities. Proper planning and control can be combined effectively with any of several costing procedures to be discussed in this chapter. Knowledge of alternative product-costing procedures is important to the understanding of the appropriate use of these costs in pricing and other decisions.

Cost-accounting systems may be classified under three general headings:

1. Job-order cost accounting.
2. Process cost accounting (either by process and/or by product).
3. Standard cost accounting (used most commonly in conjunction with the process cost accounting).

The accountant is not limited to these three systems. There are many variations and combinations which may be used. The ultimate choice of systems depends on the facts of the situation and the needs of management.

4.1 Job-Order Cost System

Costs should be accumulated by jobs when the productive process is not repetitive and when each product or group of products is more or less distinctive. Each job is given a job number or code. When material or labor costs connected with the job are incurred, they are recorded in the work-in-process account of the general ledger and in a subsidiary ledger which maintains the cost of each job. This subsidiary ledger often takes the form of a card called a job cost sheet. An example is illustrated in Figure 4.1.

Job Number_____

Description_____

Date_____   Date to Be Completed_____

Specifications_____   Bill Of Materials_____

Date	Direct Material	Direct Labor		Overhead
		Hours	Dollars	
_____	_____	_____	_____	_____
_____	_____	_____	_____	_____

Figure 4.1 Illustration of job cost sheet (subsidiary ledger).

For every cost recorded in the work-in-process account of the general ledger, an entry for the same amount is made on a job cost sheet. Thus, the work-in-process account acts as a control over the subsidiary record, the job cost sheets. The sum of the costs recorded on the individual job cost sheets should equal the balance in the work-in-process account. An example of the job cost procedure is given in Exhibit 4–1. Three different entries are recorded in the general ledger and in the subsidiary record.

Exhibit 4–1 Job Cost System Illustrated

Entry No.	Transaction	Source of Entry Data
1	Material placed into production	Summary of material requisitions
2	Direct-labor cost incurred	Labor distribution sheet of timekeeper
3	Overhead applied to product	The overhead rate is $1.60 per direct-labor hour

Summary of Material Requisitions

Date	Reqn. No.	Job No.	Amount, lb	Amount, $	Type of Material
Jan. 21	26	556	60	$ 600	Plastic powder
Jan. 21	27	557	40	400	Plastic powder
			100	$1,000	

Direct-Labor Distribution Summary

Date	Job No.	Hours	Wages	Overhead Rate	Overhead Applied (DLH × $1.60)
Jan. 21	556	700	$1,400	$1.60	$1,120
Jan. 21	557	300	600	1.60	480
		1,000	$2,000		$1,600

General Ledger Entries (x's stand for beginning balances)

Material Inventory		Manufacturing Overhead	
xxxxx	(1) $1,000	xxxxx	(3) $1,600

Payroll		Work in Processs	
	(2) $2,000	(1) $1,000	
		(2) 2,000	
		(3) 1,600	

Subsidiary Record (Job Cost Sheets)

Job Cost Sheet
Job No. 556

	Material			Labor		Overhead	
Date	Req'n. No.	Amount, lb	Amount, $	Hours	Dollars	Rate	Dollars
1/21	26	60	$600	700	$1,400	$1.60	$1,120

Job Cost Sheet
Job No. 557

	Material			Labor		Overhead	
Date	Req'n. No.	Amount, lb	Amount, $	Hours	Dollars	Rate	Dollars
1/21	27	40	$400	300	$600	$1.60	$480

The total costs recorded on the job cost sheets equal the total costs recorded in the work-in-process account.

Work in Process			*Job Cost Sheets Summary*				
			Job	Material	Labor	Overhead	Total Costs
Material	$1,000						
Direct labor	2,000		556	$ 600	$1,400	$1,120	$3,120
Overhead	1,600		557	400	600	480	1,480
Balance	$4,600		Totals	$1,000	$2,000	$1,600	$4,600

When the job is completed, the job cost sheet is taken from the work-in-process file and placed in the finished goods file. The completed cost card serves as the subsidiary ledger for the finished goods account. A journal entry is then made, transferring the total cost of the job from work in process to finished goods.

There is a column on each cost card for overhead. If the job is completed during the accounting period, the overhead can be computed for the entire job rather than on a daily basis as the labor cost is incurred. If the period ends before the job is completed, the overhead is computed at that time based in some measure of activity on that job (commonly, as in this case, direct-labor hours). The total overhead on a job is the basis for the entry transferring overhead from the manufacturing overhead account to the work-in-process account (entry 3 in Exhibit 4–1).

The job-order cost system is quite expensive to maintain, because it requires considerable clerical work to record the detailed information on the job cost sheets. The process type of cost system should be used if possible. Nevertheless, it should be recognized that the job cost system fills a need in those situations where the manufacturing operation is not repetitive.

4.2 Process Cost System

The process cost system makes no attempt to account for the costs of individual items or specific groups of items. Instead, all costs are placed into "reservoirs" and allocated to product on a systematic basis. The costs may be accumulated for different processes in the production of one product, or it may be necessary to have different "reservoirs" for different products. These "reservoirs," or places to accumulate costs, are actually work-in-process accounts. Different work-in-process accounts are set up for every major manufacturing process for each product.

Assume, for example, that a manufacturing process for a single product consists of three steps. Metal is first sheared, then formed, and then painted. Three work-in-process accounts are required. The costs flow as indicated in Exhibit 4–2. (In the chart, paint is considered a direct material, although it could be treated as overhead.)

Exhibit 4–2 Process Cost System Illustrated

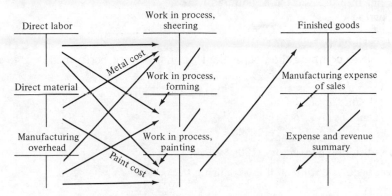

Only one overhead account is shown in the flow chart. In many cases it would be useful to set up different overhead accounts for each process. These overhead accounts are sometimes referred to as *burden centers*. The more overhead accounts, the more accurate the cost accounting tends to be; but the costs of recording the information are also increased.

If an additional product, which, say, also requires three processes, is being made, three additional work-in-process accounts, one additional finished goods account, and one or more additional overhead accounts are required. If the amount of work required for the two products were exactly the same, and the only difference were in the characteristics of the end product, no additional accounts except an additional finished goods account would have to be used.

Instead of having one work-in-process account for the shearing process, it is also possible to have three in-process accounts, one each for material, labor, and overhead. This is useful in practice.

4.2.1 Problems Peculiar to Process Cost Accounting

So far we have assumed that the amount of cost to be transferred from process 1 to process 2 is known. Actually, this type of transfer requires computations that, although simple in principle, become complicated in practice if the manufacturing process (and the cost-accounting system) is at all complicated. The procedure to be followed in computing the amount to be transferred to the next process and the amount remaining can be illustrated by a short example.

Example

Suppose that we are given the following facts relating to direct labor:

Beginning inventory	100 units ($\frac{1}{4}$ completed)
Ending inventory	100 units ($\frac{1}{2}$ completed)
Completed units during the period	500 units
Labor costs incurred during the period	$1,150
Labor in process at the beginning of the period	$75

The first step is to compute the "equivalent" units of work performed.

Total units finished	500
Plus ending inventory (200 × $\frac{1}{2}$)	100
	600
Less beginning inventory (100 × $\frac{1}{4}$)	25
Total equivalent units of labor during the period[1]	575

The second step in the solution is to compute the cost per unit of work performed during the period:

$$\text{cost per equivalent unit of labor} = \frac{\text{direct-labor costs incurred}}{\text{equivalent units of labor}}$$

$$= \frac{\$1,150}{575} = \$2/\text{unit of labor.}$$

The third step is to assume a flow of costs (FIFO, LIFO, or average). This is necessary because the cost per unit of the opening inventory rarely agrees with the cost per unit incurred during the period. In the problem being illustrated, the cost per unit of the opening inventory is

$$\frac{\$75}{100 \times 0.25} = \frac{\$75}{25} = \$3/\text{unit of labor}$$

[1] The same solution may be obtained by using a slightly different technique:

Units of labor required to *complete* the beginning inventory (100 × $\frac{3}{4}$)	75
Units of labor required to *start and complete* 400 units	400
Units of labor required to *start* the ending inventory (200 × $\frac{1}{2}$)	100
Total equivalent units of labor performed during the period	575

If a FIFO cost-flow assumption is assumed, the transfer to finished goods is computed as follows:

Opening inventory (100 × ¼ × $3)	$ 75
Required to complete the opening inventory (100 × ¾ × $2)	150
Required to start and complete 400 units (400 × 1 × $2)	800
Transfer to finished goods	$1,025

The fourth step is to compute the amount remaining in work in process. This can be done as follows:

Beginning inventory, labor in process	$ 75
Labor costs incurred during the period	1,150
	$1,225
Less amount transferred to finished goods	1,025
Amount remaining in process[2]	$ 200

The fifth step is to check the solution. This consists of adding the amount transferred to finished goods ($1,025) to the ending inventory ($200) and checking the sum ($1,225) to see that it equals the sum of the costs incurred ($1,150) and the beginning inventory ($75).

Summary: The solution consists of five steps:

1. Determine the number of equivalent units of labor performed.
2. Determine the cost per unit of work performed.
3. Assume a flow of costs and compute the transfer to finished goods.
4. Compute the ending work-in-process inventory.
5. Check the solution.

A useful review of the last three steps can be obtained by assuming a LIFO or average cost flow. The computation for the average method is given below. The reader should verify for himself that assuming a LIFO cost-flow yields an ending inventory of labor in process of $225 and transfers $1,000 to finished goods. Of course, to complete the example it is necessary to repeat this procedure for each type of labor, material, and overhead item. The value of a computerized system is obvious.

Assuming an average cost flow, we proceed as follows. The same average cost per unit is used as is used to value the amount remaining in the work in

---

[2] The $200 can also be computed (or checked) by multiplying the equivalent units of labor in the ending inventory by the labor cost per unit of labor. This can be done *if* all the ending inventory was constructed during this period.

$$200 \text{ units} \times \tfrac{1}{2} \times \$2 = \$200 \quad \text{(labor in process, ending inventory)}$$

process and to value the transfer to finished goods. The opening inventory is used in computing the average cost per unit.

$$\text{average cost per unit} = \frac{\$75 + \$1,150}{25 + 575} = \frac{1,225}{600} = \$2.04167$$

The total costs of $1,225 are split as follows:

$$
\begin{aligned}
\text{transfer to finished goods } (500 \times \$2.04167) &= \$1,020.83 \\
\text{amount remaining process } (200 \times \tfrac{1}{2} \times \$2.01467) &= \underline{204.17} \\
&= \underline{\underline{\$1,225.00}}
\end{aligned}
$$

Various compilations may occur. Some of the material may be added when the product is partially completed, or it may all be introduced at the beginning process. Part of the material may evaporate or disappear. This complicates the calculations, especially when the disappearance of material is in excess of normal. Normal spoilage or loss is spread over the good product, but abnormal spoilage is considered a loss. There are techniques for solving all these problems, which are discussed later. They are logical extensions of the techniques described here.

Process costing, unlike job-order costing, uses broad averages and applies them to large quantities of like units. Job-order costing methods concentrate on single or unique jobs, where each job or batch is different in important ways from the others.

Both process and job-order costing involve substantial clerical effort in tracing actual costs through work requisitions, work tickets, and so on. The difficulty is in part due to the emphasis on knowing the "actual cost" of product. We now turn to an alternative costing system in which predetermined costs are used to transfer units from work in process.

4.3 Standard Cost System

Standard cost systems are usually process cost systems in which accountants use set standards instead of attempting to compute an actual cost per unit for each period.[3] The major advantages of a standard cost system are that it highlights inefficiencies and allows management to manage by exception; that is, it allows management to concentrate on the areas where there are inefficiencies.

The actual labor and the actual material incurred are debited to the work-in-process accounts. The *standard labor* and *standard material* are transferred to the finished goods account. What happens to any differences between the actual costs incurred and the standard costs of work completed and in process? These differences are called *cost variances*. They are identified according to their causes and are transferred to variance accounts. For material and labor, there are two variance accounts called price and efficiency variances.

[3] Usually a standard cost system is not generally applicable to a situation where a job-order system is being used, although there are some exceptions.

Overhead is treated in a variety of ways. The following system is suggested as one of several logical procedures. A *standard* overhead rate (typically) per direct-labor hour is applied to the *actual* direct-labor hours incurred to find the amount of the manufacturing overhead incurred. This amount is transferred to the work-in-process account. The amount of overhead transferred from the work-in-process account to finished goods is found by multiplying the *standard* hours per unit of product by the *standard* overhead rate. Thus, part of the variances for overhead will be found in the work-in-process account and part in the manufacturing overhead incurred account. The nature and disposition of these variances is discussed in Chapter 5. These transfers are indicated in Exhibit 4-3.

Exhibit 4-3   Standard Cost System Illustrated

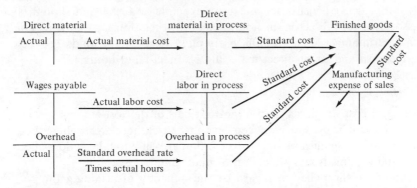

Under a standard cost system, as with the other systems discussed, the values in the work-in-process account and the finished goods account are used for determining inventory values. These values are needed in the determination of the organization's financial position and its periodic profit. But these figures, particularly on a unit basis, are also important to pricing, bidding, and other managerial decisions. Since such decisions must often be made before production is complete, the value of predetermined or standard costs is substantial. For these reasons, standard costs are commonly used in the firm's budgetary (goal-setting) process.

A standard cost system also produces cost variance between incurred costs and the standard cost at the activity level experienced. These cost variances provide one of the more important inputs to cost-control procedures, as we shall see in Chapter 5. But we need to know just how these standard costs are determined.

4.3.1 Data for Establishing Standard Costs

Perhaps the single most relied on method of estimating standard costs is to look at past experience. Trends and useful patterns of both a cyclical or seasonal nature are often revealed, together with averages through this process. The historical approach is particularly useful for estimating direct costs. However, it is common for management to place excessive reliance on the historical cost record. Past figures are supportable and apparently relieve the manager from the task of forecasting.

This is unfortunate. Often the manager's insight into the raw-materials market, the effect of economy-wide events on prices and of local events on the availability of labor, the impact of a new technology, the impact of a new intermediate goods supplier, and so on, are critical to the estimation process. The key is to estimate what future costs should be, not what these costs have been.

At times the industrial engineer, the purchasing manager, or market researcher may be able to provide useful estimates of what direct costs such as direct labor and materials should be. If indirect costs are closely related to either units of material or direct-labor hours, they may be estimated using the direct cost as the basis. Labor fringe benefits are one good example of a cost that should be closely associated with direct-labor hours. Historical relationships may also be helpful in determining whether a sufficiently close relationship holds between some indirect cost and either direct materials or direct-labor hours.[4]

4.3.2 Setting Cost Standards

The setting of cost standards is an important part of the cost-control system. These standards can be used by management to pick out those areas where there are difficulties (costs significantly in excess of standard) and to take action where action is required. This is an application of managing by exception.

What should be the policy in regard to the difficulty of attaining the cost standards? Should the standards be very difficult to attain or relatively easy to attain? Actually, there is an entire range of possibilities. The problem of setting standards is to a degree analogous to the problem of setting par for a golfer.

The theoretical standard is analogous to shooting an eighteen-hole golf course in eighteen strokes. Although this is theoretically possible, it is extremely unlikely to occur. Setting standards which are almost certain not to be attained is discouraging to workers and should be avoided.

The practical standard is analogous to shooting an 18-hole golf course in 72 (assuming that 72 is par). This 72 is difficult to attain, but a very good golfer can shoot 72 and sometimes do even better. There is more to be said in favor of this type of standard, difficult to attain but attainable, than for theoretical, impossible to attain, standards.

The normal standard is analogous to setting a par consistent with the golfer's ability (often by means of a handicap). Par for the course may be 72, but if the golfer is just a "duffer," his par may be 98, where the term "par" is used in the sense of a goal or standard of performance based on the individual's ability. The standard becomes related to the mean or expected value of the golfer's score. The use of standards that take into consideration not only the present

---

[4] Some technical procedures useful in forecasting costs are discussed in Chapter 23.

state of experience and skill of the worker but the variability in his performance as well are needed. Ideally, the skill of the worker should increase until the standard finally approaches the high level of performance called par (the 72 of the golf-course analogy); however, not everyone can shoot 72 no matter how hard he practices or how much pressure is applied from above (the learning concept discussed in Chapter 10 is relevant here). Loose standards are in a sense not standards, but they are reference points. Thus, if a golfer averages 90, he may set a standard for himself of 95 just to make sure that his variance is generally favorable. In like manner, the standards of a factory may be set so that the worker's performance is generally favorable, even though he could and should do better.

The use of standards leads to the necessity of interpreting the differences between actual costs and standard costs. (The term "standard" as used here means budgeted costs adjusted to the actual level of activity.) The analysis of cost variances could be accomplished by comparing the actual costs and standard costs and merely noting the difference. Although this would be a step in the right direction, differences between actual and standard costs have traditionally been identified with a greater degree of accuracy by the use of a technique called *variance analysis*.

Whatever the procedure of estimation, the standard set should be primarily a responsibility of the line manager involved. The use of a standard cost to establish the line manager's budget and ultimately his performance, at least in part, should be the product of discussions between the line manager and his immediate superior. The accountant is only an advisor in this process. It is a good example of the accountant's staff function as a provider of information.

4.4 Summary

In this chapter we have examined the major cost systems. Process costing is an averaging process. Accumulated costs are divided by a production measure and the resultant unit cost is used to transfer costs. Job-order costing is common where the production task differs substantively from item to item or batch to batch. Both of these systems are used to accumulate and transfer costs for the purpose of inventory valuation and product costing. Cost control under a job costing system requires that costs be recorded twice, once by job and once by department or cost center.

A standard costing system uses predetermined costs for budgeting and cost-accumulation purposes. This system is commonly combined with process costing where the latter is being used. A standard costing system provides an added dividend in that it provides data, namely cost variances, that can be used in cost-control activities. When these cost variances are accumulated in cost centers or departments, responsibility for them can be established.

Standard costs can be determined by a combination of historical perspective, expert advice, and, most important, managerial insight. Standards that represent efficient but attainable performance levels are appropriate. Allowance must be made for shrinkage, normal spoilage, and expected downtime. Final responsibility for the standard rests with the line manager and his immediate supervisor.[5] The accountant acts only in an advisory capacity to line management in the control of costs.

QUESTIONS AND PROBLEMS

4–1 The Matson Mfg. Co. specializes in producing machine tools according to specifications provided by its customers. It uses the job cost system of accounting.

Required: Enter the following information directly into the accounts in the factory ledger. Make all necessary entries on job cost sheets. All accounts not in the factory ledger are in the general ledger, which is kept by someone else. Key each item in the accounts.

  a. Materials inventory, Oct. 1 $16,500
  b. Supplies inventory, Oct. 1 $ 3,150
  c. Unfinished cost sheets, Oct. 1, as follows:

Job No.	Materials	Direct Labor		Burden (rate is $160/DLH)
1115	$1,325	400 hr	$ 800	$ 640
1118	810	250 hr	500	400
1120	765	300 hr	475	480
	$2,900		$1,775	$1,520

  d. Materials used during October were as follows:

Reqn. No.	Job No.	Cost
56	1118	$ 515
57	1120	665
58	1121	910
59	1124	720
		$2,810

  e. The balance in the manufacturing overhead account on Oct. 1 was $60 (Dr).
  f. Material purchases during October amounted to $3,890.
  g. A summary of labor costs is as follows (ignore taxes):

[5] Supplementary reading on standard costs may be found in C. Horngren, *Cost Accounting, A Managerial Emphasis*, Englewood Cliffs, N.J.: Prentice-Hall, Inc., 1972, Chaps. 4, 7, and 17.

Job No.	No of Hours	Cost
1115	50	$ 95
1118	120	215
1120	85	160
1121	65	120
1124	30	65
Total direct labor	350	$665
Indirect labor	72	115
	422	$770

h. Supplies purchased during October were $440.
i. Supplies consumed during October were $545.
j. Miscellaneous other burden charges for October were $105.
k. The burden rate is the same as in previous periods ($1.60/DLH).
l. The following jobs were completed in October and delivered to the customers: Jobs 1115, 1118, and 1120.
m. The accounts in the factory ledger are:
Materials, Inventory
Supplies, Inventory
Burden
Material in Process
Labor in Process
Burden in Process
General Ledger

The form to use for the cost sheets is as follows:

Cost Sheet
Job No. _____

Material		Direct Labor		Burden	
Requisition Number	Cost	Hours	Cost	Rate	Cost

4–2 The Labor-in-Process Company

a. Compute the equivalent units of labor performed on the following products:

Product	Beginning Inventory in Process	Completed Production	Ending Inventory in Process
1	100 units ($\frac{1}{4}$ completed)	200	None
2	——	200	100 units ($\frac{1}{4}$ completed)
3	100 units ($\frac{1}{4}$ completed)	200	100 units ($\frac{1}{2}$ completed)
4	100 units ($\frac{1}{2}$ completed)	200	100 units ($\frac{1}{4}$ completed)

b. If the labor cost incurred in making product 2 during the period was $10,000, compute the amount of labor in the ending inventory of labor in process for product 2.

c. If the labor cost incurred during the period in manufacturing product 3 was $20,000, compute the amount of labor in the ending inventory of labor in process of product 3. The beginning inventory of labor in process was $2,600. Assume a FIFO flow of costs.

4–3 The Allison Manufacturing Company produces a single product. Raw material A is committed to the production process at the start of process 1. Operating data for the period just ended are as follows:

	Process 1		Process 2	
Beginning inventories	270 lb ($\frac{1}{3}$ finished)	$1,152	160 lb ($\frac{1}{2}$ finished)	$1,972
Raw material A used	650 lb	1,170		
Direct labor and burden		5,616		3,774
Ending inventories	200 lb ($\frac{3}{4}$ finished)		90 lb ($\frac{1}{3}$ finished)	

The weight of the finished product is exactly equal to the weight of the material used.

Required:

a. How many pounds of product were transferred from process 1 to process 2 during the period? How many equivalent units of labor were performed in process 1? What is the cost per equivalent unit of labor and burden in process 1 for the period?

b. Set up "T" accounts for process 1, process 2, and finished goods, and enter therein the operating results for the period. Assume a FIFO flow.

c. What was the labor and burden cost per pound of product (cost per equivalent unit) in process 2 for this period?

d. How do labor costs for the period just ended compare with those of the preceding period for process 1? Assume that material costs were the same in each period and that a constant overhead rate is used throughout the year.

4–4 The following information applies to the only product produced by the May Company:

Work in process, January 31 inventory, 900 units, $\frac{1}{3}$ completed.
Work in process, January 1 inventory, 800 units, $\frac{1}{2}$ completed.
Product finished during January, 1,000 units.

Direct labor cost for January	$2,205
Material used during January	$3,850
Direct labor in process, January 1	$ 800
Material in process, January 1	$3,200
Overhead in process, January 1	$1,600

The material is introduced at the beginning of the production process. The labor is applied evenly throughout the production process. The overhead rate is $2 per direct-labor dollar.

Required:

a. The equivalent units of labor performed during January.

b. Units of product started during January.

c. Average cost of equivalent unit of product started and produced during January.

The following two parts assume a FIFO flow of costs:

d. The cost of goods finished during January.

e. The cost of the January 31 inventory is:

_____ direct labor in process, January 31

_____ material in process, January 31

_____ overhead in process, January 31

4–5 The Firehouse Company uses a LIFO method for inventory. The company does not use a finished goods account but transfers the cost of product sold directly from work in process to the "Cost of Goods Sold" account.

The following information applies to the month of July:

July 1, inventory of labor in process, 1,000 equivalent units which cost $2,000.

Production for July was 100 equivalent units. The direct-labor cost for the month was $300.

During the month, 900 units were shipped.

The amount of labor cost to be transferred to cost of goods sold was computed as follows:

$$\text{labor costing rate} = \frac{\text{direct-labor cost for July}}{\text{equivalent units produced}} = \frac{\$300}{100} = \$3/\text{unit}$$

$$\text{transfer to cost of goods sold} = \text{units shipped} \times \text{labor costing rate}$$

$$= 900 \times \$3 = \$2,700$$

Required: Comment on the procedure followed.

4–6 The plant manager of the Waterhouse Company is confused by accounting reports of income which have been coming across his desk. It appears recently that the more inefficient the workers are (according to the production reports), the higher the profit reported by the accounting department. Since this does not appear to be reasonable, he has called in an expert (you).

The Waterhouse Company manufactures dashboard assemblies for a large automobile producer. Beginning in July the company starts building up an inventory so that when the new model year starts in October, it can supply a steady stream of product without resorting to an excessive amount of overtime.

The company has adopted a process cost-accounting system, using actual costs. Since the stock is handled so that the oldest goods are shipped first, a FIFO assumption as to the flow of costs is followed. As is common with many manufacturers, the Waterhouse Company keeps all product in the work-in-process account until it is shipped and does not use a finished goods account (work in process is credited and manufacturing cost of goods sold is debited when goods are shipped).

The following information is made available to you for the month of September (all the information refers to direct labor in process):

Beginning work-in-process inventory (Sept. 1):		$2,250
Units of goods completed	850	
Units of goods one-half completed	100	
Units shipped during the month	100	
Ending work in process inventory:		
Units of goods completed	975	
Units of goods one-half completed	50	
Direct-labor costs for the month	$600	
Equivalent units of production during September	200	

The amount of direct labor cost transferred to cost of goods sold was computed by the following procedure:

Ending Inventory, equivalent units:

Goods completed	975
Goods in process (50 × ½)	25
Total equivalent units in inventory	1,000

Cost per unit produced during the period ($600 ÷ 200)	$3.00

Cost of ending inventory (assuming that the most recently produced goods are still in inventory) 1,000 × $3.00	$3,000

Computation of transfer to cost of goods sold:

Work in process, beginning of period	$2,520
Plus costs incurred	600
	$3,120
Less ending inventory	3,000
Amount to be transferred to cost of goods sold	$ 120

Required:
a. Why does the above procedure give misleading information?
b. If the direct-labor costs for the month had been $800 (assuming the same production), what would have been the transfer to cost of goods sold?
c. Compute the transfer to cost of goods sold, following a reasonably correct FIFO procedure.

4–7 Part I. The Stan-low Corporation makes products A and B. The company uses two work-in-process accounts, one for product A and one for product B.

The following standard costs have been established and are used in the cost accounting system:

	Product A	Product B
Material:		
Standard cost of wood	$0.20	$0.30
Standard cost of paint	—	0.02
Labor:		
Cutters (standard cost per unit)	0.40	0.60
Finishers (standard cost per unit)	0.25	0.30
Overhead rates:		
Variable (varnish, power, glue, etc.)	0.25*	0.50*
Fixed (foreman, depreciation, etc.)	0.75*	1.00*

* Per direct-labor dollar. Cutters earn $2.00 per hour; finishers, $2.50 per hour.

Required:

a. Compute the standard cost per unit for each product.
b. If the total fixed costs budgeted for the year were $30,000, and if $7,500 of these costs were allocated or identified with product A, what amount of direct-labor dollars was used in computing the fixed overhead rate? What would the fixed overhead rate be if the level of activity used to compute the rate was 200,000 units of product A?

Part II.   The following information relates to the month of May for product B:

Cost of wood used	$310
Cost of paint used	$21
Direct labor, cutters	$620
Direct labor, finishers	$290
Overhead incurred:	
Variable	$450
Fixed	$1,000
Units finished during May	950
Units in process May 31	
(units assumed to be one-half completed, labor and paint; all completed, wood)	250
Units in process May 1	
(units assumed to be one-half completed, labor and paint; all completed, wood)	150

The work in process at the beginning of May was valued at standard cost.

Required: Set up a work-in-process account for product B. Record the beginning work in process, the costs incurred, the transfer to finished goods, and the closing of the variances to an account called "Variances from Standard Costs." Overhead is to be absorbed to product, using direct-labor dollars.

4–8 The Newcastle Corporation makes one model of a product. The following information is available for the month of April:

	Actual Costs Incurred	In Process Inventory, the Beginning of the Period at Standard Cost	Goods Finished During April at Standard Cost	Goods in Process, End of Period at Standard Cost
Direct material (requisitioned)	$ 43,400	$12,000	$ 40,000	$13,000
Direct labor	84,300	20,000	80,000	20,400
Fixed overhead	21,000	5,000	20,000	5,100
Variable overhead	163,000	40,000	160,000	40,800

There were $7,500 of finished goods (500 units) in inventory at the beginning of the period. During the month of April, 20,000 units were completed and 19,000 units were shipped to customers.

The company uses four variance accounts:

Direct-material variance
Direct-labor variance
Fixed-overhead variance
Variable-overhead variance

The overhead rates used are:

$$\text{variable overhead} = \$2 \times \text{direct-labor dollars}$$
$$\text{fixed overhead} = \$0.25 \times \text{direct-labor dollars}$$

Required: Set up "T" accounts and prepare summary entries to record the given information.

4–9 If overtime is incurred in a job cost shop, how should the overtime be charged to the jobs? Does it make any difference if the job worked on during the overtime period was accepted after the regular work hours of the shop had been scheduled?

4–10 Would you want to use a fixed (that is, determined at the beginning of the budget period) or a variable basis (that is, based on some measure of actual activity) to allocate the following corporate costs to divisions?
  a. Corporate controller's costs.
  b. President's salary and staff costs.
  c. Trucking costs (assuming the corporate office handles all divisional transportation).

4–11 If a company acquires excess capacity (say it builds a boiler twice as large as is currently needed), should the cost of that excess capacity be considered a cost of product during the early periods, when that part of the capacity is not being used?

4–12 Should standard costs be used for planning purposes?

4–13 Do you think cost standards should be easy or difficult to attain? Discuss.

4–14 "Standard direct labor hours allowed for work done are superior to actual direct labor hours as an activity measure." Comment.

4–15 The Fabian Manufacturing Company, Inc. produces low-quality musical records under the brand name "Sough." Orders in units of 1,000 are accepted for specific quantities of a given record, which has been prerecorded, and are processed by order. The single process by which the records are made is a continuous one. Materials consist of only blank, labeled records that are processed to match the master record and then automatically packaged in batches of 1,000. Records are kept only of actual costs (*no* standard cost system is employed).

The accounting office was destroyed by an earthquake on April 1 and only certain facts were salvaged from the ruins (fortunately the "Artist" and the manufacturing plant were saved).

Facts known for the 1st quarter of operations:

1. Wages paid in cash since Jan. 1 $10,000 (Dr. Accrued Wages Payable)
   Wages accrued payable Jan. 1 $ 5,000
   Wages accrued payable April 1 $15,000
   (Wages are for both direct labor (at $2.50 per hr) and indirect labor (at $1 per hr)
2. Total overhead for the period $10,000
   Overhead applied ($2 per Direct Labor Hour) $12,000
3.

Orders Worked On	Completion Jan. 1	Labor Completion April 1
#10 Screech Records (1000 rec.)	0	100%
#11 Stamp Studios (2000 rec.)	0	80%
#12 Farce Films (1000 rec.)	0	?

No other orders were in process Jan. 1 or in Finished Goods.
4. Materials Stores Card.

Records				Bal Jan 1 39,000 (13,000 × $3.00)	
Date	Ref	Rec.	Issued	Balance	
1/10	#10		2000 lbs @ 3.00	11,000 @ 3.00	
2/15	#11		4000 lbs. @	7,0	
3/5	#12				

All materials enter at the beginning of the process for each order.
5. Finished goods Inventory April 1: Job #10 $15,000.

Required:
a. What was the *total labor* expense applicable to production for the quarter?
b. What was the total *direct* labor expense for the quarter?
c. How many indirect labor hours were used this quarter?
d. What is the best estimate for the dollar value of materials charged to work in process for the quarter?
e. From what accounting record would the $15,000 finished goods figure for job #10 most likely be obtained?
f. Assume (see part e) that this record was destroyed (but the $15,000 figure is known in total.) Derive the $15,000 figure. (*Hint:* Use the overhead rate given above and try to determine the hours of direct labor spent on this job.)

g. What costs are relevant to the Stamp Studio Job? (Assume the *information* supplied by the answer to part f is relevant here.)

h. Determine the labor percentage completion of the Farce Films Job.

4–16 June production data for a company that produces a single product are as follows:

Units in process — beginning	500
Stage of completion* beginning	25%
Units started	2,500
Units completed and transferred	2,000
Units in process — ending	1,000
Stage of completion* — ending	75%

    * Refers to conversion costs.

Required: Under each of the following assumptions, compute the equivalent units of material added to process during June:

a. Material is added at the beginning of processing,

b. Material is added at the end of processing,

c. Material is added when the processing is 50% complete,

d. Material is added when the processing is 20% complete,

e. Half the material is added at the beginning of processing, and the remaining half is added when the processing is 90% complete.

4–17 The Alpha Company manufactures a single product and uses a process cost system. The product is composed of Material 1 and Material 2. Material 1 is added at the beginning of the process while Material 2 is added when the process is 50% complete. Conversion costs are applied uniformly throughout the production process. The following data apply to the month of July.

	Units	Amounts
Beginning inventories (30% complete)*	100	
Material 1		$ 542
Material 2		327
Conversion costs		551
Material 1 used		2,540
Material 2 used		3,986
Direct labor		2,680
Variable overhead		1,623
Fixed overhead		5,877
Ending inventories (75% complete)*	150	
Started in July	500	
Completed in July	450	

    * Refers to conversion costs.

Required:

a. Prepare a schedule computing the equivalent units of production in July for materials and conversion.
b. Using average costing, find the cost of goods completed and transferred to finished goods, and find the cost of the ending inventory.

4–18 The Beta Company produces one product which passes through three departments. Materials are added at the beginning of processing in Department 1. Units from Department 1 are transferred to Department 2 where a second type of material is added at the beginning of the process. After the work in Department 2 is complete, the units are transferred to Department 3 where they are completed. No materials are added to the product in Department 3. Conversion costs in each department are applied evenly throughout the manufacturing process.

The following data apply to the September work-in-process:

	Units
Beginning inventory:	
Department 1 (50% complete)	500
Department 2	0
Department 3 (25% complete)	200
Ending inventory:	
Department 1 (75% complete)	100
Department 2 (80% complete)	150
Department 3	0
Department 1 began work on 2,000 units in September. There was no spoilage.	

Required: Prepare a production report by department which shows the equivalent units of production for September.

4–19 The DeBrosse Company produces a single product and uses a standard cost system. Direct materials are added at the beginning of the production process and conversion costs are applied uniformly throughout the manufacturing process. The following standards apply to the product:

Standard cost per unit:

Materials	$2.66
Direct labor and burden	3.22
Total	$5.88

Production data for February are as follows:

	Units	Cost
Beginning inventory (50% complete)	100	
Materials		$ 266
Direct labor and burden		161
Units completed	800	
Ending inventory (10% complete)	200	
Material costs incurred for Feb.		2,316
Actual direct labor and burden for Feb.		2,752

Required:
a. Compute the standard cost of units completed and the standard cost of the ending work-in-process.
b. Compute total material variance and total conversion cost variance for February.

4–20 Discuss some advantages and disadvantages of standard cost systems.

Chapter 5

Cost Control
and Variances

In Chapter 4 we discussed standard cost systems. In such systems, direct labor, direct material, and overhead are charged to work-in-process accounts using standard or actual costs. However, work in process is also carried to finished goods at standard cost. This typically results in balances being left in these accounts which represent a difference between the costs incurred and the standard cost of the output obtained. These differences are called *cost variances*.

If a standard cost-accounting system is used, the accountant has the task of analyzing these cost variances. This is the first step toward the goal of identifying the factors that caused the differences between the standard and actual costs so that important inefficiencies can be eliminated.

5.1 Cost Variances: General

A cost variance results from the comparison of an actual cost with a preset standard (or budgeted) cost. Actual costs differ from standard costs for many specific reasons (the wrong type of material was used, the material was the incorrect size, the machine was not adjusted correctly, too much material was used, and so on), but, in general, variances for labor, material, and variable overhead are classified as either "price" or "efficiency" variances. Price variances are caused by payment of a price higher or lower than the standard price (or wage rate). Frequently, the organization is not able to control the price it pays for a raw material or for labor, but there are exceptions. For example, material may be purchased from several suppliers who have different prices, different transportation costs, and different discounts for quantity purchases. In like manner, workers of several different pay grades may be able to perform a function. If only workers in the higher pay grades are employed, this may create a wage variance.

Usually the "efficiency" variance is more subject to control by management than the price variance, and where this is so, it should receive the greater attention. Efficiency variances are caused by using a different amount of real resources, such as labor hours, or material, than the amount budgeted to accomplish the task.

Overhead variances are usually divided into variable- and fixed-overhead variances. In addition to a price variance, sometimes called a fixed (or variable) overhead budget variance, and efficiency variances there are several fixed-overhead activity variances that can be used to place a dollar measure on the underutilization of capacity.

A manager must be very careful in interpreting the significance of a cost variance. For example, the significance of the material and the direct-labor variances depends on the policy concerning the tightness of the standard used. If the standard reflects an attainable level of performance (say, a normal cost standard), then an unfavorable variance of substantial size should be considered a candidate for investigation.

The variances described above are measured in dollar terms. Physical measures could also be used for the material-usage and labor-efficiency variances (although not for the spending variances). Since the standard wage rates and the standard unit prices are reasonably easy to establish, however, the dollar measures of the efficiency variances are likely to be useful.

The sign of the variance indicates whether the variance is favorable or unfavorable. (The convention of specifying a positive variance as being unfavorable is arbitrary.) It is generally (but incorrectly) assumed that an unfavorable variance reflects inefficiency and a favorable variance indicates efficiency. They may instead, for example, merely reflect changed conditions since the standards were established or, alternatively, the effects of random factors over which the manager has no control.

Frequently, cost variances, even of large sizes, are not controllable by the manager whose performance is being measured. For example, the cost of steel may increase throughout the country after standards are set, creating an unfavorable price variance for the user of the steel. But the purchasing agent of a using company does not have control over this event. For another example, an unfavorable labor-efficiency variance may reflect a power failure rather than a situation that is correctable by the company or the cost center. It is important for the manager to realize that the report of cost variances indicates places where something is causing increased costs, not that inefficiency necessarily exists. In fact, if the standard has been set incorrectly, there might not be excessive costs, but rather a difficult-to-interpret measure.

The variable-overhead variances exhibit a similarity to the material and labor variances and their interpretation is similar. For example, an unfavorable variable-overhead efficiency variance tends to show the amount of variable overhead that was incurred because of an excessive amount of direct labor. The variable-overhead budget variance indicates the difference between the variable overhead incurred and the variable overhead budgeted (the variable overhead budgeted is adjusted to the actual level of direct labor activity). However, particular variable-overhead costs may vary with other measures of activity. For example, the number of accounts receivable clerks varies with the number of billings. Also, the overhead cost may lead or lag behind the direct-labor cost. Thus, a variable-overhead budget variance may be the result of excessive expenditures or merely of the method of computation. Relationships here are often multiple and complex. The goal is an activity measure (or set of measures) that provides useful data; a measure of activity that exactly defines the amount of variable overhead is not likely to be found.

The analysis of fixed-overhead-capacity variances is somewhat more complex, and different variance breakdowns have been suggested by various authors. Unfortunately, the variances computed as by-products of product-costing techniques are often inappropriately used for control purposes as well.[1]

The fixed-overhead-capacity variances (or activity variances) are not usable for control purposes. Decisions such as pricing and output are marginal decisions, and the fixed costs of the firm should not affect those decisions if profits are to be maximized. Although avoidable fixed costs do affect decisions such as adding and abandoning a product, the relevant costs are not the historical fixed costs but rather the opportunity costs of the factors of production. It is true that the capacity variances can bring to management's attention the presence of slack resources.

We turn now to a discussion of how specific cost variances are computed and to some of the problems in their interpretation. We will discuss the following broad classifications: Labor variances, material variances, overhead variances, and mix variances.

5.2 Direct-Cost Variances

In this section we discuss labor and material cost variances. The variances include:

Labor-wage variance	$ xx
Labor-efficiency variance	xx
Total labor variance	$xxx
Material-price variance	$ xx
Material-usage variance	xx
Total material variance	$xxx

[1] See C. T. Horngren, "A Contribution Margin Approach to the Analysis of Capacity Utilization," *The Accounting Review*, April 1967, pp. 254–264, and K. Schwayder, "A Note

5.2.1 Labor Variances

A common practice is to charge (debit) the actual labor cost to a labor-in-process account and transfer from this account to finished goods (or to the next process) at standard. This means that the credit to the labor-in-process account is obtained by multiplying the standard hours of labor by the standard rate of pay per hour. The difference between the actual labor cost incurred and the standard labor applied is the labor variance.

The labor variance can then be broken up into the part caused by paying higher-than-standard rates of pay (the wage-rate variance) and the part that is caused by working an excessive number of hours (the efficiency variance).

The wage-rate variance is equal to the hours actually worked times the difference between the actual and standard wage rates:

wage-rate variance = actual hours × (actual wage rate − standard wage rate)

$$= H_A(W_A - W_S)$$

wage-rate variance = actual wages − standard cost of actual hours

$$= H_A W_A - W_S H_A$$

The efficiency variance is equal to the standard wage rate times the difference between the actual hours and the standard hours:

efficiency variance = standard wage rate × (actual hours − standard hours)

$$= W_S(H_A - H_S)$$

The wage-rate variance gives that portion of the labor variance caused by paying an amount per hour other than the standard rate. The efficiency variance discloses the extra cost incurred because of hours worked in excess of standard hours or the saving because fewer than the standard hours were worked. Note that if hours in excess of standard are worked, they are valued at standard wage rates for purposes of computing the efficiency variance. It is sometimes helpful to see the variances pictured graphically.[2] This is done in Figure 5.1.

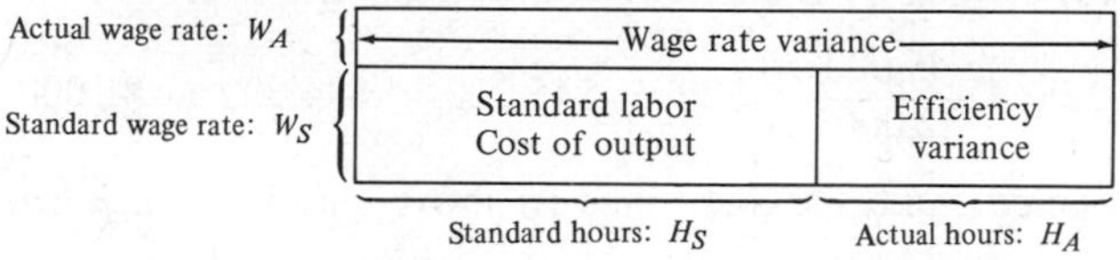

Figure 5.1   Labor wage rate and efficiency variances.

---

on a Contribution Margin Approach to the Analysis of Capacity Utilization," *The Accounting Review*, January 1968, pp. 101–104. The essential ideas in these articles are covered later in this chapter.

[2] It can be argued that the upper right-hand area, in Figure 5.1 which is caused by both the excess hours and excess wages, should be isolated as a third variance. If it can be argued that these excess hours should have been obtained at the standard rate, the present breakdown is satisfactory.

Computation of Standard Hours Worked

The total of standard hours worked is obtained by multiplying the equivalent units produced during the period by the current work standards (expressed in hours per unit). Before a product goes into production, engineers take out their boards, stopwatches, and slide rules, and compute how many hours (or minutes) of labor are required to produce each end product and each component part. If the time required to produce product A is 10 minutes, the current work standard is 10 minutes. If there are 600 units of product A produced during the period, the standard units of labor are 6,000 minutes, or 100 standard hours. Beginning and ending inventories are taken into consideration in the same manner as they were handled in computing equivalent units of product for process cost accounting. (See Chapter 4 for a discussion of equivalent units.)

Example

Given the following information, let us compute the labor variances:

Work standard per unit for product A	0.20 hr
Equivalent units of product A produced	100,000
Actual hours of direct-labor time	22,000 hr
Actual wages paid to direct laborers	$45,000
Standard wages per direct-labor hour	$2
Budgeted direct-labor hours for the period	80,000 hr

It should first be noted that the budgeted direct-labor hours do not enter into the solution of this problem. Budgeted direct hours (the budgeted level of activity for the period) do not affect the computation of labor variances. Also, solving this type of problem does not hinge on memorizing a series of formulas, but rather on an understanding of the separate variances.

WAGE-RATE VARIANCE. This is the difference between the actual and standard wage rates applied to the total hours worked. The actual wage rate is equal to the actual wages ($45,000) divided by the actual hours (22,000):

$$\text{wage-rate variance} = 22,000\left(\frac{\$45,000}{22,000} - \$2\right) = \$45,000 - \$44,000 = \$1,000$$

The $1,000 wage-rate variance is unfavorable, since an above-standard wage was paid.

EFFICIENCY VARIANCE. This is the difference between the hours actually worked and the standard hours that should have been worked to obtain the amount of output, valued at the standard wage rate:

$$\text{efficiency variance} = \text{standard rate} \times (\text{actual hours} - \text{standard hours})$$

$$= \$2(22,000 - 20,000) = \$4,000$$

The $4,000 efficiency variance is also unfavorable in this case, since extra hours above standard were required.

The figure of 20,000 standard hours of direct labor was obtained by multiplying the equivalent units produced by the work standard per unit:

$$\text{standard hours} = 100,000 \times 0.20 = 20,000 \text{ hr.}$$

The unfavorable efficiency variance may have been caused by one or a combination of factors, for example,

1. Poor-quality materials.
2. Poor quality labor.
3. Machines that have not been kept in adequate repair.
4. Improved product quality control.

To learn more, the manager must examine his operation. We do, however, have one clue already. The fact that the labor-efficiency variance was unfavorable may mean that better-than-average workers were used. If so, this would rule out poor-quality labor as an explanatory factor.

5.2.2 Material Variances

Material variances are very similar to labor variances. The variance titles change slightly, but that is about all. We now speak of a price variance instead of a wage-rate variance, and a usage variance instead of an efficiency variance, but the computations are equivalent:

Material price variance = actual quantity $\times$ (actual price $-$ standard price)

$$= Q_A(P_A - P_S)$$

Here $P_A - P_S$ may also represent actual unit purchase cost $-$ standard cost of a unit of output. The second computation is

material usage variance = standard price

$$\times \text{ (actual quantity} - \text{standard quantity)}$$

$$= P_S(Q_A - Q_S)$$

These variances are represented graphically in Figure 5.2.

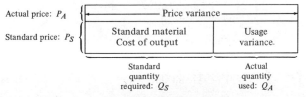

Figure 5.2　Material price and usage variances.

The standard quantity of material used is equal to the units produced times the standard material usage per unit of product. The importance of an accurate count of units produced cannot be overstated, for it is the foundation of all efficiency variance computations. Firms often have difficulty getting accurate counts because human beings are subject to accidental and intentional errors. Mechanical counts often serve as a check, but, unfortunately, they are also subject to manipulation. The best check on reported production is the inventory of finished goods. If production reports are inflated, the ending inventory of finished goods will disclose this fact.

Equally important to good production counts are reliable material usage and labor work standards. If these standards are not carefully made out at the beginning of the accounting period, they can lead to faulty financial accounting as well as a blunting of the cost accounting system as a tool for controlling costs. One way of ensuring that the standards are reasonable is for the cost accountant actually to get into the plant and learn about the production operation. In one situation where the cost accountant was using a material usage standard of 5 pounds, it should have been 0.5 pound. This error in placing of the decimal point would have been caught sooner if the accountant had been familiar with the manufacturing process and the product being made.

Example

Let us compute the material variances given the following information (the ending inventory of work in process is equal to the beginning inventory):

Material standard per unit of product	0.50 lb
Equivalent units of product produced	100,000
Actual quantity of material used	46,000 lb
Actual cost of material used	$135,000
Standard cost per pound	$3

The *material-price variance* is the difference between the actual and standard prices per unit of material applied to the actual quantity of material used. The actual cost per pound is equal to the actual cost incurred, divided by the actual quantity used:

$$\text{material-price variance} = \text{actual quantity}$$
$$\times \left(\frac{\text{actual cost incurred}}{\text{actual quantity}} - \text{standard price} \right)$$

$$\text{material-price variance} = 46{,}000 \left(\frac{\$135{,}000}{46{,}000} - \$3.00 \right)$$

$$= \$135{,}000 - \$138{,}000$$

$$= -\$3{,}000 \qquad \text{a favorable variance}$$

The *material-usage variance* is the difference between the actual quantity used and the amount that should have been used, valued at standard prices:

material-usage variance = standard price

$$\times \text{ (actual quantity } - \text{ standard quantity)}$$

material-usage variance = \$3.00 (46,000 − 50,000)

$$= -\$12,000 \qquad \text{a favorable variance}$$

The 50,000 pounds (standard quantity) was obtained by multiplying the units produced by the material standard:

$$\text{standard quantity} = 100,000 \times 0.50 = 50,000 \text{ lb}$$

If there had been changes in work in process, these changes must be taken into consideration in computing the standard usage of material.

When both the price and quantity used exceed the standard, the additional expense due to the higher price for the extra quantity may arbitrarily be assigned to the price variance (as above). An alternative approach is to use the following definitions:

$$\text{price variance} = Q_S(P_A - P_S)$$

$$\text{usage variance} = P_S(Q_A - Q_S)$$

$$\text{joint variance} = (P_A - P_S)(Q_A - Q_S)$$

This three-way breakdown of the total material variance is illustrated in Figure 5.3.

Actual price: P_A	Price variance	Joint variance
Standard price: P_S	Standard material Cost of output	Usage variance
	Standard quantity required: Q_S	Actual quantity used: Q_A

Figure 5.3   Material variance: 3-way breakdown.

If we assume that the situation described by the material example is related to the data in the labor-variance example, we can make some additional tentative observations about the labor-efficiency variance. The favorable material price variance might suggest poorer-quality materials. Further, the favorable material usage variance might be possible, given poorer materials, with good work (perhaps even extra work) by a high-quality work force. Such a high-quality work force was suggested by the unfavorable wage-rate variance. We stress that these are only guesses that are consistent with the facts: the operating manager should have a reasonable feel for the actual situation.

5.3 Overhead Variances

To analyze overhead variances, it is first necessary to separate the overhead incurred and the overhead applied to product into its fixed and variable components. The variances for fixed and variable overhead are computed individually.

The following discussion assumes that the actual overhead costs are debited to two accounts, Fixed Overhead Incurred and Variable Overhead Incurred. The overhead is applied to in-process accounts using the actual direct-labor hours worked times the rates for fixed and variable overhead. The overhead is transferred from the in-process accounts to a finished goods account using the standard direct-labor hours worked and the same overhead rates as used in the first transfer. The variances are found in the overhead incurred and the in-process accounts.

5.3.1 Variable-Overhead Variances

There are two variable-overhead variances, the budget variance and the efficiency variance. They are analogous to the price and efficiency variances encountered in labor and material. The efficiency variance occurs because the actual hours worked differ from the standard hours. A budget variance occurs when the actual variable overhead incurred differs from the variable overhead budgeted for the actual level of operations experienced.

$$\text{efficiency variance} = \text{variable-overhead rate}$$
$$\times \text{ (actual hours} - \text{standard hours)}$$
$$= V_S(H_A - H_S)$$
$$\text{budget or spending variance} = \text{actual variable overhead}$$
$$- \text{ (actual hours} \times \text{variable-overhead rate)}$$
$$= H_A(V_A - V_S)$$

The amount left in the Variable Overhead Incurred account after the transfer to the in-process account is the budget variance. The debit to the account is the actual overhead incurred, and the credit is the actual hours times the standard variable-overhead rate.

The efficiency variance is found in the Variable Overhead in Process account. The debit to this account is the same as the credit to the overhead incurred account (actual hours × variable-overhead rate). The transfer from this account is the variable-overhead rate times the standard hours; thus, the balance in the account is the variable-overhead efficiency variance.

These variances are diagrammed in Figure 5.4.

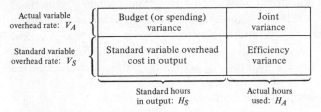

Figure 5.4 Variable overhead variances.

5.3.2 Fixed-Overhead Rates and Variances

When overhead rates are determined for product costing purposes and applied using direct labor hours, the rates are usually based on either practical or normal capacity. We shall concentrate here on physical measures (direct labor hours) of the fixed-overhead efficiency and activity variances.

Practical capacity is difficult to define, as we have seen. It is sometimes defined as the most efficient point of operations (where average variable costs are a minimum for a given set of fixed factors of production). However, many firms have relatively flat average variable-cost and average total-cost curves over a wide range of activity and thus can produce past that point with little loss of efficiency. Practical capacity can also be defined as the minimum of the average total-cost curve or the point at which the firm would operate if there were no shortage of orders. The latter makes practical capacity equivalent to the point where marginal cost equals marginal revenue. A common practice is to resort to industry usage. Thus, if the industry works 6 days a week, 20 hours a day, this becomes practical capacity. Another industry may commonly work only 8 hours a day, 5 days a week, and this becomes practical capacity. As in Chapter 3, we shall define practical capacity as the output at which long- and short-run costs are equal. If the firm wants to produce more than the amount where this equality exists, it should obtain more fixed factors of production. When a firm operates below practical capacity, as is often the case, the use of overhead rates based on practical capacity for product costing causes some of the budgeted fixed costs to be expensed.

Because practical capacity is difficult to determine, normal activity is frequently used. Normal activity has as its objective the absorption of all overhead to product in a normal year; thus it is the mean or expected activity not of one year but of several years. Some accountants maintain that a typical year should carry its own weight, and thus a normal activity concept should be used for product costing.

The use of a normal activity base implies that year-end variances are expected to average out over time. In practice the variances left at the end of each accounting period are written off or allocated between inventory and expense for costing purposes. For control purposes, however, we are not concerned with the end-of-the-year treatment.

Expected activity is an additional basis of cost absorption which is sometimes used. The expected activity is the output level anticipated for the period in question. Using expected activity to absorb fixed overhead costs results in low unit cost in periods of high expected activity and high unit costs in periods of low expected activity. This characteristic (cost being a function of expected activity) lessens the usefulness of the calculation.

The three basic fixed overhead variances are:

1. Budget variance.
2. Efficiency variance.
3. Activity variance.

The *fixed-overhead budget variance* is the difference between the budgeted and actual fixed costs for the period.

Expressed in physical units the *fixed overhead efficiency variance* (or *effectiveness variance*) is the difference in actual input hours and standard hours of output.

The *fixed overhead activity variance* is the difference between the actual input activity and practical capacity. For our purposes, however, we find it useful to break down the fixed overhead activity variance into three components (see Appendix 5B for three additional variances). A useful way to describe the relevant variances is through an examination of the schematic diagram presented in Figure 5.5. In this figure the variances are all expressed in physical units of output or input (actual or standard direct labor hours). The units could be converted into dollar measures by multiplying them by standard costs per dollar of labor, but this introduces complexities. In line with the previous discussion all undesirable variances are positive.

The *budgeted-capacity variance* (expected) is the difference between the activity level at practical capacity and the activity level budgeted at the beginning of the period (1,275 − 1,250 = 25 hours). This variance represents the difference between the expected activity level for the budget period and the practical capacity of the activity. Since the firm can produce at its practical-capacity level

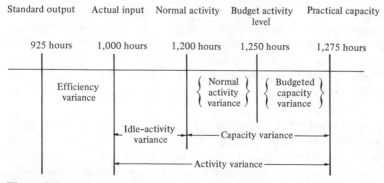

Figure 5.5   Activity levels relevant to cost control.

without expansion of facilities, the idle-capacity variance is a measure of the slack in the system. Large and persistent variances here reflect on long-range planning decisions, the ability of the marketing activity to penetrate potential markets, or perhaps changes in economic conditions. Period differences are expected. This is an *ex ante* concept. Since this is an *ex ante* concept, it should be calculated early and made available so that management may adjust its plans, if possible, to make some use of this expected idle capacity.

The *normal-activity variance* is the difference between the budgeted (expected) activity level and a normal level of activity (1,250 − 1,200 = 50 hours). Variances between the normal activity level and the expected budgeted activity are likely due to trend, cyclical, and seasonal influences. (Sometimes the normal-capacity variance and the budgeted-capacity variance are combined and called the capacity variance.)

The normal activity to be encountered over a period of several years should be one important input to the design of the plant, and thus there should be a close relationship between normal activity and practical capacity. The relationship would probably be closer than that suggested by the figures in the present example, although (because of the nonsymmetric nature of cost behavior and opportunity losses) practical capacity would be planned to exceed the normal demand for capacity. Wide differences (between normal activity and practical capacity) might reflect poor long-run activity forecasts in the past. If, on the other hand, the utilization of an asset is expected to increase through time, the budgeted (expected) activity level in the early years could easily be substantially less than the normal activity or practical capacity. The normal-activity variance and the budgeted-capacity variance together can be called, simply, the capacity variance.

The *activity variance* is the difference between practical capacity and actual input activity level (1,275 − 1,000 = 275 units). The variance represents the failure of actual activity to correspond to the practical capacity level. An unfavorable variance might be due to insufficient sales or equipment breakdowns that prevented the firm from utilizing all its capacity. The reader is warned that the terminology "activity variance" is used differently by different authors. It is useful to have a name for the difference between normal activity and actual input. This variance will be known here as the *idle-capacity variance* (1,200 − 1,000 = 200 hours).

The *efficiency variance* is the difference between the actual activity level and the standard activity level for the actual output (1,000 − 925 = 75 hours). This variance provides a measure of how effectively the actual activity was conducted. For example, an unfavorable efficiency variance may indicate poorly motivated or poorly skilled workers. Further indications of the actual problem may be sought by examining other variances, such as the labor variances. This variance is also called the effectiveness variance.

The analysis and use of variances in a given situation requires that interrelationships be considered, as well as the causes for individual variances. For example, a favorable efficiency variance, combined with a large unfavorable labor wage-rate variance and a favorable labor-efficiency variance, may indicate that a higher labor skill level than necessary is being employed.

The discussion of variances in this section is essentially a long-run analysis, since we have assumed, implicitly, that the capacity can be expanded. The definition of practical capacity requires that the possibility of expansion exist.

One additional variance is the calendar variance. The calendar variance arises because of there being an unequal number of days in the months of the year. For example, if the practical capacity for the month is 1,260, then there would be a 15 hours unfavorable calendar variance.

In the example illustrated in Figure 5.5, it is assumed that there is no calendar variance.

5.3.3 Dollar Quantification of Fixed-Overhead Variances

Traditionally, only three fixed-overhead variances are calculated in dollar terms. These simplified variances are calculated as follows (where it is necessary to first select the capacity basis: practical, or normal). These traditional variances are measured in dollars while the analysis of the previous section was in physical terms (direct labor hours).

budget variance = actual fixed costs − budgeted fixed costs

efficiency variance = fixed overhead rate

× (actual hours in input − standard hours in output)

activity variance = fixed overhead rate

× (budgeted hours − actual hours in input)

The activity variance, using dollar measures, must be consistent with the basis of the fixed overhead variance. If normal activity is used to compute the overhead rate, then normal activity must be used in computing the activity variance in dollars. One advantage of using physical measures is that this complexity is bypassed.

5.4 Graphical Approach to Overhead Variances

A graphic approach may be used to analyze the fixed and variable variances. Such solutions are especially useful for the purpose of enabling the reader to visualize the relationships of some of the variances that have been discussed. In this presentation we detail only the two variable-overhead variances and three fixed-overhead variances.

1. Variable-overhead variances:
   a. Budget (or spending) variance: includes the joint variance of Figure 5.4.
   b. Efficiency variance.

2. Fixed-overhead variances:
   a. Budget variance.
   b. Efficiency variance.
   c. Activity variance.

Consider the variable-overhead variance first. The relevant graph is Figure 5.6. Line OB in the graphic solution for the variable-overhead variances is the variable-overhead budgeted for the different levels of activity, and it is also the amount of overhead that will be applied to product for different hours of activity. Thus, for any number of standard direct-labor hours, the amount of variable overhead to be applied to product may be found by the intersection of OB and a vertical line extended up from the appropriate number of standard direct-labor hours on the horizontal axis: H_sC. The amount is OD. For any number of actual direct-labor hours, the variable overhead that should have been incurred (the budgeted amount) can be found by the intersection of OB and a vertical line extended up from the actual direct-labor hours and the horizontal axis: H_AB. The amount is OE. The difference $OE - OD$ is the variable-overhead efficiency variance. It is unfavorable because the standard hours in output are less than the actual hours worked. We have also incorporated the actual variable cost in Figure 5.6 to illustrate the budget variance FE, also unfavorable in this case.

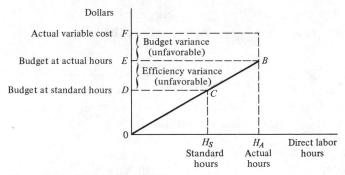

Figure 5.6   Variable overhead.

The graphical solution for fixed overhead is shown in Figure 5.7. In this case line OB has a somewhat more limited significance. It no longer represents the budgeted costs for different levels of activity. This is reasonable, since the costs are fixed over the entire range of activity being studied. Thus the line OB on the chart for fixed costs represents the amount of fixed overhead that will be absorbed by product at different levels of standard direct-labor hours.

Example
Let us compute first the fixed- and variable-overhead rates based on the following data and using normal activity. All costs listed are manufacturing costs.

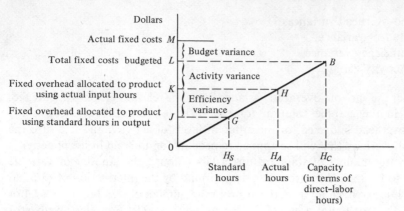

Figure 5.7   Fixed overhead.

The letters tie the discussion to Figures 5.6 and 5.7. Normal activity is equal to practical capacity.

Budgeted variable costs (for 80,000 = H_c direct-labor hours)	$20,000
Budgeted fixed costs, OL	$40,000
Normal activity, H_c	80,000 direct-labor hours

$$\text{variable-overhead rate} = \frac{20,000}{80,000} = 0.25 \text{ per direct-labor hour}$$

$$\text{fixed-overhead rate} = \frac{40,000}{80,000} = 0.50 \text{ per direct-labor hour}$$

Using these rates and the information that follows, we next compute the two variable- and three fixed-overhead variances described in Section 5.3.3.

Actual hours worked, H_A	22,000 hr
Standard hours, H_S	20,000 hr
Actual variable-overhead costs incurred, OF	$5,900
Actual fixed overhead costs incurred, OM	$40,200

The efficiency variances are given by the difference between the actual and standard hours valued at the applicable overhead rate:

$$\text{variable-overhead efficiency variance} = 0.25\,(22,000 - 20,000)$$

$$= \$500 \text{ unfavorable, } ED$$

$$\text{fixed-overhead efficiency variance} = 0.50\,(22,000 - 20,000)$$

$$= \$1,000 \text{ unfavorable, } KJ$$

The budget variances are the difference between what the overhead should have been and the actual overhead incurred. The budgeted variable overhead has to be adjusted to the actual level of operations:

$$\text{variable-overhead budget variance} = 5{,}900 - 22{,}000 \times .25 = 5{,}900 - 5{,}100$$

$$= \$400 \text{ unfavorable, } EF$$

$$\text{fixed-overhead budget variance} = 40{,}200 - 40{,}000 = \$200 \text{ unfavorable, } LM$$

The activity variance is the difference between the actual and budgeted hours valued at the fixed overhead rate:

$$\text{activity variance} = 0.50(80{,}000 - 22{,}000) = \$29{,}000 \text{ unfavorable, KL.}$$

The total overhead variance is the difference between the incurred $\$5{,}900 + \$40{,}200 = \$46{,}100$ and that applied to product at standard: $20{,}000(\$0.50 + \$0.25) = \$15{,}000$. This difference is $\$46{,}100 - \$15{,}000 = \$31{,}100$ (unfavorable). The total variance equals the sum of the five separate variances:

$$\$500 + 1{,}000 + 400 + 200 + 29{,}000 = \$31{,}100$$

The formula for the fixed overhead efficiency variance is unchanged from that for variable costs except that the fixed-overhead rate is used instead of the variable-overhead rate. The significance of the variance is changed, however. The fixed-overhead efficiency variance is not very useful. The budget variance shows the difference between actual and budgeted fixed costs. The activity variance points up the problem of not using capacity. For reasons discussed in Section 5.3.2, the activity variance will almost always be unfavorable if practical capacity is chosen as the level of activity for computing the fixed-overhead rate. It may or may not be favorable if some other basis is chosen or if the practical capacity can be exceeded.

5.5 Significance of Cost Variances

Management cannot investigate each and every variance. There must be criteria established that determine whether the variance is significant enough to be investigated. The absolute size of the variance may be one factor, the size of the variance relative to the total cost incurred in that classification may be another, and the characteristic of the cost is a third consideration. These criteria are best established by someone other than the person responsible for the operations and by someone with a knowledge of statistics, since this problem of determining significance can be handled by using statistical techniques. The use of statistical techniques in variance analysis is discussed in Chapter 19.

It should be remembered that the analysis of variances illustrated in this chapter is only the first step. Once the budget variance is computed, the causes for the variance need to be investigated in detail. Once this is done, corrective action may be undertaken. It may take some time for the corrective action to be effective; the accountant monitoring the system should keep this in mind.

5.6   Disposition of Cost Variances

This issue is relevant to product costing and financial statement preparation but not to cost control. It is essential to keep in mind the distinction between product costing and cost control.

Cost variances may be disposed of by following either of two basic procedures. They can be considered a cost of inefficiency and not a cost of product, in which case they are charged against the revenues of the period. Otherwise, they are treated as a cost of product and allocated to work in process, finished goods, and cost of goods sold. The proper procedure is to judge each variance individually and to make a decision based on the nature of the cause of the variance. In general, price variances caused by changes in the prices of goods are a cost of product and should be allocated to the product. At the other extreme, an idle activity variance caused by actually operating 100 direct-labor hours instead of the normal 800 direct-labor hours per week is not a cost of the product made but rather a loss. In between these two extremes are borderline cases where it is more difficult to determine whether the cost should or should not be considered as a cost of product. Labor-efficiency variances are an example of where the determination is difficult, depending on the tightness of the labor standards.

Of more importance than the exact treatment of specific variances is an appreciation of what is affected by the choice of procedure. Both the inventory valuation and the measurement of income are affected. The control of costs is not directly affected, since the cost variances should be analyzed in the same manner without regard to their ultimate disposition. Practical considerations, such as the costs of record keeping, may result in expensing all variances.

5.7   Summary Diagram of Flow of Entries— Standard Cost System

Figure 5.8 is an attempt to present the accounts in a typical standard cost system. Many alternative possibilities do exist, however. Note the flow of both standard costs and the setting up of the variance accounts. The illustration does not follow through to the final disposition of the variance for product-costing purposes. The reduced set of overhead variances is illustrated.

5.8   Summary

Standard cost systems are used widely, particularly in business. They facilitate the accounting for manufacturing costs and are an important aid in the

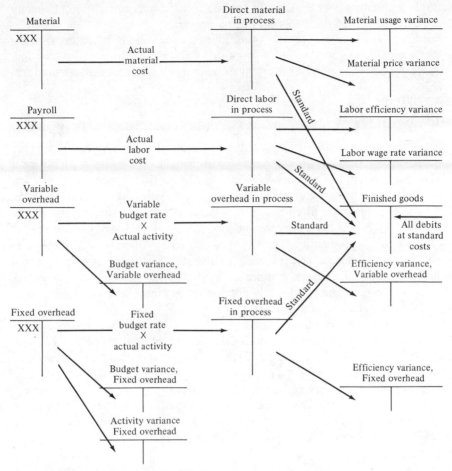

Figure 5.8 A typical standard cost system.

control of costs. If the standards have been properly set, the identification of significant cost variances is a first step toward cost control.

Perhaps the most important point to keep in mind is that two purposes are served by a standard cost system: product costing and cost control. If costs are allocated to responsibility centers, then cost variances based on standard costs form the initial step in cost control. The selection of those variances worth investigating and the determination of the causes are essential but subsequent steps.

For product-costing purposes, the first step is to measure the standard cost. Direct costs present less trouble here than indirect costs. The choice of a capacity concept to establish an overhead rate by which indirect costs are allocated to product was given a good deal of attention both here and in Chapter 3. The product costs are thereby related to long-run capacity. This is important, for example, evaluating price policies that must, over the long term, reflect capacity considerations if the firm is to continue to operate.

For control purposes, on the other hand, these overhead rates and the resultant cost variances have much less value (with the exception of the budget variances) than the cost variances derived from labor and material calculations.

APPENDIX 5A
MIX VARIANCE

In some manufacturing situations factors of production may be substituted for each other. Thus, in an emergency or during slack activity a highly paid worker may be used in a task which ordinarily requires a worker of a lower grade. In like manner, one grade of steel may be substituted for another grade. This type of transaction gives rise to mix variances. A mix variance is defined as a variance which is caused by the substitution of one factor of production for another factor of production. The variance caused by differences in wage rates (or prices) can be determined relatively easily, but the change in efficiency that results from the substitution is more difficult to establish since the necessary information to compute it is usually not available. Hence it is often difficult to measure the total effect of a shift in mix.

The mix variance can be illustrated by the use of a shift in direct labor. The mix variance is computed by multiplying the number of direct-labor hours which are shifted by the difference between the standard wage rate for the workers who were transferred and the standard wage rate for the task. Several other possible definitions of mix variance would be equally reasonable; thus there is no implication that this is the only correct method of computation. There is too much jointness connected with the incurrence of these variances to allow precision in the method of computation. In general:
mix variance =

> units shifted (standard cost of units shifted − standard cost of task)

Example
Assume there are two types of workers, "skilled" and "unskilled," working on two processes, grinding and assembly. The standard cost information and the facts for March are given in Exhibits 5A–1 and 5A–2.

Exhibit 5A–1   Standard Costs for One Unit of Product

Process	Type of Worker	Standard Hours	Standard Wage Rate	Totals
Assembly	Unskilled	4	$2.00	$ 8.00
Grinding	Skilled	6	3.00	18.00
				$ 26.00

Exhibit 5A–2   Actual Costs for Month

Type of Worker	Actual Hours	Actual Wages	Actual Wage Rate
Unskilled	380	$ 836	$2.20
Skilled	610	2,074	3.40
		$2,910	

Assume that there are skilled workers on the assembly line for 10 hours (the total hours worked on assembly operations are 390 and on grinding 600). There are 100 units of products manufactured. The standard cost is $2,600 and actual cost is $2,910; thus, there is an unfavorable variance of $310.

The computation of variance is as follows.

EFFICIENCY VARIANCE: the standard wage rate times the difference between standard and actual hours worked:

Assembly	$2(400 − 390) =	$20 favorable
Grinding	$3(600 − 600) =	0
		$20 favorable

WAGE-RATE VARIANCE: the actual hours times the difference between the actual and standard wage rates (for both types of workers, the actual hours worked by that type of worker is used):

Skilled	610(3.40 − 3.00) =	$244 unfavorable
Unskilled	380(2.20 − 2.00) =	76 unfavorable
		$320 unfavorable

MIX VARIANCE: the number of hours shifted, multiplied by the difference between the standard wage rate for the men shifted and the standard wage rate for the task performed:

$$10(3.00 − 2.00) = \$10 \text{ unfavorable}$$

TOTAL VARIANCE: the algebraic sum of the three variances:

Efficiency	$ 20 favorable
Wage Rate	320 unfavorable
Mix	10 unfavorable
	$320 unfavorable

(Note that nothing is said about whether the 100 units were produced more quickly or whether some other advantage was obtained; nor is the value of the advantage, if any, given.)

APPENDIX 5B
FURTHER FIXED VARIANCES

Figure 5.9 may be used to illustrate three variances in addition to those described in the chapter. The first addition is an ex post budgeted activity level of 1,150 hours. This measure represents the level of activity that would have been set after the budget period given the changes which occurred during the period. It is a hind-sight figure and gives the budget for the actual conditions which the organization faced. Two variances of note can be added to the chapter analysis with this additional activity level: the forecast variance and the production variance.

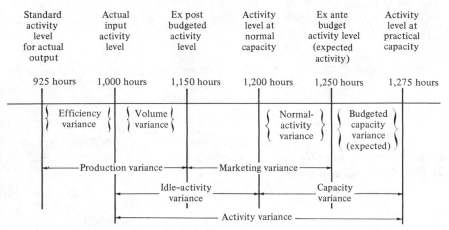

Figure 5.9   Fixed overhead variance analysis.

The (*marketing* or *forecast*) *variance* is the difference between the ex ante and ex post (or revised) budgeted activity levels (1,250 − 1,150 = 100 units). This variance is typically a result of disruptions in marketing plans, but it may be due to inaccurate economic projections or difficulties such as strikes. This variance has an expected value of zero when the ex ante budget is prepared. It is meaningful in evaluating current results.

The *production variance* is the difference between the ex post budgeted activity level and the standard activity level needed to produce the actual output (1,150 − 925 = 225 units). This variance is in part a measure of how effective the production process has been. The variance is a function of the productive apparatus of the firm. For some reason the actual activity of the firm did not equal the revised (ex post) sales budget even though the revision was below the initial budget estimate. There may be many reasons for this variance, including some reasons that are not attributable to the production department. For example, changes in raw-material quality or labor skills might be involved. This variance is made up of two parts: a volume variance and the efficiency variance.

We have already discussed the efficiency variance. The volume variance is the difference between the ex post budgeted activity level and the actual input activity level (1,150 − 1000 = 150 hours). This variance represents the failure of actual activity to reach the revised lower budget. This could be due to poor scheduling or equipment breakdowns. It is also possible that changes occurred too late in the period to allow a change in production scheduling.

QUESTIONS AND PROBLEMS

5–1 The Bobb Company makes one product. The following data are accumulated for the month of July. Overhead is absorbed, using direct-labor hours.

	Standard	Actual	Budgeted
Hours of direct labor	95,000	90,000	100,000
Dollars of direct-labor cost	$190,000	$185,000	$200,000
Pounds of material A used	76,000	75,000	80,000
Dollar amount of material A used	$228,000	$228,000	$240,000
Variable manufacturing overhead		$82,000	$100,000
Fixed manufacturing overhead		$47,500	$50,000
Units of equivalent product	38,000	38,000	40,000

Required: Compute the material, labor, and overhead variances.

5–2 The Thrower Company produces one product. For the month of March, the following information is accumulated:

	Actual Hours and Tons	Standard Hours and Tons	Actual Cost	Standard Cost per Unit
Direct labor	10,500 hr	10,000 hr	$21,500	$ 2.10/hr
Direct material	550 tons	540 tons	52,250	100.00/ton

	Budgeted Overhead for Year	Actual Overhead for March
Variable	$216,000	$15,200
Fixed	72,000	6,200

The overhead is budgeted for average (normal) activity of 144,000 hours of direct labor per year.

Required:
a. Compute the labor and material variances.
b. Compute the overhead variances.
c. Show the overhead variances graphically.

d. Assuming no beginning or ending balances in work in process, set up necessary "T" accounts to show the entries that would be made to record the manufacturing costs and variances. Set up a separate "T" account for each variance.

5-3 The Pitcher Company produces one product. For the month of March, the following information is accumulated:

	Actual Usage	Standard Hours and Tons	Actual Cost	Standard Cost per Unit
Direct labor	11,000 hr	10,000 hr	$22,500	$ 2.10/hr
Direct material	530 tons	540 tons	52,650	100.00/ton

	Budgeted Overhead for Year	Actual Overhead for March
Variable	$288,000	$20,900
Fixed	144,000	13,200

The overhead is budgeted for average (normal) activity of 144,000 hours of direct labor per year and 12,000 hours per month.

Required:

a. Compute the labor and material variances.

b. Compute the overhead variances.

5-4 The Auburn Company manufactures one product, Bypo. The standards for one unit of Bypo are as follows:

10 lb of material X at $1/lb	$10
3 hr of direct labor at $3/hr	9
Overhead	
Fixed: $2/DLH	6
Variable: $1/DLH	3
Total standard cost for one unit of Bypo	$28

Material X is added at the beginning of the manufacturing process. Overhead is budgeted on the basis of direct-labor hours.

The inventory of work in process on February 1 consisted of 900 units of Bypo, $66\frac{2}{3}\%$ complete with regard to labor and overhead. A purchase of 92,000 pounds of material X was made during February at a cost of $1.05 per pound. During the month, 26,000 hours of direct labor were worked at an average wage of $3.10 per hour. February plant capacity was 30,000 direct-labor hours. Actual fixed overhead costs amounted to $63,000 during February, and actual variable overhead costs amounted to $26,000 during the month.

During February, 8,900 units of Bypo were completed. The inventory of work in process as of February 28 consisted of 1,000 units of Bypo, 80% complete with regard to labor and burden.

The entire 92,000 lb was used during February.

Required: Compute labor, material, and overhead variances for the month of February. Indicate whether the variances are unfavorable (debit) or favorable (credit).

5–5 The I. C. Thelite Company has accumulated the following information in an effort to explain the differences between standard and actual cost for the month of March. Overhead is absorbed, using standard direct-labor hours. All the actual costs given are for March. There is no beginning or ending balance in work in process.

Production for March

Product	Equivalent Units Produced	Direct-Labor Standards	Standard Direct-Labor Cost per Hour	Material Standards	Standard Material Cost per Ton
A	900,000	6.0 min/unit	$2.10	1.0 lb/unit	$100.00
B	800,000	4.8 min/unit	2.20	3.0 lb/unit	200.00

Actual Direct Labor and Material

Product	Direct-Labor Hours	Direct-Labor Dollars	Material, tons	Material, $
A	80,000	$164,000	530	$ 54,500
B	70,000	190,000	1,248	259,000

Budget Information

Product	Budgeted Fixed Cost, March	Budgeted Production March	Budgeted Variable Overhead, March	Budgeted Direct-Labor Hours, March
A	$150,000	1,000,000	$200,000	100,000
B	340,000	850,000	170,000	68,000

Additional Information

Product	Actual Fixed Cost, March	Actual Variable Cost, March
A	$148,000	$210,000
B	343,000	168,000

Required: Prepare an analysis of all variances. Overhead is applied to product, using direct-labor hours.

5–6 The Carter Corporation makes one product, widgets, and uses a standard cost system to record the costs of making that product. On December 1, manufacturing inventory accounts had balances as follows:

Finished goods	$18,000	1,000 units
Work in process, labor	1,000	500 units one-half completed
Work in process, material	5,000	500 units completed as far as material is concerned
Work in process, overhead	1,000	overhead rate $2.00/DLH

The standard cost of a widget is:

Direct-labor	$ 4
Direct-material (20 lb of material)	10
Overhead:	
Fixed	3
Variable	1
	$18

The current work standard is 2 direct-labor hours per unit of product. The fixed-overhead rate is $1.50 per direct-labor hour, and the variable-overhead rate is $0.50 per direct-labor hour.

The normal activity for a month is 200,000 direct-labor hours, and the overhead rates are based on normal activity. The fixed manufacturing costs budgeted for a month are $300,000, and the variable manufacturing overhead costs are $100,000.

The following transactions took place during December:

Direct-labor costs incurred (180,000 hr of work)	$ 380,000
Material requisitioned and used (1,800,000 lb)	1,150,000
Fixed overhead incurred	320,000
Variable overhead incurred	95,000
Selling expenses incurred	1,000,000
Administrative expenses incurred	800,000
Income taxes	100,000
Sales on account (95,000 widgets)	4,800,000

During the month of December, the plant completed 100,000 units of product. The work in process on December 31 consisted of 400 units, 50% completed as far as labor and 100% completed as far as material.

Required:
a. Record in "T" accounts the transactions of December, including the adjusting entries.
b. Give the ending inventories in finished goods and work in process.
c. What additional information should be obtained for purposes of controlling costs?

5–7 A corporate controller was pleased that the overhead variances for the year were very small. He said, "This shows that we effectively predicted costs and activity in setting our overhead rates." Comment on this statement.

5–8 Each December the Kracked Bat Company prepares a series of budgets for the coming year. The complete budget has the following components:

Sales and selling expenses
Production budget
Material and labor budgets
Manufacturing overhead budget
Cash budget
Projected financial statements

The Kracked Bat Company's only products are baseball bats. The bats are all produced at one plant. There are four sales offices. The company uses a LIFO procedure for pricing inventory and cost of goods sold expense.

Part I. Sales and Selling Expense Budgets
The sales and selling expense budgets are prepared by the sales department with the assistance of the controller's office. The sales forecasts are based on reports from the salesmen and information from the company economist, whose task it is to incorporate into the forecast such things as changes in prices, population, age of the population, and income. The following projections were made for the year:

Sales Projections for Year

Sales District	Number of Bats	Sales	Budgeted Selling Expense
New England	500,000	$1,500,000	$20,000
Middle West	300,000	900,000	18,000
South	150,000	450,000	10,000
South West	50,000	150,000	12,000
	1,000,000	$3,000,000	$60,000

Required: What additional information should be contained in the completed sales budget and selling expense budget?

Part II. Production Budget

The production department receives from the sales department a breakdown of forecasted sales by months.

Sales Projections for Year by Months (number of bats)

January	200,000	July	vacation
February	200,000	August	60,000
March	100,000	September	60,000
April	100,000	October	100,000
May	50,000	November	40,000
June	50,000	December	40,000

The company follows a policy of stabilizing employment throughout the year. If it did not follow this policy, it would probably lose its skilled workers to other plants in the area. Studies and experience indicate that the plant can produce 60,000 bats per month when it is operating without overtime and employing only the basic work force. By working overtime and adding temporary workers, production can be upped to 120,000 bats per month. The entire plant and sales force is given a month's vacation in July. Normal activity for budget purposes is 100,000 bats per month.

There will be a January 1 beginning inventory of 180,000 bats. The company tries to keep a basic minimum inventory of 20,000 finished bats, and it builds up the inventory to 180,000 bats as of the beginning of each year. Where there is conflict between inventory control and employment policy, the stabilized employment policy has priority.

Required: Plan the production (number of bats to be produced) in each month.

Part III. Material and Labor Budgets

The material and labor standards for the type of bat being produced are as follows:

Wood (standard rough weight)	2 lb
Standard cost per pound	$0.10
Standard cost of wood used in bat	$0.20
Direct labor:	
Cutters	0.25 hr at $2.00/hr = $0.50
Finishers	0.50 hr at $3.00/hr = 1.50
Standard direct-labor cost per bat	= $2.00

Required: Compute the total direct labor and material to be used during the year, and for each of the first three months of the year.

Part IV. Manufacturing Overhead Budget

The manufacturing overhead costs are budgeted as follows:

Fixed Overhead	
Equipment depreciation	$ 24,000
Salaries of supervisors	180,000
Building rent	96,000
Manufacturing labor, indirect	36,000
Manufacturing supplies	24,000
	$360,000

Variable Overhead (for normal activity of 1,200,000 bats per year)	
Indirect labor	$ 96,000
Power	$ 24,000
Indirect supplies	48,000
	$168,000

Required:

a. What additional information should be presented in the detailed budget?

b. Compute the fixed- and variable-overhead rates to be used.
   Overhead is to be absorbed using direct-labor hours.

c. What is the standard overhead per unit of product?

Part V. Cash Budget

The only sources of cash in the next period are sales and the collections of accounts receivable. Past experience indicates that the following schedule of collections holds true:

Collections in month of sale	20%
Collections in month following sale	70
Collections in second month following sale	9
Uncollectible accounts	1
	100%

The accounts receivable balance as of January 1 is expected to consist of the following items:

Source	Accounts Receivable	Expected Uncollectibles
December sales	$32,000	$ 400
November sales	3,000	300
October sales	1,000	1,000
September sales	500	500
	$36,500	$2,200

Payments of cash are expected to be equal to the sum of

Selling expenses
Cost of direct material used
Direct-labor cost incurred
Out-of-pocket overhead costs

There is a cash balance of $100,000 on January 1.
No income tax payments are due in the coming year.
Required: Prepare a statement of forecasted sources and applications of cash for the year.

Part VI. Projected Financial Statements
The January 1 position statement is expected to include the following items:

Assets		Equities	
Cash	$100,000	Accounts payable	$200,000
Accounts receivable	36,500	Capital stock	400,000
Allowance for uncol-		Retained earnings	154,300
lectibles	(2,200)		
Inventories	400,000		
Equipment	300,000		
Accumulated deprecia-			
tion	(80,000)		
	$754,300		$754,300

Required: Prepare a projected income statement for the year and a projected position statement (as of December 31). Assume that the income tax rate is

50% and that the taxable income (if any) is the same as the income per books.

Part VII. Budgets and Variances

Assume that certain price (wage) and usage (efficiency) variances can be forecasted. Which of the budgets will be affected by these items? Explain briefly.

Part VIII. Actual Costs of January

The following events occurred during January:

Bats produced		125,000
Cutters worked 30,000 hr and earned		$ 75,000
Finishers worked 62,000 hr and earned		$250,000
Cost of wood used (260,000 lb)		$ 28,000
Fixed overhead:		
Equipment depreciation	$ 2,000	
Salaries of supervisors	15,000	
Building rent	8,000	
Indirect labor	4,500	
Indirect supplies	2,500	
		$ 32,000
Variable overhead:		
Indirect labor	$ 9,000	
Power	2,000	
Indirect supplies	5,000	
		$ 16,000
Selling expense		$ 5,000

Required:

a. Compute the material price and usage variances; labor-efficiency and wage-rate variances; variable-overhead budget and efficiency variances; and fixed-overhead budget, efficiency, and idle-capacity variances.

b. Assuming that all the bats produced could be sold for $3 per bat, analyze the results of operations for January. What actions could be taken to improve the profit picture?

5-9 The Universal Corporation uses a flexible budget procedure to control variable-overhead costs. Each month the actual cost incurred is plotted, using direct-labor hours as a measure of activity. At the end of the year, the points are plotted and a regression line is calculated. The equation of the line is determined in order to obtain the fixed and variable components of the cost. This equation is used as the basis for the flexible budget for the next year.

Required:

a. Comment on the effectiveness of the procedure followed.

b. How could the procedure be improved? Could the monthly plottings of cost be used for cost-control purposes? Explain.

5–10 The Hall Corporation has made an analysis of how the salaries of foremen should react to changes in activity.

	Foremen's Salaries
From plant shutdown to 20,000 direct-labor hours per month	$4,000 (monthly)
From 20,000 direct-labor hours to 22,000 direct-labor hours per month	$4,000 + ($0.50 per direct-labor hour in excess of 20,000)
From 22,000 direct-labor hours to 23,000 direct-labor hours per month	$5,000 (monthly rate)

There is a core of foremen who would be retained even if the plant were temporarily closed. If production required more than 20,000 hours of direct-labor hours per week but less than 22,000, then these foremen could handle the extra work by taking overtime. If the direct-labor hours increased above 22,000 hours, it is expected that a new foreman would be hired.

The actual costs for the first quarter were as follows:

	Direct-Labor Hours per Month	Foremen's Salaries
January	20,400	$4,800
February	22,400	5,600
March	19,600	4,900

Required:

a. Plot the budgeted costs and the actual costs for the first quarter.

b. Comment on the level of foremen's salaries for each of the first three months.

5–11 The Small Automobile Company (sales, $1 billion per year) is very much concerned with the control of indirect labor. To help control this cost, the following report is prepared monthly:

PLANT ——— DEPARTMENT ——— MONTH ———

Code Number	Account Title	Budgeted for Month	Actual Exp. for Month	Variance	Budgeted for Year	Actual Exp. for Year

This report is expensive to prepare ($400,000 per year), and it has several weaknesses. The timing of the report is not good. It is distributed 20 working days after the end of the month. Some executives feel that by the time they receive the report, it is too late to take action.

Another difficulty has to do with sick leave and vacations. If the person who goes on sick leave or vacation is replaced by a temporary worker, this appears as a variance, since the wage cost of this extra worker has not been budgeted for the month. This annoys executives who have to explain why they had an unfavorable variance.

The company has a procedure whereby the wage rates are strictly tied to the type of work being done. A higher grade of labor cannot be used for a job other than that approved without the personnel department's written permission. Changes in wage rates (increases in wages) are also strictly controlled, requiring the permission of the head of the department, the immediate supervisor, the personnel department, and the budget control officer.

Since wage rates are so well controlled, wage-rate variances only appear because of authorized wage-rate changes not yet incorporated into the budget figure. The significant variances in labor expense are caused by an excessive number of hours worked in proportion to the amount of direct-labor activity budgeted.

An analyst in the budget control group has suggested that the present report be replaced by a report that would compare the budgeted manpower with the actual manpower (a head-count basis). Overtime would be controlled by a separate but accompanying report. These reports could be distributed on the second working day following the end of the month.

Required: Assuming that you are controller of the Small Automobile Company, what action will you take?

5–12 A flexible budget is a budget that adjusts the indirect labor (and other variable-overhead costs) to the actual level of activity. This is necessary if variable indirect costs are to be effectively controlled. Usually, direct-labor hours, direct-labor dollars, machine hours, or some other one basis is used to adjust all indirect costs. In recent years the weakness of this procedure has been noted. Many indirect costs will not vary directly with direct-labor hours. In the long run, there may be a good correlation, but in the short run there may be leads and lags. For example, the receiving department may have to expand to receive raw material before the direct-labor force is expanded. The accounts receivable department may not have to expand, although the direct-labor force has been expanded.

To secure better control of indirect labor, attempts have been made in recent years to obtain types of work measurement more immediately related to the work than direct labor. For example, the accounts payable labor cost is related to the number of invoices processed.

Required: Name several types of indirect labor and the measures of work that can help to control these indirect labor costs.

5-13 The Sell-More Company followed a strict budgeting procedure with respect to advertising expenditures. The president of the firm received a forecast of sales from the sales vice-president and a forecast of expenses from the controller. He computed the profit without deducting advertising expense and compared it to a budgeted profit (based on a reasonable return on investment). The difference between the two profits was then allocated to advertising (assuming that the expected profit was greater than the budgeted profit).

Required: Comment on the policy described above.

5-14 The College Textbook Company was regularly faced with accept or reject decisions concerning the possible printing of books. To make this decision, it employed a projected income per copy of the book. In computing this projected income, no general overhead was assigned, and editorial work on the book was excluded. Included were the printing costs and advertising and distribution costs of a direct nature (the salaries of the salesmen were excluded).

Required: Comment on the policy described above.

5-15 The following information applies to a day's production:

Units of good product started and finished	5,000
Standard material per unit	2 lb
Actual material used	11,000 lb
Standard price per pound of material	$3.25/lb
Actual price per pound of material	$2.35/lb

Required:
a. Compute the material-usage variance.
b. Compute the material-price variance.
c. Compute the total variance from standard cost.
d. Part of the variance was caused by a higher price paid for units that should not have been used. Compute this amount. Compute a price and usage variance to accompany it so that the total variance is equal to the answer of part c. Explain the difference in results in relation to parts a and b and discuss the value, if any, of the refinement in calculation.

5–16 Using average total cost, average variable cost, marginal cost curves, and any other curves that you think useful, indicate on a diagram the practical capacity of a plant.

5–17 (Relates to Appendix 5A.) Prepare an analysis of cost variances from the following information:

Process	Workers	Standard Hours	Standard Costs per Hour	Total
1	Jones	1	$3.00	$ 3.00
2	Smith	3	4.00	12.00
				$15.00

During January, Jones worked 40 hours and Smith worked 180 hours. Jones earned $130 and Smith $765. There were 50 units of product produced. All of Smith's and Jones's time was assigned to this product. Smith filled in and worked on process 1 for 8 hours.

5–18 Prepare as complete an analysis of cost variances as possible from the following information:

Standard Costs per Unit	
Direct labor (5 hr @ $4)	$20.00
Material (20 lb at @ $2)	40.00
Variable overhead ($1.50 × 5)	7.50
Fixed overhead ($3 × 5)	15.00
	$82.50

Budget Information for the Year	
Variable overhead	$150,000
Fixed overhead	300,000
Normal activity for year	100,000 direct-labor hours
Practical activity for year	120,000 direct-labor hours

The actual results of January's operations were as follows:

Variable overhead	$11,000
Fixed overhead	$26,000
Actual activity	8,000 direct-labor hours
Actual production	1,450 units
Actual labor cost	$33,600
Actual material cost (30,000 pounds)	$66,000

5–19 Analysis of cost variances. Complete the list below:

No.	Item	Amount
1.	Variable overhead rate per standard hour.	85c
2.	Fixed overhead rate per standard hour.	
3.	Total overhead rate per standard hour for product costing.	
4.	Total overhead incurred.	$11,425
5.	Total variable cost incurred at actual hours worked.	
6.	Total fixed overhead incurred	
7.	Actual hours worked.	7,000
8.	Standard hours of (or allowed for) work done.	6,500
9.	Standard hours at normal capacity.	
10.	Overhead applied to product using standard rates only.	$10,400
11.	Budget variance-fixed.	$425 F
12.	Budgeted variable overhead for actual hours.	
13.	Budgeted fixed overhead.	
14.	Budget variance-variable.	100 F

5–20 Krocks and Potts Company

Memorandum
To: The Controller
From: Thebos
Subject: Price Variance Ball Clay: April

I note that the total material variance for the month of April amounted to $1,050 despite continuance of our normal production level of 36 units. Can you give me any explanation of why this occurred?

The data in the controller's records indicate

1. Equivalent units of work (material, Ball Clay) in mixing: April		36
2. Standard pounds of Ball Clay required per unit		875
3. Standard purchase price per April budget		$0.80/lb
4. Purchases of Ball Clay (30,000 lbs)		$23,100
5. Requisitions by Mixing Department (@ average April price)		35,000 lb
6. Inventories of Ball Clay at Average Prices		
April 1	30,000 lbs	$21,900
May 1	25,000 lbs.	$18,750

The periodic inventory method is used to value raw materials and to cost out requisitions on a FIFO basis.

Required: As controller write a brief reply to the boss. In your response indicate (a) how the $1,050 figure was derived, (b) what—if any—modifications you would make to this figure, (c) and any reasons that might explain (regardless of your personal knowledge of their actual occurrence) the price variance.

SUPPLEMENTARY READING

A.A.A., *A Statement of Basic Accounting Theory*, The American Accounting Association, 1966.

ANTON, H. R., and P. A. FIRMIN, *Contemporary Issues in Cost Accounting*, Boston: Houghton Mifflin Company, 1966.

BENSTON, G. J., *Contemporary Cost Accounting and Control*, Belmont, Calif.: Dickenson Publishing Company, Inc., 1970.

DEMSKI, J. S., "An Accounting System Structured on a Linear Programming Model," *The Accounting Review*, October 1967, pp. 701–712.

———, "Analyzing the Effectiveness of the Traditional Standard Cost Variance Model," *Management Accounting*, October 1967, pp. 9–19.

———, "Decision-Performance Control," *The Accounting Review*, October 1969, pp. 669–679.

DOPUCH, N., J. G. BIRNBERG, and J. DEMSKI, "An Extension of Standard Cost Analysis," *The Accounting Review*, July 1967, pp. 526–536.

FELTHAM, G., "The Value of Information," *The Accounting Review*, October 1968, pp. 684–696.

FRANK, W., and R. MANES, "A Standard Cost Application of Matrix Algebra," *The Accounting Review*, July 1967, pp. 516–525.

HORNGREN, C. T., "A Contribution Margin Approach to the Analysis of Capacity Utilization," *The Accounting Review*, April 1967, pp. 254–264.

———, *Cost Accounting: A Managerial Emphasis*, 3rd ed., Englewood Cliffs, N.J.: Prentice-Hall, Inc., 1972, Chap. 9.

IJIRI, Y., *Management Goals and Accounting for Control*, Amsterdam: North-Holland Publishing Company, 1965.

———, and R. JAEDICKE, "Reliability and Objectivity of Accounting Measurements," *The Accounting Review*, July 1966, pp. 474–483.

NATIONAL ASSOCIATION OF ACCOUNTANTS, Research Reports Nos. 11, 15, 17, 22, and 28.

RONEN, J., "Capacity and Operating Variances: An Ex Post Approach," *Journal of Accounting Research*, Autumn 1970, pp. 232–252.

SHWAYDER, K., "A Note on a Contribution Margin Approach to the Analysis of Capacity Utilization," *The Accounting Review*, January 1968, pp. 101–104.

———, "Relevance," *Journal of Accounting Research*, Spring 1968, pp. 86–97.

SORTER, G. H., "An Events Approach to Basic Accounting Theory," *The Accounting Review*, January 1969, pp. 12–19.

Part II

Special Topics in Cost Accounting and Control

Chapter 6

Some Behavioral Aspects of Cost Control

The traditional approach to cost control has involved the comparison of actual results with budgeted or standard amounts that represent goals for management. For many years considerable attention has been given to improving the means by which such analyses could be used. Standards and the analysis of variances were used to increase the ability of management to exercise control over performance. The development of cost centers and the decentralization of decision making were in large part responses to the need for the subcomponents within a firm that had control of specific resources and could therefore be evaluated in light of their utilization of these resources. Central to these developments was the assumption that the more sophisticated the system, the greater the likelihood of success in controlling costs and improving performance. Indeed, there was perhaps a tendency for many firms to expect desirable results merely from the use of the techniques alone.

The importance of measuring and maintaining performance has not diminished. But in recent years attention has focused on a new dimension that has had and will continue to have a profound impact on the activity of the accountant: the motivational aspects of human activity. Although the importance of interpersonal relationships and individual behavior is not a new area of study and its impact on organizations and groups has been under examination for many years, it is only recently that the results have begun to have an impact on managerial accounting theory and practice.

There has developed an increased recognition of the importance of the organizational—and human—resource assets of the firm.[1] If management uses only conventional measures of revenues, expenses, profits, cost variances, and output, it is possible that short-run economic gains may be achieved at the expense of long-run goals. Failure to consider the impact of control techniques on the individuals responsible for the activity of the firm may adversely affect employee morale, loyalty, trust, and motivation.

Present methods of evaluation often fail to consider how people are motivated. Cost control and other reports measuring performance are often used primarily for punitive purposes. Several authors have found that there is a strong asymmetrical reward system connected with performance reports.[2] The fact that the budget is exceeded is more important than how much it is exceeded. Equally important, reports may be required and investigations conducted when there are unfavorable variances; these investigations are frequently followed by reprimands and recommendations for corrective action to be taken, while favorable reports do not elicit an offsetting favorable response. Control systems may lead to reports of losses but they usually fail to show the opportunity costs of ventures foregone. The result is conservative behavior on the part of managers, often substantially more conservative than top management desires. These comments suggest that the design of control techniques should include the motivational aspects of human activity as a paramount consideration.

Organizations arise from the needs of individuals to cooperate to achieve personal goals otherwise unattainable or reached with less difficulty by organizations. These personal goals usually include social and psychological goals as well as economic ones; in fact, the former are often more important than the latter. Each individual is in turn expected to contribute toward the realization of the organization's goals—often the goals of its dominant members.

Since many of the managers will have goals that differ substantially from the goals of the organization and since these goals will be multidimensional, it is imperative that means be found to obtain goal congruence. Means must be found by which a diverse set of individuals with a diverse set of goals can be motivated to seek the goals of the organization.

6.1 The Budget

The primary mechanism for obtaining goal congruence is the budget process. A budget is a quantitative expression of the goals the organization wishes to achieve and the costs of attaining these goals. The overall or master budget summarizes the budgets of the various subcomponents. In a manufacturing organization this summary includes sales estimates, production plans, and the costs of the supportive activities, such as distribution, purchasing,

[1] See R. Likert, *The Human Organization*, New York: McGraw-Hill Book Company, 1967.

[2] For an example, see D. H. Woods, "Improving Estimates That Involve Uncertainty," *The Harvard Business Review*, July–August 1966, pp. 91–98.

finance, and administration. In a not-for-profit organization, the master budget will include a cost budget that reflects the service requirements placed on the organization. In all organizations the master budget provides an overall view of the financial resources and plans of an organization.

Reaching the objectives involves obtaining resources, their effective utilization, and the delivery of an output (or service) to consumers. The budgeting process serves several purposes:

1. It exposes situations in which plans of subcomponents are inadequate to attain the total organization's objectives. It forces planning.
2. It allows a reiterative process to bring the goals of the organization and the subcomponents into agreement.
3. It provides a means of communicating organization goals down through the organization, and subunit operational limitations up through the organization.
4. It provides a basis for financial planning, subunit coordination, resource acquisition, inventory policy, scheduling, and output distribution.
5. It yields a basis by which activity can be monitored, with actual results being compared to the planned results. One result may be an improvement in the planning process.

Successful operating organizations generally have strong financial and operational planning and budgeting systems. Many organizations have moved to computerized budget systems through which the periodic master budget is quickly obtained and updated during the operating cycle. This increases the ability of management to respond in an appropriate and timely manner to environmental changes.

Despite the ability to quantify and computerize the budgetary process, the human element remains as an inexact, difficult to predict, component of the process. The success of the budget system ultimately depends on people. People must accept the budget system and work sympathetically within it if the system is to be successful. Failure to understand and act consistent with this fact has led the budget process to be regarded with suspicion and as a managerial tool of manipulation in many organizations. The system must be designed carefully and be implemented intelligently if the positive aspects of the budget process are to predominate employee attitudes.

6.1.1 Types of Budgets

Budgets may be classified by either the time period to which they apply or the purpose for which they are prepared. A budget may be prepared to cover any range of time from a month up to multiyear periods. The longer budget periods incorporate long-run strategic plans. They are continually updated and modified as new information becomes available. However, the more common operational budget period is one year, with the budget broken down into months and quarters. Ideally, the yearly budgets are continuously updated so that a yearly budget for the next 12 months is always available.

One component of the master budget is a set of forecasted financial statements. Underlying these financial statements are separate detailed operating and financial budgets. The operating budget may contain a sales budget, a production budget, an expense budget, a purchasing budget, and so on. Even these budgets can be further subdivided to yield plans for each operational unit, such as a division, plant department, or cost center. The financial budget includes a cash budget of day-to-day and week-to-week operating needs, a capital-expenditure budget, and typically a budgeted statement of sources and uses of funds. When combined, these budgets imply a new financial position for the end of the period and an income statement for the period.

The starting point in the budget process is an estimation of prices, unit sales, and hence revenues. Given a sales forecast and data concerning the productive capabilities of the organization, it is possible to determine (1) if present productive capacity is sufficient or whether new facilities are required, (2) inventory needs, (3) labor and material requirements, and (4) delivery schedules. This information, together with data on collection-of-accounts experience and payment terms, is sufficient to estimate cash and funds flows, including tax payments, expenses, investments in machinery or short-term securities, and related items. Once this information is in hand, management can determine whether the organization's goals can be met or whether new strategies must be devised to alter present expectations. For example, the promotional (advertising and sales) budget may be increased to increase the expected unit sales.

In a not-for-profit organization the production objective may be imposed from outside. In this case, the organization's problem is to determine how the objective can be met within the cost limitations imposed on it. A governmental organization may use the budget to support a request for appropriations in order to fulfill the goals which have been set for it.

An important observation at this point is to note the interaction of all aspects of the organization in the budget process. For a profit-making organization, the estimation of unit sales is a critical factor and the basis for the entire operating plan. Just how the sales forecast is made is a subject discussed at length in marketing and operations management courses. We will not attempt to go into it here.

6.1.2 Administering the Budget

As we have indicated, the budget process represents a building process. Given the initial statement of management's goals and their interpretation into operational objectives for the subunits, each cost center or department formulates its budget plan. These budget plans become a part of the plant's (or division's) budget and so on up the line. This process is illustrated in Figure 6.1.

Once the budget process is complete, these same budget figures become the

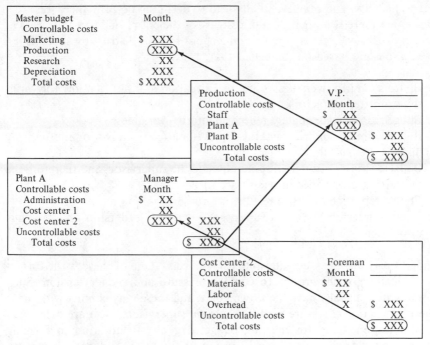

Figure 6.1   The budget process.

basis of cost-control procedures, performance measurement, and feedback evaluation on the budget process itself. To accomplish this important activity, responsibility for the budget is assigned to a budget director. Alternatively, the responsibility for the budget may be assigned to the controller or treasurer (this is likely in a small organization). The budget director acts in a staff position and is responsible for a continually updated budget. Those in senior line positions and often a staff economist work closely with the budget director in budget preparation. The procedures of this group should be formalized into a budget manual. This tends to assure that the process will not be heavily influenced by changes in personnel.

One of the more inportant outputs of the budget process is the report that goes to department heads summarizing actual results. This feedback process assists operating managers to evaluate performance and to formulate future budget inputs. If this feedback is timely, it also helps the operating manager to react to problems and opportunities, and in adapting his behavior to changing environmental conditions.

6.1.3 The Budget and Behavior

The budget consists of a set of specific goals and gives the appearance of inflexibility. It is a source of pressure that can, if it becomes too great, create mistrust, hostility, and may eventually lead to declining performance. Research suggests that there is a great deal of distrust of the entire budgetary process at the supervisory level.[3] There are several reasons for this distrust by supervisors. These reasons are based on the beliefs that:

1. Budgets tend to oversimplify the real situation and fail to allow for variations in external factors.
2. Budgets do not adequately reflect qualitative variables.
3. Budgets simply confirm what the supervisor already knows, or alternatively distorts the true situation.
4. Budgets are too often used to manipulate the supervisor, and therefore the indicated performance measures are suspect.
5. Budget reports emphasize results, not reasons.
6. Budgets interfere with the supervisor's style of leadership and are thus unwelcome.

Budgets may also produce unwanted side effects.[4] One of these is the formation of small informal groups to combat pressure and reduce tension. Such informal groups usually have their own goals, and these may conflict with those of the organization. Pressure is most acute on supervisors, who are compelled to accept responsibility for meeting budgeted goals. In addition to forming informal groups, they may try to shift responsibility to other departments or to question the validity of the budgeted data. Such a situation makes it difficult for the accounting staff functions to be discharged effectively.

Sometimes a supervisor may even be able to distort successfully the measurement process. This might be done by overt manipulation of the data or by actions which improve his immediate performance but harm the firm in the long run; for example, a foreman might delay needed maintenance.

A second undesirable side effect that can develop from the budgeting process is the overemphasis on departmental performance as compared with firm performance. Important interdepartment dependencies and economies may be ignored or overlooked in a quest for optimization of the performance as reported.

A third effect is the perhaps undue publicity given to individual performance, particularly to "failure." The extensive exposure given to performance reports across departments for comparative purposes may increase friction among supervisors as well as between supervisors and the accounting staff.

A fourth and particularly noxious consequence of the budget and performance-evaluation process can be a stifling of initiative. Individuals are often

---

[3] C. Argyris, *The Impact of Budgets on People*, New York: The Controllership Foundation, 1952. The study is admittedly old, but there is no more recent evidence that would cause its conclusions to be suspect.

[4] On these and related issues, see M. E. Wallace, "Behavioral Considerations in Budgeting," *Management Accounting*, August 1966, pp. 3–8.

discouraged from trying something new when the established ways have a large chance of success and new methods portend a greater degree of uncertainty. Churchill, Cooper, and Sainsbury found that workers who were audited conformed more closely to company policy than those who were not. Furthermore, they did so even when there were more efficient alternatives available.[5]

The problems associated with the budgeting process do not mean that the process should be scrapped, but rather that careful consideration is required if it is to have the desired effect. Ideally, the budget provides a plan for achieving a goal or goals that have been accepted by the participants. If the budgeted amounts are reasonable, the projected achievement levels may then become the aspiration levels of the supervisors who must also obtain acceptance of the budget by members of their activities. If the goal aspired to is reached, the manager will experience subjective feelings of success, and if it is not reached, he will experience subjective feelings of failure.[6] The manager, according to the aspiration literature, will extend a disproportionate amount of energy to achieve his aspiration level.[7] It seems, then, useful to investigate various proposals for securing conformance between aspiration levels and firm goals as expressed in budgets.

6.2 Variable Budget Standards

One of the early empirical studies dealing with the interactions of budgets, aspiration levels, and performance in an accounting context was conducted by Stedry.[8] His pioneer study, although subject to question in several areas, highlighted the importance of the acceptance of the goals or standards and the relationship between the level of difficulty implied by the standard and the resulting performance.

Stedry used several groups in controlled experimental situations. Some of these were given budgets and some were not. Among those given budgets, some were asked to set their own goals prior to receiving the budgets and some were given the budget first. Finally, budget levels were varied; high, medium, and low budgets were used.

The groups that were told a goal existed but were never told its amount performed better than those who were told their budgeted amounts initially. Of

[5] N. C. Churchill, W. E. Cooper, and T. Sainsbury, "Laboratory and Field Studies of the Behavioral Effects of Audits," in *Management Controls*, edited by Bonini, Jaedicke, and Wagner, New York: McGraw-Hill Book Company, 1964.

[6] See K. Levin, T. Dimbo, L. Festinger, and P. Sears, "Level of Aspiration," in *Personality and the Behavioral Disorders*, edited by J. M. Hunt, New York: Ronald Press, 1944, pp. 333–378.

[7] On this and several other points here, see S. W. Becker and D. Green, "Budgeting and Employee Behavior," *The Journal of Business*, October 1962, pp. 392–402.

[8] A. C. Stedry, *Budget Control and Cost Behavior*, Englewood Cliffs, N.J.: Prentice-Hall, Inc., 1960.

those told their budgets first, those groups with attainable (medium at best) goals performed better than those given high (difficult to attain) goals. Stedry also found an interaction effect between the setting of the individual's aspiration levels and the imposed budgets.[9] A high budget led to the best performance in those groups setting their aspiration level after receiving the budget, and it led to the lowest performance when given to those groups that set their aspiration level first.

The level of the budget also had an impact on aspiration levels. Groups given budgets with goals less than their aspiration level tended to lower their aspiration level. Such behavior may have led to performance substantially below the abilities of the individuals and the level that was attained without a goal being set. The report on actual performance also influenced the aspiration level, the aspired level tending toward the actual level.

Stedry concluded that budgets should be developed consciously considering the motivational effects. By properly adjusting the budget given to an individual in light of his past performance, he could be motivated toward better performance. He recognized that it would be necessary to consider each individual separately and that it would be necessary for the manager to achieve his aspiration level part of the time.

Although perhaps intuitively appealing, the use of individual budgets to motivate individual managers suffers from several limitations. In the first place, this approach would require a dual record system. Records must be kept of actual performance and expected performance for evaluation and decision making. Simultaneously, a separate set of records must be kept in order to provide the manager with budget levels and performance reports that would achieve the desired motivational results. Since actual results affect aspiration levels, and budgets would be expected to exhibit certain relationships to one another over time, it would seem that two sets of records would be necessary.

Not only is this dual reporting system an additional cost, but it could lead to undesirable results in terms of trust, morale, and performance if it became general knowledge.[10] In addition, a problem may develop if two individuals with similar tasks under similar conditions discover that they are being measured against different standards. This would be a particularly touchy subject with labor unions, which are not sympathetic toward techniques that hint of manipulation. It appears doubtful that the dual reporting system would remain privy to top management alone. Hence, one could accept the basic hypothesis advanced by Stedry, and even admire a motivational system such as he proposes, yet find the problems of implementation insurmountable.

---

[9] Stedry, however, defined aspiration level in terms of the goal hoped for rather than the goal aimed for. There is also a question as to the long-run validity of his essentially short-run study.

[10] Another cost would involve hiring trained psychologists to establish workable means of measuring accurately each employee's aspiration level, assuming that it could be done at all.

The importance of motivation in obtaining goal congruence sends us scurrying elsewhere for insights. Fortunately, students of psychology have been worrying about these issues from some time. We turn now to a cursory examination of some of the more relevant literature.

6.3 Motivation

A primary behavioral problem in achieving an organization's goals is one of motivation. Contrary to the assumptions implicit in much cost accounting literature, superiors are seldom in positions of absolute authority and hence are not able to achieve their ends by decree. The consent and cooperation of those in subordinate positions must be attained. Also, it must be recognized that information is not always perfect. For example, a subordinate may have reason to withhold or alter the data transmitted. Moreover, it is unrealistic to assume that even correct information is always accurately processed.

Perhaps the most questionable assumption of traditional control theory is the assumed indifference of the subordinate to his task and to the goals of the organization. The attitude of the subordinate is assumed basically to be negative. The traditional response to this assumption has been that financial rewards combined with an authoritative control system are required. Yet in recent times we have witnessed an increased awareness of the factors of pride in a job well done, the importance of job content, and other positive factors as variables that can play an important role in achieving goal congruence.

Recent accounting thought has begun to explore the work of several writers in psychology for clues to motivational success. Chief among these is the work of Abraham Maslow and his hierarchy-of-needs-based theory of motivation.[11] Others, including Cyert and March (goals achieved through subordinate efforts), McGregor (Theory X, Theory Y), Herzberg (stressing the job content as distinct from its context), and Skinner (positive reinforcement), have made substantive contributions. None of the theories advanced by these writers has achieved universal acceptance, yet all have contributed to a better understanding of the motivational process.

Dopuch, Birnberg, and Demski have nicely summarized the contributions of these authors to what we know about motivation[12]: "People as a group may behave according to general rules. However, exactly how each person will react to any given factor is not known. Some individuals function best in a structured situation; others do not. Some prefer a precise statement of goals; others would prefer to shape their own. Each individual produces best in the environment that best fits his personal needs."

---

[11] For the references to this and the following works, the reader is referred to the supplementary readings at the end of this chapter.

[12] N. Dopuch, J. Birnberg, and J. Demski, *Cost Accounting: Accounting Data for Management's Decisions*, New York: Harcourt Brace Jovanovich, Inc., 1974; pp. 306–307.

6.4 Participatory Management

The theory behind participatory management is that if there is participation in the setting of goals, the established levels of accomplishment and the required sacrifices to achieve it will be accepted as the goals of the participants.[13]

Participation by itself will not necessarily lead to better performance, however. One problem with the participatory technique is that it may be quite difficult to realize in practice. Argyris describes what he calls pseudo-participation on the part of the supervisor.[14] The supervisor must first perceive that his input is desired and then he must supply his knowledge and expertise to the questions at hand. He must really become involved, not just go through the motions.

Consider, for example, the following comment: "We bring them in (supervisors of budget areas), we tell them that we want their frank opinion, but most of them just sit there and nod their heads. We know they're not coming out with exactly how they feel. I guess budgets scare them."[15] Here is a case where the supervisors do not perceive that their opinions are really desired. The result is a failure of the budget and control process before it begins. Knowledge of this attitude should be a signal to the accounting department of a possibly serious breakdown in the trust and respect of the supervisors for the accounting function. If true, it will almost certainly impair the effectiveness of that department.

It is possible that participation in decisions will cause all levels of employees to join together in a concerted effort to reach and attain the organizational goals (which the employees helped set). The spirit of cooperation that is implicit in participatory management is very attractive to a layman compared to a coercive type of managerial environment implicit in the conventional organizational arrangement. Also, participatory management is not inconsistent with the basic motivations and workings of the free enterprise system, which is aimed at giving all parties an opportunity to exercise their initiative and freedom of choice. It extends the same principles within the organization that are present external to it.

Unfortunately, pushed too far a participatory management can result in too much discussion and delay and not enough action. Too often events do not wait for organizations to fully explore all alternative decisions.

If all parties affected by a decision concur with the decision, then that is ideal, but this is likely to be rare. Even if all parties participate in decisions, we are likely to find unreconcilable differences. In fact, participation might accentuate these differences.

[13] Becker and Green, *op. cit.*, p. 397.
[14] Argyris, *op. cit.*
[15] *Ibid.*, p. 28.

In the future there will probably be a mixture of authoritarian and participatory management. Considerable thought will have to be applied to determine which decisions should be made in an authoritarian manner and which in a participatory manner.

6.5 Other Methods

There are other means of obtaining goal congruence. Mention has already been given to the idea of independently auditing the performances of supervisors and others (examined by Churchill, Cooper, and Sainsbury). An appealing suggestion is the use of an audit technique to evaluate the means by which decisions are made. In other words, managers could be evaluated, at least in part, on the basis of the principles and techniques used in decision making rather than on the consequences of the decisions alone. The method emphasizes the reasonableness of the decision, given the information available at the time the decision had to be made.

Quite often a good procedure can lead to a poor result when decisions must be made under uncertainty. Moreover, poor decision making can occasionally work out for the best. The firm that did not construct a plant in downtown San Francisco just prior to the great earthquake because the payback period was 7 years rather than an arbitrarily imposed limit of 5 years should congratulate itself on its good fortune, not on its decision making. The managerial audit technique due to Churchill, Cooper, and Sainsbury is one means of implementing this approach. The emphasis is placed on the process and procedures rather than solely on the results obtained.

Still another means of motivating employees is through incentive plans. Several firms have gone so far as to adopt group plans that reward the entire group for gains achieved by a member of that group.[16] Some observers believe this may provide a means of circumventing the problems of isolating individual performance in an age characterized by technological dependence.[17] In the opinion of these observers, individual standards may increasingly give way to group standards.

Group standards could be one means of treating the very real problem of goal congruence among technologically oriented employees. These individuals often perceive their goal as recognition among those of similar talents in professional organizations. They may be more interested in securing a position in a firm composed of men with similar talents than in working toward the goals of the firm for which they are presently employed.

Finally, we should not overlook the positive incentives that accrue to challenging and enjoyable jobs, and to opportunities to learn and advance.

---

[16] The individual may be rewarded separately as well.

[17] A well-known example here is the Scanlon Plan. See F. C. Lesieur (ed.), *The Scanlon Plan*, Cambridge, Mass.: The MIT Press, 1958.

These very real incentives contribute to the needs of the subordinate as well as to obtaining the goals of the organization.

6.6 Future of Behavioral Theory in Cost Control

The history of cost control has been marked by the view that the primary incentive for employees is an economic one. Furthermore, employees have been implicitly viewed, at best, as indifferent and, at worst, as wasteful, lazy, and purposefully inefficient. Modern behavioral theory, on the other hand, recognizes a whole host of goals in addition to the economic one. It recognizes that individual behavior is essentially adaptive, problem-solving, and decision-oriented; and that this behavior is constrained by limited knowledge, limited cognitive ability, and changing value structures. Hence, individuals tend to adopt "satisficing" behavior (or constrained optimization behavior) patterns.[18]

Managerial accounting has traditionally been viewed as the primary means of controlling and reducing costs. Yet organization theorists have argued for some time that this traditional view, with its emphasis on cost variances and the budgeted income and the implied behavioral implications, produces or reinforces the responses of indifference, inefficiency, hostility, and conflict which management wishes to avoid.[19] In this regard Katz, Maccoby, and Morse found that management may be more effective when it concentrates on the organizational needs of the firm rather than directly on profit requirements.[20] Although a conclusive statement that a reduction in undesirable responses by employees can be attained by moving toward approaches more consistent with a modern behavioral model cannot be made because of the lack of reliable empirical data, there is a strong presumption that this may be the case.[21]

6.7 Summary

This section contains a list of suggestions for improving the goal congruence and hence the control function. No claim for originality is made here

---

[18] See E. H. Caplan, "Behavioral Assumptions of Management Accounting," *The Accounting Review*, July 1966, pp. 496–509; and "Behavioral Assumptions of Management Accounting—Report of a Field Study," *The Accounting Review*, April 1968, pp. 342–362.

[19] See Argyris, *op. cit.*; M. Haire, *Psychology in Management*, New York: McGraw-Hill Book Company, 1956; R. Likert, *New Patterns of Management*, New York: McGraw-Hill Book Company, 1961; and D. McGregor, *The Human Side of Enterprise*, New York: McGraw-Hill Book Company, 1960.

[20] D. Katz, N. Maccoby, and N. Morse, *Productivity, Supervision and Morale in an Office Situation*, Institute for Social Research, University of Michigan, 1950; and D. Katz, N. Maccoby, G. Gurin, and L. G. Floor, *Productivity, Supervision and Morale Among Railroad Workers*, Institute for Social Research, University of Michigan, 1951.

[21] See Caplan, "Behavioral Assumptions of Management Accounting—Report of a Field Study," *op. cit.*, for a similar conclusion.

(or elsewhere in this chapter for that matter). The ideas have been borrowed liberally from the numerous sources, some cited here or on previous pages.

1. Continued attention should be given to the problem of accounting for human resources.[22] Measures are available by which aspects such as trust and loyalty can be measured. Changes in these measures may provide indications of the effects of different policies.

2. Communication and feedback devices need reexamination. It is important for individuals to learn about their success or failure. More frequent feedback is required than is generally now supplied.[23,24] If performance equals or exceeds expectations, aspirations will improve and increased efficiency can be obtained. If performance is slightly below expectations, feedback is needed so that employees will continue to work for the budgeted goals. If performance is substantially below expectations, budgetary revisions downward may be in order to prevent the frustrations associated with failure to reach aspiration levels, which in turn leads to lower future performance. These comments suggest that the feedback and budget cycle should be tied to aspiration levels and their changes rather than to an arbitrary time cycle where economically feasible.[25] The time dimension is important, however, in the short run, factors may not be controllable by the manager that are under his control over the long run.

A related point concerns the matching of the input and output data with the period budget. This suggests that time periods be used for which useful input and output figures can be developed. The figures must be valid not only from a measurement point of view, but in addition they must be related. In other words, the input-activity measures must be related to the output-activity results if the resulting feedback is to be of any value. The problem of measurement and reporting time lags is one that needs attention on this score. The accounting function has a significant role to play in creating believable data.

3. Accountants should work more closely with behavioral scientists. Furthermore, they should learn more of this area themselves. Encouragement should be given to those on the job to obtain this training. Such an approach will accelerate a total-system's view of the accounting function, a step that will facilitate more goal-oriented control techniques.

4. Participation schemes should be introduced into organizations with due consideration for the implementation problems entailed. Where such plans exist, consideration should be given to improving their effectiveness. When this is done

[22] See, for example, R. L. Brummet, E. G. Flamholtz, and W. C. Pyle, "Human Resource Measurement—A Challenge for Accountants," *The Accounting Review*, April 1968, pp. 217–224.

[23] See Becker and Green, *op. cit.*, pp. 399–400.

[24] The problem of data abundance, an outgrowth of EDP and the increased likelihood of mistakes, omissions, and a decline of skepticism of the data provide related problems.

[25] *Ibid.* See also J. L. Child and J. W. M. Whiting, "Determinants of Level of Aspiration: Evidence from Everyday Life," in *The Study of Personality*, edited by H. Brand, New York: John Wiley & Sons, Inc., 1954, pp. 145–158.

a system of participation with some goals imposed will improve the setting within which effective control can be exercised. This, it should be emphasized, is a necessary but not sufficient condition for effective control. The accounting department still needs to develop and cultivate the trust of the line positions through better measurement techniques if it is to help the line managers do a better job.

QUESTIONS AND PROBLEMS

6–1 Should decisions be made to optimize the well-being of a segment of an organization as a whole?

6–2 Are quantitative measures of dollars of expected profit (or rate of return or present value) good and sufficient bases for making business decisions?

6–3 Is cost accounting the best means of implementing a cost-reduction program?

6–4 Who has responsibility for repair department costs?

6–5 Of the several possible objectives of a cost-accounting system, which are most likely to be successfully achieved?

6–6 Should cost standards be hard or easy to attain?

6–7 Are people more motivated by threats of punishment or by the offer of rewards for accomplishment?

6–8 Assume you have been directed by the president of your firm to improve profits by 10%. What alternatives do you have?

6–9 What methods might be used to motivate development and research department personnel toward achieving the firm's objectives?

6–10 How should a class in, say, cost control, tackle its own motivation problem?

6–11 Every six months the production manager, I. Makit, and the purchasing manager, D. LeGrump, determine the raw material and other input needs of the production department. LeGrump knows that he is responsible for meeting the general purchasing schedule once it is set up and agreed to by Makit and himself. Eight weeks ago Makit advised LeGrump that he noticed that the supply of one essential input was running low and that he would need the next batch of raw material on time (in accordance with the original production schedule) in four weeks. LeGrump found that the regular supplier could not make delivery in accordance with this schedule. He called a number of places and finally found a supplier who accepted the four-week commitment.

LeGrump followed up by mail and was assured by the supplier that he would receive the material in time. The matter was so important that LeGrump called again a week in advance and was again assured that the material would arrive in time.

The day before the material was to be used LeGrump checked once again and found that the shipment had not been received. Inquiry revealed that the shipment had been misdirected by the railroad and was still in Chicago, 500 miles away, and would not be received for 2 days.

The material was finally obtained but only after considerable extra expense (only a part of which is recoverable) and substantial downtime.

Where do you believe the responsibility lies, and who should bear this cost?

6–12 The Spede Manufacturing Company owns a trucking fleet, has its own utility services, and maintains a repair shop. These are all operated as profit centers. The trucking division had been complaining to the utility division that its wires at one point in the road were too low and did not give the larger trucks enough clearance. The repair shop agreed to make the changes, but wanted to know whether the costs of the adjustment were to be charged to the utility division or the trucking division. Both the divisions refused to accept the $1,500 cost of making the adjustment, and the repair shop refused to perform the task unless it could charge the costs of making the adjustment to one of the two divisions. One day the top of a truck caught the wires and ripped them down. The cost of repairing the lines was $2,500, and there was an additional cost to the firm of $4,000 because of the disruption of service. Investigation disclosed that the truck had failed to clamp down its top properly and the extra 2 inches of height caused the catching of the wire. The trucking division and the utility division both refused to accept the $2,500 repair charges.

Required: Assume that you are the controller in charge of the accounting for the three service divisions (repair, trucking, and utility). What would be your next step? What is the proper role of responsible accounting in determining the blame for this situation?

6–13 The following letter was received by a new controller. Write a reply.

THE KROCKS AND POTTS COMPANY
(MAKERS OF FINE DINNERWARE)
SCURRY, OHIO

Controller   Today
13 Morningside Avenue
Sashay, Ohio

Dear Controller:

I hesitate to write to you even before your arrival, but a problem has come up in the controller's division about which you should be informed.

As you know, we have recently overhauled our entire organization and brought in a number of new people. One of these new people is Ben Pole, who has taken over our Putter, Pennsylvania, activities. Ben is a good man and well suited to our decentralized activities.

About the time that we hired Ben, U. U. Pusher, one of our extremely bright and young staff members, took over our new performance analysis staff. This staff operates out of the controller's office.

It is Pusher's duty to prepare reports showing budgeted performance, actual performance, and explanations of any differences for both divisions of the plant. Pusher has a staff of two men, one for each division, who operate out of our main plant. They have consulted and are acquainted with their respective division's line and staff executive personnel as well as with the operation.

Until yesterday we thought all was going well. Yesterday afternoon, however, Ben Pole stormed into my office quite unhappy about the whole setup.

I can't recall his exact words, but the gist of his comments indicate that he feels Pusher's staff is usurping his responsibilities. He feels they snoop around asking too many questions and generally waste his staff's time. Ben feels it is his job to analyze and explain his division's performance.

From your experience, can you think of any reason for Ben's position, and what would you suggest we do, if anything, about his complaint?

> Sincerely,
> I. M. Thebos
> Manager

6–14[26]

Memo
To: Controller
From: Thebos
Subject: Budgets

Ben Pole has sent me the following budget report, which applies to his manufacturing supervisor:

Period	1	2	3	4	5	6
Budget	$39,000	$40,000	$39,500	$38,000	$38,500	$38,500
Actual	41,000	39,500	38,000	39,000	38,500	38,250
Variance	2,000U	500F	1,500F	1,000U	0	250F

The supervisor has a substantial number of men and a large amount of equipment under his control. He is paid a "base" salary which is actually somewhat low for his type of work. However, we have a rather liberal bonus plan which pays him an additional $1,000 per month each time he makes his budget and 2% of the saving (amount below budget).

We have been quite pleased so far with the continued improvement in the supervisor's performance and wonder if this might not be a model for the rest of our operations. What do you think?

I. M. Thebos

Required: Write a reply.

6–15 The following is a condensation of an actual case. In a particular plant a mistake was made on a customer's special order. The goods were returned at a cost of $3,000, which was paid by the manufacturer. The allocated costs to these

---

[26] This problem, as well as 6–11 and 6–13, was suggested by problems in C. H. Horngren, *Cost Accounting: A Managerial Emphasis*, Englewood Cliffs, N.J.: Prentice-Hall, Inc. 1962.

goods was $100,000. The customer was so unhappy that he decided to take his entire business elsewhere. This business had been growing and amounted to about 4% of the manufacturing firm's total billings over the past fiscal year.

There developed a strong argument over which segment of the firm should receive the charge for the error and how large the charge should be.

There seemed to be general agreement that the problem was poor workmanship. The manufacturing department argued that they had been on overtime the whole period and that the extra workers hired for this particular job were not able to do the job. The personnel department countered by saying that under the tight labor markets, this was the best that could be done and that management knew this when it accepted the special order. Both agreed that the inspection department should have located the error if it had done its job properly. Inspection maintained that perhaps it could have caught the problem even though it was unusual but even if it had it would have saved only the small transportation expense. Further, its equipment and procedures would have to be changed substantially if the firm wished to assure that defects such as the present kind would be detected by the inspection department.

The plant manager finally gave up. He decided to charge the error to no department. He explained "I thought it might be best to put the whole thing in a loss account, otherwise someone would be hurt."

a. What is the most important issue here?

b. If you were the controller what advice would you give the plant manager? (Indicate the priority attaching to your suggestion.)

6–16 In a behavioral study Stedry hypothesized that if an individual were at least moderately discouraged, the difference between actual and aspired to cost levels would increase because the individual would then allow actual costs to rise. Do you agree or not, why?

6–17 The president of Nifty Novelties Company, a wholesaler, presents you with a comparison of distribution costs for two salesmen and wants to know if you think the salesmen's compensation plan is working to the detriment of the company. He supplies the following information for the month of June.

	Salesmen	
	Smith	Brown
Gross Sales	$25,000	$15,000
Sales returns	2,000	500
Cost of goods sold	18,000	9,000
Reimbursed expenses (e.g., entertainment)	600	200
Other direct charges (e.g., samples)	400	500
Commission rate on gross sales dollars	5%	5%

a. What inappropriate sales practices might be encouraged by basing commissions on gross sales?

b. Is there information to support the president's concern? What additional information would be useful before any decisions are made?

(Adapted from the 1966 Uniform C.P.A. examination.)

6–18 Some accountants argue that budgets have motivational impact and should therefore be changed from period to period and from person to person for motivational reasons. Comment.

6–19 "Static budgets have no use if large deviations from the budgeted activity level are expected." Comment.

6–20 Suppose a control system is based on the following premise. It is better to set a standard of 10 hours knowing it will take 15 to do the job than to set 15 hours as the standard if it would then take 16 hours. It is better to do the job in 15 hours than in 16. Do you agree?

SUPPLEMENTARY READING

ARGYRIS, C., "Human Problems with Budgets," *The Harvard Business Review*, January–February 1953, pp. 97–110.

——, *The Impact of Budgets on People*, New York: The Controllership Foundation, 1952.

BECKER, S. W., and D. GREEN, "Budgeting and Employee Behavior," *The Journal of Business*, October 1962, pp. 392–402.

BENSTON, G., "The Role of the Firm's Accounting System for Motivation," *The Accounting Review*, April 1963, pp. 347–354.

BRUNS, W. J., "Accounting Information and Decision Making: Some Behavioral Hypotheses," *The Accounting Review*, July 1968, pp. 469–480.

——, and D. T. DeCOSTER, *Accounting and Its Behavioral Implications*, New York: McGraw-Hill Book Company, 1969.

CAPLAN, E. H., "Behavioral Assumptions of Management Accounting," *The Accounting Review*, July 1966, pp. 496–509.

——, "Behavioral Assumptions of Management Accounting—Report of a Field Study," *The Accounting Review*, April 1968, pp. 243–362.

CYERT, R., and J. MARCH, *A Behavioral Theory of the Firm*, Englewood Cliffs, N.J.: Prentice-Hall, 1963.

DECOSTER, D., and J. FERTAKIS, "Budget-Induced Pressure and Its Relationship to Supervisory Behavior," *Journal of Accounting Research*, Autumn 1968, pp. 237–246.

HERZBERG, F., B. MAUSNER, and B. SNYDERMAN, *The Motivation to Work*, New York: John Wiley & Sons, Inc., 1959.

HOFSTEDE, G., *The Game of Budget Control*, New York: Van Nostrand Reinhold Company, 1967.

LIKERT, R., *The Human Organization, Its Management and Value*, New York: McGraw-Hill Book Company, 1967.

MARCH, J. G., and H. A. SIMON, *Organization*, New York: John Wiley & Sons, Inc., 1958.

MASLOW, A., *Eupsychian Management: A Journal*, Homewood, Ill.: Richard D. Irwin, Inc., 1965.

McGREGOR, D., *The Human Side of Enterprise*, New York: McGraw-Hill Book Company, 1960.

————, "An Uneasy Look at Performance Appraisal," *The Harvard Business Review*, September–October 1972, pp. 133–139.

SCHIFF, M., and A. LEWIN, "The Impact of People on Budgets," *The Accounting Review*, April 1970, pp. 259–268.

SKINNER, B., *Science and Human Behavior*, New York: Free Press, 1953.

STEDRY, A. C., *Budget Control and Cost Behavior*, Englewood Cliffs, N.J.: Prentice-Hall, Inc., 1960.

WALLACE, M. E., "Behavioral Considerations in Budgeting," *Management Accounting*, August 1966, pp. 3–8.

Chapter 7

Inventory Valuation
and Decisions

Inventory valuation is somewhat complex because management wishes to accomplish two quite separate purposes: to make inventory-level decisions and to provide data for financial reporting to internal and external parties. The objective of decisions concerning inventory levels is to minimize the cost associated with inventories. One relevant cost in this connection is the opportunity cost of lost sales. A second relevant cost is the inventory carrying cost, which can be determined using the average inventory value and the per dollar cost of carrying inventory.

Financial reporting, on the other hand, requires not only useful measures of inventory values at the beginning and end of the period but also data that lead to meaningful income figures. The dual information requirement for external reporting makes the simultaneous attainment of meaningful figures for both inventory values and income measures difficult. A theoretical approach to this problem and a practical alternative are suggested.

Management also has the task of measuring performance for evaluation purposes and to control costs. Here the question of inventory valuation is joined by the question of determining the responsibility for cost incurrence. The approaches used for external reporting are not necessarily useful for internal performance measurement and cost control.

7.1 Inventory Costs and Internal Decision Making

The establishment of optimal inventory levels is one part of determining the current asset portfolio and is one of the more important decisions the firm must make on a continuing basis in relation to its operations. Recent years have seen the development of several formal models for inventory control.

Implementing these models requires a good deal of data that the accountant should be in a position to supply. Unfortunately, however, accountants have frequently lacked familiarity with the models and hence have failed to accumulate the relevant data.

The number of companies using formal and sophisticated inventory models is not nearly so large as the recent deluge of writing on the subject might indicate. Nevertheless, the simple economic-order-quantity model, the EOQ model, with some of its extensions, has been used with success by a number of companies. Furthermore, the future will no doubt see increased use of the simple models as well as an introduction of more complex models. The range of models is extensive, and it is not the task of this book to develop the theory of inventory control. Fortunately, however, the data requirements of the simpler models are reasonably constant across situations. It is these general data requirements that are examined here.

7.1.1 Reasons for Holding Inventories

Inventories are held for essentially three reasons: transactions, precautionary, and speculative. If a firm knows the demand for its products, the output of its productive process, and the availability of the factors of production with certainty, and if input prices will not change, then it will have only a transactions reason to hold inventory. If, on the other hand, uncertainty exists concerning demand, the output of the productive process, or the supply (and timing) of the input factors, then a precautionary motive for holding inventory arises. This motive occurs when, for example, there are opportunity costs associated with stock-outs.

When input prices can be expected to change, the opportunity to speculate on the expected increase or decrease in prices exists. In general, formal inventory models do not include this possibility. Nevertheless, management should be aware of the fact that optimal inventory levels do depend to some degree on expected input price movements. For example, if prices of input factors are expected to fall, a firm should consider allowing its inventory to decline in the expectation of replacing it at a lower price later. The firm would, however, be limited in its actions by inventory needs for both transactions and precautionary purposes. The savings arising from lower prices would be augmented by the carrying costs avoided with a lower inventory and decreased by the increased likelihood of stock-outs.

7.1.2 Inventory Costs

The relevant inventory costs are suggested by the equation for the economic order quantity, EOQ, for the inventory model involving stock-out costs for inventory items that can be back-ordered and a given time period, T^1:

$$\text{EOQ} = \sqrt{\frac{2C_1 D}{C_2}\left(\frac{C_2 + C_3}{C_3}\right)} \tag{7.1}$$

where

C_1 = order cost (per order)

C_2 = storage cost (per unit per time period T)

C_3 = stock-out cost (per unit per time period T)

D = total demand (expected during time period T)

The costs associated with inventories arise from the processes of acquiring and carrying them, and from being out of stock. The costs of acquiring inventories include the incremental costs of placing and receiving orders as well as the incremental cost of setting up production. These costs also include inspection, shipping, handling, returning inferior goods, setup costs, and paying bills. Carrying costs are composed of storage costs such as rent, insurance, costs of spoilage and obsolescence, taxes, and the opportunity cost of the funds tied up in the inventory. Stock-out costs include the costs of lost goodwill during the stock-out.

It is, or should be, the accountant's task to supply the cost data suggested above. He must be cognizant not only of what data are needed but also of the likely measurement errors associated with his figures. If this information is available, the sensitivity of the optimal solutions can be examined.

Data relevant to stock-out costs are difficult to obtain with accuracy. Permanently lost sales and declines in goodwill are very difficult to estimate, and hence the figures used are usually very unreliable. Bias and lack of objectivity are both present in most cases. The costs of special orders, although somewhat easier to obtain, also present problems, since they are often influenced by the time when the order is made and the conditions, such as the required delivery time and size, which surround the order.

The determination of acquisition costs is also difficult. In part this is true because these costs are common to other activities as well. Inspectors may inspect output as well as input, for example. Furthermore, several variables usually influence the incremental level of these costs, and hence some technique which can isolate the effect of each variable, such as multiple regression analysis, is required to obtain adequate estimates of these costs.

[1] See C. W. Churchman, R. L. Ackoff, and E. L. Arnoff, *Introduction to Operations Research*, New York: John Wiley & Sons, Inc., 1957, pp. 205–206. The basic EOQ model is $\text{EOQ} = \sqrt{2C_1 D/C_2}$. If there are price breaks at certain quantity levels, or if prices are expected to change through time, the solution is more complex.

Carrying costs are perhaps the easiest to estimate, although even here the opportunity-cost measure of holding inventories is subject to a wide estimation range. Typically, carrying costs are estimated as a percentage rate per dollar of average-inventory investment based on actual, estimated, or expected figures for the component costs. Determination of the proper percentage requires, initially, an estimate of the component costs making up C_2.

But how should the average-inventory investment be measured? In theory it should represent the funds tied up in the inventory investment. Two alternative measures of this value would be the replacement cost or net sales value of the inventory. Raw materials and often finished goods have reasonably active markets from which replacement or net sales values, respectively, can be estimated. This is not generally the case for partially finished items, which typically constitute the largest segment of inventories for most manufacturing-oriented firms. In this case the inventory values may be estimated by using the cost of the resources committed to the goods in process. A question then arises concerning the inclusion of fixed costs in these inventory values.

7.1.3 Fixed Costs and Inventory Decisions

The adherents of including only variable costs argue that fixed costs would be incurred in any event, and thus they are period costs and not inventoriable. This argument has some validity but falls short of proving the case for using only variable costs. A fixed cost may not be as inevitable or as nonrelevant as the statement suggests.

Consider the wages of a plant manager and the depreciation of the plant. These are fixed costs, but it is possible that if there were no intention of producing the product the plant could be sold or diverted to producing another product. The plant manager could be switched to another job. Fixed costs are relevant costs of product when there are opportunity costs connected with the factors of production, which in turn give rise to the fixed costs. Thus the value of the plant manager's services, if he were performing other tasks, represents the opportunity cost of the plant manager working on the present product. In like manner, the funds which would result from the sale of a plant or the net revenue that would result from other uses of the plant are the opportunity costs of using the plant to make the present product. It may be reasonable to substitute the wages of the plant manager and the depreciation of the plant for the opportunity costs of these factors of production, and to consider these costs as inventoriable. The exclusion of fixed costs from inventory tends to result in an understatement of inventory, since no estimate is being made for the opportunity costs of the factors of production which lead to costs that are classified as being fixed.

In many cases the factors of production that give rise to fixed costs do not have alternative uses; their opportunity costs are zero. These fixed costs are time-period costs and are not inventoriable: they would be incurred even if production ceased. The variable (or incremental) costs incurred in producing the units of product are the only inventoriable costs in this case.

An alternative approach to inventory valuation would abandon the concept of cost entirely in favor of a present-value or present-benefit basis. Using this approach the value of an inventoriable item would be the smaller of the item's net sales value or its replacement cost.[2] This approach can be summarized by the relationship

$$I = \text{Min}(C, S) \tag{7.2}$$

where I is the inventory value; C is the replacement cost, measured using current, opportunity, or avoidable cost; and S is the net sales value of the item to be inventoried. I is equal to the minimum of C or S. The inventory value cannot exceed the net sales value, although it may be less. Similarly, the inventory value cannot exceed replacement cost.

For an example, assume that the variable cost of an item in stock was $80, the cost (in economic terms) of replacing the item in the next period is expected to be $85, and the net sales values is $100. Under these assumptions, the inventoriable value would be $85. If to alter the assumptions slightly, the net sales value remains at $100 but the replacement cost is $110, the inventory estimate is $100. On the other hand, if the replacement cost is $60, then $60 is the inventory value of the item. Finally, if there is no opportunity to replace the item during the next period, but it could be expected to be sold, then the net sales value of the item, $100, would be the inventory value of the item.

Since the inventoriable cost is likely to exceed variable costs, it could be said that some fixed costs are being inventoried. However, using the present benefit procedure for inventory valuation purposes, there is no need to know the actual cost, since valuation is based on future benefits, not past costs.

The discussion can also be related to the reasons for holding inventories. If future variable costs are expected to increase, the replacement cost of the item rises and hence so does the inventoriable value (assuming that the net sales value exceeds the higher replacement cost). This reflects the speculative reason for holding inventory. Also, if failure to produce today is expected to result in lost future sales because of limited capacity and if replacement cost is higher than net sales value, the inventoriable value is the net sales value. This is the precautionary motive for holding inventory. Finally, inventory held for transaction purposes would also lead to a direct application of expression (7.2).[3]

---

[2] The approach is similar but not identical to that proposed by G. H. Sorter and C. T. Horngren, "Asset Recognition and Economic Attributes—The Relevant Costing Approach," *The Accounting Review*, July 1962, pp. 391–399; and C. T. Horngren and G. H. Sorter, "Direct Costing for External Reporting," *The Accounting Review*, January 1961, pp. 84–93.

[3] Alternatives to producing inventory would be to acquire additional productive facilities and employees or, possibly, to subcontract. The least-cost alternative should be chosen.

It is important to emphasize that the present-value approach rests on subjective judgments and hence is unlikely to receive wide acceptance. Yet it can be argued that procedures presently being used to estimate the value of goods-in-process inventory are also subjective. Any procedure adopted must find its justification in the fact that it leads to reasonable estimates of the relevant figures at acceptable cost.

7.1.4 Additional Factors

As the basic EOQ model is extended, the effect of lead times in ordering and quantity discounts on purchases are two of several complications that are introduced. The incorporation of lead times and an uncertain demand rate create the need for a safety stock. Safety stocks add to expense and it becomes necessary to balance this cost against the cost of stock-outs.

7.1.5 Inventory Cost Changes and Control

The inventory EOQ formula and the associated total cost equation also provide the manager with the means of evaluating the sensitivity of costs to the decision. For example, if a different value for the decision variable is inserted, the new total cost can be computed. It is also possible to compute the total cost if the inventory policy is adjusted to reflect an expected change in a cost variable. Where several costs vary at once and probability distributions for these changes might be estimated (perhaps several distributions would be required for one or more of the cost variables to take dependencies into account), computer simulation techniques can be used to estimate the total cost and make the comparisons suggested in this paragraph.

7.2 Inventory Costing and Financial Reporting

Recent years have witnessed an increasing application of marginal analysis to decision making and the reporting of only variable costs on income statements for internal-performance evaluation. The increased attention to variable costs has produced a continuing argument among accountants concerning the appropriateness of valuing inventories on the basis of variable costs alone for financial reporting and hence influencing external decision making. The approach can be referred to as variable costing.[4]

The term *variable costing* is used in two ways: (1) it can refer to a method of accounting that considers fixed costs as costs of the time period and treats only

---

[4] The terms *direct costing* or *marginal costing* are frequently used instead of variable costing. They all refer to a procedure that considers fixed costs an expense of the time period and only variable costs as costs of product.

variable costs as inventoriable costs; and (2) variable costing may refer to a system of internal reporting and analysis for decisions which differentiates between fixed and variable costs. The distinction is central to an important issue in cost accounting: whether costs are being computed for the purpose of inventory valuation for internal decision making and control or for the purpose of reporting to outsiders.

In this book the term "variable costing" is used only when the discussion concerns inventory valuation for reporting financial position and income. The distinction between fixed and variable costs is useful for decision making, but the necessity to determine the nature of costs for purposes of decision making is not dependent on, although it may be influenced by, the method of accounting for fixed costs for financial reporting purposes. The additional problem in reporting is that the inventory value is a variable in the computation of period income.

Under generally accepted procedures of financial accounting, all or a portion of the fixed costs are absorbed as costs of product, and the financial income reported for a period is affected not only by sales and efficiency but also by the amount of production and by the change in inventory. Thus the reported income of a period may be increased not only by more sales or improved efficiency but merely by producing more and putting the excess into inventory. This can be illustrated with an example.

Example

Assume that a company sells 5,000 units at $8 each in both March and April. The production costs are identical for both months. They are:

> Fixed Costs $90,000 (per month)
>
> Variable Costs $1 (per unit)

Production for March was 10,000 units and for April 20,000 units. The normal activity for both months is 15,000 units.

A variety of income statements (see Table 7–1) are possible for the two months, depending on the policy regarding the accounting for the fixed costs.

It is important to note that the "actual" cost procedure and the normal-costing procedure give the same reported income if the unabsorbed overhead is allocated back to the product sold and to the ending inventory and a LIFO cost flow is assumed. Both procedures result in the reported income of the period being a function of the level of production as well as of sales.

Frequently, activity variances in financial reporting are handled as expenses of the period in which they are incurred instead of being considered as costs of product to be allocated to the costs of goods sold and to the ending inventory. Using one procedure they are included with other expenses of the period and allowed to affect the reported income. In the second procedure they are sub-

Table 7–1   Income Statement Using Actual Costs and Normal-Activity Costing

	"Actual" Costs		Normal-Activity Costing (overhead variance allocated to product)	
	March	April	March	April
Sales	$40,000	$40,000	$40,000	$40,000
Less: Variable costs	5,000	5,000	5,000	5,000
Fixed costs	45,000*	22,500†	45,000‡	22,500§
	$50,000	$27,500	$50,000	$27,500
Income (loss)	($10,000)	$12,500	($10,000)	$12,500

* The fixed cost per unit produced was $90,000/10,000, or $9 per unit. There were 5,000 units sold; thus the fixed costs charged to expense were $45,000. The remainder are inventoried.

† The fixed cost per unit produced was $90,000/20,000, or $4.50 per unit. There were 5,000 units sold; thus, the fixed costs charged to expense were $22,500. This statement assumes a LIFO cost flow.

‡ On the basis of normal activity the fixed cost per unit was $90,000/15,000, or $6 per unit. There were 10,000 units produced in March; thus, the fixed cost absorbed by product was $60,000 and the unabsorbed fixed cost was $30,000. Half of the unabsorbed overhead, $15,000, is charged to inventory and half to expense, since 5,000 units were sold and 5,000 units remain in inventory. Thus, the total fixed-cost charge to expense was $15,000 of allocated, unabsorbed overhead and $30,000 of normal overhead (one half of the absorbed fixed costs of $60,000).

§ During April production was 20,000 units; thus there was $120,000 = $6(20,000) of fixed overhead absorbed to product. There was a favorable activity variance of $30,000 = $6 (20,000 − 15,000). The fixed cost charged to expense was the number of units sold times the normal-overhead rate of $6 (this assumes a LIFO flow of costs), minus 5,000/20,000 of the $30,000 activity variance.

tracted from the reported operating income so that income is not affected by the level of activity. The results are shown in Table 7–2.

The second normal-costing procedure gives equal reported incomes for the two months if attention is focused on a subtotal before the deduction of the activity variance. However, this might result in the reporting of income for all 12 months but a reported loss for the year when the activity variance is taken into consideration.

The last procedure illustrated for these facts is variable costing (see Table 7–3). When this process is followed, all fixed costs are accounted for as expenses of the period in which they are incurred, and only variable costs are considered to be inventoriable.

Under variable costing the reported incomes of the two periods are the same. This is consistent with the fact that the sales and efficiencies of the two periods

Table 7–2   Income Statements with Different Treatment of the Idle-Activity Variance

| | Normal-Activity Costing (activity variance included as an expense) | | Normal-Activity Costing (activity variance subtracted from the reported operating income) | |
	March	April	March	April
Sales	$40,000	$40,000	$40,000	$40,000
Less: Cost of goods sold*	35,000	35,000	35,000	35,000
Activity variance	30,000	(30,000)		
	$65,000	$ 5,000		
Operating income (loss)	($25,000)	$35,000	$ 5,000	$ 5,000
Less: Activity variance			30,000	(30,000)
Income (loss)			($25,000)	$35,000

* The $35,000 is equal to $5,000 variable cost and $30,000 fixed overhead.

were exactly the same and that the only difference in the two periods was the level of production. While the other methods all arrived at a reported income for one period and a loss for the other, the variable-costing procedure shows the same loss for both periods. The total reported loss is also larger than in the other methods.

Table 7–3   Income Statement: Variable Costing

| | Variable Costing | |
	March	April
Sales	$40,000	$40,000
Less: Variable costs	5,000	5,000
Excess of revenues over variable costs	$35,000	$35,000
Less: Fixed costs	90,000	90,000
Income (loss)	($55,000)	($55,000)

Accounting theoreticians generally feel that income should not be a function of production or of the level of inventory that is carried (especially where the higher the inventory, the higher the resulting income). They do not wish to recognize revenue at the production stage except in special cases where the sale is certain and the production period is long (shipbuilding and extractive industries offer examples). Generally, they hold that a completed legal sale is necessary to justify the recognition of revenue. It is paradoxical that these accountants, who are so careful about when to recognize revenue, often allow income and asset values to be distorted by procedures which indiscriminately permit the inclusion of fixed costs in inventory values. If fixed costs are included in inventory, under conventional accounting procedures, then the income is affected by changes in inventory and changes in production, as well as by the level of sales and efficiency.

The primary advantage of variable costing is that reported income is not directly affected by changes in inventory and changes in production. To increase reported income, either total sales must increase or some meaningful change must be achieved in the cost–revenue relationship. The fixed costs of production of the period are not inventoried but are charged to expense. Thus the final reported income figure is not influenced by fluctuations in inventory levels. This is desirable since an increase in inventory may indicate increased efficiency, but, on the other hand it may reflect inefficiency, since excess inventory gives rise to additional handling, storage, and carrying costs, which are undesirable. Also, increasing inventory levels may suggest the existence of marketing problems. Unfortunately, the inventory values obtained by omitting fixed costs may give little indication as to the real value or even the inventory's cost (when the value excludes the opportunity costs of fixed factors of production). Hence, such values are unlikely to be useful in the models discussed in Section 7.1.

A policy of including only variable costs as costs of inventory biases the valuation of the inventory in the direction of being less than the actual value of the inventory either in terms of net sales value, value in use, or replacement cost. This conclusion is based on the assumption that some fixed factors of production are in scarce supply and have alternative uses; thus, they have opportunity costs. The allocation and absorption of fixed costs to inventory may be incorrect because they are based on historical costs, but the inclusion of fixed costs can be considered as an attempt to include an estimate of the opportunity costs of the factors of production that conventionally result in fixed-cost charges.

Another argument advanced in favor of inventorying fixed costs is the concept of matching expenses with the revenues which they help earn. If the fixed costs are valid costs of product (as is suggested above), it is argued that they should not be considered an expense until the product is sold. The accounting treatment of the variable- and fixed-cost factors identified as costs of product should be the same.

7.2.1 Criteria for Judging Financial Reporting Procedures

What is good financial reporting? The decision whether or not to use variable costing for financial reporting must be decided by whether or not it is good reporting. There follow three criteria that can be used in deciding what shall constitute good financial reporting. These are:

1. Is it in accordance with generally accepted accounting practice and conventions as set forth by professional organizations and governmental bodies?
2. Is it in accordance with good accounting theory?
3. Is it useful for decision making?

Too frequently the first two criteria are cited as the determining factors in choosing the proper method. The third criterion is neglected or assumed to be automatically covered by accounting practice or basic accounting theory. This assumption is unwarranted.

If accounting practice is to be the determining criterion, then change is impossible, since by definition what is being done is correct. The accounting practice in effect today is of interest, but a statement of convention should not be used as evidence that a procedure is correct or incorrect. The fact that an official pronouncement approves absorption costing does not of itself determine whether variable costing is a reasonable procedure or not.

The criterion of accounting theory should not be discarded lightly. The authors of the past 70 years have contributed tremendously to raising the level of accounting practice. The fact that thought-provoking writings have been produced by such men as Cole, Hatfield, Paton, and others makes accountants reluctant to modify time-honored concepts. But it must be recognized that these men changed accounting practice, advocated further changes not accepted, and certainly did not intend to freeze accounting thought. To quote an accounting authority as a justification for an accounting procedure is meaningful only to the extent that the logic of the authority continues to be applicable. It does not actually show one or another position to be sound. Even when a logical argument can be presented in favor of a given position, it does not follow that yet another position is unsound.

It is useful for decision making? There are times when it is useful to inventory fixed costs and there are other times when these costs should be excluded. One means of achieving this result is to use the present-benefit approach discussed in Section 7.1.3. However, the same factors of subjectivity and complexity that work against its use for valuing work-in-process inventories also make unlikely its acceptance for financial reporting. In practice, the accountant typically has only three alternatives available:

1. Dividing the total costs incurred during the period by the number of units produced to obtain the unit cost (absorption costing).
2. Using a standard-overhead rate based on a predetermined level of activity, for example normal activity, and considering any activity variance as a cost of the time period. (To distribute the variance to product would make this procedure the equivalent of the first procedure.)
3. Inventorying only variable costs.

All three procedures give the same inventory and income results if, in every period, all of the product produced were sold. However, these assumptions seldom describe the actual situation, for some of the product produced is usually not sold. The problem is made even more complex by the fact that production as well as the amount sold changes from period to period.

Since whichever method is used makes no attempt to judge fixed costs in terms of their applicability to future cost reduction or incremental revenue production, none of the choices is optimal. Recognizing the limitations imposed by restricting the set of alternatives, a reasonable choice at least for determining income is the third one. The first two procedures result in the incomes of successive periods being affected by the changes in production and the changes in inventory. With the second procedure, not only is income affected by changes in production, but by using a predetermined overhead rate based on normal activity, the company can show a deceptively high income figure with very low sales. (If the fixed overhead is overabsorbed to product, and the activity variance is favorable, this reduces the expenses and increases the income of the period assuming that inventories increase.)

If variable costs alone are inventoried, the unit value of the inventory is unaffected by fluctuating productions levels. This is the variable-costing solution. Under variable costing the inventory presented in the position statement would include only variable costs. An additional advantage of this procedure is that, in the absence of input price changes or changes in efficiency, the inventory reported in the position statement would reflect changes in the physical units on hand. This may be preferred over fluctuations in the cost per unit caused by variations in the level of production. The fluctuation occurs if the cost per unit is determined by dividing the actual costs by actual production, or by distributing the idle-activity variance back to inventory and the cost of product sold. The disadvantage of variable costing for financial reporting is that the inventory figures are usually meaningless indicators of actual value.

How important is the fact that inventory figures do not represent actual values? What decisions would be made differently because of the exclusion of fixed costs from the inventory position? Even in the computation of financial position, variable costing often gives information that is generally as useful for decision making as absorption costing. But the present-benefit argument that fixed cost should sometimes be included as a cost of product still remains.

7.2.2 Alternative Valuation Procedure

A paradoxical situation may often exist where inventory values may best be approximated by absorption costing which includes fixed costs, while income is best measured by variable costing so that fluctuations in productive activity are eliminated. This section suggests a means by which both objectives can be accomplished. Income is measured by an accounting procedure that considers all fixed costs as expenses of the time period. Thus the fluctuations in income caused by changes in production and inventory are eliminated.

To avoid an understatement of inventory values, the often unwanted by-product of a variable-costing procedure, the inventory is presented at full cost, using the methods of absorbing overhead to product.[5,6] The fixed overhead in the inventory of the present period is compared to the amount of fixed overhead in the inventory of the previous period, and the change is recorded in the retained earnings account. The change in fixed costs included in inventory at the end of the period appears in the reconciliation of retained earnings, but does not affect the reported income of the period.

A reconciliation is needed, however, since both absorption and variable costing assume that income is being measured in terms of the difference between revenues and expenses of the period. If income were to be redefined in terms of the change in the stockholders' equity at the beginning and end of the accounting period, excluding new capital and capital distributions, the need for the special adjustment to retained earnings would be eliminated. If production is treated as increasing the well-being of the stockholders, this fact would then be reflected in the income statement. However, as long as accountants consider realization of income to be accomplished only by a completed sale, and historic cost to be the basis of asset accounting, then the basic inconsistency between absorption and variable costing will continue to exist, and with it a need for reconciliation of the two conventions.

A possible objection to the suggested procedure is that it makes use of the retained-earnings reconciliation to adjust the amount of fixed costs remaining in inventory and considers the fixed costs an asset after they have been expensed. Against this objection can be balanced an improved measure of income compared with that of generally accepted accounting procedures, as well as an improved valuation of inventories and presentation of financial position compared with that under variable costing. The following example shows how the suggested procedure works. The results from the suggested procedure are also compared with those from conventional accounting and variable costing.

Example

The AC Company produces one product. The budgeted and actual fixed manufacturing costs of each year are $10,000. The standard and actual variable manufacturing costs are $2 per unit. The company has normal capacity of 10,000 units and uses normal capacity to absorb fixed overhead to product (the fixed-overhead rate is $1 per unit). Assume no work-in-process inventories.

At the beginning of the year the company had the position statement given in Table 7–4.

---

[5] Understatement here implies that the variable cost of production is less than the market value or reproduction cost of the inventory.

[6] The method need not be restricted to valuing inventories at full cost. Some other figure could be used to obtain the desired inventory value.

Table 7-4 Position Statement as of January 1: AC Company

Other assets	$40,000	Capital stock	$20,000
Finished goods		Retained earnings	20,000
	$40,000		$40,000

During the year the company finished 10,000 units of product and sold 4,000 units for $3.10 per unit. During the following year the company finished 2,000 units and sold 4,000 units, also at $3.10 per unit. Assume that the only expenses are costs of manufacturing.

Under the suggested procedure, the reports in Tables 7-5, 7-6, and 7-7 could be prepared.

Table 7-5 Income Statements: AC Company

	Year 1		Year 2	
Sales revenues (4,000 × $3.10)		$12,400		$12,400
Manufacturing costs:				
Variable costs (4,000 × $2)	$ 8,000		$ 8,000	
Fixed costs	10,000	18,000	10,000	18,000
Operating loss		($ 5,600)		($ 5,600)

Table 7-6 Position Statement: AC Company

	Dec. 31 Year 1	Dec. 31 Year 2		Dec. 31 Year 1	Dec. 31 Year 2
Other assets	$22,400	$20,800	Capital stock	$20,000	$20,000
Finished goods	18,000	12,000	Retained earnings	20,400	12,800
	$40,400	$32,800		$40,400	$32,800

Table 7-7 Retained Earnings Reconciliation: AC Company

	Dec. 31 Year 1	Dec. 31 Year 2
Retained earnings, January 1	$20,000	$20,400
Less: Operating loss for year	5,600	5,600
	$14,400	$14,800
Plus: Adjustment for changes in amount of fixed costs in inventory	6,000	(2,000)
Retained earnings, December 31	$20,400	$12,800

The fixed costs are charged to expense in the period in which they are incurred. However, generally accepted accounting principles consider the cost of manufactured goods to include a *pro rata* share of the fixed manufacturing costs incurred. Thus, the inventory and retained earnings are adjusted for the amount of fixed costs considered to be associated with the goods in inventory (six tenths of $10,000 in year 1 and four tenths of $10,000 in year 2).

Since the second year begins with $6,000 of fixed costs in inventory and ends with $4,000, a credit of $2,000 to inventory, and a debit of $2,000 to the retained-earnings account is required. The accounting entries would be:

	Year 1	Year 2
Retained earnings—adjustment for amount of fixed costs in inventory		$6,000 $2,000
Finished goods—fixed costs	$6,000	$2,000

These entries adjust the amount of fixed costs included in inventory to be consistent with the number of units in inventory as of December 31. They do not affect the income of the period or future periods.

This procedure accomplishes several goals. The inventory is stated at full historic cost, thus satisfying the concern with the omission of fixed costs often needed for meaningful inventory values that results from using variable costing. On the other hand, the incomes of the two periods are equal, as would be expected for two accounting periods where the revenues were equal, where the total number of units sold were the same, and where there were no changes in efficiency. Under the conventional variable-costing procedure, the income statements would be exactly the same as above, but the inventories would include only the variable costs. The income statements under absorption accounting are given in Table 7–8. Generally accepted accounting procedures

Table 7–8   Income Statements Using Absorption Accounting: AC Company

	Year 1	Year 2
Revenues	$12,400	$12,400
Manufacturing costs:		
Standard cost of product	12,000	12,000
Activity variance—loss	0	8,000
Total expenses	$12,000	$20,000
Net income (loss)	$ 400	($ 7,600)

lead to the interesting (although misleading) conclusion that there is an income of $400 in year 1, and a loss of $7,600 in year 2, when the only difference between the two years is the level of production.

We must recognize that this does not reduce at all the problem of obtaining a useful inventory value number for either financial reporting or decision making. For example, in obtaining values for financial reporting, there may be problems of joint costs to be considered (see Chapter 8). For decision making, we should still like a value measure that could be used in deciding whether further processing is desirable, method of sale, price to charge, and so on.

7.2.3 Variable Costing and Internal Reporting

It is not unusual for firms to prepare financial reports for purposes of evaluating performance in divisions, departments, cost centers, or for other activities. Often these reports are prepared to focus attention on the contribution of the activity and hence use a variable-costing approach. The method is most appropriate when a department's performance goal is profitability.

As will be discussed in Chapter 17, not all segments of an organization should have a profit goal. For some, cost minimization subject to an assigned output goal (in terms of quantity and quality) is more appropriate. In these cases cost control is the primary long-run objective of internal reporting. The variable costs, however, may only approximate the controllable costs. Differences occur to the extent that expenditures that are fixed in relation to the level of activity are nevertheless under the control of the department manager.

Internal reports can create problems in performance evaluation and thereby in motivation if they are prepared to reflect inappropriate goals or if they include costs over which the manager is not able to exercise control. Dependencies between cost centers and fuzzy lines of responsibility for decisions and expenditure authorization contribute to the difficulties. Although not ideal for this purpose, variable costing is an improvement over full-costing methods. Problems in motivation are more subtle, and the reader is referred to Chapter 6 for a discussion of the issues involved.

A common error is to assume that a method of reporting on performance for external purposes is equally relevant to internal performance measurement and cost-control needs. The two objectives must be considered separately.

7.3 Summary

Developments in inventory decision models suggest new areas for cost accumulation and analysis. Typically, the accountant can do more to understand these models and to provide the necessary cost data.

One of the data requirements for determining optimal inventory levels is the cost of holding inventories, and this is based on the value of resources tied up in inventories. Although net realizable values and market-replacement cost data are often available for finished goods and raw materials respectively, work-in-process inventories are harder to value. Often some cost approach is used. The present-benefit approach is one alternative to the use of cost. Problems of implementing this technique stem, however, from its subjectivity. Nevertheless, the present-benefit approach would be more useful if it could be implemented.

Similarly, inventory values are also necessary inputs to external decision making because of their relevance to asset values and reported income in financial statements. The subject is a separate one from internal decisions involving inventory control but involves many of the same elements. Inventory valuation for financial reporting deals with the dual problem of establishing useful inventory and income figures.

One problem here is to separate the cost of product and the cost of idleness as the use of productive facilities fluctuates. The concept of present benefits is again a possibility, but implementation problems exist. It is likely that either a variable-costing or absorption-costing technique will generally be used. The use of variable costing creates a problem in that inventories are undervalued, and income is distorted by the level of production using absorption costing. A method is suggested in the chapter to mitigate the inventory-valuation problem created by using variable-costing techniques to determine income.

QUESTIONS AND PROBLEMS

7–1

   a. What three fundamental data needs exist affecting the problem of inventory valuation? What data are necessary for financial reporting but are not needed for inventory-level decisions?

   b. How should reports be prepared for internal performance evaluation?

   c. Why are there differences between inventory-cost data for (1) inventory-level decisions, (2) financial reporting to outsiders, and (3) internal performance measurement?

7–2 Suppose that cash and cashlike assets (short-term securities for example) are considered as an inventory. Using the EOQ equation (7.1), what would the symbols mean?

7–3 In decisions involving the level of cash and cashlike assets to hold, what related decisions involving cash must be considered?

7–4 Three costs of an inventory policy, C_1, C_2, and C_3 (ordering costs, storage costs, and stock-out costs, respectively), are usually treated as linear functions of the inventory quantity (i.e., as constant per unit per time period over a rather wide range). Consider now several components of these costs and decide how they vary with inventory quantity over the relevant range. Also suggest methods of estimating each.

A. Order costs
   1. Clerical processing labor
   2. Inspection labor
   3. Forms and materials
   4. Transportation

B. Storage costs
   1. Insurance
   2. Taxes
   3. Obsolescence and breakage
   4. Warehouse costs (light, heat, labor)
   5. Interest in investment

C. Stock-out costs
   1. Special order filling
   2. Lost goodwill

7–5 Three names (variable costing, direct costing, and marginal costing) are used for the accounting procedure which for financial reporting purposes expenses all fixed costs and considers only variable costs to be inventoriable. Which name do you consider most appropriate and why?

7–6 What advantages for financial reporting does the use of absorption costing using normal activity have over the use of actual costs and actual activity as the basis of overhead absorption?

7–7 When does the use of normal activity and overhead absorption result in a distortion of the measure of income? How can this be corrected?

7–8 Is the use of variable costing reasonable from the point of view of financial accounting?

7–9 May cost factors which are conventionally classified by the accountant as being fixed ever be considered a cost of product from an economic point of view?

7–10 Should revenues be recognized as the production takes place or when the product is sold? Should income be a function of the level of production rather than sales? Should the cost per unit for reporting inventory levels and determining income for products be a function of the level of production?

7–11 Company Y produces one product which it sells for a price of $4.80 per unit. The production costs are as follows:

Fixed costs per year $150,000
Variable costs per unit $1

Normal activity is 100,000 units per year. At the beginning of 1968 the company has the following position statement:

Position Statement January 1, 1976

Other assets	$50,000	Capital stock	$30,000
Finished goods*	25,000	Retained earnings	45,000
	$75,000		$75,000

* Represents 10,000 units ($10,000 of variable costs and $15,000 of fixed costs).

The information for the years 1976–1978 is as follows:

Year	Sales (units)	Sales ($)	Production (units)
1976	50,000	240,000	80,000
1977	50,000	240,000	40,000
1978	50,000	240,000	120,000

The manufacturing costs of each year were as indicated previously.

Required

a. Prepare income statements for the three years, using normal activity as the basis of overhead absorption.

b. Prepare income statments for the three years, using variable costing as the basis of overhead accounting.

c. Prepare retained earnings reconciliations for the three years, assuming that inventory is presented on the position statements using normal activity as the basis of overhead absorption while variable costing is used for measuring the income of the period.

d. Prepare a position statement as of December 31, 1978.

7–12 Company Y produces one product, which it sells for $5.00 per unit. The production costs are as follows:

Fixed costs per year	$200,000
Variable costs per unit	$1

Normal activity is 100,000 units per year. At the beginning of 1976 the company has the following position statement:

Position Statement January 1, 1976

Other assets	$45,000	Capital stock	$30,000
Finished goods*	30,000	Retained earnings	45,000
	$75,000		$75,000

* Represents 10,000 units ($10,000 of variable costs and $20,000 of fixed costs).

The information for the year 1976 is as follows:

Year	Sales (units)	Sales ($)	Production (units)
1976	50,000	250,000	140,000

The manufacturing costs were the same as specified above. The company uses a LIFO inventory procedure.

Required

a. Prepare an income statement using normal activity as the basis of overhead absorption. Allocate idle-activity variances to inventory and cost of goods sold. Assume a LIFO flow of costs.
b. Prepare an income statement using variable costing as the basis of overhead accounting.

7-13 Explain the difference between the reported income and the incomes of $100,000 budgeted for sales of 10,000 units (see the accompanying break-even chart).

THE GRIPPER COMPANY
INCOME STATEMENT
FOR MONTH ENDING JULY 31, 1976

Sales (10,000 units sold for $10 apiece)		$100,000
Expenses:		
Manufacturing cost of sales (see note 1)	$60,000	
Selling expenses:		
Variable $10,000		
Fixed 15,000	25,000	
Administrative expenses	5,000	
		90,000
Income (before taxes)		$ 10,000

Note 1:		
Standard cost:		
Material	$ 8,000	
Labor	15,000	
Variable overhead	3,000	
Fixed overhead (based on a fixed-overhead rate		
of $2 per direct-labor dollar)	30,000	
		$ 56,000
Material usage, price and labor		
efficiency, and wage-rate variances	$19,000	
Activity variance (favorable)	15,000	4,000
		$ 60,000

Note 2: The budgeted fixed costs for the month were:		
Manufacturing overhead	$25,000	
Selling	12,000	
Administrative	5,000	
	$42,000	

The budgeted variable selling expense is 10% of sales.

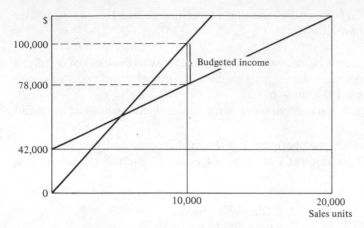

7–14 The Capable Company includes its activity variance based on normal capacity in its cost of sales. The income statements for January and February were as follows:

Sales	January	February
Sales	$900,000	$900,000
Less: Manufacturing cost of sales	750,000	950,000
Manufacturing margin	$150,000	$(50,000)
Less: Selling and administrative expenses	25,000	25,000
Net income	$125,000	$(75,000)

During the month of January the company produced 500,000 units of product and sold 300,000. During the month of February the company produced and sold 300,000 units.

The variable costs of manufacturing are $1.50 per unit. There were no spending (expense) or efficiency variances during either of the two months. The fixed costs budgeted and incurred for each of the two months were $500,000. The normal capacity of the plant is 500,000 units (used for determining the fixed-overhead rate).

Required: Present comparative income statements for the two months which would be more useful in appraising the results of operations during these months.

   a. Using direct costing.

   b. Using absorption costing.

7–15 The can industry is an industry in which there are fluctuations in production and sales, owing to the seasonal nature of the products being canned. The United States Can Company has two plants, one in San Francisco and one in New York. The physical characteristics of the plants are similar, and the results of operations of the two plants are compared each month to judge the performance of the two managements. The March income statements of the two plants were as follows:

	San Francisco Plant	New York Plant
Sales	$1,000,000	$1,000,000
Less:		
Manufacturing cost of sales	$ 700,000	$ 800,000
Selling and administrative expenses	200,000	200,000
Total expenses	$ 900,000	$1,000,000
Net income	$ 100,000	0

Each plants sells their product for the same price. During the month of March, both plants sold and shipped 20,000,000 cans. The production for the month at the two plants were as follows:

	San Francisco Plant	New York Plant
Opening inventory (number of cans)	50,000	50,000
Production during month	30,000,000	20,000,000
	30,050,000	20,050,000
Cans shipped during month	20,000,000	20,000,000
Ending inventory	10,050,000	50,000

The San Francisco plant built up its inventory in March in anticipation of the canning season, which begins in April on the West Coast. The East Coast canning season begins in the middle of May.

The standard cost card for the type of can sold in March discloses the following information:

Standard Cost Card (for both plants): Can No. 4593

	Cost per 1,000 Cans
Direct material	$20
Direct labor	4
Overhead:	
Variable	1
Fixed	10
	$35

For both plants the manufacturing fixed costs budgeted for the month were $300,000. There were no spending (budget) or efficiency variances.

All selling and administrative expenses were of a fixed nature.

Required: Write a report relative to the operations of the two plants during the month of March. Explain the differences in income and prepare a revised statement which would be more useful in appraising the results of the operations of the two plants.

7–16 For several months management has been puzzled by fluctuations in the income reported by the New York Plant. The results for February, March, and April were as follows:

	February	March	April
Sales	$1,000,000	$1,000,000	$500,000
Less manufacturing cost of sales	$1,000,000	$ 800,000	$250,000
Selling and administrative expenses	200,000	200,000	200,000
Total expenses	$1,200,000	$1,000,000	$450,000
Net income (loss)	$ (200,000)	$ 0	$ 50,000

There has been no change in sales price during the three-month period. During the months of February and March, the plant sold and shipped 20,000,000 cans. In April it shipped one half that total. The production for the three months was as follows:

	February	March	April
Opening inventory	20,050,000	50,000	50,000
Production during month	———	20,000,000	40,000,000
	20,050,000	20,050,000	40,050,000
Cans shipped during month	20,000,000	20,000,000	10,000,000
Ending inventory	50,000	50,000	30,050,000

The standard cost card for the type of can sold discloses the following information:

	Cost per 1,000 Cans
Direct material	$20
Direct labor	4
Overhead:	
Variable	1
Fixed	10
	$35

The fixed manufacturing costs budgeted for each of the months were $300,000. There were no spending (expense) or efficiency variances during the three months.

All selling and administrative expenses were of a fixed nature.

Required: Present comparative income statements for the three months which would be most useful in appraising the results of operations for the three months.

7–17 The Can Company of New York has decided to use a variable costing procedure for internal accounting reports. Following this procedure, all fixed costs will be considered a cost of the period, and only variable costs will be inventoried.

Manufacturing costs incurred	
Variable manufacturing costs	$500,000
Fixed manufacturing costs	$250,000
Selling costs incurred	
Variable selling costs	$50,000
Fixed selling costs	$80,000
Administrative costs incurred	
Fixed administrative costs	$100,000
Number of cans produced	25,000,000
Number of cans sold	24,000,000
Revenues from sales	$1,000,000

Required

a. Prepare two income statements, one following conventional overhead absorption accounting techniques, the other using variable (direct) costing. Assume that there was no beginning inventory of finished goods and that the fixed overhead absorption rate is $10 per 1,000 cans. Except for fixed overhead, actual costs are used in determining the cost of product.

b. Prepare two additional income statements, one assuming that the fixed overhead absorption rate is $5 per 1,000 cans and that the company does not close out the activity variance monthly; the other assuming that the plant uses normal activity of 20,000,000 cans as the basis for computing the fixed overhead rate, an absorption rate of $12.50 per 1,000 cans, and the company does close the variance account monthly to cost of goods sold.

c. Is it possible to use absorption costing and still retain the benefits of variable costing? Explain.

7–18 Some accountants state that fixed costs should not be considered a cost of product (should not be inventoried), since these costs will be incurred regardless of production or sale. These items should be treated as period expenses.

Required: Name several costs that can be considered as fixed costs and which would *not* be incurred unless there was *intent* of producing the product.

7–19 Company X has sales of $200,000 in both May and June (this represents 50,000 units at $4 per unit). The production costs for each of the two months are as follows:

Fixed costs per month	$150,000
Variable costs per unit	$1

The production for May was 50,000 units and for June 150,000 units (the plant operated at capacity). The May 1 finished goods inventory is zero.

Required: Prepare income statements for May and June based on:
a. Actual costs and actual activity for the month.
b. Overhead absorption using normal activity of 100,000 units as the basis of overhead absorption.
c. Overhead absorption using practical capacity of 150,000 units as the basis of overhead absorption.
d. Variable costing.

7–20 The ABC Company was organized on January 1, 1974.

	Financial Position		
	Jan. 1, 1974	Jan. 1, 1975	Jan. 1, 1976
Cash	$10,000	$ 6,000	$20,000
Inventories	0	15,000*	5,000†
	10,000	21,000	25,000
Capital stock	10,000	10,000	10,000
Retained earnings	0	11,000	15,000
	$10,000	$21,000	$25,000

* Includes $3,000 of fixed overhead.
† Includes $1,000 of fixed overhead.

Required:
a. What were the reported incomes for 1974 and 1975 assuming that no dividends were declared?
b. What would have been the income if variable costing had been used in the two years?

7–21 The annual report of a corporation had the following note:

Inventories are priced, for the most part, at the lower of cost or market of materials plus direct labor and other direct costs, including overhead; however, in continuation of practices adopted by certain companies merged into the Corporation in prior years, overhead has been omitted from a portion of the inventories. The omission of such overhead ($6,826,618 this year and $5,609,148 last year) resulted in a reduction in net income (after taxes of approximately $600,000) for this year.

Required: Comment on the procedure followed. How was the $600,000 probably computed?

SUPPLEMENTARY READING

BRUMMET, R. L., "Direct Costing: Should It Be a Controversial Issue?" *The Accounting Review,* July 1955, pp. 439–443.

CHURCHMAN, C. W., R. L. ACKOFF, and E. L. ARNOFF, *Introduction to Operations Research,* New York: John Wiley & Sons, Inc., 1957, Chaps. 8, 9, and 10.

DOPUCH, N., "Mathematical Programming and Accounting Approaches to Incremental Cost Analysis," *The Accounting Review,* October 1963, pp. 745–753.

HADLEY, G., and T. M. WHITIN, *Analysis of Inventory Systems,* Englewood Cliffs, N.J.: Prentice-Hall, Inc., 1962.

HEPWORTH, S. R., "Direct Costing: The Case Against," *The Accounting Review,* January 1954, pp. 94–99.

HORNGREN, C. T., and G. H. SORTER, "Direct Costing for External Reporting," *The Accounting Review,* January 1961, pp. 84–93.

KAPLAN, R., and G. L. THOMPSON, "Overhead Allocation via Mathematical Programming Models," *The Accounting Review,* April 1971, pp. 352–364.

SHILLINGLAW, G., "The Concept of Attributable Cost," *Journal of Accounting Research,* Spring 1963, pp. 73–85.

SORTER, G. H., and C. T. HORNGREN, "Asset Recognition and Economic Attributes —The Relevant Costing Approach," *The Accounting Review,* July 1962, pp. 391–399.

Chapter 8

Joint Costs
and Joint Products

This chapter is concerned with two similar but basically different types of cost: joint costs and indirect costs. Joint costs relate to a situation in which the factors of production by their basic nature result in two or more products. The jointness results from there being more than one product, and these multiproducts are the result of the method of production or the nature of the raw material and not of a decision by management to produce both (management may find the production of one of the resulting products uneconomical and drop the "finishing" process). An example of a joint cost is the cost of a barrel of crude oil purchased by a refining company. Several products, including gasoline, fuel oil, tar, and chemicals, result from the processing of a barrel of crude oil, and these products all have a common cost, the cost of oil. By the nature of the raw material (or the productive process) several products result; thus the costs are "joint" to these products. Frequently, in joint-cost situations, it would be uneconomical to produce a single product.

Indirect costs, on the other hand, result from the production of more than one product, but the decision to use the factors of production to produce several products is a decision of management. Any indirect cost factor could be directed to the production of one product instead of several products. A railroad is an example of a productive process which may lead to indirect costs, with the cost of the rails being an indirect cost to both freight and passenger travel. Unfortunately, the distinction between joint and indirect costs is often blurred, since both may be involved at once.

172

Another example of indirect costs occurs if a plant produces beer cans and soda pop cans, since some of the same equipment may be used to produce both products yet both need not be produced. Another example is the machinery used in processing timber: the cost of the logs, on the other hand, is a joint cost.

There are, then, two types of costs (joint and indirect) that cannot be directly identified with the end products when two or more types of products are being made. It might be said that these costs are common to all of the products; in fact, the term "common costs" is sometimes used to describe both of these types of costs.

Products resulting from joint costs are called joint products if they are approximately of equal importance to the firm. Products of relatively small importance to the business are called by-products. The by-product may be of considerable absolute value, but it is still a by-product as long as it results from the production of the main product. An example of a by-product is the scrap metal resulting from the production of an airplane. This scrap has considerable value in absolute amount, but compared to the value of the primary product, airplanes, it is of small value. The scrap results from the airplane production process and hence satisfies the definition of a by-product. If the value of the end product were nearly equivalent to the value of the scrap produced, the scrap metal would be considered a joint product by accountants, though common usage might still refer to it as a by-product.

In practice, the distinction between a joint product and a by-product is primarily a result of accounting convention and of minimal use to management in decision situations. The remainder of this chapter deals with the problems of determining output decisions for joint products and establishing their inventory values. Some interesting results for the accounting problem of inventory valuation can be developed by first considering the decision problem.

8.1 Joint Costs and Decision Making

Suppose that a firm makes two products, call them A and B, from a raw material that costs $2 per pound and that weighs 10 pounds. The 10 pounds of raw material yields one unit of A at 4 pounds and one unit of B at 6 pounds. The direct finishing costs are $1.25 per pound of A and $0.50 per pound of B. Indirect finishing (joint processing) costs that apply to both A and B amount to $0.70 per pound of the raw material. These facts are summarized in Table 8–1.

Table 8–1 Summary Statistics: Products A and B

	A	B
Weight of product resulting from 10 lb of raw material (cost $20.00)	4 lb	6 lb
Direct-finishing costs	$1.25/lb	$0.50/lb
Indirect-finishing costs $7 (applies jointly to A and B)		

Both the direct and indirect finishing costs indicated above are of an incremental nature. (Any purely fixed costs have been omitted since they do not affect the production decision to be made.)

Neither cost, that of A or B, can be determined with certainty since they have common costs of $20 for material and $7 for processing costs. However, the cost of making both A and B can be determined. It costs $35 to manufacture 4 pounds of A and 6 pounds of B.

Also, if the company made just A and did not finish B, the costs would be $32 (made up of $20 plus $7 plus $5). If it made just B and did not finish A, the costs would be $30 (made up of $20 plus $7 plus $3).

Raw material	$20
Joint-processing costs	7
Direct costs of A ($1.25 × 4)	5
Direct cost of B ($0.50 × 6)	3
	$35

From the above information, several initial conclusions can be drawn that do not depend on an allocation of joint costs and are theoretically sound:

1. If the revenues from the sale of A plus B are in excess of $35, the firm should produce. (It does not follow that if the revenues are less than $35, it should not produce.)
2. If the revenues from the sale of A are greater than $32, the firm should produce A. It should not finish B unless the revenues arising from the sale of B are in excess of $3, the direct cost of finishing B.
3. If the revenues from the sale of B are greater than $30, the firm should produce B. It should not finish A unless the revenues arising from the sale of A are in excess of $5, the cost required to finish A.
4. If the revenues from the sale of A and B are both less than $30 for each product and, in total less than $35, the firm should not produce either A or B.

Although products A and B are joint products, since they are made from a common raw material, the manufacturer may choose not to produce one or the other or both. Thus, a chemical company may find that it is commercially sound to produce one joint product but that the use for another of the joint products has decreased, with a resulting decrease in price, so that production is no longer economically sound.

8.1.1 Determining the Price of Joint Products

It is frequently assumed that the pricing policy for joint products requires a cost allocation of an arbitrary nature. This is not true. It is possible to establish a theoretically sound framework for determining price and output decisions for joint products.

The example of the preceding section dealing with products A and B produced in fixed proportions may be used. These products will be assumed to have independent demand curves (average-revenue or price curves). (See Figure 8.1.) The demands for the two products may be independent or mutually dependent, but for simplicity it is assumed here that the prices and total sales at different prices of the two products are independent of each other. The only assumption made is that the demand curves slope downward to the right (the number of units sold increases as the price is decreased).

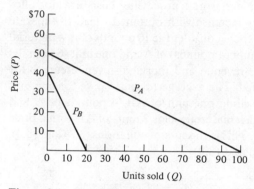

Figure 8.1   Demand curves for two joint products.

To continue the numerical example (recall that each unit of A weighs 4 pounds and each unit of B weighs 6 pounds), let

$$Q_A = 100 - 2P_A \tag{8.1}$$

and

$$Q_B = 20 - 0.5P_B \tag{8.2}$$

be the demand equations where Q and P stand for quantity and price respectively and the subscripts designate the product. Solving equations (8.1) and (8.2) for P_A and P_B yields

$$P_A = 50 - 0.5Q_A \tag{8.3}$$

and

$$P_B = 40 - 2Q_B \tag{8.4}$$

Using equations (8.3) and (8.4), the total-revenue equations, R_A and R_B, are obtained by multiplying price by quantity:

$$R_A = P_A Q_A = 50Q_A - 0.5Q_A{}^2 \tag{8.5}$$

$$R_B = P_B Q_B = 40Q_B - 2Q_B{}^2 \tag{8.6}$$

Since, economically, optimal solutions are a result of equating marginal revenue with marginal cost, the next step is to obtain the marginal-revenue expressions for each product. This is done by differentiating equations (8.5) and (8.6) with respect to Q_A and Q_B, respectively. This yields

$$MR_A = \frac{dR_A}{dQ_A} = 50 - Q_A \qquad (8.7)$$

$$MR_B = \frac{dR_B}{dQ_B} = 40 - 4Q_B \qquad (8.8)$$

Equating marginal revenue with marginal cost, however, is not so easily accomplished, since the joint raw material and processing costs are not allocatable to the products, and yet they increase with output. Instead of separate demand curves for the two products, then, consider the 10 pounds of raw material as making one product, namely, one unit (4 pounds) of A and one unit (6 pounds) of B. Call this product AB. Average-revenue and marginal-revenue curves for this new product can then be obtained. The average-revenue curve for one unit would consist of the revenue from selling one unit of AB (4 pounds of A and 6 pounds of B). Thus, 20 pounds of raw material yields 2 units of AB with a price of $50 - 0.5 (2) + 40 - 2 (2) = \$85$. This is the sum of equations (8.3) and (8.4). Symbolically, adding equations (8.3) and (8.4):

$$P_{AB} = 90 - 2.5Q_{AB} \qquad (8.9)$$

The only cost curve shown in Figure 8.2 is the marginal-cost curve. The curve is assumed to be a horizontal line; thus, it also serves as an average variable-cost curve.

Figure 8.2 suggests that the optimal solution to the problem of setting the output level is Q_{AB} units, where the units are expressed in terms of 4 pounds of A and 6 pounds of B. At that output, the prices charged result in average

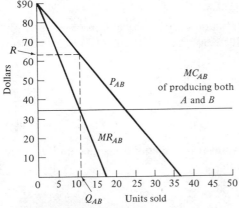

Figure 8.2   Marginal analysis for two joint products.

revenues of R. Note that R is not the price, since Q_{AB} units are not sold, but rather units of products A and B are sold. To find the prices at which the units are sold, it is necessary to return to Figure 8.1 and find the prices for A and B that clear the market of the number of units that will be produced. The price of A times the number of units of A, plus the price of B times the number of units of B, is equal to R times Q_{AB} (the number of units) from Figure 8.2.

The same solution can also be obtained using equations (8.7) and (8.8). Again, consider a single unit of A (4 pounds of A) and a single unit of B (6 pounds of B) to be the result of processing one unit of raw material (10 pounds). Then the revenue of the joint product AB is given by

$$R_{AB} = 50Q_A - 0.5Q_A{}^2 + 40Q_B - 2Q_B{}^2$$

Now since one unit of AB yields one unit of A and one unit of B

$$Q_{AB} = Q_A = Q_B$$

and:

$$R_{AB} = 50Q_{AB} - 0.5Q_{AB}^2 + 40Q_{AB} - 2Q_{AB}^2 = 90Q_{AB} - 2.5Q_{AB}^2$$

Taking the derivative we obtain:

$$MR_{AB} = 90 - 5Q_{AB} \tag{8.10}$$

(Note this is also the sum of equations (8.7) and (8.8).)

Equating the marginal revenue to the marginal cost of completing both product yields

$$90 - 5Q_{AB} = 35 \tag{8.11}$$

Both the joint costs and the direct costs of finishing are incorporated in the $35 marginal cost figure of equation (8.11). Solving equation (8.11) yields eleven for Q_{AB}. In other words, the initial solution is to produce 11 units of both A and B. The prices to be charged are obtained from equations (8.3) and (8.4) using $Q_A = Q_B = 11$. The prices are

$$P_A = 50 - 0.5Q_A = \$44.50 \tag{8.12}$$

$$P_B = 40 - 2Q_B = \$18.00 \tag{8.13}$$

It would be in error to assume that the problem is solved. Several complications should be noted. When the marginal revenue of B falls below $3 per unit of B (that is, marginal revenue is $3 for 6 pounds or 1 unit of B), then B should not be finished, and the marginal-cost curve for the product A plus B should take this into consideration by elimination of the $3 of finishing costs. This occurs, using equation (8.8), when B equals $9\frac{1}{4}$ units (or 55.5 pounds). In like manner, when the marginal revenue of A falls below $5 per unit of A (that is, marginal revenue is $5 for 4 pounds or 1 unit of A), then A should not be finished, and the marginal-cost curve should take this into consideration. This occurs, using equation (8.7), when A equals 45 units (180 pounds).

While marginal revenue equals marginal cost for the production level found and the determined prices, this is not necessarily the optimum solution. Since the direct costs of finishing are not common to both products, to have an optimal solution the marginal revenues for each product separately must exceed their marginal-finishing costs. The marginal revenues are given by equations (8.7) and (8.8):

$$MR_A = 50 - Q_A = 50 - 11 = \$39 \tag{8.14}$$

$$MR_B = 40 - 4Q_B = 40 - 44 = -\$4 \tag{8.15}$$

The marginal revenue of B is less than its finishing cost of \$3 and, indeed, here it is negative. If the marginal revenue of each product had equaled or exceeded its finishing cost, the solution given by solving equation (8.11) would have been optimal. But this is not the case.

Equating the marginal revenue of product B to its finishing cost yields

$$40 - 4Q_B = 3$$

and solving indicates that only $9\frac{1}{4}$ units of B should be finished. The rest should be sold for whatever can be obtained for them (possibly as scrap) at the split-off point.[1] The $9\frac{1}{4}$ finished units of B should be priced, using equation (8.4), at

$$P_B = 40 - 2Q_B = 40 - 2(9\tfrac{1}{4}) = \$21.50.$$

Equating the marginal revenue of B with its marginal-finishing cost means that the costs of the joint raw material and processing costs of the last unit must be recovered by product A. Therefore, the marginal cost of producing a unit of A is \$20 + \$7 + \$5 = \$32. Now, equating marginal revenue and marginal cost for product A yields

$$MR_A = MC_A \qquad 50 - Q_A = 32 \qquad Q_A = 18 \tag{8.16}$$

The optimal quantity of product A is 18 units, and, using equation (8.3), it should be priced at $50 - 0.5Q_A = \$41$ per unit.

Summarizing, the optimal solution is to produce and sell 18 units of product A at \$41 per unit (or \$41/4 = \$10.25 per lb). The production will yield 18 units of product B, of which $9\frac{1}{4}$ units should be finished and sold for \$21.50 per unit (or \$21.50/6 = \$3.58 per lb). The remaining $8\frac{3}{4}$ units of B should be disposed of at the split-off point without finishing them. If an integer solution is required, 9 units should be finished.

Summarizing, the steps necessary to solve this joint price–output problem for any number of products are:

1. Derive the total- and marginal-revenue functions for each product.
2. Add the marginal-revenue functions to obtain a single marginal-revenue

---

[1] It is interesting to note that in this case the same product may be both a by-product and a joint product. However, if B can be sold at a profit as a by-product, this would reduce the number of units finished. For example, if the incremental profit from the sale of 1 unit of B at split off is \$5, only 8 units of B would be finished. $40 - 4Q_B = 3 + 5$ and $Q_B = 8$.

function which assume equivalent units of all products will be sold (4 pounds of A and 6 pounds of B are made equivalent units in the example).
3. Set the joint-marginal revenue equal to the joint-marginal cost (where the joint-marginal cost equation is obtained in the same way) and solve for the quantity of the joint product.
4. Determine the marginal revenue for each separate product using the equations determined in step 1 and the quantity determined in step 3.
   a. If the marginal revenue for all separate products is equal to or greater than the direct-finishing costs, the solution obtained in step 3 is optimal.
   b. If the marginal revenue less finishing costs for a product is negative, equate the marginal-revenue function for that product to its finishing costs to determine the optimal output. Steps 1 through 4a must be repeated for all products with nonnegative marginal revenues using the relevant costs.

The analysis given here includes the case where the production involves by-products since the same dependencies in output and profits exist.

The reader may object to a pretense of accuracy in the solution offered, since all the information necessary for this solution is seldom known in practice. The objection has merit, but the importance of the presentation is not in terms of its being applied exactly as illustrated but rather in terms of a method of reasoning. This reasoning shows that the allocation of joint costs is not essential to a clear and definite solution to the problems of output and pricing of joint products.

8.2 Inventory Valuation and Joint Costs

The first fact to note concerning the accounting for joint costs is that the joint costs cannot be split up and identified with certainty to several joint products. There is no single right way to split the cost of a barrel of crude oil among the products made from it. The total cost of a barrel is known, but the costs of the several products processed from it cannot be known with certainty. The same is true of the indirect costs.

Having recognized the impossibility of the job, the accountant is still faced with the necessity of determining inventory values. As Chapter 7 showed, these figures are required for external and internal decision making. They may also affect performance evaluation through their effect on the computed contribution of the several products. Procedures must be established for determining reasonable values for reporting joint-product inventories.

8.2.1 Net Revenue and Cost Allocation

Several methods of allocating joint costs are possible. One method would use the sales value at the split-off point, if it were known. This is the preferred approach. A second possible method of joint-cost allocation is to take the expected sales value of the finished products and allocate the costs so that they are proportionate to the gross sales value. An objection to this procedure is that different products may require different finishing costs to prepare them for the market. If the finishing costs are subtracted from the sales value, then it would also be reasonable to charge each product with an amount of the common cost in proportion to those amounts. This gives us a third method. The assigned cost would then be in proportion to the net sales value of the products of the firm.

For an example of the latter two methods, suppose that a raw material costs $200 per unit and that three joint products are made from each unit. The characteristics of the three products are given in Table 8–2.

Table 8–2 Product Characteristics: Three-Product Example

Product	Pounds	Sales Revenue	Percent of Total	Finishing Costs	Net Sales Value	Percent of Total Value
A	70	$130	26.5	$30	$100	25
B	20	210	43.0	50	160	40
C	20	150	30.5	10	140	35
		$490			$400	

Using the net sales value to prorate the $200 of costs, product A would be charged with 25%, or $50; product B with 40%, or $80; and product C with 35%, or $70. A different allocation of the common costs results if the gross sales revenue of each product is used.

If the units are sold for the predicted prices, it is interesting to look at the income statements resulting from the use of net sales value to prorate the $200 of costs. The results are given in Table 8–3. The percentage of gross profits to

Table 8–3 Unit Income Statements: Net-Sales-Value Method: Direct Material and Finishing Costs Not in Proportion to Sales Value

	Product A	Product B	Product C
Sales	$130	$210	$150
Finishing costs	30	50	10
Cost of raw material	50	80	70
Total expenses	$ 80	$130	$ 80
Gross profit	$ 50	$ 80	$ 70
Gross profit as percent of sales	38.5	38.1	46.7

sales for all three products differs. Now assume that there were no unequal finishing costs, but that the net sales value was actually the sales price and that all finishing costs were necessary to both and were included in the $200 figure. This results in the direct materials and finishing costs being in proportion to the sales value. The income statements are given in Table 8–4.

Table 8–4   Unit Income Statements: Net-Sales-Value Method: Direct Material and Finishing Costs in Proportion to Sales Value

	Product A	Product B	Product C
Sales	$100	$160	$140
Less: Raw material and finishing costs	50	80	70
Gross profit	$ 50	$ 80	$ 70
Gross profit as percent of sales	50	50	50

Note that the ratio of gross profits to sales is now the same for all three products, a result of the method of computing the allocation of the common costs. The percentages will be different only where there are direct material or finishing costs which can be directly identified with the end product, and where these costs are not in proportion to the net sales value of the product. The tendency of the joint-cost allocations to result in an equal ratio of gross profit to net sales values warns against placing excessive faith in profit figures for product lines resulting from arbitrary joint-cost allocations.

Where the gross-sales-value method is used for the information presented in Table 8–2, the income statements in Table 8–5 result. There is an increase in the apparent contribution per unit of product C.

Table 8–5   Unit Income Statements: Gross-Sales-Value Method

	Product A	Product B	Product C
Sales	$130	$210	$150
Finishing costs	30	50	10
Costs of raw materials	53	86	61
Total expenses	$ 83	$136	$ 71
Gross profit	$ 47	$ 74	$ 79
Gross profit as a percent of sales	36.2	35.2	52.7

Both methods make implicit assumptions about the importance of finishing costs in generating a contribution to fixed costs and profits. The gross-sales-value method assumes that all costs are equally effective in generating a contribution to fixed costs and profits. The net-sales-value method, on the other hand, assumes that the finishing costs generate sufficient revenues to cover themselves only; they are implicitly assumed to contribute nothing toward fixed costs and profits. Neither assumption is likely to be in accord with the facts.

The preceding methods of cost allocation are probably the most reasonable methods, but many other methods are used in practice.[2] One common method is to allocate the costs on a physical measure. For example, the pounds of product in the above illustration could be used. This would result in product A receiving 70% of the $200 common costs despite the fact that its net sales value is only $100. This does not seem to be a reasonable procedure, since the allocations are made on a basis completely unrelated to the value of the product. Managers have traditionally felt that costs are incurred with the expectation that they will be recovered. This has led them to favor methods involving relative sales values to allocate joint costs since such methods assures that all end products will show some profit under normal market conditions.

8.2.2 By-products

Assume that in addition to the products, A, B, and C, there is another product, Z, which is relatively small in value (perhaps scrap metal that is accumulated and sold to scrap dealers). Assume that 50 pounds of Z is generated from each unit of raw material, that Z sells for $0.40 per pound, and that it costs $0.10 per pound to dispose of it.

Each unit of raw material results in 50 × $0.40, or $20 of the sales value of Z. But preparing Z costs $0.10 per pound, or $5. The net value of the scrap is $20 less $5, or $15. One reasonable accounting procedure for by-products is to remove from the total manufacturing costs the net value of the by-product (the sales value less the finishing and disposal costs) and set it up in a by-product inventory account.

The by-product inventory is priced at its sale price (net of preparation cost). This procedure results in the by-product showing neither a profit nor a loss unless there is a change in the price of the by-product after it has been transferred to inventory. It does, however, implicitly recognize revenue prior to sale. Decisions on the disposition of by-products should not be made on the basis of this information.

---

[2] A. A. Walters has described a joint-cost model where demand is in the form of a joint-probability distribution for a given price. (Up to this point the amount demanded for different prices was assumed known.) The specific model presented by Walters is limited by his assumptions that price is fixed at the beginning of the marketing period and held throughout the period and that product is impossibly expensive to store; but he does show that under certain conditions the allocation of fixed cost based on *expected* sales is reasonable. See A. A. Walters, "The Allocation of Joint Costs," *American Economic Review*, June 1960, pp. 419–432.

If the dollar value of the by-product becomes significant in size, then the procedure described above can distort the relative performance of the by-product compared to the primary products, since it now tends to show no profit for the by-product when it is sold. It could then be treated as a joint product.

A common practice is not to assign any material costs to the by-products. If the amounts are small, this procedure can be excused, since the errors are not material. However, the procedure is not theoretically sound.

An alternative method of allocating common costs is suggested by the use of such costs in a decision-making context (this method is, however, not presently in use). Consider products C and D, which have the same characteristics as products A and B of Section 8.1. The marginal revenues of the individual products can be used to obtain the inventory values. Suppose, in harmony with Figure 8.2 (but not the numerical example), that the marginal revenues of both products are equal to or exceed their finishing costs.

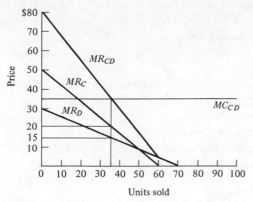

Figure 8.3   Determining marginal revenue of product.

Figure 8.3 shows the marginal-revenue curves of product C and product D as well as the combined marginal-revenue curves. The marginal-cost curve includes finishing costs. The total marginal cost of the two products at the point of optimal output is equal to $35. It is reasonable to divide the marginal cost into two parts based on the marginal revenue of each product. At the optimal level of output the marginal revenue of D in this example is $15, and the marginal revenue of C is $20; the marginal revenue and the marginal cost of the joint product is $35. Dividing the $35 of cost between D and C results in $15 being allocated to D and $20 to C. This procedure is somewhat different from earlier methods of allocation, which based the allocation on the price (average revenue) less any finishing costs. The two procedures would be equivalent if the average-revenue curve were horizontal, since the average-revenue and marginal-revenue curves would then coincide.

If a firm has one unit of D and one unit of C in inventory at the end of a period, and if these units would otherwise be produced next period, then the value of these units is the cost that can be saved (less holding costs) from not making these units in the next period. The value of these units is the marginal cost of the units to be produced in the next period. But since marginal revenue will be equated to marginal cost, the marginal-revenue figures can be used to split the marginal costs. If the productive facilities are not available in the next period, or if the demand will expand so that without the existing inventory of finished products the total demand would not be met, then the value of the units in the inventory would depend on the revenues they could earn and not on their costs of replacement. (The actual costs are sunk and are not relevant to the decision to sell.)

The numerical example given previously in Section 8.1 led to a marginal revenue for A of $32 and for B of $3. These would become the unit inventory values for any marginal units of product.

Two final points might be made:

1. Suppose that the raw material has been purchased and all of product A has been sold while some product B is still on hand (A and B are joint products). If the firm could not economically store any more B nor sell B, then the cost of product A is the entire cost of the raw material. The cost (and value) of B's raw material is zero.

2. If the firm has purchased a small amount of raw material and the analysis is similar to that presented in Figure 8.3, it is reasonable to split the cost of the raw material between D and C, using the expected marginal revenues of the products. These costs would be relevant for decision making (although the price would be set by reference to the average-revenue curves), since they give a reasonable estimate of both the cost and value of the last units made.

8.3 Summary

Common costs arise when the factors of production lead to two or more products. Although it is not possible to determine a precise cost for each product, it is possible to make economically sound price and output decisions.

The decision-making techniques also suggest an additional means of valuing inventories. The procedure uses the marginal revenue of the joint products to allocate costs. It does not make the unrealistic implicit assumptions concerning the revenue-generating ability of specific costs that are made by the gross-sales-value and net-sales-value methods. However, since it uses marginal revenues, it can only be used for small amounts of product.

QUESTIONS AND PROBLEMS

8-1 It is sometimes said that joint-cost allocations are worthless, since they cannot be used for decision making. Comment.

8-2 The costs of operating and maintaining a building are common costs with several products resulting. Do you think that it is useful to allocate building-department costs to operating departments and to product lines?

8-3 Distinguish between joint costs and indirect costs.

8-4 Distinguish between joint products and by-products from an accounting point of view.

8-5 Assuming the presence of joint costs, what types of decisions may be made using cost-revenue information?

8-6 A firm makes two products which are normally of equal value. Because of a temporary overabundance of one product, it is sold for scrap at a net of $0 per unit. How should the cost of the raw material be allocated during that period of overabundance?

8-7 Is it reasonable for the accountant to allocate joint costs to different products despite the fact that it is acknowledged that it is an impossible task to prove that the allocation is "the" correct allocation?

8-8 The Fidler Company has an accounting problem resulting from the production of joint products. How much of the raw material and other joint costs of $3,000 should be assigned to each of the joint products A, B, and C?

Joint Products	Pounds*	Sales Value (price × units)	Direct-Finishing Costs
A	150	2,000	400
B	50	3,000	900
C	200	4,000	1,700

* Product resulting from one unit of raw material and joint cost of $3,000.

Required: Compute a reasonable allocation of the $3,000 to the three joint products, using the net sales values.

8-9 Referring to problem 8-8, assume that a by-product is produced which has a value of $100 (per $3,000 of joint costs) and processing costs of $20. Compute the allocation of the $3,000 to the joint products and to the by-product.

8-10 Referring to problem 8-8, assume that the market prices of the factors of production remain unchanged but that the sales prices of the joint products A, B, and C change to $2,500, $2,000, and $1,000 for A, B, and C, respectively. What would be your decision relative to producing and selling each type of product?

8-11 The Capital Corporation stamps a component part, which shall be called X. From a roll of steel 100 feet long it is expected that 50 units of X will be obtained. The cost of 100 feet of the steel is $25, and the standard material cost of a unit of X has been set at $0.50. X utilizes approximately 90% of the total metal.

In April 1976, an engineer found that by cutting the metal scraps from the production line of X into easily handled shapes, a product Y could be made. For the remainder of 1976, Y's were made from this scrap. It is estimated that one unit of Y could be obtained per foot of steel. Y utilized approximately one tenth of the total metal; the cost per unit was established at $0.025. To record the manufacture of 1 million units of Y from 1,000,000 feet of steel, the following journal entry was made for the material component of Y (a standard cost system was in use for material):

Inventory—Y	$25,000	
Material		$25,000

To record the manufacture of 500,000 units of X, the following entry was made:

Inventory—X	$250,000	
Material		$250,000

Required: Comment on the procedure followed.

8–12 The AC Company has an extensive scrap operation, since the pieces of metal resulting from stamping operations have a high value on the scrap market. Total scrap sales amount to approximately $4,000,000 per year. The total sales of the corporation are approximately $1 billion per year. The expenses of operating the scrap-processing center (where the scrap is sorted and baled) are approximately $300,000 of direct costs.

The controller has argued that the scrap operation should be charged with part of the cost of raw material; the production manager, who is in overall charge of the scrap operation, argues that it should not be charged, since there is no reasonable method of assigning material costs to the operation.

Required: Comment on the positions of the controller and the production manager. What, if any, are the accounting problems?

8–13 A raw material is used to produce two products. One unit of raw material costing $8.50 is turned into 1 unit of A and 1 unit of B. Additional information is as follows:

Joint cost of processing raw material	$ 4
Direct cost of finishing product A	8
Direct cost of finishing product B	12

The price–quantity relationships of the two products are:

$$Q_A = 40 - \tfrac{1}{2}P_A \qquad Q_B = 80 - 4P_B$$

where Q is the number of units demanded in one day with price P.

Required:
a. How many units of raw material, product A, and product B should be processed daily?
b. If there were one unit each of A and B remaining in the finished-goods inventory, what would be the inventory value of those units?
c. Suppose that $P_A = 16$, $P_B = 18$ regardless of the firm's output and either product can be sold for $7 at the split-off point. What should the firm do?

8-14 The Auston Company purchases a raw material for $50 per unit that is turned into two products, A and B. The joint costs of processing are $30. After the two products are separated it costs $14 to finish A and $6 to finish B. One unit of A and one unit of B are obtained from each unit of raw material.

The following quantity–price relationships are expected to continue into the future (they relate the units of demand for a month):

$$P_A = 200 - \tfrac{1}{2}Q_A \qquad P_B = 150 - 2Q_B$$

a. What price and what output for each of the two end products would maximize profits?
b. Assuming that one unit of unfinished A and 20 units of unfinished B are on hand at the end of a month, how should these be valued?

8-15 The following summary is from W. J. Baumol et al., "The Role of Cost in the Minimum Pricing of Railroad Services," *The Journal of Business*, October 1962.

SUMMARY

1. In the determination of cost floors as a guide to the pricing of particular railroad services, or the services of any other transport mode, incremental costs of each particular service are the only relevant costs.
2. Rates for particular railroad services should be set at amounts (subject to the regulation of maximum rates and to legal rules against unjust discrimination) that will make the greatest total contribution to net income. Clearly, such maximizing rates would never fall below incremental costs.
3. Pricing which is not restricted by any minimum other than incremental cost can foster more efficient use of railroad resources and capacity and can therefore encourage lower costs and rates. This same principle applies to other modes of transportation.
4. The presence of large amounts of fixed costs and unused capacity in railroad facilities makes it especially important that railroad rates encourage a large volume of traffic.
5. Reduced rates which more than cover incremental costs and are designed by management to maximize contribution to net income do not constitute proof of predatory competition.
6. "Fully distributed" costs derived by apportioning unallocable costs have no economic significance in determining rate floors for particular railroad services. The application of such a criterion would arbitrarily force the railroads to maintain rates above the level which would yield maximum contribution to net

income and would deprive them of much traffic for which they can compete economically. For similar reasons, restriction of railroad minimum rates according to the "full cost of the low-cost carrier" is economically unsound.

Required: Comment on the conclusions.

8–16 The following argument can be found in the source for problem 8–15.

"Fully Distributed" Cost,
An Invalid Basis for Minimum Pricing

The relevant incremental costs constitute all the cost information pertinent to the determination of floors in the pricing of particular railroad services. "Fully distributed" cost, measured by some kind of arbitrary statistical apportionment of the unallocable costs among the various units or classes of traffic, is an economically invalid criterion for setting minimum rates, from both a managerial and a regulatory standpoint. No particular category of traffic can be held economically responsible for any given share of the unallocable costs. Whether any particular rate is above or below some fully distributed cost is without real economic significance for minimum pricing.

Stated differently, the appropriate aim of the railroads is to determine that margin above incremental costs, traffic volume considered, at which a rate produces the maximum total contribution toward fixed costs and net income. Fully distributed costs cannot serve this vital economic purpose. They present an entirely false picture of traffic profitability. Their use would drive away great quantities of profitable, volume-moving traffic now handled at rates below fully distributed costs.

Required: Is the statement valid for a manufacturing firm?

8–17* The High and Dry Company uses a joint process in the production of turpentine and methanol (wood alcohol). Joint costs amount to $1,200 per 1,000 gallons of output. The process produces 75% turpentine and 25% methanol. Added processing costs to make the products ready for sale are turpentine, 20¢ per gallon; methanol, 30¢ per gallon. Turpentine sells for $1.40 per gallon and methanol sells for $2.10 per gallon.

Required:

a. What joint costs per batch should be assigned to the turpentine and methanol, assuming that joint costs are assigned on a physical-volume basis?

b. If joint costs are to be assigned on a net sales-value basis, what amounts of joint cost should be assigned to the turpentine and to the methanol.

c. Prepare product-line income statements per batch for requirements a and b.

8–18* Refer back to the High and Dry Company problem. Suppose the company has discovered an additional (top-secret) process by which the methanol (wood

---

* Problems 17, 18, and 19 are adapted from C. Horngren, *Cost Accounting: A Managerial Emphasis*, Prentice Hall, 1972.

alcohol) can be converted from a poisonous liquid into a pleasant-tasting alcoholic beverage. The new selling price would be $6 per gallon. The additional processing would increase separable costs 90¢ a gallon, and the company would have to pay taxes for 20 percent on the new selling price. Assuming no other changes in cost, what is the joint cost applicable to the wood alcohol? Use the net sales value method. What costs are necessary to determine whether the new process should be used?

8–19* The J. Products Company produces both A and B from a joint process. During one period, their cost up to the point of separation was $40,000. There were no additional costs beyond this point. The production of A was 10,000 units, while 20,000 units of B were produced. A's selling price is $5, and B sold for 20¢ per unit.

Required:
a. If the inventory at the end of the period was 5,000 units of A and 10,000 units of B, what valuation figure should be used for the total inventory (that is, A and B together)?
b. If the ending inventory was 5,000 units of A and 5,000 units of B, what would be the valuation of A for balance sheet purposes? The valuation of B? Use the net sales value method.
c. If there is no ending inventory of A and B (that is, all the units were sold during the period), what allocation of cost would be made to A and B?

8–20 The Microtheory Company uses a joint process for the production of three goods: A, B, and C. For each unit of raw material, one unit of each of the three end products is obtained. The total joint costs of both purchasing the raw material and processing it into the intermediate stages of the three goods is $20. The additional costs of finishing the products are: A, $10; B, $20; and C, $20. The company has done a study of price-quantity relationships for the three goods, and it is believed that over the relevant range of output (50,000–100,000 units of each product) the following demand functions will apply for the next period:

$$P_A = 200 - Q_A$$
$$P_B = 400 - 2Q_B$$
$$P_C = 260 - 2Q_C$$

In each case, the Q's represent 1000's of units.

What quantity of each product should be produced for the next period, and what should the prices be? (The intermediate products have no scrap value.)

SUPPLEMENTARY READING

BAUMOL, W. J., et al., "The Role of Cost in the Minimum Pricing of Railroad Services," *The Journal of Business*, October 1962, pp. 1–10.

HARTLEY, R. V., "Decision Making When Joint Products Are Involved," *The Accounting Review*, October 1971, pp. 746–755.

MANES, R., and V. L. SMITH, "Economic Joint Cost Theory and Accounting Practice," *The Accounting Review*, January 1965, pp. 31–35.

NATIONAL ASSOCIATION OF COST ACCOUNTANTS, *Costing Joint Products* (Research Ser. 31), 1957.

PFOUTS, R. W., "The Theory of Cost and Production in the Multi-product Firm," *Econometrica*, October 1961, pp. 650–658.

SHUBIK, M., "Incentives, Decentralized Control, the Assignment of Joint Costs, and Internal Pricing," *Management Science*, April, 1962, pp. 325–343.

WALTERS, A. A., "The Allocation of Joint Costs," *The American Economic Review*, June 1960, pp. 419–432.

WEIL, R. L., "Allocating Joint Costs," *The American Economic Review*, December 1968, pp. 1342–1345.

Chapter 9

Analysis of Nonmanufacturing Costs

Traditionally, cost accountants have primarily concerned themselves with manufacturing costs. In recent years an increasing amount of attention has been directed to the control and analysis of distribution and other nonmanufacturing costs. This has occurred partly because of the increased relative importance of these costs as a percentage of total costs and partly because of the introduction of formal decision-making models in this area.

This chapter examines several types of nonmanufacturing costs, including distribution costs, administrative costs, and research costs. Attention is also given to the impact of the Robinson–Patman Act on cost record keeping in this area.

The techniques used for decision making and control of manufacturing costs are, in large part, also relevant to nonmanufacturing costs. Thus, the notions of cost-variance analysis, cost–volume–profit analysis, budgeting, and performance evaluation are all appropriate in some degree to the present subject material. However, the benefits are more difficult to measure in the area of nonmanufacturing costs than they are with manufacturing costs.

9.1 Distribution Cost Analysis and Control

The distribution function generally begins before the manufacture of the product and continues after the cash is collected. Under this broad time horizon, distribution costs typically include:

1. The costs (including advertising costs) of promoting customer goodwill and obtaining sales.
2. The costs of handling and storing the completed product and of shipping it to the customer.
3. The costs of recording and collecting the amounts owed to the company by its customers.
4. Handling the returns and servicing guarantees (a more generous guarantee being a way to enhance the saleability of the product).

The purpose of the distribution function can be taken as maximizing the long-run contribution to fixed costs and profits.[1] Thus, the analysis of distribution costs should be directed toward decisions that can be made to improve the overall contribution. This implies that such costs should be broken down by product line, customer type, salesmen, geographical location, and so on. The classification in Table 9–1 suggests some of the possibilities:

Table 9–1   Possible Breakdowns of Distribution Costs

Sales Outlets (customer type)	Methods of Selling
Wholesalers	Mail order
Retailers, independent	Company salesmen, outside
Discount houses	Company salesmen, inside
Chain stores	Manufacturers' agents

Product Line	Graphical Location
Line I	Cities over 1,000,000
Product *A*	Cities over 100,000
Product *B*	Cities over 10,000
Product C	Cities under 10,000
Line II	or
Product *D*	Sales districts, counties, states,
product *E*	countries

Historical cost figures should be carefully analyzed. In the first place, the data may reflect arbitrary cost allocations and costs that would not be altered by the decision being contemplated (the contraction or expansion of some activity, for example). Second, future costs are relevant, and historical data only provide reliable indications of the future when conditions remain essentially unaltered. In the determination of future costs, the use of modern statistical techniques of experimentation and decision making can be particularly helpful.

---

[1] Short-run goals may include market penetration and establishing markets for new products. Performance evaluation should take cognizance of these short-run goals when they are operative and considered consistent with long-run profit maximization.

Distribution costs are usually common to several functions and, therefore, allocation must often be made on a relatively arbitrary basis. In decision making and control, it is important to recognize the common nature of these costs and the effect of this commonality on decisions.

9.1.1 Decision Making and Distribution Costs

Many decisions in the distribution area are made intuitively, and it is unlikely that distribution cost analysis will completely eliminate the necessity of making such decisions in this manner. For example, it will probably never be possible for the accounting department using historical costs to tell the marketing staff that they are spending too much or too little on advertising and prove that an alternative amount is optimal. On the other hand, the accounting department can tell top management that the revenues of a product are not recovering the manufacturing and distribution costs—including advertising—directly associated with the product. This may lead indirectly to a decision concerning advertising.

In the type of cost analysis being considered, it is useful to think of three layers of costs:

1. Direct costs are costs that can be directly identified with the product, division, geographical unit, etc.
2. Allocated costs with traceable benefits are costs that cannot be directly identified but which have a close correlation with the activity of a unit. For example, costs of writing bills may be affected by the number of lines on an invoice.
3. Allocated costs with indirect benefits are costs that cannot be directly identified and that have little correlation with the activity of a unit. For example, the benefits derived from the sales manager's salary may not be closely identified with any one product line and thus must be arbitrarily allocated to several product lines.

In addition to the above three distinctions it is often useful to know if the cost is fixed or variable. These classifications take on different meanings in the analysis of distribution costs from that of manufacturing costs. In manufacturing-cost analysis, interest centers on how costs react to changes in manufacturing activity. With distribution costs, interest centers on how costs react to changes in sales or a given type of promotional effort. An example of a variable-distribution cost is a salesman's commission. An example of a fixed cost is the salary of the sales manager. The problem is complicated, however, by the fact that costs may be fixed in one sense, but not in another. Thus advertising costs may be fixed by a managerial decision, but in order to increase sales it may be necessary to increase the amount spent on advertising.[2] On the other

---

[2] Advertising is often treated as a residual factor in budgeting. This treatment implicitly assumes that advertising is a function of sales and does not acknowledge the effect of advertising on sales.

hand, a given amount of advertising may result in increased sales if the sales price is lowered. Thus advertising may be considered fixed when the firm is considering a change in sales price, or the firm may vary both advertising and sales price at once.

The decisions made with the help of distribution-cost analysis are varied. Among some of the more important are:

1. Setting prices of the product.
2. Expanding, contracting, or abandoning product lines or sales effort.
3. Expanding, contracting, or abandoning specific customer outlets or geographical locations.
4. Establishing warehouses and supply points.
5. Determining the relative merits of different sales efforts (including performance of salesmen).
6. Media selection.

The above decisions require cost and revenue information classified in several ways. For example, where possible, each cost must be identified as to product line and geographical location. Also of interest is the relation of the cost to any particular type of sales outlet, its functional classification (delivery, warehousing, billing, collecting, sales, etc.), and its natural classification (labor, supplies, utilities, etc.). Costs that cannot be directly identified with product lines, geographical locations, and so on, present a problem. Should they be allocated? All costs may be allocated, but the manager should carefully distinguish among the direct costs, the allocated costs with traceable benefits, and the allocated costs that have no close relation with the unit to which the cost is being allocated.

For example, assume a situation where the Tall Bottle Company makes four different types of bottles. Management is reviewing the profitability of the milk bottle line. The income statement for the most recent period is given in Table 9–2. Assume further that all the fixed costs are unavoidable and would be incurred even if the product were abandoned, and that the $2,500 of allocated costs

Table 9–2   Milk Bottles Income Statement (for year ending December 31)

Sales	$30,000	
Less: Manufacturing costs of goods sold (includes fixed costs of $3,000)	25,000	
Gross margin		$5,000
Less: Distribution costs directly identified with product (includes fixed costs of $2,000)	$ 6,500	
Allocated costs	2,500	9,000
Net loss		($4,000)

includes $1,000 of costs that are variable and closely related to the sale of milk bottles (these include delivery expense, which is allocated by weight, bulk, and mean distance of the deliveries).

What action, if any, should management take? If the income statement is rearranged, management will find that the sale of milk bottles is contributing $2,500 to the recovery of common and fixed costs, and should not be abandoned. This is shown in Table 9–3. Allocated costs in the amount of $1,000 are considered relevant to this decision.

Table 9–3   Milk Bottles Income Statement: Revised

Sales		$30,000
Variable costs:		
Manufacturing	$22,000	
Distribution ($1,000 + $4,500)	5,500	37,500
Contribution to recovery of fixed costs		$ 2,500
Fixed costs		
Manufacturing	$ 3,000	
Distribution	3,500	6,500
Net loss		($ 4,000)

The fact that the product is recovering more than the variable costs does not mean that no action is required. A company may recover variable costs every day right up until it has to file bankruptcy papers. The analysis does indicate, however, that assuming the fixed costs are unavoidable, the company is better off with the milk bottle business than it would be without it. It is possible that more or less selling effort is required or that the price should be raised or lowered. The income statement presented shows that management should not be complacent. It does not indicate the nature or the direction of managerial action.[3]

In recommending a decision not to drop the product, neither the unavoidable fixed costs nor the allocated costs not closely related to the product were considered. If some of the fixed costs could be avoided by the dropping of the product, these costs become relevant to a decision to abandon.

If the problem were changed so that there were the option to sell the milk bottle portion of the business, then most of the fixed costs could be avoided. The price that could be obtained for the business becomes a type of opportunity cost. The problem might then be solved by implementing the theory of capital budgeting (see Chapter 13). The procedure would be to compare the present value of the cash flows resulting from retaining the business to the present value of the cash flows that would result from the sale of the business.

[3] The possibility of allocating effort in other directions should also be considered.

Recent years have also witnessed the introduction of operations research models to distribution decisions. The advertising function is one of several in the distribution area in which formal mathematical models have been used.[4] For example, programming and statistical decision-theory models have been applied to the media selection and message effectiveness problems. Typically the models attempt to minimize cost subject to a constraint on the minimum total service provided. Although a substantial portion of the costs, such as the cost per unit of an advertising medium, are externally set, there is a tendency to ignore the associated internal costs. This is particularly true for the cost of supportive activities, accounting for example, which can be allocated only to the advertising function on relatively arbitrary bases. The allocation should include even the fixed costs of providing service where such costs may be considered as opportunity-cost approximations for using the committed resources.

Formal mathematical models have been used to make other distribution decisions as well. The location of warehouses and the establishment of supply centers provide examples. Costs play a central role in all these decisions. Hence it behooves the managerial accountant to understand these models and the cost-information requirements they entail.

There are a variety of decisions and they often require different arrays of cost information. Not all costs are relevant for all decisions. Costs to be especially watched are costs that are fixed but avoidable, and costs that are common to many products or other units. The inclusion or exclusion of these costs depends on the exact nature of the decisions. Neither the inclusion nor exclusion of indirect or common costs should be automatic.

9.1.2 Distribution Cost Control

The control of distribution costs is especially difficult, since in contrast with many manufacturing type operations, there is no easily measurable and assignable output. Also, standards of performance are much more difficult to set. Nevertheless, it is sometimes possible to set standards that are effective enough to assist in the control of distribution costs.

For purposes of cost control, it is useful to separate distribution costs into those involved with obtaining sales and those involved with filling orders. The techniques of control are somewhat different.

Control of Order-Filling Costs
Order-filling costs include the costs of order processing, storage, packing and shipping, billing, credit, and collection. The use of task analysis and work-measurement techniques can be valuable in setting standards for budgeting and controlling costs of this type.

---

[4] See D. W. Miller and M. K. Starr, *Executive Decisions and Operations Research*, Englewood Cliffs, N.J.: Prentice-Hall, Inc., 1964, Chap. 9.

Where the action is repetitive and of a uniform nature and the benefits easily measured, the setting of the standards is relatively well defined. Thus the billing department may be judged on how much it costs to turn out invoices, with due consideration for the characteristics of the invoices. The shipping and receiving departments may be judged on the number of items handled and the weight of the items or by delays that it causes in production or breakage or some combination of these. The credit and collection departments may be effectively controlled in a manner similar to that used in the control of manufacturing costs.

Consider the situation in a billing department. Suppose that a firm employs 20 individuals in the billing department. Each can handle (the standard at normal activity levels) 500 billings per week. The 20 employees are all paid $200 per week. Suppose that in a given week, 9,700 billings were made. If the 20 employees had worked at the standard rate, the expectation would be that 10,000 billings would have been made. What is the explanation of the difference of 300 billings?

An analysis similar to that of Chapter 5 is relevant. In the first place, it is necessary to know how the standard was determined, since this affects the interpretation of the variance. Suppose that the standard was established on the basis of normal activity. Under these conditions the actual sales level may explain some of the variance. For example, there may have been 9,700 billings requiring processing. Alternatively, the employees may have been inefficient in performing their jobs (assuming that more than 9,700 billings required processing). Or, alternatively, the bills may be more complex than the average bills. The activity variance in this case is 10,000 − 9,700, or 300 billings. An analysis of these factors can assist in week-to-week activity evaluation and, it is hoped, lead to better performance.

It should be noted that the approach, or attitude, taken by management toward cost control can influence cost-reduction programs. Cost savings are not likely to be achieved in areas where costs are considered by management to be uncontrollable.

Suppose that in the above example 9,700 billings actually required processing. Even when activity and expectations match, there may still be valuable information available for cost control. Since the work force could process 10,000 billings, there is presently overcapacity in the billing task—at least for the week in question. But this may represent only a necessary safety factor to handle variable-activity levels. It would be useful to know the standard-activity level and the activity's variability. The cost of the difference between the normal capacity, 10,000 billings, and the actual output level in this case, 9,700 billings, is $120: $200/500 (10,000 − 9,700), or, alternatively, the cost of billing is $4,000/10,000, or $0.40. Since 300 billings less than 10,000 were processed, the cost of the idle capacity is $0.40(300), or $120. This amount might represent the investment required to maintain a stable work force necessary to meet fluctuating activity levels. On the other hand, it might indicate opportunities for cost savings over the longer run. Management must decide the employee level for each task and whether it wishes to meet peak activity levels by hiring part-time employees, by overtime, by delays, or by shifting employees from other tasks. Each reasonable alternative should be examined in terms of its cost, considering a full cycle of activity and the frequency associated with the various activity levels. If this has not been done previously, large cost variances suggest that it may be profitable to consider the alternatives.

The process (controlling the cost of billings) would involve the concept of work measurement. It should be mentioned that work measurement may often be a difficult task. In distribution-cost control, the difficulties may center about the diversity of tasks performed by individuals of a group or, instead, on the difficulty of isolating an output measure (such as the number of billings). Sometimes work measurement is difficult because of the nature of the output. For example, how should the output of the market research staff be measured for cost-control purposes or how should the output of the legal or economic-analysis staff be computed?

Control of Order-Getting Costs

Controlling the costs of selling is complicated by the fact that the effectiveness of the costs in gaining sales is affected by variables beyond the control of the sales department, such as general business conditions, the action of competitors, the design of the product, the price of the product, and changing habits of consumers. In the control of selling costs, the quantitative measures must sometimes be tempered by qualitative judgments as to whether the sales department or a particular salesman is doing a "good" job. Furthermore, the measurement and control of costs becomes more complex as advertising becomes more general, selling more personal, products more interrelated, and as economic conditions change more quickly. Thus, control of institutional advertising cost is not facilitated by allocating it to specific products.

Companies frequently use measures such as selling cost per order, or selling cost per call, or calls per day, as control devices. But there is a danger in comparing salesmen where the geographical and economic characteristics of the different sales areas differ considerably. Used with discretion, however, these measures can be useful in forming impressions of how effectively a salesman is performing. An analysis of the trends may also be helpful.

Control of order-getting costs is more effective in the cost-planning stage than in the implementation stage. Still, *ex post* implementation analysis is important as a step in improving resource allocation. Analysis can highlight those areas (product line, selling method, advertising medium, etc.) where the contribution is large, either on a unit basis or in total, and thus identify possibilities that may deserve greater (or less) effort on the part of the firm. A comparison of actual costs to the figures used in decision making can help determine the limitations of the decision model or provide cost information for future decisions.

9.1.3 Distribution Costs and Financial Reporting

The greatest portion of distribution costs is considered to be an expense of the time period in which the costs are incurred, and little attempt is made to assign these costs to the periods which benefit from their incurrence. Thus advertising costs are generally considered an expense in the period in which the advertising medium appears rather than a cost allocated over the periods that benefit from the advertising. In like manner, the selling costs connected with obtaining unfilled orders are only infrequently carried over to the period in which the order is filled. These are considered to be conservative accounting procedures and thus desirable. But, in part, the accounting treatment reflects the impact of taxes. Since such expenses are deductible for tax purposes, they are usually treated as tax expenses in the earliest period permitted by law. For simplicity and consistency this treatment is then typically used in the firm's financial records regardless of its effect on the data supplied to external decision makers.

9.2　Administrative Costs

A distinction between administrative and distribution costs is somewhat artificial, at least from an analysis and control point of view. All of what has been said concerning distribution costs is relevant, at least in part, to administrative costs. Those distinctions that can be drawn are essentially ones of degree and not of substance.

Administrative costs are basically fixed in the short run (some authors would refer to them as "programmed"). In this sense they are similar to promotional expenditures. Few of these costs exhibit any variability with short-run changes in the physical activity of the firm.

As was true in the case of distribution decisions, formal models have also been applied in recent years to several problems in the administrative area. These include problems of the optimal-sized work force, the related problems of absenteeism, pay incentive plans, vacations, and so on. Once again these decisions usually center on cost considerations, since the contribution of administrative activity to profit and fixed costs is extremely difficult to establish. The decisions, when formalized, are often based on minimizing the expected cost to perform some given level of service.

Often an analysis of cost behavior is important since management needs to know what improvement in costs can be obtained by the introduction of corrective action: management needs a cost–benefit analysis. For example, if the relationship between the absentee rate and total-period costs were known, and if the effect of various strategies (such as a bonus for a good employment record) on the absentee rate could be estimated, then decisions among several strategies to lower absenteeism would be facilitated.

The accountant can assist in these decisions if he recognizes problem areas, often a result of cost analysis, and understands the types of formal and informal analysis that could be applied. He is then in a position to analyze cost behavior, predict the effect of strategic variables on costs, and thereby assist in the initiation and implementation of administrative cost-reduction programs.

Control is again usually achieved in the planning stage through the use of budgets based upon the type and amount of service anticipated for the period in question. However, some tasks, including clerical activities, lend themselves to the use of standards based on some measure of task activity. Where this is the case, the control methods found in the production area can be applied. Generally, however, administrative services are rendered indirectly to many different departments, and in addition it is practically impossible to establish input–output relationships that permit overall evaluations. These facts make the control and evaluation of administrative costs one of the more difficult areas.

The tendency of new administrative services, regardless of their actual value, to become permanent once initiated argues strongly for a full analysis of suggested new activities. The same types of stringent criteria should be applied to the benefits associated, or alleged to be associated, with new administrative services before they are adopted, as are applied to other more easily evaluated activities in the firm. However, objective measures of the benefits may not always be available.

9.3   Research-and-Development Cost Analysis and Control

Once again much of what has been said about distribution and administration costs is relevant to the research and development area. Nevertheless, there are additional factors that call for some discussion.

The difficulty of measuring the results or output of an activity are perhaps most pronounced in this area. Usually it is only over an extended period of time involving several years that some indication of the success of research and development activities can be obtained. Further, benchmarks against which to measure the effectiveness of research and development activities are not easily established. Conditions may change appreciably over time, and the difficulty of disentangling a research department's contribution from that of sales, production, and so on, makes it difficult to use historical data. Also, information concerning similar activities in other firms is neither easily obtained nor adjustable to permit comparisons.

The use of budgets as a control mechanism is common but suffers from several shortcomings. First, there is usually a strong incentive built into the control system to stay within budgeted levels. Such budgets, however, reflect an amalgamation of research activities and are therefore unrelated to specific projects or the advantages to be obtained thereform.

Second, department managers are often moved up to higher positions. Hence, they may be motivated more by the easily seen short-run budget controls than by the long-run research contribution to the firm, which is more difficult to evaluate. Finally, research and development budgets, like many promotional expenditures, have an indirect impact on the level of sales and thereby on cash flows. Thus they interact with the very factors that often determine the budgeted level for research. This interrelationship, although indirect, is nevertheless important. Research and development expenditures (like promotion expenditures) should not usually be treated as residual budget allocations made after production and similar outlays have been determined. Indeed, in most industries the single most important activity affecting the future prosperity of the firm is the success of its research and development activities.

Given the importance of research and development and the unreasonableness of short-run evaluations, the emphasis should be placed on creating a climate where research has an optimal chance of success. In accomplishing this objective, it is important to consider the unusual character of the creative individual, the frustration of delays resulting from inadequate facilities or lack of adequate assistance, the need for praise that such individuals usually demonstrate, their desire for some pure (or free) as well as specific-objective research, the importance of minimizing paperwork and reports, and the tendency for many creative individuals to be unconcerned with time and cost considerations.

A useful approach to control and, indirectly, analysis is to organize the research department by projects. Each project should be under the supervision of someone in the department. The supervisor then takes responsibility for administration and personnel evaluation. Cost control is achieved through the comparison of periodic reports listing percentage completion, expenditures of time and resources, as well as estimates of time and resources needed to finish the project, with initial project estimates. Typically it will be necessary to subdivide projects into well-defined subtasks in order to maximize the effectiveness of this control procedure.[5] Even the mere fact that control is considered important, if attempted in a reasonable way, can often encourage real savings in both costs and time.

9.4   Service Organizations and Departments

Some organizations are entirely of a service nature. In this case service is the final product. Examples include: utilities, education, insurance and financial services, transportation, recreation, lodging, spectator sports, legal services, consulting, communications, personal services, and health-care organizations. Service departments are also found in manufacturing firms. These departments are distinguished by the fact that they supply service to other parts of the organization but not directly to ultimate consumers. Examples

---

[5] The ability to form projects and to divide them into distinct and ordered subtasks suggests that the techniques of PERT and PERT-Cost might be applicable at least to certain specific-object research. See Chapter 21.

include: power, maintenance, repair, engineering, cafeteria, administration, and building and grounds. This section discusses some of the costing issues related to the direct and indirect control of service costs.

9.4.1 Service Organizations

In service organizations it is first necessary to distinguish the services offered. Seldom does a service organization offer only a single service. Whether these services are provided in a market context or offered by not-for-profit organizations, it is important to know their cost. Pricing, cost control, and performance evaluation are all fundamentally tied (but not limited) to cost measures.

The methods we have discussed in earlier chapters, and which we will discuss in future ones, are all equally relevant to the costing problems of service organizations. Standard costs of such operations can be estimated and combined to obtain costs for various activities. For example, in banking, a number of tasks, such as opening an account and posting entries, can be studied and costed. These tasks can then be combined in determining the cost of servicing a checking or commercial account, for example. Types of customers (or activities) can be evaluated for profitability, and departments can be monitored over time to assure that their costs remain in control.

In order to cost the final output of service organizations it is necessary, as with manufacturing organizations, to allocate common costs. For this reason it is necessary to find meaningful relationships between the various activities performed by the organization and the requirements of the final service to be provided. Cause-and-effect relationships are desirable where they exist.

The bases traditionally used include physical identification, service supplied, capacity provided, actual benefits received, ability to recover costs, and fairness or equity. Sometimes combinations of these bases are appropriate.

Physical identification is preferable where a direct relationship between the final product and the input activities exists. This is common in the manufacture of physical goods, where direct materials can be physically traced to the product. It is not nearly as relevant for service operations; however, it can be used to allocate the use of physical items to final service operations. This would be true, for example, of blood transfusions and intravenous feedings in a hospital.

Service supplied is appropriate to such activities as repair, engineering, and power. Charges can be made at standard rates based on efficiency considerations for such service. Typically this charge can be made when the service is requested. However, the fixed costs of establishing and maintaining these indirect service activities must be allocated as well. Separate cost-allocation rates for these fixed costs based on the needs of the operating departments that justified incurring the fixed costs are appropriate. The idea of practical capacity suggests itself as a useful measure. If, on the other hand, these departments are equipped to meet peak activity levels, these levels should be used to allocate the fixed costs.

A key point in the discussion of cost allocation is that different allocation rates are often appropriate for the fixed- and variable-cost components of indirect service departments. A second key point is that the cost allocation need not reallocate all costs either from a costing or control point of view. Inefficiencies should be detected where they occur if control is to be attained. This can occur only if the costs caused by the inefficiency remain in the offending department. For planning and for control, flexible budgets based on realistic activity measures (that is, those measuring cost incurrence) should be used. Standard, predetermined unit prices and rates (not actual costs) are required. Fixed- and variable-cost components are best handled separately. Finally, the costs reallocated to one activity should not be influenced by those allocated to some other activity.

The use of benefits received is often a convenient basis of allocating service costs. The limitation is that it utilizes input, not output. The method is often applied to property taxes, building depreciation, and related items. Cause and effect are hard to establish, yet long-run operations require these expenditures. The result is that such costs are often allocated on the basis of the revenue-producing ability of the final product. The implication is that these expenditures have added value to the final product, but this is often not the case. The method is in many respects a fallback position when other more convincing criteria are lacking.

The ability to recover costs and fairness criteria are also arbitrary bases that leave the thoughtful manager at the least uneasy about the usefulness of the final cost allocations. They should be avoided except perhaps for costing in cost-plus contracts, where prior agreement is obtained on how the cost allocations are to be made.

Where substantive damage will not be done, that is, in the case of relatively small cost allocations, similar costs may be grouped and allocated using a single base.

Service organizations face the need of establishing a basic charge unit. Consulting organizations typically use time with different hourly rates for different service types. Hospitals cost several types of service, including room, laboratory, and surgical. Airlines base their rates on miles traveled and type of flight as well as special services provided.

9.4.2 Allocation of Service Department Costs

Whether an organization is service-oriented or produces a physical product, the costs are allocated for product-costing purposes. (Allocation, it should be remembered, is not typically useful for control purposes. Allocation based on actual services, such as repairs, is an exception.) Figure 9–1 illustrates a simple situation that is nonetheless complex enough to illustrate how service department costs can be allocated.

Three basic methods may be used to allocate service department costs: (1) direct allocation, (2) stepwise allocation, and (3) a mathematical solution.

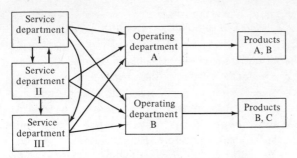

Figure 9.1   **Service department cost allocation.**

In the direct method, service department costs are allocated directly to operating departments. The fact that one service department renders service to another is ignored.[6] This method is the most commonly employed approach. Stepwise allocation recognizes the service given by one service department to another. The method can become quite involved where reciprocal services (indicated by the arrows between Service Departments I and II in Figure 9–1) are involved. The problem of selecting the order in which the service departments should be allocated must be established. The most common solution is to allocate the costs of that service department first which services the greatest number of other service departments. An alternative (which could also be used in cases where no choice is indicated by the first solution) is to select first that service department with the largest total value to be allocated.[7]

There follows an example illustrating both the direct and the stepwise approaches (see Tables 9–4, 9–5, and 9–6). A single base will be used in each

Table 9–4   **Data for Cost Allocation**

| | Service Activity Measure | | | | | |
| Service Department | Service Department | | | Operating Department | | Total Units |
	I	II	III	A	B	
I		100	100	600	200	1,000
II	20		40	30	30	120
III				75	25	100

[6] A simultaneous equation solution is possible which implicitly considers reallocation. This is the "Mathematical solution" to be discussed later. The presence of high-speed computers facilitates obtaining this solution.

[7] Other methods, not widely used, include selecting for initial allocation the department that gives the greatest percentage of its service to other service departments versus operating departments; and the one that has the greatest net service due to other service departments over what is due to it.

department for simplicity, although we emphasize that separate rates are appropriate for the fixed- and variable-cost components. Indeed, more than one rate might be appropriate within each cost category. Only the allocation from the service departments to the operating department is illustrated.

Costs (000 omitted):

Service Department	
I	$ 800
II	600
III	900
Operating Department	
A	$1,000
B	1,200

The service activity measures may be the same or different from service department to service department. For example:

Service Department	Activity Measure
Power	Kilowatt-hours
Maintenance	Employee-hours
Building and grounds	Square footage

Table 9–5   Direct-Method Allocation

Service Department	Operating Department			
	A		B	
	Ratio	Amount	Ratio	Amount
I	$\frac{6}{8}$	$ 600	$\frac{2}{8}$	$ 200
II	$\frac{3}{6}$	300	$\frac{3}{6}$	300
III	$\frac{3}{4}$	675	$\frac{1}{4}$	225
Direct costs		1,000		1,200
Total Costs		$2,575		$1,925

The ratios for the direct method are determined as follows for Operating Department A:

Service Department I	$600 \div (600 + 200) = \frac{6}{8}$
Service Department II	$30 \div (30 + 30) = \frac{3}{6}$
Service Department III	$75 \div (75 + 25) = \frac{3}{4}$

Table 9–6   Stepwise-Method Allocation

| | Service Department | | | | Operating Department | | | |
| | II | | III | | A | | B | |
Service Department	Ratio	Amount	Ratio	Amount	Ratio	Amount	Ratio	Amount
I	$\frac{1}{10}$	$ 80	$\frac{1}{10}$	$ 80	$\frac{6}{10}$	$ 480	$\frac{2}{10}$	$ 160
II*			$\frac{4}{10}$	272	$\frac{3}{10}$	204	$\frac{3}{10}$	204
III†					$\frac{3}{4}$	939	$\frac{1}{4}$	313
Direct		600		900		1,000		1,200
Total		$680		$,1252		$2,623		$1,877

* $600 + $80 is allocated.
† $900 + $80 + $272 is allocated.

Explanation of Table 9–6

1. Service Department I is allocated first since it has more cost to allocate than II. Both service two other service departments.
2. The rates are 100/1,000, 100/1,000, 600/1,000, and 200/1,000.
3. Service Department II is allocated second (department III is not allocated to I or II).
4. The rates are 40/100, 30/100, and 30/100.
5. The amount allocated by II is $600 direct + $80 from I.
6. The rates for Service Department III are: 75/100 and 25/100.
7. The amount allocated by III is: $900 direct + $80 from I + $272 from II.

9.4.3 Reallocation: A Mathematical Solution

As described above, an allocation problem arises when one service department services another service department and is serviced in turn by that department. The allocation of overhead in this type of situation may be solved by the use of algebra for an exact solution. The solution is relatively simple unless the number of departments involved becomes large.

The usefulness of this computation (in effect an allocation and reallocation) is limited. It usually serves no function relative to the control of costs. It does result in a more logical allocation of costs to the operating departments, and thus leads to improved unit-cost computations. In many cases a reasonable solution can be obtained through bypassing the mathematical solution and using one of the two procedures illustrated above.

To simplify the explanations we shall assume there are only two service departments and two operating departments.

Example

Assume that the Building Department cost should be allocated as follows (percentages are based on use of floor space):

20% to Repair Department
70% to Operating Department 1
10% to Operating Department 2

The Repair Department should be allocated as follows (percentages are based on this period's repairs):

80% to Building Department
20% to Operating Department 1

The costs incurred in the Building Department were $5,960. The costs incurred in the Repair Department were $2,000. Computation of the total costs of the Building and Repair Departments and the allocation of these costs to the two operating departments is as follows. Let

B = total building costs (costs incurred directly in the Building Department plus the allocation from the repair shop)

R = total repair costs (costs incurred directly in repair shop plus the allocation from the Building Department)

Then

$$B = 5,960 + 0.8R$$
$$R = 2,000 + 0.2B$$

The next step is to solve for B and then R.

$$B = 5,960 + 0.8R$$
$$= 5,960 + 0.8(2,000 + 0.2B)$$
$$= 5,960 + 1,600 + 0.16B$$
$$0.84B = 7,560$$
$$B = \$9,000 \text{ ("total" Building Department cost)}$$
$$R = 2,000 + 0.2B$$
$$= 2,000 + (0.2 \times 9,000)$$
$$= \$3,800 \text{ ("total" Repair Department cost)}$$

The results are shown in Table 9–7.

Table 9–7　Allocation of Building and Repair Department Costs

| Dept. | Total Cost | Allocated to: | | | |
		Op. 1	Op. 2	Building	Repair
Building	$ 9,000	$6,300 (70%)	$900 (10%)		$1,800 (20%)
Repair	3,800	760 (20%)		$3,040 (80%)	
	$12,800	$7,060	$900	$3,040	$1,800

The total of Building Department cost ($9,000) and Repair Department cost ($3,800) is greater than the total cost incurred in the two departments ($7,960). This occurs because of the reallocation of building cost to the Repair Department and then repair cost back to the Building Department, and so on. The total overhead allocated to the operating departments is $7,960, which is equal to the costs incurred in the two service departments ($5,960 plus $2,000).

The journal entries to record the allocation of the Service Department costs will be similar to the following:

Overhead—Repair Department	$1,800	
Overhead—Operating Department 1	6,300	
Overhead—Operating Department 2	900	
Overhead—Building		$9,000
Overhead—Building	3,040	
Overhead—Operating Department 1	760	
Overhead—Repair Department		3,800

(These entries are typically made only in the subsidiary records.)

Appendix 9A describes a matrix formulation for cost allocations that is consistent with the above simplified example.

9.5　Robinson–Patman Act

The Robinson–Patman amendment to the Clayton Act concerns itself with unlawful price discriminations.[8] Price discrimination is considered unlawful where the effect "may be to substantially lessen competition or tend to create a monopoly in any line of commerce." The law is administered by the Federal Trade Commission.

The primary purpose of the act is to make it easier to establish a violation

---

[8] For a more complete description of the Robinson–Patman Act, see H. E. Taggart, "Cost Justification: Rules of the Game," *Journal of Accountancy*, December 1958, pp. 52–60; and H. E. Taggart, *Cost Justification* (Michigan Business Studies, Vol. 14, No. 3), Ann Arbor: University of Michigan, 1959; and supplements No. 1 and 2, 1964 and 1967.

and more difficult to achieve a defense than was the case under the Clayton Act. For a firm to be subject to the act, several conditions must be satisfied. These conditions are that the prices "must:

1. Occur in interstate commerce.
2. Be related to "commodities of like grade and quality."
3. Have the requisite effect on competition.
4. Be other than price changes occurring because of market conditions such as seasonal clearances.
5. Not be justified as a means of meeting an equally low price of a competitor.
6. Not be justified by cost differences of equal or greater magnitude."[9]

Defenses by firms faced with suits under the Robinson–Patman Act have attempted to show that one or more of these six conditions are not satisfied. In general, this has been very difficult to do. The concept of interstate commerce has been expanded until this section of the law offers little if any defense. Goods can be considered of like grade and quality even though they are not identical. Once price differences have been established, the presumption of at least a potentially undesirable effect on competition is nearly automatic, and it has been extremely difficult to rebut this charge by the defense of meeting an equally low competitor's price.[10]

Complaints involving distress merchandise have been rare, and thus this sort of activity is unlikely to bring action by the Commission. This is important since, contrary to normal legal proceedings, a defendant under the Robinson–Patman Act is presumed guilty unless he can successfully establish a defense. Furthermore, if the firm is unable to establish a successful defense, it may be subject to treble damages. These facts suggest that it is desirable not to come under the investigatory scrutiny of the Commission.

In fact, the most successful defense against a complaint brought by the Federal Trade Commission under the Robinson–Patman Act has been by cost justification of the price differences. Even in this area success is an elusive goal. While about 50% of the cost defenses made in public proceedings have been at least partially successful, relatively few cases have reached the stage of public proceedings.[11] Most of the complaints have been settled by informal hearings before the Commission's staff. The number of successful cost defenses in informal hearings, however, is not known, since the results of such hearings are not available to the public.

The reasons for the limited use of the cost defense stem in part from the time-consuming nature of the work involved and the expense of making cost-justification studies. Perhaps even more important is the difficulty anticipated in

[9] Taggart, *Cost Justification, op. cit.*, p. 548.

[10] The meeting-of-competition defense has been used successfully by only one firm in public proceedings, and this defense took 17 years.

[11] Taggart, *Cost Justification, op. cit.*, pp. 544–545. Only 22 defendants have pleaded this defense in 22 years, while in the year 1957 alone the Commission issued 22 complaints.

convincing the Commission or, more accurately, the Commission's accountants that adequate cost justification exists. Nevertheless, the fact that cost calculations have been accepted in both formal and informal proceedings is evidence that this defense is not completely illusionary.

An analysis of the cases that have been open to the public suggests several basic principles that are valuable for firms faced with potential complaints by the Federal Trade Commission. Perhaps most important in this list is recognition of the fact that any cost-justification defense must convince the Commission's accountants. One important means of accomplishing this objective is to provide evidence of having considered the price differentials in light of the related costs prior to offering the prices to customers. Cost analyses prepared in advance and, perhaps, if possible, after consultation with the Commission, could provide evidence of this good faith. Since the effect of the Commission's actions can be severe, the best talent available should be put on the job. This is not a place for the second team.

Several additional points can also be gleaned from the public cases.[12] They include:

1. Time has been the only satisfactory means of allocating labor services.
2. Sales dollars cannot be used to allocate overhead.
3. Differential costing is not acceptable.
4. Cost methods and classifications already in use by a firm need not be accepted by the Commission.
5. Management cost estimates are not acceptable.
6. Sampling methods may be used, but samples must be demonstrably representative. (Small samples are suspect.)

The generally acceptable principles enumerated above are few in number. Several additional principles also are relevant to the treatment of specific cost items. The interested reader is referred to the materials authored by Taggert (see footnote 8) and the report of the Advisory Committee (Appendix A to the Taggert book) for specific examples.

Perhaps the best summary of this section is given by Taggert when he writes that "the cost defense, with all its complexities and uncertainties, is the most practical and available [defense against a complaint under section 2(a) of the Robinson–Patman Act]. And the conclusion to be derived from studying the recorded cost-defense cases is that the best time to prepare to offer the cost defense is before a complaint is issued."

Example
Ten thousand units of a product are being produced and sold at a price of $10. The product costs $5 per unit (variable costs are $3, and fixed costs are

[12] The reader is referred to Taggart, *Cost Justification, op. cit.*, particularly Chapters 20 and 21.

$2 per unit and $20,000 in total). An order for 10,000 more units can be obtained if they are sold at a price of $8 per unit.

Should the order be taken, from the point of view of economic considerations (assuming that the order will not reduce the present sales)? Since the price per unit of $8 exceeds the variable cost per unit, the additional business is desirable from an economic point of view.

Should the order be taken from the point of view of legality under the Robinson–Patman Act? Can the $2 difference in price be explained by a "saving" of $2 in fixed costs? The answer is no. The defense would be rejected. If the company wants to accept the business, it will have to change its basic price to all customers to $8 per unit, or change the price for the order to $10 per unit, or find another defense. One possible defense would be to show that the fixed costs of $20,000 should reasonably be allocated to the other sales. For example, assume that the $20,000 is related to packaging equipment which will not be used with the new order, since shipment will be in bulk. In this case a price difference might be justified by real cost savings.

9.6 Summary

If X dollars are expended for direct labor, it is not difficult for the accountant to suggest that Y units of product should be forthcoming. The benefits of the expenditures are concrete and relatively easy to measure. If significantly less than Y units of product results, there is cause for suspecting some type of inefficiency.

With costs of the kind treated in this chapter the cause-and-effect relationship is not as easily measured. Two salesmen may be doing equally good work, but one has a better territory and so is making more sales. Or, the automobile traffic in one city may be heavier than in another, resulting in fewer calls per day for one salesman than another. In one year the advertising campaign may be considered a big success, but in the second year sales decrease and it is a complete failure. Are sales declining because of changes in the quality of advertising, changes in styling of the product, changes in prices, changes in actions of competitors, or because of a general business recession? Is a salesman efficient if he reduces his selling expense, or is he just making fewer telephone calls and traveling less?

There are too many variables connected with distribution and administration costs for the accountant to offer definitive advice in this area. He can report magnitudes of expense and sales and break these down in various ways, but it is generally rash to draw conclusions and recommend decisions about performance on this information. It would be better for the accountant to obtain the assistance of a statistician and by the use of experimental and statistical techniques attempt to determine the impact of the several types of costs on sales and profits. For example, by varying the advertising expenditures in one market area while not changing the expenditures in other areas, management may obtain some insight into the effectiveness of the advertising. It would seem desirable for the accountant to supplement his skills in this field. Service department costs may be allocated for product-costing purposes, but allocation is seldom useful for cost-control purposes. Concepts of standard costs are used as with other types of costs. The allocation of service department cost to operating departments is typically accomplished using the direct method, although the stepwise method is common as well.

The accountant should be alert to the relationship of nonmanufacturing costs to activity variables and to other variables that can be manipulated by the firm. An example involving the relationship of total cost to the absentee rate is discussed in Section 9.2. The accountant is in an excellent position to observe cost behavior and analyze alternatives for cost reduction. Further, the accountant should be familiar with the cost requirements of formal models that have been subject to increasing use in decision making involving nonmanufacturing activities. In particular, he should be cognizant of the importance and subsequent difficulties associated with measuring the relevant indirect costs required by these models.

In some cases cost control may be achieved by the same methods that are used in the area of production costs. Generally, however, output measures and standards are not easily established. Therefore, control tends to be exercised more through comparing budgeted and actual costs. Management must also be particularly alert to the necessity of designing the elements of these indirect-control systems so that they motivate employees toward achieving the goals of the firm.

APPENDIX 9A
MATRIX FORMULATION FOR COST ALLOCATIONS

Let $a_{ii}X_i$ be the total overhead cost of ith department, a_{ij} be the percentage of the j department cost allocated to the ith department, and B_i be the actual cost incurred directly in the ith department. Then

$$a_{11}X_1 = B_1 + 0 + a_{12}X_2 + a_{13}X_3 + \cdots + a_{1n-1}X_{n-1} + a_{1n}X_n$$

$$a_{22}X_2 = B_2 + a_{21}X_1 + 0 + a_{23}X_3 + \cdots + a_{2n-1}X_{n-1} + a_{2n}X_n$$

$$\vdots \qquad\qquad\qquad\qquad\qquad\qquad\qquad\qquad\qquad \vdots$$

$$a_{nn}X_n = B_n + a_{n1}X_1 + a_{n2}X_2 + a_{n3}X_3 + \cdots + a_{n,n}X_{n-1} + 0$$

Isolating the B_i on the right-hand side and then utilizing matrix notation we have

$$AX = B$$

where

$A = n \times n$ matrix consisting of the a_{ij} coefficients

$X = n \times 1$ column vector whose components are the total cost of each department

$B = n \times 1$ column vector consisting of the costs directly incurred in the departments

Solving for the X vector (the total allocated costs of the departments) by premultiplying by A^{-1} (the inverse), we have:

$$X = A^{-1}B.$$

QUESTIONS AND PROBLEMS

9–1 It has been said that the primary function of the accountant relative to distribution costs is to record the costs so that the information is available for analysis. Comment on this proposition.

9–2 Why is distribution-cost analysis more difficult than manufacturing-cost analysis?

9–3 Is it possible for fixed-distribution costs to be avoidable?

9–4 How would you allocate billing department costs to different product lines?

9–5 How would you allocate shipping department costs to different product lines?

9–6 Are advertising expenditures properly considered expenses in the period in which the advertising is distributed?

9–7 Would it ever be reasonable to consider costs associated with selling to be an asset at the end of a period rather than an expense?

9–8 As a business manager, would you want an income statement for a product line which included allocations of joint distribution and manufacturing costs not controllable by the manager in charge of the product line?

9–9 Stenographic pools that handle all dictation and typing required by executives are common. On the one hand, money can be saved by cutting down on the total number of typists and/or stenographers required. On the other hand, a pool eliminates private secretaries, and executives generally dislike pools in part for convenience reasons and in part because private secretaries are often considered status symbols. How would you analyze the problem of whether or not to have a stenographic pool? Assume that the pool does not presently exist.

    a. How would you estimate the costs and savings?

    b. What other factors should be considered?

9–10 The Elson Company is considering a suggestion to allocate national magazine advertising costs to sales territories on the basis of circulation of the media weighted by an index of relative buying potential in each territory. Is this a good method for decision making involving:

    a. Whether to discontinue an unprofitable territory?

    b. Measuring the performance of a district sales manager?

    c. Controlling advertising costs?

9–11 A firm is considering the purchase of a special type of duplicating machine. Two of the costs that must be estimated are service and operating costs (other than material used in duplication). Service is supplied at a fixed monthly fee but operating costs are not. How would you estimate the total of these costs?

9–12 The Automated Tank Company reports the following results for operations in the past two years:

	19X0	19X1
Sales revenues	$3,000,000	$3,300,000
Cost of sales	1,500,000	2,250 000
Gross margins	$1,500,000	$1,050,000
Operating expenses	900,000	300,000
Net profit	$ 600,000	$ 750,000

During 19X1, $675,000 of depreciation expense on manufacturing equipment was transferred from operating expense to cost of sales since management felt that the decrease in the value of manufacturing equipment should be considered a cost of the manufactured product. There has been no essential change in either the manner in which operations are conducted or in prices.

The Company is considering two alternatives:

1. An intensive sales campaign expected to increase sales by $750,000. This effort will necessitate nine additional salesmen at a salary of $12,000 each.
2. Opening a new branch which is expected to increase sales by $675,000. The operating costs for the new branch include rent, $4,500; office employees, $30,000; branch manager (who is presently employed at the home office and whose present duties would be allocated to other present employees), $25,000, and other expenses, $10,000. All figures are yearly.

Required: Which alternative do you favor and why? Assume that the figures are accurate as given.

9–13 How should service department costs be treated from a cost-control and decision-making viewpoint?

9–14 The Winter Company is considering offering one of its customers a quantity discount, but the president of the firm is concerned about the possibility of the government bringing action under the Robinson–Patman Act. The usual method of shipment for the Winter Company is to pack its product individually in boxes and ship by truck. If a customer would be willing to buy in larger quantities (such as 1,000 units), larger containers could be used. In fact, it would be possible to ship the product loose in a railroad freight car. The estimated packing saving would be $0.20 per unit.

Required: Would the cost savings described be acceptable grounds for having price differentials for customers who ordered in 1,000-unit lots?

9–15 The Fall River Paper Company sells to two different customers. One customer is charged a price of $2 per unit and the other customer is charged a price of $3 per unit. In defense of its pricing policy, the following schedule was prepared by the company.

| | Unit Revenue and Cost Schedules for Selling to: | |
	Company A	Company B
Net margin*	$1.00 100%	$2.00 100%
Distribution costs (allocations based on net margin	0.60 60%	1.20 60%
Net income	$0.40 40%	$0.80 40%

* Net margin is after deducting the cost of product sold, $1.

Since the profit per dollar of net margin was the same for sales to both companies, the Fall River Paper Company argued that it was reasonable to charge Company A a price of $1.00 and Company B a price of $2.00.

Required: Comment on whether the price differentials are justified. What additional information would you want to know?

9–16 Since the cost defense against a charge of illegal price discrimination provided by Section 2(a) of the Clayton Act as amended by the Robinson–Patman Act has proved largely illusory in practice, the prudent company would be well advised to charge the same price on commodities of similar grade and quality. Do you agree with this statement? Is so, why? If not, why not?

9–17 The Re-allocation Corporation has two operating departments and two service departments.

The Building Department should be allocated as follows:

10% to Utility Department
45% to Operating Department 1
45% to Operating Department 2

The Utility Department should be allocated as follows:

50% to Building Department
40% to Operating Department 1
10% to Operating Department 2

The costs incurred in the Building Department were $90,000; in the Utility Department, $10,000.

Required:

a. Compute the allocation of the service departments and prepare journal entries to accomplish the allocation to the operating departments. Use the "mathematical" solution.
b. Discuss the usefulness of the allocation from the point of view of controlling costs and determining unit costs of product.

9–18 Consider education as a product. What are the direct costs to a university of facilitating the education of a student?

9–19 Comment as required:

a. A single base for reapportionment of one service department's costs is not theoretically justifiable.

   Do you agree? If not, why not? If so, then why is a single basis the common method for reallocation of such costs?
b. What differences exist between the allocation of service department costs for setting predetermined overhead rates and the actual end-of-period allocation of such costs?

9–20 The Havid Crimson Corporation is an organization that mass-produces certain standardized-quality products that are consumed by large businesses. Each of its two main products is produced in a separate department. Product "Embiary" is manufactured in the Beeskule Department, which employs 60 laborers, and product "Jaydee" is manufactured in the Ellskule Department, which employs 65 laborers.

A recent financial squeeze has caused management to desire to know the "full cost" of its products. This information will then be used in an attempt to justify proposed higher prices. Therefore, they want to have the costs of their service departments allocated to the operating departments.

The manager of Buildings and Grounds reported that in the last period 25,000 man-hours were spent taking care of the Beeskule Department and 20,000 man-hours were used by the Ellskule. The employee cafeteria require 5,000 man-hours for maintenance. The total actual expenses of Buildings and Ground was $150,000 during that period and this division employed 25 people.

It was reported by the Utilities manager that his division, which employed 10, had total expenses of $120,000 during that period. It was further reported that Buildings and Grounds had consumed 30,000 kilowatt-hours of power; the cafeteria had used 10,000 kilowatt-hours; the Beeskule used 40,000 kilowatt-hours; and the Ellskule used 40,000 kilowatt-hours.

The manager of the cafeteria reported that his total expenses for this period were $80,000.

Required: Given that the manufacturing expenses for the Beeskule and the Ellskule were $230,000 and $310,000, respectively, compute the total costs allocating those of the service departments in the step-wise manner. Allocate first by number of departments serviced and second using department cost.

9–21 Given the service relationships in the following table, allocate costs to the producing departments using the following methods (parts *f** through h* are optional):

From: \ To:	O.D.A.	O.D.B.	S.D.1	S.D.2	S.D.3
Operating Dept. A	100%	—	—	—	—
Operating Dept. B	—	100%	—	—	—
Service Dept. 1	30%	30%	—	10%	30%
Service Dept. 2	20%	40%	20%	—	20%
Service Dept. 3	50%	20%	20%	10%	—
Total Period Costs	$40,000	$35,000	$10,000	$4,500	$9,500

    a. Without regard for one service department's service to another.

    b. Allocating the service department costs to all departments in order of the department which yields the greatest percentage service to operating departments.

    c. Allocating the service department costs to all departments in order of the number of other departments serviced.

    d. Allocate the service department costs to all departments in order of the service department with the most cost to be allocated.

    e. Repeat d using least cost to establish the allocation order.

    f*. Allocate service department costs using a simultaneous equation approach which considers implicitly the reallocation of service department costs. This is done by solving the allocation among service departments first.

    g*. Allocate the service department costs in order of which service department has the greatest absolute difference between what is owed to it by other service departments less what it owes other service departments.

    h*. Repeat g using the inverse order to allocate the costs of service departments

    i. Which solution do you believe best and why?

* Optional.

SUPPLEMENTARY READING

Antitrust Laws, Report of the Attorney General's Committee, 1955, Washington, D.C.: Government Printing Office, particularly pp. 155–186 and pp. 170–176.

CHARLES, A., W. W. COOPER, J. K. DEVOE, D. B. LEARNER, and W. REINECKE, "A Goal Programming Model for Media Planning," *Management Science*, April 1968, pp. 423–430.

EDWARDS, C. D., "20 Years of the Robinson–Patman Act," *The Journal of Business*, July 1956, pp. 149–159.

JONES, R. L., and H. J. TRENTIN, "Budgeting General and Administrative Expenses: A Planning and Control System," *Management Bulletin 74*, New York: American Management Association, 1966.

KING, W. R., "Performance Evaluation in Marketing Systems," *Management Science* July 1964, pp. 659–666.

TAGGART, H., *Cost Justification*, Bureau of Business Research, Ann Arbor: University of Michigan, particularly Chaps. 20 and 21 and App. A.

Chapter 10

Learning Curves and Cost Behavior

Conventional economic theory assumes that both the average-variable cost and the marginal cost per unit of product are concave-upward functions. Furthermore, the marginal-cost curve intersects the average-variable cost curve at its minimum. These classic relationships are illustrated in Figure 10.1.

The shape of the marginal-cost curve reflects initially increasing efficiency with increasing output followed by increasing marginal costs resulting from inefficiencies. Constant efficiency, a condition often assumed in accounting analyses, would be reflected by a horizontal marginal-cost curve.

The analysis as traditionally made mixes together two factors that should be considered separately. These include the time rate of production and the total number of units produced.[1] The marginal cost per unit might, on an a priori basis, be expected to increase as the time rate of production increases or, perhaps, to exhibit a cost-behavior pattern similar to that in Figure 10.1 with the horizontal axis relabeled in terms of the units produced per unit of time.

In many situations, such as the production of a new product, however, the learning phenomenon tends to reduce the marginal cost as the cumulative output increases. If the rate of production is increased so that the incremental unit cost is increasing (decreasing efficiency) but learning is also taking place simultaneously, it is

[1] See J. Hirshleifer, "The Firm's Cost Function: A Successful Reconstruction?", *The Journal of Business*, July 1962, pp. 235–255, and A. Alchian, "Costs and Outputs," in M. Abramovitz, *The Allocation of Economic Resources: Essays in Honor of B. F. Haley*, Stanford, Calif.: Stanford University Press, 1959.

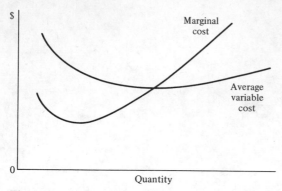

Figure 10.1 Average-variable and marginal-cost curves: traditional economic analysis.

difficult to predict the shape of the marginal-cost curve.[2] This in turn has implications for decision making and for accounting.

That average labor time per unit of output declines, at least in the early stages of a new process, has been generally known for many years.[3] The observation that the rate of improvement exhibited regularities for similar activities even across firms and repeated itself for new but similar projects was an important factor in making the effects of the learning phenomenon predictable.

10.1 Learning-Curve Model

Industrial analyses indicate that the nature of the learning phenomenon can be described as a constant percentage reduction in the *average* direct labor input time required per unit as the cumulative output doubles. For example, assume a cost reduction rate of 20% and the first unit takes 125 hours. Then the average for 2 units should be 100 hours, 0.8(125), a total of 200 hours for both. The second unit takes 75 hours to produce. Four units would take an average of 80 hours each, 0.8(100), or a total of 320 hours. This means that 120 hours, 320 − 200, must be expended in total to produce the third and fourth units. One minus the percentage reduction due to learning is known as the learning rate. The learning rate in the present example is 1 − 0.2 = 0.8, or 80%.

Mathematically, the learning curve effect can be expressed in exponential equation form as

$$Y = aX^b \qquad (10.1)$$

[2] If a steady state has been reached or the learning effect is exhausted, the more conventional analysis depicted in Figure 10.1 applies.

[3] Initial applications were made in the airframe industry on the basis of regularities observed as early as 1925. See M. A. Requero, *An Economic Study of the Airframe Industry*, Wright-Patterson Air Force Base, Ohio: Department of the Air Force, October 1957, p. 213, and T. P. Wright, "Factors Affecting the Cost of Airplanes," *Journal of Aeronautical Science*, February 1936, pp. 122–128.

where

Y = *average* number of labor hours required for X units
a = number of labor hours required for the first unit
X = cumulative number of units produced
b = *index* of learning equal to the log of the learning rate divided by the
 log of 2 (for the present example, $b = -0.322$)[4]

Since Y is the average number of labor hours required for X units, the total number of hours required for X units is given by

$$YX = aX^{b+1} \tag{10.2}$$

The learning effect can be graphed. The average number of labor hours required for X units as expressed by equation (10.1) is graphed on arithmetic scales in Figure 10.2 and on log scales in Figure 10.3. Equation (10.1) is linear on the log chart, since

$$\log Y = \log a + b \log X \tag{10.3}$$

is a linear equation.[5]

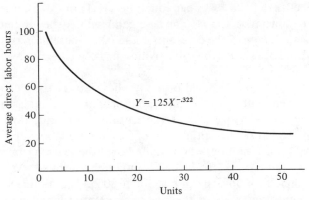

Figure 10.2 Average labor hours required for X units.

An appealing alternative but equivalent mathematical description of the learning-curve model given by equation (10.1) is obtained by altering the form of the formula to incorporate the learning rate explicitly. The result for the present example is

$$Y = a(0.8)^{\log_2 X} \tag{10.4}$$

[4] This can be shown as follows. If the first unit takes a hours, then the average for 2 units is $0.8a$ hours according to the model. Since $X = 2$, equation (10.1) gives $0.8a = a(2)^b$. Taking logs (all to the base 10) $\log 0.8a = \log a + b \log 2$. Simplifying $b = \log 0.8/\log 2$.

[5] See J. E. Howell and D. Teichroew, *Mathematical Analysis for Business Decisions*, Homewood, Ill.: Richard D. Irwin, Inc., 1963, pp. 159–163 for a formulation solving for marginal cost rather than average.

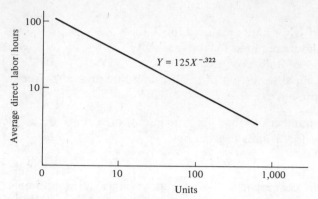

Figure 10.3   **Average labor hours required for X units.**

where the symbols retain their same definitions.[6] The problem with the model in this form is that it is necessary to recompute the exponent at each step.

10.1.1 Determining the Parameters of the Model

In order to use the model as defined by either equations (10.1) or (10.5), it is necessary to estimate the parameters a and b.[7] The data gathered may be plotted on log-log paper and estimates made of the constants a and b.[8] It is useful in this stage to collect data on subactivities since the subactivities may often be involved in future production.

The manager is well advised to be skeptical of the applicability of the slope coefficient obtained from the data. Significant variations are common in empirical studies.[9] Previous work suggests that the learning rate and, thus, also the slope, are directly related to the initial ratio of machine to labor input hours. Where this ratio is 3 machine hours to 1 labor hour, the learning rate tends to be near 90%. When the ratio is 1 to 1, the learning rate is around 85%, and when it is 1 to 3, machine to labor, the rate is about 80%. The decline in these figures is intuitively appealing, since as the relative amount of labor in an activity increases, the opportunities for learning increase.

---

[6] Mathematically, using equation (10.3) and the fact that
$$b = \log 0.8/\log 2$$
$$\log Y = \log a + (\log X)(\log 0.8) \log 2$$
$$= \log a + \log 0.8 \exp (\log X/\log 2)$$
$$= \log a + \log 0.8 \exp (\log X \log_2 10)$$
$$= \log a + \log 0.8 \exp (\log_2 X)$$

[7] This can be solved algebraically or graphically.

[8] The value of a is the intercept on the vertical axis, the value of Y (or Y') when X is zero. The value of b is the slope of the line; the ratio of the change in the log of the average time to the change in the log of the output.

[9] See N. Baloff, "The Learning Curve—Some Controversial Issues," *Journal of Industrial Economics*, July 1966, pp. 275–282.

As an example, consider a company that acts as a subcontractor for parts used in the space program. Assume that the company has been requested to bid on a contract for 750 units required in the assembly of the reentry mechanism of a new space capsule. Thus, the firm is interested in the expected cost of the contract. The company had recently produced 250 of the items at the following costs as indicated by the accounting records.

Direct materials	$10,000
Direct labor (5,000 hours @ $5)	25,000
Tooling (can be reused)	3,000
Variable overhead	5,000
Fixed overhead (billed on the basis of one fourth of direct-labor cost)	6,250
Total cost	$49,250

The company has retained a partial record of the total time required to produce the 250 units. The data are first unit, 120 hours; 15 units, 735 hours; 100 units, 2,724 hours; 250 units, 5,000 hours.

The learning effect applies only to the direct-labor time and perhaps to the variable-overhead time if it is a direct function of the direct-labor time. Plotting the labor-time data on a log-log scale after converting it to averages suggests a straight line with an intercept of approximately 120 hours. Since the relationship appears to be linear using averages, the model of learning suggested by equations (10.1) or (10.3) can be used with b established by solving equation (10.1) for $Y = 20$ when $X = 250$ and $a = 120$. (A least-squares technique could also be used.) This gives:

$$Y = aX^b$$
$$20 = 120(250)^b$$

Hence

$$\frac{\log 20 - \log 120}{\log 250} = b$$

or

$$b = -0.325$$

Assume, from this analysis and what the manager knows about the labor intensity of the process, that he concludes that an 80% learning rate is appropriate. (Recall that the b value for an 80% learning rate is -0.322.) With these data he may use equation (10.2) to estimate the total direct-labor hours required for the additional 750 units, or he may reason as follows. Given an 80% learning rate for the time required for the average unit, a doubling of the quantity produced results in a 20% reduction in the average time per unit. Given an average time of 5,000/250 = 20 hours for 250 units, the average time for 500 units is 0.8(20) = 16 hours and the average time for 1,000 units is 0.8(16), or 12.8 hours. The total time required for the 750-unit contract would be 1,000(12.8) or 12,800 hours, less the 5,000 hours put in on the initial 250 units, a requirement of 7,800 additional hours. Assuming the hourly wage rate remains constant, variable overhead remains at 20% of direct labor, and other costs change proportionally, the marginal costs of the new contract would be

Direct materials	$30,000
Direct labor (7,800 hours @ $5)	39,000
Tooling	0
Variable overhead	7,800
Total marginal cost	$76,800

The firm may still choose to incorporate a fixed-overhead element, but the anticipated incremental costs of the 150-unit order are $76,800. This is less than twice the accounting cost of the initial 250 units, although the new contract is three times as large.

10.1.2 Use of Learning Curves in Decision Making

An additional example of the use of learning curves in estimating costs for decision making is useful at this point.[10] An aircraft company was faced with a cutback in orders resulting from a stretch-out procurement program by the Air Force. Its reaction was to consider canceling various subcontracts and doing this work in its own plant.

One such subcontract involved 372 landing-flap assemblies. However, before canceling the subcontract, the aircraft company wished to consider the costs of the two alternatives.

The aircraft company had already produced 165 similar assemblies, the last of which took 445 hours. This put the company well along its learning curve. Extrapolating the curve indicated a total labor input of 111,000 hours for the 372 additional units. In contrast, the subcontractor, while apparently a more efficient producer of this item in the long run, was just getting started on its learning curve. Extrapolating its curve indicated that the subcontractor would be able to produce its one hundred sixty-fifth assembly with only 402 hours, 43 hours less than the aircraft company had needed. Nevertheless, since at the decision time its curve was much higher the total hours required to produce 372 assemblies by the subcontractor was predicted to be 164,000 hours, or 53,000 more than required by the aircraft company.

The short-run, lower-cost choice was to cancel the subcontract and to do the

---

[10] The example is adapted from one in an article by F. J. Andress, "The Learning Curve as a Production Tool," *The Harvard Business Review*, January–February 1954, pp. 87–97.

work internally. In the long run, assuming that future cost characteristics are known with certainty and there is enough additional work of an identical nature, it would have been cheaper to continue the contract since the subcontractor could do the job with less labor after getting out as far as the aircraft company on its learning curve. The decision hinged on the expected future demand for this type of landing-flap assembly. (Note that a change in assembly type probably moves both firms back on their learning curves.) In the case described, the future demand was uncertain and difficult to predict. Hence, the aircraft company elected to cancel the subcontract and take advantage of the present savings, which amounted to over $300,000.

10.1.3 Difficulties in Obtaining the Data

Perhaps the most serious limitation to using learning curves is in obtaining valid data on which to base their computation. For example, suppose that a firm decreases the planned labor input into a product by increasing the use of purchased parts. The result may be a decline in the actual labor used per unit, but it would not be due to learning. There is a shift of the required labor input to the supplier. Indeed, the effect of ignoring such facts may simultaneously give an apparently declining learning curve coupled with increasing unit cost. A given learning curve relates to one manufacturing process, and if the process is changed the learning curve may no longer apply.

The learning-curve phenomenon measures only direct labor. Thus, if more time is spent in, say, designing the product or process, there may again be an apparent increase in learning as reflected by the curve without a decline in total cost. The direct labor is merely shifted to indirect labor or overhead. A similar effect occurs if supervisory labor or new equipment replaces direct labor.

Declines in the labor input can also occur when there are changes in the materials used. Better materials can reduce labor input without necessarily lowering cost. A similar result can be obtained if there is a change in the labor mix. Better but more expensive labor can cause an artificial learning effect. These factors can work in the opposite direction as well. For example, a tight labor market may lead to poorer labor quality. Both the effect of new and poorer labor diminishes the learning effect, yet costs may decline if the wages are sufficiently low. Changes in labor mix, overhead, and the associated factors of production, then, can considerably confound the learning-curve effect.

10.2   Learning-Curve Applications

The applicability of learning curves is, as has been previously indicated, more important in cases where the labor input in an activity is large and the activity is complex. Since the curve is steepest at its start and since new projects cause recycling, the learning effect is also more pronounced where the rate of product or process innovation is high. Finally, if learning is expected and planned for, greater use of this phenomenon can be made. Indeed, if learning is encouraged and expected, a climate may be created where it can and will occur. An interesting example was supplied by Conway and Schultz, who showed that when a new group of workers were put on a task already far down its learning curve, the fresh approach brought by the new group produced a new learning cycle.[11]

Andress suggests that conditions conducive to learning are ideal in the electronics, home appliance, construction, shipbuilding, and machine shop areas.[12] On the other hand, he suggests that industries which are capital-intensive such as petroleum refining, "would find the learning curve of little value."[13] Hirschmann finds, however, that a significant learning effect also exists, although to a lesser degree, in heavily capital intensive industries.[14] He attributes this to the removal of bottlenecks, relaxing preset safety margins, and technological resourcefulness generally.

Next we will suggest several areas where the effects of learning curves would be useful to decision making.

10.2.1 Pricing

Since learning curves permit better cost predictions, it seems that they should be employed in pricing decisions. In some cases involving government contracts, consideration of learning-curve effects is required. The question is not whether learning curves will be used but what the appropriate parameters are.

An extension of the pricing use of learning-curve data is in buying from a supplier. Sometimes a supplier will experience high initial outlays resulting in part from the fact that the supplier is at the early stages of its learning curve relative to the job. A purchasing firm might be willing initially to pay a higher price if the supplier agrees to and subsequently lowers the price per unit.[15]

10.2.2 Work Scheduling

Learning curves increase a firm's ability to predict their required labor input and make it possible to forecast labor needs. They also allow the development of production and delivery schedules with greater accuracy. These, in turn, permit the firm to do a better job of scheduling maintenance and overhead activity, quality control, material purchasing, and promotion. Better forecasting and scheduling result in lower costs through better cost control and improved customer relations.

[11] R. W. Conway and A. Schultz, "The Manufacturing Process Function," *Journal of Industrial Engineering*, January–February 1959, p.48.

[12] Andress, *op. cit.*, pp. 95–97.

[13] *Ibid.*, p. 96.

[14] W. B. Hirschmann, "Profit from the Learning Curve," *The Harvard Business Review*, January–February 1964, pp. 125–139.

[15] See Andress, *op. cit.*, pp. 94–95, for an example.

10.2.3 Capital Budgeting

One of the more important aspects in capital-budgeting problems is the amount of cash flows. The learning effect suggests that unit costs are likely to begin high and taper off. This is in contrast to the steady-state, constant unit cost usually assumed in capital-budgeting analysis. Furthermore, the learning curve permits improved estimates of production levels that can be attained and thus has implications for cash flows. These modifications can be particularly important where the project start-up period is large relative to the life of the project.

10.2.4 Motivation

Costs are often controlled using standards and variances from standards. If these standards are set without regard to the learning phenomenon, meaningless initial and unfavorable variances may occur, with resulting motivational impact. Performance reports that show large unfavorable variances, about which the manager can do nothing and which he may even expect, can lead to a deleterious effect on his aspiration level and thereby on performance. Sometimes this is resolved by admitting the learning effect through arbitrary adjustments or allowances or by making no evaluations until the process "settles down." It would be an improvement to recognize the learning effect in the standard where possible.[16]

The same problems arises when the investigation of an out-of-control process leads to corrective action. The time over which the corrective action takes effect often covers several cost-reporting periods. During this period, costs may even rise for a while before the learning effect takes hold. Simultaneously, management will be keeping close tabs on the reaction of costs to new procedures. Hence it is necessary for management to be cognizant of the influence of learning during this period and to use standards that consider it, if standards are to be used.

A similar effect is apparent in evaluating divisional performance. Large activities in early phases of activity will experience relatively higher costs and lower output than at later stages. This should be considered when a division manager's performance is evaluated.

10.2.5 Overtime Decisions

Hiring more workers is not likely to be an easily reversible decision. Once locked into the cost structure, this cost may be difficult to change in the short run. Hence, if an organization is near the beginning of its learning curve, it may prefer to work overtime rather than hire additional workers who will not be needed later.

---

[16] Even such decisions as establishing piecework incentive rates should be made considering the learning effect.

10.2.6 External Reporting

Learning influences profits through its effects on cost and output. When these effects are important, some attention should be given to them on the firm's annual report. For example, *The Wall Street Journal* in early 1967, reporting on the consolidation of all subsidiaries by the Phillips Petroleum Company in which it held over a 50% interest, stated that "the effect of this [consolidation] will be to reduce earnings from what they would be without such consolidation, because most of the companies being consolidated are ones that are under construction or in the start-up stage, and which therefore are expected to show losses this year." [17]

Assume a situation in which these early losses were expected when the decision to undertake the construction was made. If financial reports are to be an aid in evaluation and are to be consistent with decision making, some attempt should be made to separate nonrecoverable losses from costs that are incurred as part of the learning process. Where there is good reason to believe that learning will take place, an argument can be made for capitalizing some or all of a firm's early losses as assets rather than mislead investors into believing that the financial situation is unfavorable. Admittedly, this procedure could be misused by managers wanting to defer losses that are likely to be nonrecoverable. It would have to be applied with care.

10.3 Summary

The concepts of learning curves have many applications. They should be used in cost control, labor planning, and even financial reporting. The true nature of the learning curve associated with a new product or process will never be known a priori. However, a reasonable assumption of its shape is better than the implicit assumption of no learning at all.

QUESTIONS AND PROBLEMS

10–1 Modify the following statement so that it is more accurate: "Marginal costs will tend to increase as more units are produced."

10–2 What conditions may cause the average variable cost to decline as:
  a. Output per unit of time increases?
  b. Cumulative output increases?

10–3 Accept as a premise that the average labor hours required per unit is reduced 20% as the quantity produced doubles. Is it correct to say that "This implies a situation where the second unit requires about 80% as much direct labor as the first; the tenth 80% as much as the fifth, and so on?"

---

[17] Reported in N. Baloff and J. N. Kennelly, "Accounting Implications of Product and Process Start-ups," *Journal of Accounting Research*, Autumn 1967, p. 142.

10–4 If an 80% learning model is assumed to apply and labor costs $5 per hour, how much should it cost in direct labor to produce 100 units if the first unit takes 80 hours?

10–5 In plotting learning-curve data, why is log-log paper particularly useful?

10–6 "Learning curves are relatively easy to estimate; however, their influence tends to be of very marginal value." Evaluate this statement.

10–7 Suggest 5 decisions for which the learning effect may be important.

10–8 The Sharp Company subcontracts some aircraft parts to the Doit Company because of the greater familiarity of the latter with the task. The manager of Sharp notes that Doit has an 85% learning curve, whereas Sharp has an 80% curve. However, Doit is far down the curve. Sharp would start at the top of its own curve if it made the part and hence would incur large initial costs. But since it would not need to pay freight or profit to Doit, the manager believes that Sharp, at least from a learning-curve viewpoint, should not subcontract. Do you agree? Why?

10–9 The Boxer Company makes parts for ship navigation systems. It has previously made about 10,000 parts exactly like the type ordered by the government for a new type of submarine. A new government order calls for 10,000 parts. The company's records yield the following cost data for the 10,000 parts made to date:

Direct materials	$ 1,000,000
Direct labor (800,000 hours at $8/hr)	6,400,000
Setup costs (no labor)	60,000
Variable overhead ($4.00/DLH)	3,200,000
Fixed overhead (allocated at $1.00/DLH)	800,000
Total costs	$11,460,000

Assuming an 80% learning rate on the average time required as production doubles and no change in unit-of-labor costs per hour, estimate the company's additional costs from accepting the order.

10–10 What is the most significant feature about the learning curve that makes it useful?

10–11 Assume a learning rate of 80%; that is, the average number of labor hours required per unit is reduced 20% as the quantity produced doubles.
Required:
a. If the first 100 units require 100 hours, how many total hours will be required to produce 200 units? How many additional hours are required for the second 100 units?
b. Suppose the firm has an opportunity to bid on a contract that will raise its total output from 200 to 500 units. How many labor hours will be involved?

10–12 Discuss how learning-curve techniques may be used in setting standards for control.

10–13 What costs might one expect to be associated with a particular learning curve?

10–14 Does an 80% learning curve denote a higher rate of improvement than a 70% curve? Explain. Which curve has the more negative slope? (Assume that the first unit would be produced in the same amount of labor using either curve.)

10–15 Draw a graph of an 80% learning curve that reaches a steady-state (i.e., no more learning takes place) after 32 units have been produced. (Assume that the first unit requires 100 direct labor hours.) Use arithmetic scales.

10–16 Using the following costs:

Direct labor	5.00 per hour
Other variable manufacturing costs	4.00 per direct labor hour

and assuming an 80% learning curve is applicable, compute the labor and labor-related costs associated with (assume the first unit produced required 100 labor hours):

    a. the production of three additional units after the first unit has been completed;

    b. the production of eight units after the eighth unit has been completed.

10–17 Easy Run Motors, Inc., produces electric motors, which it sells to manufacturers of household appliances. The company is currently producing 150 units of a model that a single firm is purchasing for $35 per unit. Variable production costs associated with the 150 units are expected to total $3,000. The firm that is purchasing the 150 units has expressed an interest in contracting for an additional 450 units if the selling price per unit is reduced to $22 per motor. Assuming that all variable production costs fluctuate with labor hours and that a 90% learning curve is applicable, should Easy Run lower the price? (Assume that all other variable costs and expenses associated with the product would total $5 per unit.) Learning applies to the average time per unit.

10–18 Manual Machine Company has received an invitation to submit a bid for the production of 800 private-label vacuum cleaners. The company knows that the competition for this contract will be keen and it would like to find the minimum price it could charge for the 800 units. The planning department of the company has estimated the costs of producing the first 100 units as follows:

Direct labor 400 hours @ $5.00	$2,000
Direct materials 100 units @ $20 per unit*	2,000
Other variable manufacturing costs @ $4.00 per direct labor hour†	1,600
Nonvariable manufacturing costs	4,000
Set-up costs	5,000

    * Each additional 100 units of direct material can be purchased at a 10% discount from the previous 100 until the minimum cost per unit reaches $14.58.

    † Varies with direct labor.

The nonvariable manufacturing costs and the set-up costs are not expected to change as the units produced are increased from 100 to 800, and selling and administrative expenses associated with the product are negligible. Assuming that a 90% learning curve is applicable to average direct labor per unit, what is the lowest price per unit Manual Machine could offer?

10–19 Estimate the total cost (outlay) to produce an order for 250 parts given the following information on 750 identical parts which have just been finished.

Total Cost 750 Units	
Material cost* @ $100 per unit (average)	$ 75,000
Direct labor (53,250 hours @ $4)	213,000
Variable O.H.† @ 2 per D.L.H.	120,000
Set-up costs (required for every 250 units)‡	75,000
Tooling costs (required for every 500 units)‡	46,000
Fixed O.H. (allocated)	173,000
Total	$702,000
Total time for the first 125 units	15,630 hrs.
Total time for the first 250 units	24,985 hrs.
Total time for the first 500 units	40,082 hrs.

* It is estimated that material costs will decline by ten per cent on a unit basis for future units made.

† Based on, and variable with, direct labor hours.

‡ No labor involved. Same level expected.

NOTE: *Indicate the learning rate you used and show how you obtained it.* You may assume some noise in the data and hence use a "rounded" rate.

10–20 Suppose that prior to the production of a certain item an 80% learning curve is believed to apply to the average labor hours involved in the process with the first unit to be produced estimated at 100 direct labor hours. Indicate how the following events would tend to alter the estimate of the learning curve. Specifically, would the following events result in (a) a shift in the estimated learning curve with no change in the shape of the curve; (b) a change in the shape of the estimated learning curve; or (c) no change? (Treat each event independently of all previous events.)

    a. The estimated number of direct labor hours required for the first unit is revised from 100 to 150.

    b. The estimated learning rate is changed from 80% to 90%.

    c. The depreciation that will be applied to the manufacturing equipment used in the process during the production period is increased by 10%.

    d. The estimate of the hourly wage for direct laborers is increased from $5.00 to $5.25.

e. A new machine is purchased which will replace 10 direct laborers. This new machine was not considered in estimating the 80% learning curve.

SUPPLEMENTARY READING

ANDRESS, F. J., "The Learning Curve as a Production Tool," *The Harvard Business Review*, January–February 1954, pp. 87–97.

BALOFF, N., "The Learning Curve—Some Controversial Issues," *Journal of Industrial Economics*, July 1966, pp. 275–282.

CONWAY, R. W., and A. SCHULTZ, "The Manufacturing Progress Function," *Journal of Industrial Engineering*, 1959, pp. 39–53.

HIRSCHMANN, W. B., "Profit from the Learning Curve," *The Harvard Business Review*, January–February 1964, pp. 125–139.

JORDAN, R. B., "Learning How to Use the Learning Curve," *N.A.A. Bulletin*, January 1958, pp. 27–40.

LUNDGREN, E. F., and J. V. SCHNEIDER, "A Managerial Cost Model for the Hiring Overtime Decision," *Management Science*, February 1971, pp. 399–405.

TAYLOR, M. L., "The Learning Curve—A Basic Cost Projection Tool," *N.A.A. Bulletin*, February 1961, pp. 21–26.

TEICHROEW, D., *An Introduction to Management Science*, New York, John Wiley & Sons, Inc., 1964, pp. 159–163.

WYER, R., "Learning Curve Techniques for Direct Labor Management," *N.A.A Bulletin, Conference Proceedings*, July 1958, pp. 19–27.

Chapter 11

Control of Spoilage

In the usual production process some product is likely to be rejected as not being usable or saleable. The control of this spoiled product is sometimes neglected and the cost of spoilage is buried in the cost per unit of acceptable product. Spoilage is also confused with scrap. There are important differences, and each should be controlled separately. Scrap results from the fact that the raw material being processed is not of the exact length, width, or thickness required for the product being made. Thus, there is some part of the raw material which is not usable in making the product. Spoilage results either when the raw material being processed or the finished item is discovered to be unusable because of defects in workmanship or material. Like scrap, the spoilage occurs after the raw material has entered the production process, but spoilage is not inherent in the design of the product or in the characteristics of the raw material. With sufficient care, spoilage could be avoided entirely or at least reduced to very small amounts. This reduction in spoilage will have a cost. Scrap may also be reduced and controlled, but there is likely to be a "skeleton" in a process where pieces are punched from a metal strip, or bar ends when bar stock is being cut into pieces. Spoilage occurs because of carelessness or the inevitable likelihood of errors or faulty material; the amount of spoiled product may be normal or abnormal in quantity, just as scrap may be normal or abnormal. Defining what is normal spoilage is a management responsibility. The figure should be reviewed periodically, since new techniques, better inputs, or improved controls may lead to a reduction in the normal level.

The procedure followed in accounting for spoilage depends on whether or not a standard cost accounting system is being used. The following discussion is divided into two parts: a description of spoilage (1) when a standard cost accounting system is being used, and (2) when an actual cost, process-cost accounting system is being used. Our concern here is in estimating the amount of spoilage and its present and potential cost to the organization. We are not interested here in the accounting entries regarding spoilage but in its control.

11.1   Standard Cost System—Spoilage

Cost accounting for spoilage using a standard cost accounting system is relatively simple, especially where normal spoilage is incorporated into the standards. Following this procedure the cost of normal spoilage is not reported separately. The unit standard cost of product includes the cost of normal spoilage and is not affected by the actual amount of spoilage. Assume, for example, that normal spoilage in a manufacturing process is 25% of the good product. Thus with the production of 80 units of good product, 20 units of spoiled product are expected. By adding 25% to each of the unit standard costs, a new standard can be obtained that incorporates the cost of normal spoilage:

	Standard Cost per Unit (without spoilage factor)	Standard Cost per Unit (with spoilage factor)
Direct material	$1.00	$1.25
Direct labor	0.50	0.625
Overhead (rate is $0.50 DLD)	0.25	0.3125
	$1.75	$2.1875

The total standard cost for 80 units of good product is $2.1875 times 80, or $175. It is also equal to 100 units times $1.75 (the standard cost, not considering normal spoilage, times the total units, including the normal spoilage). The $2.1875 is applied to only good products while the $1.75 cost is applied to both good product and normal spoilage.

At the end of each period it is necessary to compute the normal spoilage (25% of the good product) and determine whether the actual spoilage is higher or lower than normal. If the actual spoilage is different from the normal spoilage, the difference might be helpful in the analysis of labor efficiency. For example, a decline in spoilage to less than normal may result from workers being especially careful, which in turn may result in an unfavorable efficiency variance. The decrease in spoilage may or may not be desirable, depending upon the additional cost. Thus, the breakdown of spoilage into normal and abnormal spoilage should be an integral part of cost variance analysis. While the analysis and control of spoilage can be carried out using just the physical-unit measures, it is useful to have dollar measures to evaluate the importance of spoilage to the costs of the organization.

Example

Suppose that normal spoilage is 25% of the good product. Standard direct labor is $0.80 per unit (the standard includes a normal spoilage factor). In July 1,100 units were produced, of which 800 were good units and 300 were spoiled. The direct-labor costs were $700. In August 950 units were produced, of which 800 were good and 150 spoiled. The direct-labor costs were $900. The analysis of these facts is as follows.

Analysis of July Performance:

Actual spoilage	300 units	
Normal spoilage	200	
Spoilage: unfavorable	100	
Standard direct labor (800 × $0.80)		$640
Actual direct labor		700
Unfavorable labor variance		$ 60

Analysis of August Performance:

Actual spoilage	150 units	
Normal spoilage	200	
Spoilage: favorable	50	
Standard direct labor (800 × $0.80)		$640
Actual direct labor		900
Unfavorable labor variance		$260

The August analysis should also include a computation showing the saving in material and variable overhead resulting because the spoilage was less than expected for the period.

On the basis of both logic and theory, normal spoilage is rightly considered to be a cost of product, using either a standard cost or an actual cost system. This is so even though the exclusion of normal spoilage from the standard costs may be recommended on the basis of practicality and ease of handling.

11.1.1 Standard Cost—Credit for Spoiled Work

The standard cost of production of the time period is equal to the standard cost per unit (with a spoilage factor) multiplied by the units of good product obtained, or it can be obtained by multiplying the units of good product plus the spoiled units for which the department was not responsible. This latter procedure gives the department credit for labor performed on spoiled units if the spoilage did not occur because of any action which occurred in the department. If, for example, a part requires three processes (shearing, forming, and painting), detection of spoilage may take place after any of the three processes. Assume that enough raw material is placed into production to make 100 units of product and that 100 units of product are made, but that 20 of the units are found to be defective after the first process, the shearing process. Normal spoilage for shearing is zero. The standard costs of the product are:

	Standard Cost (assuming that normal spoilage is zero)
Direct material—metal	$1.00
Direct material—paint	0.20
Direct labor—shearing	0.50
Direct labor—forming	0.80
Direct labor—painting	0.10
	$2.60

The standard overhead rate for all three operations is $0.50 per direct-labor dollar, that is, $0.70, [0.5(0.50 + 0.80 + 0.10)] per finished unit. Assume that there is no change in the work in process inventory.

Since all the spoilage is abnormal, one reasonable procedure is to charge $1.75 per unit, or $35 total, to spoilage expense for the 20 spoiled units detected after the shearing operation.

Direct material	$1.00
Direct labor—shearing	0.50
Overhead ($0.50/DLD)	0.25
Unit cost of spoiled product	$1.75

Some firms only charge the direct costs to spoilage and do not absorb any overhead in this charge, and some firms charge only the variable costs. The latter procedure is based on a desire to isolate the incremental costs associated with the spoilage. Where there is a shortage of productive facilities, it is reasonable to include the opportunity cost of the fixed facilities in the product cost if these costs are to be used for decision purposes.

Assume that the shearing department is arbitrarily given credit for the spoiled product exactly as if the product were good, and that the direct-labor costs of the shearing department during the period were $50. Since 100 units of product passed through shearing, it could be argued that the standard labor cost of the operation was $50 (the total units produced times the standard cost per unit of

$0.50). Assuming no wage-rate variance, the labor-efficiency variance is zero. But in order to have effective control over the operation, the amount of spoilage which took place should be analyzed. Was it normal and within the allowed spoilage for the operation? Was it caused by the workers in the shearing operation, or were the spoiled units caused by the purchased metal? Could the spoilage have been avoided prior to the work that was performed on the raw material?

In order to reduce spoilage in the future, the spoilage must be classified by the causes and by the responsible department or operation. For example, the spoilage in this example might be classified as follows:

> Company Responsibility:
>> Caused in shearing department
>> Caused in forming department
>> Caused in painting department
> Vendor Responsibility:
>> Incorrect dimensions
>> Insufficient strength

If the vendor was responsible, the spoilage should be reported to the accounts payable section and the purchasing department so that steps may be initiated to recover damages from the supplier and, perhaps, to examine alternative sources of supply.

In the example being studied, the shearing department was not responsible for the spoilage which was detected after the shearing operation, and it is therefore reasonable for the labor efficiency of the shearing department not to be affected by the fact that 20 units of products were rejected. The labor-efficiency variance of zero is correct. If the shearing department were responsible for the spoilage, it would be reasonable not to count the spoiled product in computing the standard hours (or dollars) of work performed during the period. If this were done, an unfavorable labor variance would appear. For example, the 80 units of good product times the $0.50 standard for shearing labor gives a standard labor figure of $40. But the actual labor was $50; thus, there was an unfavorable labor variance of $10 (the 20 units of product spoiled were not included in the department in computing the standard product of the period.) Since the shearing department caused the spoilage, it receives no credit for the work performed on the spoiled product.

Following the theory which excludes abnormal spoilage from the cost of good product, the cost of the spoilage would appear on the income statement as $35 (20 units times $1.75 per unit). The figure reported for spoilage would be different if the fixed overhead were not reported as a cost of spoilage (that is, if only the incremental costs were included in the standard), or if the spoilage was caused by materials or parts supplied by vendors. In the latter case, an attempt should be made to recover all, or a portion of, the spoilage from the vendor. The spoilage could be set up as a receivable for the amount that there is a reasonable chance of collecting from the vendor. If only the cost of the material or the part which was defective can be collected, not the wasted labor and overhead, the latter costs should be expensed as spoilage costs.

There are thus several paths which can be followed in accounting for spoilage costs under a standard cost accounting system. Further, we have argued that it is important to control spoilage as part of the standard cost system, and to take spoilage into consideration in analyzing labor-efficiency and material-usage variances if cost control is to be effective.

11.2 Process Cost Accounting—Actual Costs

Where a standard cost-accounting system is not being used, the same problems in controlling spoilage exist as with a standard cost system, although the computations tend to become somewhat more complex. The computations frequently are so involved that it is possible (in fact, likely) that the manager will lose sight of the objectives of the computations. The prime objective is the control of costs, implemented here via the control of cost per unit of product and control of the amount of spoilage.

Should spoilage be considered a cost of product in computing the "actual" cost of product? In the standard cost section of this chapter, the expected normal spoilage is considered a cost of product, but abnormal spoilage is a cost of inefficiency. It is computed separately rather than being hidden with other cost items in the cost of product sold. Any computations developed for the present case should also result in the actual normal spoilage incurred being included as a cost of product and abnormal spoilage being considered a cost of inefficiency and thus an expense of the period.

We shall find it useful in our discussion of process cost accounting using actual costs to define the cost per unit algebraically. Let

Q = number of good units

S = number of spoiled units

n = normal spoilage percentage

nQ = expected normal spoilage

T = total labor cost

L = actual labor cost per good unit

k = cost of an equivalent unit of labor

Then

$$k = \frac{T}{Q + S} \qquad (11.1)$$

The actual cost per good unit of product is defined to be

$$L = \frac{(Q + Qn)k}{Q} = (1 + n)k \qquad\qquad \text{if } S \geq nQ \qquad (11.2)$$

and

$$L = \frac{(Q + S)k}{Q} = \frac{Q + S}{Q} \times \frac{T}{Q + S} = \frac{T}{Q} \qquad \text{if } S < nQ \qquad (11.3)$$

Equation (11.3) applies where the actual spoilage is less than normal spoilage and all costs are assigned to the good product. In the case where $S \geq nQ$, equation (11.2) should be used, and some of the costs are assigned to abnormal spoilage rather than to product.

The formulas given by equations (11.2) and (11.3) are definitional and hence would change if the definition of actual cost were changed.

Example 1

Assume a situation where 80 good units and 20 spoiled units are produced, and that the normal spoilage is 25% of the good units produced. The actual total labor costs incurred were $50. What are the labor costs per unit and the total labor costs to be applied to product? The cost per equivalent unit of labor, including normal spoilage, is $0.50 ($50 divided by 80 plus 20). The labor cost per unit of good product is $0.625 (equal to $50 divided by 80 units). The total labor cost applied to good product is $50. Since there is no abnormal spoilage, all the actual labor is considered a cost of product.

Cost of good units	80 × 0.50	$40
Cost of normal spoilage	20 × 0.50	10
Total cost of good product		$50

$$\text{labor cost per unit of good product} = \frac{\$50}{80} = \$0.625$$

Using equation (11.1) we find

$$k = \frac{T}{Q + S} = \frac{50}{100} = \$0.50$$

Since $S \geq nQ$, we may use equation (11.2) to find L:

$$L = (1 + n)k = (1.25)(0.50) = \$0.625$$

which is the same labor cost per unit of good product as we obtained above.

Example 2

If the actual total labor cost remains at $50 but, to alter the example, the number of spoiled units is zero and the number of good units is 100 (normal spoilage is still defined to be 25% of the good units produced), the cost per equivalent unit of labor remains $0.50 ($50 divided by 100). However, the labor cost per unit of good product is now only $0.50 ($50 divided by 100), and the total labor cost applied to good product is again $50, although there are now 100 units of good product.

Cost of good units	100 × 0.50	$50.00
Cost of normal spoilage	0 × 0.50	0
Total cost of good product		$50.00

$$\text{labor cost per unit of good product} = \frac{\$50.00}{100} = \$0.50$$

Since $S < nQ$, we may use equation (11.3) to find L:

$$L = \frac{T}{Q} = \frac{50}{100} = \$0.50$$

As long as $T = \$50$, $Q = 100$, and S is less than 25 units, L will be $0.50. Normal spoilage is considered to be a cost of product.

Example 3
Next assume production of 72 good units and 28 spoiled units, so that the abnormal spoilage is 10 units (the normal spoilage is 25% of 72, or 18 units). The actual total labor costs are again $50, and if abnormal units are included, the cost per equivalent unit of labor is again $0.50. What is the labor cost per good unit? It is $0.694 (equal to $50 divided by 72).

One hundred units were produced (72 plus 28). Dividing the labor cost, $50, by the total units produced, 100, gives a cost of $0.50 per equivalent unit of labor.[1] The cost of good units produced should include the cost of the 72 good units and the cost of normal spoilage.

Cost of 72 units (72 × $0.50)	$36
Cost of normal spoilage (18 × 0.50)	9
Total cost of good product (72 units)	$45
Cost of abnormal spoilage (10 × 0.50)	5
Total labor costs	$50

The cost per unit of good product, excluding the abnormal spoilage, is again $0.625 per unit (equal to $45 divided by the number of good units, 72). As long as the actual spoilage is equal to or greater than 25% of the good product, the cost of the good product will be $0.625.

[1] The examples assume no change in work in process. If the work in process changes, it is necessary to compute the equivalent units of labor performed, taking any changes into consideration.

Using the algebraic formulations:

$$k = \frac{T}{Q + S} = \frac{5}{100} = \$0.50$$

and since $S \geq nQ$:

$$L = (1 + n)k = (1.25)(0.50) = \$0.625$$

This agrees with the results that we obtained earlier. It should be remembered, however, that the quality of the product and control of labor efficiency are accomplished through control of the amount of abnormal spoilage.

This illustration has been simplified by considering only labor costs. For full control, similar computations would have to be made for material and overhead. Also it has been assumed that the inspection point is at the end of the manufacturing process, and thus as much labor is incurred for the spoiled units as for the good units. It is possible for an inspection point to occur prior to the point where the labor effort on the product is completed. In such cases the equivalent units of labor performed on the spoiled product may be less than the amount of work performed on the good product.

Consider the last example (72 good units and 28 spoiled units), but assume that the inspection for spoilage takes place when 70% of the labor has been performed. Further, we shall continue to assume that there are no beginning or ending work-in-process inventories. The total equivalent units of labor are no longer 100 but rather 91.6, and the cost per equivalent unit of labor becomes $0.546.

Good product (72 units carried to completion)	72.0
Normal spoilage (18 × 70%)	12.6
Good product	84.6
Abnormal spoilage (10 × 70%)	7.0
Equivalent units of labor	91.6

$$\text{cost per equivalent unit of labor} = \frac{\$50}{91.6} = \$0.546$$

Cost of 72 units (72 × $0.546)	39.31
Cost of normal spoilage (12.6 × $0.546)	6.88
Cost of good product	46.19
Cost of abnormal spoilage (7 × $0.546)	3.82
Total labor costs	$50.01

$$\text{cost per unit of good product} = \frac{\$46.19}{72} = \$0.64$$

If we define E to be equivalent units of work performed, then we also have to redefine k:

$$k = \frac{T}{E} = \frac{50}{91.6} = \$0.546 \qquad (11.4)$$

In the example the actual spoilage exceeds the normal spoilage. We can, however, modify equation (11.2) to take into consideration the fact that only 70% of the work was completed on the spoiled units.

$$L = \frac{(Q + 0.7Qn)k}{Q} = (1 + 0.7n)k \qquad (11.5)$$

$$= [1 + 0.7(0.25)](0.546) = 1.175 \times 0.546 = \$0.64$$

Frequently, the complication created by not finishing work on the spoiled items may be eliminated by having the inspection point considered a paypoint. The product passing through the inspection point is treated as a completed product relative to that paypoint, even though additional work may be necessary. However, there is still a problem if spoilage can occur both before and after the inspection point.

If the convention is adopted that considers only normal spoilage a cost of product, but all spoilage is included in computing the cost per equivalent unit of labor, changes in the amount of spoilage affect neither the unit cost of product nor the cost per equivalent unit of labor. This is reasonable from the point of view of accumulating costs for inventory where we do not want costs of inefficiency to be inventoried.

11.2.1 Determining Normal Spoilage

The determination of normal spoilage is necessary since normal spoilage is considered a cost of product and is, therefore, inventoriable. Abnormal spoilage is expensed. From the point of view of control the determination of normal spoilage is needed if the amount of abnormal spoilage is to be known.

Normal spoilage should be determined by applying a percentage representing the normal spoilage per good unit to the number of good units produced. Assume that normal spoilage is 25% and 100 units of raw material are placed into production. If the output is 80 good units and 20 units are spoiled, the normal spoilage is determined by multiplying the 80 units of good product by the normal spoilage percentage of 25% to obtain 20 units. There is no abnormal spoilage in this situation. It would be incorrect to argue that a percentage of 20% applied to the input of 100 units also gives a normal spoilage of 20 units and thus the procedure of applying a given percentage to the input is equally correct. The weakness of this position can be seen by assuming that 200 units of raw material were required to produce 80 good units where the normal spoilage is 25% of the good units. The normal spoilage for 80 units of good product does not change: it is still 20 units (not 0.2 times 200). If the 25% figure is applied to the good product of 80 units the normal spoilage remains 20 units, and the abnormal spoilage increases by 100. This is consistent with the fact that an extra 100 units of raw material were required to produce 80 units of good product.

The correct procedure for computing the normal spoilage is to apply the percentage of normal spoilage to the good product completed during the period. The abnormal spoilage is computed by subtracting the normal spoilage from total spoilage. Using input as the base for the computation of normal spoilage can give an incorrect measure of normal spoilage, as we have just illustrated.

11.2.2 Interpretation of Normal Spoilage

For the computations made in this chapter, we have defined normal spoilage in terms of one number, a percentage of good product. Normal spoilage may be thought as the mean (or expected) amount of spoilage. Assuming that the number of spoiled units may be approximated by a normal probability distribution, we would expect actual spoilage to exceed this value 50% of the time.[2] The next step would be to obtain an idea of spoilage variability by estimating the standard deviation of this distribution. This may be accomplished using past data, perhaps adjusted for management's subjective judgments. Having determined the standard deviation, the probability of any amount of spoilage occurring can be computed.

Example
Assume, based on past data, that normal spoilage (the mean or expected spoilage) per 100 units is 18, and the standard deviation is 6 units. The actual spoilage is 30 units.

The actual spoilage is 2 standard deviations from the mean $[(30 - 18)/6 = 2]$. The probability of a deviation of this size or larger (above or below the mean) is 0.0456, and the probability of this level of spoilage or a larger level is 0.0228 (one half of 0.0456).[3] Thus, the spoilage of this period was a very unlikely event and should probably be investigated subject to the costs of investigation and potential savings.

11.3 Summary

Control procedures that make use of cost per unit or efficiency variances are incomplete unless control is also exercised over the amount of

---

[2] Spoilage is, in fact, a discrete variable, but continuous approximations are often quite adequate in estimating discrete probabilities. We also note that the statement holds for any symmetrical distribution. (In such distributions the mean and the median are identical, and it is the median that divides the distribution into two equal portions.)

[3] Since the normal curve represents a continuous probability function but measurement here is discrete (number of defective units), we might calculate actual spoilage to be $(29.5 - 18)/6 = 1.83$ standard deviation units. Normally this correction for continuity can and will be ignored.

spoiled product. Spoilage should be rigorously controlled and the control should be coordinated with the control of labor costs, since labor efficiency may be increased at the expense of an increase in spoilage unless labor and spoilage are controlled jointly.

The computations of cost of product are complicated by the fact that the cost of product should reasonably include the normal spoilage but not the abnormal spoilage. The abnormal spoilage should be considered a cost of the period arising from inefficiency or, perhaps, other causes. A further computational complication occurs because normal spoilage should be based on the good-product output rather than the input. In some cases the application of an incorrect procedure does not result in material differences, but, logically, normal spoilage should be a function of the good product, not the amount of input. Although a rough control of spoilage may be implemented by a report of the physical number of units spoiled, a more refined report of the incremental costs of the spoiled units, and the amount of spoilage above normal in dollar amount, should be made. Above all, the control of spoilage is a matter of balancing the costs of spoilage with the costs arising from careful production procedures. A procedure that results in little or no spoilage, and little or no product, may be equally as bad as a procedure that results in too much spoilage with a large amount of production. A reasonable amount of spoilage may be acceptable to obtain optimal production levels.

To control labor, it is necessary to control both labor-efficiency variances (or actual cost for equivalent units of labor) and spoilage. If only one or the other is controlled, it is possible that undesirable incentives will arise from the control procedure. For example, the cost per unit of labor may be decreased by an increase in work tempo, and this in turn may result in increased spoilage.

QUESTIONS AND PROBLEMS

11–1 Distinguish between scrap and spoilage.

11–2 Should spoilage be considered a cost of product and thus inventoriable or a cost of inefficiency and thus an expense of the period?

11–3 With an "actual" cost system, if normal spoilage is considered a cost of product, how is the cost per good unit affected by changes in efficiency?

11–4 How is normal spoilage computed assuming that the input and output are given?

11–5 In computing standard hours of work performed by a work group, how would you handle the work found to be spoiled?

11–6 Assume that actual spoilage was significantly below normal spoilage. What other information would you desire before assuming a high level of efficiency?

11–7 What costs are relevant in computing the "real" costs of spoilage?

11-8 The normal spoilage in a manufacturing process is 10% of the good product. The standard cost per unit, without a spoilage allowance, is:

	Standard Cost per Unit (without spoilage)
Direct material	$2.00
Direct labor (1 hour)	3.00
Overhead (the rate is $4.20/DLH)	4.20
	$9.20

In July 1,000 units were produced, of which 900 were good units. The actual direct-labor costs were $3,300. There were no wage-rate variances.

Required
a. Compute the standard costs per unit, including normal spoilage in the costs.
b. Analyze the spoilage and direct-labor cost for the month.

11-9 Assume the same basic situation as in problem 11-8. In August 1,000 units were produced, of which 800 were good units. The actual direct-labor costs were $2,400. There were no wage-rate variances.

Required
a. Analyze the spoilage and direct-labor costs for the month.
b. Compare the operations of July and August (problem 11-8 gives the data for July).

11-10 The normal spoilage of a manufacturing process is 0.10 of the good product. Inspection takes place at the end of the production process. The data for three months were as follows:

	Total Equivalent Units of Labor	Good Units	Spoiled Units	Total Labor Costs
March	99	90	9	$79.20
April	99	99	0	79.20
May	99	80	19	79.20

Required:
a. For each of the three months compute the labor cost per equivalent unit of product and the cost per good unit.
b. Compute the abnormal spoilage for each of the three months.

11-11 The normal spoilage of a manufacturing process is 25% of the good product. The inspection for spoilage takes place when 60% of the labor has been performed. In September, 115 units were processed, of which 80 complete units were good. The direct-labor cost for the month was $3,535.

Required:
a. Compute the cost per equivalent units of product and the cost per good unit.
b. Compute the abnormal spoilage and the direct-labor cost of the abnormal spoilage.

11–12 The normal spoilage is 10% of the good product or 9.09% of the input (assuming that the spoilage is normal). Compute the normal and abnormal spoilage for each of the months shown.

	Input	Good Product
March	88	80
April	100	80
May	500	80
June	500	100

11–13 The normal spoilage is estimated to be 10% of good product; this is the mean or expected value of the spoilage. The standard deviation of the spoilage is 2%. Assume the percentage of spoiled units is normally distributed. During the first three months of the year the actual spoilage was as follows:

	Good Product	Actual Spoilage
January	1,000	120
February	1,500	195
March	2,000	160

Required:
a. For each month compute the probability of the spoilage being as large or larger than the spoilage incurred.
b. For January and February compute the probability of unfavorable spoilage that is as large or larger than the amounts actually incurred.

11–14 The grinding department of Spoilow Company has experienced a spoilage rate in the past months on a particular product that has averaged 20% of the good units. The foreman of the department notes that this spoilage rate is the highest for any department in the company. He believes that he can reduce this normal spoilage rate to 10% by adding seven more workers to his department. Assuming that you are the plant manager, what would you tell the foreman?

11–15 Jones Manufacturing Company produces a single product which begins processing in Department 1 and completes production in Department 2. In

January, Department 2 began work on 1,000 units and transferred 1,000 partially completed units to Department 2. The total Department 1 production cost associated with the 1,000 units was $5,000, and Department 2 costs incurred were as follows:

Direct materials	$2,000
Direct Labor	500
Overhead	1,000

Assuming that inspection occurs at the end of Department 2 processing and that normal spoilage is 25% of the good units, compute the cost per unit of good product and the total cost of abnormal spoilage for January in each of the following situations (there was no beginning or ending inventory for January):
  a. The number of good units completed was 1,000.
  b. The number of good units completed was 800.
  c. The number of good units completed was 500.

11–16 The standard costs per thousand units of a single product (without the spoilage factor) produced by a company are as follows:

Direct materials	20 lbs @ $0.10	= $ 2.00
Direct labor	10 hours @ $5.00 =	50,00
Overhead	10 hours @ $0.55 =	5.50
Total		$57.50

In the production process, the materials are added at the beginning, and all other costs are assumed to be incurred evenly throughout the manufacture. Inspection occurs when the production process is 70% complete, and normal spoilage is 25% of the good units.

The following data apply to the December production process:

Beginning work in process	0 units
Completed and transferred	1,000,000 units
Spoilage	400,000 units
Ending work in process—50% complete 600,000 units	

Required:
  a. Compute the standard cost of the abnormal spoilage.
  b. Compute the standard cost of the units completed and transferred.

11–17 Sauce Italiano Company makes a popular brand of spaghetti sauce, which is sold in supermarkets in 8-ounce cans. In making one batch of sauce, 100 lbs of ingredients are mixed together, and the mixture is cooked for several hours. During the cooking, the mixture loses 20% of its initial weight. If the mixture is not carefully watched during cooking and canning, spoilage may occur that would be detected after all the saurce is canned. Past experience suggests that the number of eight-ounce cans spoiled through improper processing is normally distributed with a mean of 5% of the good cans and a standard deviation of 1% of the good cans. In March, 500 batches of sauce were begun and 72,500 good cans of sauce were produced. Assuming that there was no beginning or ending work-in-process for March, determine:

a. the cost per good can of sauce if the total cost associated with cooking and canning the 500 batches was $25,000.
b. the probability that spoilage this great could occur if the spoilage process were actually distributed according to the normal distribution given above.

11–18 The Limelight Corporation produces a single product and uses a process cost system. During November the company began production on 12,000 units. Inspection for spoilage occurs when the products are about 75% complete, and normal spoilage is 20% of the good units. During November, 9,500 units were completed, and the units still in processing were 25% complete. Assume that there was no beginning inventory, that materials are added at the beginning of production while conversion costs are applied uniformly through the manufacture, and that the November costs incurred were as follows:

Materials	$12,600
Conversion costs	40,050
Total	$52,650

All spoilage during November was normal.

Required: Find the cost of the completed units and the cost of the units in the ending inventory.

11–19 Rockaway Corporation manufactures a product that is inspected when the production process is 60% complete. At inspection, all defective units are destroyed. Normal spoilage is 10% of the units that pass inspection. Direct materials are added at the beginning of the manufacturing process, whereas labor and overhead are applied at a constant rate throughout the production. There was no beginning inventory for July, and the ending inventory was 50% completed. Production and cost information for July is as follows:

Costs incurred in July:	
Direct materials used	$ 5,200
Direct labor	21,315
Overhead	9,555
July Production Information:	
Units started	8,000
Units passing inspection	6,500
Units in ending inventory	500

Required:
a. Compute the cost of the units that were completed.
b. Compute the cost of the units in the ending inventory.
c. Compute the cost of the abnormal spoilage.

11–20 A manufacturing company produces a single product and uses a process-cost basis for determining product costs. Materials for the product are added at the beginning of the process while labor and overhead costs are assumed to be added evenly throughout the production. The beginning inventory for May was one-half complete with respect to labor and overhead, and the ending inventory was one-fourth complete. Inspection occurs when complete, and normal spoilage is 10% of the good product. The company uses average cost for determining unit costs of the product. The following information applies to the May work in process:

Beginning inventory:	
Materials	$ 948
Labor	1,544
Overhead	690
Costs incurred in May:	
Materials	$11,400
Labor	36,225
Overhead	7,007
Inventory and production information:	
Units in beginning inventory	1,000
Units completed	8,000
Units in ending inventory	800
Spoilage	1,000

Required:
a. Compute the cost of the goods completed.
b. Compute the cost of the ending inventory.
c. Compute the cost of the abnormal spoilage.

SUPPLEMENTARY READING

STANLEY, H., "Standard Costs for Manufacturing," New York: McGraw-Hill Book Company, 1960, pp. 275–280 and 303–308.

Chapter 12

Cost–Price–Volume Decisions

Decisions involving price, volume, and cost can be split into two classifications: those decisions made after the capital assets necessary for production have been acquired, and those made in connection with the acquisition of the necessary capital assets. It is important to distinguish between the two situations, since considerations which are relevant for one may not be relevant for the other. Applying the same procedures in both situations can lead to incorrect decisions. This chapter reviews the pricing and output decisions in the case when the capital assets are already owned. The problems of decision making when the capital assets have not yet been acquired are capital-budgeting decisions. These decisions are examined in Chapters 13, 14, and 15.

12.1 Price–Volume Decisions

Assume that the Scot Company owns a new plant which is fully equipped with the latest model machinery to make lawn mowers. What price should it charge? At what output should it produce? What cost and profit decisions can it make? These decisions are examined in reverse order.

What profit decisions can be made? The answer is none. The company decides on a price and an output; it attempts to produce the goods efficiently. If the planning process is effective and is efficiently carried out, a profit may result. But management does not "plan" profits. In this situation it cannot say that it needs a profit of 20% on an investment of $1 million and therefore must have a profit of $200,000. The profit is a result of planning and the execution of the plans, but it is a residual of these plans and not the result of a "profit decision."

The cost decisions of the Scot Company are somewhat less limited. The firm can budget costs for various levels of output, can attempt to control costs and improve efficiency, and can use inventories to stabilize production. However, the basic cost structure is determined by the characteristics of the machinery and plant purchased. Whether overtime is necessary is a decision to be made in each period, but to some extent the decision was made when the plant was built. If the demand for the product is high enough, it will be necessary to incur overtime; but the decision that determined the size of the plant and in turn resulted in the necessity to incur overtime was made in a previous period.

The pricing decision is one of the most important decisions made by management, and one of the most misunderstood. Two pricing methods commonly used which are subject to criticism are the *cost-plus* and the *desired-return-on-investment* methods of pricing.

12.1.1 Cost-Plus and Return-on-Investment Pricing

With the cost-plus method of pricing, the cost of the product is computed and a "reasonable" or "fair" profit is added to obtain the price. If a government cost-plus contract is in hand, this is a justifiable procedure; but in a competitive situation (as in bidding for a government contract) it may lead to undesirable results.[1] One difficulty is in computing unit cost and involves deciding on the level of activity which should be used to absorb fixed costs to product. A second problem is in determining unit price and involves deciding on what constitutes a "reasonable" profit. But perhaps of most importance is the fact that the entire cost-plus procedure is not theoretically sound.

To illustrate the problem of determining unit cost, assume that the Scot Company can produce 10,000 lawn mowers per month when operating at capacity. The monthly fixed costs are $200,000, and the variable costs are $30 per lawn mower. What is the cost of one lawn mower? One reasonable answer is $50 (the variable costs of $30 plus fixed costs of $20). The absorption of fixed costs is based on capacity. But suppose that the company expects to produce and sell only 5,000 lawn mowers during the month. Are the unit costs to be used for pricing then $70 (the variable costs of $30 plus fixed costs per unit of $40)? Carrying this issue to its illogical conclusion, if only one unit is to be produced, the total cost per unit would be $200,030, or at the opposite extreme $30, if the fixed costs are not considered as part of the unit cost.

With cost-plus a reasonable profit is added to the unit cost. The desired-return-on-investment pricing method focuses attention on return on investment

---

[1] For some results in this area, see S. Colantoni, R. Manes, and A. Whinston, "Programming, Profit Rates and Pricing Decisions," *The Accounting Review*, July 1969, pp. 467–481.

instead of income. It has no advantage over the cost-plus procedure, and retains the disadvantage of requiring the computation of unit cost. There is no objection to a company attempting to recover all costs and to earn as much profit as it can in a competitive environment. But this desire does not necessarily mean that all costs will be recovered, or that the company will earn a profit.

12.1.2 Standard Price

One method of handling the pricing problem is to base the absorption of fixed costs on normal activity without regard to the expected or actual level of operations. This procedure is better than adjusting the cost per unit and the price upward as the output decreases. In fact, it can be used to set a sort of "standard" price which must be obtained to maintain the productive facilities and earn a selected return on the capital employed. Nevertheless, it is not always desirable to set a standard price. In some situations the firm may be able to charge more than the standard price (for example, if it is introducing a new product for which there is little if any competition as yet), while in other situations it may be desirable or necessary to set a price less than the standard price. Competition, for example, may prevent the use of the standard price. In fact, a complementary product may be priced below its direct-variable costs to increase sales of a related product. Camera and film is one example. Another example is the pricing of razors by a company which also manufactures razor blades.

12.1.3 Determining Price and Output: The Economic Solution

The theoretical solution to the problem of output and price is an exercise in the application of economic theory. For this reason it is useful to digress for a moment to examine the major differences in assumptions between the behavior of costs as economists see them and as accountants generally consider them. Figure 12.1 plots total variable, total fixed, and total costs first from the economist's point of view (Figure 12.1a) and then from the accountant's point of view (Figure 12.1b). Figure 12.2 represents the same breakdown for unit costs,

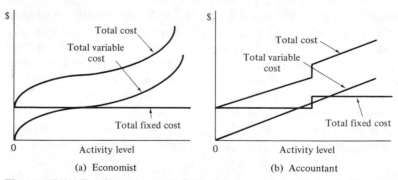

(a) Economist   (b) Accountant

Figure 12.1 Total cost curves from (a) an economist's and (b) an accountant's viewpoint.

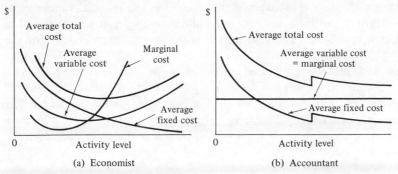

Figure 12.2 Unit-cost curves from (a) an economist's and (b) an accountant's viewpoint.

assuming a single measure of activity.[2] Both figures are simplified to highlight the major differences.

A substantive difference involves the range of activity graphed. The economist graphs a broader range of possible activity and changes in efficiency. The accountant, on the other hand, is usually concerned only with a limited range of activity. Over this range, fixed costs are constant except perhaps for occasional discrete upward jumps. Furthermore, within a wide range the accountant's assumption of linearity for the variable-cost activity relationship is usually an adequate approximation.

The differences in the curves are a function of different assumptions and they need not be considered as conceptual differences. Given an identical problem, there would be essential agreement among them on the relevant-cost curves involved (one remaining difference would be that the economist includes the cost of equity capital as a cost but the accountant excludes it).

With these distinctions in mind, the discussion now turns to the resolution of the price–output decision from the vantage point of economic theory. There is a tendency to dismiss the analysis which follows by suggesting that the solution is akin to determining the number of angels that can dance on the head of a pin. Rather than pretend to present a procedure that permits the determination of the exact price that will maximize profits, this section develops a theoretically sound guide for determining price and output. The principles are correct, even though in many situations they cannot be applied with exactness because of incomplete information: the procedure, then, is a normative one.

Before the cost curves of economic theory can be very useful, it is necessary to add the revenue function to the analysis. The economist typically assumes that units sold (and therefore output activity indirectly) increase as price decreases (accountants often assume a constant price over the expected or relevant range of activity), and that the number of units of product that can be sold at different

---

[2] A failure to specify whether total or per unit costs are under consideration can lead to useless discussions and often to erroneous conclusions.

prices is known. Usually it is assumed that the lower the price, the more units will be sold. Although this is not always a valid assumption, it will be useful in the illustration to follow. (The assumption is, however, not necessary for the theory being developed.)

It is possible to plot the number of units that can be sold at all feasible prices. This curve is called the average-revenue or price curve. It shows the price or average revenue per unit necessary to sell the associated number of units. The average-revenue curve (AR) in Figure 12.3 slopes downward to the right because it is assumed that the number of units sold increases as the price decreases.

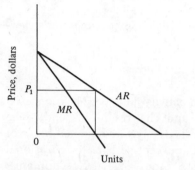

Figure 12.3   Revenue curves.

A marginal-revenue curve (MR) is also plotted in Figure 12.3. This curve shows the amount of revenue added by the sale of one additional unit. It slopes downward to the right since it is necessary to reduce the price to sell an additional unit. It is below the average-revenue curve since every time the sales price is reduced, the price of all previous units also has to be reduced.

No useful decisions can be made with just the revenue curves, but it is interesting to note that when the price is P_1 (Figure 12.3) the marginal revenue is zero, and that with a lower price the marginal revenue becomes negative. This means that a further reduction in price results in a reduction in total revenue. With zero costs, a price of P_1 constitutes the minimum price that the firm could charge without losing money on the next unit of product sold.

If the marginal-cost curve is added (see Figure 12.4), additional conclusions can be drawn. This curve shows the amount of cost that is added by the production and the sale of one additional unit of product. For example, if it costs $300 to produce and sell 100 units and $305 to produce and sell 101 units, the marginal cost of the one-hundred-first unit is $5. The accountant is accustomed to talk of variable, or incremental, costs. In this case the incremental cost of one more unit is $5. The shape of the marginal-cost curve indicates that the firm is at first operating under increasing efficiency (the marginal cost decreases) and then reaches a point where the efficiency decreases (the marginal cost increases). If constant efficiency is assumed, the marginal-cost curve becomes a horizontal line.

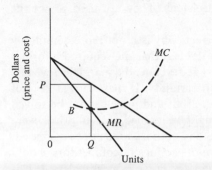

Figure 12.4   Determining output and price.

The point where the marginal-cost curve intersects the marginal-revenue curve (point B in Figure 12.4) is very important. This intersection determines the optimal output (Q units) and optimal price (P).

If the company is producing less than this level of output, one more unit of production and sale results in additional revenue greater than the additional cost (the marginal revenue is greater than the marginal cost). Thus, as long as the value of the marginal-revenue curve is greater than the value of the marginal-cost curve, it is profitable to increase output. The point where the two curves intersect is the optimal level of output. But assume that a decision is made to increase production by still another unit. Figure 12.4 shows that if production is increased beyond Q units, the additional cost is greater than the additional revenue. Thus, there is no profit incentive to increase output and sales beyond Q units.

What price will maximize profits? To sell Q units it is necessary to charge a price P. This is determined by constructing a vertical line through the point B where marginal cost equals marginal revenue until it intersects the average-revenue line and then horizontally to the vertical axis. This determines the price necessary to sell Q units and thus maximize profits. If a lower price is charged, more than Q units are purchased, but the additional revenue earned by these additional units is less than the additional costs of producing them. If a price greater than P is charged, the number of units sold is less than Q, and marginal revenue is greater than marginal cost. Only an output of Q units sold at a price of P maximizes profits.

Several additional remarks can be made. The optimal output is determined directly by the intersection of the marginal-cost and marginal-revenue curves. The price necessary to achieve this optimum is determined indirectly by this same intersection. The marginal-revenue curve in Figure 12.4 implies the average-revenue curve in the same figure, and hence once point B is known, the optimal price can be determined. Also, the only costs that enter into the decision are those costs which vary with output. This is a difficult thought to digest; but it is true that costs which are constant in total and do not vary with output should not enter into the pricing decisions. They are used to set the standard but not the selling price.[3]

Since the logic of the above analysis is correct, why is it not more commonly used in practice? The reasons are related to the fact that the required information is often incomplete. Seldom can the average-revenue, the marginal-revenue, and the marginal-cost curves be known with certainty. If these curves are not known, then the solution to the problem of output and price cannot be solved with absolute accuracy. For example, it might be argued that if prices were reduced, competitors would also reduce prices and output would not be increased. When plotting a firm's average-revenue curve the actions of competitors should be taken into consideration. If this is not done, the curve is meaningless. If it is done, the objection just mentioned is not applicable.

12.2 Break-even Analysis

The break-even point is located where the total cost curve intersects the total revenue curve, or equivalently where total revenue equals total cost. Conventional break-even analysis represents total revenue and total cost with straight lines. This assumes that output and sales can be increased without changing price (at least, the effect of price changes are not shown) and that the firm operates at the same efficiency at all levels. Thus, to increase profit it is necessary merely to increase the number of units sold. The conventional analysis is illustrated in Figure 12.5.

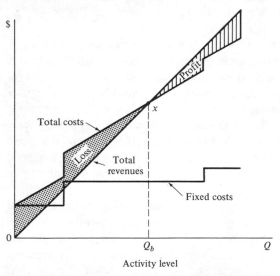

Figure 12.5   Conventional break-even analysis: Constant selling price.

---

[3] The standard price is that price needed to cover both variable and fixed costs and yield a selected profit margin.

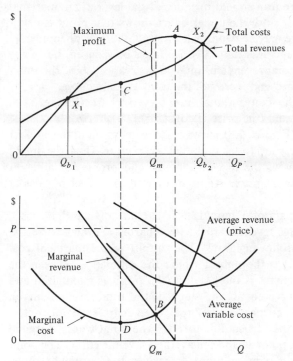

Figure 12.6 Break-even analysis: Changing selling prices. Units sold and the prices at which they are sold (moving to the right the price decreases and the units sold increase).

Several comments might be made concerning Figure 12.5. First, fixed costs are assumed to have two-step increases over the relevant output range. It is common for the accountant to assume that the total-expense line can be approximated by a straight line between these steps. The point X represents the break-even point and the activity level Q_b the break-even activity level.[4] The curves are drawn down to zero activity even though the nature of the relationships is suspect in this region. These relationships may be established using the correlation-regression techniques that will be discussed in Chapter 23.[5] The break-even line is of limited value over ranges where no data points exist. A very low activity level is an example of such a region.

If the firm relaxes the requirements that the quantity sold can be increased with the price remaining unchanged and that the efficiency be/constant, the plottings of total revenue and total costs are no longer straight lines. This later type of situation is illustrated by the break-even chart in Figure 12.6. Figure 12.6

[4] Note that when fixed costs jump, it may be possible to have more than one break-even point.

[5] Jumps in the fixed costs within the data range can obscure the true relationship. In particular, the slope coefficient will be underestimated when a linear relationship is assumed.

is useful in explaining why the firm should produce at the level where marginal cost equals marginal revenue, since the upper chart shows that profit is maximized. It also shows that there may be two break-even points. This phenomenon results from the fact that to increase output, price must be reduced, but if the price is reduced sufficiently, total revenue ultimately decreases. Thus, the total-revenue curve slopes downward and recrosses the total-expense curve.

The horizontal axis of the conventional break-even chart (Figure 12.5) showed the number of units sold (the price is constant). The horizontal axis of the revised break-even chart (Figure 12.6) shows that the net result of the number of units sold and the price necessary to sell that number of units. Thus, the break-even chart of Figure 12.6 shows the revenues, costs, and profits for different levels of units sales and different prices (though for only one level of sales at each price).

Beneath the break-even chart of Figure 12.6 is a chart of marginal costs, marginal revenues, and average revenues. If the two charts are drawn correctly, they are interrelated in the following ways. The output where marginal cost equals marginal revenue, Q_m, is the output where the difference between the total-revenue and total-cost curves is the greatest (the profit is maximized and the slope of the total-cost curve equals the slope of the total-revenue curve). The price, P, at which profit is greatest on the break-even chart is the price determined by the intersection of the vertical line through the point where marginal cost equals marginal revenue, point B, and the average-revenue curve. The point where total revenue reaches a maximum, point A, is where the marginal revenue is equal to zero. The marginal-cost curve reaches a minimum at the point where the total-cost curve changes from concave downward to concave upward. Finally, the two break-even points, Q_{b_1} and Q_{b_2} (neither of which appears in the lower graph), bracket the optimal level of activity.

The presentation of a break-even chart with changing prices is not meant to suggest that the conventional break-even chart with its assumption of constant prices is not useful. In many cases it is useful. However, if the need is for a chart showing the results of using different possible price–quantity relations, a figure similar to Figure 12.6 could be used.

A common practice of managers is to draw a break-even chart assuming the present price and to show that a decrease in price requires greater sales in order to break even. There is no question that the lower the price, the higher the break-even point in terms of units sold and total revenues.[6] The lowest conceivable break-even point is a price equal to the sum of the variable costs of one unit and the total fixed costs. Thus, only one unit would have to be sold to break even. But would that unit be sold?

A careful look at Figure 12.6 shows that the optimal price and output are determined by reference to the marginal-cost, marginal-revenue, and average-revenue curves. The effect on the break-even point is not considered, nor should

[6] The argument assumes no gains in efficiency.

it be. The conventional break-even analysis is inadequate for determining the optimal price and output. For example, Figure 12.7 shows a break-even chart with two possible revenue lines, R_1 and R_2, which are the result of two prices, P_1 and P_2. All other things being equal, the price that leads to the revenue line R_1 appears more desirable, since it gives a lower break-even point and higher profits at every point of output. However, it is impossible to determine the better of the two prices until the probable revenues to be earned following each of the two suggested price policies are inserted. Assume that with price P_1, which results in the revenue curve R_1, the firm operates at the break-even point B; but with price P_2 the firm sells an amount equal to capacity, Q. In this case, price P_2, which results in line R_2, is the more desirable, even though the indicated break-even point with that price is higher. The fact that a larger dollar amount of sales (or of units sold) is needed to break even does not indicate that the break-even point is harder to attain. Again, a price equal to the sum of the variable cost per unit and the total fixed costs gives the lowest break-even point, but it may be difficult to sell that one unit necessary to break even.

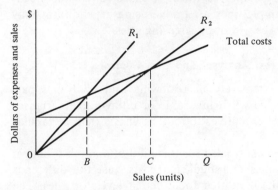

Figure 12.7 Comparing two selling prices.

It is also important to recognize that break-even analysis is essentially an *ex ante* static analysis. The initial *ex ante* diagram cannot easily be used to explore changes in the activity levels over time. This is the result of the irreversibility of efficiency changes and the sticky nature of costs to decreases in activity levels. It is also important to note that the level of fixed costs is not relevant to the decision.

12.2.1 Changes in Costs and Sales Price

If the firm is selling its product to an optimal price (marginal revenue equals marginal costs) prior to a change leading to increased efficiency (in the form of decreased marginal costs), then the profitable action is for the manager to decrease his price and increase his output. This is not done altruistically to share the increased profits with the consumer but rather to increase the profits of the firm. Inspection of Figure 12.6 (particularly the lower portion) shows that any lowering of the marginal-cost curve results in the optimal output being increased, and in a lower price in order to sell these extra units. The profits of the firm are increased by the amount of the increase in the area between the marginal-revenue and marginal-cost curves from the origin to their intersection.

The same result can also be derived from the upper portion of Figure 12.6. A decline in the marginal cost due to an increase in efficiency results in a decrease in the slope of the total-cost curve at all points and a lowering of the curve. (The marginal cost is the slope of the total-cost curve.) The slope of the cost curve now equals the slope of the total-revenue line at a point above Q_m. Thus, the optimal output is increased and a lower price is required to sell the larger output.

Other factors may, however, prevent a price decrease. The response of competitors must be considered. Secondly, in an inflationary economy the increased efficiency may merely delay a further price rise in response to increased prime costs already experienced or expected.

If a change is made in selling expenditures, it can be expected that the break-even chart will change. For example, increased advertising expenditures may enable the firm to increase its prices without decreasing sales.

12.2.2 Break-even Charts, *Ex post* Analysis, and Cost Control

Break-even charts are used extensively in reviewing and analyzing past results, since they show at a glance when favorable or unfavorable variances exist. Frequently it is easier to get executives to look at charts than at tabular presentations.

One popular type of break-even chart used for this kind of analysis is shown in Figure 12.8. Instead of revenues and budgeted costs, just the difference between the two (budgeted profit) is plotted for different levels of sales. The actual profit for the period (a month here) is marked on the graph; the location of the actual profit in relation to the budgeted profit determines whether the budgeted profit for the actual level of activity was attained. In Figure 12.8 the

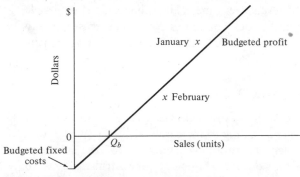

Figure 12.8   Budgeted and actual income.

profit for January is more than budgeted and the profit for February is less than budgeted. One explanation could be that expenses were not reduced rapidly enough in face of sales decline. The expected variability around the line as determined perhaps from a correlation-regression analysis would be useful in evaluating the significance of the observed deviations.

An alternative presentation would show only the budgeted costs for the different levels of sales and the actual expenses for the different time periods. Such a graph is shown in Figure 12.9. Such a graph would be useful to a manager with responsibility for costs but not revenues.

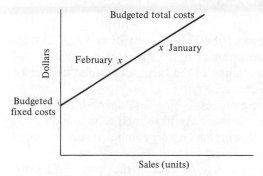

Figure 12.9   Budgeted and actual costs.

In addition to showing the budgeted and actual total costs, it is desirable to break down the totals by types of cost, by departments, and by product lines. Charts may be prepared for any of these breakdowns, so that the budgeted and actual results may be compared for any level of operations. Also, for many costs, measures of activity other than sales are more appropriate as explanatory variables. Indeed, several variables may be employed using the correlation-regression techniques described in Chapter 23. Graphs can then be constructed to illustrate the net effect of each independent variable. Thus, the direct-labor costs incurred might be plotted against the number of units of product actually produced or machine hours used, while the wage costs of accounts payable clerks are plotted against invoices processed or hours worked. For each cost classification one or more appropriate measures of activity should be determined. An examination of these charts can direct efforts toward areas where possible savings can be achieved.

12.2.3 Break-even Analysis Under Uncertainty

Assume two different break-even charts as shown in Figure 12.10. The slope of the line gives the contribution margin per unit. Situation (b) may be interpreted to be the same as situation (a) except that the profit line results from a higher price or lower variable cost. Is the higher price in situation (b) more desirable than the price in situation (a)? The break-even point is lower, but this

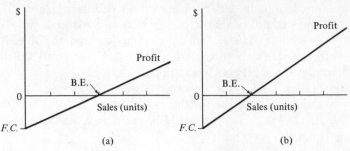

Figure 12.10   Break-even charts for two different prices for the same product.

is an inevitable result of a higher contribution margin; however, it assures nothing about the likelihood of occurrence of the different possible profits following either pricing policy. The change in the break-even point cannot be used as the criterion in making the decision.

A more reasonable decision-making process would first establish for a given price policy the probability function, showing the likelihood of selling different amounts of product.[7] See Figure 12.11, where such a distribution is superimposed on a break-even chart. The left-hand vertical axis still records dollars while the right-hand vertical axis gives the probability of sales at that point.[8] The dis-

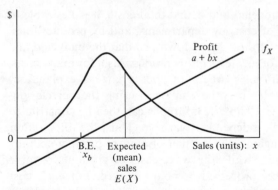

Figure 12.11   Break-even chart with a probability distribution over demand superimposed.

[7] In this chapter the probability distribution of the number of units sold is assumed to be the same as the number of units demanded. The possibility of the firm's being unable to fill an order because demand is in excess of the number of units on hand, with the result that the customer buys elsewhere, could be allowed for but the solution to this problem then becomes more complex because it combines pricing, production, and inventory decisions. The separation of pricing, production, and inventory decisions is unrealistic, but it is helpful in understanding one segment of the decision. Also, while optimizing a segment of the firm may not be the ideal solution, it is frequently an important feasible solution.

[8] If a continuous probability function is used, the vertical axis gives the probability density.

tribution is assumed to be continuous and unimodal, but it is not assumed to be normal or even symmetrical.[9]

The probability density function for demand (and thus sales) shows the relative likelihood of each level of sales. The total area under the curve is equal to 1, and the area over any sales interval is equal to the probability that sales will be in that interval. Such a curve could be developed from historical data, and it might be substantially modified for circumstances the decision maker believes now exist which are not adequately reflected by the historical data.

If the choice is made to produce, the profit, Y, for a given price policy is $Y = a + bx$, and the expected profit is obtained by taking the expectation[10]:

$$E(Y) = a + bE(X)$$

The term a is equal to or less than zero and measures the negative of the fixed costs. If the decision maker chooses not to produce, the return is zero in all cases. Thus, he need only compute the expected profit associated with the decision "produce" and take the action to produce if the expected profits exceed zero. He is basing his decision on the expected profits.[11] It is assumed that the fixed cost represents the opportunity costs of using the production facility in the best alternative manner or that they have not yet been committed.

A decision can be made on the basis of the expected state (such as expected demand) value whenever the payoff functions for the actions are linear functions. For example, suppose that the payoffs for two different decisions involving linear payoffs, where x stands for sales, are given by

Action	Payoff
1: Produce	$a_1 + b_1 x$
2: Don't produce	$a_2 + b_2 x$

where $b_1 > b_2$ and $a_1 < a_2$ to assure that the two lines cross and the actual

[9] Normality is introduced later, but it is not required for this step of the analysis.

[10] Equivalently, the expected income is equal to the product of the income at each level of sales and the probability density of that level of sales integrated over all sales levels, that is, by

$$\int_0^\infty (a + bx) f_x(x) dx \tag{12.1}$$

Sometimes the evaluation of the integral given by this expression becomes rather complex, and it is therefore useful to know that the decision can be made on the basis of the expected level of sales when the payoff function is linear.

[11] The assumption is implicitly made that the monetary values represent relevant measures of the impact of the outcomes on the manager (in more technical terms, the decision maker's utility for money is linear).

value of x is independent of the two actions. Then the indifference sales level, x_b, is found by setting the two equations equal and solving. This yields

$$x_b = \frac{a_2 - a_1}{b_1 - b_2} \qquad (12.2)$$

Action 1 is more desirable than action 2 if its expectation is greater:

$$E(a_1 + b_1 X) > E(a_2 + b_2 X)$$

or

$$a_1 + b_1 E(X) > a_2 + b_2 E(X)$$

or

$$b_1 E(X) - b_2 E(X) > a_2 - a_1$$

Thus action 1 is more desirable if

$$E(X) > \frac{a_2 - a_1}{b_1 - b_2} = x_b \qquad (12.3)$$

Equation (12.3) indicates that if the expectation is greater than the indifference level, the expected payoff from action 1 exceeds that from action 2. Action 2 is more desirable if the expected value of X is below x_b. This result is independent of the shape of the distribution; it depends only on the value of the expectation. For the present example, the payoffs from the decision to produce are represented by the equation for action 1 with slope greater than zero while the payoffs for the decision not to produce are represented by a line coincident with the X-axis and a slope of zero.

The expected level (the mean) of sales may not, however, always be easy to determine. The modal value of sales is the most likely level, and the median value is that level of sales for which the odds are equal that it will or will not be exceeded. These two values are perhaps relatively easy to visualize and discuss with the manager. Mean sales has no such simple interpretation or visualization. Furthermore, for skewed distributions such as the one in Figure 12.11, the mean tends to be slightly larger than the median. If median sales exceed the indifference level in this case, the decision to take action 1 is still best since the mean exceeds the median. But if median sales are less than but close to the indifference level, the best decision may not be clear. Experience with moderately skewed distributions indicates that as a general rule of thumb the median falls about two thirds of the distance from the mode toward the mean.[12] Using this general relationship, the mean can be estimated for moderately skewed distributions by the formula $E(X) = \text{mode} + \frac{3}{2}(\text{median} - \text{mode})$. If the probability distribution can be assumed to be symmetrical, the mean, median, and mode are identical and the decision process is again simplified.

---

[12] This is a result of using Pearson's coefficient of skewness.

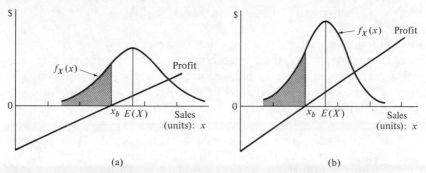

Figure 12.12 **Break-even charts for two different prices for the same product and different demand distributions.**

Turning now to the choice between the two prices whose profit functions are graphed in Figure 12.10, a decision is obtained by examining the expected profits, since both payoff functions are linear. However, a different probability distribution applies to each price decision because price influences the amount sold. The distributions for the example illustrated in Figure 12.12 assume that a lower price, case (a) increases the likelihood of larger sales levels. In this situation both distributions are assumed to have different means and variances. Since expected sales exceed the indifference or break-even level in both cases, a choice should be made between the two prices based on expected profits. Thus, a solution can be obtained by evaluating expression (12.1) for both price situations and selecting the price that yields the larger expected profit. Equivalently, the expression for the expected profit given by equation (12.4) can be used.[13]

$$\text{expected profit} = E(Y) = b[E(X) - x_b] \tag{12.4}$$

where b is the slope of the profit function (the contribution margin per unit), $E(X)$ is expected sales, and x_b is the break-even sales volume in units.

Equation (12.4) states that the expected profit associated with any price is given by the product of the contribution margin with the amount by which expected sales exceed the break-even sales volume.

Example

Assume that the contribution margin per unit is $2 in case (a) and $2.50 in case (b), fixed costs are $100,000, and expected sales are 60,000 units in case (a) and 46,000 units in case (b); then the break-even sales level (x_b) is 50,000 in case (a) and 40,000 in case (b). The expected profits are $E(Y) = 2(60,000 - 50,000) =$ $20,000 in case (a) and $E(Y) = 2.50(46,000 - 40,000) = $15,000$ in case (b). The lower contribution margin is preferred.

[13] If $Y = a + bX$, then $E(Y) = a + bE(X)$. At the break-even point, $Y = 0$, $a = -bx_b$. Therefore, $E(Y) = -bx_b + bE(X) = b[E(X) - x_b]$.

If $E(X) < x_b$, equation (12.4) would be negative (that is, an expected loss would be indicated).

In most practical problems there are other uncertainties (although typically of a lesser magnitude). Thus, there is uncertainty concerning the various costs that will be experienced (even if suitable measures could be agreed on), the performance of the employees, the lives of the equipment, and so on. Introduction of these complexities is considered by the authors to be beyond the scope of this volume.[14]

The probability distributions can be used to obtain measures of riskiness associated with each price distribution. The shaded areas in Figure 12.12(a) and (b) represent the probability of failing to achieve the break-even level of sales. If the previous example is used, now assuming normality, and that the standard deviation of the sales distribution $\sigma(X)$, is known, this area can be obtained from a table of the normal probability distribution function.[15,16] Assuming $\sigma(X) = 10,000$ and using Table I in the appendix,

$$P(x < x_b) = P\left(\frac{x - E(X)}{\sigma(X)} < \frac{x_b - E(X)}{\sigma(X)}\right)$$

$$= P\left(z < \frac{50,000 - 60,000}{10,000}\right) = P(z < -1) = 0.1587$$

The choice between alternatives might be based on the size of these probabilities where expectations were considered inadequate. It is not clear, however, just how much of a difference in these probabilities is needed to compensate for a larger expectation. It is a matter of judgment on which most managers would experience some difficulty.

12.2.4 Nonlinear Profit Functions

In the previous example profit is assumed to be a linear function of unit sales; that is, profit plotted against sales is a straight line. In this situation the profit resulting from expected (mean) sales could be used in decision making, since it is equal to the expected profit. Whenever the profit plotted against sales is a straight line, mean sales can be used in computing expected profit, or, equiva-

[14] The interested reader is referred to R. K. Jaedicke and A. Robichek, "Cost–Volume–Profit Analysis Under Conditions of Uncertainty," *The Accounting Review*, October 1964, pp. 917–926.

[15] An alternative and theoretically superior means of incorporating riskiness into the analyses is to use utility theory to determine the payoffs. The analysis so far assumes that the utility function is linear with money and that decisions can therefore be made using expected values. If true, the risk measures derived here are not relevant. Determining and using utilities is still, however, more of an art than a science.

[16] If $E(X)$ and $\sigma(X)$ are known or can be estimated and are finite, this probability can be estimated using Tchebychev's inequality for cases where the probability density function is not normal.

lently, the profits of the different possible sales weighted by the probability of their occurrence could be used.

The following example assumes that profit is not a linear function of sales.

Example

Assume that the probability mass function for sales is given in Table 12–1.

Table 12–1   Probability Mass Function for Sales

Sales (units)	P(sales)	Column 1 × Column 2 (units)
1,200	0.30	360
700	0.50	350
0	0.20	0
		Expected unit sales = 710

The expected profit is computed in Table 12–2. There is an expected loss of $1,000; thus, the decision being considered is not desirable. The mean sales of

Table 12–2   Expected Profit

Sales (units)	Profit*	P(sales)	Column 2 × Column 3
1,200	$20,000	0.30	$6,000
700	0	0.50	0
0	(35,000)	0.20	(7,000)
		Expected profit =	($1,000)

* The profit figure for different levels of sales are assumed to be the result of economic analysis and are not given by a linear function of sales.

710 units cannot be used to make the decision because profit is not a linear function of sales in this example. Also, the sales distribution is skewed.

12.2.5 Changes in Product Mix

Break-even analysis is at its best when there is a set price and only one product is being sold. The problems of price changes have been discussed and a reasonable solution suggested. The problem of product mix is more complex. Not only may the total output vary, but also the amount of each product sold may change from period to period. If the different products have different profit margins, the profit per dollar of sales will differ for each product and the break-even point becomes a function of the mix of sales.

One possibility is to draw break-even charts by product line. The costs that can be identified directly with the product line are plotted to obtain a break-even point of direct costs (direct in terms of the product line). On top of these costs, in order to obtain another break-even point, the costs that are assigned to the product as the result of indirect-cost allocations may be plotted.

If one break-even chart is desired for a company that produces several different products, the assumption of a normal product mix might be made and this assumption clearly indicated on the chart. In any event, the usefulness of a break-even chart for the company as a whole decreases as the number of products made by the firm increases.

12.2.6 Changes in Inventory

A break-even chart implicitly assumes that the fixed costs incurred by the firm are charged against the revenues of the period. This is consistent with a variable-costing procedure which charges only variable costs to product but is not consistent with normal cost-accounting procedures (except when there are no changes in inventory and cost variances are charged against the income of the period).

Assume that a firm is using a cost-accounting system with overhead absorption based on normal activity. If there is an increase in inventory during the period, then some of the fixed costs incurred during the period are applied to the goods in inventory and are not deducted from the revenues of the period. If the resulting income is compared to the budgeted income (the amount the firm expects to earn according to the break-even chart), the reported income is greater, all other things assumed to be equal. There are two solutions to this problem. One would be to use variable-costing procedures that inventory only variable costs in computing the income of the period. The second would be to adjust either the budgeted income of the break-even chart or the income which is a result of the cost-accounting system for such changes in the inventory.

12.2.7 Uniform Cost Control

Break-even analysis assumes that constant attention is given to cost control over the range of activity considered. This may not, in fact, be the case. For example, in times when business is expanding rapidly, management may tend to emphasize volume with a resulting decrease in attention to cost control. Poorer materials and workers with marginal skills may be used at the same time that prices and wages are rising. Labor turnover increases. Simultaneously, selling prices may increase together with a shift of the entire demand schedule to the right. It is also not uncommon for selling expenses per order to decline, although total selling costs may rise. An increase in the break-even point will occur if variable costs per unit increase more than the selling price.

12.2.8 Fixed Costs

The break-even sales volume is determined in part by the level of fixed costs. The question arises as to how these costs should be measured. Many possibilities exist, including historical cost allocations, adjusted historical costs, current costs, replacement costs, and so on. The choice may be viewed implicitly as an approximation of the opportunity costs of using the fixed factors of production. In the conventional analysis historical costs are used. Thus, a given percentage change in the fixed-cost factor changes the break-even level of activity by the same percentage. This is true if

$$bx_b = a \tag{12.5}$$

where b is the unit contribution margin per unit assumed to remain constant, x_b the break-even sales level, and a the fixed cost. A change of y per cent in fixed costs yields a new fixed-cost level of $(1 + y)(a)$. If equality is to be maintained in equation (12.5), then

$$(1 + y)bx_b = (1 + y)(a)$$

or

$$b[(1 + y)x_b] = (1 + y)(a)$$

This means that the break-even level of activity also increases by y per cent, given b constant.

12.3 Profit–Value Ratio

Break-even analysis is closely related to capital-budgeting decisions involving expansion of capacity or changes in the production function. For example, should a company produce aluminum if it is currently in the chemical industry, or, alternatively, should it expand its productive capacity for aluminum if it is currently in the aluminum industry but finds its productive capacity too small?

Before expanding the productive facilities for a present product, or adding a new product, management must decide as to the relative desirability of the different profit possibilities of the different product lines. These are normal capital-budgeting decisions, and the discounted cash-flow capital-budgeting procedure is a proper method of analysis for this type of problem.

Some companies, however, prefer to use a different technique in deciding which product is worthy of additional sales effort and productive capacity. The procedure makes use of the ratio of the variable margin to sales (the excess of revenues over variable costs, divided by sales). This ratio is called by various names, but the exact title is unimportant. The terminology PV ratio (PV standing for profit–value) is used here.

The PV ratio fails as a guide to the type of decision being considered for two reasons. First, it relies on the excess of revenues over variable costs for the present manufacturing process. The manufacturing process being considered for the additional productive capacity may make use of a different degree of automation and thus may have a different PV ratio. The PV ratio fails to take into consideration the capital outlays required by the additional productive capacity and the additional fixed costs that are added (for example, the additional accountants, quality-control personnel, and foremen who will be required for the operation and whose salaries may become fixed costs). Second, the PV ratio fails to consider the number of units sold, or which can be sold.

Inspection of the PV ratios of products can suggest profitable product lines that might be emphasized and unprofitable lines that should be reevaluated and possibly eliminated from the company's offerings. But until the analysis is broadened to take into consideration all incremental costs incurred and revenues generated as well as their likelihoods because of the expansion, a decision cannot be made as to whether or not to expand the line.

The PV ratio is a questionable device for decision making, but it does give an indication of the relative profitability of the different profit lines, if all other things are equal. For example, an automobile manufacturer may make 10 models of his low-priced car. Should a car be pushed by salesmen because of the high PV ratio? If the fixed costs connected with producing additional cars are truly fixed, the car with the highest PV ratio may be the most desirable car to sell. But even here the conclusion may not be correct, for the PV ratio generally uses average revenues and average-variable costs. The decision is one which should be made using marginal analysis.

The use of PV ratios defined in terms of marginal profits per marginal dollar of costs can lead to reasonable decisions. But even this ratio should not be used in decisions that are of a nonmarginal nature (such as one involving plant expansion). The PV ratio as generally computed is useful for forming impressions, not making decisions.

12.4　Summary

It is possible to arrive at a standard price of a product by computing the cost of product and adding a reasonable profit. The cost of product should include fixed-overhead elements determined using normal activity to compute the overhead rate. A standard price is a reasonable target. In the long run the price of the product must be close to the standard price to attract additional investment to the industry. With incomplete knowledge as to the characteristics of the demand curve (because of uncertainty as to the reaction of competitors and customers to price changes), it may be sensible for a firm to charge a standard price for its product. A "fair" profit resulting from the use of a standard price may be more attractive to management than the dangers accompanying a price reduction justified using the argument that the firm is attempting to find the sales volume which equates marginal cost and marginal revenue. Failure to predict correctly the firm's demand curve (average-revenue curve) can result in a situation where the additional costs are greater than the additional revenues. Why was the price reduced? Because it was thought that the increase in the number of units sold would be greater than actually resulted (the elasticity of demand was overestimated). Thus keeping the present price may be an economically valid decision if the element of uncertainty which accompanies any price change is taken into consideration. The theoretical solution to the problem of determining the optimal price requires a knowledge of the number of units likely to be sold at different prices and the marginal costs for different levels of output. The theoretical solution does not prevent the selling price from being greater than the marginal costs, but it does mean that the fixed costs do not enter into the decision.

Frequently prices are set with reference to other factors than those mentioned in this chapter. Long-run considerations may enter into the decision: for example, the effect a price may have on customer goodwill, or the possibility of competitors entering the market if the price is too high. These factors may lead to setting a price lower than the price which would maximize short-run profits.

Break-even analysis can be broadened from its conventional use to take a variety of factors into account. Methods are suggested in the chapter for dealing with uncertainty about demand, changes in product mix, and so on. Nevertheless, the method often makes substantive assumptions, such as constant-cost efficiency and no change in inventories, both of which limit its application.

The output and pricing decision may be made to maximize profits, but a firm does not know if it is going to make a profit. It may very well be that it will be minimizing a loss. To determine whether a profit will be made, it is necessary to compare the average cost and average revenue, or total cost and total revenue. But the pricing and output decisions may still be made without knowing whether or not a profit will be earned.

QUESTIONS AND PROBLEMS

12–1 In a situation where a corporation desires a 20% return on the plant assets it owns, would it be correct to start the budgeting process by computing the necessary profit and then conceiving decisions which will lead to the desired profit?

12–2 Assume that the cost-accounting system produces a cost per unit of $50. What questions may be raised relative to this cost measure?

12–3 In establishing an optimal price, should the firm take into consideration fixed costs of production?

12–4 The conventional break-even analysis shows total cost and total revenues as straight lines. What are the assumptions and limitations of using straight lines in this type of analysis?

12–5 Explain how the following curves are interrelated:
  a. Total revenue and marginal revenue.
  b. Total cost and marginal cost.

12–6 Discuss the following statement: "If you lower your price, the break-even point will increase."

12–7 Assuming that a firm is currently pricing its product optimally, should it change its price if it is able to shift its average variable-cost curve downward? Assume that the average-revenue curve slopes downward.

12–8 An automobile executive wants to expand the sales of his deluxe model, since its ratio of gross margin to sales is higher than that of any other model. This expansion would require additional plant facilities. Discuss.

12–9 A corporation has fixed costs of $250,000 and variable costs of $2 per unit. The company is attempting to choose the best of three possible prices. The prices, mean sales, and the standard deviations of sales are as follows:

Prices	$2.50	$3.00	$3.50
Mean sales (units)	600,000	280,000	100,000
Standard deviations	40,000	30,000	20,000

Required: Based on expected monetary values, what price should be charged? (Compute the effected profit for each of the three prices and choose the price with the highest expected profit.) What is the break-even volume and what choice of price is best using expectations?

12–10 (Ref. to problem 12–9).

Required:

For each possible price, what is the probability of operating at less than break-even?

12–11 The ABC Corporation is about to market a new product which has fixed costs of $100,000 and variable costs of $3 per unit at a level of production of 100,000 units. (There are changes in efficiency for different levels of sales.) The company is considering selling at a price of $4 per unit. The probability distribution of sales as estimated by the sales manager and the expected profit for the different levels of sales are:

Sales	P(sales)	Profit Given Sales
50,000	0.10	(25,000)
100,000	0.50	0
150,000	0.30	40,000
200,000	0.10	75,000

Required:
a. Compute the mean sales.
b. Compute the expected profit.

12–12 The demand for a product is said to have an elasticity greater than 1 if a decrease in the sales price of the product will result in an increase in total revenues. The Roger Corporation has hired an economist who has come up with the following schedule, which shows that the elasticity of the product being sold by the Roger Corporation is greater than 1 (the demand is relatively elastic). The capacity of the plant is 150,000 units per year.

	Present Policy	If Price Is Reduced 10%	If Price Is Reduced 20%
Price per unit	$ 1.00	$ 0.90	$ 0.80
Unit sales (per year)	100,000.00	120,000.00	150,000.00
Fixed manufacturing costs (per year)	15,000.00	15,000.00	15,000.00
Variable manufacturing costs	0.50 (per unit)		

Required:
a. Compute the total revenues following the three alternatives.
b. What are the break-even points?
c. What price should the firm charge?

12–13 A corporation has fixed costs of $250,000 and variable costs of $2 per unit. The company is attempting to choose the best of three possible prices. The prices, mean sales, and the standard deviations of sales are as follows:

Price	$ 2.50	$ 3.00	$ 3.50
Mean sales (units)	500,000.00	280,000.00	200,000.00
Standard deviation	20,000.00	30,000.00	40,000.00

Required: Based on the expected monetary values, what price should be charged? Compute the break-even points for the three prices.

12–14 The Akron Company has two plants producing the same product and wants to know how the production decision should be made if it wishes to continue to split production between the two plants. Assume that the product of the plants is sold in a perfectly competitive market.

An economist has been hired as a consultant. He suggests that each plant should produce so that their marginal cost equals marginal revenue (which in turn is equal to the price of the product).

Required: Comment on the recommendation.

12–15 The Akron Company has two plants producing the same product on a government order for 1,000 units. It wants to know how to split production between the two plants.

Required: How should the decision to split the production be decided?

12–16 In August 1965 Ford of England slowed its production of automobiles and shifted to a 4-day work week. It was suggested that the company increase its export of cars. The company stated that a good export position required a strong home market, since large production reduces unit costs. If the sales in the home market slow down, unit costs rise, putting pressure on export sales prices (for a more complete report, see *The New York Times* of August 24, 1965).

Required: Comment on the company's point of view.

12–17 The accompanying diagram combines a traditional break-even analysis with a probability density function for demand.

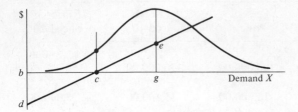

a. Give an expression using the letters in the graph for the unit contribution margin.
b. Give the break-even output.
c. Should this firm produce? Why or why not?
d. Assuming that the density function is normal, give an expression for the expected profit, that is, the total expectation, considering both the possible losses and gains.

12–18 The accompanying graph illustrates several average-cost curves and a revenue curve under the condition of perfect competition.

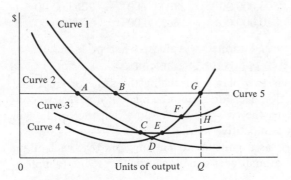

a. Name the five curves.
b. Indicate the break-even point.
c. Indicate the maximum-profit point.
d. What area represents the total profits of the firm when it is producing at its optimal output level?

12–19 "Costs are a function of output increasing when output increases and decreasing when output decreases." Comment.

12–20 The American Dynamics Company experienced an increase in its break-even volume as sales expanded sharply over the period 1962–1968. This occurred despite the fact that their prices were increased enough to cover the direct increases in unit variable cost resulting from increases in direct material prices wage rates, and related items. Can you suggest a reason for this occurrence?

12–21 One way to estimate fixed-cost levels is to fit a regression equation to the cost data and use the intercept term (the constant in the equation) as a measure of fixed costs. Is this a good procedure?

12–22 The Brake-Even Company

The Brake-Even Company manufactures two general types of brakes, automobile and truck brakes. The management of the Brake-Even Company is concerned because of the fluctuations in income which have been experienced in the past few years. Some members of management have also suggested that one of the product lines should be dropped.

The company has made an analysis of its sales and income by product line (each of the products is organized as a department for manufacturing and sales purposes).

Year	Quarter	Sales of Brakes		Income Before Taxes	
		Auto	Trucks	Auto	Trucks
1976	1	$2,000	$ 500	$200	$(450)
	2	2,400	·600	440	(440)
	3	3,200	1,200	920	(380)
	4	1,500	2,000	(100)	(300)
1977	1	2,100	1,500	260	(350)

All dollar figures in thousands.

An analysis of the expenses associated with the sales of the product disclosed the following information:

	Auto Dept.	Truck Dept.
Variable costs per dollar of sales, 1976:		
Material	$ 0.10	$ 0.25
Direct labor	0.21	0.50
Variable overhead	0.05	0.10
Variable selling expenses	0.04·	0.05
	$ .0.40	$ 0.90
Fixed costs for 1976:		
Directly Associated with the department:		
Avoidable (foremen's salaries, etc.)	$1,600,000	$ 80,000
Unavoidable (depreciation of special equipment, etc.)	400,000	320,000
Allocated from other departments (including administrative costs)	2,000,000	1,600,000
	$4,000,000	$2,000,000

The unavoidable costs cannot be avoided by sale of the equipment, since the removal costs would approximately equal the sales price. General overhead would not be reduced by elimination of any one of the product lines.

For internal reporting purposes, the company charges all fixed costs to the period in which they are incurred, and only variable costs are considered a cost of product.

Required:
a. Prepare an analysis explaining the fluctuations in income.
b. Make recommendations as to the desirability of continuing the sale and production of any of the products.
c. Prepare a break-even chart for the auto department. Explain the difficulties connected with preparing one break-even chart for the company as a whole.
d. Assume that during the first quarter of 1977 the auto brakes were sold at a price of $20 per unit. If the price were dropped to $15 per unit, 200,000 would be sold (according to the company's economist). Is the reduction in price desirable? Assume that the variable costs are $8 per unit.

12–23 The New York Company manufactures folding chairs for sale to clubs, commercial establishments, and individual consumers. The sales for the past several years have been cut back to 40% of capacity. At this level, the company produces 60,000 chairs, which it sells at an average price per chair of $2.10. Total costs at the 40% level are made up of $54,000 for fixed items and $90,000 for variable items. Variable costs are known to change exactly in proportion to output.

Required:
a. If the average selling price remains the same as it has been in the past, at what level of activity will the company break even?
b. What would the company's profit be if it could operate (and sell) at capacity?
c. Assume that the company computes the fixed cost per unit, using capacity level of operations. What is the average total cost per unit?
d. Assume that a new customer offers the New York Company $1.70 per unit for its product. Provided that there are no effects on sales to old customers (and no legal complications), should the New York Company accept an order for 40,000 chairs? Briefly justify your answer.

12–24 A profit-volume or P/V graph is sometimes used in place of or along with the break-even chart. An example of such a graph is given here.

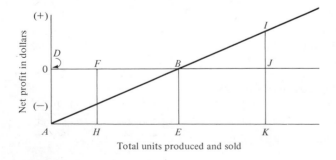

Required: Answer the associated questions and be precise.
a. What does *JK* represent?
b. What is represented by the point *E*?
c. What is represented by *IJ*? (be precise)
d. What is represented by *GH*?
e. What does *IK* ÷ *AK* represent?
f. What does *IJ* ÷ *DJ* represent?
g. If variable cost per unit decreases (other factors constant) what would happen to the ratio *IJ/DJ*? Why?
h. If fixed costs were to increase but sales prices were also increased to the extent necessary to retain the prior breakeven, what would be the effect on profits at a level of output (sales) *K* and how would this appear on the graph?
i. Order the following in terms of their *absolute* effect on the slope of the line *AB*. (Give a 1 to the greatest change and a 3 to the smallest change.)
  1. Variable cost per unit declines 10 per cent
  2. Selling price per unit declines 10 per cent
  3. Fixed costs decline 10 per cent
j. What, in your opinion, is *the* most significant limitation to traditional break-even analysis and why do you think so?

12–25 The following diagram combines a traditional break-even analysis with uncertainty concerning demand. The probability distribution of sales is skewed to the right. The letter e represents median sales (a figure as likely to be exceeded as not reached).

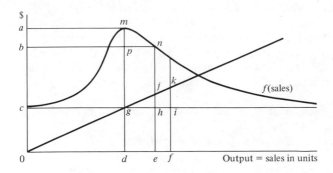

Using the letters to represent *points* on the graph,
a. Can you give an expression for the unit price? If so, do so.
b. Give an expression for the unit contribution margin in this graph.
c. What is the break-even output level?
d. Indicate, in some way, the probability that the firm will fail to make a profit. (Define any new symbols used.)
e. The *expected* (profit, loss) is best approximated by what line segment?

12–26 Consider the following breakeven chart where cost is given on the left ordinate and the probability density function (p.d.f.) of sales on the right.

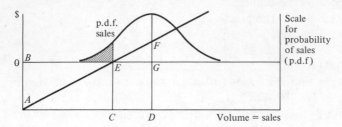

a. What does the slope of the line AE represent?

b. What is the output volume (also assumed sales) at the breakeven?

c. What does the darkened area represent?

d. Give an expression for expected profit that is independent of the form of the p.d.f. (assume D equals expected sales).

SUPPLEMENTARY READING

CHARNES, A., W. W. COOPER, and Y. IJIRI, "Breakeven Budgeting and Programming to Goals," *Journal of Accounting Research*, Spring 1963, pp. 16–43.

COLANTONI, S., R. MANES, and A. WHINSTON, "Programming, Profit Rates and Pricing Decisions," *The Accounting Review*, July 1969, pp. 467–481.

DEARDEN, J., *Cost and Budget Analysis*, Englewood Cliffs, N.J.: Prentice-Hall, Inc., 1962.

IJIRI, Y. and H. ITAMI, "Cost–Volume Relationship and Demand Information," *The Accounting Review*, October 1973, pp. 724–737.

JAEDICKE, R. K., and A. ROBICHEK, "Cost–Volume–Profit Analysis Under Conditions of Uncertainty," *The Accounting Review*, October 1964, pp. 917–926.

JOHNSON, G. and S. SIMIK, "The Use of Probability Inequalities in Multiproduct C-V-P Analysis Under Uncertainty," *Journal of Accounting Research*, Spring 1974, pp. 67–79.

MANES, R., "A New Dimension to Breakeven Analysis," *Journal of Accounting Research*, Spring 1966, pp. 87–100.

NATIONAL ASSOCIATION OF ACCOUNTANTS, *Research Reports Nos. 16, 17, 18, 23, and 37.*

SAMUELS, J. M., "Opportunity Costing: An Application of Mathematical Programming," *Journal of Accounting Research*, Autumn 1965, pp. 182–191.

VICKERS, D., "On the Economics of Break-even," *The Accounting Review*, July 1960, pp. 405–412.

Part III

Capital Budgeting
and
Related Topics

Chapter 13

Introduction to
Capital Budgeting

Capital budgeting is the process of deciding whether or not to commit resources to projects whose costs and benefits are spread over several time periods. The problem is to relate the benefits to the costs in a reasonable manner which is consistent with an objective of maximizing the stockholders' well being.

There are many possible methods of relating a stream of future earnings or cost savings to the cost of obtaining them. Among these, four methods (cash payback, return on investment, rate of return, and present value) are defined and evaluated in this chapter. The focus of our attention is on taking the time value of money into consideration. In this chapter we shall not be concerned with the method by which the investment is financed.

13.1   Cash Payback

The cash payback of an investment is the period of time required to recover the initial investment. Thus, if an investment of $10,000 yields $5,000 in net cash proceeds in each of the first two years of use, it would have a cash payback of two years. Available investments may be accepted or rejected according to the length of their payback periods. An investment with a payback of two years might be considered desirable while an investment with a payback of three years is rejected. Some firms incorrectly accept or reject investments on the basis of duration of the payback period alone; in fact, for many years payback has been the most common method of capital budgeting.

281

13.2   Return on Investment

The return on investment is equal to the forecasted average income divided by the average investment. This computation is based on the entire life of the investment. Rather than the average investment (that is, a figure based on the depreciated plant assets) some companies use the initial investment (undepreciated plant assets). Although the choice is not critical in performance evaluation if all comparisons use the same procedure, it may be important in particular investment decisions.

13.3   Rate of Return or Yield

The rate of return is that rate of discount (interest) that equates the present value of the cash flows to zero. This rate is found by trial and error using different rates of interest. That rate of interest that equates the algebraic sum of the present value of all cash outlays and the present value of all cash proceeds to zero is the *rate of return* or the yield of the investment.

It is desirable to understand the implications of the term rate of return of an investment. If an investment requires an outlay of \$173.55 and yields a net cash flow of \$210 at the end of two years, the rate of interest that equates the present value of \$210 and an immediate outlay of \$173.55 is the investment rate of return. Equivalently, the following equation can be solved for r:

$$210(1 + r)^{-2} - 173.55 = 0$$

$$(1 + r)^{-2} = 0.8264$$

Using Table III at the back of the book, r is found to be 0.10. The rate of return is 0.10, since, using this rate, the algebraic sum of the present value of the cash outlays and the present value of the cash proceeds is zero.

Another interpretation of the rate of return is that it is the rate of growth of the investment. Thus, the investment may be imagined to grow as follows:

Original investment	\$173.55
0.10 return on \$173.55	17.36
Investment plus interest	\$190.91
0.10 return on \$190.91	19.09
Final value of investment	\$210.00

A third interpretation of rate of return is that it is the highest rate of interest that an investor could pay for borrowed funds to finance the investment being considered and be no worse off than if he did not undertake the investment. This interpretation assumes a conventional investment, that is, an immediate outlay followed by periods of cash flows into the firm. It also assumes that the funds generated by the investment are used to repay the debt plus interest.

If the investment results in several unequal cash proceeds, the analysis is the same, although the computations become more complex. Assume, for example, that an investment requires an immediate outlay of $2,810.65 and has an expected life of two years. The forecasted net cash savings or proceeds for the first year are $1,000 and for the second year, $2,000. What is the rate of return and what are the implications of the rate of return? The solution for the rate of return requires a trial-and-error approach. (If an interest rate results in the present values being positive, a higher rate of discount is used.) After several tries the situation shown in Exhibit 13–1 is obtained. (Note that the sum of the present values is zero.)

Exhibit 13–1   Rate of Return Calculations

Year	Proceeds (outlays)	Present Value of a Dollar Discounted at 4%	Present Value of Cash Proceeds
0	($2810.65)	$1.00000	($2,810.65)
1	1000.00	0.961538	961.54
2	2000.00	0.924556	1,849.11
			0

At a rate of discount of 4%, the present value of the cash proceeds is equated to the cost of the asset, $2,810.65. Thus the rate of return is 4%. But what does this mean? The asset that cost $2,810.65 earns 4% the first year, and then $1,000 is withdrawn; the remaining investment again earns 4% and then $2,000 is withdrawn; at this time there will be zero investment left. The asset earned a 4% return during its life. The calculations in Exhibit 13–2 show that the investment generates sufficient cash flows to pay for the funds used to make it if those funds cost 4%.

If the income of the period and the investment at the beginning of the period are properly measured, then the return on investment of each period of its life will equal the rate of return of the investment. This is 4% in the example.

The rate of return of an investment is frequently used to determine the desirability of an investment. Either the investments are ranked in order of desirability according to their rates of return (the ranking may be spurious), or all conventional independent investments with a return greater than some selected hurdle rate are accepted and all other investments are rejected.

Exhibit 13–2   Rate-of-Return Computations

Original investment funds required: loan	$2,810.65
	× 0.04
Interest first year	$ 112.43
Original debt	+2,810.65
Debt owed at time 1	$2,923.08
Cash proceeds withdrawn to pay debt	−1,000.00
Debt beginning of second year	$1,923.08
Interest second year	× 0.04
	76.92
Debt beginning second year	+1,923.08
Debt owed at time 2	$2,000.00
Cash proceeds withdrawn to pay debt	−2,000.00
Debt remaining	$ 0.00

There is a relation between the rate-of-return and payback approaches. This relationship is illustrated by transforming the mathematical equation for the present value of a level annuity. The present value of an annuity of A dollars for n periods at a rate r per period is

$$P = A \frac{1 - (1 + r)^{-n}}{r} \tag{13.1}$$

Dividing by P and multiplying both sides by r, equation (13.1) can be written as

$$r = \frac{A}{P} - \frac{A}{P} \frac{1}{(1 + r)^n} \tag{13.2}$$

The first term on the right-hand side of equation (13.2) is the reciprocal of the payback period, since P is the initial investment. The second term is the payback-period reciprocal multiplied by the present-value factor for n periods. The larger the effective rate and the life of the investment, the closer the right-hand side approximates the reciprocal of the payback period. Note that the payback reciprocal is slightly larger than the rate of return for a project with a finite life.

For a project with constant benefits and an unlimited life, the rate of return would be equal to the payback-period reciprocal. In practice, this payback reciprocal is a reasonable estimate of the rate of return when the project life is at least twice as long as the payback period and each year's benefits are the same. Nevertheless, requiring short payback periods is equivalent to requiring a higher rate of return, and this in turn tends to cause the rejection of otherwise acceptable projects.

13.4 Present Value

Under the present-value method, cash outlays and cash proceeds are both discounted back to the present period using an appropriate discount rate. If the present value of the cash flows is positive, the investment is considered eligible for further consideration. If the present value of the cash flows is negative, the investment should not normally be undertaken. (A positive present value does not mean that the project will be undertaken, however, since better alternatives may exist, or the risk of the investment may be considered to be too great.)

What is the significance of discounting cash flows back to the present? Assume that a firm with a cost of money of 10% is considering an investmen which promises to return $11,000 at the end of one year in exchange for an immediate cash outlay of $10,000. The present value of $11,000 discounted back one period at a 10% rate of interest is $10,000. The present value of the outlays is also $10,000; thus, the net present value of the investment is zero. This means that the firm could be just as well off not borrowing from investors and not investing in the project. The cost of borrowing the $10,000 is $1,000, which is equal to the income the investment will earn ($11,000 less $10,000). On the other hand, the firm will be no worse off investing in the project. The investment yields a return equal to the required return and no more. In fact, the rate of return of the investment is 10%, which is equal to the required return.

Now change the illustration by assuming an investment which promises to earn proceeds of $20,000 at the end of period 1 and costs $10,000. The present value of the proceeds is $18,182; the outlay is $10,000. The net present value of the investment is $8,132. This $8,132 is the amount that the firm could afford to pay in excess of the cost of the investment (while paying the cost of borrowing) and still be no worse off than if it had not made the investment. For example, assume that it paid $18,182 for the investment and the cost of borrowing is 10% of $18,182, or $1,818. Thus, the total outlays would be $20,000 ($18,182 plus $1,818) an amount equal to the expected cash proceeds. The outlay of $18,182 today is equivalent to proceeds of $20,000 one year hence. The computations take into consideration interest of 10% either by discounting the $20,000 back to the present or by accumulating the $18,182 to the end of the year.

The net present value of the investment is the estimated profit (unrealized, thus not recognized for accounting purposes) at the time of purchase. It is also the amount the firm could pay in excess of the purchase price for the investment but because of fortuitous circumstances does not have to pay.

In the last example we illustrated the present-value with an investment that had an immediate outlay of $10,000 and earned cash proceeds after one year of $20,000. The net present value using a 10% discount rate was $18,182. It is helpful to plot the net present value of the investment over a wide range of discount rates. The resulting graph is called a present-value profile. An example is shown in Figure 13.1.

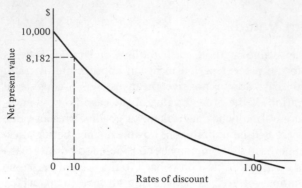

Figure 13.1   Present value profile: $10,000 Investment.

The rate of return of the investment is the intersection of the graph with the
x axis. In this example the rate of return is 100%.

13.5   Evaluating the Methods of Decision Making

The example described in Exhibit 13–3 is used to test the four methods
that have been proposed. There are three investment proposals, and the investment decisions suggested by the different procedures are compared. The relationships to other investments are ignored except as they are incorporated in the
discount rate.

Exhibit 13–3   Cash Flows for Investments A, B, and C

Investment Proposed	Initial Outlay (period 0)	Cash Proceeds (period 1)	Cash Proceeds (period 2)
A	$10,000	$10,000	0
B	10,000	1,000	$11,000
C	10,000	5,762	5,762

The cash-payback method would identify investment A as being the most
desirable, since it has a payback time of one period. The weakness of this position is indicated by the fact that investment A returns its orginal investment, but
that is all. The cash-payback method fails as an all-purpose device for making
investment decisions, since, among other factors, it does not take into consideration the life of the investment after the payback period. Another weakness,

not illustrated by the above example, is that the payback method fails to take into consideration the timing of proceeds during the payback period. Thus, while the payback periods of investments B and C are approximately the same, the cash inflows for investment C are more desirable from a timing point of view because they come earlier than those of investment B.

The return on investment for A is zero; thus A is eliminated from consideration if the return-on-investment method is used. The return-on-investment computations for the other two investments are given in Exhibit 13–4.

Exhibit 13–4   Return on Investment Calculations for Investments B and C

Investment	Outlays	Total Proceeds	Net Income	Average Income	Average Investment	Return on Investment (%)
B	$10,000	$12,000	$2,000	$1,000	$5,000	20.0
C	10,000	11,524	1,524	762	5,000	15.2

The return-on-investment computations shown in Exhibit 13–4 indicate that investment B is more desirable than investment C. But the return-on-investment procedure also fails to take into consideration the timing of the proceeds. A dollar of proceeds earned in period 2 is given the same weight as a dollar earned in period 1. This failure to take the timing of the proceeds into consideration is one reason the return-on-investment approach should not be used as a general method of making investment decisions.

When the rates of return of the two investments B and C are computed, both are found to be 10%. The rate of return of investment A is zero. Before deciding that investments B and C are equally desirable, consider the present value of the two investments, using several interest rates (different assumed costs). At a 10% rate of interest the present values of both investments are zero; thus, the investments are equally desirable (this occurs because the rate of return is equal to the rate of discount being used). This is the same result as was obtained using the rate-of-return procedure. With a discount rate of less than 10%, investment B has a higher present value; but both investments have positive present values. At a rate of interest higher than 10%, investment C has a higher present value than B, but both investments have negative present values. While the rate-of-return and the present-value methods may give different rankings to investments, they lead to the same accept or reject decisions.

Ignoring risk considerations, if the rate of return of a normal investment is greater than the required return, the investment is accepted; if the rate of return is less than the required return, it is rejected. The same accept or reject decisions are obtained when the required return is used as a rate of discount and the present values of the investments are compared to $0 as are obtained by computing the rate of return on each investment and comparing that rate to the required rate.

Are the rankings obtained using the present-value or the rate-of-return method the "correct" rankings? Unfortuately, a ranking of investments frequently appears to be correct but is actually only a function of the method used and the assumptions made. Fortunately, for most investment decisions a firm does not have to rank investments, but only has to choose those investments which have a yield greater than the firm's cost of money. If the investments are mutually exclusive, however, it may be necessary to choose that investment which is the best of a group. This can be done, since the failure to undertake a mutually exclusive investment does not invalidate the choice of the discount rate.[1]

13.5.1 Mutually Exclusive Investments: Timing and Scale Problems

Mutually exclusive investments are investments which compete with each other; that is, of several investments being considered; only one can be undertaken because of their nature.

A firm may need a tanker to transport oil but may not yet have determined the size or number of tankers which is best. Tankers of all sizes and shapes are in this case mutually exclusive investments. Another illustration of mutually exclusive investments would be brick and wood as the basic materials for building a plant. The initial costs and maintenance costs through the years would be different.

Assume that investments B and C are mutually exclusive investments and that both have 10% rates of return and are otherwise equally desirable. Which is the more desirable, assuming a cost of money of 6%? The present values of the cash flows of the two investments are given in Exhibit 13–5, which illustrates the importance of the timing of the cash flows. The present value of the cash flows for investment B is greater than the present value of the cash flows for investment C.

The rate-of-return method may not give correct rankings of mutually exclusive investments, because the method fails to consider effectively the timing of the cash flows (it assumes that funds can be reinvested to earn the rate of return). Mutually exclusive investments with unequal lives provide an example. The rate-of-return method implicitly assumes, when the two investments are compared, that the proceeds for the investment with the shorter life can be reinvested at the same rate of interest as the rate of return. The present-value method assumes that the proceeds are invested at the cost of money. The later assumption is usually more reasonable. In any case, the expected situation should be considered explicitly.[2]

---

[1] If an independent investment with a rate of return greater than the required return is rejected, the use of that required return to compute the present values is invalid.

[2] Two assumptions that may be important in the present example are those of equal initial outlays and equal lives for investments B and C.

Exhibit 13–5 Comparison of Investments B and C at 6%: The Timing Problem

Investment B

Period	Cash Flows	Present-Value Factor	Present Value
0	($10,000)	$1.0000	($10,000)
1	1,000	0.9434	943
2	11,000	0.8900	9,790
			$ 733

Investment C

Period	Cash Flows	Present-Value Factor	Present Value
0	($10,000)	$1.000	($10,000)
1	5,762	0.9434	5,436
2	5,762	0.8900	5,128
			$ 564

Considering only the incremental cash flows gives the benefit to be gained by the firm from selecting one investment over another (see Exhibit 13–6).

Exhibit 13–6 Incremental Cash Flows and Their Present Values: Investments B and C

Period	Cash Flows B	Cash Flows C	Cash Flows B − C	Present-Value Factor	Present Value B − C
0	($10,000)	($10,000)	0	1.0000	0
1	1,000	5,762	($4,762)	0.9434	−4,493
2	11,000	5,762	5,238	0.8900	4,662
					$ 169

Figure 13–2, which gives the present-value profiles of investments B and C, shows that if the appropriate rate of discount is 6%, then investment alternative B is preferred to C.

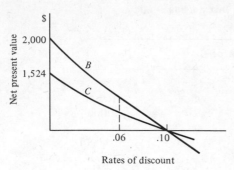

Figure 13.2   Present value profile: Investments B and C.

Exhibit 13–7 illustrates a second problem involving mutually exclusive invest-ments: the scale problem. The rate-of-return criterion indicates that investment X is superior to investment Y. However, imagine that the differences between the cash flows of investments X and Y are the cash flows of an investment Z. Thus investment Z would have outlays of $20,000 in period 0 and proceeds of $23,000 in period 1, a rate of return of 15%. Assuming a cost of money of 6%, invest-ment Z is desirable. The fact that the cash flows of investment Z are actually the difference between the cash flows of investments X and Y would indicate that investment Y is more desirable than X, since by investing an amount $20,000 greater than investment X, a return of 15% may be earned. The rate-of-return method may be used here to evaluate the incremental benefits, but it is awkward to employ if there are many investment possibilities (an elimination tournament is required). Thus the present-value method is to be preferred. This example illustrates the scale problem (that is, the original investments are of different sizes and it is necessary to consider this difference).

Exhibit 13–7   Rate of Return for Investments X and Y: The Scale
              Problem

Investment	Initial Investment Period 0	Cash Proceeds Period 1	Rate of Return (%)
X	($10,000)	$12,000	20.0
Y	(30,000)	35,000	16.7

An additional difficulty with using the rate-of-return method is that some investments may have more than one rate of return. This occurs if, after an outlay, there are periods of positive cash flows followed by periods of negative cash flows (for example, when there are removal costs at the end of the invest-ment's life). This result can also occur with mutually exclusive investments. When an investment has more than one rate of return, it is easier to reach a decision using the present value method than with the rate-of-return method.

13.5.2 Comparability of Life

The present-value method gives the correct decision in judging mutually exclusives investments with unequal lives, but it may be necessary to consider what happens after the asset with the shorter life is discarded. Assume a simple example where there are two mutually exclusive investments C and D with the characteristics given in Exhibit 13–8. Investments C and D may be different types of equipment, with investment C having a life of one year and investment D a life of three years.

Exhibit 13–8   Cash Flows for Investments C and D

	Initial Investment	Cash Proceeds		
Investment	Period 0	Period 1	Period 2	Period 3
C	($10,000)	$12,000		
D	(10,000)	5,000	$5,000	$5,000

With a cost of money of 10%, the present values of the cash flows of investments C and D are given in Exhibit 13–9. Investment D would seem to be the more desirable investment; however, this analysis is incomplete since it fails to take into consideration what will be done at the end of the first year if investment C were selected. The present-value method assumes reinvestment at 10%. But suppose that after one year, equipment of type C (or similar equipment) will again be purchased. Where it is likely that investment C will be repeated at the beginning of periods 2 and 3, the cash flows in Exhibit 13–10 would occur for investment C. The present value of the cash flows as now presented is $2,488 for investment C; thus, C is more desirable than D. Where the mutually exclusive investments have unequal lives, the reinvestment, possibly in similar equipment, must be taken into consideration.

**Exhibit 13–9   Present Value of Cash Flows
for Investments C and D**

Investment	Present Value of Cash Flows
C	$ 909
D	2,434

Exhibit 13–10   Cash Flows for Investment C Modified

Investment	Initial Investment Period 0	Cash Flows		
		Period 1	Period 2	Period 3
C	($10,000)	($10,000)	($10,000)	
		12,000	12,000	$12,000

Sometimes it may be difficult to find a common comparison time for two or more mutually exclusive investments. In some situations the lowest common multiple of the lives of the investments results in a length of time longer than the life of the longest lived of the alternatives. For example, consider the relative merits of two types of equipment, one of which has a life of three years and the other of eight years. In a situation of this nature, the equivalent return per year, the returns for perpetuity, or the present value of the investment for 24 years could be computed. These three methods of computation all lead to the same decision. Alternatively, an attempt to forecast investment alternatives may be both feasible and appropriate.

Example
Assume that two pieces of equipment have the characteristics given in Exhibit 13–11 and that reinvestment in similar equipment may be assumed. An interest rate of 10% is used.

Exhibit 13–11   Cash Flows for Investments E and F

Investment	Expected Life (years)	Initial Cost	Net Cash Proceeds per Year
E	3	$10,000	5,000
F	8	30,000	6,500

Exhibit 13–12 shows the present-value calculations for these two investments. The net-present-value results cannot be used directly to compare the two investments, since their lives are not identical. This problem can be solved by taking the lowest common multiple of eight and three, 24 years, and computing the expected value assuming reinvestment. An alternative is to compute the present value of each alternative and then find an equivalent yearly annuity. Since cash inflows are often difficult to associate with a given investment, this second approach is often used with cost data to find the equivalent cost per year of doing a given task. The investment with the smaller equivalent cost is preferred.

Exhibit 13–12 Present Value of Cash Flows for Investments E and F

Invest-ment	Expected Life (years)	Initial Cost	Net Cash Proceeds per Year	Present-Value Factor	Present Value of Proceeds	Net Present Value
E	3	($10,000)	$5,000	2.4869	$12,435	$2,435
F	8	(30,000)	6,500	5.3349	34,677	4,677

The task is to find the level annuity, R, which when discounted at 10% equals $10,000 in present value for investment E. If $B(n, r)$ is the appropriate discount factor for a level annuity of n years at rate $r = 0.10$, then

$$B(n, r)R = \$10,000$$

From Table IV, $B(3, 0.10) = 2.4869$. Hence

$$2.4869R = \$10,000$$

and

$$R = \$\ 4,021$$

This is the three-year annual equivalent of $10,000 at 10%. It is the equivalent yearly payment an investor would be willing to substitute for an immediate outlay of $10,000. For investment F the comparable figure is $5,623.

$$B(8, 0.10)R = 5.3349R = \$30,000$$

and

$$R = \$5,623$$

The two investments can now be compared. See Exhibit 13–13. Investment E is preferred to F.

Exhibit 13–13 Comparison of Investments E and F

Investment	Annual Benefits	Annual Equivalent Costs	Annual Net Benefits
E	$5,000	$4,021	$979
F	6,500	5,623	877

It was assumed in this example that continued reinvestment in the selected alternative would ensue. We might be interested in comparing these two investments in perpetuity, then. To find the value for perpetuity, multiply the equivalent value per year by the present value of a perpetuity. The general formula for the present value of a perpetuity of $1 a period is:

$$\text{present value of a perpetuity} = \frac{1}{r}$$

where r is the appropriate rate of interest.

Since r is equal to 0.10, the factor in this example is 10. The present value of using E forever is 10(979), or $9,790. The present value of using F is 10(877), or $8,770. Since the equivalent yearly annuity of both alternatives is being multiplied by a constant factor of 10, the relative merits of the alternatives are not changed.

Investment E remains more desirable than F. Many factors have been omitted from this analysis, however, such as flexibility and the likelihood of the future returns. More important, we have also assumed that the equipment will be replaced in kind. If other assumptions are more reasonable, they should be evaluated.

The cash-payback method can be rejected because neither does it take the entire life of the investment into consideration, nor does it consider the time pattern of the cash flows. The return-on-investment method fails to consider the timing of the proceeds, and thus has severe limitations. The rate-of-return method gives acceptable reject or accept decisions for conventional independent investments except in the special situation where there are several rates of return for an investment. However, the rate-of-return procedure may incorrectly rank mutually exclusive investments, for two reasons. In the comparison of two mutually exclusive investments it implicitly assumes reinvestment of proceeds at the same rate of return, and it fails to take into consideration the size of the investment being considered. For these reasons the present-value method should be used as the prime method for making investment decisions.

13.6   Cash Flows for Investment Decisions

One of the important details of capital budgeting that is frequently neglected in discussions of the subject is the computation of the cash flows used in the analysis. The generally used term *cash flows* is not adequately defined. This is a serious omission, since cash flows are the basis of the computations. The term is used in this book to describe a procedure that measures the change in cash in each period. Alternatively, the capital-budgeting analysis could be based on the change in working capital or the change in funds: The two methods may be equated to each other if receivables and payables of the future are recorded today at their present value. Properly used, there is no material difference between the two procedures.

13.6.1 Cash-Flow Estimation

The cash-flow procedure assumes that the moment of cash disbursement or cash receipt is the moment at which the change in financial position associated with the investment should be measured. It may be argued that only when the cash is disbursed has the firm suffered any disutility, since only then are real resources, which could be engaged in other earning activities, restricted to this project. For example, the cash may be invested in government securities and interest may thus be earned; but the disbursement of cash either requires that the securities be sold, thus the interest otherwise earned is lost, or that new interest-bearing debt be issued, in which case the costs connected with having debt outstanding are incurred. In like manner, it is argued that until the sales result in cash, which the firm can then put to other uses, there is no real benefit from the transaction. Thus, the making of the legal sale and the creation of an account receivable is not important for purposes of analyzing the investment decision; what is important is the receipt or disbursement of cash.

For each period in the life of the investment it is necessary to compute the change in cash resulting from the investment being considered. Exhibit 13–14 indicates how this might be accomplished for one such period.

Exhibit 13–14   Computation of Forecasted Cash Flow for 1980 for Investment G

Sales (as recorded by accountant) (1)		$100,000	
Less: Manufacturing costs of goods sold (2)	$40,000		
Expenses of selling and administration (3)	20,000	60,000	
Net revenue after expenses			$40,000
Less: Investment outlays (4)	...		
Decrease in revenues from other products (4)	...		
Opportunity costs of factors of production (4)	$ 5,000		
Income tax caused by investment	10,000	$ 15,000	
Less: Changes in working capital and noncash expenses (5)			
Decrease in current liabilities (change the sign for an increase)	$ 4,000		
Increase in current assets (including non-cash expenses)	8,000	12,000	
Miscellaneous uses of cash			27,000
After-tax cash flow			$13,000

Explanation of entries

1. Sales on the accrual basis were $100,000.
2. This is the expense figure taken from the income statement. Usually it is not equal to the out-of-pocket cost of production because of changes in the level of inventories and the inclusion of costs not using cash. These items are picked up as adjustments. (See item 5.)
3. Selling and administration expenses for which a current liability was incurred (or cash disbursed) and which are due to investment G.
4. Investment-type outlays, decreases in revenues from other products (increases due to product complementarily would be positive), and

opportunity cost (including the use of executive time) associated with this venture are deducted as cash outlays, even though there may not be a cash disbursement, since they represent inflows lost elsewhere. The increase in income taxes associated with the investment is calculated after the deduction for any depreciation related to the investment under consideration.

5. The adjustment for the changes in working capital is necessary in order to determine the amount of cash needed to finance these items. The $4,000 is the result of a decrease in current liabilities (using cash). The $8,000 is an increase in current assets (for example, a $33,000 increase in accounts receivable and a $10,000 decrease in inventories) less the amount of fixed costs ($15,000) converted into inventory and cost of goods sold for which no cash disbursement is made, such as depreciation.[3] Note that $33,000 − $10,000 − $15,000 = $8,000.

An increase in current liabilities would be subtracted from the deductions; that is, it would be added to the cash-flow stream. There would be some "expenses" that would not actually utilize cash, since they would be financed out of current liabilities. Thus, the increase in current liabilities is subtracted.

A side computation would be necessary to compute the income taxes of the period associated with this investment. There may be differences between the cash-flow computations and the computations for tax purposes. The person making these computations should be familiar with the tax code or have access to expert tax advice. The accountant is a central figure in all the calculations suggested in this subsection.

13.6.2 Fund Flow Versus Cash Flow

The concept of cash flow is relatively simple. The objective in each time period is to compute the change in the cash account caused by investing or not investing in the asset under consideration. This cash-account explanation is easy to understand, and with practice not difficult to apply, although the opportunity-cost concept with the possibility of no explicit cash outlay weakens the cash-account analogy.

The cash-flow procedure seems, however, to ignore the beneficial effects of other changes which may be of significance. For example, assume that in the first operating period it is expected that sales will be $10,000 (all on account) to be collected at the end of period 2, and that the total expenses (including income

---

[3] For example, assume fixed costs in year n of $15,000, for which the cash disbursement was made some years ago, variable costs of $1 per unit, production of 15,000 units, sales of 17,000, and an inventory of 6,000 units at $3 per unit at the start of the year. Under these conditions, assuming all fixed costs are absorbed to product, the cost of sales would be (using FIFO) $3(6,000) + $2(11,000) = $40,000. The inventory increase would be $2(4,000) − $3(6,000) = − $10,000. The $40,000 is deducted as cost of sales and the $10,000 is added to the cash flow as the change in inventory. The $15,000 of fixed cost are also added as a noncash expense.

taxes) are $7,000, all resulting in immediate cash disbursements. There are no other changes expected in the first time period except an increase in depreciation of $1,000 caused by the investment. The total changes are:

Increase in accounts receivable	$10,000
Decrease in cash	7,000
Increase in depreciation	1,000
Increase in retained earnings	2,000

The cash-flow procedure would indicate a negative cash flow of $7,000. The computations would be

Sales	$10,000
Less: Out-of-pocket expenses	7,000
Net revenue after expenses	$ 3,000
Less: Increase in current assets (exclusive of cash)	10,000
After-tax cash flow	($ 7,000)

The negative cash flow of $7,000 correctly measures the change of the cash account. But the measure seems to fail to take into consideration other events that have occurred, such as the increase of $10,000 in accounts receivable and the increase of $2,000 in retained earnings. However, in the next period the $10,000 will be collected, and the cash inflows of that period will be increased by $10,000. But since there is a time delay before collection, the sales of the first period should be recorded—but recorded at the present value of $10,000, not $10,000.

Instead of computing the cash flow, the fund flow could be computed, where fund flow is defined as the change in working capital caused by the investment being considered. In the present example the fund flow of the first year would be:

Sales	$10,000
Less: Out-of-pocket expenses	7,000
Increase in funds	$ 3,000

The fund flow is a positive $3,000, which is the same as the sum of the cash flows of the two periods. The two procedures yield different figures if the time value of money is included in recording the events, that is, if the cash flow of $10,000 in the second time period is discounted back two periods. However, the differences can be reconciled by computing the fund flow on the basis of the present value of the sales of $10,000. This is done in Exhibits 13–15 and 13–16. For example, at the end of year 1 and assuming a time value of money of 0.10, the present value of the $10,000 to be collected one year hence is $9,091.

Exhibit 13–15   Investment Evaluation: Cash Flow

Period	Cash Flow	Present-Value Factor	Present Value
0	$ 0	1.0000	$ 0
1	− 7,000	0.9091	− 6,364
2	10,000	0.8264	8,264
		Net present value =	$ 1,900

Exhibit 13–16   Investment Evaluation: Fund Flow

Period	Fund Flows	Present-Value Factor	Present Value
0	$0	1.0000	$ 0
1	9,091 − 7,000 = 2,091	0.9091	1,900
2	0	0.8264	0
		Net present value =	$1,900

The net present value of the investment is $1,900 by either technique. Despite that fact that the cash-flow and fund-flow approaches can be reconciled, the former is used almost exclusively for investments since it is easier to apply.

13.6.3 Absolute and Marginal Cash Flows

A complication arises in the computation of cash flows when a new process is being considered to replace the present process. Should the absolute revenues be used (the revenues that would be earned if there were no present process) or the marginal revenues (the incremental revenues that would be earned in excess of what could be earned using the present process)? One possibility is to compute the present value of each alternative method (including abandonment of the project) and choose the method with the highest present value. This bypasses the question of whether the absolute or incremental revenues are appropriate.

Another possible procedure is to determine if the present method would still be undertaken if there were no possibility of improved methods. If the project should be abandoned, the relative proceeds could not be used. For example, train transportation may be more efficient than truck transportation, but it may be that a truck cannot pay its way; thus a comparison of train with truck is invalid in determining whether a train is economically feasible. If the present method is economically sound, assuming no change in method, the old method can be compared with the new method and the net savings computed. If the present value of the savings is greater than the present value of the outlays, the new method should be adopted.

13.6.4 Cash Flows and Taxes

The cash flows should be on an after-income-tax basis. This means that the taxable income of each period must be determined, and that the amount of income tax arising because of the investment should be computed and included as a decrease of the cash proceeds or, possibly, as an increase in liabilities.

Some interesting things occur when both the time value of money and taxes are both included in the analysis. For example, it may be more desirable for a company to allow an account to become a bad debt and claim it as a tax deduction than to try to collect it in the future. Suppose it would cost $2 to collect a $5 account two years hence. With a cost of money of 10%, the present value of the account is ($5 − 2)(0.8264) = $2.48. The present value of the tax deduction, in the presence of taxable income and with a tax rate of 52%, is $0.52 per dollar of deduction, or $0.52(5) = $2.60.

An important complication in computing income taxes arises from the opportunity to use accelerated depreciation to compute taxable income allowed under the Internal Revenue Code. With new depreciable property the company will probably choose either the twice-straight-line-declining-balance method, or the sum-of-the-years'-digits method. It is difficult to generalize as to which procedure will be better, because the answer is a function of the amount of the salvage, the life of the investment, and the firm's cost of money. Another complication is the fact that the firm has an option at any time to switch from the twice-straight-line to the straight-line method of depreciation. Since the twice-straight-line procedure generally reaches a point where a switch-over is desirable, this privilege should be taken into consideration. The theoretically sound answer to the question of which depreciation method is more desirable to a firm must be solved by computing the present value of the tax deductions that result from following the allowed procedures. The procedure resulting in the highest present value is more desirable.[4]

The amount of depreciation allowable for tax purposes is the relevant figure, not the amount of depreciation to be taken for book purposes. The latter amount does not directly affect the investment decision. However, the cash flows are needed, and since the income tax affects the cash flows and is in turn affected by the amount of depreciation allowable for tax purposes, depreciation allowed for taxes is of relevance to investment decisions.

13.6.5 Problems in Cash-Flow Analysis

Some of the difficulties in the use of the present-value method come from the problem of predicting the relevant cash flows. This problem stems in part from the interrelationships which often arise between existing or proposed projects

[4] Davidson and Drake found that the sum-of-the-years'-digits method maximized the present value of future tax reductions, other things equal, for longer-lived asset lives. S. Davidson and D. F. Drake, "The 'Best' Tax Depreciation Method—1964," *The Journal of Business*, July 1964, pp. 258–260.

because of the use they make of limited resources. The problem also reflects the uncertainty inherent to both the external factors, such as demand, and internal factors, such as the project life, that attend any investment. In addition, the classification of costs and knowledge of cost behavior available to the accountant is central to good predictions.

Sophisticated forecasting methods are of help, but the essence of the problem remains. The forecasting problem is one reason that the payback method is still in wide use.

A desirable feature of many capital-investment projects is the opportunity for the manager to adjust the commitment of resources to a project as information concerning its success is received. This might be thought of as the manager's reaction to the resolution of a project's uncertainty over time. A crude measure of the importance of reducing this uncertainty is the size of the investment and a measure of the rate at which the project's uncertainty is expected to be resolved is supplied by the payback period. This use, and the manager's desire for early information confirming the wiseness of his decision and the asymmetric payoff function typically applied by organizations in evaluating his success, are strong reasons for the continued use of the payback method in practice. Failure to reach goals is often punished more than equivalent success is rewarded (see Chapter 6 and also Section 13.7.2). It should be noted, however, that even in practice payback should only be used as one of several constraints in accepting a project rather than as the sole criterion.

13.6.6 The Cost of Money

Determining the cost of money for a firm is difficult, and this section is no more than a brief survey of the problem. The cost of money is the rate of discount to be applied to future cash flows. This carries with it an implicit assumption that funds may be borrowed or lent at this same rate.

We believe that the rate of interest used in the compound-interest formula to discount for time should not be used to adjust for risk as well as for taking the time value of money into account. If this argument is accepted, the discount rate used for computing the present value of an investment should be closer to a default-free interest rate than to that rate required by the common stockholders.

Although it may properly be argued that the default-free rate is appropriate to compute present values, for purposes of this book and considering the desire to find a workable approach to decision making, the use of the firm's borrowing rate to take the time value of money into consideration is reasonable. A more complete prescription is beyond the scope of this book.[5]

One reason for a firm not using a single discount rate to allow for two problems (time and risk) is that it is usually not clear to the decision maker just what implicit risk assumptions are made by the choice of a particular discount rate. This is true of both the assumed degree of risk and its time pattern.

[5] For a more complete discussion, see H. Bierman, Jr., and S. Smidt, *The Capital Budgeting Decision*, New York: Macmillan Publishing Co., Inc., 1975.

If the default-free time value of money is used in the initial evaluation of outcomes from various decisions, another step is necessary to adjust the cash flows for the riskiness of the situation using probabilities.

13.6.7 Present-Value Index

The present-value index is a variant of the present-value approach. Its appeal lies in the fact that seemingly it can be used to rank investments. Unfortunately, the ranking is frequently neither useful nor correct. The index is computed by dividing the present value of the cash proceeds, exclusive of the initial investment, by the investment. The term profitability index is also used to describe this calculation.

Example
The X Company has a cost of money of 10%. Assume that an investment has the following cash flows:

Period 0	Period 1	Period 2
($1,500)	$1,000	$1,000

The present value of the $1,000-a-period, two-period cash proceeds is $1,736. The present-value index is 1.16:

$$\text{present-value index} = \frac{1,736}{1,500} = 1.16$$

One rule to use with an independent investment is: If the index is larger than 1, accept the investment. This rule is sound. However, if the index is greater than 1, the net present value is also positive, and the computation of the present-value index is unnecessary.

A second rule is this: Rank mutually exclusive investments by their indices, and choose the investment with the highest ranking. This rule may lead to incorrect decisions because of problems related to either the scale of the investment or the classification of cash flows.

Example (The Scale Problem)
Assume two mutually exclusive investments with the cash flows given in Exhibit 13–17 and a cost of money of 0.1. Which is the more desirable?

Exhibit 13–17   Cash Flows for Investments J and K and the Present-Value Index

Investment	0	1	2	Present-Value Index
J	($1,500)	$1,000	$1,000	1.16
K	(3,100)	2,000	2,000	1.12

The index indicates that investment J is preferred to K. However, a computation of present values shows that K is better (a net present value of $372 for K compared to $236 for J). The present-value index is a ratio of benefits to outlay and fails to consider the scale of the investment. The other ratio measures, such as return on investment and rate of return, also fail to consider scale. This point can be seen more clearly by looking at the incremental investment resulting from moving from investment J to K. Label this investment K − J:

Investment	0	1	2	Present-Value Index
K − J	($1,600)	$1,000	$1,000	1.08

The present value of the incremental investment is positive (thus the index is greater than 1) and the incremental investment is desirable. The problem of scale can be solved by comparing pairs of investment, but this is unnecessary since the problem is more easily resolved by using present values. Also, the problem of the classification of cash flows still exists.

Example (Classification of Cash Flows)
The second difficulty with the present-value index is that it requires a distinction between deductions from cash proceeds and investment-type outlays. Assume the two mutually exclusive investments given in Exhibit 13–18. The present-value index ranks L over M, but inspection of the cash flows of the investments show that the difference is a result of classifying the two $1,000 outlays of M as investments rather than as deductions from cash proceeds. Any procedure depending on arbitrary classifications is resting on an unreliable foundation, and for this type of decision, the problem can be avoided.

Exhibit 13–18   Cash Flows and Present Value Index for Investments L and M

	Cash Flows			
Investment	0	1	2	Present-Value Index
L	($1,500)	$1,000	$1,000	$\dfrac{1,736}{1,500} = 1.16$
M	(1,500)	(1,000) 2,000	(1,000) 2,000	$\dfrac{3,472}{3,236} = 1.07$

There are some who argue that the present-value index ranks independent investments. This ranking may not be reliable. In addition to the difficulties described above, if the company does not intend to accept all independent investments with a positive present value (or an index greater than 1), it can be argued that the discount rate is not appropriate and the index ranking is not reliable, since the index is not computed using the opportunity cost of money. It is not claimed here that the present-value method may be used to rank independent investments. It is claimed only that the present-value method leads to correct decisions involving choices between mutually exclusive investments and gives correct accept or reject decisions when it is applied to independent investments.

13.6.8 Nonconstant Cash Flows

The present value of an investment can be computed by projecting the cash flows of each period. Instead of following this detailed procedure, a firm may wish to know the present value of the cash flows with different assumptions of rates of growth or decay applied to the projection of the initial period. The formulas for computing these present values are relatively easy to apply. Formula (13.3) gives the present value of the positive cash flows assuming a continuous rate of growth g. [See Appendix 13A for the derivation of equation (13.3).] To find the net present value of the investment, the initial outlay must be subtracted. All the formulas assume a zero tax rate, or, alternatively, that the cash flows are on an after-tax basis. The assumptions are as follows:

1. Constant rate of growth through time.
2. Cash flows continue forever.
3. In growth situations r exceeds g; otherwise, the present value is infinitely large.

These assumptions give:

$$\text{present value} = \frac{A}{r - g} \tag{13.3}$$

where A is the cash flow of the first period, g the rate of growth (if flows are declining, the rate of growth is negative), and r equals the rate of discount (continuously compounded).

Example
For increasing cash flows, assume that A equals \$100, g equals 0.06, and r equals 0.10 (in this situation r is assumed to exceed g):

$$\text{present value} = \frac{\$100}{0.10 - 0.06} = \frac{100}{0.04} = \$2,500$$

Example

For decreasing cash flows, assume that A equals $100, g equals −0.15, and r equals 0.10:

$$\text{present value} = \frac{\$100}{0.10 - (-0.15)} = \frac{100}{0.25} = \$400$$

If g equals 0 (that is, constant cash flows), equation (13.3) gives the present value of a perpetuity:

$$\text{present value} = \frac{\$100}{0.10} = \$1,000$$

A table of values per dollar of initial cash flow can be developed. First, formula (13.3) is revised to read:

$$\text{present value} = \frac{A}{X} \tag{13.4}$$

where X is equal to r − g (g is negative if the cash flows are declining). A table of values of $1 divided by X for different values of X can now be developed. See Exhibit 13–19.

Exhibit 13–19   Partial Table of Values

Values of X	Values of $1/X
1.00	1.00
0.50	2.00
0.25	4.00
0.20	5.00
0.10	10.00
0.05	20.00
0.04	25.00
0.03	33.33
0.02	50.00
0.01	100.00

13.7 Review Process for Capital-Budgeting Decisions

After the capital-budgeting decision has been made, two control problems remain:

1. Controlling the amount of funds spent purchasing or constructing the investment.
2. Reappraisal of the investment decision once the investment starts operating.

13.7.1 Controlling Investment Expenditures

Capital expenditures are difficult to control since each investment project is usually unique, and neither standards nor past experience can be used in establishing the probable expenditure of funds. When the actual costs differ from the amount originally estimated, the question remains whether the difference is caused by a bad original estimate, by changes in the prices of labor and material, or by inefficiency. The action taken by top management to prevent recurrence of the variance depends on the cause of the variance. Random uncontrollable events can also cause a difference from the estimate, further complicating the analysis. The reasons the actual expenditures exceed the budgeted expenditures are related to all the above items, and it will frequently be impossible to isolate the causes with reasonable accuracy.

For capital investments, actual costs should be compared with budgeted costs. The estimated times related to preparing the investment for operation should also be controlled.

During installation or construction, reports of the percentage completion, the over or under cost expenditure relative to the budgeted costs for the stage of completion, the estimated costs to complete, the time taken relative to the time budgeted for the stage of completion, and the estimated time to complete can enable management to take corrective or cost-saving action (possibly by changing the construction schedule). Any report should include the probable completion date. A delay in completion of an investment may be costly since interest payments have to be made even if the operations have not yet begun. Thus, there are strong incentives to meet the planned date of completion. An expected delay in completion should be explained and differences between actual and budgeted costs may require investigation, whether favorable or unfavorable.

If the actual costs are overrunning the budgeted costs significantly (say, by 20%), it may be necessary for the person in charge of the project to request additional funds. The decision to invest additional funds in the project is again a capital-budgeting decision, and the request should be treated like any other request. The funds already expended are sunk costs, and thus are not relevant to the decision concerning whether or not to invest further funds in the project.

Control of capital expenditures is an extremely inexact procedure since it is often difficult to establish benchmarks of performance. However, an estimate of cost is made and defended by the sponsor and the director of a project. This estimate is, at least in part, the basis of the decision to invest; it should be made with care and only after detailed investigation. It is reasonable to use this cost as the benchmark. Large variances should be explained, not shrugged off by saying, "The estimate must have been off." The reason the estimate was off should be reviewed. Furthermore, comparisons of actual and budgeted costs are useful in signaling the necessity for management action.

At a minimum, review of purchase or construction costs gives an incentive for project sponsors to make careful estimates and for those in charge of construction to have an incentive to control costs and completion times of both the overall job and the subactivities.

13.7.2 Review of Operating Results

The sponsor of a capital-budget request makes an estimate of revenues and expenses of the future in order to jusitfy the proposed expenditure. If the rate-of-return or the present-value approach is used, a key item forecasted is the net cash proceeds. After the investment has been placed in operation, the actual results should be compared to the estimate information (which formed a basis of the capital-budgeting decision), and the variances should be explained. Similarly, a director of the construction or installation of a project should be held accountable for the construction cost and time budget. The selection of items that can be reviewed varies, depending to some extent on the method used to make the capital-budgeting decision.

The budget request usually contains an estimate of the cash-payback period (the length of time required to recover the original investment). A comparison of the actual payback period and the expected payback period is one way of measuring the results of operations and the efficiency of the budget process, but there are several difficulties. The payback period is probably of several years' duration; thus there will be a period with no appraisal of the decision to invest. Also, the appraisal is limited to the payback period; after that period there is no further appraisal. These difficulties might lead instead to a comparison of actual and predicted cash proceeds of each period. The use of cash proceeds eliminates waiting for the cash-payback period to end in order to start the appraisal, and it also corrects the one-shot characteristic of the cash-payback method of review.

The comparison of actual and predicted cash proceeds is a useful method of reappraising capital-budgeting decisions, but it cannot be used in all circumstances. Where the projected cash flow is an incremental value (as when equipment is being replaced), it may not be possible to determine the actual relative cash flow, since the costs of using the required equipment after replacement are unknown.

Income (the difference between revenues and expenses) is probably the most widely accepted and used measure of performance, and the return on investment (income divided by investment) is the second. But unless they are carefully used, both these measures are inferior to the use of cash proceeds as a means of reappraising capital-budgeting decisions.

By using cash proceeds the problem of allocating the cost of an investment to specific periods of use is avoided. If income is being used to measure performance, the depreciation cost of the investment must be computed and used as a revenue deduction, since income cannot be computed without taking into consideration the cost of using the investment. Useful measures are difficult to obtain.

Another popular method of measuring performance is the return on investment. There are two variants of the procedure. Investment can be defined as the gross investment (the accumulated depreciation is not subtracted) or the net investment (the accumulated depreciation is subtracted). There are many difficulties in using return on investment. One of the more important is that with constant (and in some cases decreasing) proceeds, the asset may have an increasing return on investment if the straight-line method of depreciation (or any of the decreasing-charge methods of depreciation) is used together with the net-investment method.

It is possible to develop a method of depreciation that allows income and return on investment to be used in appraising capital-budgeting decisions without the distortion introduced by the other depreciation procedures. If such a method of depreciation is not used, the analyst faces the difficult task of disengaging the effect of the depreciation method from the effect of the efficiency or inefficiency of the operations and the capital-budgeting process.[6]

Capital-budgeting expenditures should also be controlled during the construction period, and the investment decision must be reappraised once operations have begun. The best means of appraising the decision to invest and the operation of the investment after completion is a comparison of the actual and expected cash proceeds; but this is not always possible. The projected incomes and return on investment may also be used, but, if so, it is desirable that depreciation charges be handled with care. In many cases reappraisal of the decision is not possible by any of the above methods. For example, an investment that improves the product and prevents lost sales cannot be directly appraised, since the level of sales without the expenditure is unknown.[7]

Finally, capital-budgeting decisions are made under uncertainty. A good decision may turn out to be unsuccessful and still have been the correct decision. For example, most investors would pay $1 for an investment which had a 0.9 probability of an immediate return of $1,000 and a 0.1 probability of $0. However, if the event with a 0.1 probability occurred, the investment appraisal would cause the investment to appear to have been undesirable.

13.8 Summary

This chapter has focused on the making of investment decisions and the control and evaluation of investment expenditures. The most widely used

---

[6] See Bierman (1961) and Dyckman (1967).

[7] The decision to make the improvement should have included estimates of the savings and, thus, implicitly, of the opportunity costs. Evaluations of this and similar projects should at least compare results with those anticipated when the decision was made.

methods, payback and return on investment, are found to be inferior to the discounted cash-flow procedures, rate of return, and present value. For mutually exclusive investments, the present-value method is more easily applied and thus is superior to the rate-of-return method.

As long as it is assumed that the cash flows are known, the present-value method deals very well with the choice of the acceptable independent investments and the selection of the best of a collection of mutually exclusive investments.

Reappraisal of the capital-budgeting decisions should result in three benefits:

1. The presentation of better information on capital-budget requests.
2. An incentive for the operating departments to meet the income goals which they set on the request form in applying for the authority to make a capital expenditure.
3. An incentive for those charged with the installation or construction of the project to conform with the cost and time budgets given them.

APPENDIX 13A
DERIVATION OF PRESENT-VALUE FORMULAS WHEN CASH FLOWS CHANGE AT A CONTINUOUS RATE

Derivation of the formula, present value $= A/(r - g)$ for changing cash flows is as follows. Assume that r is larger than g:

$$\text{present value} = \int_0^\infty Ae^{gt}e^{-rt}\, dt$$

$$= A \int_0^\infty e^{(g-r)t}\, dt$$

$$= \frac{Ae^{(g-r)t}}{g-r}\bigg|_0^\infty = 0 - \frac{A}{g-r} = \frac{A}{r-g} \qquad (13.3)$$

Instead of assuming that the growth in flows continues for an infinite time period, it may be more appropriate to assume that the growth continues only for the life of the investment, say s periods, and that there is no salvage value. Formula (13.3) becomes [8]

$$\text{present value} = A\left[\frac{e^{(g-r)s} - 1}{g - r}\right] \qquad (13.5)$$

[8] The values of e^{-x} may be obtained from Table V.

Example

Assume that A equals \$100, g equals 0.06, r equals 0.10, and s equals 20 years:

$$\text{present value} = 100\left(\frac{e^{(0.06-0.10)20} - 1}{+0.06 - 0.10}\right)$$

$$= 100\left(\frac{e^{-0.8} - 1}{-0.04}\right)$$

$$= 100\left(\frac{0.499 - 1}{-0.04}\right)$$

$$= 100\left(\frac{-0.551}{-0.04}\right) = \$1,378$$

Previously, when it was assumed that the growth continued for an infinite time period, a present value of \$2,500 was obtained. Thus, the assumption of growth for a finite time period, even if it is of lengthy duration, gives significantly different results from the simpler, but more inexact, assumption of infinite duration. In a situation where there is a decay rate instead of a growth rate, the assumption of an infinite life does little harm, since the value of the cash flows is decreasing rapidly. Continued growth and positive salvage values can be added to the analysis.

The derivation of the formula, when growth is assumed to continue for a finite time periods and there is zero salvage value, is:

$$\text{present value} = \int_0^s Ae^{gt}e^{-rt}\,dt$$

$$= A\int_0^s e^{(g-r)t}\,dt$$

$$= \frac{Ae^{(g-r)t}}{g-r}\bigg|_0^s = A\,\frac{e^{(g-r)s} - 1}{g-r}$$

QUESTIONS AND PROBLEMS

13–1 Explain how the cash flow of a typical period should be computed. Should interest payments be deducted? Do all the deductions require an explicit cash outlay?

13–2 How would a cash-flow computation differ from a fund-flow computation?

13–3 If the present value of the absolute cash flows of an investment is negative, is it possible for the present value of the relative cash flows of the investment to be positive (that is, the cash flows resulting from this investment being compared to an alternative)?

13–4 What are some difficulties involved in reviewing capital-budgeting decisions?

13–5 In making investment decisions, what other factors than those discussed in this chapter must be taken into consideration?

13–6 Compute the rate of return of the following investment:

0	$-3,477
1	1,000
2	1,000
10	10,000

13–7 An investment costs $1,000 and promises to return $1,210 two periods from now.

  a. Determine the rate of return of the investment.
  b. Explain in three different ways what is meant by the term *rate of return*. Use this example as the basis of your explanation.

13–8 Compute the net present value of an investment that costs $800 and promises to return $1,000 three periods from now. Assume that the time value of money is 0.05 per year. Explain what is meant by the term *net present value of an investment*.

13–9 Compute the rate of return of the following investment:

0	$-2,621
1	1,000
2	1,000
10	10,000

13–10 There are two mutually exclusive investments:

	Cash Flows			
Project	Period 0	Period 1	Period 2	Yield
A	$-10,000	—	$11,664	0.08
B	-10,000	$5,608	5,608	0.08

You are to advise a client. What information do you need to choose between the two investments? Should the client be indifferent?

13–11 Compute the net present value of an investment that costs $800 and promises to return $1,000 three periods from now. Assume that the time value of money is 0.10 per year.

13–12 Assume that two pieces of equipment have the following characteristics:

Equipment	Expected Life	Initial Cost	Operating Cost per Year
X	5	$43,295	$4,500
Y	8	60,000	4,000

Required: Assuming a cost of money of 0.05, which piece of equipment is the more desirable if both can do the same job equally well? Ignore taxes and uncertainty.

13–13 The Auction Company uses a discount rate of 0.05. The following information applies to a projected investment (ignore taxes):

Time 0
Initial outlay of $1,000,000

Time 1	
Net revenue from sales (all cash sales)	$1,080,000
Interest paid	50,000
Net change in bank balance	$1,030,000

Required: Should the investment be accepted?

13–14 A product is currently being manufactured on a machine that results in incremental costs of $7.50 per unit. The rate of production expected in the future is 10,000 units per year, and the sales price per unit is $8.50. It is expected that the old machine can be used without repair for the next ten years.

An equipment manufacturer has agreed to accept the old equipment as a trade-in for a new version. The new machine would cost $200,000 plus the trade-in and would result in incremental costs of $5.50 per unit. It has an expected life of 10 years, and an expected salvage of $10,000 at that time. The old equipment could be sold on the open market now for $55,000. Ten years from now it has an expected salvage of $1,000. Ignore income taxes. The appropriate time-discount rate for this company is 0.05.

Required: What do you recommend the company do?

13–15 Assume the same situation as in problem 13–14 except that the resale price of the old equipment is now $100,000.

Required: What do you recommend?

13–16 The Electrolite Company has a cost of money of 0.10. The following two mutually exclusive investments are available (two machines which do the same task). The task will be continued in the foreseeable future.

	X	Y
Initial cost	− $10,000	−$20,000
Other costs per year	− 2,000	− 1,000
Estimated life years	15	20

Required: Which machine should be purchased? Ignore taxes.

13–17 The cost of money of the Blair Company is 0.10. The following mutually exclusive investments are available (ignore taxes):

Project	Period 0	Period 1	Period 2	Yield
		Cash Flows		
W	− $10,000	$6,545	$6,545	0.20
X	− 10,000		14,400	0.20
Y	− 10,000	12,000		0.20
Z	− 30,000	19,400	19,400	0.19

Required: For each of the following pairs of mutually exclusive investments, pick the better of the two.

a. W and X   b. W and Y   c. Y and X   d. W and Z   e. Z and Y

13–18 Which of the following three pieces of equipment is the more desirable? Assume that the investments are mutually exclusive.

Type of Equipment	Initial Outlay	Life	Labor Savings per Year	Yield
A	$ 5,000	1	6,000	0.20
B	16,761	5	5,000	0.15
C	42,883	7	10,000	0.14

The cost of money of the firm is 10%. Assume a tax rate of zero.

13–19 Assume that two pieces of equipment have the following characteristics:

Equipment	Expected Life	Initial Cost	Operating Cost per Year
X	5	$43,295	$4,500
Y	8	60,000	4,000

Required: Assuming a cost of money of 0.08, which equipment is the more desirable? What assumptions are you making? Ignore taxes.

13–20 Assume that two pieces of equipment have the following characteristics:

Equipment	Expected Life	Initial Cost	Operating Cost per Year
X	3	$10,000	$4,500
Y	4	12,000	4,000

Required: Assuming a cost of money of 0.05, which equipment is the more desirable? Ignore taxes.

13–21 Assume the cash flow of the first year is $1,000,000 and that the rate of discount is 0.08. What is the present value of the cash flows assuming that the
a. Cash flow decreases by 0.02 per year?
b. Cash flow is constant and continues forever?
c. Cash flow increases by 0.03 per year forever?
d. Cash flow increases by 0.09 per year forever?

13–22 Assume that the cost of money is 0.10 and the first period's cash flow is $10,000. Compute the present value of cash flows assuming that
a. The $10,000 continues for perpetuity.
b. The $10,000 decays at the rate of 0.15 per year.
c. The $10,000 grows at the rate of 0.08 per year.

13–23 Some persons prefer to compute the present value of the cash flows of an investment, while others prefer to compute the terminal value. Will the choice of the method affect the acceptability of an investment?

13–24 The Happy Valley Mattress Company plans to close down one of its plants. The plant building was purchased 60 years ago for $500,000 and has been depreciated on a no-salvage, straight-line basis to a present book value of $200,000. The best offer for the plant building at this time is an offer of $288,000. If the plant is continued in operation for five more years, the after-tax accounting income will be $63,000 per year. At the end of five years, the plant would be sold for $100,000. If the plant were sold today, it would be possible to reduce certain expenditures, for example, general administration, by $20,000 per year for the five years. Under all alternatives the equipment would be retained for standby use. The cost of moving the equipment if sold now or later is $16,000. Assuming a 50% tax rate on all types of income, and considering the after-tax time value of money to be 16%, what decision should be made? Assume depreciation for tax purposes is the same as for book purposes.

13–25 The controller of the Waditap Company has asked a member of his staff to prepare a report on the company's equipment-replacement procedure. One of the comments made by the staff member reads as follows:

Present procedure overestimates the profitability of replacement proposals because the investment in inventory, receivables, and working-cash balances is ignored. We have two dollars invested in these assets for every dollar invested in equipment, and, therefore, the average annual investment as computed (with the previously suggested changes) should be tripled in calculating the rate of return on investment.

Evaluate this statement.

13–26 Given a 20-year project with a payback period of 5.1 years, determine the project's rate of return assuming that the cash inflows are uniform over the project's life and the total investment is made immediately.

13–27 Given the limitations of payback, why do you think it is so widely used in practice?

13–28 An organization is considering purchase of a small computer in order to reduce the costs of its manual operations. At the present time, the manual system in use involves the following direct cash expenses per month.

Salaries	$7,500
Payroll taxes and fringes	1,700
Supplies	600
	$ 9,800

Existing related furniture and equipment are fully depreciated in the accounts and for income taxes. The cost of the new computer, including alterations, installation, and accessory equipment, is $100,000. The *entire amount* can be depreciated for income-tax purposes on a double declining balance basis at the rate of 0.20 per year. The computer is expected to be obsolete in 3 years at which time it is expected to have a salvage value of $20,000. (This is treated as a cash inflow at the end of year 3.) Current equipment has zero salvage value.

Estimated annual costs of the new system are:

Salaries (supervisor)	$15,000
Salaries (other)	24,000
Payroll taxes and fringes	7,400
Supplies	7,200
	$53,600

Required:

a. Compute the cash savings using a 40% tax rate.

b. Should the computer be purchased assuming a 20% cost of debt before taxes?

13-29 Consider the following two mutually exclusive investments:

		Cash Flows		
Investment	Cost	Year 1	Year 2	Yield
A	($10,000)	$ 5,608	$ 5,608	0.08
B	($10,000)	—	$11,664	0.08

What decision should the firm make?

SUPPLEMENTARY READING

BIERMAN, H. "Depreciable Assets—Timing of Expense Recognition," *The Accounting Review*, October 1961, pp. 613–618.

———, and S. SMIDT, *The Capital Budgeting Decision*, New York: Macmillan Publishing Co., Inc., 1975.

DEAN, JOEL, *Capital Budgeting*, New York: Columbia University Press, 1951.

DYCKMAN, T., "Discussion of Accelerated Depreciation and Deferred Taxes: An Empirical Study of Fluctuating Asset Expenditures," Empirical Studies in Accounting Research: Selected Studies 1967, pp. 124–138.

HAMMOND, J., "Better Decisions with Preference Theory" *The Harvard Business Review*, November–December 1967, pp. 123–141.

HERTZ, D., "Investment Policies that Pay off," *The Harvard Business Review*, January–February 1968, pp. 96–108.

HESPOS, R., and P. STRASSMAN, "Stochastic Decision Trees for the Analysis of Investment Decisions," *Management Science*, August 1965, pp. 244–259.

HILLIER, F. S., "The Derivation of Probabilistic Information for the Evaluation of Risky Investments," *Management Science*, April 1963, pp. 443–457.

LUTZ, F., and V. LUTZ, "The Theory of Investment of the Firm," Princeton, N.J.: Princeton University Press, 1951.

MAGEE, J., "How to Use Decision Trees in Capital Investment," *The Harvard Business Review*, September–October 1964, pp. 79–96.

QUERIN, G. D. *The Capital Expenditure Decision*, Homewood, Ill.: Richard D. Irwin, Inc., 1967.

ROBICHECK, A. A., and S. C. MYERS, *Optimal Financing Decisions*, Englewood Cliffs, N.J.: Prentice-Hall, Inc., 1965.

Chapter 14

The Lease-or-Buy Decision

An important example of a capital-budgeting decision is the lease-or-buy decision. Should land, a plant, or a piece of equipment be bought or leased?[1]

There is at least one very good reason why leasing might be mutually beneficial to both parties. This is where the lessee (the tenant) has a temporary need (as when a firm rents a building for a temporary excess of inventory) or when a need is recurring but each occurrence is for a short period of time (as when the firm needs only one hour of computer time per day; thus the firm should prefer to share a computer on a lease basis rather than buy one). With most of the other reasons why a firm might want to lease, it is not apparent that both parties benefit. Nevertheless, a leasing arrangement may be desirable because of the different expectations of the lessee and the lessor. If the lessor expects a computer to have a life of 10 years and the lessee expects a life of 5 years, it would not be surprising to find that they can arrange a lease contract which both parties consider beneficial, but it may be that only one party actually benefits. The same could be true if both parties estimated different salvage values or if they used a different cost of money.

Accounting methods and practices also contribute to an incentive to lease. The omission of leases from the balance sheets of many corporations, which results in an understatement of assets and

[1] For other considerations, see Albert H. Cohen, "Long Term Leases," *Michigan Business Studies*, Vol. 11, No. 5, Ann Arbor: University of Michigan, 1954; Robert N. Anthony and Samuel Schwartz, "Office Equipment: Buy or Rent?" Boston: Management Analysis Center, Inc., 1957; "Leasing in Industry," *Study in Business Policy*, No. 127 of the National Industrial Conference Board, 1968; R. F. Vancil, "Lease or Borrow: New Method of Analysis," *The Harvard Business Review*, September–October 1961, pp. 122–136.

liabilities and an overstatement of the return on investment, is one such factor, even though expert analysts will almost invariably restructure performance measures to include the effects of leases. Leases can also make investments seem to be desirable that would otherwise not pass the rate-of-return requirement by the firm (this will be illustrated later). Taxes are another institution that might contribute to an incentive to lease.

Some of the advantages to the lessee are disadvantages to the lessor. Thus the payment flexibility (assuming the lease can be canceled) in the lease is a disadvantage from the point of view of the lessor. Whether or not the lessee has flexibility depends on the terms of the lease, and flexibility should not just be assumed. The flexibility of a lease is somewhat balanced by the fact that the lessee does not have any residual value in the asset being leased.

A lease contract might also cover maintenance and servicing of the equipment leased. One advantage of such a contract is that it sets a maximum for this cost, thus, in a sense, reducing the risk. However, such a provision also sets a minimum cost, since it precludes the possibility of incurring less costs than the amount specified by the contract. Generally a maintenance arrangement could be obtained with or without a lease. This should be considered as a separate issue. Statements that leases are less risky to the lessee than debt to the borrower and hence are less likely to cause bankruptcy than debt should not be automatically accepted; rather, they stand or fall depending on the terms of the lease.

A lease is a form of debt financing and serves a function similar to that of other types of debt. In some situations it may be the only type of financing available, or it may be the cheapest type of financing. In any event, since it is an alternative source of capital, its cost must be compared to the cost of other sources. Unless the lessor can borrow at a lower cost than the lessee, there is no inherent reason why the firm acting as lessor should have a lower real cost of money. A contract may occur because of different perceptions of the cost of money. These different perceptions may lead to lease terms that are desirable from the point of view of the lessee while also seeming to be desirable to the lessor.

The analysis begins by assuming that the terms of the lease require that the lease payments be made for the duration of the lease; hence the lease is a form of implicit debt (this is a financial lease). The procedure does not apply to a lease which can be canceled readily (an operating lease). Such leases are discussed later in this chapter.

14.1 Borrowing or Leasing

First it is necessary to establish the importance of the question of the rate of interest. The decision frequently depends on the rate of interest that is chosen. We will ignore tax complications in this section.

Assume that the choice is between borrowing $50,000 from a bank (and an immediate outlay of $50,000) or paying $18,360 a period on a lease for three periods. Assume that the tax rate is zero. With a zero rate of interest the present value or cost of the immediate outlay is $50,000, and the present value or cost of the rental payments is $55,080 ($18,360 times 3, the number of payments). The immediate outlay is a better choice than the three payments of $18,360 a period.

Now increase the rate of interest. The present value of the rental payments becomes smaller as the rate of interest is increased. The cost of the immediate outlay remains the same. At a rate of interest r^*, the present values of the two cost streams are equal, while for larger rates of interest, the present value of the rental payments is less than the $50,000 initial outlay. This is shown graphically in Figure 14.1.

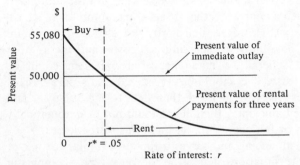

Figure 14.1   Rent versus buy with different interest rates.

If the appropriate borrowing rate is less than r^*, the decision should be to buy the equipment, since the present value of the immediate outlays resulting from purchase is less than the present value of the rental payments. If the rate of interest (cost of debt) is greater than r^*, the decision should be to rent the equipment. In this example r^* equals 0.05. In other words, the present value of the yearly payments of $18,360 is $50,000 at 5%. Thus 5% is the implicit rate of interest of the lease. Assume that the rate of interest r (the cost of bank borrowing) is equal to 0.04. The present value of the lease payments is

$$\$18,360 \times 2.77509 = \$50,951$$

and the firm would prefer to buy and borrow compared to renting the equipment. If the cost of debt is greater than 0.05, the decision should be to rent rather than to purchase.

A possible interpretation of the above procedure is that the present outlay or debt equivalent of the three lease payments of $18,360 at 4% is $50,951. Since the present debt equivalent of leasing is more than $50,000, the company should buy and finance the acquisition through borrowing at 4% (the present value of the debt would be $50,000).

The firm has implicitly assumed that the equipment is desirable and should be financed with debt, and the only question is the form of the debt, leasing or bank borrowing. The advantage of bank borrowing also can be shown if the bank agrees to accept repayment of the $50,000 loan at 0.04 interest in equal annual payments. Each payment to the bank, the first payment due one period from now, would be for $18,017. Given the choice between a series of three debt (bank) payments of $18,017 or three lease payments of $18,360, where the lease is the legal equivalent of debt, the manager should choose the bank payments of $18,017.[2] There may be other characteristics of the leasing contract that should be considered, however, before a final decision is reached.

14.2 The Investment Decision

The above discussion and Figure 14.1 show that the relative desirability of leasing or borrowing and buying depends on the cost of debt. But the basic investment decision has not yet been considered.[3]

Assume that the investment considered for purchase (and described in Section 14.1) earns proceeds of $21,000 a year for three years, and that the weighted average cost of capital is 15%. Table 14–1 presents the decision to purchase the asset using the firm's weighted average cost of capital to discount the cash flows.

Table 14–1   Investment with No Borrowing

Period	Cash Flows	Present Value (15%)
0	($50,000)	($50,000)
1	21,000	18,260
2	21,000	15,880
3	21,000	13,810
		($ 2,050)

The present value of the cash flow is negative, and the investment would be rejected *if* the cost of capital is used as the discount rate. The cash flows for the leasing alternative are shown in Table 14–2.

Table 14–2 shows that leasing has a positive present value and the firm, using conventional procedures, might conclude that leasing is desirable and buying is not desirable. But in the previous section it was concluded that borrowing at 0.04 was superior to leasing. How can it be that the first analysis presents buy–borrowing to be superior to leasing and the analysis of Tables 14–1 and 14–2 shows leasing to be acceptable but buying not to be acceptable?

[2] To avoid implying a bias against leasing, assume that the debt rate is 0.06. Leasing has a present value of $18,360 × 2.6730, or $49,076, and leasing would be more desirable than bank borrowing with a present value of $50,000 and an annual cost of $18,706.

[3] The general method of analysis presented in this chapter was brought to the authors' attention by William D. McEachron.

Table 14–2   Investment (Lease)

Period	Investment and Proceeds	Lease Payments	Cash Flow	Present Value (15%)
0	$ 0		$ 0	
1	21,000	($18,360)	2,640	$2,296
2	21,000	(18,360)	2,640	1,996
3	21,000	(18,360)	2,640	1,736
				$6,028

The paradox arises because a cost of capital of 15% is used to accomplish the discounting in Table 14–1 (the present value of the cash flows in Table 14–2 is positive as long as the rate of discount used is positive). To reconcile the two presentations, assume that the cost of bank borrowing is 0.05 (recall that this is also the implicit interest being charged on the lease). Assume that a loan of $50,000 can be obtained, the terms being that the loan can be repaid at the rate of $18,360 per year for three years (an interest rate of 5%). The cash flows from the investment and the borrowing to finance the investment are shown in Table 14–3.

Table 14–3   Investment with Borrowing

Period	Investment and Proceeds	Proceeds from Borrowing	Net Cash Flow	Present Value (15%)
0	($50,000)	$ 50,000	$ 0	$ 0
1	21,000	(18,360)	2,640	2,296
2	21,000	(18,360)	2,640	1,996
3	21,000	(18,360)	2,640	1,736
				$6,028

The present value of the cash flows in Table 14–3 is positive, and the indication is that the investment and borrowing should be undertaken. The positive present value was obtained by incorporating the borrowing of $50,000 and the repaying of the debt into the analysis of cash flows. Table 14–3 gives results for buying and borrowing that are identical to the results for leasing contained in Table 14–2.

Any conventional investment with a yield greater than the cost of borrowing can be made to appear acceptable by incorporating into the cash-flow analysis a sufficient amount of debt financing. This is true for leasing or for borrowing from a bank or for other sources of debt capital.

Table 14–3 presents the same present value of cash flows as Table 14–2. This arises because of the zero tax rate and the assumption that borrowing an explicit

amount of funds carries the same interest rate as the implicit borrowing connected with a lease.

If the lease payments (a form of debt) are included for the lease analysis
(Table 14–2), the debt (bank borrowing) should also be included in the analysis
as shown in Table 14–3 rather than using the analysis in Table 14–1. The buy
analysis of Table 14–1 excludes debt, and a comparable analysis should be made
for the lease alternative. With a lease the borrowing is implicit in the contract;
such implicit borrowing must be eliminated if it is excluded from the buy analysis.
This can be done by finding the immediate payment that is equivalent to the
lease payments. With an interest rate of 5%, the implicit interest cost in the lease,
the immediate-payment equivalent to a series of three payments of $18,360
each is $50,000 (the present value of the annuity, with 5% as the rate of discount).
Thus, instead of considering three outlays of $18,360, these can be replaced by
one outlay of $50,000. The cash flows are given in Table 14–4.

Table 14–4 Lease Payments
Converted into an
Equivalent
Immediate Pay-
ment

Period	Cash Flow
0	($50,000)
1	21,000
2	21,000
3	21,000

This series of cash flows is identical to the one presented in Table 14–1, and
the same decision should be made in both cases. The cash flows related to the
implicit borrowing for the lease situation have been eliminated by computing
the immediate-payment equivalent for the lease payments and by considering
this payment equivalent to an investment type of outlay. The two investments
are now comparable and, in this case, identical.

Two problems have been highlighted by the lease analysis presented. One is
the necessity of making the lease and buy–borrow alternative comparable.
The debt cannot be included in the lease analysis and excluded in the buy–
borrow alternative. There is the choice of including the debt for both alternatives (Tables 14–2 and 14–3) and obtaining the cash flows to the stock equity, or
excluding it from both alternatives (Tables 14–1 and 14–4). But regardless of the
treatment of the debt in the investment analysis, there remains the question of
the rate of interest to be used in discounting the cash flows. If 15% is used as the
discount rate, the investment is not acceptable regardless of how it is financed.
(See Tables 14–1 and 14–4.)

322   Capital Budgeting and Related Topics

With no taxes, and if a borrowing cost of 5% is appropriate, the cost of debt and the cost of leasing are equal, and if the cost of debt is used for discounting the investment cash flows for time, including or excluding the debt gives identical present values.[4] Furthermore, both are acceptable if the cost of money were 0.05. This is shown in Table 14–5.

Table 14–5   Comparison of Omitting and Including Financing Costs

	From Table 14–1 Investment with No Borrowing		From Tables 14–2 and 14–3 Investment with Debt Flows Included	
Period	Cash Flows	Present Value (0.05)	Cash Flows	Present Value (0.05)
0	($50,000)	($50,000)	0	0
1	21,000	20,000	$2,640	$2,514
2	21,000	19,048	2,640	2,395
3	21,000	18,141	2,640	2,280
		$ 7,189		$7,189

In the illustration being considered the alternatives of purchasing outright (borrowing funds at a cost of 0.05) and leasing are equivalent. This does not have to be the case; in fact, with the introduction of income taxes and with different estimates of risk and the life of the asset, and different time-value costs for bank borrowing and lease payments, it would rarely be the case that the lease and buy alternatives would give exactly the same present values.

14.2.1 Income Taxes

The income tax complication is relevant to the investment decision. Accelerrated depreciation for tax purposes tends to make buying more attractive than leasing since leasing implicitly assumes an increasing-charge depreciation pattern. However, the effect of income taxes must be computed, it cannot be assumed. The present investment provides a useful example because the two alternatives are identical before tax considerations.[5] Suppose in the present example that the lease payments of $18,360 per period are separated into implicit interest and principal using the implicit cost of leasing of 0.05. The schedule for a loan of $50,000 with a contract interest rate of 5% is shown in Table 14–6. This is also the schedule of debt retirement that could be used for the buy–

---

[4] The cost of leasing is equal to the cost of debt if the present value of the lease payments, using the cost of debt as the discount rate, is equal to the cost of the asset.

[5] The alternatives are identical since the implicit interest in the lease is equal to the interest payments for the buy–borrow case.

Table 14–6 Separation of Lease into Interest and Principal Payments

1 Period	2 Debt Balance: Beginning of Year	3 Interest (5%) on Debt Balance	4 Rent (Debt Retirement) $18,360 − Interest	5 Depreciation in Buy–Borrow (Straight Line)
1	$50,000	$2,500	$15,860	$16,667
2	34,140	1,707	16,653	16,667
3	17,487	873	17,487	16,667
4	0			

borrow alternative, since the interest costs of leasing and borrowing are equal in this example.

In signing a lease, contract services are expected from the asset leased. The periodic payments for these services are "rent" costs plus an amount paid to cover the interest cost on the money tied up in the project. Table 14–6 separates these two costs. The amount paid for rent is as shown in column 4 of Table 14–6. This is the counterpart of depreciation which a firm would incur if it purchased the asset outright. Since in the present example the interest is the same with buy–borrow or a lease and the schedule of "rent" is increasing, either a straight-line or decreasing-charge method of depreciation, with taxes, will make buy-borrowing more attractive than leasing with a positive cost of money.

The income tax for the buy–borrow alternative is calculated in Table 14–7 and the present values of the net cash flows are calculated in Table 14–8.

Table 14–7 Buy–Borrow: Computation of Income Tax

Period	Gross Proceeds	Depreciation	Interest	Taxable Income	Income Tax (40%)
1	$21,000	$16,667	$2,500	$1,833	$ 733
2	21,000	16,667	1,707	2,626	1,050
3	21,000	16,667	873	3,460	1,384

Table 14–8 Buy–Borrow: Computation of Present Value of Cash Flows

Period	Gross Proceeds	Income Tax	After-Tax Cash Flow	Present Value (0.05)	Present Value (0.03)
1	$21,000	$ 733	$20,267	$19,302	$19,677
2	21,000	1,050	19,950	18,095	18,805
3	21,000	1,384	19,616	16,944	17,951
				$54,341	$56,433

Leasing gives after-tax cash flows of $1,584 per year, ($21,000 − $18,360) $(1 − 0.4) = \$1,584$, and income taxes of $1,056 each year. The total tax payments are equal in total, but the timing of the tax payments is more favorable under the buy–borrow alternative. The present values of the lease alternative for the different interest rates are $4,314 with a rate of 0.05 and $4,481 with a rate of 0.03. The 0.03 rate is the after tax rate: $0.05(1−.4)$.

This analysis does not indicate, however, whether the investment is still acceptable. The present value of the cash flows resulting from the better alternative, the buy–borrow alternative, is $54,341 or $56,433 depending on whether 0.05 or the after-tax borrowing rate $0.03 = 0.05 − 0.4(0.05)$ using a 40% tax rate is used as the discount rate. With both discount rates the decision would be to accept, since the present value of the cash flows after taxes is positive with either rate compared to the $50,000 cost. With a discount rate of 0.15, the decision would be to reject, since the present value after taxes is less than $50,000. With any nonnegative discount rate the present value of leasing is positive if the analysis of Table 14–2 is used.

Without taxes the use of a 0.05 interest cost for both leasing and bank borrowing resulted in the same present value for leasing and buy–borrow. With taxes and the remainder of the assumptions unchanged, buy–borrow has an advantage compared with leasing if the same borrowing rate is used for both. This arises because the lease arrangement implicitly includes an increasing depreciation charge while the tax law allows a constant or decreasing charge. The present values of the buy–borrow alternative will be higher than the present value of the cash flows associated with leasing, if the costs of leasing and borrowing, without taxes, are equal, and the lease payments are equal and begin at time 1 (the same time that debt payments are made).[6] If any of these conditions are not valid, calculations must be substituted for generalizations.

In all normal cases, buy–borrow will be enhanced by the use of accelerated depreciation. Normally there would be differences in the two alternatives before taxes, the leasing cost would not equal the borrowing cost, the salvage value would differ from zero, and so on. In these cases, it is necessary both to establish the present value of both alternatives and to evaluate any nonmonetary factors involved before a choice could reasonably be made.

14.2.2 Estimating the Life of the Equipment

In the present example it was assumed that the life of the equipment is known to be three years. Actually, the life of the equipment may not be known with certainty. Any equipment purchased is constantly being challenged by new and more efficient models, and sooner or later it will be replaced by one of these newer models. Thus the life of the equipment being considered is uncertain. The

---

[6] For the statement to hold for any discount rate, the financing cash flows implicitly included in the lease analysis also have to be included in the buy–borrow alternative (or be excluded from both).

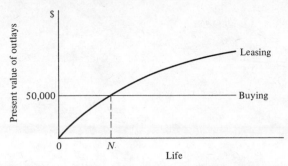

Figure 14.2   **Present value of cash outlays with a flexible lease.**

accounting records may be helpful in estimating the likelihood of various life estimates.

Figure 14–2 shows the different present values of the lease payments and purchase outlays for different assumptions as to the life of the investment (although the lease might be terminated at any time). With a life of zero periods, the lease payments would be zero, since no payments would have to be made. The purchase outlay would be $50,000 for all possible lives. If the life of the investment is expected to be zero, or close to zero, it is more desirable to lease.

As the life of the equipment is assumed to increase, the present value of the lease payments increases since they are paid for longer and longer periods of time. Finally a point is reached where the present value of the lease payments is just equal to the cash-purchase outlays, and it is a matter of indifference whether the firm purchases or leases. This occurs at N years in Figure 14.2. If the life is longer than N years, the present value of the lease payments exceeds the cost of purchasing, indicating that it is desirable to buy. This is consistent with the common-sense conclusion that, all things being equal, the longer the economic life of the equipment, the more desirable it is to purchase the equipment.

In the example illustrated in Figure 14.2, it is assumed that the lease is flexible and that it would be void if the equipment is not satisfactory: hence the zero outlay with a zero life. If the lease was not flexible and there was a firm commitment to make the lease payments even if the equipment turned out to be unusable, the graph should show the minimum present value of the lease payments associated with each assumed life.

If the equipment has been determined to be desirable, the firm must decide whether to buy or lease. But frequently it will be necessary to include the positive cash flows to determine whether the equipment itself is desirable. Figure 14–3 repeats the analysis where the present value of the cash flows is negative up to a life of b years for buying and c years for leasing.

14.2.3   Incorporating Uncertainty

Given the relationships in Figure 14.3, would it be desirable to lease or buy? It would be possible to arrive at a decision if the manager felt that the equipment

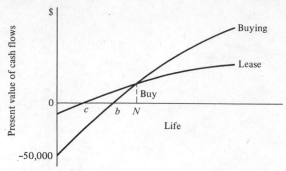

Figure 14.3   Lease versus buy with different possible lives.

was likely to last more than N years. A somewhat more exact procedure would be to compute the probabilities of the equipment lasting a different number of years. Each present value could then be weighted by the probability of its lasting that long in order to obtain a weighted present value.

Example

Assume that analysis indicates an uncertain life for a piece of equipment and that management foresees the probabilities of its having different lives, as shown in Table 14–9.

Table 14–9   **Probability Mass Function for Equipment Life**

Life	Probability
0	0.00
1	0.05
2	0.50
3	0.25
4	0.20
5	0.00
	1.00

The present values of cash flows for buying and leasing for different assumed lives and a new example are given in Table 14–10.

If management merely considered the most likely life of two years, the decision would be to lease (a present value of $10,000 versus a present value of zero). However, a more correct procedure is to multiply the conditional present values for each possible life by the probability of that life occurring.[7] This is done in Tables 14–11 and 14–12.

[7] The analysis assumes that decisions can be made using expected values or, in other words, a linear utility function for money. Chapter 16 considers the case where the monetary values do not reflect the impact of the events on the decision maker.

Table 14–10 Present Values of Buy and Lease Alternatives

Assumed Life	Present Value (buy)	Present Value (lease)
1	($30,000)	0
2	0	$10,000
3	30,000	20,000
4	60,000	30,000

Table 14–11 Computations: Expected Value of Buying

1 Assumed Life	2 Probability	3 Conditional Present Value (buy)	4 Expected Present Value (column 2 × column 3)
1	0.05	($30,000)	($ 1,500)
2	0.50	0	0
3	0.25	30,000	7,500
4	0.20	60,000	12,000
		Expected value of buying =	$18,000

Table 14–12 Computations: Expected Value of Leasing

1 Assumed Life	2 Probability	4 Conditional Present Value (lease)	4 Expected Present Value (column 2 × column 3)
1	0.05	0	0
2	0.50	$10,000	$ 5,000
3	0.25	20,000	5,000
4	0.20	30,000	6,000
		Expected value of leasing =	$16,000

The expected value of buying is higher than the expected value of leasing; thus the decision should be to buy. Where there is some probability that the equipment will have a long life, even where the most likely life is short, it will be necessary to compute the expected value of leasing and purchasing rather than to rely on the decision reached by computing the present values by assuming the most likely life.

If a subjective probability density function over the possible lives is relevant, the better alternative is found in general by multiplying the equation for the payoffs from a given alternative by the equation for the relevant probability density function, integrating and picking the larger expected value. If the payoff equations are linear, or nearly so, the choice can be made by selecting the alternative with the largest payoff for the expected life of the equipment.[8]

14.3 Lease or Buy—Land

An organization which owns land cannot recover the cost of the land through tax deductions unless it sells the land. A corporation which rents land can deduct the rental payments for tax purposes. Assume a cost of borrowing of 5%. If a firm buys land for $2,000,000, it has an immediate outlay of that amount, and there is an explicit interest cost of $100,000 per year before taxes or $52,000 after taxes. If a firm rents the same land for $100,000 per year, under a 48% tax rate, there is again a net cash outlay of $52,000 (the $100,000 reduces taxes by $52,000). The present value of the outlays of $52,000 per year for perpetuity with an after-tax interest rate of 2.6% is $2,000,000. With the facts as given, the cost of renting the land with a lease extending for perpetuity is equal to the cost of the land outright ($2,000,000). This assumes no speculative advantage in owning land.

14.4 Other Considerations

The analysis has been presented as if the only factor which should be considered is the size and timing of the cash flows. Frequently, there are nonquantitative factors which might be brought into the analysis. For one thing, the owning of equipment does result in risks (and possibly satisfactions) of ownership. The problem of servicing the equipment may exist, although this may frequently be solved by entering into a service contract with the manufacturer or an equipment-servicing agency. Hence, it is necessary to evaluate these factors to the extent that they result in a net advantage to the otherwise less attractive alternative.

The possibility of more profitable investments is not relevant here. This consideration is incorporated into the analysis by means of the discounting procedures followed in making the decision. If "better" investments are available, they should also be accepted. In some cases money values can be estimated for qualitative factors by asking how much the manager would pay for them. This determination can be made by asking whether the advantage, in present-value terms, of the more attractive alternative outweights the net qualitative advantages (if any) of the less attractive option.

[8] The expected life for the present example (in which the payoffs are a linear function of the life) is 2.60 years. Since this exceeds the intersection value, leasing and buying are equally desirable when N equals 1.5 years, the optimal alternative is to buy. Note that if the expected life were less than point c in Figure 14.2, neither the buy–borrow nor the lease alternative would have been attractive.

14.5 Summary

The buy-versus-lease decision is different from the normal capital-budgeting decision, since the economic analysis for the lease alternative incorporates the financing in the cash flows, unless an adjustment is made to eliminate the financing element. This means that the widely accepted practice of evaluating an investment using the firm's weighted average cost of capital cannot be used to evaluate the buy alternative if this amount is then to be compared to the present value of the net cash flows of the lease.

Most important, the buy-or-lease decision raises interesting questions about the choice of a rate of discount and the computation of the cash flows (whether or not financing flows are included in the analysis).

The procedure recommended in this chapter can be summarized as follows. If present-value methods indicate that buying the equipment is appropriate, the question remaining is one of how to finance the purchase: by lease or bank borrowing. This question can be answered by finding the interest rate that equates the lease payments to the purchase price. If this rate is less than the borrowing rate, the firm should lease.

Such features as the possibility of early lease cancellation and the effect of taxes are omitted from the above procedure but can be added. Furthermore, if there are other qualitative factors of importance, these must be considered before a final decision is reached. The chapter also describes a statistical decision theory method for handling the problem of uncertain project life in lease-buy decisions.

It is important for the accountant to be familiar with the necessary inputs to the lease–buy decision, such as the relevant cash flows, appropriate tax rates, the effect of depreciation on taxes, and information on expected project lives, if he is to provide data relevant to the decision maker.

QUESTIONS AND PROBLEMS

14–1 What are the differences and similarities between a debt contract and a lease contract?

14–2 "Leasing is more desirable than purchasing because of the tax advantage." Discuss.

14–3 Recognizing that part of the lease payment is for interest, and interest is deductible for tax purposes (as is the entire amount of the lease payment): Is it reasonable to exclude the interest in computing the taxable income of the period (that is, not deduct it in computing the income tax for the cash projection)?

14–4 One method of analyzing leases uses both the cost of capital and the cost of debt. Can two rates of discount be used? Does this suggest a general problem?

14–5 "To determine whether a contract is acceptable, discount the cash flows using the cost of capital." Is this reasonable if the contract is a debt contract? A lease contract?

14–6[9] The Elcor Company can contract to make three lease payments of $10,000 each for the use of a piece of equipment. The first payment is to be made immediately and the other payments are to be made in successive years. Assume that the cost of debt is 0.05.

Required: Determine the debt equivalent of the lease payments.

14–7 Referring to problem 14–6, if the equipment being leased could be bought for $28,000, should it be purchased or leased? Assume that the firm can borrow funds at 0.05 and the equipment is going to be obtained. Assume a zero tax rate for problems 14–7 to 14–11.

14–8 Assume that a piece of equipment costs $28,000 and has related cash flows of $10,200 per year for three years. The cash flows are received at the *beginning* of each year. Using a cost capital of 0.10, is the investment desirable? Should the cost of capital be used?

14–9 Assume that $18,000 could be borrowed with the funds being paid back as follows:

Period	Payments
0	
1	10,000
2	10,000

Referring to problem 14–8, is the investment now desirable? Assume that the initial cash flow could also be used toward the purchase price.

14–10 Referring to problem 14–8, if the company could lease the equipment for $10,000 per year, first payment due immediately, would the equipment be desirable? Assume a cost of debt of 0.05.

14–11 Referring to problem 14–8, if the company could lease the equipment for $9,000 per year with the first payment due immediately, would it be desirable to lease the equipment? Assume that other debt costs 5%.

14–12 The Dundee Company is considering leasing a piece of equipment. There are three lease payments of $10,000 due at the end of each of the next three years. The equipment is expected to generate cash flows of $10,500 per year. Assume that the after-tax cost of debt is 0.05 and the income tax rate is 0.52. The after tax cost of capital is 0.10.

Required
a. Compute the debt equivalent of the lease payments.
b. Prepare a schedule showing a breakdown of the lease payments into interest and "rent."

[9] Problems 14-6 to 14-11 are related and should be done consecutively.

   c. Compute the income tax of each year and the cash flows after tax of leasing. Include the "rent" but exclude the "interest" component of the lease payment.

   d. Compute the present value of the cash flows using a 0.10 after–tax rate.

   e. Should the firm lease the equipment using this calculation?

   f. With lease payments of $10,000 per period, what will be the after-tax cash flow each year? Is the present value of this flow positive?

14–13 Assume that the equipment described in problem 14–12 can be purchased at a cost of $27,232.

Required: Should the equipment be purchased? Use the sum-of-the-year's-digits method of depreciation for tax purposes and a 10% after-tax discount rate.

14–14 Assume that the life of a piece of equipment is uncertain but that management believes that the probabilities of it having different lives are as follows:

Life	Probability
0	0.00
1	0.20
2	0.30
3	0.40
4	0.10
	1.00

The present values of cash flows for buying and leasing for different assumed lives are as follows:

Assumed Life	Present Value (buy)	Present Value (lease)
1	$(10,000)	$(2,000)
2	0	4,000
3	11,000	10,000
4	23,000	16,000

   Required: Is it more desirable to buy or lease?

14–15 A company is planning to purchase a machine for $60,000. In order to do so, however, it will have to borrow the money at 6% interest. The machine would last for 10 years and would have no residual value. The president of the company believes that perhaps a 10-year leasing arrangement might be better than purchasing the machine, but he is not certain as to what is a reasonable rental payment. Assuming a zero tax rate and that all lease payments would be payable at the end of each year, should the company buy or lease?

14–16 An equipment leasing firm has offered Quality Furniture manufacturers a lease on a new machine. The lease would be for six years and would be non-cancellable. Lease payments would total $7,000 per year and would be paid at the beginning of each year. The machine would save Quality an estimated $8,000 each year. Quality has a policy of rejecting all investments that return less than the 10% weighted average cost of capital. Quality could purchase the same machine elsewhere for $32,000, but it would have to borrow the money at 6% interest. Assume that all savings generated by the machine accrue at the end of each year, and assuming zero taxes. If purchased, the machine would last for six years and would have no residual value.

Required: Should Quality acquire the machine, and, if so, should it lease or buy?

14–17 Lathe-Maker Company wants to acquire a new machine being sold by Lessor Company for $108,705. The machine would have a useful life of 10 years. Instead of purchasing the machine, Lathe-Maker could lease the same machine from Lessor at $15,000 per year with each payment due at the beginning of the year.

Required: What is the before-tax interest rate implicit in the lease contract?

14–18 An electronics firm is considering the acquisition of a new machine. The machine would cost $50,000 and would last five years. Alternatively, the machine could be leased for $12,000 payable at the end of each year. If the machine were purchased, it would generate cash flows of $13,000 per year for six years after which it would have no residual value. The financial vice-president of the corporation reasoned that since the cash flows for each year were always greater than the required lease payment, there was nothing to lose in leasing the equipment. Is he correct? Why or why not?

14–19 A manufacturing company is considering leasing a special machine for three years with each payment of $7,000 due at the beginning of the year. The machine is expected to generate net cash flows of $8,000 at the end of each year. The company believes that it could instead purchase the machine which would have a useful life of three years and no residual value. In order to purchase the machine, however, the company would have to borrow money at 10% interest, and that the tax rate is zero. The company uses the 10% as the discount rate in making accept or reject decisions.

Required:
a. What is the highest price the firm should pay for the machine?
b. Should the company lease the machine if the answer in (a) is the purchase price?

14–20 Funtime Toy Makers are planning to introduce a new toy, and they need a special machine for the production. Research by the sales department indicates that the toy could remain on the market either four years, five years, or six years depending upon a number of factors. The company has definitely decided to introduce the toy, but it needs to determine whether to purchase the machine or whether to lease it. The company could buy the machine for $40,000, and it would have a life of six years. By the end of the fourth year, the company believes that the machine would have been used to such an extent that it could not be sold, even though, with proper maintenance, it could still be used within the company for two years. Funtime could, however, acquire a four-year lease for the machine, and after the initial four years, Funtime would have an option to renew the lease each year for another one-year period up to a maximum of six years total. The lease would require a $10,000 payment at the beginning of each year. Assume that Funtime can borrow at 6%, and ignore all tax considerations.

Required:

a. Show how the decision would vary depending upon the assumed length of the equipment's usefulness to the company.

b. Assuming that the sales department believes that the toy's life cycle is equally likely to be four years, five years, or six years, is leasing or buying more desirable? (The decision to acquire the machine has already been made.)

SUPPLEMENTARY READING

GANT, D. R., "Illusion in Lease Financing," *The Harvard Business Review*, March–April 1959, pp. 121–142.

GRIESINGER, F. R., "Pros and Cons of Leasing Equipment," *The Harvard Business Review*, March–April 1955, pp. 75–89.

HERTZ, D., "Risk Analysis in Capital Investments," *The Harvard Business Review*, January–February 1964, pp. 95–106.

MCEACHRON, W. D., "Leasing a Discounted Cash Flow Approach," *The Controller*, May 1961, pp. 214–219.

VANCIL, R. F., "Lease or Borrow—New Methods of Analysis," *The Harvard Business Review*, September–October 1961, pp. 122–136.

———, *Leasing of Industrial Equipment*, New York: McGraw-Hill Book Company, 1963.

Chapter 15

Other Capital-Budgeting Decisions

The present chapter investigates the issues associated with several common capital-budgeting decisions faced by firms. The controller generally plays a substantial role in accumulating the data relevant to such decisions, assisting in the analysis, control, and execution of the projects, and in the evaluation of their success. The four particular decisions selected for examination are illustrative of a wide spectrum of the decisions he may influence. They include:

1. The optimal-plant-size decision.
2. The make-or-buy decision.
3. Foreign investments and the effect of inflation.
4. Debt refunding.

15.1   Optimal Plant Size

The process of choosing the optimal size of a plant is both an interesting theoretical exercise and a question that has important practical significance. Different-sized plants have different efficiencies for different levels of operations, require different timing and amounts of cash outflows, and generate different (both as to timing and amount) streams of cash proceeds. The incomes of future periods are affected by the plant-investment decisions made today.

The problem of optimal plant size is an example of a special type of capital-budgeting decision. The investments are mutually exclusive; if one investment plan is accepted, the others are rejected.

In the examples that follow it is assumed that both the relative proportions and the absolute amounts of the factors of production affect the efficiency of the plant. Thus references to changes in size assume that these proportions also change. All theoretically possible plans are being considered.

Two investment decisions have to be made. One is whether production is desirable at all. The other is choosing which of several investments can do the best job of production. For example, what size of plant should be constructed? If one plant investment is undertaken, all alternative plants will be rejected. Since the alternatives are mutually exclusive, the investment with the highest yield (rate of return) or present-value index (ratio of present value of cash proceeds to investment) may not be the most desirable. The problem can be resolved by using the present-value method. Sometimes more complex alternatives are involved. For example, a small plant might be expanded later, however, at a larger cost than if the larger capacity were built initially.

15.1.1 Graphic Solution

The accepted theoretical procedure is to plot a series of average total-cost curves for all possible plant sizes and all possible combinations of the factors of production. A smooth curve, called an envelope curve, results, which just touches the cost curve of the most efficient plant for each output. (It does not touch the lowest point or minimum-cost point of the curves except for the lowest of all the average total-cost curves.[1])

In Figure 15.1 there are three plants (or combinations of plants), which give cost curves ATC_1, ATC_2, and ATC_3 for plants 1, 2, and 3, respectively. Plant 2 is the most efficient plant if output is not a constraint, as evidenced by the fact

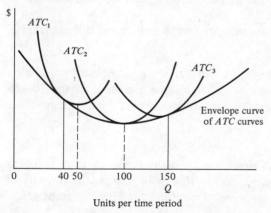

Figure 15.1   Optimum plant size for different outputs.

[1] See J. S. Bain, *Price Theory*, New York: Holt, Rinehart and Winston, Inc. 1952, pp. 117–120. See also E. H. Chamberlin, *The Theory of Monopolistic Competition*, Cambridge, Mass.: Harvard University Press, 1950, pp. 230–259.

that it shows the lowest average total cost. But if 40 units are to be produced, plant 1 is the most efficient. At 150 units, plant 3 is the most efficient. Note that 40 units is not the most efficient point of operations for plant 1. It could actually produce 50 units at a lower average total cost per unit than it could 40 units. Nevertheless, plant 1 is the most efficient plant to produce 40 units. The plant which could produce 40 units at its minimum average total-cost point would not be more desirable, since at 40 units its cost would be greater than plant 1's cost.[2]

If it is desired to build a plant to produce 100 units, plant 2 would be the choice, for at 100 units of production plant 2, which is the most efficient of all the plants, would be operating at maximum efficiency, that is, at the point of minimum average total cost. If the decision were based on a desired production of 150 units, plant 3 would be chosen; but plant 3 would operate at a higher minimum average total cost than plant 2 producing 100 units.[3] (Production is for a given time period.)

15.1.2 Quantitative Solution

Plants of different capacities are mutually exclusive investments. To choose the best of mutually exclusive investments of equal life, the firm can compute the present values of the cash flows of all investment possibilities; the investment with the greatest present value is the best investment. This method does not explicitly use incremental costs, but they are implicit in the solution.

Assume that the forecast for the demand for a product is such that the firm desires to produce 70 units per period as efficiently as possible. The management must choose one of the two following alternatives:

1. A plant that can produce 50 units per period at its most efficient level of output (see ATC_1) in Figure 15.1.
2. A plant that can produce 100 units per period at its most efficient level of output (see ATC_2) in Figure 15.1.

Both plants can produce the expected needs, but the most efficient production capacity of the plant selected may be either less or greater than the 70-unit requirement; thus, management must determine the optimal plant size given the objectives of the firm.

Example

The expected (forecasted) cash flows are given in Table 15–1. A two-year life is assumed and taxes are ignored. At a 0.10 cost of money, the capacity of 100 units per period is the more desirable, since it has the higher present value.

---

[2] Depending on the discreteness in plant size, plant 1 may be optimal for 50 units if no plant can be built with a lower average total cost for this level of output.

[3] The concept of optimal plant size is frequently confused with optimal size of the firm. There are similarities, but the discussion here is limited to the narrower interpretation of what is meant by "plant."

Table 15-1   Present Value of Cash Flows for Two Plants

Plant: Described by Most Efficient Output Level	Cash Flows*			Approximate Rate of Return	Present Value (0.10)
	0	1	2		
50	($20,000)	$15,000	$15,000	0.32	$6,033
100	(35,000)	25,000	25,000	0.27	$8,388

* The net cash flows at a production level of seventy units reflects a higher operating efficiency for the larger plant size and higher initial costs.

The lower rate of return is misleading, since it ignores the fact that the incremental investment is desirable. The analysis in Table 15-2 indicates that the incremental investment is desirable using a 0.10 discount rate.

The analysis in the previous section is correct as far as it goes, but it is incomplete, since it considers the costs for only one level of output. Differences in costs may arise from the operation of the alternative plants at different percentages of their capacity. If probabilities are put on the different output requirements, the expected cost of the different sized plants can be computed.

Table 15-2   Incremental Analysis for the Larger Plant

Investment	Cash Flows			Approximate Rate of Return	Present Value (0.10)
	0	1	2		
Incremental investment	($15,000)	$10,000	$10,000	0.12	$2,355

Example

A motor company is considering building an assembly plant. The decision has been narrowed down to two possibilities: a larger plant at a cost of $1 million or a smaller plant for $764,500. The company desires to choose the best plant at a level of operations of 100,000 cars per month. Both plants have an expected life of 10 years and are expected not to have any salvage value at the time of their retirement. The cost of money is 10%. Income taxes are ignored for simplicity. The relevant facts are given in Table 15-3.

Table 15-3   Yearly Costs for 100,000 Cars per Month

	Large Plant	Small Plant
Initial cost	$1,000,000	$764,500
Direct labor: First shift	500,000	260,000 per year
Second shift		300,000 per year
Overhead	80,000	70,000 per year

Table 15–3 assumes that the large plant will have economies of scale, that is, labor efficiencies in terms of the hours of labor necessary to assemble a car. The small plant will have savings on service (for example, heating). The yearly incremental advantage of the larger plant is indicated in Table 15–4. The present value of savings of $50,000 per year is the present value of an annuity of $50,000 for 10 years at 10%: $50,000 × 6.1446 = $307,230.

Table 15–4   Yearly Incremental Advantage per Month of the Larger Plant (100,000 Cars per Month)

	Saving (Dissaving) per Year of Using the Larger Plant
Direct labor: First shift	($240,000)
Second shift	300,000
Overhead	(10,000)
Saving per year of using the larger plant	$ 50,000

The incremental present value of the larger plant can be compared to its incremental cost. The present value of the savings ($307,230) resulting from use of the larger plant is $71,730 greater than the $235,000 (that is $1,000,000 − $764,500) of additional outlays required, indicating that the larger plant is more desirable than the smaller plant.[4] However, there are some important elements of the problem which have not yet been considered. What is the probability of activity being less (or more) than the expected level? How much of the overhead presented in the example is fixed and how much variable? How badly does the company need elbow room for the possibility that the demand will be greater than expected? How important is it to retain flexibility in order to respond to new information?

Are the costs of possible idle-capacity losses arising from high fixed costs balanced by the ability of the large plant to produce more goods when needed? The small plant is designed to be worked at overtime. If demand increases, the production of the small plant may be increased somewhat by working three shifts as well as on holidays; but the basic fact still remains that the large plant has more reserve capacity. The large plant, however, is more vulnerable to decreases in production since certain costs continue whether the plant produces or not and it costs more.

It is necessary, then, to consider the desirability of the investment not at just one activity level but rather over its entire range of operations.[5] This can be

---

[4] The savings could be computed on a monthly basis and discounted (with an appropriate adjustment of the rate), but this refinement would not alter the result.

[5] A realistic complication, not considered here, would be to include the cost of expanding the small plant together with ways of gathering and evaluating information on future demand once operations begin.

accomplished by weighting the present value of cash flows for different operating rates by the probability of the flows occurring.

Example

Assume that the demand can be approximated by five discrete levels (see Table 15–5). For different levels of operation, the incremental present value of a large plant compared to a small plant is indicated in columns 3 and 4 of Table 15–5. Also shown is the probability of the different levels of demand occurring, as estimated by the marketing department. By multiplying the probability by the present value, an expected (or weighted) present value is obtained. Since the expected present value of the incremental investment is positive, the larger plant is still desirable.

Table 15–5 Expected Present Value of Incremental Plant Investment: 10-Year Life

Level of Operation Cars per Month	Probability of Demand Level	Present Value of Incremental Investment	Expected Present Value
0	0.10	($235,500)	($23,550)
50,000	0.15	(100,000)	(15,000)
100,000	0.25	71,730	17,933
150,000	0.35	100,000	35,000
300,000	0.15	200,000	30,000
	1.00	Expected present value =	$44,383

If the probabilities on the lower two production levels were large enough, either no plant or the smaller plant would have been preferable.[6] In some industries firms may use inventories of finished goods as a means of reducing the investment in the plant. By following a policy of building up a finished goods inventory in anticipation of higher demand, firms may employ plants of a smaller capacity than would otherwise be needed. Although omitted for simplicity, tax effects are relevant to the incremental-advantage computation.

15.2 Make-or-Buy Decisions

The make-or-buy decision may take several forms:

1. To make or buy a product (or a component) the firm is not currently making.
2. To continue to make or begin purchasing a product the firm is currently making.
3. To make more or less of a product than the firm is currently making.

[6] Note that the expected level of activity should not be used for decision purposes in this case because the payoff function given in column 3 is not a linear function of activity.

The three variants of the make-or-buy decision could all be considered capital-budgeting decisions, or they could be considered as incremental-cost-and-revenue decisions with interest a relevant factor. Whether they are treated in one manner or the other depends to some extent on the relative importance of the required investment. Where the investment is large, it is reasonable to consider the make-or-buy decision just as the firm would consider other decisions involving the investment of resources.

15.2.1 Where Significant Resources Are Involved

Consider initially a situation where new plant facilities, including a building or equipment, are required in order to make a product. Thus, the initial investment is significant. In addition to the investment in plant facilities, there is an investment in working capital, for example, cash outlays for rent, financing of material purchases, and so on. First, the series of cash outlays is determined on the assumption that the firm makes the item. This series of cash outlays should be discounted back to the present. The series of cash outlays resulting from making the product would then be compared to another series of cash outlays resulting from purchase. If the present value of this second series of outlays is less than that of the first, the decision (*ceteris paribus*) should be to purchase the product. If the present value of the first series of outlays is less, then the decision should be to invest in the new facilities and make the item.

Costs not requiring cash outlays are included if there is an alternative opportunity connected with using the facilities which give rise to these costs. Thus, a piece of equipment may already be owned, but if making the new product results in another product not being made, there is an opportunity cost connected with making the new product, even though there may not be an out-of-pocket outlay connected with the equipment.[7]

Example

The cost of new equipment needed to produce an item being considered is $25,000. The equipment has an expected life of five years. Other outlays in the beginning of the first period are $1,000. Cash outlays for the next five years are expected to be $2,000 per year if the product is made. If the product is purchased, outlays of $10,000 per year will be required. The cash outlays are assumed to be made at the end of each year. The firm has a cost of money of 10%. The cost of purchasing is an annuity of $10,000 for five years. The value of this annuity at 10% is $10,000(3.7908) = $37,908. The cost of making the product is $25,000 + $1,000 + $2,000(3.7908) = $26,000 + 7,582 = $33,582. The present value of making the product is less than the present value of purchasing the product; thus, the decision should be to make it. A final decision should not be reached without considering the impact of taxes.

[7] In determining the savings from making the product, consideration should be given to the decrease in unit cost that results from the learning process. See Chapter 10 on this point.

This problem is somewhat similar to the problem of buying or leasing discussed in Chapter 14, although the debtlike characteristics of a long term contract are not present. In the buying-or-leasing decision, the possibility of different service lives was considered. This procedure would also apply to the make-or-buy decision. In the above example, if the part were to be used for only four years, and if the equipment had no other use or salvage value, the decision would be to buy the part.

15.2.2 No Resources Required

Next assume a situation where there is and will be idle capacity in the plant and in the machinery presently owned (the opportunity cost of these facilities is therefore zero), and that there is no significant investment in working capital required. In this case the firm could compute the incremental costs connected with producing the product. Note that the incremental costs are used. The traditional accounting costs (which may include an allocation of fixed-overhead costs which would be incurred in any event) are not relevant. Since there may be more than one unit produced, the marginal cost of one unit is also not relevant; the incremental costs are relevant.

Example

The Creighton Company is attempting to determine whether to make or buy a component part presently being produced. The cost of purchasing the part would be $10 per unit. There is and will be excess capacity in the plant, and there is and will be free machine time. The cost of the product in the most recent time period was:

Direct labor	$ 3.00
Material	4.50
Fixed overhead (allocated)	2.50
Variable overhead (identified with product)	1.00
	$11.00

Assume that the fixed overhead would be incurred in any event, and thus there are outlays of only $8.50 identified with the manufacture of the product. The amount would be less if some of the variable overhead were the result of an arbitrary allocation. Since the product could not be purchased for less than $10, it would seem desirable to make the product at an incremental cost of $8.50. If the assumption of free machine time and idle-plant capacity were removed, some or all of the fixed costs might be included. In fact, it is conceivable that the opportunity costs used for decision making are higher than the accounting costs.

In this example the assumption is made that the product is already being produced. This assumption is not necessary to the analysis, except that it lends an air of reliability to the cost information relative to making the product.

Exactly the same analysis is appropriate if the product were not currently in production. The rule to follow is to include only those that are incremental to the decision—those costs incurred only if the product is made. Income lost if the product is made is also an incremental cost. Once again consideration should be given to taxes. In considering the decision to buy, for example, the firm should decide what is to be done with the unused equipment. If it can be disposed of, the tax effects of early retirement are relevant.

In the solution just suggested, interest is not considered. Generally speaking, the making of any product requires the commitment of new capital resources; thus, interest should be taken into consideration. One method of incorporating interest is to compute the present values of the cash flows of the several alternatives. A second possibility is to compute the relevant costs per unit and include an interest cost per unit. The complete exclusion of interest in the analysis of inventory decisions or the computation of product costs would result in a bias toward investment in work in process rather than in plant and equipment. This is not desirable. All investments involving resource allocations should be placed on a comparable basis by the recognition of interest costs incurred.

15.2.3 Other Factors

The firm should also take into consideration qualitative factors such as the advantages and disadvantages of having several sources of supply, the quality of the product and the possibility of improvements in the product, the possibility of better uses of managers, and the risks of the industry the firm is entering.[8] The quantitative analysis may not enable the firm to make the final decision independently of other information, but it supplies a very important factor in making the decision—the answer to the question of the direct impact of the make-or-buy decision on the profitability of the enterprise. Furthermore, the decision maker may be able to decide whether the quantitative difference between two alternatives should be sacrificed for the qualitative advantages of the previously less attractive choice.[9]

15.3 Inflation

When inflation is present, it must be considered in computing the "real" cost of borrowing (the real interest rate) to the firm. The real rate is lower than the stated or contractual rate (the nominal rate) when there is inflation. The real rate should not be used in discounting cash flows for capital budgeting unless the cash flows are expressed in dollars of constant purchasing power.

[8] Sometimes the qualitative factors can be given quantitative values by asking, for example, how much might be paid to obtain the safety features of a given alternative.

[9] Costs are also influenced by learning, and this effect may be quite important for new facilities or equipment. See Chapter 10.

Let

A = amount borrowed
S = amount to be repaid (A plus the amount of interest)
p_0 = price index at the beginning of period
p_1 = price index at end of period
r = real interest rate
S^* = amount to be repaid in terms of constant, beginning-of-period dollars

$$S^* = S\frac{p_0}{p_1} \tag{15.1}$$

Hence, to convert the amount to be paid at the end of the period into beginning-of-the-period purchasing power, S is multiplied by the ratio of the price indices. The formula and examples below assume that money is borrowed for a period of one year. Solving for the real interest rate:

$$A = \frac{S^*}{1+r} \qquad A(1+r) = S^* \qquad r = \frac{S^*}{A} - 1,$$

and, using equation (15.1),

$$r = \frac{Sp_0}{Ap_1} - 1 = \frac{Sp_0 - Ap_1}{Ap_1} \tag{15.2}$$

Example

$$A = \$1,000$$
$$S = \$2,000$$
$$p_0 = 100$$
$$p_1 = 150$$

The nominal interest rate here is $S/A - 1 = 2 - 1 = 1.00$:

$$S^* = S\frac{p_0}{p_1} = \$2,000\left(\frac{100}{150}\right) = \$1,333$$

$$r = \frac{S^*}{A} - 1 = \frac{1,333}{1,000} - 1 = 1.333 - 1 = 0.333$$

or

$$r = \frac{Sp_0}{Ap_1} - 1 = \frac{2,000}{1,000}\frac{100}{150} - 1 = 1.333 - 1 = 0.333$$

Although the nominal (stated) interest rate on the loan is 1, the effective or "real" rate is 0.333.

Example

$$A = \$1,000$$
$$S = \$1,200$$
$$p_0 = 100$$
$$p_1 = 130$$

The nominal interest rate is 0.20:

$$S^* = S\frac{p_0}{p_1} = 1,200\left(\frac{100}{130}\right) = \$923$$

$$r = \frac{S^*}{A} - 1 = \frac{923}{1,000} - 1 = -0.077$$

(a negative real interest rate).

The real rate is negative in this case, indicating that the lender will suffer a real loss.

Example

$$A = \$1,000$$
$$S = \$1,200$$
$$p_0 = 100$$
$$p_1 = 110$$

The nominal interest rate is again 0.20:

$$S^* = 1,200 \times \frac{100}{110} = \$1,091$$

$$r = \frac{S^*}{A} - 1 = \frac{1,091}{1,000} - 1 = 0.091$$

This may be the most typical case. The real rate is positive but substantially less than the nominal rate.

Now define i to be the rate of inflation and k to be the nominal interest rate. Then by definition

$$i = \frac{p_1}{p_0} - 1$$

and the nominal rate is

$$\frac{S}{A} - 1 = k,$$

or

$$1 + k = \frac{S}{A}.$$

We can rewrite (15.1) divided by A as

$$\frac{S}{A} = \frac{S^* p_1}{A p_0}.$$

Since

$$\frac{S^*}{A} = 1 + r \quad \text{and} \quad \frac{p}{p_0} = 1 + i,$$

we have:

$$1 + k = (1 + i)(1 + r)$$

For example, using the above information,

$$i = \frac{110}{100} - 1 = 0.10$$

and

$$1 + r = \frac{1 + k}{1 + i} = \frac{1.20}{1.10} = 1.091$$

$$r = 0.091$$

With continuous time discounting and continuous inflation, then

$$k = i + r$$

15.3.1 Capital-Budgeting Implications

Assume that the price level is expected to double in the next 12 months. There is an interest rate of 100% demanded by the banks (that is, for every dollar borrowed, two must be paid one year later). The one-year investment described in Table 15–6 is being considered. Using the indicated interest rate of 100%, the investment (which has a rate of return of 40%) should be rejected. With a real interest rate of $r = (Sp_0/Ap_1) - 1 = [2,000(100)/1,000(200)] - 1 = 0\%$, the investment would seem to be desirable; however, this would be an incorrect use of the real interest rate. If the funds were borrowed at a cost of 100%, the cash flows would be as given in Table 15–7.

Table 15–6   Investment Cash Flows

Period	Cash Flows
0	$-1,000
1	1,400

Table 15–7   Cash Flows from Investment and Borrowing

Period	Investment	Borrowings	Difference
0	$-1,000	$ 1,000	$ 0
1	1,400	-2,000	-600

The above analysis indicated that this investment is not desirable if the funds are obtained by borrowing at 100%.[10] The same conclusion could be reached by adjusting the $1,400 to the beginning of the period purchasing power. Thus,

[10] It should not be implied that if the present value of the differences were positive the investment would be acceptable. Canceling debt against the investment can be used to show that the investment is not acceptable (if the difference is negative); it cannot be used to show that it is acceptable. However, it would be eligible for further consideration.

$1,400(100/200) = $700, which leads to a reject decision with an immediate outlay of $1,000, since the net present value is negative using the real interest rate of zero.

Still another way to evaluate this investment is to examine the position of the firm at the end of the year. If it does not accept the investment, it will have experienced no change in the real value of its net assets except that due to inflation. If it accepts the investment, its net assets will experience the same effect as well as be reduced by $600, the excess of the loan repayment over the net cash inflows generated by the investment.

An investment must earn a return equal to the cost of money, with both the interest rate and the cash flows unadjusted for the change in the price level. If the interest rate is adjusted to reflect the effective cost of the money with due regard for inflation, and if this is used as the rate of discount, the cash flows must be adjusted into dollars of the same purchasing power. In the example being explored, the real rate is zero. The cash flows in terms of beginning-of-period dollars are given in Table 15–8.

Table 15–8   Cash Flows from Investment: Present Period Dollars

Period	Cash Flows	Adjustment Factor	Adjusted Cash Flows (beginning-of-period purchasing power)
0	$-1,000	—	$-1,000
1	1,400	$\dfrac{100}{200}$	700

The present value of the cash flows is again negative (at a zero rate of discount, the present value is a negative $300).

15.3.2 Foreign Investments

Many firms are expanding operations overseas. In most respects these investments are very similar to those made at home. Yet there are important differences that must be considered. These include different social customs and their impact on the market as well as on employee behavior, problems in the stability of foreign governments, restrictions on a firm's actions, including the movement of capital in and out of the country, availability of a trained labor market, capable suppliers and production facilities, tax policies, foreign-exchange rates, different market distribution systems, and the likelihood of inflation and currency devaluation, to mention but a few.

Continuing the example of the previous section, would the present investment be desirable in a foreign country if the funds were obtained from another country (say the United States), where the real and nominal cost of money is 0.10? If $1,000 is borrowed, $1,100 will have to be returned to investors. If the initial conversion rate between dollars and the foreign currency is 1 to 1, assuming a doubling of the foreign price level and no change in the purchasing power of the dollar, so that the exchange rate becomes 2 for 1, the $1,400 of foreign currency will convert back to $700 U.S. dollars. This is less than the $1,100, that is, $1,000 + 0.1 ($1,000), required to make this a desirable investment. Thus, the investment is again deemed undesirable.

But suppose inflation in the host country is only 10%, the nominal cost of borrowing abroad, the nominal rate is 20%, and the cost of money in the United States 10%.[11] The real rate abroad is 0.091, $[1,200(100)/1,000(110)] - 1$, and the adjusted net cash flow at the end of the first year would be $1,400(100/110) = 1,273$. Discounting at the real rate, 0.091, gives approximately $1,168 or $168 as the net present value, which shows that the investment is now desirable if financed abroad. Given an exchange rate of 1 to 1 at the start and 1.1 to 1 at the end of the period, the $1,400 converts to $1,273 U.S. dollars.[12] Discounting gives $1,157 or a net present value of $157. Since the real cost of money in the United States exceeds the real rate abroad, the project should be financed abroad. Restrictions on capital flows, if present, might add to the argument to finance the investment abroad.

If the funds are already in the foreign country and cannot be removed, it may be necessary to invest them in absolutely undesirable investments to minimize the loss. That is, it may be better to undertake an undesirable investment than to have the funds eaten away by inflation at an even more rapid rate.

Example
Consider now another fictitious example involving different capital costs in different countries. Suppose that the Clark Manufacturing Company is considering building plants in each of four different countries. The cost of money for the company in each country is given in Table 15–9.

The cost of money for the Clark Company in the United States is 0.06. What rate of discount and what capital-budgeting procedure should the company use

Table 15–9   Borrowing Cost by Country

Country	Cost of Money per Year
United States	0.06
Britain	0.08
Japan	0.10
Brazil	0.40

[11] Assume, further, no inflation in the United States.

[12] Exchange rates may not move in such a way that they precisely reflect relative inflationary conditions. The actual rate (or rate expected) might be used. A further refinement would consider the probability distributions of both the future rate of inflation and the exchange rate.

in evaluating investments in the four countries? For ease in exposition, assume that the investment has a life of one year and that the cash flows given in Table 15–10 are available in each country. Assume further that each foreign investment must be financed in the host country.

**Table 15–10   Foreign Investment Cash
Flows Expressed in Host
Country Currency**

Beginning of Year 1	End of Year 1
(100,000)	120,000

The above cash flows are expressed in the currency of each respective country. For an investment in the United States, and assuming a cost of money of 0.06, the present value is $- \$100,000 + (\$120,000/1.06) = \$13,200$.

The positive net present value of \$13,200 indicates that the investment is acceptable, or, more exactly, it indicates that the investment is worthy of further consideration. The riskiness of the venture and qualitative factors should be considered before the investment is finally accepted. Following the above method of analysis and using the capital cost of each country in turn, the investments would be undertaken in all countries except Brazil. (The assumption is made that the capital costs represent the return for the time value of money and do not include an adjustment for risk.[13])

Now assume the same facts as above except that 40% of the investment must be financed by funds from the United States. It is now necessary also to consider possible currency depreciation. The procedure is illustrated using the numbers associated with the Japanese investment and assuming that the exchange rate between yen and dollars over the year now changes from 1 yen to 1 dollar, to 1.25 yen to 1 dollar, perhaps reflecting a relative inflation of 25% in Japan as compared to the United States.

There are two problems. The first is the choice of the rate of discount to use, and the second is the necessity to adjust for currency depreciation. A seemingly reasonable discount rate is obtained by taking a weighted average of the two sources of funds (from the United States and Japan):

	Cost	Proportion of Funds	Weighted Cost
U.S. dollars	0.06	0.40	0.024
Japanese yen	0.10	0.60	0.060
			0.084

---

[13] Portfolio implications of the several investment opportunities are also ignored in this analysis.

Discounting the 120,000 by 0.084 gives $120,000/1.084 = 110,700$. Since the cost of the investment is 100,000, the investment has a positive net present value and seems to be acceptable. However, the above analysis is not correct for two reasons. The 0.084 does not consider the end of period conversion rate or the opportunities available in Japan. At the end of the first year, if the plant is built the investment will yield 120,000 yen. The investment is financed as shown in Table 15–11.

Table 15–11 Financing of Japanese Investment

	Initial Loan	Interest	Total Repayment Required
Yen	60,000	6,000	66,000
Dollars	$40,000	$2,400	$42,400

The total yen available after repayment of the Japanese loan is

$$120,000 - 66,000 = 54,000$$

The expected value of the 54,000 yen converted to dollars is

$$\frac{54,000}{1.25} = \$43,200$$

This amount is received at the end of period 1. The firm can compare the $43,200 to the $42,400, the repayment required at home, or it may discount the $43,200 to the present time using the U.S. borrowing rate and compare it to the amount invested, $40,000:

$$\frac{\$43,200}{1.06} = \$40,750$$

Using either comparison, the investment is marginally acceptable. Here again the next step is to incorporate the riskiness of the investment and, perhaps, other qualitative factors. With a projected exchange rate of 1.4 yen to 1, the investment would be rejected. The computational procedures are:

1. Compute the cash flows in the currency of the land where the investment is being made.
2. Include in the cash flows the funds from foreign sources which can be borrowed to finance the investment, interest on these funds, and the repayment of this debt.
3. Convert the net cash flow that is available for return to the United States for each time period using the expected conversion rate for the time period.
4. Discount these dollars using the borrowing rate in the United States.
5. Finally, consider the investment further if the net present value is positive.

If, instead of borrowing funds, financing in the foreign country is in the form of stock equity funds, the analysis is comparable but the end-of-the-period debt repayment is omitted. For an example of foreign equity financing, assume that 60% of the capital is to be obtained from foreign stock equity sources and the rest from U.S. borrowing. The analysis is given in Table 15–12, again assuming a 1-to-1 exchange rate between yen and dollars at the start of the period. The 48,000 yen converts to $38,400 (48,000/1.25), which is inadequate to justify the project for further consideration. Thus, the same investment that was accepted when financed by debt earning 0.10 is rejected when the investment is financed entirely by stock because of the increased share of returns that go to the foreign investors. The cash flow measured in terms of yen leads to an acceptable investment. When the yen are converted to dollars, the investment is not acceptable if it is financed with 60% foreign stock equity funds and 40% U.S. dollars.

Table 15–12   Net Cash Flows from Japanese Investment Stock Financing

	Beginning of Year	End of Year
Investment flows	$ – 100,000	120,000
Foreign equity financing	+ 60,000	
	$ – 40,000	120,000
Returns allocated to foreign equity investors (0.6 × 120,000)		72,000
Net cash flow	$ – 40,000	48,000

Intuitive evaluations of the cash flows of foreign investments can be unreliable. It is necessary to include systematically the domestic and foreign borrowing rates, the type of foreign capital to be obtained, and the exchange rates at the relevant dates.

15.4   Debt Refunding

A company with debt outstanding should periodically review the possibility of refunding the debt to take advantage of favorable changes in current interest rates. The problem of refunding has sometimes been treated as if it were a problem separate from other decisions being made in the firm, but actually it is a capital-budgeting decision under uncertainty. To simplify the analysis, the question is limited here to whether or not to replace a debt obligation with another debt contract. The possibility of substituting stock equity securities is passed to avoid complications.

15.4.1 Under Certainty

Assume that the IOU Company has $100,000 of debt outstanding that pays 6% (that is, $6,000) interest annually. The bond-issue cost and bond discount of the old debt are assumed to be zero to simplify the explanation when taxes are considered. The maturity date of the securities is 10 years from the present. Assume that a new 10-year security could be issued that would yield 4% per year. The issue costs would be $8,000, and the bond redemption penalty on the old bonds would be $4,000. Ignoring tax considerations, should the old bonds be replaced with new securities?

The solution using the current effective interest rate is as follows:

1. Determine the interest savings per year resulting from the new contract:

Annual interest of old debt	$6,000
Annual interest of new debt	4,000
Savings per year	$2,000

2. Compute the present value of the savings per year, using the current effective yield. Present value of $2,000 per year for 10 years using a 4% discount rate: $2,000(8.111) = $16,222.

3. Compare the present value of the savings with the present value of the outlays:

Present value of savings	$16,222
Present value of outlays	12,000
Present value of net savings	$ 4,222

Since the net savings are positive (the present value of the savings is greater than the present value of the outlays minus the bond issue cost plus the redemption premium), the refunding of the old investment should be undertaken.

A possible criticism of the above solution centers on the choice of the effective rate of interest of the new security as the appropriate rate of discount for determining the present value of the savings per year, instead of using the corporation's cost of capital or some other discount rate.

The refunding of a bond issue requires an investment of resources today just like any other capital-investment decision. If the cost of capital is used to determine the worth of capital investments, should the same criterion be used in determining whether this refunding should be undertaken?[14] The $12,000 of issue costs and redemption penalty necessary to accomplish the refunding is an

---

[14] It is still an unresolved issue whether the cost of capital should be used to take account of risk in evaluating investments. However, many firms do use their cost of capital and if it is used the problem described will appear.

investment analogous to other investments, but there are several differences. The benefits (savings) promised by this investment are more certain than those available from most investments. The refunding operation reduces the real total debt outstanding (the present value of the debt burden is less) and the decrease is the relevant measure of the value received. The use of the effective rate of interest of the new security to find the present debt equivalent of the series of interest savings (the difference between the interest paid with refunding and the interest which would have to be paid if the bonds were not refunded) is consistent with finding the present value of the new debt.

Continuing the above illustration, assume that the cost of capital is 12% and that this rate is used to discount the cash flows connected with the refunding operation. The computations would be as follows:

1. Compute the present value of the savings per year, using the cost of capital as the appropriate rate of discount: $2,000(5.65) = $11,300.
2. Compare the present value of the savings with the present value of the outlays.

Present value of savings	$11,300
Present value of outlays	12,000
Present value of dissavings	$ (700)

Since the present value of the outlays is greater than the present value of the savings, it would seem that the refunding should not take place. The previous solution using the effective rate of interest of the debt suggests that the refunding should take place. If the previous solution is accepted, bond refunding will have a priority over conventional alternative investment opportunities.

The use of the current bond yield rate may give a more reasonable solution since the outlay required actually reduces the amount of debt outstanding. In decisions involving the issue or retirement of debt the yield rate of the new debt is appropriate for discounting the cash flows resulting from the debt. Use of the bond yield rate in refunding is predicated on the assumption that refunding is desirable if it returns more than that yield. Ordinarily a firm has other uses for the cash required for the refunding, and these other uses would yield more than the bond yield rate, but these investments will have different risk characteristics from the outlays for refunding. They do not result in an improved capital structure. In the above example, the present value of the debt was reduced by $16,222, the present value of the interest savings; the net savings were $4,222. Furthermore, the certainty of the savings is greater than with the average investment.[15]

[15] Theoretically for other investments, it would be appropriate to use the current interest rate and make a separate adjustment for uncertainty. The decision maker could then decide whether the improvement in capital structure was worth the difference between the savings from refunding and the best alternative use of funds.

15.4.2 Tax Issues

For a more complete solution of the refunding decision the income tax effect must also be included. Whether or not particular items are deductible for tax purposes in the year of refunding depends on the exact nature of the transactions and on the tax regulations. If the retirement and issue are separate transactions (there is not an exchange), the costs of retiring the old bonds, including the redemption premiums and the book loss resulting from writing off unamortized bond discount and bond issue costs, are all deductible for tax purposes at the time of retirement.[16] However, the costs of issuing the new bonds have to be written off over the life of the new bonds.

Example (*continued*)

Assume a tax rate of 40%. Should the bonds described earlier be refunded? It is necessary to include the tax effects for each year.

1. There will be a saving equal to 40% of the bond redemption costs of the old securities in the year of issue:

    tax saving in year 1: 0.40($4,000) = $1,600

2. Taxes for each year will be decreased by 40% of the portion of the bond issue costs (of the new issue) allocated to the period:

    allocation of bond issue costs to each year $8,000/10 = $800

    tax savings occurring each year $800(0.40) = $320

3. The interest expense will be reduced by $2,000, and thus taxes will increase by 40% of this reduction, or by $800.

Interest decrease	$2,000
Loss on tax deduction	800
Net saving on interest expense	$1,200

4. The net savings each year will be:

After tax savings on interest	$1,200
Savings on taxes	320
Net saving per year	$1,520

Using 4%, the before tax cost of debt and discounting the tax savings of the first year for one year, the present value of the savings will be:

Present value of net savings at 4%	$1,520(8.111) = $12,329
Tax savings first year at 4%	1,600(0.962) = 1,539
Present value of savings, allowing for taxes	$13,868

[16] This is typically a reason for attempting to establish them as separate transactions.

The introduction of income taxes makes the refunding somewhat less desirable in this case. The refunding would cost $12,000, and the present value of the savings is $13,868. In the same situation, without income taxes, the present value of the savings is $16,222. But the effect of income taxes on the solution cannot be assumed to always be in the same direction, since it depends on the size of redemption premiums, the bond-issue costs of the new issue, and the unamortized bond-issue costs and the discount of the old issue which are deductible in the year of refunding rather than later. It can be properly argued that the after-tax interest cost of 2.4% $[0.04(1 - 0.4)]$ should be used to accomplish the discounting for time since the cash flows are on an after tax basis. The use of this discount rate gives:

Present value of net savings	$1,520(8.983) =$	$13,654
Tax savings first year	$1,600(0.980) =$	1,568
Present value of savings, allowing for taxes		$15,222

The solutions suggested here are based on the assumption that the future tax rates will be the same as the present rate of 40%. If a change in rates is expected, this should be incorporated into the solution.

15.4.3 Extension of Maturity of Debt and Changes in Interest Rates

New issues often extend the maturity of the debt; that is, they push the date of repayment further into the future. All other things being equal, this is desirable, since it reduces the payment pressure accompanying a debt of early maturity.

How does a firm place a dollar value on the fact that the maturity date of the debt is now 1990 instead of 1985? One compromise procedure is to incorporate this factor as a qualitative factor to be considered in favor of refunding if refunding is not clearly advantageous following the quantitative analysis. Alternatively, a monetary value could be estimated and incorporated into the analysis.

15.4.4 Bond Discount

What is the relevance of an unaccumulated bond discount to the refunding decision? The book value of the liability is not relevant to the refunding decision, except through its effect on income taxes. This situation is analogous to the analysis of equipment replacement, where the book value of the asset being replaced is not relevant to the decision while the tax basis is relevant. Since the bond discount is a valuation account to the face value of the debt, it is not relevant to the refunding decision. This is true no matter how the discount has been accumulated through the years. What is relevant is the impact of the promise to pay an amount in n years and the promise to pay interest for n years. The present value of these promises represents the true liability; the liability recorded on the company's books does not. The computations of the preceding sections appraising refunding were made without reference to the accounting records to determine the balance in the discount account. Whether a book gain or loss will be suffered in the year of refunding as a result of the decision is not relevant to making the decision, if the appropriate computations indicate that refunding is desirable, and if the decision is being made on an economic (cash flow) basis.

The presence of bond discount on the books may result in a loss on retirement of the outstanding bonds. This should be taken into consideration in computing the tax savings of the first year. Since it will increase the tax loss, the presence of bond discount, which is deductible for tax purposes, increases the tax saving and makes refunding more desirable.

15.5 Summary

This chapter described the application of capital-budgeting techniques to the optimal-size-plant, the make-or-buy, the evaluation of investments with inflation and foreign investments, and the bond-refunding decisions. The wide range of decisions discussed illustrates the multitude of possibilities that exist for applying capital-budgeting procedures. Any decision where the results (cash outlays or inflows) are spread out through time is susceptible to solution by using these tools.

QUESTIONS AND PROBLEMS

15–1 Distinguish between determining the optimal size of a plant and the optimal size of a firm.

15–2 Is it better to build a small plant and work it intensively (with overtime and double time) or to build a large plant and sometimes have idle capacity?

15–3 Is the plant which offers the highest rate of return (yield) the most desirable plant (in a set of mutually exclusive alternatives)?

15–4 Assume that a firm has two alternatives:
  a. Plant A promises to earn a net present value of $10 million with certainty (assume that this is a cost-plus government contract). Instead of plant A, a larger plant, plant B, could be built.
  b. Plant B may earn a net present value of $50 million (this outcome has a 0.5 probability) or it may return a negative net present value of $20 million (this outcome also has a 0.5 probability).
Which of the two plants is preferable? Assume that the firm's yearly earnings have averaged $5 million per year.

15–5 To make a product, inventories must be increased by a total of $5 million for each year. Should this be considered a cash outlay? Should it be considered as part of the investment to make the product?

15–6 Would you expect the relevant costs for decision making (such as the make-or-buy decision) to be higher or lower than the accounting costs computed on an absorption-costing basis?

15–7 In making the bond-refunding decision, should the present value of any interest savings be computed using the cost of capital?

15–8 How does the presence of discount on the bonds which are presently outstanding affect the bond-refunding decision?

15–9 If the new debt will extend the maturity of the debt, how does this affect the bond-refunding decision?

15–10 What are the uncertainties connected with the bond-refunding decision?

15–11 If the present value of the savings are larger than the present value of the outlays connected with refunding, should the decision be to refund? Explain.

15–12 The Tin Can Company must choose between two plants. One is large and has sufficient capacity for working efficiently at the higher ranges of possible sales estimates. The other plant is smaller and is more efficient at lower range of sales, but is less efficient if sales are high. The net present values of the two plants are shown with different assumed budgeted sales levels. The probability of attaining that level of sales is also shown.

Level of Expected Sales (as a % of budgeted sales)	Probability	Present Value	
		Large Plant	Small Plant
150	0.10	$50,000,000	$40,000,000
100	0.70	35,000,000	30,000,000
50	0.20	(10,000,000)	20,000,000

Required: Which of the two plants should the company build based on the information presented?

15–13 The Ashcot Company has $10 million of debt outstanding which pays 0.05 (that is, $500,000) interest annually. The maturity date of the securities is 20 years from the present. Assume that a new 20-year security could be issued which would yield 0.04 per year. The issue costs would be $800,000 and the call premium on redemption of the old bonds is $100,000. Assume a zero tax rate for this company. The cost of capital for the firm is 0.10.

Required: Should the present bonds be refunded?

15–14 (See problem 15–13.) If the corporate income tax marginal rate is 0.52, is the refunding desirable? Use 0.04 as the discount rate in making these computations.

15–15 (See problem 15–13). How would your answer be modified if the maturity date of the new issue were 30 years instead of 20 years?

15–16 The Bond Company has $10 million of debt outstanding which pays 0.06 annually. The maturity date of the securities is 20 years from the present. Assume that new securities could be issued which would have the same maturity date. The issue costs of the new securities would be $2.7 million; there is no call premium on the present debt. Assume a zero tax rate.

Required: Determine the rate of interest or yield rate of new securities at which the firm would just break-even if they refunded. Determine this rate to the nearest percent.

15–17 The Alcott Company operates in a foreign country and has found that it can borrow money at an indicated interest rate of 0.20. It is considering borrowing $1.5 million for a period of one year. The current price index is 150 and the price index is expected to increase to 180 at the end of the year.

   a. What is the expected real interest rate of the borrowed money?

   b. If the $1.5 million can be invested in the foreign country to yield $1.7 million at the end of one year, is the investment acceptable? Assume that the company uses a 0.10 cost of capital for investment decisions in the United States.

   c. If the 1.5 million is already on hand in the foreign country and if there are exchange restrictions preventing the withdrawal of the funds, is the investment described in part b acceptable?

15–18 The Cranston Company operates in a foreign country and has found that it can borrow money at an indicated interest rate of 0.30. The current price index is 100 and the price index is expected to increase to 120. What is the real interest rate?

15–19 In recent years in most countries a 0.15 return after taxes would generally be considered an excellent rate of return. If the cash flows projected for an investment in a country with a large amount of inflation promised a return of 0.15, the investment might not be acceptable from an economic point of view. Explain why this difference exists.

15–20 The Raymon Chemical Company is considering whether to build a small plant or a large one to manufacture a new product with an expected market life of ten years. The key variable is demand, which may be high in the initial two-year introductory period or low. Demand in the last 8 years will be dependent on the level in the first 2 years.

The market demand estimates are as follows:

Situation	Initial Period 1st 2 years	Future Period last 8 years	Probability
A	High	High	0.6
B	High	Low	0.1
C	Low	High	0.0
D	Low	Low	0.3

Estimates of the relevant income and costs are:

1. Cost of large plant $3,000,000
2. Cost of small plant   1,300,000
3. Cost of expanding small plant to large plant capacity
   in 2 years   2,200,000

The large plant will earn $1,000,000 of cash flows per year with high demand and $100,000 with low demand. The small plant will earn $450,000 of cash flows with high demand and $400,000 with low demand unless it is expanded in which case it will earn $700,000 with high demand and $50,000 with low.

Required:

a. What alternatives does Raymon have?
b. Is the level of sales in the initial first 2 years an accurate indicator of the level of sales in subsequent periods?
c. Which alternative should Raymon accept? Assume a 0.10 rate of discount.

15–21 A product is currently being manufactured on a machine. It has variable costs of production and sale of $7.50 per unit. The rate of production expected in the future is 10,000 units per year, and the sales price per unit is $8.50. It is expected that the old machine can be used without repair for the next ten years.

An equipment manufacturer has agreed to accept the old equipment in a trade-in for a new version. The new machine lists for $200,000 but would cost $170,000 with the trade-in and would result in incremental costs of $5.50 per unit. It has an expected life of ten years, and an expected salvage of $10,000 at that time.

The old equipment could be sold on the open market now for $30,000. It has an expected salvage of $1,000 ten years from now.

The product can be purchased in a semifinished state for $7.00. Direct (and variable) finishing sales expenses are estimated at $1.00 per unit. If the product is bought in semifinished form the machine is not needed. Ignore income taxes. The appropriate time-discount rate for this company is 0.05.

Assuming the company intends to market the product in question, what alternatives are available to the company and which should it elect? (Support your choice with relevant calculations.)

SUPPLEMENTARY READING

BIERMAN, H., and S. SMIDT, *The Capital Budgeting Decision*, New York: Macmillan Publishing Co., Inc., 1975.

DEAN, JOEL, *Capital Budgeting*, New York: Columbia University Press, 1951.

GUPTA, S., and J. ROSENHEAD, "Robustness in Sequential Investment Decisions," *Management Science*, October 1968, pp. 18–29.

HAMMOND, J., "Better Decisions with Preference Theory," *The Harvard Business Review*, November–December 1967, pp. 123–141.

HERTZ, D., "Investment Policies That Pay Off," *The Harvard Business Review*, January–February 1968, pp. 96–108.

HESPOS, R., and P. STRASSMAN, "Stochastic Decision Trees for the Analysis of Investment Decisions," *Management Science*, August 1965, pp. 244–259.

HILLIER, F. S., "The Derivation of Probabilistic Information for the Evaluation of Risky Investments," *Management Science*, April 1963, pp. 443–457.

LUTZ, F., and V. LUTZ, *The Theory of Investment of the Firm*, Princeton, N.J.: Princeton University Press, 1951.

MAGEE, J., "Decision Trees for Decision Making," *The Harvard Business Review*, July–August 1964, pp. 126–138.

———, "How to Use Decision Trees in Capital Investment," *The Harvard Business Review*, September–October 1964, pp. 79–96.

QUERIN, G. D., *The Capital Expenditure Decision*, Homewood, Ill.: Richard D. Irwin, Inc., 1967.

ROBICHECK, A. A., and S. C. MYERS, *Optimal Financing Decisions*, Englewood Cliffs, N.J.: Prentice-Hall, Inc., 1965.

Chapter 16

Utility and
Capital Budgeting

Solutions to capital-budgeting decisions frequently assume that the cash flows of all periods are known with certainty. If this assumption is not explicitly made, an implicit assumption of a mean value is made, that is, the expected value, or what might be called, inaccurately, the best guess of the cash flows. The solution generally accepted among academic authors and a growing number of businessmen is that the present-value method gives the most useful information. If the present value of the cash flows is positive, the investment is acceptable if it is independent of other investments. If a set of investments are mutually exclusive, the investment with the largest net present value is the most desirable, assuming that the investment periods under consideration are comparable.

Many business firms use the cost of capital (a weighted average of the cost of interest-bearing debt and the cost of stock) as the discount rate applied to the expected value of the cash flows. This means of solution can be criticized on two counts. First, the use of the cost of capital incorporates an implicit allowance for risk of a very special nature which is compounded through time. But risk does not necessarily increase at a compound rate through time. Second, it is not always appropriate to consider, as this approach implicitly does, only the expected value of the cash flows and to ignore the other possible values. The notion of risk really has two parts. One involves the fact that more than one event may occur. This is uncertainty. The other is that the impact of the outcomes on the manager or investor may not be adequately represented by the associated monetary values. This chapter presents a method for separating these two factors so that they may be more appropriately handled. In this respect this chapter departs from the discussion in Chapters 13–15, where the terminology "cost of money" was used explicitly to avoid this problem.

16.1 Investment Decisions Under Uncertainty

The present-value method gives information that helps management decide to accept or reject independent investments and to choose the best of mutually exclusive investments. Under conditions of certainty and where the amounts involved are not too large, this information is sufficient for management to make its decisions. But under conditions of uncertainty involving large amounts of money, the present-value procedure does not yield a sufficient measure of the desirability of an investment. The capital-budgeting method should take risk attitudes into consideration.[1] Utility theory combined with probability theory provides a possible approach.

Assume that an investor or manager is offered the choice between two alternatives (or gambles), call them A and B[2]:

Alternative A	Alternative B
0.50 probability of $1,000 0.50 probability of $0	1.0 probability of $X

For the investor or manager to be *indifferent* between alternatives A and B, what value of X should be inserted in the description of alternative B? If it is less than $500, he is somewhat averse to gambling in this situation.[3] If X is more than $500 the manager requires something for forsaking the opportunity of winning $1,000. The expected monetary value of alternative A is $500. If the manager is indifferent between alternative A and $500 certain, the manager's utility function is linear in this range of values.

The point of indifference for many investors and managers occurs when X is less than $500.[4] That is, they are willing to accept a certain sum of less than $500 in place of the gamble represented by alternative A. Questions similar to the above may be used to determine the entire utility function. For example, assume the following relationship:

$$U(\$X) = 0.5U(\$0) + 0.5U(\$1,000)$$

where $U(\$X)$ is the utility of X dollars. •

[1] Another consideration is the timing of the information. This will not be discussed here.

[2] Any investment under uncertainty may be thought of as a gamble.

[3] Someone adverse to gambles is someone who would equate a gamble to a certain value less than the gamble's monetary expectation.

[4] If a manager makes decisions on expected monetary values, an increase in the amounts involved may tend to elicit the indicated response.

Arbitrarily setting the utility of $0 to be zero and the utility of $1,000 to be 1, and assuming that the value chosen by the manager for X is $300:[5]

$$U(\$300) = 0.5(0) + 0.5(1) = 0.5$$

The utility of $300 is equal to 0.5. Now suppose that the manager is given a chance on a gamble involving $1,000 or $300, both with probabilities 0.5. The monetary expectation of this gamble is $650, but assume that the manager is adverse to risk and is willing to accept as little as $500 for certain in place of the gamble. Therefore,

$$U(\$500) = 0.5U(\$1,000) + 0.5U(\$300) = 0.5(1) + 0.5(0.5) = 0.75$$

The utility of $500 is 0.75. By asking the manager a variety of similar questions, the entire function can be determined.[6] See Figure 16.1 for an assumed utility function.

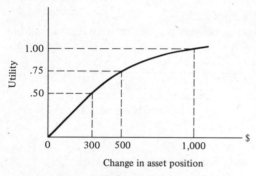

Figure 16.1   A utility function.

The horizontal axis measures the change in the asset position. The vertical axis measures the utility of the change. The utility function shows the utility of different possible changes for an individual. The utility function should be checked for validity before it is used. This might be done by asking questions concerning gambles implied by the function. Preciseness should not be expected, but perhaps a usable utility function may be obtained. If the utility function is linear, expected monetary values are a reasonable measure of the desirability of an investment. This is not the case for the present manager: he is adverse to risk. The marginal utility to this manager for large gains is positive and decreasing.[7]

---

[5] The first two utility values chosen are arbitrary; that is, the origin and interval scale are not unique. Technically a utility function is unique up to a linear transformation. The choice of a utility of zero for an outcome at least as bad as the worst outcome in the decision situation and unity for an outcome at least as favorable as the best outcome in the decision situation are common but not necessary choices.

[6] The reader is referred to Appendix 16A for an explanation of the procedure's logic.

[7] It is generally assumed that the utility function is bounded from above (that is, it approaches a maximum amount).

16.2   Using the Utility Function

Consider again alternative A, described in Section 16.1 as having a 0.5 probability of $0 and a 0.5 probability of $1,000. Assume that the utility of these uncertain payoffs can be read from the utility function of Figure 16.1 (say the utilities are zero and 1, respectively). The expected utility is 0.5, 0.5(0) + 0.5(1.0), in this case. The next step is to determine the certainty equivalent of the gamble. The certainty equivalent is $300 (the utility of $300 is 0.5). The certainty equivalent can be obtained from the graph by entering the vertical axis at 0.5 and finding the value of the asset change on the horizontal axis that has a utility index of 0.5.

The expected monetary value of alternative A is equal to $500, 0.5($1,000) + 0.5(0). Its certainty equivalent is $200 less than the expected monetary value; thus, the manager attaches a $200 discount for risk to this alternative.

The discount for risk arises because the monetary values of $1,000 and $0 do not adequately represent the impact of these changes on the manager. If they did, there would be no discount. Thus, if the utility function were linear, the expected monetary value of alternative A would have a certainty equivalent of $500. Uncertainty alone then is not sufficient to produce a discount for risk: there must also be an aversion to risk. The information could be presented as follows:

Expected monetary value of alternative	$500
Certainty equivalent	300
Discount for risk	$200

The general procedure for one gamble may be summarized as follows:

1. Determine the utility of each discrete event (say, possible earnings of $0 and $1,000).
2. Compute the expected utility of the alternative by weighting the utilities of each event by the probability of occurrence.
3. Find the asset change with the same utility as the expected utility. This is the certainty equivalent.
4. Compute the expected monetary value of the investment. Compare the expected monetary value and the certainty equivalent to obtain the discount for risk.

16.3   Complex Alternatives

Instead of one gamble with a 0.5 probability of $1,000 and a 0.5 probability of $0, assume that there is an opportunity to enter into two identical gambles (A_1 and A_2) of this nature. Suppose that the manager must decide to reject both or engage in both—he cannot accept one gamble and reject the other. Assume that the utility function given in Table 16–1 is now relevant.[8]

Table 16–1   Assumed Utility Function

Dollars	Utility Measures for Changes in His Asset Position
$ − 400	0.00
− 200	0.40
0	0.60
75	0.685
200	0.75
300	0.80
500	0.86
600	0.88
800	0.91
1,000	0.95
1,600	0.98
2,000	1.00

Suppose that the manager must pay $400 for the opportunity to engage in this double gamble. The double gamble has three possible outcomes. The outcomes together with the expected utility of the total gamble are given in Table 16–2. The outcomes of the two gambles are independent.

Table 16–2   Expected Utility Computation: Double Gamble

1 Outcome	2 Probability of Outcome	3 Utility of Outcome	4 Column 2 × Column 3
$ − 400	0.25	0.00	0.000
600	0.50	0.88	0.440
1,600	0.25	0.98	0.245
		Expected utility =	0.685

The certainty equivalent for this gamble from Table 16–1 exceeds zero and the gamble would be accepted. This can be determined by comparing the expected utility of the gamble, 0.685, with the utility of $0, which is 0.60. The fact that the certainty equivalent exceeds zero implies that the investor would be willing to pay something to engage in this gamble. If the utility function were

[8] A utility function can be developed either for the various asset positions of the decision maker or for changes in the asset position. The latter is done here. It is often assumed that the function so obtained is relevant over a range of initial asset positions for the given decision maker.

more completely specified, a good approximation of this amount could be determined.

Suppose, however, that the two identical gambles are separable and that each requires an investment of $200. An immediate decision is still required for each investment. Three alternatives exist: accept one gamble, accept both gambles, or reject both gambles. The expected utility of accepting both gambles has been calculated in Table 16–2 to be 0.685. The utility of rejecting both gambles is 0.60, the utility of $0 net change. The utility from selecting only one of the component gambles is

$$0.5U(-\$200) + 0.5U(+\$800) = 0.5(0.40) + 0.5(0.91) = 0.655$$

which is less than the utility of undertaking both gambles.

The certainty equivalent of this double gamble is $75. The expected utility of accepting double gamble is the greatest of the three choices. The reader may be surprised that the single-gamble alternative yields a lower expected utility given a manager with an aversion to risk. This result is due to the nature of the assumed utility function and the fact that each gamble is relatively desirable.

As a final possibility, suppose that the constituent gambles follow one another and that a decision can be made concerning gamble A_2 after the result of gamble A_1 is known. Since a single gamble here has an expected utility of 0.655, which exceeds the utility of doing nothing, 0.60, gamble A_1 should be accepted. Whether gamble A_2 should be accepted depends on the change, if any, in the investor's utility function due to the results of gamble A_1. If the utility function for changes in his asset position is essentially unaffected by the result of the first gamble, the second gamble will also have a utility index of 0.655 and be acceptable.

In none of the above cases is it correct to assume that the expected utility of immediately accepting both gambles A_1 and A_2 is twice 0.655 (the utility of one of the two constituent gambles). This would incorrectly assume that $U(A_1 + A_2) = U(A_1) + U(A_2)$, a condition that holds only for linear utility functions. It is also incorrect to assign the double gamble a certainty equivalent of twice the certainty equivalent of one of the constituent gambles, since this assumes that $E[U(A_1 + A_2)] = E[U(A_1)] + E[U(A_2)]$. This relation also holds generally only for linear utility functions.

The components of a gamble cannot usually be separated, evaluated, and then recombined. This has relevance to the investor considering several investments simultaneously and to the manager involved in selecting a set of capital projects at a point in time.

The general procedure is to:

1. List all the possible monetary outcomes.
2. Determine the probability of each outcome.
3. Assign utility measures to each outcome.
4. Compute the expected utility of the gamble.

The sum of money with this expected utility is called the certainty equivalent. Decisions between alternatives can be made using the expected utilities or the certainty equivalents.

Example

Ask yourself how much you would be willing to pay for one of the gambles described above. Also ask yourself the minimum amount you would be willing to accept for certain rather than gambling (one gamble). Compare your answers.

16.4   Time Discounting

Most investments differ from the gamble described above, since the benefits do not occur instantaneously but are spread out through time. The situation involving the double gamble could, for example, be thought of as a two-period investment the outlay occurring in period 0, the first gamble in period 1, and the second gamble in period 2. Instead of dealing with immediate amounts, the investor must concern himself with inflows and outflows that take place over different time periods. In addition, the outcomes connected with the investment will require utility measures.

The theory dealt with so far in this chapter is not easily applied to long-run investments where the cash flows are significantly separated in time, and where the date of resolution of the uncertainty is very important. Where the date when the outcome is known is important, the necessary time adjustments cannot be adequately made by discounting, because some evaluations depend upon information obtained near the resolution date. Further, some alternatives permit strategic information to be obtained earlier than do others. Although progress is being made on these issues, practically useful and theoretically satisfying methods are not yet available.

16.4.1 Independent Cash Flows

One method that has appeal and that offers a reasonable approximation requires that all cash flows for a given project first be discounted for time. If, for the moment, the yearly cash flows can be considered as independent events, a computation of the present values of all possible cash flows together with their probabilities can be made. After converting the present value of the cash flows associated with each possible set of events into utility measures, a decision can be based on the expected utility calculations.

There remains the problem of choice of the rate of interest to use in the discounting. In computing present values, managers frequently use the cost of capital. The possibility of the cash flow not being realized and the reaction of the investor to this possibility are assumed to be effectively incorporated into the analysis using this rate. The use of the cost of capital (which implicitly incorporates a risk allowance) is assumed to take "normal" risk into consideration. With the proposed procedure, the possibility that the cash flow will not occur is taken into account by the probabilities, and the investor's reaction to the monetary amounts involved is taken into account by means of the utility function. Thus, it is now appropriate to use a default-free measure for time discounting, say, the interest rate associated with long-term government securities. This rate, combined with an explicit statement of the probabilities, is a more effective way of incorporating uncertainty into the analysis than using different rates of discount for different investments or ignoring uncertainty entirely.[9]

Table 16–3 Investment Cash Flows

Period	Proceeds
0	($400) outlay
1	0.5 probability of $0 and 0.5 probability of $1,000
2	0.5 probability of $0 and 0.5 probability of $1,000

Assume a situation where the investment consists of the cash flows given in Table 16–3 (assume that the cash flows of each period are independent). In Figure 16.2, the investment under consideration is represented by a tree diagram. Using a default-free discount rate of 0.05, the figures after the colons show the present values of the possible results. The probability of each final outcome in this case is $0.5(0.5) = 0.25$.

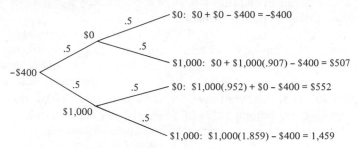

Figure 16.2 Investment tree diagram.

Now, if the monetary values calculated at the end of the tree are valid measures of the impact of the outcomes on the decision maker, the expected value of the

[9] Some authors prefer to consider risk in terms of the variance (and sometimes higher moments) of the return distribution. This method is perhaps easier from the point of view of calculations, but it does not provide a clear indication of just how the risk is being weighted. In part this is because risk has two elements: the uncertainty of the cash flow, a probabilistic problem, and the inability in some cases to measure the impact of events on the decision maker with a single quantitative measure, money, a utility problem.

investment, $0.25(-\$400) + 0.25(\$507) + 0.25(\$552) + 0.25(\$1,459) = \$539$, can be used as the value of this investment in decision making. Since the net expected value is positive, the investment is desirable.

If, on the other hand, the amounts are too large to be treated in this manner, or if other considerations are involved, the monetary outcomes might be converted into utilities. Assume that the utilities of Table 16–1 apply for the present decision maker. Approximation yields the values in Table 16–4. The expected utility of the investment exceeds the utility of the decision maker's present asset position $[U(\$0) = 0.60]$, and therefore the investment is desirable.

Table 16–4   Expected Utility Calculations

1 Net Present Value	2 Utility	3 Probability	4 Column 2 × Column 3
$ – 400	0.00	0.25	0.00
507	0.86	0.25	0.2150
552	0.87	0.25	0.2175
1,459	0.97	0.25	0.2425
		Expected utility =	0.6750

The advantage of this procedure is that it takes into consideration both the probabilities of different events occurring and the reaction of management to the possible events. Large negative present values would have relatively small (possibly negative) utility measures and thus would be appropriately weighted in computing the expected utility of the investment.

The expected utility of the investment is 0.675. Using Table 16–1, the change-in-asset position which has a utility of 0.675 can be approximated. The value is about $70; that is, $U(\$70)$ is approximately 0.675. This means that the manager should be willing to sell this investment opportunity for $70. Furthermore, using the expected monetary values of the investment and a discount rate of 0.05, the investment has an expected net present value of $529. The discount for risk is therefore $459 based on the amount of uncertainty and attitudes toward risk.

Expected monetary value (present value with 0.05 as rate of discount)	$529
Certainty equivalent of net present value	70
Discount for risk	$459

The $459 is the amount deducted from the present value of the investment because the monetary values of the outcomes are not valid indicators of the impact of the outcomes on the decision maker.

16.4.2 Dependent Cash Flows

In the previous examples it was assumed that the cash flows of the second period were independent of the results of the first period; the results of the second gamble were independent of the results of the first gamble. Now assume that the dependency in Table 16–5 exists. The relevant tree diagram is given in Figure 16–3. The expected value of the cash flows is

$$0.5(\$-400) \mid 0.5(\$1,459) = \$529$$

which is equal in amount to the previous expectation. From an expected monetary calculation the investment is still desirable. If utilities are computed, the expected utility of this investment, again using Table 16–1, is

$$0.5(0) + 0.5(0.97) = 0.485$$

Since the utility of the decision maker's present asset position, $0 net change, is 0.6, the investment is not desirable. The change in decision from the previous situation is due to the assumed dependency in the cash flows and the risk aversion of the investor.

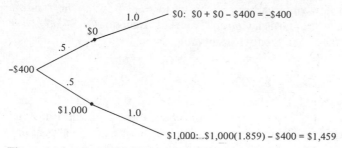

Figure 16.3   Compound investment diagram.

Dependencies of the type illustrated tend to lead to the probability of larger profits and larger losses; the more moderate possibilities are eliminated. This reduces the desirability of the investment if the utility function is one which reflects increasing marginal aversion to losses and decreasing marginal utility to gains, as is the case for the function in Table 16–1.

Table 16–5   Investment with Dependent Cash Flows

Period	Proceeds
0	($400) outlay
1	0.5 probability of $0 and 0.5 probability of $1,000
2	Same cash flows as period 1

16.4.3 Continuous Probability Distributions

Most of the examples developed in this chapter assume that only two events are possible in each of the operating periods. The possible number of events can be increased to as large a number as desired. In fact, the number of events may be infinite; instead of a series of discrete probabilities (a probability mass function), a probability density function may be relevant. With a density function, earnings may take on any value within certain limits.

The procedure using a probability density function is essentially the same as previously illustrated with one modification. Because the utility function is difficult to express mathematically, it may be easier to simulate the expected utility of the earnings of each time period.

Assume, for example, that the net cash flows of a period are normally distributed, with a mean of $10,000 and a standard deviation of $3,000. The simulation procedure is as follows. Take a number, say, d, from a table of standard normal deviates (or have an electronic computer generate the number). The number d is the number of standard deviations from the mean. It is necessary to convert the number d to a cash-flow observation:

$$Y = \overline{M} + d\sigma$$

where Y is the cash-flow observation, $\overline{M}$ the mean cash flow, d the random observation, and σ the standard deviation. Say that d is equal to -1.5, $\overline{M} = \$10,000$ and $\sigma = \$3,000$; then the first observation is

$$Y = 10,000 - 1.5(3,000)$$
$$= \$5,500$$

The $5,500 earnings would then be discounted back to the present. The cash flow for each period would be computed with separate random selections and discounted back to the present and the present value summed for one trial life. This assumes that the cash flows of each period are independent.

The utility function for the manager (see Figure 16.1, for example) could be used to determine the utility for the net present value of each draw (this is sometimes referred to as a Monte Carlo simulation). The process would be repeated for many trials, and the utility for each trial (each trial leading to a present value) would be recorded. The sum of these utilities divided by the number of observations gives the average utility of the uncertain earnings. The last step is to convert the average utility to a certainty equivalent in the same manner used to find the certainty equivalent of $70 for the expected utility of 0.675. Enter the vertical axis at the value of the average utility and read the value on the horizontal axis which has that value of utility. An investment with an expected utility greater than $U(\$0) = 60$ would be an acceptable investment. Furthermore, the expected utilities could be used to make a choice between two investments.

It is not necessary to assume that the earnings are normally distributed. Other continuous probability distributions could be used (though often with more difficulty).

16.4.4 Mathematical Solution

If the cash flows of each period are considered to be independent of one another, it is possible to obtain mathematically a distribution of the net present value of the investment and to use this as the basis of the expected utility computation.

Assume that the appropriate rate of discount is r, the cash flow of period i is Y_i, and the variance of the cash flows of the ith period is σ_i^2. The mean value of the cash flows of the ith period is $\overline{Y}_i$, and the mean value of the distribution of net present values is

$$\text{mean} = \sum_{i=0}^{n} (1 + r)^{-i}\overline{Y}_i \tag{16.1}$$

The variance of the net-present-value distribution (with independent cash flows) is given by

$$\sigma^2 = \sum_{i=0}^{n} (1 + r)^{-2i}\sigma_i^2 \tag{16.2}$$

It should be noted that the discount factor in equation (16.2) is raised to an exponent equal to twice the number of periods. For example, consider the values in Table 16–6.

Table 16–6   Characteristic of an Investment

Period	Mean-Value Cash Flow	Standard Deviation of the Cash Flow
0	$-1,600	100
1	1,000	200
2	2,000	300

The mean value of the distribution of the present value is equal to the present value of the mean values of each period. This value is computed in Table 16–7 using a 0.05 rate of discount.

Table 16–7   Calculation of Mean Value

Period	Mean Value	Discount Factor	Present Value
0	$-1,600	1.0000	$-1,600
1	1,000	0.9524	952
2	2,000	0.9070	1,814
		Mean =	$ 1,166

The computation of the variance of the distribution of net present values is similar to the mean calculation except that the discount factor is raised to twice the period rather than the number of the period. The calculations are given in Table 16–8.

Table 16–8   Variance Calculation

Period	Square of Standard Deviation	Discount Factor $(1 + r)^{-2t}$	Product
0	10,000	1.0000	10,000
1	40,000	0.9070	36,280
2	90,000	0.8227	74,043
		Variance =	120,323

The square of the standard deviation (or the variance) is equal to 120,323. The standard deviation is therefore equal to approximately 347. With the standard deviation and the mean value of the probability distribution, it is possible to determine the utility of this investment by the simulation method illustrated in Section 16.4.3.

16.5   Law of Large Numbers and Investments

An approximate statement of the law of large numbers is that if the probability of a success is p on any one trial, and if a large number of trials are performed, the proportion of successes will differ from p by a very small amount. If a fair coin is tossed, the probability of a head is 0.5, but after tossing the coin once there is a 0.5 probability that the proportion of heads observed so far is zero (that the coin came up tails). If the coin is tossed 1 million times, the proportion of heads will be very close to 0.5. Even though the number of heads will no doubt differ from 500,000, the number of heads divided by the number of tosses will be close to 0.5.

This law of probability can be applied to investment analysis. Consider drilling for oil. If an independent organization raises enough capital to drill one well, the probability of an economic well may be 0.1, and the probability of the equivalent of a dry well may be 0.9. Taking into consideration the entire range of possibilities, the distribution of outcomes may appear as in Figure 16.4.

Figure 16.4 shows a high probability that the one well will be nonproducing. If, instead of an independent driller, one of the major oil companies drills 500 wells during the year, the probability distribution of the possible events is different. There is a very small probability that all 500 wells will be dry, and there is an even smaller probability that all 500 will be producers. Figure 16.5

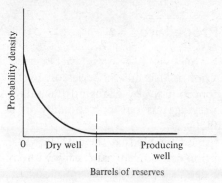

Figure 16.4   Drilling one well.

shows how the probability distribution of barrels of reserves per well will change; a very important observation is that the variance of the reserves per well decreases as the number of wells drilled increases. The variance of the distribution of the proportion of successful wells drilled also decreases as the number of wells drilled increases.

By drilling a large number of wells, an oil company can eliminate the rather large possibility of complete failure that is present with drilling a single well. Furthermore, an expert can predict the proportion of producing wells to be found by drilling 500 wells and come reasonably close to his prediction (the deviation from his prediction will be small). The same manager's prediction about the results of drilling any one well could be completely off; that is, the well could be dry, or it could be a producer, Thus, in one sense, the drilling of a large number of wells decreases the risk associated with drilling for oil.

It is possible that an investor would not be willing to finance completely the drilling of one well where only one well was to be drilled, but would be willing to participate in the drilling of the 500 wells to the extent of buying 1/500 of the ownership. For this reason large oil companies may be considered reasonable investments by individuals who are essentially conservative in their investment policies.

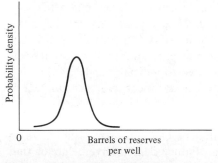

Figure 16.5   Drilling 500 wells.

16.6   Appraisal of the Procedure

The procedure described in this chapter has several weaknesses. First, it assumes that the same utility function is relevant for series of investments. This weakness can be corrected conceptually by changing the utility function as investments are accepted. Carrying this out operationally in a meaningful manner is likely to be quite difficult.

The assumption was made in all except one example that the cash flows of each period were independent. This assumption can be changed readily without damaging the basic analysis, although the details of calculation are modified. However, the decision process becomes much more complex if the acceptance of one investment changes the expected cash flows of other investments and if it is recognized that the acceptance of one investment affects the willingness of an investor to accept further investments.

The suggested procedure for solving decision problems involving several time periods offers a method of incorporating attitudes toward outcomes that is more effective than just using the one cash-flow figure, as is done in the conventional present-value procedure. Making decisions on the basis of monetary expectations is reasonable if the dollar amounts involved are small. The underlying assumption is that the utility function is linear with respect to money when the dollar amounts are small. However, if the amounts are large in relation to the magnitude of operations of the entity making the decision, then expected utility is usually more appropriate for making decisions than expected monetary values. This can also be true if other factors surrounding an investment are important and not measurable in terms of marginal adjustments in the cash flows.

One by-product of the utility approach is that it permits a default-free discount rate to be used in computing the present value. This eliminates the necessity of computing the cost of capital. More important, the risk of an investment is brought directly and systematically into the analysis (though separate from the time discounting).

Despite the fact that the determination of the utility function for the manager(s) of a corporation is not well defined, it is still desirable that some assumption relative to the utility function be made and that decisions be made that are consistent with that function. If this is not done, it is implicitly assumed that the utility function is linear. No organization has a utility function which is linear over all possible outcomes; thus the technique presented in this chapter has relevance to all organizations. The measure used to indicate the desirability (or acceptability) of the investment is incomplete unless it incorporates the impact of the outcomes on the firm.

An individual's aversion to risk seems to be related to amounts that are large in comparison to the size of expenditure that he can authorize rather than to the financial position of the firm.[10] This can induce conservative behavior that

[10] R. O. Swalm, "Utility Theory-Insights into Risk Taking," *The Harvard Business Review*, November–December 1966, pp. 123–135.

the firm would like to prevent.[11] The accountant should be aware of the behavioral effects of cost control techniques on the type of decisions made by the manager. Control techniques should be designed to motivate the behavioral pattern desired by the organization.

It is also useful to bring the uncertainty of the cash flows into the decision by dealing explicitly with the probabilities implicit in the problem. Although difficult, it is necessary to estimate the probabilities of the relevant events. If the information-processing system of a firm only presents a point estimate of the uncertain cash flow, the extent of the confidence of the person or persons responsible for the estimate is not known by the receiver of the information. The use of such terms to describe uncertainty as *optimistic, reasonable chance*, and *quite likely* are susceptible to various interpretations and hence lead to difficulties in implementation.[12]

The discussion of uncertainty and utility in this chapter has not systematically considered the "portfolio" question, although the assumptions of independence and dependence of the cash flows for the two-time-period situation was very close to the portfolio question. Investments may be related to each other so that if one is successful, the other is successful (this is described as statistical dependency with positive correlation). The opposite extreme is where the success of one investment is accompanied by failure of the other (the investments are dependent and negatively correlated). The third situation is where the results of the investments are independent of each other (the investments have zero correlation). The risk associated with an investment is a function of how it relates to the other investments of the firm. An apparent risky investment may not be at all risky when it is considered in relationship to other investments of the firm. On the other hand, while a firm might willingly undertake a single investment of a given kind, it might reasonably hesitate to undertake several, all of which are positively correlated with each other. Although this is an extremely important area, a complete analysis is beyond the coverage of this book. In addition to the portfolio of investments of the firm, the fact that investors also have portfolios of investments affects the decisions of the corporation.

16.7 Capital-Asset Pricing Model and Capital Budgeting

The theoretical finance literature is currently being rewritten in terms of the capital-asset pricing model. In addition, investors are applying the model

---

[11] On reason for this behavior lies perhaps in corporate control procedures that tend to be unduly hard on failures versus the rewards for success.

[12] See D. H. Woods, "Improving Estimates That Involve Uncertainty," *The Harvard Business Review*, July–August 1966, pp. 91–98, and J. S. Hammond, "Better Decisions with Preference Theory," *The Harvard Business Review*, November–December 1967, pp. 123–141, for further discussions of these issues.

in making investment decisions, and the next step will be for finance officers to apply the capital-asset pricing model to the decisions of their firms.

The capital-asset pricing model leads to a conclusion that investors have available a market basket of risky securities and can also invest in other securities with no risk of default. The risk preferences of an investor dictate a specific combination of the market basket of risk securities and the default-free security. In equilibrium, the return of any security must be such that the investor expects to earn a basic return equal to the return on a default-free security plus an adjustment that is heavily influenced by the "covariance" of the security's return and the market's return.

If the covariance of a security is positive, the equilibrium return of that security will be larger than the default-free return. If the covariance is negative, the equilibrium return will be smaller than the default-free return. A covariance is positive if the two random variables, the returns here from investments j and m, have a positive correlation (see Figure 16.6a) and negative if they have a negative correlation (see Figure 16.6b). It can be shown that β_j, the slope of the regression lines of Figure 16.6, is

$$\beta_j = \frac{\text{Cov}(j, m)}{\sigma_m^2} \tag{16.3}$$

where

$\text{Cov}(j, m) = $ covariance of r_j and r_m and equal to $E(r_j - \bar{r}_j)(r_m - \bar{r}_m)$

$\sigma_m^2 = $ variance of r_m

If we define $\bar{r}_j{}^*$ to be the equilibrium-required expected return for investment $_j$, it can be shown that

$$\bar{r}_j{}^* = r_f + (\bar{r}_m - r_f)\beta_j \tag{16.4}$$

where r_f is the return on a default-free security and $\bar{r}_m$ is the expected market return. Note that if β_j is negative, the $\bar{r}_j{}^*$ equilibrium required expected return will be less than the return of the default-free security.

Equation (16.4) implies that β_j and its components are the only relevant risk factors. Only the extent to which the security's return is correlated to the market's return affects the necessary risk adjustment. The "nonsystematic" risk

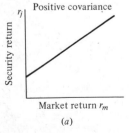

(a)   (b)

Figure 16.6.

which is independent of the market fluctuations is not relevant, since it has been assumed the individual investor has diversified his investments so as to eliminate this type of risk.

The objective of capital budgeting is to select alternatives that will maximize the value of the common stock. While the above formulation is based on a one-period model, a multiperiod procedure can be developed that is very much similar to the net-present-value procedure except that the "present-value" factors are replaced by "prices" for each event in each time period that take both time value and risk into consideration.[13] The proposed procedure makes use of the capital-asset pricing model. The computations take into consideration how the cash flows of the investment vary with the overall market conditions. A nondiversified investor may also be interested in "nonsystematic" risk, that is, the risk of an investment independent of the market fluctuations. A solution to this problem requires an approach similar to that suggested earlier in this chapter.

16.8 Summary

Large-sized investments cannot be made as if the cash flows are known with certainty when this assumption is not valid. The use of expected monetary value is not likely to be appropriate except for investments involving relatively small commitments of resources.

One solution is to evaluate investments using utility analysis. Even when all the results occur in one time period, the application of utility analysis is difficult because of the necessity of deriving a utility function for the person or persons making the investment. The analysis becomes more complex when the consequences are spread through time. Nevertheless, utility analysis offers insights into the making of capital-budgeting decisions under conditions of uncertainty and is, therefore, a valuable tool.

A reader may ask why these concepts, which are so useful in making rational capital-budgeting decisions, are introduced so late in the book. Several other chapters have already discussed the same general type of decision problem. The explanation is that much information can be obtained from the computations that assume certainty. Also, present corporate practice frequently fails to use to the fullest extent possible even the present-value method. Hence, decision making in the area of internal investments can be improved by the wider use of the present-value method. However, the goal is to incorporate information about uncertainty and utility into the analysis, and so produce a measure which enables decision makers to separate investments into acceptable and unacceptable classifications. The need for incorporating utility considerations into the analysis for major investments leads to a procedure similar to that described in

---

[13] See H. Bierman and S. Smidt, *The Capital Budgeting Decision*, 4th ed., New York: Macmillan Publishing Co., Inc., 1975, for more complete explanations of the calculations.

this chapter. There remains the difficulties (and costs) of obtaining meaningful utility functions.

If the formal utility analysis is rejected, it should be apparent to the reader that no one measure of investment desirability is sufficient for investment appraisal. It is necessary to know how the investment may fare under a wide range of circumstances and how the investment's performance is tied to the performance of other investments, already undertaken and currently being considered.

APPENDIX 16A
UTILITY FUNCTIONS AND GAMBLES

In Section 16.1 a portion of a utility function is derived for an investor. The procedure used rests on some psychological assumptions, several of which have been challenged in the literature. One very important assumption is that if two gambles involve the same two prizes, the decision maker prefers the gamble with the larger probability of winning the larger prize.

The technique used to determine a utility function in essence reduces all gambles so that they involve only two reference outcomes or prizes. These outcomes may be given arbitrary utility indices of zero and 1. The reference outcomes are selected so that the larger is at least as favorable as any outcome in the gamble being considered and the smaller is at least as unfavorable as any outcome.

In the example described in Section 16.1, the two reference outcomes are $1,000 and $0. These outcomes may be assigned utility indices of 1 and zero, respectively. Now suppose that the decision maker is offered a fifty-fifty gamble on $1,000 or $300 versus a gamble involving $1,000 and $0 with probabilities of 0.7 and 0.3, respectively. The fifty-fifty gamble can be simulated by a box-and-chip analog. Suppose there are 100 chips in a box, 50 marked "win $1,000" and 50 marked "win $300." One chip will be selected and the payment indicated will be made. Now the investor in Section 16.1 indicated that he is indifferent between $300 and a fifty-fifty gamble involving prizes of $1,000 and $0. Thus, the 50 chips marked "win $300" could be divided in half, with 25 marked win $1,000 and 25 marked win $0. There would now be 75 chips marked "win $1,000" and 25 marked "win $0." In this manner the original gamble is converted into a gamble involving only the reference outcomes with a probability of $0.50 + 0.25 = 0.75$ of winning $1,000.[14] Since 0.75 exceeds 0.7 and the outcomes are identical, the initial gamble ($1,000 or $300 each with probability 0.5)

---

[14] The choice of zero and 1 permits probability numbers to serve as utilities. Recall that 0.75, the chance of winning in the reference gamble, was the utility of the certain monetary amount of $500 found to be equivalent to the same gamble in Section 16.1. Other choices besides zero and 1 could be used if desired.

must be preferred. The expected utility calculations give the first gamble an expected utility of 0.75:

$$0.5[U(\$1{,}000] + 0.5[U(\$300)] = 0.5(1) + 0.5(0.5) = 0.75$$

and a utility to the second gamble of 0.7, since

$$0.7[U(\$1{,}000)] + 0.3[U(\$0)] = 0.7(1) + 0.3(0) = 0.70$$

Thus the expected utility method also leads to a preference for the first gamble.

QUESTIONS AND PROBLEMS

16-1 A company estimates the expected cash flow of year 5 to be $10,000. If this figure is used in the investment analysis, what assumption (or assumptions) is (are) being made?

16-2 What is the maximum amount you would pay for a gamble that involved the following two alternatives?

Alternative 1: 0.5 probability of $1,000
Alternative 2: 0.5 probability of $0

What does this imply about your utility function?

16-3 For you to be indifferent between the following two gambles, what value of X must be inserted?

Gamble A	Gamble B
0.5 probability of $1,000 0.5 probability of $0	1.0 probability of X

What does this imply about your utility function? Compare your answer to the answer you gave to problem 16-2.

16-4 Why might you expect the utility function for earnings (or for money) to have an upper bound? Why might you expect it to have a lower bound?

16-5 Some suggest that risk should be taken into consideration by the use of a risk discount rate which is added to the default-free interest rate. This assumes that risk causes the cash forecast of a period to be worth a given fixed percentage less than an equal amount of cash in the previous period (this is in addition to the interest factor). Is this a good way of incorporating risk into the analysis? Can you think of a situation where the risk of future cash flows is less than the risk associated with cash flows of immediate time periods?

16–6 Would the utility function of a firm change after making an investment? Why?

16–7 When is it reasonable for a firm to base decisions on the expected monetary values and to ignore utility considerations?

16–8 In obtaining a utility function for a corporation, how would you handle the situation where different corporate executives had different utility functions?

16–9 If the analysis did not try to incorporate utility considerations into the investment analysis, would the investment decisions of the firm still be affected by the utility functions of the individual corporate executives? Assume some degree of decentralization.

16–10 If the firm is small enough for the president (and owner) to make all the decisions, is it necessary to make a formal analysis using utility functions. Explain.

16–11 The following utility function of Mr. Jay will be used for problems 16–11 and 16–12.

Change in Net-Asset Position	
Dollars	Utility Measures
$ – 3,000	– 3,000
– 1,000	– 1,000
– 600	– 500
– 500	– 350
0	0
100	100
500	150
1,000	200
2,000	350
4,000	500
9,000	680
10,000	700

Assume there is a gamble which has a 0.5 probability of $10,000 and 0.5 probability of $0.

Required:
a. What is the utility measure of the gamble?
b. What is the amount Mr. Jay would be willing to accept for certain to cause him to be indifferent to the two choices?
c. Would Mr. Jay be willing to pay $1,000 for this gamble?
d. What is the expected monetary value of the gamble?
e. What is the risk discount?
f. Would you describe Mr. Jay as financially conservative?

16–12 Assume that there is a gamble which has a 0.5 probability of $4,000 and 0.5 probability of $1,000.

Required:

a. What is the utility measure of the gamble?

b. What is the amount Mr. Jay would be willing to accept for certain to cause him to be indifferent to the two choices?

c. Would Mr. Jay be willing to pay $1,000 for this gamble?

d. What is the expected monetary value of the gamble?

e. What is the risk discount?

16–13 The following problem attempts to illustrate the simulation of the mean utility of a cash flow which has a normal probability density function.

The earnings of a period are normally distributed with a mean of $100,000 and a standard deviation of $20,000. Assume that the following values of *d* were obtained from a table of standard normal deviates.

d
0.40
1.35
−0.83
2.50

The following values were obtained from the utility function:

Dollars	Utility Measures
$ 0	0
83,400	10,000
108,000	15,000
110,000	16,000
127,000	19,000
150,000	20,000

Required:

a. Compute the four earnings observations.

b. Using the utility function, determine the utility observation for each earning observation.

c. Determine the mean utility.

d. Determine the certainty equivalent.

16–14 Assume that the following utility function applies to the Arnot Corporation.

Change in Net-Asset Position

Dollars: Present Value	Utility Measures
$ 20,000	−400
− 10,000	−100
0	0
7,200	80
8,600	90
10,000	100
18,600	140
20,000	150
30,000	190
35,800	200
40,000	220
60,000	240

a. Would the corporation accept an investment which requires an outlay of $10,000 and will either be a complete failure or generate cash flows of $30,000 within a week if each possibility has a 0.5 probability?

b. What would be your recommendation if the probabilities were 0.65 of failure and 0.35 of success?

16–15 Assume the same utility function as in problem 16–14.

a. Should the Arnot Corporation undertake the following investment? Assume that a 0.05 discount rate is appropriate.

Period	Cash Flow
0	$ − 10,000
1	$0 with 0.5 probability
	$30,000 with 0.5 probability

b. What would be your recommendation if the probabilities were 0.6 of failure and 0.4 of success?

16–16 Assume the same utility function as in problem 16–14. The Arnot Corporation has been offered an investment which costs $20,000. The investment has 0.5 probability of not generating any cash the first day and 0.5 probability of generating $30,000. It can also generate $0 or $30,000 with the same probabilities the second day (the outcomes are independent of the day). Should the firm accept the investment?

16–17 Assume the same situation as in problem 16–16 except that the transactions take place in successive years instead of days. The discount rate is 0.05. Should the firm accept the investment?

16–18 Assume the same investment as in problem 16–16, except the cash flows of the second day will be the same as the first day (the outcomes are dependent). Should the firm accept the investment?

16–19 Assume that the expected cash flows of an investment are as follows:

Period	Mean Value	Standard Deviation
0	$-8,000	$500
1	10,000	1,000
2	10,000	2,000

Compute the mean, variance, and standard deviation of the net-present-value distribution assuming that the cash flows of each period are independent. Use a 0.05 rate of discount.

16–20 Determine whether the following investment is acceptable.

Period	Cash Flows
0	($1,000)
1	0.5 probability of $2,100 cash flow
	0.3 probability of $1,050
	0.2 probability of $0

The firm has a cost of money of 0.05. The utility function of the corporation has the following values (interpolate if you need other values):

Dollars: Present Value	Utility Measures
$-1,000	-300
0	0
500	50
1,000	70
1,050	75
1,300	85
1,500	90
2,000	100
2,100	101
3,000	125

SUPPLEMENTARY READING

BIERMAN, H., and S. SMIDT, *The Capital Budgeting Decision*, New York: Macmillan Publishing Co., Inc., 1975.

DEAN, JOEL, *Capital Budgeting*, New York: Columbia University Press, 1951.

HAMMOND, J., "Better Decisions with Preference Theory," *The Harvard Business Review*, November–December 1967, pp. 123–141.

HERTZ, D., "Investment Policies That Pay Off," *The Harvard Business Review*, January–February 1968, pp. 96–108.

HESPOS, R., and P. STRASSMAN, "Stochastic Decision Trees for the Analysis of Investment Decisions," *Management Science*, August 1965, pp. 244–259.

HILLIER, F. S., "The Derivation of Probabilistic Information for the Evaluation of Risky Investments," *Management Science*, April 1963, pp. 443–457.

LUTZ, F., and V. LUTZ, "The Theory of Investment of the Firm," Princeton, N.J.: Princeton University Press, 1951.

MAGEE, J., "How to Use Decision Trees in Capital Investment," *The Harvard Business Review*, September–October 1964, pp. 79–96.

QUERIN, G. D., *The Capital Expenditure Decision*, Homewood, Ill.: Richard D. Irwin, Inc., 1967.

ROBICHECK, A. A., and S. C. MYERS, *Optimal Financing Decisions*, Englewood Cliffs, N.J.: Prentice-Hall, Inc., 1965.

Part IV

Measuring Performance

Chapter 17

Factors in
Measuring Performance

The ability of management to react optimally to change is limited by the timing and the nature of the amount of information available, the continuous nature of change, lack of familiarity with operations of other units, and by the difficulty of predicting with certainty the ripple effects of decisions made and actions taken. As a partial solution many firms resort to some degree of decision decentralization. It is inefficient to attempt total decision control from the top level of a large firm. Decision making is delegated from top management to lower-level personnel to take advantage of the familiarity with operations and the availability of information at different activity levels. This delegation may involve the authority to make nearly all the operating decisions (including buying materials externally) or, alternatively, the authority may be limited to a small range of decisions.

Concurrent with decentralization of control and decision making there arises a need to control these decision-making subunits to assure that their actions are consistent with the goals of the total entity. Subactivities, if left on their own, tend to suboptimize by failing to consider economies and diseconomies external to their own activity.

Control may be achieved through goal setting and performance evaluation. The type of goal set and the manner in which performance is evaluated should depend on the degree of decision making delegated. As decentralization increases, the measures used to evaluate the performance should become more general. Thus, where authority is delegated to determine the complete mix of inputs used in production and the sale of a product, as might be true of a division, the evaluation of performance is characterized by focusing on a measure such as net contribution or perhaps return on investment. Where this is not the case, cost may often be used.

The evaluation and control mechanism is influenced by the organizational structure of the firm. The specification of the firm's organizational structure and its accounting system must both be considered when designing an evaluation system. The accounting system should provide performance measures that reflect the consequences of decision making for the activity and hence allow top management to evaluate these decisions in light of the firm's goals. There should be incentives for subactivity managers to improve their performance.

How can the performance of a member of management be measured? The first step is to establish the objective or objectives of the activity over which he has authority. The second step is to see how well these objectives are met. The prime objective of the firm is assumed here to be maximization of profits. Perhaps a more realistic way to phrase the objective is to describe it as profit maximization subject to constraints (for example, continuity of existence). Profit in this definition includes the opportunity cost of invested funds as a cost.

The extent of success in attaining objectives may be assessed quantitatively or qualitatively. The qualitative criterion includes such things as relations with superiors and subordinates, training of subordinates, professional attainments, civic activities, and ability to get things done. The qualitative factors are relevant in judging performance, but are traditionally more the province of the industrial psychologist than of the accountant. It should be recalled, however, that the means used to evaluate an individual affects his motivation and, thereby his attainment of corporate objectives. Thus, it is important for the accountant to understand and work with the behavioral scientist in designing control reports and performance-measuring techniques. This chapter considers, however, only quantitative measures of performance. The reader interested in a further examination of the qualitative factors is referred to Chapter 6. Quantitative factors that provide useful information include:

1. Costs and cost variances.
2. Physical production (quantity and quality).
3. Sales.
4. Income.
5. Return on investment.
6. Investment turnover.
7. Income per dollar of sales (operating rate).
8. Share of market.
9. Rate of growth.
10. Changes from period to period of any of the above measures.

17.1   Single Measures of Performance

There is danger in seeking out the one best measure of performance and using it to the exclusion of all other measures. Frequently, a single measure cannot do the job satisfactorily, since a measure that is useful for one purpose is not useful for another. The fact that a golf drive went 250 yards is useful in judging the force with which the ball was hit, but knowledge of the total distance covered is not sufficient to conclude whether the drive was good or bad. Information relating to the starting point and to location and distance of the hole is needed before this type of evaluation can be made.

Most of the quantitative measures just listed are not above unintended distortion or manipulation. The manipulations may be a product of figure juggling or the result of managerial actions designed to obtain the result looked for by superiors, even though the end result may not be consistent with the end objectives of the corporation. It is important to ensure, to the extent possible, that the measure of performance being used does improve performance and that the measure of performance is consistent with the basic objectives of the firm. To obtain a valid measure of performance, several measures may be needed and then judgment should be applied to weighing the importance of each measure. If this is not done, the result may not measure performance but rather the ability of a clever manager to obtain a favorable performance report.

The measures of performance used should be influenced materially by the nature of the responsibilities of the manager (or organization) whose performance is being measured. Where possible, items which are not controllable by the manager should be excluded from the measure. A second principle is that the methods used by a manager in decision making and control rather than the actual results should be evaluated, since the results are often a product, in part, of factors over which he has no control or influence. Uncertainties can cause excellent decision making to yield unsatisfactory results and vice versa.

The performance measure adopted should indicate how well the manager or organization is meeting predetermined objectives. To accomplish these objectives, more than one measure of performance will usually be required, and different measures will be needed for different situations, firms, and organization levels.

The subsections of Section 17.1 discuss some of the limitations of several of the measures listed earlier. Section 17.2 considers the task of developing appropriate measures for different organizational levels.

17.1.1   Investment Turnover

Investment turnover may be defined as the sales of a period divided by the average investment:

$$\text{investment turnover} = \frac{\text{sales}}{\text{average investment}} \qquad (17.1)$$

The investment turnover gives an indication of how intensively the investment is being used. If more sales are generated, the turnover increases. Taken by itself, the investment turnover is not a good measure of a manager's performance, since total sales and turnover can be increased by increasing selling effort, lowering selling price, or by a random change in general economic conditions. An increase in turnover may not reflect more efficient use of resources by the manager whose performance is being measured it may reflect factors that are not controllable. However, when used with other measures, investment turnover may be helpful in pointing out a cause of decreased profits, namely, less intensive use of the resources committed to the operation.

17.1.2 Operating Rate

The operating rate is the operating profit per dollar of sales:

$$\text{operating rate} = \frac{\text{operating profit}}{\text{sales}} \tag{17.2}$$

The operating rate gives an indication of the efficiency of operations, but only an indication, since in addition to efficiency the profit per dollar of sales is affected by:

1. Changes in the level of sales.
2. Changes in the product mix sold.
3. Changes in the price of the products sold.
4. Changes in the costs of materials and services used to produce the products sold.
5. Accounting methods of determining operating profit.

If each of the above influences is isolated and the effect of each computed, then the operating rate is useful. The inclusion or exclusion of income taxes for performance measurement is not crucial as long as the same procedure is followed for the different operating localities being compared. If attention is focused on the operating rate, without proper analysis, incorrect conclusions may be drawn as to the causes of the changes in the rate. For example, assume the following situation:

	Period 1	Period 2
Sales	$1,000,000	$1,500,000
Income	50,000	300,000
Operating rate	5%	20%

Here the operating rate increased from 5% to 20%. Does this reflect increased efficiency?[1] To answer this question it is first necessary to know what the income should be for sales of $1,500,000. It may be that the income should be $400,000 for sales of that level, and instead of being "good," the operating rate of 20% for sales of $1,500,000 reflects inefficiency. The increase in the operating rate may have occurred merely because of the increase in sales, for which the sales manager should receive primary credit. Moreover, assuming increased, even maximum, efficiency at this output, the increase in income could still have been attained at the expense of future periods. In other words, a good case can be made for the argument that to maximize profitability (a long-run notion) the firm cannot maximize accounting income in any single period. For example, research and development tends to reduce short-run profit measures. The effects of the factors responsible for the change in the operating rate should also be examined for their long-run effects. Taking advantage of short-run opportunities can have adverse long-run consequences.

In another situation, sales may not have changed at all, but the opening rate may change because different products are sold. For example:

	Period 1	Period 2
Sales	$1,000,000	$1,000,000
Income	100,000	200,000
Operating rate	10%	20%

Does this situation reflect increased efficiency? Maybe not; it may indicate merely a change in the composition of sales from low-margin items to high-margin items. This may or may not reflect on management's efficiency in production. It may, for example, indicate increased efficiency on the part of a manager responsible for sales-promotion decisions (a change in sales mix). On the other hand, it may merely reflect a fortuitous market phenomenon.

Discussion of these and similar problems arising with the use of the operating rate could be expanded. But the problems cited, which are illustrative, must be given attention and must enter into any analysis of the operating rate.

17.1.3 Return on Investment

The return-on-investment (ROI) method of measuring performance is said to have several desirable features. First, it provides a single, comprehensive figure that incorporates the impact of a large number of events on the division or other activity unit. Thus, it is useful for comparing different divisions. Furthermore, since it measures how effectively the division's assets are used to generate profits, it compels managers to acquire only those investments that improve the expected return. To attain these advantages, ROI must be used carefully.

[1] The term *efficiency* is used here to describe a situation where the assets of the firm are being employed to maximize, on a long-run basis, the contribution for a given level of output.

The return on investment may be computed by dividing income by average investment or by multiplying the investment turnover (sales divided by average investment) by the operating rate (income divided by sales):

$$\text{ROI} = \frac{\text{sales}}{\text{average investment}} \times \frac{\text{operating profit}}{\text{sales}} = \frac{\text{operating profit}}{\text{average investment}} \quad (17.3)$$

Just how important these three percentages (investment turnover, operating rate, and return on investment) are considered to be by management is difficult to guess. There are indications that they are thought to be important devices for measuring efficiency of utilization of resources. Dearden, for example, writes that "...nearly every major decentralized company in the United States today uses some adaptation of return on investment for measuring division performance."[2]

The return on investment as a measure of performance is only as good as the numbers used to compute it. It should not come as a surprise to anyone familiar with accounting that the problems of measuring sales, income, and average investment are numerous.

Measuring sales is often spoken of as the problem of revenue recognition. Is revenue to be recognized when the order is received, the product made, the product shipped, or the cash received? Since most companies are on the accrual basis of recognizing revenue, the revenue is recognized when the goods are shipped or the services performed. Only in relatively rare cases does this method of accounting cause difficulties in computing the investment turnover. For example, a shipbuilding firm that uses the accrual method and recognizes revenue only on a completed sale might have a low investment turnover in a period of great activity if no ships were delivered during this period. This specific difficulty might be readily solved by shifting to a production basis (percentage of completion basis) of revenue recognition, but the general problem of revenue recognition does exist.

The problems of measuring the income of a corporate entity are many, and they increase when attention is focused on the component parts of an organization. The main problems are the pricing of transfers and the splitting of common costs. These problems become important when the component parts of the company are compared to each other. Accounting procedures, which are generally accepted from a financial point of view, may result in a report of income that is worth little from the point of view of comparing different operating units. The report of income can be qualified by footnotes, but these qualifications tend to be lost when attention is focused on the return on investment.

Some of the problems of income measurement that are particularly relevant for the purpose of measuring return on investment are:

1. Revenue recognition and the matching of expenses with revenues.
2. Treatment of repairs and maintenance costs.

[2] J. Dearden, "The Case Against ROI Control," *The Harvard Business Review*, May–June 1969, p. 124.

3. Accounting for inventory. (During periods of fluctuating prices income will be affected by the choice of the inventory-valuation basis, FIFO, LIFO, average cost, and so on, as well as by changing inventory levels.)
4. Treatment of nonproductive supplies. (Should they be expensed when purchased or should they be inventoried?)
5. Choice of depreciation procedure. (Are subunits using depreciation procedures that permit meaningful comparisons of their calculated return on investment?)
6. Adjustments for changes in price level.
7. Allocation of common cost, especially central office expenses.
8. The effect of changes in the level of production on income (caused by absorption costing combined with changes in production).

Fortunately, theories and techniques have been developed to handle all these problems. Unfortunately, the theories and techniques are frequently not applied uniformly to all plants and all divisions of a company. One plant may use LIFO and another FIFO. One plant may use straight-line depreciation, another may use some method of accelerated depreciation. For any of the eight items listed, examples can be presented showing two plants or divisions (assumed to have the same physical characteristics) that will have different returns on investment, the differences being caused entirely by the accounting methods, and not by variations in efficiency.

Measuring Average Investment
Many of the problems of measuring average investment are directly related to the problems of income measurement. The list is shortened here to focus attention on the three important problems:

1. Valuing long-lived assets.
2. Valuing inventories.
3. Allocation of assets administered directly from the central office.

There are three problems associated with the valuation of long-lived assets. First, what items should be capitalized and what items charged to expense? This is particularly troublesome with repairs, maintenance charges, and any large expenditures for developing new procedures or products. For example, in the oil industry, should the costs of digging dry wells and producing wells be treated as assets or as expenses?

The second problem is to decide what to do about depreciation. Should the accrued depreciation be subtracted in computing the average investment? This is a troublesome question, to which there is no one simple answer. However, several observations may be made. With constant revenues and maintenance charges, an asset will have an increasing return on investment through the periods of use if either straight-line depreciation is used (and the accumulated depreciation is subtracted), or any one of the decreasing-charge methods of computing depreciation is used (and the accumulated depreciation is subtracted). With the above assumptions, the depreciable asset has an equal return on investment through the periods of use only if a compound-interest method (an increasing-charge method) of computing depreciation is used. But this method complicates the analysis of income (revenues of the later periods are charged with larger and larger depreciation charges), and it is not generally used by industrial firms (see Chapter 18 for an alternative).

If straight-line depreciation is used, a common result is for the investment to show a low initial return and an increasing return over time as the investment base declines. This phenomenon tends to discourage new investments that might decrease the rate of return simply because they are new.

Return on investment as conventionally computed does not provide a reliable check on investment performance. Discounted cash-flow techniques and portfolio considerations are involved in selecting investments. The accounting measures of profit (even ignoring tax problems) are not generally designed to be consistent with investment decision methods. As a result, the calculated return on investment differs from the projected rate of return even though actual cash flows are precisely as estimated.[3]

Nearly all firms use some measure of book value for the fixed assets included in the investment base. Market values, although theoretically more correct, seem to present too many implementation problems for practical use. Some firms use gross book values rather than the net figures discussed here. When gross book values are used, the return on investment is more likely to be increased by scrapping old assets. Moreover, if group depreciation methods are in use, no loss is recognized on retirement.

The third problem of valuing long-lived assets for purposes of determining the average investment is possibly the most important, particularly in periods of rapid inflation. What should be done about the fact that the unit used to measure the investment in long-lived assets is the dollar when the dollar has different meanings in different years? The purchasing power of the dollar has changed significantly over time. If the return-on-investment measure is to have significance, the effect of unexpected changes in the price level has to be included.

The problem of measuring the value of inventories is related to the fact that LIFO is accepted for accounting purposes. Under this procedure, the oldest goods purchased are the last goods to be charged as an expense. This means that if LIFO is used, the inventory value often represents goods dating back to the moment of introducing LIFO. In any event, the inventory resulting from the use of LIFO rarely gives an indication of the actual cost of the inventory, nor does it give an indication of its present value.

Other problems of measuring inventory include writing down obsolete or

[3] See also Chapters 13 and 18.

spoiled items, taking a meaningful physical inventory, and, in the case of a manufacturing firm, deciding what costs are inventoriable.

When assets are administered directly from the central office, should these assets be allocated for purposes of computing the return on the investment of a division or plant? This is the cousin of the familiar problem of common costs and could be termed the problem of common assets. If there are reasonable grounds for allocating the asset, it should be allocated. For example, if the payroll is paid out of a centrally administered payroll fund, the cash held in this fund should be considered an asset assignable to the individual plants. In this example the take-home pay of the workers of each plant would seem to be a reasonable basis for allocation.

Some companies do not allocate cash administered by the central office. This is not harmful if all the operating units being compared have like characteristics, but if they are unlike (one plant having a large amount of long-lived assets, another a larger number of workers), the failure to allocate cash may give misleading results.

Return on Investment and Decision Making

The usefulness of return on investment for decision making or performance evaluation is limited. Among the more questionable uses of the return on investment approach are:

1. Capital-budgeting decisions (including equipment replacement, capacity expansion, research, buying versus leasing, making versus buying, introducing new product lines, or other new activities).
2. Pricing decisions.

The objection to return on investment as a guide for capital-budgeting decisions results from the fact that the procedure ignores the time shape of earnings and the discounting of future earnings back to the present. The present-value approach to capital budgeting is not perfect, but it is to be preferred over the return-on-investment method (see Chapter 13).

It is sometimes suggested that pricing decisions should be made with one eye on the return on investment, and that an "optimal" return on investment should be the goal. It is well to keep economic principles in mind. A company may set a price, but the buyers determine how much is purchased; that is, each product has a demand curve. The fact that a set return on investment is desired does not mean that it will be attained by changing the price. The successfulness of a change in price depends on the demand curve, which in turn depends on the degree of competition to be found in the industry and among industries as well as the preferences of consumers. Theoretically, a price should be established that equates marginal revenue and marginal cost. If profits can be increased by raising or lowering prices, this decision can be reached without looking at the return on investment.

17.1.4 Measuring Divisional Performance

A very difficult and interesting problem is caused by the use of return on investment to measure the performance of a division. Assume that a high return on investment is considered desirable, and that division A has a return on investment of 35% and division B a return on investment of 20%. Division B may actually be the better-managed division. If division A is rejecting all investment proposals of less than 35%, this leads to a high return on investment but a less-than-optimal amount invested in the division from the point of view of the firm as a whole, assuming that the firm has a cost of money of less than 35%. It is not desirable for a division to employ a very high cutoff rate for investments while the home office has a great quantity of idle cash which it wants invested.

The conflict of interests created by the use of a single measure of performance is not unique to return on investment. For example, a grocery chain might employ profit per dollar of sales as a measure of a store manager's efficiency. Since certain items in the store have profit margins below the "standard required" margin, some store managers would stock a small amount and allow these items to run out on busy days so that the profit per dollar of sales figure would not be decreased. Although this would decrease the profit of the store, it may still be done, since the major emphasis is on the objective of earning the required profit per dollar of sales. The significant ratio for decision making here should have been the total contribution per unit of floor (or shelf) space if, as is likely, floor space represents the scarce resource of the store.

One method of counteracting the distortions just described is to include the rate of growth among the measures of performance. Since growth for growth's sake is not desirable, growth in income rather than in sales is suggested. If income is growing at the same time that return on investment is maintained at the desired level (or even increased), then, at least according to the quantitative measures, the manager is doing a reasonable job. Including the rate of growth in the performance measures puts the spotlight on the manager who is willing to be satisfied with the status quo. Balancing growth against return on investment ensures that the manager will not be obsessed with growth in sales at the expense of profits, or return on investment at the expense of growth.

Example

Assume that the income and investments of successive years are as follows:

Year	Operating Profit	Average Investment
1975	$10,000	$100,000
1976	11,000	110,000
1977	14,300	125,000

The growth rates in operating profits are:

1975–1976: $\dfrac{1,000}{10,000} = 10\%$

1976–1977: $\dfrac{3,300}{11,000} = 30\%$

1975–1977: $14,300(1 + r)^{-2} = 10,000$

$$(1 + r)^{-2} = \frac{10,000}{14,300} = 0.6993$$

$$r = 19.5\%$$

The returns on investment are:

1975: $\dfrac{10,000}{100,000} = 10\%$

1976: $\dfrac{11,000}{110,000} = 10\%$

1977: $\dfrac{14,300}{125,000} = 11.4\%$

The manager is accomplishing growth and an increase in the return on investment simultaneously. It is still possible, however, that the investment decisions being made may not be taking full advantage of the individual opportunities available or may not be making adequate allowance for the interrelationships among the existing and proposed investments. Investment policies, which are based on "portfolio" considerations, need to be examined in light of the return and risk goals of the firm as a whole, remembering the constraints within which both the firm and the division must operate.

All assets should not be expected to earn the same return since the required profitability may well differ among assets even in a single division. The return appropriate to different divisions need not be the same nor need it be identical to the average rate earned across the entire company. If performance is measured using a single rate, decisions that are inconsistent with the overall goals of the firm are likely.

17.2 Measuring Performance on Different Levels of Organization

The proper measures of performance are related to the degree of decentralization present and are a function of the level of organization under consideration. Several organizational levels are considered in this subsection. They include:

1. Department or cost center.
2. Plant.
3. Division.
4. Company.

17.2.1 The Department

The term *department* is used here interchangeably with cost center or burden center. Assume that the performance of a manager such as foreman or department head is to be measured.

A manager's task is to accomplish a set objective with a minimum of cost. Recognizing that he could accomplish his task with more dispatch with the incurrence of more cost, he compromises between cost and time. Thus, a controller might be able to prepare the reports two days sooner by hiring 10 more accountants or using a more powerful computer but still not hire the additional accountants or use the computer because the costs would be greater than the value of the expected benefits. To say that costs are too high must mean either that there is gross inefficiency and waste of resources or that the benefits to be obtained are less than their cost even if the costs are administered effectively.

In a research and development department, the quantitative measurement of costs is reasonably accurate while the measurement of the benefits is very inaccurate. Hence, it is very difficult to control or measure the performance of this type of department with purely quantitative measures (see Chapter 9). On the other hand, both the direct costs and the benefits of a production department may be determined with relative accuracy, the indirect costs with less accuracy. The benefits in this case are the units produced. Generally, the costs are measured in terms of the labor, material, and overhead which are used by a department. The physical product may be converted into the amount of labor, material, and indirect costs which should have been used (the standard costs of the product) and the cost-control techniques suggested in Chapters 1–5 can then be used.

It is also necessary to control the scrap or spoilage that results from the manufacturing process. A high production level with low costs per unit may be desirable, but not if it results in large amounts of rework or unusable product. This undesirable outcome may be prevented by excluding bad units in computing the production of the period (if the bad production was caused within the department) and by carefully controlling the amount of spoilage.

The main pitfall in measuring the performance of a foreman is one that applies to all levels of management, namely, the inclusion of items not controllable by the person whose performance is being measured. The foreman should be held accountable for costs that can be directly identified with his department and over which he can exert control. The measure of performance, for example, for the foreman of an operating department should not include the insurance on the machinery used in the department. Although this cost may be directly identified with the department, it is not a cost item controllable by the foreman.

17.2.2 The Plant

We will assume in this discussion that the plant manager has no control over the sale of the product but that he is concerned with all phases of its production.[4] When attempts are made to compute a profit and a return on investment for the plant under these conditions, it is quite likely to be the case that this computation will be dysfunctional and may even be misleading. The profit of the plant is a function of the level of sales, the sale price, and the cost of product. If the plant manager has control over the last item only, his performance should be measured only by the cost of product, or perhaps better, by the costs incurred in relation to the level of production.

Computing a profit for a plant is generally thought to supply both a measure of performance and an incentive. It may approximately accomplish this goal during prosperous periods, but in periods of slack activity it supplies an excuse for the plant manager. He can blame the poor showing on low unit sales or a low sale price. While these two items are probably the more dramatic of the causes of low profits, there may also be inefficiencies that should be corrected.

A suitable measure of the performance of the plant manager is similar to the measure of performance of the foreman. His task is to complete a good product at as low a cost as possible. Thus the same measures used at the department level are also appropriate at the plant level. A desirable situation is one in which the costs of production of one plant may be compared to the costs of similar plants.

In addition to the quantitative measures centering around the costs of production, the overall evaluation of performance should include the quality of the work performed and the timeliness of production, that is, ability to meet production schedules. Although sometimes difficult to quantify, these factors can be extremely important in relation to the maintenance of the firm's profits. Evaluation should also consider any geographic and time differences involved in profit-figure comparisons.

Since the authority of the plant manager is broader than that of the department head, more costs incurred in the plant are controllable by him. In fact, any out-of-pocket expenditures originating in the plant are usually subject to his control, and thus should be used in measuring his performance. Should expenses such as depreciation of plant and equipment be included in the computation of the cost of product? While the plant manager may not have had a voice in the original purchase of these assets, he does control their use, and the opportunity costs of these assets may well be included, perhaps as a separable item. The measure of the opportunity cost would be the incremental revenues that would have resulted from the best alternative use of the assets.

[4] Even though the production manager does not control sales, he can indirectly influence the level of sales. Availability of a product of good quality will lead to satisfied customers which in turn will influence the demand schedule. While the production and inventory control policies of the plant manager can influence sales, it is not desirable to measure his efficiency on the basis of sales, or a figure which is influenced to a great extent by the level of sales.

17.2.3 The Division

The measurement of the performance of the division manager who does not control sales is exactly analogous to that of the plant manager. The use of costs of production is a better measure of performance than a fictitious profit figure. When the division manager has control of the selling effort but not the level of plant investment, a different measure of performance is required, for example, the difference between revenues and costs controllable at the division level.

Where the division manager also controls the level of investment, the measuring performance is further broadened. The division then becomes an entity very similar to a small corporation, and many of the measures of performance relevant for corporate organizations can be used. These may include total sales, profits, return on investment, investment turnover, operating profit per dollar of sales, share of market, and changes in any of the above items.

Two problems that are encountered with a division but not with a separate corporation are the problem of common costs (costs of the central office incurred in servicing several divisions) and the problem of pricing transfers to and from other divisions. These subjects are discussed in Chapter 19.

In measuring the performance of a division, the allocations of central office costs should in general be excluded. The division manager has no control over these costs, and while the division may benefit from the incurrence of the expenses, it may do more harm than good to include these costs in divisional income statements and computations of return on investment. On the other hand, it may be desirable to inform the division that it is billed a standard amount for central office services, and that for the corporation to be profitable, these costs must be recovered. If services such as engineering or consulting are requested by a division from the central office, a charge based on a standard (or market) fee would be appropriate to reflect the use of scarce corporate resources.

17.2.4 The Company

The measures of performance used in the case of a division that controls its sales force can be used for the company. Several problems are eliminated, such as transfer pricing and allocation of overhead costs, but the many problems of financial accounting remain. For example, should variable costing be used so that effects of changes in inventory are eliminated? In computing the return on investment, should the investment be net of depreciation? What methods of inventory flow and depreciation should be used? There are no shortages of accounting problems.

There are other problems as well. If, for example, decreased sales are a result of general business conditions, does this absolve the company president from the blame of having a bad year? The president is responsible for how well the company does, but he cannot control the business cycle.

Perhaps the most common performance measures at the overall corporate level are those which reflect profitability. Chief among these measures is the return-on-investment measure. We have already given this measure substantial attention in this chapter, and we have pointed out some of the problems of its use, including problems of measurement.

A related measure of profitability also in general use is *residual income*. Residual income measures operating income less an imputed interest cost for the assets employed by the organization. Residual income directs the manager to maximize the return above a charge for the assets used. The two methods are compared:

a.	Operating income	$100,000
b.	Less imputed interest at 15% on assets utilized	75,000
c.	Operating assets	$500,000
	ROI ($a \div c$)	20%
	Residual income ($a - b$)	$ 25,000

Since different values are obtained, different conclusions may easily result, but both measures take into consideration the amount of assets used. The performance measure should consider this factor.

Determining residual income necessitates a selection of the appropriate interest rate to use in charging implicit interest. The choice of a rate tends to be based in practice on some concept of the average required return, or cost of capital. Not only is this a difficult value to determine, but it may not be appropriate to use to estimate the capital cost on incremental investments with risk characteristics quite different from those implicit to the asset mix the organization already has. Other measurement problems have been discussed above in connection with our discussion of return on investment.

The residual income approach has an advantage in that it avoids the objective of maximizing ROI by rejecting investments when the added investments (adjusted for risk) exceed the return needed to justify their purchase, but, if obtained they would reduce the reported ROI. However, we found in Section 17.1.4 that the ROI method could be augmented with a growth measure applied to operating income to avoid this problem. An alternative to both measures would be to concentrate on contribution margins.

17.3 Measures for Improving Performance

Good performance measures provide the manager with figures that he can use to control operations. However, performance measures often represent the combined results of many subsidiary variables. Where possible it is helpful to provide the manager with indicators of the economic value of the scarce resources to the subactivity: the opportunity costs of the scarce resources.

These measures of opportunity cost provide the means by which the manager can make better decisions concerning which activities to push and which resources are in short supply. In some cases the opportunity cost of resources can be obtained by noting the increase in contribution that can be achieved by switching one unit of a scarce resource to its best alternative use. The opportunity cost of other factors can be estimated by determining the contribution obtainable if another unit of the resources were available. Shadow prices resulting from the solution of mathematical programming formulations are measures of opportunity cost and may facilitate resource-allocation decisions.[5]

Results of mathematical programming formulations are also relevant to control. If decisions are made using a linear programming model, the original solution adopted before the operating plan is implemented may be compared with a revised solution based on changes occurring in the data input to the model during the operating period. The value of the objective function using the now nonoptimal activity-level with the new data can be determined and compared with the value of the objective function under the new optimal solution. The difference represents the gain from altering the program. If this difference exceeds the change-over cost, consideration should be given to altering the activity levels.

If it is too late to make the adjustments, the revised solution compared to the initial solution provides a rough measure of the forecasting error and the maximum amount that might be expended on improving this activity. The difference between the actual results and the revised or *ex post* solution is an estimate of the opportunity cost associated with the actions taken. The differences or variances can be examined using the methods described in Chapters 4 and 5.

It is important to make a distinction between the performance of managers and the performance of the investment in an organizational subunit such as a plant or division. Managers should be evaluated on the basis of those costs, programs, and decisions under their control. A division may prove unsuccessful regardless of the efforts of its management.

The exceptional manager is often shifted to the department or plant where troubles are plentiful. He may be able to improve the performance to acceptable levels and, despite this heroic accomplishment, never achieve the return experienced by a segment of the organization facing better economic conditions. If top management relied solely on profit-performance comparisons to judge management (such performance measures—adjusted for the opportunity cost of the able manager—are appropriate inputs to evaluating the investment), skillful managers would be reluctant to accept such trouble-plagued assignments. Contribution compared to past levels might be one useful measure of the manager's performance (coupled with effects on morale, training, etc.), while some measure of investment return would be relevant to evaluating the unit's investment performance.

[5] Using the dual of the profit-maximization form of the problem, the optimal value of each ordinary or structural variable represents the increase in contribution if the associated activity is increased by one unit. The optimal value of each slack variable shows the decline in contribution if that activity is expanded by one unit. See Chapter 20 for a discussion of linear programming in cost analysis.

17.4 Summary

The quantitative measures of performance may assist in measuring performance, but they are not the complete answer. If enough measures are used, always in reference to trends and changes, and with such factors as general business conditions considered, a reasonable indication of the performance of the management team can be obtained. For example, the use of share market can be a measure of performance when business conditions change, but this has to be supported by an analysis of changes in prices and selling expenditures to make sure the market gain did not result in decreased profits. In addition to the record of performance, an analysis of the decision-making technique used by the manager would be extremely useful in evaluating management.

QUESTIONS AND PROBLEMS

17-1 From the annual reports of three companies in the same industry, compute the
a. Operating rates.
b. Investment turnover.
c. Return on investment.
Describe the difficulties of using the computations. Would the same difficulties persist if you had access to the corporate records?

17-2 What additional measure is required for evaluating performance in a profit center that is not required in a cost center?

17-3 To what extent can quantitative measures reflect the performance of a manager? Would it be reasonable to rely exclusively on quantitative measures?

17-4 What factors may affect the investment turnover, operating rate, and return on investment?

17-5 Should accumulated depreciation be deducted in computing the investment for purposes of computing return on investment?

17-6 What are the difficulties of measuring the performance of a research and development department?

17-7 In a manufacturing firm, how would you measure the performance of the departmental foreman, department head, plant manager, division manager, personnel manager, sales manager, and the president of the firm?

17-8 *The Deep Well Machine Company*
The Deep Well Machine Company has 20 divisions and is highly decentralized. Each division makes its own decisions as to price, output, and investments.

One of the primary means of measuring performance used by the company is the return-on-investment chart. Using a series of these charts, the performance of each division through time is noted as well as the comparison of each division with each other division.

Top management is very enthusiastic about the charts, since they show the relationship of profit to sales (operating profit per dollar of sales), sales to investment (the investment turnover), and the return on investment (profit divided by average investment).

The charts are relatively easy to construct since each return-on-investment curve is a smooth curve. Thus only three or four points have to be plotted for each return-on-investment value and a curve drawn to connect the points.

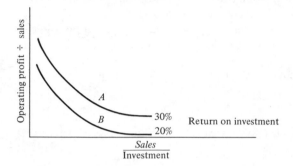

Required: Comment on the effectiveness of these charts as control devices. Is division A more efficient than division B if the cost of money to the firm is 0.15? Explain.

17–9 The ABC Company has a policy of accepting only investments that have yields equal to or in excess of 0.10. It also pays out as dividends 60% of its earnings. Assuming that investments are financed entirely with stock equity funds generated from operations, at what minimum average rate would you expect the earnings of this firm to grow? Assume further that there are many investments available that yield 10%.

17–10 Managers are usually evaluated on their actual performance. What alternatives are there and what is your evaluation of them?

17–11 Explain how the use of ROI as the sole measure of performance for divisions within a company can produce results exactly opposite from those desired.

17–12 Compare and contrast ROI and residual income as performance evaluators. List some advantages and disadvantages associated with each measure.

17–13 How is it possible for some companies to have very low profit margins and high returns on investment while other companies have very high profit margins and low returns on investment? Explain this phenomenon in terms of the formula for ROI.

17–14 The executives of a large company are attempting to construct measures that will be useful in evaluating the performance of machining department foremen. One problem facing the executives is deciding which variables will be included in the measures. They feel that no variable should be used in performance evaluation unless the variables can be affected by actions on the part of the foremen. The following list includes many of the variables that the executives have considered. State whether each variable is controllable or not controllable by the foremen.

1. Rework expenses
2. Lubricant expenses
3. Building rent
4. Supplies expenses
5. Repairs and maintenance expenses
6. Freight-in costs for materials
7. Direct labor rates
8. Overtime expenses
9. Payroll taxes
10. Taxes on building and equipment
11. Insurance on building and equipment
12. Depreciation on equipment
13. Idle time
14. Clean-up labor
15. Heat in building

17–15 The following financial information applies to three companies in the same industry. Fill in the blanks.

	Company A	Company B	Company C
Sales	1,000,000	1,500,000	_____(e)
Income	_____(a)	125,000	400,000
Average investment	_____(b)	1,000,000	_____(f)
Investment turnover	2	_____(c)	1.5
Return on investment	5%	_____(d)	10%

17–16 A small firm has an operating rate of .06 and an investment turnover of 3.
Required:
a. Compute the return on investment.
b. If sales are $100,000, what is the average investment?
c. If the president of the firm wishes to increase the return on investment without increasing the average investment, what major approaches are open to him?

17–17 The following data applies to two divisions in the same company:

	Division A		Division B	
	Operating Profit	Average Investment	Operating Profit	Average Investment
Year 1	$50,000	$500,000	$15,000	$ 90,000
Year 2	60,000	550,000	10,000	100,000
Year 3	65,000	600,000	20,000	150,000
Year 4	70,000	700,000	14,000	140,000

Required:
a. Compute growth rates in operating profits for each division for each year.
b. Compute the return on investment for each division for each year.
c. Based upon a and b, which division has performed better? Do you need to qualify your answer? Why or why not?

17–18 In order to achieve a return on investment of 15% next year, a divisional manager of a large, diversified company is considering a price increase from $4 to $5 on each unit of the single product manufactured by his division. The applicable financial information projected for next year is as follows:

Average investment	$400,000
Variable cost per unit	3
Fixed expenses	100,000
Tax rate	40%

Required:
a. How many units must the division sell in order to achieve a 15% ROI for next year?
b. Compute the investment turnover and the operating rate associated with the 15% ROI.

17–19 The following information concerns two divisions within a large manufacturing firm:

	Division A	Division B
Operating income	$ 500,000	$ 2,500,000
Operating assets	2,500,000	25,000,000

Required:
a. Compute the return on investment for each division.
b. Compute residual income using:
   i. 5%

    ii. 10%

    iii. 15%

    iv. 20%

c. Based upon a and b, which division has the better performance?

17-20 Brightbulb Manufacturing Company, a subsidiary of Acme Lighting, has prepared a schedule of investments that are proposed for the coming year. The following data apply to the investments:

Project	Required Investment	Projected First Year Incremental Operating Income
A	$1,000,000	10,000
B	1,000,000	40,000
C	1,000,000	150,000
D	2,000,000	200,000
E	2,000,000	200,000
F	2,000,000	250,000
G	2,000,000	300,000

The firm presently employs assets totaling $30,000,000, and with no additional investments the firm would expect operating income for the next year to total $5,000,000.

Assume that each project is independent of all others; that is, the fact that one project will be adopted will not affect the projected incremental operating income for any other project considered here or presently in use.

Required:

a. Assuming that the president of Brightbulb knows he will be evaluated on the basis of the maximum ROI he delivers for the year, what project or projects will he select (use $30,000,000 plus the project investments as the base for computing ROI)?

b. Assuming that the president will be evaluated on the basis of next year's residual income using a 10% imputed interest charge, what project or projects will he select?

c. How might the use of a one-year evaluation period affect the long-run performance of the firm?

SUPPLEMENTARY READING

BIERMAN, H., JR., "A Further Study of Depreciation," *The Accounting Review*, April 1966, pp. 271–274.

COUGHLAN, J., "Contrast Between Financial-Statement and Discounted-Cash Flow Methods of Comparing Projects," *N.A.A. Bulletin*, June 1960, pp. 5–20.

DEARDEN, J., "The Case Against ROI Control," *The Harvard Business Review*, May–June 1969, pp. 124–135.

DEMSKI, J. S., "The Decision Implementation Interface: Effects of Alternative Performance Measurement Models," *The Accounting Review*, January 1970, pp. 76–87.

———, "Predictive Ability of Alternative Performance Measurement Models," *Journal of Accounting Research*, Spring 1969, pp. 96–115.

FURLONG, W., "Risk Income and Alternative Income Concepts," *N.A.A. Management Accounting*, April 1967, pp. 25–29.

HENDERSON, B., and J. DEARDEN, "New System for Divisional Control," *The Harvard Business Review*, September–October 1966, pp. 144–161.

MAURIEL, J., and R. ANTHONY, "Misevaluation of Investment Center Performance," *The Harvard Business Review*, March–April 1965, pp. 98–105.

SHWAYDER, K., "A Proposed Modification to Residual Income—Interest Adjusted Income," *The Accounting Review*, April 1970, pp. 299–307.

SOLOMONS, D., *Division Performance: Measurement and Control*, New York Financial Executive Research Foundation, 1965.

THOMPSON, P., and G. DALTON, "Performance Appraisal: Management Beware," *The Harvard Business Review*, January–February 1970, pp. 149–157.

Chapter 18

Return on Investment and Performance Evaluation

After an investment decision has been made and the investment has been acquired, there is the necessity of evaluating the performance of the investment. To reduce possible misunderstanding, the term *asset* could be used in place of *investment*, since this evaluative process applies to all assets.

Sometimes it is impossible to evaluate an isolated investment (or asset), and it is necessary instead to evaluate the utilization of groups of assets because of their jointness. Thus, the recommendations of this chapter are not always applicable with the degree of accuracy indicated. One necessary condition for the application of the proposed present methods is that the costs and benefits of the investment be measurable in dollar terms.

18.1 Definition of the Problem

Previous chapters have recommended the use of discounted cash flows in making investment decisions. However, after the asset has been acquired, performance evaluation is likely to be based on measures of income and return on investment. A component of both measures is depreciation. The primary objective of this chapter is to present a method of depreciation to be used in performance evaluation that is consistent with the cash-flow procedure used in the investment decision-making process.

409

Define:

$V(t)$ = present value of the cash flows of an investment at the end of period t

$V(0)$ = present value at the end of period 0 or the beginning of period 1

$D(t)$ = depreciation for the tth period

$Y(t)$ = income for the tth period

$N(t)$ = net revenues for the tth period (revenues less costs other than depreciation)

$r(t)$ = return on investment for the tth period computed using the beginning of the period investment.

Then $D(t)$ is equal to

$$D(t) = V(t - 1) - V(t)$$

if there is no additional external investment; $r(t)$ is equal to

$$r(t) = \frac{Y(t)}{V(t - 1)}$$

and $Y(t)$ is equal to

$$Y(t) = N(t) - D(t)$$

To avoid complications, the following example assumes that the actual decrease in value for each period is the same as the expected decrease.

Example

Assume that an asset costs $17,355 and has net cash flows of $10,000 per year for two years. The cash is received at the end of each period. The time value of money is 10%. The yield of the investment is 10% (the present value of $10,000 for two years at 10% is $17,355). Actual and expected cash flows are both $10,000.

The investment has the values, decreases in values, and performance measurements given in Table 18–1 for the two years of its existence. The values of $Y(t)$ are:

$$Y(t) = N(t) - D(t)$$
$$Y(1) = 10,000 - 8,264 = 1,736$$
$$Y(2) = 10,000 - 9,091 = \quad 909$$

Using this depreciation procedure, the returns on investment of each period (proceeds less depreciation divided by net investment) are the same percentage and equal to the yield of the investment as anticipated upon purchase.

If the straight-line method of depreciation were to be used instead, as is common in accounting, the results in Table 18–2 are obtained. The return on investment increases from an unsatisfactory (in that it is less than cost of money) 7.7% to a pleasing 15.4% for a situation in which the cash proceeds that were used to predict the expected yield of 10% actually occur.

Table 18–1   Characteristics of Investment

Period t	Investment, End of Period: $V(t)$	Depreciation $D(t)$	Income: $\$10,000 - D(t)$: $Y(t)$	Return on Investment $r(t)$
0	$17,355	—	—	—
1	9,091	$8,264	$1,736	10%
2	0	9,091	909	10%

There is a deficiency in a system that forecasts one thing and when the fore-casted event actually occurs reports something different. The present investment promises a 10% return and constant proceeds, but only if the reporting method suggested in this chapter is used will the reported return be consistent with the rate used in the decision model. Hence, in a situation where the benefits are constant, the depreciation used in evaluating the investment should not be straight-line depreciation if return on investment is to be used in performance evaluation. Furthermore, accelerated depreciation would further distort the measurement problem. In fact, only one depreciation schedule will be consistent, in the present sense, with a given investment. And this schedule may not be related to any of the common depreciation schemes presently used by accountants.

Table 18–2   Return-on-Investment Calculation

Period	Investment, End of Period	Depreciation $D(t)$	Income $\$10,000 - D(t)$	Return on Investment
0	$17,355.00	—	—	—
1	8,677.50	$8,677.50	$1,333.50	7.7%
2	0	8,677.50	1,333.50	15.4%

It is now necessary to be more explicit about what is meant by the term *cash proceeds* and to distinguish between the amount that is needed for purposes of computing depreciation and the amount that is used in the basic investment analysis. The objective is to develop a timetable of depreciation that is internally consistent with the decision, and at the same time gives reasonable measures of income and return on investment.

18.2   Time-Adjusted Revenues and Expenses

The use of cash proceeds in computing depreciation is correct only in the unlikely set of circumstances where the time-adjusted measures of revenues and expenses coincide with the cash-flow computations. If the two are different for any period, it is desirable to explain the difference and, if possible, to reconcile the two sets of numbers.

To avoid confusion with accounting practices that may not be accurate enough for these purposes, it is desirable to use the terms *time-adjusted revenues* and *time-adjusted expenses* to describe items that appropriately take into consideration the time value of money.

The inadequacy of using the cash-proceeds revenue approach to compute depreciation rather than time-adjusted net revenues can be illustrated by a short example.

Example

An investment costs $8,264, and will repay $10,000 after two years. The time value of money is 10% and $8,264 is the present value of the expected $10,000 receipt two years hence. The use of the cash-proceeds approach results in the schedule given in Table 18–3 and the income statements given in Table 18–4. Note that in period 2, the net depreciation-appreciation deduction is $10,000 − $909 = $9,091.

Table 18–3 Investment Appreciation Cash Flows, and Income

	Period 0	Period 1	Period 2
Cash flows at end of period	$ −8,264	$ —	$10,000
Investment at beginning of period		$8,264	$ 9,091
Appreciation of investment (interest): 0.10 × investment		827	909
Depreciation		—	(10,000)
Investment at end of period		$9,091	$ 0
Income recognized using cash proceeds		$ 827	$ 909
Return on beginning of year's investment		10%	10%

Table 18–4 Income Statements Using Cash Proceeds and Accrual Basis

	Period 1	Period 2
Cash flows	$ 0	$10,000
Plus: Appreciation	827	909
	$827	$10,909
Less: Depreciation	—	10,000
Income	$827	$ 909

In both period 1 and period 2 the return on investment is 10%. Now add the information that the cash flow of $10,000 at the end of two periods is the result of a sale on account at the end of period 1. The value of the receivable at the time of the sale is $9,091. Using accrual accounting, this $9,091 is recognized as revenue in period 1, and there is an apparent large profit in period 1 and large loss in period 2, as illustrated in Table 18–5.

Table 18–5   Income Statements Using Time-Adjusted Revenues

	Period 1	Period 2
Sales revenue—accrued	$9,091	
Interest revenue—implicit on receivable		$ 909
Total revenue	$9,091	$ 909
Cash-flow appreciation (depreciation)	827	(9,091)
Net income (loss)	$9,918	($8,182)

It is necessary to refine the depreciation procedure. Rather than basing the depreciation on the cash proceeds, the calculation must be based on the time-adjusted net revenues (revenues less the expenses exclusive of depreciation, all adjusted for the timing of the receipts and disbursement of cash). The analyst must be careful to separate the basic investment that gives rise both to cash and to increases in accounts receivable and other secondary investments that may arise. The account receivable in the present example is such a secondary investment.

The basic investment has a value of $8,264 at the beginning of period 1, and zero value at the end of that period. The depreciation of the first period is therefore $8,264. The receivable has a value of $9,091 at the end of period 1 and a value of $10,000 at the end of period 2. Based on the difference in the value of the receivable at the beginning and end of the second year, the receivable appreciated $909 during period 2. This information is the basis of the schedule given in Table 18–6. In this example the depreciation of the investment for a

Table 18–6   Time-Adjusted Investment and Return on Investment

	Period 1	Period 2
Time-adjusted revenues	$9,091	$ 0
(Depreciation) appreciation	(8,264)	909
Income	$ 827	$ 909
Investment beginning of year	$8,264	$9,091
Return on investment	10%	10%

period is based on the decrease in value of the asset during the period; but it is necessary to define how to compute the values at the several moments in time and the decreases in value. The manager making the investment decision is not concerned with how the accountant measures the revenues of each period, and he may erroneously assume that the cash-flow estimates can be used as the basis for computing the value decreases.

This assumption does not affect the investment decision since the present value of the cash proceeds and the present value of the time-adjusted revenues and expenses are identical. It is only when the analysis shifts from the overall profitability of the investment to a period-by-period profitability analysis that the difference between the cash-flow depreciation and the time-adjusted revenues and expense depreciation makes a difference (and then only if the cash flows are not equal for each period to the time-adjusted net revenues).

The cash-flow depreciation procedure incorrectly combines the analysis of two assets, the original investment and the account receivable acquired as a result of the original investment. Using accrual accounting, cash-flow depreciation does not necessarily match revenues and the expenses of earning those revenues. A significant economic event has occurred when a sale takes place and the business has a legal claim against the customer. The accountant properly recognizes revenue at the moment of sale. Since the revenue is recognized before the cash is received, it is also appropriate to incorporate this consideration into the depreciation calculation. This may be accomplished by defining the depreciation in terms of the decrease in value of the original investment, where the value is measured by discounting the future net time-adjusted revenues.

To illustrate, consider an investment of $2,645 that provides cash flows of $2,000 at the end of period 1 and $1,000 at the end of period 2. The present value of these two cash flows at 0.10 is also $2,645. Add the information that in period 1 the cash sales are $2,000 and the charge sales are $600, and that the charge sales to be collected a year later have a present value of $545 at the end of period 1 (that is, they are discounted at 10%). There are $400 of cash sales at the end of period 2. The time-adjusted revenues and present values are given in Table 18–7.

The present values of the basic investment and the decreases in its values are given in Table 18–8, where the $364 figure for year 1 is the value of the second year's cash sales at the end of the first year. The $2,281 of depreciation for period

Table 18–7   Time-Adjusted Revenues and Present Values

	Period 1	Period 2	Total
Time-adjusted revenues	$2,545	$ 400	
Present-value factors	0.9091	0.8264	
Present value at time 0	$2,314	$ 331	$2,645

Table 18–8 Present Value of Basic Investment and Decreases in Value:
Time-Adjusted Revenue Method

End of Period	Value of Basic Investment	Decrease in Value (depreciation)	Present Value of Accounts Receivable	Appreciation of Receivable
0	$2,645	—	—	—
1	364	$2,281	$545	—
2	0	364	—	$55

1 may also be computed by taking the difference between the present value of the first period's revenues and the appreciation of the second period's revenues in period 1. The present value of the first period's revenues consists of $1,818 in cash sales, $2,000(0.9091), plus $496 in credit sales, $600(0.8264), a total of $2,314. The initial value of period two's cash sales is $331, that is, $400(0.8264). This initial value appreciates by $33 during the first period, $331(0.10). The difference of $2,281 (which is $2,314 − $33) is the first year's depreciation.

The income statements for the two years are given in Table 18–9 (ignoring rounding errors). Note that there are two assets at the end of the first year, a receivable worth $545 and the remaining machine investment of $364. The results of period 2 are divided into two parts, since there are two assets earning income, the basic investment and the derived accounts receivable.

Table 18–9 Time-Adjusted Income Statements for Investment

	Period 1	Period 2 Investment	Period 2 Receivable	Total Period 2
Time-adjusted revenue	$2,545	$400		$400
Depreciation	2,281	364		364
Appreciation			$ 55	55
Income	$ 264	$ 36	$ 55	$ 91
Investment at start of period	$2,645	$364	$545	$909
Return on investment	10%	10%	10%	10%

18.2.1 Reconciliation of the Two Depreciation Methods

It would be disconcerting if two depreciation schedules (and equivalently two value-decrease schedules) result from the same set of economic data. Continuing the previous example, and using the cash-flow method, the schedule of values and decreases in value given in Table 18–10 is obtained.

**Table 18–10   Present Value of Basic Investment
and Decreases in Value: Cash-
Flow Method**

Time	Value	Decrease in Value
0	$2,645	—
1	909	$1,736
2	0	909

Using the time-adjusted revenues there is depreciation of $2,281 for year 1 and
$364 for year 2. The differences arise because in using the time-adjusted revenue
method the increase in the accounts receivable is recognized as a depreciation
of the primary asset. In like manner, the cash-flow depreciation of period 2
recognizes the decrease in the receivable that has already been recognized under
the time-adjusted revenue method in period 1. Table 18–11 attempts to reconcile
the two depreciation schedules.

**Table 18–11   Reconciliation of Depreciation: Time-Adjusted
Revenue Method and Cash-Flow Method**

Period	Cash-Flow Depreciation	Conversion of Investment to Receivable	Time-Adjusted Net Revenue Depreciation
1	$1,736	$ 545	$2,281
2	909	− 545	364

18.2.2 Yields Greater Than the Time Value of Money

All the examples to this point assume that the net present value of the investment is zero; that is, the yield of the investment equals the time value of money
for this firm. Now assume that the yield is greater than the time value of money.

Example

An investment is expected to give an adjusted net income of $10,000 at the
end of period 1 and $20,000 at the end of period 2. (It can also be assumed that
these are cash flows, with the cash flows and time-adjusted net revenues being
equal.) The cost of the investment is $25,619 (the investment has a 10% yield).
The firm's time value of money is 5%.

If 5% is used as the discount rate, a value of $27,664 is obtained at time zero
and the results of operations given in Table 18–12 are relevant. The investment
that cost $25,619 has an immediate value increment to $27,664 (an increase of
$2,045) and that value then earned 5% over its life.

Table 18–12   Results of Operations: 5%

Period	Investment, End of Period	Depreciation	Income	Return on Investment
0	$27,664			
1	19,048	$ 8,616	$1,384	5%
2	0	19,048	952	5%

If the $25,619 had been used as the basis of the accounting and if a 10% time-value factor had been used, the results would appear as in Table 18–13. A difficulty with using this schedule is that the time value of money has been defined to be 5%, and the value of the investment at time 0 is $27,664, not $25,619. As a compromise, the two procedures might be combined as in Table 18–14.

Table 18–13   Results of Operations: 10%

Period	Investment, End of Period	Depreciation	Income	Return on Investment
0	$25,619			
1	18,182	$ 7,437	$2,563	10%
2	0	18,182	1,818	10%

Table 18–14   Combining the Results

Period	Income Using 5%	Portion of Income Unrealized (at time of acquisition) Profit Realized During Period	Total Realized Income (income using 10%)
1	$1,384	$1,179	$2,563
2	952	866	1,818

The income using 5% might be used for purposes of performance evaluation for the manager operating the investment and the total income using 10% might be reported to stockholders where there is more of a requirement for obtaining objective evidence before reporting income. That is, income should not be reported externally at the time of purchase just because the decision maker is optimistic about the prospects. On the other hand, the schedule based on the 10% return could be used. If the manager makes propitious investments, the measure of his performance should reflect the increase in the return he is able to make. In other words, deviations from expected results or, in this case, from the required minimal return, appear as improved rates of performance.[1]

18.3 Imputed Interest

As a supplement to the return-on-investment calculation, the effect of the utilization of assets can be incorporated into the measurement of performance by deducting implicit interest from the operating income of the period. Thus, if $40,000,000 of assets are utilized during a period and if the interest cost is 0.05, an implicit interest charge of $2,000,000 can be deducted from the operating income. If the operating income were $3,000,000, it would be $1,000,000 after the deduction of the implicit interest. This is the residual income approach. Thus management might be told:

1. The return on investment was $3,000,000/$40,000,000 = 0.075.
2. The amount of $1,000,000 was earned over and above the implicit interest cost charged on the assets utilized.

There are two difficulties with the procedure of charging implicit interest. The most important is that it may be that not all the interest cost of a period should be an expense. For example, an asset may be purchased today at a cost of $10,000 with a promised return of $11,025 two years from now. At 5% there is an interest cost of $500 after one year, but this is not an expense but rather an increase in the value of the asset. After one period the cost basis of the asset should be adjusted to $10,500; the cost basis includes the implicit interest cost of $500.

The difficulty can be solved by allocating the interest cost between the assets and expenses of the period. This allocation requires judgement, but there is no escaping the need for the allocation if the firm is going to avoid a distortion in incentives.

The second difficulty follows from the first. If the cost basis of the asset is adjusted from $10,000 to $10,500 and then to $11,025, no operating income is reported when the expected revenues of $11,025 are earned.

There is no income above the implicit interest cost of $1,025 and the $10,000 explicit cost of the asset. However, the other side of the implicit interest cost of $1,025 is implicit interest revenue. This revenue should be recognized during some time period if the implicit interest cost is recognized. The income statement should have at least three subtotals:

---

[1] The fact that depreciation taken for taxes has implications for cash flows through its effect on tax obligations adds another dimension to the problem that is not considered here. One appealing means of dealing with this complication is to consider the tax-payment deduction associated with an asset because of depreciation as a separable asset.

Revenues	$xxxxx
Less: Expenses	xxxxx
Operating income	$xxxxx
Less: Implicit interest cost	xxxxx
Income after interest cost	$ xxx
Plus: Implicit interest revenue	xx
Change in stockholders' equity	$ xxx

Example

The facts in Table 18–15 relate to a firm with a cost of money of 0.05. The cost of the asset is $18,594. First the depreciation and operating incomes of the two time periods are computed in Table 18–16 in accordance with the depreciation method developed earlier in this chapter. The returns on investment are 0.05 for both years. If the firm computes the implicit interest cost for the two years, its net income is as given in Table 18–17. To complete the procedure, the

Table 18–15   Revenues and Expenses by Periods

	Period 1	Period 2
Revenues	$25,000	$25,000
Less: Out-of-pocket expenses	15,000	15,000
	$10,000	$10,000

Table 18–16   Depreciation and Operating Income

t	$V(t)$	$D(t)$	Operating Income
0	$18,594		
1	9,524	$9,070	$930
2	0	9,524	476

Table 18–17   Net Income Calculated

	Period 1	Period 2
Operating income	$930	$476
Less: Implicit interest cost		
0.05 × 18,594	930	
0.05 × 9,524		476
Income	$0	$0

Table 18–18   Operating Results by Periods

	Period 1	Period 2
Revenues	$25,000	$25,000
Less: Out-of-pocket expenses	$15,000	$15,000
Depreciation	9,070	9,524
	$24,070	$24,524
Operating income	$930	$476
Less: Implicit interest cost	930	476
Income after interest	$ 0	$ 0
Plus: Implicit interest revenue	930	476
Change in stockholders' equity	$ 930	$ 476

implicit interest revenue of the two time periods should be added. The complete presentation of operating results is given in Table 18–18. Taking the last line and dividing by the investment at the beginning of the period, a return on investment of 0.05 is obtained for both years.

The above procedure is somewhat awkward since interest is already taken into account in the depreciation computation and the deduction of the implicit interest is redundant. There is at least as much information in the $930 operating income figure, the changes in this number, and the return on investment as there is in the $0 income after-interest measure.

Now suppose that the capital consumption of a period is defined "To be equal to the present value of the expected future benefits of that period."[2] Thus, the basic capital consumption for period 1 is $9,524 and for period 2, it is $9,070. It is now necessary to compute the interest cost and implicit interest revenue as associated with the two investments of $9,524 for the first period and $9,070 for the second period. Table 18–19 identifies the implicit interest costs and rev-

Table 18–19   Implicit Interest Cost and Revenues by Period

	Investment	Interest in Period 1	Interest in Period 2	Total Implicit Interest Cost
Cost of period 1's revenue	$9,524	$476	...	$ 476
Cost of period 2's revenue	9,070	454	$476	930
Total interest revenue		$930	$476	$1,406

[2] The concept of capital consumption used here may be reconciled to the depreciation notions discussed earlier in this chapter by suitable adjustments for interest costs and revenues.

Table 18–20   Income Statements by Periods

	Period 1	Period 2
Revenues	$25,000	$25,000
Less: Out-of-pocket expenses	$15,000	$15,000
Capital consumption	9,524	9,070
	$24,524	$24,070
Operating income	$ 476	$ 930
Less: Implicit interest cost	476	930
Income after interest cost	$ 0	$ 0
Plus: Implicit interest revenue	930	476
Net change in stockholders' equity	$ 930	$ 476

enues of the two time periods. The related income statements are supplied in Table 18–20. The returns on investment for both time periods are again 0.05.

Using different procedures it was possible to obtain constant returns on an investment of 0.05 for the two periods. One strong warning is necessary. A wrong combination of interest calculations and depreciation method will result in meaningless income measures. The interest and the depreciation calculations must be consistent with each other.

18.4   Interest As a Cost of Product

Through the years accountants have argued as to whether interest was a cost of an inventoriable nature similar to material and labor costs. Although the question is theoretically interesting and there are arguments both pro and con, it is subordinate to the primary question of how interest should be incorporated into the decision-making process. The following sections review briefly the technique for incorporating interest into the manufacturing accounts.

A method suggested for incorporating interest into the accounts is to compute the interest on the assets utilized and allocate this interest to departments and absorb it into the cost of product. Assuming a value of money of 6% and assets of $100,000, the entries to accomplish the inclusion of interest are as follows[3]:

---

[3] Depreciable assets should be excluded from the asset total on which interest is being computed if interest is being taken into account via the depreciation method.

Implicit Interest Cost		Implicit Interest Revenue	
(1) 6,000	(2) 6,000	(3) 5,000	(1) 6,000

Manufacturing Costs		Income	
(2) 6,000	(4) 5,000	(4) 5,000	(3) 5,000

Explanation of entries

1. Records the interest cost and the interest revenue earned on the funds tied up in assets ($100,000 × 6%). Part of the credit would be to "interest payable" if there is debt outstanding.
2. Records the transfer of the $6,000 implicit interest to the manufacturing account.
3. Transfers $5,000 of the interest revenue to the income account.
4. Transfers $5,000 of the manufacturing costs to the income account (five sixths of the inventory has been used).

The above entries assume that five sixths of the goods worked on during the period were sold and thus five sixths of the interest is expensed during the period. For the portion of manufactured product still on hand, it has been decided not to recognize interest revenue since the funds are invested in goods not yet sold. Since five sixths of the goods worked on during the period were sold, and one sixth are still in inventory, it is conservative to recognize only five sixths of $6,000, or $5,000, as income for the period. Interest cost of $5,000 appears as revenues (the net effect of implicit interest on the income of the period being zero). The $1,000 balance in implicit interest revenue could be formally closed to the manufacturing account (or inventory accounts) or merely subtracted from the inventories. The net effect of recognizing implicit interest on income in the manner indicated is zero.

The question of whether interest should be considered a cost of product and treated in a manner comparable to costs of material and labor is less important than how the interest cost of the resources committed to a project may be incorporated into the decision-making process. It is suggested that computing the present value of cash flows will frequently be a reasonable and adequate method of accomplishing this objective.

If it is desired to present a unit cost of product for decision making and measuring performance, the cost of product should include interest cost on the incremental assets. For assets already owned, the cost measure used should be the interest on the opportunity cost of employing the resources in other projects. Thus, interest on the increase in working capital which is required by the project would also be relevant. But where the machinery and equipment have other uses than the one being considered, the opportunity cost of the equipment should be used as the measure of cost.

18.5   Implicit Interest and Break-even Analysis[4]

Implicit interest also has an impact on traditional break-even analysis. One of the differences between most economic and accounting approaches to break-even analysis concerns the treatment of the cost of money. The economists include it as a cost, the accountants do not. The latter, however, evaluate (or leave it to management to evaluate) profits in terms of the required return on investment that is implied relative to the cost of money to the firm. Thus, both recognize the importance of the cost of money but consider it at different points in the analysis.

The cost of money can be incorporated into conventional break-even analysis (which assumes constant price, linear variable cost, constant inventory levels, etc.) by discounting the relevant cash flows. Figure 18.1 assumes that there are fixed costs. The traditional break-even volume, computed using a zero interest rate, is at an activity of x_1. The fixed cost is OA dollars. Introducing a positive rate of interest causes the discounted value of the total revenues to decline for a given activity level. The same is true for total costs. If the fixed costs were all incurred over the same period and under the same timing assumed for the revenue and variable-cost flows, the fixed costs would drop to OB and the break-even activity level would remain unchanged. This is illustrated by the dashed line, with the same slope as the line labeled "Total cost: $r > 0$" emanating from point B.

But if the fixed costs are incurred at the start of the period, the break-even point is affected by the discounting.[5] The result is a revised break-even point,

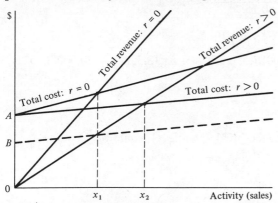

Figure 18.1   The effect of incorporating the cost of money into the break-even analysis.

[4] The development here follows R. Manes, "A New Dimension to Break-even Analysis," *The Journal of Accounting Research*, Spring 1966, pp. 87–100. The reader is encouraged to read the original article.

[5] The costs of an investment can often be converted into annual costs by leasing. Additional costs are incurred in the process due to the postponement of payment, and these costs are among those that traditional break-even analysis ignores if the asset is purchased.

x_2, which exceeds the break-even point, ignoring the cost of money. In the following example there is a long-lived asset servicing several periods.

Example
Assume a situation with the following characteristics:

Variable cost per unit	$0.50
Sales price per unit	$2
Fixed costs of initial investment	
(assume the investment is avoidable)	$100,000
Life of proposed activity	5 years
Annual fixed operating outlays	$20,000
Salvage value of investment after 5 years	$0
Assumed cost of money	0.15

Let $B(5, 0.15)$ be the present value of a 5-year annuity with a 0.15 cost of money. Then

$$B(5, 0.15) = \frac{1}{(1 + 0.15)} + \frac{1}{(1 + 0.15)^2} + \frac{1}{(1 + 0.15)^3}$$

$$+ \frac{1}{(1 + 0.15)^4} + \frac{1}{(1 + 0.15)^5}$$

$$= \frac{1 - (1 + 0.15)^{-5}}{0.15} = 3.3522$$

The break-even level is given by x_b, where

$$100,000 = [(2-0.50)x_b - 20,000]B(5, 0.15) = 1.5x_b(3.3522) - 20,000(3.3522)$$

and

$$x_b = 33,227 \text{ units per year}$$

If the interest rate were ignored, the break-even level would be

$$\frac{100,000 + 5(20,000)}{5} = 1.50x_b$$

and x_b equals 26,667 units per year.

The effect of adding the cost of money in this case increases the break-even quantity by nearly 25%.[6]

---

[6] The method used here can be extended to include the effect of taxes, depreciation policy, growth or decline in future sales, and the effects of inflation. This would take the analysis further afield than the authors wish to go. The interested reader is referred to Manes, *op. cit.*, for a discussion of these points.

18.6 Summary

The difficulties in performance evaluation include all the problems of measuring unit costs, income, and assets. Any evaluation of performance must consider the limitations of the measures being used as the basis of the evaluation.

The examples have illustrated the computation of depreciation in situations where the cash flows of a period differ from the time-adjusted net revenues of a period because of the presence of sales made on account. In situations where there are expenses not requiring the immediate disbursement of cash because of the possibility of delaying payment (current liabilities may be increased), an analysis analogous to that associated with the accounts receivable would be appropriate.

The chapter also examines briefly the effect of implicit interest on revenues and product cost. Interest also affects break-even analysis, increasing the break-even level over that obtained in traditional analysis.

APPENDIX 18A
CAPITAL-ASSET PRICING MODEL APPLIED TO
COST–VOLUME PROFIT ANALYSIS

For many years cost–volume profit analysis has included considerations of uncertainty. This appendix is an attempt to apply capital-asset-model theories to corporate decisions affecting both operations and capital structure.

Figure 18A.1 shows the conventional break-even analysis under conditions of uncertainty. The decision maker can compute the expected profit, the expected loss associated with the undesirable outcomes, and the probability of undesirable outcomes (for example, the probability of a loss). If desired, the variance and standard deviations of the outcomes can also be computed.

Figure 18A.2 applies to capital-structure decisions and is comparable to Figure 18A.1. It shows the returns on investment for two different capital structures for different amounts of earnings before interest. Instead of return on investment, we could just as easily show the earnings per share that result for different capital structures.

If Figure 18A.2 is rotated counterclockwise 90 degrees and then combined with Figure 18A.1, we have Figure 18A.3, which shows the effect of changing the operating characteristics or capitalization on the return on investment. If desired, given a probability distribution on sales, a probability distribution of return on investment can be derived. For example, if sales are Q_1 units, the earnings before interest will be X_1 and the return on investment will be r_1.

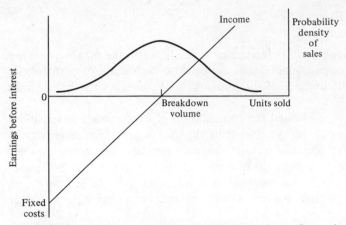

Figure 18A.1   Break-even analysis under uncertainty: Operating leverage.

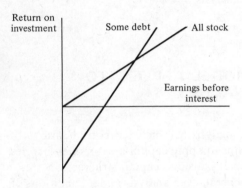

Figure 18A.2   Break-even analysis with different capital structures: Financial leverage.

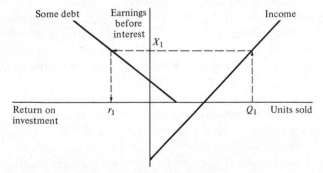

Figure 18A.3   Operating and financial leverage.

Capital-Asset Pricing Model and Capital-Structure Decisions

A basic understanding of the capital-asset pricing model will be assumed, although aspects of the model will be reviewed without proof. Let

X = earnings before interest

$\bar{r}_j$ = required expected return for investment j where $\bar{r}_j = \dfrac{X}{S}$

r = default-free return

$\bar{r}_m$ = expected return from investing in a market portfolio

$\beta = \dfrac{\text{Cov}(r_j, r_m)}{\text{Var}(r_m)}$

S = total capital of the firm

It has been proved that in equilibrium,

$$\bar{r}_j = r + (\bar{r}_m - r)\beta \tag{A18.1}$$

If with a firm of size S, B of debt is substituted for common stock so that $S = B + S_B$, where S_B is the new amount of common stock, and r_{jB} is the new return on common stock investment, the new beta, β_B, is [7]:

$$\beta_B = \frac{\text{Cov}(r_{jB}, r_m)}{\text{Var}(r_m)} = \frac{E((X - \bar{X})/S_B)(r_m - \bar{r}_m)}{\text{Var}(r_m)}$$

$$= \frac{(S/S_B)E(r_j - \bar{r}_j)(r_m - \bar{r}_m)}{\text{Var}(k_m)} = \frac{S}{S_B}\frac{\text{Cov}(r_j, r_m)}{\text{Var}(k_m)} = \frac{S}{S_B}\beta \tag{A18.2}$$

Defining $\bar{r}_{j_B}$ to be the required return with B of debt, then, by definition:

$$\bar{r}_{j_B} = r + (\bar{r}_m - r)\beta_B \tag{A18.3}$$

Substituting $(S/S_B)\beta$ for β_B in (A18.3):

$$\bar{r}_{j_B} = r + (\bar{r}_m - r)\frac{S}{S_B}\beta \tag{A18.4}$$

Since we defined $S = B + S_B$, we can rewrite (A18.4):

$$\bar{r}_{j_B} = r + (\bar{r}_m - r)\beta + (\bar{r}_m - r)\frac{B}{S_B}\beta \tag{A18.5}$$

[7] It is assumed that payments to debtholders are a constant rather than a random variable. Thus, if Y is defined to be the earnings of stockholders, $Y - \bar{Y} = X - \bar{X}$ where X is the earnings before interest.

where

$$r = \text{default-free return}$$

$$(\bar{r}_m - r)\beta = \text{adjustment for operating risk}$$

$$(\bar{r}_m - r)\frac{B}{S_B}\beta = \text{adjustment for the financial risk arising}$$
from the capital structure

Capital-Asset Pricing Model and Operating Risk

Let

$$p = \text{price per unit}$$

$$b = \text{variable costs per unit}$$

$$F = \text{fixed costs of operations}$$

$$Q = \text{units sold (this is a random variable)}$$

$$X = \text{earnings before interest}$$

Then

$$X = Q(p - b) - F$$

and

$$X - \bar{X} = (Q - \bar{Q})(p - b)$$

We want to write $\text{Cov}(r_{j_B}, r_m)$ in terms of Q:

$$\text{Cov}(r_{j_B}, r_m) = \frac{p - b}{S_B} E[(Q - \bar{Q})(r_m - \bar{r}_m)]$$

$$= \frac{p - b}{S_B} \text{Cov}(Q, r_m)$$

We can now write β_B in terms of Q:

$$\beta_B = \frac{\text{Cov}(r_{j_B}, r_m)}{\text{Var}(r_m)} = \frac{p - b}{S_B}\left[\frac{\text{Cov}(Q, r_m)}{\text{Var}(r_m)}\right]$$

Figure 18A.4 shows how the operating and financial decisions may be combined to determine the optimal mix of financial and operating risk and return. Figure 18A.4 also shows the derivation of point A that results from B_1 of debt and a given method of operations that results in $E(Q_1)$ units sold and $E(X_1)$ of earnings before interest. It also results in $\text{Cov}(Q_1, r_m)$ that defines a $\text{Cov}(r_{j_B}, r_m)$ which in turn helps define point A. In the lower right-hand quadrant $\text{Cov}(Q, r_m)$ is converted into $\text{Cov}(r_{j_B}, r_m)$. The $\text{Cov}(Q, r_m)$ could just as well have been used to compute $\bar{r}_{j_B}$, the required return.

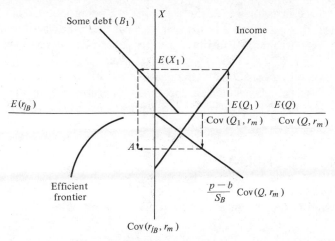

Figure 18A.4   Trading off risk and return.

Assuming that the curve labeled "Efficient Frontier" represents feasible points, point A is inferior to other financial and operating combinations that have been used to map the efficient frontier. Not all points on the efficient frontier are equally desirable (but they are better than all points to the right of the frontier or interior to it). The point that maximizes the value of the firm is the optimum point, and the decisions leading to that point would be the optimum decisions.

Overview of the Analysis

It is well known that firms make operating decisions (such as deciding on the extent of mechanization or pricing decisions) and also capital-structure decisions. These decisions affect the expected profits and the risk of the firm. The above procedure can be used for separating the operating and financial risks, and it can also be used for including them jointly in making decisions that maximize the value of the firm. There are some firms that undertake very risky investments but would not think of using debt in their capital structure. There are other firms that use a great deal of debt but would not consider an investment that introduces significant risk.

The above analysis suggests that risk is a well-defined characteristic that results from either investments or capital structure, or both, and that the combined result is the important consideration, not the presence of financial or operating risk considered in isolation. Although the above is a partial analysis, since tax considerations have not been explicitly considered, it does point the way to a method of analysis that shifts attention from the partial effects of piecemeal decisions to a consideration of the global effects of sets of interacting decisions. One very important assumption that has been made is that the capital-asset pricing model applies to the firm for which the decisions are being made. The model applies if the firm's investors are well diversified, or if the nondiversified investors are willing to accept the maximization of market value as the corporate goal.

Finally, it should be noted that consistent with the above assumption, the risk measure that is relevant is the covariance of the firm's operations with the market return, not the variance. This has important implications relative to the type of information to be reported by the accountant.

QUESTIONS AND PROBLEMS

18-1 An asset costs $18,594 and will earn proceeds of $10,000 per year for two years. The cash is received at the end of each period. The time value of money is 0.05.

Required:
a. Compute the yield of the investment.
b. Compute the depreciation in the value of the asset, the income, and the return on investment for each of the two years of life.

18-2 An asset costs $27,665 and will earn proceeds of $10,000 in year 1 and $20,000 in year 2. The time value of money is 0.05.

Required:
a. Compute the yield of the investment.
b. Compute the depreciation in the value of the asset, the income, and return on the investment for each of the two years of life.

18-3 An asset costs $28,118 and will earn proceeds of $20,000 in year 1 and $10,000 in year 2. The time value of money is 0.05.

Required:
a. Compute the yield of investment.
b. Compute the depreciation in the value of the asset, the income, and the return on investment for each of the two years of life.

18-4 An asset costs $20,000 and earns proceeds of $11,000 in year 1 and $10,500 in year 2. The time value of money is 0.05.

Required:
a. Compute the yield of the investment.
b. Compute the depreciation in the value of the asset, the income, and return on investment for each of the two years of life.

18-5 An asset costs $20,000 and will earn proceeds of $12,000 in year 1 and $11,000 in year 2. The time value of money is 0.10.

Required:
a. Compute the yield of the investment.
b. Compute the depreciation in the value of the asset, the income, and the return on investment for each of the two years of life.

18-6 An asset costs $18,594 and will earn cash proceeds of $10,500 per year for two years; the first payment is to be received two years from now. The sales of $10,500 will be made at the end of periods 1 and 2 and the collections at the end of periods 2 and 3. The time value of money is 0.05.

Required: Compute the depreciation, the income, and return on investment for each year of the life of the investment.

18–7 An asset costs $27,665 and will earn proceeds of $10,500 in year 2 and $21,000 in year 3. The time value of money is 0.05. The sales will be made at the end of periods 1 and 2 and the collections at the end of periods 2 and 3.

Required: Compute the depreciation, the income, and return on investment for each year of life.

18–8 An asset costs $17,355 and will earn proceeds of $10,000 per year for two years. The cash is received at the end of each period. The time value of money is 0.05.

Required:

a. Compute the yield of the investment.

b. Compute the depreciation, income, and return on investment.

18–9 An asset costs $25,619 and will earn proceeds of $10,000 in year 1 and $20,000 in year 2. The time value of money is 0.05.

Required:

a. Compute the yield of the investment.

b. Compute the depreciation, income, and return on investment.

18–10 Assume that the Alstar Company is considering the investment described in 18–9. The company uses a straight-line method of depreciation for financial accounting purposes and management is very sensitive to the effect that an investment will have on income and earnings per share.

Required: Should the company undertake the investment assuming that the cash flows are known with certainty and 0.05 is an appropriate discount rate?

18–11 Accountants typically ignore implicit interest in break-even analyses. What is the effect of this behavior? Is the effect important?

18–12 A recent proposal in the literature suggests that a firm may want to consider its growth rate of income as reflected in its published accounting statements in its decision making.[8] In particular, the firm may select among investments subject to limitations placed on the minimum percentage growth in earnings to be reported. Is it reasonable for a firm to be concerned about its reported growth in income? What problems do you see in using the suggested procedure? What remedies might you suggest?

18–13 Consider a situation in which a firm has received the first order from a new customer. Assume that:

1. The firm has excess capacity at the present time.
2. The marginal revenues exceed variable costs.

[8] See E. Lerner and A. Rappaport, "Limit DCF in Capital Budgeting," *The Harvard Business Review*, September–October 1968, pp. 133–139.

3. There are no externality problems.
4. The problems of cost justification under the Robinson–Patman Act can be ignored.
5. The new customer is likely to maintain purchases in periods when unexpected declines occur in the orders from other customers.

Present arguments, from a risk standpoint, for accepting the order as well as from the traditional marginal viewpoint.

18–14 Is the variance of an investment the best measure of the risk of that investment?

18–15 Does a project with uncertain returns necessarily add to the firm's overall risk?

18–16 Can you argue from a risk standpoint that a firm with several divisions might be justified in using different rates of return for each?

Questions and problems 18–17 to 18–23 require an understanding of Appendix 18A.

18–17 Figure 18A.1 shows the earnings before interest plotted as a function of units sold. Write the equation for earnings. Indicate on a graph the slope and the Y-axis intercept.

18–18 Figure 18A.2 shows the return on investment as a function of the earnings before interest for different amounts of debt. Let k_i be the interest rate on the debt. Assume zero taxes. Write the equation for the return on investment on common stock as a function of earnings.

18–19 Write an equation for return on investment in terms of earnings quantity.

18–20 For what values of units sold will the stockholders be indifferent as to capital structure?

18–21 Assume that the β of a company with zero debt is 1. What will the β be if the company switches to 0.5 debt?

18–22 Assume that the default-free rate is 0.08, the expected return from the market portfolio is 0.12, and the facts of problem 18–21 apply.
   a. What is the required expected return before the change in capital structure?
   b. After the change?

18–23 The following relationship was developed in the chapter:

$$\beta_B = \left[\frac{p - b}{S_B}\right]\left[\frac{\text{Cov}(Q, r_m)}{\text{Var}(r_m)}\right]$$

If $(p - b)$ can be increased by a decrease in b (the variable costs), what will be the effect on β_B? Is this good or bad?

18–24 A major business on the West Coast decided to install a "Watts" telephone line to reduce phone costs. A Watts line is obtained for a fixed fee per month. The firm uses a cost-center approach to performance evaluation.

a. How should the monthly cost to the firm be allocated to the various cost centers for performance measurement purposes? (Presently, costs are allocated to the division in which the extension on which the call originated is located. This is prior to installing the Watts line.)
b. How should the firm evaluate the Watts line to decide whether to keep the line or not?
c. Is this analysis (in a and b) relevant to a not-for-profit activity? If not, why not?

SUPPLEMENTARY READING

BACKER, M., "Additional Considerations in Return on Investment Analysis," *N.A.A. Bulletin*, January 1962, pp. 57–62.

BIERMAN, H., JR., "A Further Study of Depreciation," *The Accounting Review*, April 1966, pp. 271–274.

COUGHLAN, J., "Contrast Between Financial-Statement and Discounted-Cash Flow Methods of Comparing Projects," *N.A.A. Bulletin*, June 1960, pp. 5–20.

DEMSKI, J. S., "The Decision Implementation Interface: Effects of Alternative Performance Measurement Models," *The Accounting Review*, January 1970, pp. 76–87.

———, "Predictive Ability of Alternative Performance Measurement Models," *Journal of Accounting Research*, Spring 1969, pp. 96–115.

DYCKMAN, T. R., BIERMAN, H., and T. CRICHFIELD, "Depreciation Policy and Decision Making," in *Conference on Topical Research in Accounting*, New York University, 1975.

FAMA, E. F., "Risk, Return, and Equilibrium: Some Clarifying Comments," *Journal of Finance*, March 1968, pp. 29–40.

HAMADA, R. S., "Portfolio Analysis, Market Equilibrium, and Corporation Finance," *Journal of Finance*, March 1969.

HORNGREN, C. T., "Report of the Committee on Management Decision Models," *The Accounting Review*, Supplement 1969, pp. 43–78.

MANES, R., "A New Dimension to Breakeven Analysis," *Journal of Accounting Research*, Spring 1966, pp. 87–100.

RUBINSTEIN, M. E., "A Mean-Variance Synthesis of Corporate Financial Theory," *Journal of Finance*, March 1973.

SHARPE, W. F., "Capital Asset Prices: A Theory of Market Equilibrium Under Conditions of Risk," *Journal of Finance*, September 1964, pp. 425–442.

SHWAYDER, K., "A Proposed Modification to Residual Income—Interest Adjusted Income," *The Accounting Review*, April 1970, pp. 299–307.

SOLOMONS, D., *Division Performance: Measurement and Control*, New York: Financial Executives Research Foundation, 1965.

Chapter 19

Transfer Pricing

Since the end of World War II two interesting business phenomena which are in many respects contradictory have accrued. One is the large number of business combinations (mergers and acquisitions) which have resulted in an increase in the complexity of business organizations. The other is the increased use of decentralization or divisionalization as a means of controlling large corporations. Many of these corporations are the result of business combinations. Thus firms seek the advantages of being large and small, simultaneously.

The desirability of decentralization arises in part from a planning point of view. The underlying rationale stems from the limitations on human cognitive ability. This position has been advanced by Hayek and Von Mises in their defense of the price system, and later by March and Simon as the principle of bounded rationality.[1] The desirability of decentralization was eloquently expressed by Hayek in describing the role of the price system:

As decentralization has become necessary because nobody can consciously balance all the considerations bearing on the decisions of so many individuals, the coordination can clearly not be affected by "conscious control," but only by arrangements which convey to each agent the information he must possess in order effectively to adjust his decisions to those of others. And because all the details of the changes constantly affecting the conditions of demand and supply of the different commodities can never be fully known, or quickly enough be collected and

[1] F. Hayek, *The Road to Serfdom*, Chicago University of Chicago Press, 1944; L. Von Mises, *Bureaucracy*, New Haven: Yale University Press, 1944; and J. G. March and H. A. Simon, *Organizations*, New York: John Wiley & Sons, Inc., 1958.

disseminated, by any one centre, what is required is some apparatus of registration which automatically records all the relevant effects of individual actions, and whose indications are at the same time the resultant of, and the guide for, all the individual decisions.

The advantages of decentralization have also been advanced from a motivational prospective. Argyris and Likert, among others, maintain that decentralization permits factors that motivate middle and lower management to play a more important role.[2] Others, including Dean, emphasize improved control through better knowledge of the strength and weakness of specific company activities.[3] Regardless of the reasons for decentralization, the existence of several divisions with interrelated activities creates a need for performance evaluation. Often one division sells to another, and this complicates the evaluation process since the arm's length transaction found between firms in the market is lacking.

19.1 Need for Transfer Prices

If an automobile company buys its glass from an independent glass company, the price is set by market forces. The automobile executives can determine the cost of glass by looking at purchase invoices. If the automobile company creates a glass division to manufacture all its glass, a transfer-pricing problem is created. The assembly division "buys" from the glass division. The price of the units sold is set by management and this price is not usually a market price.

The price has an important effect on the glass division's profits (since it affects revenues) and the profits of the assembly division (since it affects costs), but the price does not directly affect the profits of the company as a whole, although there may be indirect effects by way of the decisions made from the accounting information which incorporates the transfer prices.

19.2 Conflict of Interests

It is assumed that the basic goal is profit maximization for the corporation as a whole. Decentralization attempts to gain that goal by having division managers act in the interest of their own divisions. To the extent possible, the intracompany pricing method should be consistent with the goals of maximizing the profits of the company and the division. Transfer prices can have an important impact on the profits of the divisions involved. Moreover, these prices affect

[2] C. Argyris, *Personality and Organization*, New York: Harper & Row, Publishers, 1957; and R. Likert, "Measuring Organizational Performance," in *Studies in Personnel and Industrial Psychology*, edited by E. A. Frishman, Homewood, Ill.: The Dorsey Press, 1961.
[3] J. Dean, "Decentralization and Intercompany Pricing," *The Harvard Business Review*, 1955, pp. 65–74.

decisions involving the acquisition and utilization of the organization resources. Ideally, transfer prices should guide the managers of the organization's subunits to maximize the incomes of the organization as a whole.

It does not always follow that a division manager acting to maximize the profits of his division will be acting to maximize the profits of the corporation. Hirshleifer and Cook have both supplied illustrations where the rational actions of the division manager (consistent with maximizing the profits of the division) are not consistent with maximizing the profits of the company.[4] In part this is because one division may be able to act as a monopolist in its dealings with other divisions. A division may also attempt to alter activity decisions made in the central office by modifying its cost structure. Furthermore, it is possible for one division to affect external economies (by using up an overabundant resource or encouraging a cost-benefiting technological change) or diseconomies (by using a scarce corporate resource or changing the reward structure) in other divisions.[5]

Do the gains arising from simulated competition and decentralized authority exceed the losses arising from decisions aimed at maximizing division profits rather than corporate profits? The answer to this question is avoided here by assuming there is agreement that an intracompany pricing scheme should be used and that it should facilitate the maximization of corporate profits rather than divisional profits. Nevertheless, many executives would object to the weakening of decentralization by a procedure that overrules decisions made at the division level because of the claim that the decisions were not consistent with the maximization of the profits of the company. In some firms, at least, the degree of decentralization is limited. For example, Whinston found in two firms that little authority was decentralized when it came to output and type-of-product decisions, although substantial authority for cost control was delegated.[6] Division managers are rarely, if ever, given the option to acquire or dispose of large segments of the division's capital assets, nor are they able to control the disposition of their earnings. In such a situation it is not clear that a manager can be held responsible for the profitability of current operations, since he is not responsible for the methods of production and sale. An excellent example involves the allocation of service department costs. This allocation is essentially a form of transfer price for services received which represents an imposed value on the part of central management.

---

[4] J. Hirshleifer, "On the Economics of Transfer Pricing," *The Journal of Business*, July 1956, pp. 172–184; P. W. Cook, "New Technique for Intracompany Pricing," *The Harvard Business Review*, July–August 1957, pp. 74–80; see also J. R. Gould, "Internal Pricing in Firms Where There Are Costs of Using an Outside Market," *The Journal of Business*, January 1964, pp. 61–67.

[5] See Chapter 20 for a further discussion on these points.

[6] A. Whinston, "Price Guides in Decentralized Organizations," in *New Prospectives in Organization Research*, edited by W. Cooper, H. Leavitt, and M. Shelly, New York: John Wiley & Sons, Inc., pp. 409–417.

19.3 Transfer-Price Alternatives

The intracompany prices may be established in several ways. These include:

1. Market price (determined by printed price lists, invoices, price quotations, or other evidence).
2. Marginal cost.
3. Variable costs (perhaps used as a substitute for marginal costs because of the difficulty of determining the marginal-cost curve).
4. Full cost (either actual or standard and including or excluding a "reasonable" profit).
5. Negotiated price.
6. Prices determined by the central office.

The transfer-pricing problem has frequently been approached from the point of view that only one procedure is correct. This chapter attempts to show that any of the above alternatives may be reasonable and that the choice of method can be made only after determining the purpose for which the information is to be used. At its best, accounting information is raw material, which, to be useful to management, must be processed. Without analysis, any intracompany pricing scheme may lead to faulty information and decisions.

Although there is no single best transfer-pricing method for all situations, a general rule can be given that yields a useful first approximation. The transfer price should equal the division's marginal (often, approximately the variable) costs directly associated with production and transfer, plus any opportunity costs to the total organization. The rule is easier to state than apply. The marginal costs are essentially the easily established prime costs of materials and direct labor for which reasonably recent cash payments have been made. It is more difficult to establish the indirect costs directly associated with the goods or service transferred which should be included.

In a perfect intermediate market, the opportunity cost can be estimated as the market price less the aforementioned out-of-pocket costs. But perfect intermediate markets seldom exist. Opportunity costs will generally depend on the extent of competition in the market, the existence of idle capacity (which reduces production costs), volume effects on production, alternative facility uses, and interdependence among divisions. Approximations and negotiations will, then, usually be required. Division managers must be careful not to create more problems for the organization than are solved in attempting to formulate transfer prices.

If there is no intermediate market, the opportunity cost is zero and a transfer price equal to marginal (variable) cost results from the general rule. But managers are typically reluctant to transfer goods and services at marginal cost, since it tends to reduce the division's performance measure. Such transfer prices may cause behavioral responses that destroy many of the advantages otherwise attained by decentralization. We shall also find in Section 19.5 that under certain conditions the marginal price rule is insufficient to obtain an optimal solution when no intermediate market exists.

We close this section with an example of the problems that can arise to compound the determination of a useful transfer price. Suppose that division A is considering purchasing intermediate goods from division B at a market price of $500 per unit. Division B's marginal cost is $490. An outside supplier wishing to obtain the business offers to supply the goods at a price of $480 to A. Division C now supplies B at a price of $100 per unit. Division C's marginal costs are $40 per unit. The $100 is included in B's marginal cost of $490.

Division A would prefer to buy from the outside at a cost of $480 (which is less than B's marginal costs and less than the price B is charging). The net cost to the firm of buying would be $480 on each unit. But if A buys from B, the marginal cost to the firm is only $40 + (490 − 100) = $430. The firm is better off if A buys from B even though B's "marginal cost" is more than the cost of buying.

19.4 Uses of Divisionalized Data

What are the uses of the accounting data of the decentralized operating units? The intracompany prices are the basis of the revenues of one division and the costs of the other; thus, the pricing method directly affects the basic reports of the operating units. These reports may be used for:

1. Measuring the performance of division management.
2. Decision making, including:
   a. Make-or-buy decisions.
   b. Pricing policy for the end product.
   c. Output decisions of components and end products.
   d. Capital-budgeting decisions and decisions to drop products.
3. General financial information, including:
   a. Determination of income of the corporation.
   b. Determination of financial position of the corporation.

The use of the report dictates which one or more of the intracompany pricing methods best fills the needs of management.

19.4.1 Measuring Performance

The best method of intracompany pricing for purposes of evaluating the divisional management of the selling division is market price. In the absence of an easily determined market price, it may be necessary to use negotiated prices or a combination of market and negotiated prices. The use of market price simulates the market conditions which the divisions would face if the divisions were separate corporate entities rather than subdivisions of one business organization.

While market price may be the most desirable method, it cannot always be easily applied. For one thing, there is the problem of determining the market price. Anyone who has purchased an automobile knows that market price is not always equal to list price. Industrial prices are also confused by special terms of payment, freight absorption, quantity concessions, and so forth.

Even if it can be assumed that the market price can be determined, the question still remains as to whether it is a fair price for internal purposes. For example, the manufacturing division may have a more-or-less captive market, and so have less selling expense than the firms setting the market price. Should the manufacturing division get the entire benefit of these savings?

A troublesome problem also exists when there is no market price. For example, if one division conducts research that is applicable to another division, at what price should the research be sold? Here the sale price must be negotiated or possibly arbitrated. In a research type of operation there is frequently no market price, and costs incurred are not the primary factor in setting the value of the research.

In the absence of market price, any reports or measures resulting from the intracompany price are even more arbitrary than the normal accounting report. Do such reports and measures of efficiency do more harm than good? A management faced with recurring situations where intracompany transfers cannot be priced objectively should reconsider the pros and cons of decentralized accounting reports aimed at measuring income and return on investment. In situations of this nature, the use of other measures of performance than those suggested should be investigated. The use of standard costs is one possibility.

Assuming that the objective is to measure performance, there are several reasons for not basing the transfer price of the manufacturing division on cost. The use of variable costs (or marginal costs) would almost automatically lead to a deficit for the supplying division. The use of full cost, with or without a reasonable profit, would be better than variable costing. The prime difficulty is the determination of the cost of the product. Should actual or standard costs be used? Are inefficiencies to be passed on to the purchasing division? The use of cost as the basis of the transfer price places a large burden on the cost accounting department. A by-product of a transfer-price system based on cost often is a welter of arguments and hassels on what is cost.

While it is suggested that the selling division use a market price to compute its revenues, the marginal costs of the selling division should be used to determine the cost to the buying division. The use of marginal costs to determine the transfer price to the buying division is a necessary but not a sufficient condition for optimal output decisions.

19.4.2 Decision Making

Four general types of decisions are considered. These are:

1. Make-or-buy.
2. Pricing of an end product.
3. Level of output.
4. Capital-budgeting decisions and decisions to drop products.

All these decisions should be made on the basis of either marginal or differential cost techniques from the point of view of the corporation as a whole. Hirshleifer has shown systematically that the pricing and output decisions must be solved with the use of marginal costs of the several divisions, but the individual division's best interests may not be the same as those of the corporation. Neither full costs nor market prices can be used as transfer prices in making these decisions. However, the marginal costs should be compared with the relevant market prices in arriving at a final decision.

The make-or-buy decision requires knowledge of those costs which can be avoided by purchasing the product. This requires a cost breakdown that is not supplied by the market price. The same type of information is required for the decision as to whether or not to drop a product. These are nonmarginal decisions and must be made on the basis of differential-revenue and cost techniques.

The transfer pricing used in capital-budgeting decisions made by a division buying components from another division should be based on the incremental cash inflows and outflows that result from the investment. These flows are tied to variable and semivariable cost, not to the market price of intermediate products purchased from other divisions of the company.

Thus for some decision-making purposes (make-or-buy, capital budgeting, or abandoning a product), the differential costs of the goods transferred from division to division should be known. For decisions such as pricing or output, the marginal costs of the product must be used to determine optimal solutions.

19.4.3 General Financial Accounting

The general financial accounting reports require that inventories be recorded at cost to conform to generally accepted accounting principles. This cost is full cost, including manufacturing overhead but not including any element of unrealized profit (that is, profit not realized by sale to a party outside the corporate organization). This requires that the accounting group in the central office be supplied with unit cost of product by the selling division. The element of divisional profit (or loss) must then be eliminated from the inventory of the purchasing division and the income of the selling division in preparing consolidated financial statements.

19.4.4 Comparing Methods

No single method of transfer pricing can fill the needs of a decentralized corporation. The uses of the information and the methods that best accomplish the objectives of relevant reporting are summarized in Table 19–1.

Table 19–1 Transfer Pricing and Decision Usage

Use	Method of Pricing
Measuring performance	Market price (negotiated price if market price is unavailable) and marginal cost
Decision making	Marginal cost, variable cost (as a substitute for marginal cost), and differential cost
Generally accepted financial accounting	Full cost of product (excluding intracompany profits)

No pretense of absolute correctness has been made for any of the pricing methods. The admitted inaccuracies must be weighed against the unmeasurable gains resulting from having decentralized operations and decision making. The greater the significance of the intradivisional transfers, the more unreliable are the income measures of the divisions.

As we have already suggested, it may be useful to transfer from one division at a price different from that used to transfer to another division. Dual systems can be useful to prevent behavior that is not congruent with the organization's goals. Similarly, one transfer-pricing system might be used for making production and investment decisions while another is used for performance evaluation.

Business considerations beyond those of production and investment may also be relevant to transfer-pricing decisions. Differences in tax rates, tariffs, and conversion rates among countries can have an overriding impact on the transfer price selected. Similar considerations can also influence transfer prices within a country. For example, to maximize tax deductions based on percentage-depletion allowances in the extractive industries, firms may wish to use very high transfer prices among subsidiaries. Again, different transfer prices are suggested for different objectives. Since internal performance measurement can be accomplished separate from the requirements of external financial reporting, multiple transfer-pricing systems may be appropriate within a single firm.

19.5 Economics of Transfer Pricing[7]

The solution to the transfer-pricing problem has sometimes been expressed in naive terms, as if the use of the marginal costs of the selling division

[7] This section is more difficult and will require more time than the previous sections.

(or a competitive price, or a negotiated price) would enable managers to make correct decisions and measure performance. For example, marginal (or variable) cost is often suggested as the proper transfer price when there is no intermediate market. There is no simple solution to the problem of pricing products sold within the company; the solution is complex and requires rigorous analysis. One meaningful analysis presented in the business literature has been made by Hirshleifer, and the analysis which follows is based on his article in *The Journal of Business*.[8] There are, however, several places where Hirshleifer's articles differ in detail and method from the present approach; thus the reader is encouraged to refer to the original Hirshleifer articles. An alternative approach involves the ideas of mathematical programming.

To simplify the initial explanations of the Hirshleifer approach as much as possible, the following assumptions are made:

1. A manufacturing division makes a product which has no intermediate market; that is, it must be sold to the distribution division.
2. The price of the product sold by the distribution division is set by purely competitive forces, and the company cannot influence the price. The average revenue or price line is horizontal, hence the same line also measures the marginal revenues.

These assumptions are not essential to the basic analysis and are relaxed later.

19.5.1 Optimum Output Under Perfect Competition

The first objective is to determine the optimal output for the firm. (Remember that the firm does not have a pricing problem since it faces a price set by purely competitive forces.) Figure 19.1 shows the solution of this problem. A marginal-cost curve is drawn for the marginal costs of the distribution division (curve

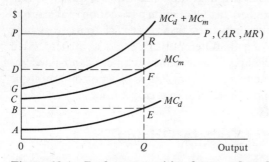

Figure 19.1 Perfect competition for an end product: No intermediate market.

[8] Hirshleifer, *op. cit.* Also see a later article by Hirshleifer, "Economics of the Divisionalized Firm," *The Journal of Business*, April 1957, pp. 96–108.

MC_d) and the marginal costs of the manufacturing division (curve MC_m). A curve may be drawn representing the total marginal costs of the firm ($MC_d + MC_m$). The intersection of this total marginal-cost curve with the price line, PP, determines the optimal output of the product. At that point the marginal costs of the product are equal to the marginal revenue of the product since the marginal revenue is equal to the price. The optimal output is OQ.

The firm maximizes its profits if OQ units are produced, since production of fewer units means that not enough would be produced to make marginal revenues equal to the marginal costs. Production of more than OQ units means that for each additional unit produced, the costs to the firm are greater than the additional revenues.

The next problem is to determine a reasonable transfer price that will result in the division arriving at the optimal output decision. The manufacturing division should transfer to the distribution division at its marginal cost OD. If the manufacturing division transferred at a higher price, the autonomous distribution division would decrease final sales, since the marginal costs of some of the sales would be greater than the division's marginal revenues. A transfer price of OD (the marginal cost of the manufacturing division) will result in an optimal output for the firm. It will be shown, however, that marginal-cost pricing by itself may not be sufficient to ensure that the firm arrives at the optimal output OQ. Other constraints may be necessary.

If the goods are transferred at the marginal cost OD, the profits of the distribution division are equal to the area ABE and the profits of the manufacturing divisions are given by the area CFD, which in sum equals the total profits of the firm, area PGR. The curve of average revenues for the manufacturing division coincides with the marginal-cost curve (since the transfer price is equal to the marginal cost).

19.5.2 Distribution Division As a Monopolistic Buyer

Can the distribution division, by limiting output and acting as a monopolistic buyer, maximize its own profit at the expense of a maximum profit for the firm? Figure 19.2 shows the distribution division acting monopolistically. Assume that a curve AR_d is drawn which shows the net average revenue of the distribution division (the difference between the price, P, of the end product and the price P_m which must be paid to the manufacturing division). The curve MC_m and the curve P_m follow exactly the same path since the marginal cost to the manufacturing division represents the minimum price necessary to draw forth an additional unit of product, and P_m is that price.

The curve AR_d passes through point E at an output of OQ units (the optimal output for the firm), since the firm is operating under perfect competition and its average revenue is equal to its marginal revenue. Thus, AR_d is equal to $P - P_m$, $AR - P_m$, and $MR - P_m$; and, at an output of OQ, it is equal to the marginal cost of the distribution division.

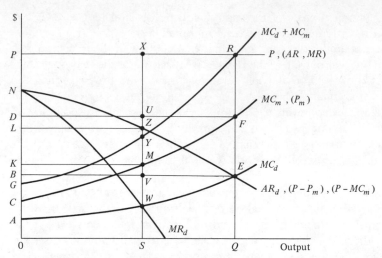

Figure 19.2 Perfect competition for an end product: No intermediate market. Distribution division as a monopolistic buyer.

In addition to the net average-revenue curve, AR_d, the marginal-revenue curve, MR_d, for the distribution division may be drawn. If the distribution division restricts sales to OS and pays the manufacturing division a price equal to the marginal cost OK of the manufacturing division, the distribution division will be maximizing its own profits, since MR_d equals MC_d. The profits of the firm decrease, since the output OS is less than the optimal output OQ. The profits of the distribution division are increased at the expense of the manufacturing division and the overall well-being of the firm. Note that the transfer price OK is the marginal cost of the product, but that in this case the use of marginal cost does not lead to optimal output for the firm.

19.5.3 Manufacturing Division As a Monopolistic Seller

It is shown in Figure 19.2 that the profits of the distribution division may be increased if that division acts as a monopolistic buyer. Similarly, the manufacturing division can increase its profits by acting as a monopolistic seller. This is also adverse to the interests of the firm, since the firm's total profits will be decreased.

Figure 19.3 shows the results of the manufacturing division acting as a monopolist. Suppose that the manufacturing division correctly assumes that the distribution division requires a net revenue equal to its marginal cost if the division is going to increase its sale of the product. Thus, the curve MC_d may be labeled R_d, indicating that this is the minimum net revenue or net price required by the distribution division.

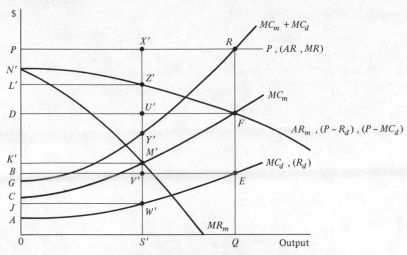

Figure 19.3 The manufacturing division as a monopolistic seller.

A net average-revenue curve $P - R_d$ or AR_m may be drawn for the manufacturing division, showing the net average revenue to that division. (This is the difference between the price curve of the firm, P, and the average-revenue curve for the distribution division.) A curve may then be drawn representing the marginal revenue to the manufacturing division, MR_m. The manufacturing division will produce OS' units since at that quantity of output the marginal cost $S'M'$ of manufacturing equals the marginal revenue.[9] The manufacturing division will, however, charge a transfer price equal to OL', which is greater than OK', the marginal cost of manufacturing. The output OS' that results from this price is less than the optimal output OQ, and the overall profits of the firm are again less because of the actions of the manufacturing division aimed at increasing its own profits.

Thus, the distribution and manufacturing division could enter into a form of competition that might not be desirable in terms of maximizing the profits of the firm as a whole. This analysis argues against allowing the divisions to "battle it out" or negotiate prices. The division with the better poker player may win out to the detriment of the firm as a whole. But even if the manufacturing division charges a price equal to its marginal costs and does not act as a monopolist, this does not ensure an optimal output, since the distribution division may be acting as a monopolistic buyer. Both the selling and buying divisions (the manufacturing and distribution divisions) must be coerced to take the interests of the firm into consideration if the profits of the firm are to be maximized: a way must be found to assure an output of OQ units.

[9] The primes indicate that the point has the same interpretation as in the previous section, but a different value. Thus, OS and OS' are output levels under different monopolistic behavior; $OS \neq OS'$.

19.5.4 Constant Marginal Costs

Assume now a situation where the marginal costs of both the manufacturing and distribution divisions are constant. The firm can expand its facilities without a significant (measurable) change in efficiency. This assumption has the effect of making the MC_m and MC_d lines horizontal (see Figure 19.4).

A necessary condition for the firm to produce is

$$MR \geq MC_m + MC_d \tag{19.1}$$

With perfect competition $MR = P$, and therefore for the firm to produce it is necessary that $P \geq MC_m + MC_d$. If the inequality holds, the firm should produce as much as possible.

The distribution division may again act as a monopolist. If so, its average revenue curve is equal to

$$AR_d = P - MC_m = P - P_m$$

where P_m is the price it must pay to the manufacturing division and P is the price of the final product. The average-revenue curve is horizontal and so therefore is the marginal-revenue curve. The optimal solution for the distribution division is still to produce as much as possible as long as strict inequality in equation (19.1) holds.

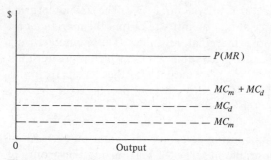

Figure 19.4   Constant marginal costs: Perfect competition.

The manufacturing division receives a price equal to its marginal cost of MC_m and incurs marginal costs of MC_m (with constant marginal cost it will have zero profit). The distribution division shows a profit of $(P - P_m - MC_d)$ per unit which is greater than zero if the strict inequality in equation (19.1) holds. Just as the distribution division can act as a monopolistic buyer, so the manufacturing division can act as a monopolistic seller. The results are symmetrical. The distribution division shows no profit and the manufacturing division shows a profit of $(P - P_d - MC_m)$ per unit.

With constant costs for both the manufacturing and distribution divisions, the profits of the firm will be maximized by maximizing output if the strict inequality in equation (19.1) holds. Given strict inequality in equation (19.1) and the fact that both divisions will produce only if their profits are not negative, the transfer price, P_m, must satisfy the relationship

$$P - MC_d \geq P_m \geq MC_m$$

Optimal output will be reached even if one division acts as a monopolist.

19.5.5 Relaxing the Assumptions of Perfect Competition

Relaxing the assumption of perfect competition, the firm may determine the price at which its product is sold. For example, to increase production and sales, the firm may decrease its sale price. Therefore, instead of a horizontal line, the average-revenue curve of the firm slopes downward to the right, and the firm has a marginal-revenue curve that is below the average-revenue curve. The optimal output for the firm may be obtained from a graph similar to the one in Figure 19.1, except that the price line (average-revenue curve) is not horizontal, and a marginal curve can be drawn for the end product. The intersection of the total marginal-cost curve and the marginal-revenue curve determines the optimal output.

Constant Marginal Costs: Imperfect Competition
Consider first the case of constant marginal costs. In this situation the previous conclusions are altered only slightly (see Figure 19.5). The optimal solution for the firm is an output of OQ units (where the firm's marginal cost equals its marginal revenue) and a price of OR. This output will be attained even though one of the divisions acts as a monopolist. If the distribution division acts as a monopolist, $P_m = MC_m$ and the cost per unit to the distribution division is

$$P_m + MC_d = MC_m + MC_d$$

Hence, its output remains unchanged at OQ. Alternatively, the average and marginal revenue curves for the distribution division can be constructed as before. The result is the same: an output of OQ units.

The profits of the distribution division equal the profits of the firm and are represented by area $RSUT$ in Figure 19.5. The manufacturing division shows

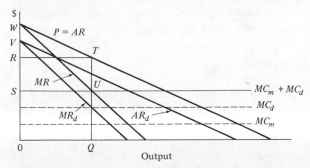

Figure 19.5 Constant marginal costs: Imperfect competition.

zero profits. If the manufacturing division acts as a monopolist, its profits will be $RSUT$ and the distribution division will show no profit. The zero profits occur because of the constant marginal cost curves.

As was true for the case of perfect competition, the optimal activity is achieved with constant costs, despite the efforts of one division to act as a monopolist. If the transfer price to the manufacturing division satisfies the inequality $P - MC_d > P_m > MC_m$, say to assure the manufacturing division a profit, the optimal output will not be reached. With perfect competition and constant marginal costs, optimal output could still be reached.

In order for the firm's profits to be maximized, the firm must assure that the distribution division sells OQ. Using a transfer price of $P_m = MC_m$ is sufficient to accomplish this objective in this case.

Increasing Marginal Costs: Imperfect Competition

Consider now the case where marginal costs are increasing for both divisions. If it is desired to find the optimal output for each division with the aim of maximizing its income instead of the income of the firm, a diagram similar to Figure 19.2 may be used. The average revenue of the distribution division would again be obtained by subtracting the price curve of the manufacturing division (P_m) from the average-revenue curve of the end product. A marginal-revenue curve similar to the MR_d curve is obtained. The distribution division acting as a monopolistic buyer could restrict output to the intersection of this marginal-revenue curve and its marginal-cost curve.

The best transfer price for decision making is the marginal cost to the manufacturing division; but the use of marginal cost does not ensure that the purchasing division will not act as a monopolistic buyer. Centralized action is required to ensure that the optimal output is attained. One means of obtaining the desired output level is for central management to establish the output levels of the divisions. Another means would be for it to establish a price for all purchases by the distribution division from the manufacturing division equivalent to OD in the example graphed in Figure 19.2. Still another means of achieving the maximum output is for the central office to provide a subsidy payment to the division acting as a monopolist. The subsidy payment schedule would shift the marginal-revenue curve of the monopolistic division to coincide with its average-revenue curve as determined without the subsidy.

19.5.6 Competitive Intermediate Markets

Up to this point it was assumed that the product could be sold only to the distribution division. Suppose that the intermediate product can also be bought or sold by the manufacturing division in a purely competitive market at a price p, and that the end product is sold in a purely competitive market at a price P. Figure 19.6 shows that the manufacturing division should produce OQ_m units of product (use the second quadrant of Figure 19.6) and that the distribution

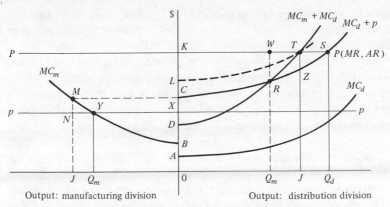

Figure 19.6   Competitive intermediate and final markets.

division should sell OQ_d units. The unit output of the manufacturing division does not have to equal the units sold by the distribution division.

The curves are explained as follows:

$$P, AR, MR = \text{price curve of the end product}$$

$$p = \text{market price of the intermediate product}$$

$$MC_m = \text{marginal-cost curve of the manufacturing division}$$

$$MC_d = \text{marginal-cost curve of the distribution division}$$

$$DRT \text{ or } MC_m + MC_d = \text{sum of the marginal-cost curves of the manu-facturing and distribution divisions; the marginal-cost curve } DRT \text{ is based on the assumption that the product of the manufacturing division must be sold to the distribution division and the distribution division must buy from the manufacturing division}$$

$$CRS = \text{sum of } MC_d \text{ plus } p, \text{ the marginal cost of the distribution division and the intermediate price of the product; the curve is based on the assumption that all products produced at a marginal cost of less than the competitive price } p \text{ have a marginal cost to the distribution division equal to the opportunity cost } p$$

$$DRS = \text{sum of } MC_d + MC_m \text{ up to } Q_m \text{ and } MC_d + p \text{ thereafter; it is the marginal-cost curve for the firm}$$

The manufacturing division would produce OQ_m units since if it produced more, its marginal cost would then exceed the market price p. The distribution division would not pay in excess of the market price p to the manufacturing division, since it could purchase the product in the market for that price. Thus, the marginal-cost curve of the distribution division would be the sum of the marginal costs of the distribution division, MC_d, plus p, the effective cost of the intermediate product. The transfer price should be p, the competitive price, which is also the marginal cost of the manufacturing division at an output of OQ_m. The distribution division would buy OQ_m from the manufacturing division, $OQ_d - OQ_m$ from outside, and obtain a profit of $CRSK$. The profits to the manufacturing division are BYX.

The marginal-cost curve of the firm is given by DRS, the sum of the marginal costs of the two divisions up to an output of OQ_m and $p + MC_d$ thereafter. The profits to the firm are therefore $DRSK$. (Note that since $DRSK = CRSK + DRC$, $BYX = DRC$.)

If the additional requirement were made that the distribution division could sell only the product of the manufacturing division, the competitive price p of the intermediate product would not be relevant to the decision.[10] The relevant costs would be the marginal costs of the manufacturing division and the marginal costs of the distribution division. The solution would be similar to the solution illustrated in Figure 19.1. Referring to Figure 19.6, the output would be OJ and, using the same marginal cost of OX as the transfer price, the manufacturing division would show a profit of $BYX - YNM$.

Restricting the distribution division to selling only the product of the manufacturing division reduces the number of units sold by the distribution division from OQ_d to OJ. The number of units sold by the manufacturing division increases from OQ_m to OJ. There is a loss in profit to the manufacturing division and also a loss in profit is suffered by the distribution division. The total loss of profit to the firm is the area RST. The profits of the firm decline from $DRSK$ to $DRTK$. The transfer price may be the marginal cost to the manufacturing division, but the distribution division is being penalized (as is the firm) by management's restricting the distribution division to selling only products made by the manufacturing division. The loss is partly due to the greater cost of the $OJ - OQ_m$ units and partly to a smaller output. If the transfer price used were to be the new marginal cost for OJ units, OC, the new marginal-cost curve for the distribution division would be LT, output would still be OJ, and company profits $DRKT$. The only result would be a shift of profits to the manufacturing division of $YXCM = CRTL$. Since the manufacturing division has no control over its sales level if it is forced to sell OJ units, it would be appropriate to evaluate the manager as though he were managing a cost center rather than a profit center.

[10] This would restrict total output to OJ and the profits of the firm to $DRTK$.

19.5.7 Transfer Pricing and Decision Making

The limitations of transfer pricing for decision making should be carefully noted. The fact that using marginal costs as the basis for the transfer prices may not lead to the optimal output decision at the division level has been discussed. Indeed, there is no one method of transfer pricing that can be used for all varieties of decision making and performance evaluation.

Consider the problem of whether or not to drop Division B which sells parts to Division A. Assume that the transfer-pricing system uses marginal costs, that a computation of the income of Division B manufacturing component parts indicates that the income computed in accordance with accounting procedures is negative, and that a computation of the contribution of Division A to the recovery of fixed costs directly identified with Division B indicates that the division is not making any contribution. Should Division B be abandoned? Not necessarily. The production of parts may have the effect of increasing the profits of Division A that utilizes the component part and would otherwise have to purchase it on the open market at a higher price. Thus, to determine whether Division B should be dropped, it is necessary to look beyond the information obtained from using transfer pricing to the effect of the abandonment on the income of the entire firm. The case illustrated in Figure 19.6 would be an example if the area YNM exceeded the area BYX, and the firm sells only products made by the manufacturing division using a transfer price of OX.

19.5.8 Transfer Pricing and Performance Measurement

Difficulties of applying the transfer prices to decision making have been noted. There is also an interesting paradox that may result from the use of marginal cost for transfer pricing. If the marginal costs of one division are constant (its marginal-cost curve is a horizontal line with no increase as production increases), this division shows no profit if the marginal cost is used as the transfer price. (See Figure 19.7 as well as 19.4 and 19.5 and assume that there is no intermediate market for the product.) The profit of the distribution division is ABC, which is equal to the area DEP, the profit of the firm. The manufacturing division makes no profit if it charges a price that is equal to its marginal cost and its marginal-cost curve is horizontal.[11] This emphasizes the importance of using a market price to evaluate the manufacturing division as discussed in Section 19.4.1.

A division can determine which type of marginal-cost curve maximizes profits under a given transfer system based on marginal costs. Although this may not be consistent with the firm's objective of maximizing company profits, in certain cases inefficiencies that increase marginal costs may actually be desirable from the point of view of, say, the selling division. The use of marginal cost as a transfer price for the product of the manufacturing division provides no incentive for this division to reduce its costs.

---

[11] The same result occurs in the situation where both divisions have constant costs and one acts as a monopolist.

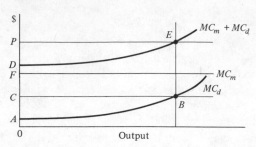

Figure 19.7   Transfer pricing and constant efficiency.

19.6 Summary

Attempting to administer the separate components of one industrial firm as if they were separate competing entities frequently results in the necessity for the use of transfer prices for accounting purposes and for decision making. The economic analysis of transfer pricing indicates that the solutions can become extremely complex if the demand and the production of the products are dependent on each other (technological dependence may also be introduced). However, several observations may be made:

1. Marginal cost and the competitive prices of the product being transferred are not necessarily equal. There is an entire schedule of marginal costs, so that this equality, or the appropriateness of the marginal cost, should not be assumed.
2. The use of marginal costs for transfer pricing does not ensure that the company is operating at its optimal output since divisions may act to maximize their own profits to the detriment of the profits of the company (this is also possible if competitive prices are used).
3. The use of marginal-cost transfer pricing may result in weird actions, such as attempting to decrease efficiency or to have an increasing marginal-cost curve to increase divisional profits (by increasing marginal costs and thus increasing the transfer price of the product).
4. The transfer-pricing procedures does not generally give good results for nonmarginal decisions such as abandoning a plant and make-or-buy decisions (these decisions require a differential-cost and revenue analysis).

The choice of the transfer-pricing method depends on the information available; for certain decisions transfer prices are not useful at all. The extent to which transfer prices are an artificial compromise should be recognized by the user, so that he may be alert to those cases where they cannot be used for decision-making purposes.[12]

[12] Several complications have been omitted from the discussion. Among these are situations of demand dependence for the intermediate and end products, and cost or technological dependence. See Hirshleifer (1957) for discussions of these items.

It is likely that in many cases firms have created profit centers which require the use of transfer prices when cost centers would have been a more effective means of controlling costs and measuring performance. The use of a profit center requires that revenues be computed, and this in turn requires the use of prices where there may not have been an arm's length transaction; in fact, the profit center may not be able to control the number of units sold. Consider a parts division of an automobile company making components of a new model when there is no replacement market. The parts division cannot control the number of units sold, and the transfer price cannot help but be somewhat arbitrary. In a situation of this type, it might be more desirable to measure the performance of the parts division by the cost of the product rather than by a fictitious profit figure at least two steps removed from the correctly measured variables (that is, those which are controllable by the parts division).

The first question raised by management must be whether the use of transfer prices is appropriate at all. Only if the answer to this question is yes should the questions of the method of computing and controlling the transfer price be raised.

If an intermediate market exists and there are no important demand or cost dependences, market price will lead to the maximization of both divisional and company profits. On the other hand, if such intermediate markets do not exist, analysis is required to determine the best transfer price. Such prices require some nonmarket imposition that inevitably reduces the division manager's independence. The decision of what transfer-price system to use requires a consideration of the expected savings gained in more appropriate operational decisions versus the expected losses from reduced decentralized operations. Such losses reflect, for example, behavior changes when a manager no longer perceives independence of operation. This factor, coupled with a justified skepticism of the correctness of large-scale centralized models, has led most firms to employ market prices as transfer prices.

QUESTIONS AND PROBLEMS

19–1 Under a marginal-cost transfer-pricing arrangement, will a division manager acting to maximize the profits of his division also be maximizing the profits of the corporation?

19–2 What are the advantages and disadvantages of centralization and decentralization of authority?

19–3 What are some of the possible methods of establishing transfer prices? Describe where each might be used to advantage.

19–4 Explain why a distribution (buying) division may act as a monopolistic buyer. Explain the effect on the firm.

19–5 Explain why a manufacturing division (selling division) may act as a monopolistic seller. Discuss the effect on the firm.

19–6 If the transfer price is set equal to the marginal cost of the manufacturing division, will this lead to decisions which will maximize the profits of the firm?

19–7 Assuming the use of marginal cost as the basis of final prices, are transfer prices useful for such decisions as abandoning a division?

19–8 Assuming that a division is performing research for other divisions, at what price should it transfer its completed research? (Assume that the research is one of several products made by the division.)

19–9 If both the distribution and manufacturing divisions act monopolistically, what is the effect on the firm?

19–10 The Regulite Company has two divisions (manufacturing and distribution) acting as profit centers. Since it is a small company, it feels that its price is set by its competitors but that it can sell all it can produce at a price of $100 per unit. The average variable costs for the two divisions are

$$AVC_m = 40 \qquad AVC_d = 10 + 0.005Q$$

The manufacturing division has $5,000 and the distribution division $1,000 of fixed costs. In addition, the corporate headquarters allocates $3,000 of its costs to manufacturing and $2,000 to distribution.

Required:
  a. What is the optimum level of production for the firm? What would be the profit of the firm? What is the marginal cost of manufacturing at the optimal output?
  b. If you were in charge of the distribution division, what price would you offer the manufacturing division? What output would result? What would be the profits of the distribution division?
  c. Do the profit figures provide useful performance measures? Explain.

19–11 Suppose that the average variable costs for the two divisions of the Regulite Company in problem 19–10 are

$$AVC_m = 8 + 0.01Q \qquad AVC_d = 62$$

There are no fixed costs.

Required:
  a. What is the optimum level of production for the firm? What would be the profit of the firm? What is the marginal cost of manufacturing at the optimal output?
  b. If you were in charge of the distribution division, what price would you offer the manufacturing division? What output would result?
  c. What is the effect in part b on the firm's profits?
  d. What profits are shown by the distribution division? Under these assumptions, would the profit figures provide good performance measures?

19–12 Suppose that the average variable costs for the two divisions of the Regulite Company in problem 19–10 are

$$AVC_m = 8 + 0.01Q \qquad AVC_d = 2 + 0.005Q$$

There are no fixed costs.

Required:

a. What is the optimum level of production for the firm? What would be the profit of the firm? What is the marginal cost of manufacturing at the optimal output?

b. If you were in charge of the distribution division, what price would you offer the manufacturing division? What output would result?

c. What effect is there on company profits? Are the profit figures of the divisions good indicators of performance?

19–13 Suppose that the average variable costs for the two divisions of the Regulite Company in problem 19–10 are

$$AVC_m = 8 + 0.01Q \qquad AVC_d = 2 + 0.005Q$$

The price is $100 - 0.01Q$, and there are no fixed costs.

Required:

a. What is the optimum level of production for the firm? What is the marginal cost of manufacturing? What is the profit of the firm?

b. If you were in charge of the distribution division, what price would you offer the manufacturing division? What output would result?

c. What is the effect on company profits in part b? Are the profit figures good indicators of performance?

19–14 (Refer to problem 19–13.) If the manufacturing division were to act as a monopolist, at what price would it sell its product to the distribution division? What output would result? Which division acting monopolistically had the greater impact? Why?

19–15 The Elston Company used the market price of a competitive producer for an identical product as the internal transfer price. The manufacturing division claimed that it should be permitted to charge a higher price. The market price was based on a vendor with a more modern and more efficient plant. The manager of the manufacturing plant was forced to operate with an outdated and inefficient plant. Further, he had no authority to make capital investments or otherwise modernize his plant. He believed that he was being penalized for something beyond his control and claimed the practice created bad "managerial psychology." The vice-president for finance ruled that "since the primary objective of the intracompany pricing system was to provide a means of measuring performance against known competitive levels, competitive practice with regard to cost and price must be followed."

Comment on this situation in terms of the use to which the performance measures are being put and the appropriateness of the procedure. Can you think of other reasons besides the efficiency of the plant that might cause other divisions under similar plans to object?

19–16 Using Figures 19.2 and 19.3, determine the profits and the change in profits for the firm and for each division.

19–17 If the firm in Figure 19.6 restricts the distribution division to selling only products made by the manufacturing division, what output will result and what areas represent the profits to each division and to the firm? (Assume that marginal cost is used as the transfer price.)

19–18 In the example discussed in the chapter and illustrated in Figure 19.2 and 11.3, under which situation is output most restricted? How can you tell in general which division acting as a monopolist will have the greater effect?

19–19 Assume that the top management of the Argon Company requires all divisions to have their activities audited periodically by the Internal Auditing Division. At what price should the audit services be charged to the divisions?

19–20 Figure 1 is a reproduction of Figure 19.6 of the text.

The figure describes the case of competitive intermediate markets. Give the appropriate areas or points to each question.

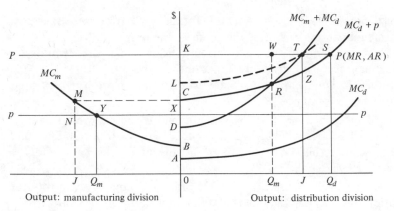

Figure 1

a. Optimal output level for the firm in units.
b. Optimal output for the manufacturing division in units.
c. Total profit to the manufacturing division at an output and sales level of Q_m units if it acts optimally at this level.
d. Optimal output if the firm is restricted to selling only the output of the manufacturing division.
e. Profit to the distribution division under d above. (Give the area on each side of the line KO corresponding to this profit.)

19–21 Suppose a firm's demand function is given by $P = 100 - X$ where P is price and X is output. The marginal cost functions are:
 Manufacturing division: 20
 Distribution division: $20 + X$.

a. What is the optimal firm output and the price per unit at this output?
b. What is appropriate transfer price?
c. What are the profits to the firm and to each division under a?

d. If the distribution division acts as a monopolist, answer questions a and c and give the resulting transfer price.

e. If the manufacturing division acts as a monopolist answer question a and give the resulting transfer price.

19–22 Consider a decentralized firm with constant marginal costs that is operating under imperfect competition.

a. What condition(s) are necessary for the firm to produce?

b. If one of the divisions acts as a monopolist will the firm's optimal output level be reached?

c. If a transfer price equal to the manufacturing division's marginal cost is used will optimal output be reached? Explain.

d. Can a profit measure of some kind be used in performance evaluation for the manufacturing firm if marginal cost is used as a transfer price?

e. What happens if the price to the manufacturing division exceeds its marginal cost but is less than the market price of the finished unit less the distribution division's marginal cost?

SUPPLEMENTARY READING

BAUMOL, W. J., and T. FABIAN, "Decomposition, Pricing for Decentralization and External Economies," *Management Science*, September 1964, pp. 1–32.

COOK, P. W., "New Technique for Intracompany Pricing," *The Harvard Business Review*, July–August 1957, pp. 74–80.

GODFREY, J. T., "Short-Run Planning in a Decentralized Firm," *The Accounting Review*, April 1971, pp. 286–297.

GOULD, J. R., "Internal Pricing in Firms Where There are Costs of Using an Outside Market," *The Journal of Business*, January 1964, pp. 61–67.

HASS, J. E., "Transfer Pricing in a Decentralized Firm," *Management Science*, February 1968, pp. 310–331.

HIRSHLEIFER, J., "Economics of the Divisionalized Firm," *The Journal of Business*, April 1957, pp. 96–108.

———, "On the Economics of Transfer Pricing," *The Journal of Business*, July 1956, pp. 172–184.

NATIONAL INDUSTRIAL CONFERENCE BOARD, *Interdivisional Transfer Pricing*, Studies in Business Policy No. 122, 1967.

ONSI, M., "A Transfer Pricing System Based on Opportunity Cost," *The Accounting Review*, July 1970, pp. 535–543.

RONEN, J., and R. COPELAND, "Transfer Pricing for Divisional Autonomy," *Journal of Accounting Research*, Spring 1970, pp. 99–112.

SOLOMONS, D., *Divisional Performance: Measurement and Control*, New York: Financial Executives Research Foundation, 1965.

WHINSTON, A., "Price Guides in Decentralized Organizations," in *New Prospectives in Organization Research*, edited by W. Cooper, H. Leavitt, and M. Shelly, New York: John Wiley & Sons, Inc., 1962, pp. 405–448.

Part V

Advanced Models and Techniques Useful in Managerial Cost Accounting

Chapter 20

Cost Determination: The Use of Linear Programming

This chapter has two objectives. One is to describe the use of linear programming techniques to solve a wide range of managerial problems. Second, we want to use the linear programming solution as the basis of defining a useful concept of cost that we can apply to fixed factors of production.

It has long been agreed that sunk costs, or costs that are not avoidable (they will be incurred independently of managerial actions with respect to the decision being considered), are not relevant to the decision. Thus, the managerial economist has discussed the non-relevance of such costs as building depreciation (while recognizing the relevance of opportunity costs) at the same time that the accountant has allocated depreciation costs to different processes and products. With the development of linear programming, there has evolved a new technique for quantifying the opportunity costs associated with the use of fixed factors of production. This technique gives rise to measures which, interestingly, were originally called *accounting prices* but now are more commonly called *shadow prices*. These prices are by-products of the solution to the *dual* formulation of the basic linear programming decision problem that is called the *primal*.

In this chapter we discuss the formulation of linear programming problems and illustrate the solution process with graphs. More realistic and complex problems than those illustrated in this chapter would be solved using the simplex method of solution.[1] Linear programming problems are well suited to being solved on electronic computers and canned programs are generally available.

20.1 The Primal

Linear programming is a technique designed to optimize the allocation of scarce resources. The objective is to maximize some function (for example, profits) or minimize some function (for example, costs). The maximization (or minimization) is accomplished subject to a set of constraints. It is assumed here that the relationships are all linear. In many situations this is close enough to the real-world facts to make the results useful.

The function being maximized (or minimized) is called the objective function. If we let f be the amount of profits and A_i be the net contribution of the ith product and X_i be the number of units of the ith product, we can write

$$f = A_1 X_1 + A_2 X_2 + \cdots + A_N X_N$$

or

$$f = \sum_{i=1}^{N} A_i X_i$$

The A_i are all constants (sales price less direct variable costs traceable to the product) and the number of units, X_i, are decision variables. Suppose that $N = 2$ and that the contributions of each product are

$$A_1 = \$4 \text{ per unit} \qquad \text{and} \qquad A_2 = \$2 \text{ per unit}$$

If it is decided to produce $X_1 = 5$ units and $X_2 = 10$ units, we obtain

$$f = A_1 X_1 + A_2 X_2$$
$$= 4(5) + 2(10) = \$40$$

If we add constraints, the above solution may change. For example, assume that product X_1 requires 6 hours of time on machine 1 and product X_2 requires 2 hours, but there are only 8 hours of machine time available. Mathematically we have the following constraint (written in the form of an inequality):

$$6X_1 + 2X_2 \leq 8$$

If only product X_1 is produced, at most $\frac{8}{6}$, or $1\frac{1}{3}$, units can be made per period. If only product X_2 is produced, then at most $\frac{8}{2}$, or 4, units can be made. Combinations (for example, one unit of each) are also possible.

Table 20.1 shows several possible production alternatives and the resulting profits. The greatest profit shown in the table results when 4 units of X_2 are

[1] For more complete explanations of the material in this chapter, see H. Bierman, Jr., C. P. Bonini, and W. H. Hausman, *Quantitative Analysis for Business Decisions*, Homewood, Ill.: Richard D. Irwin, Inc., 1973, pp. 199–289.

Table 20-1   Production Alternatives and Profits

X_1	X_2	Total Hours	$f = 4X_1 + 2X_2$
0	4	8	$f = 2(4) = 8$
1	1	8	$f = 4(1) + 2(1) = 6$
1.33	0	8	$f = 4(1.33) = 5.32$

produced. This gives a total profit of $8. It turns out that this is also the maximum profit. No other feasible solution produces as much profit, as we will show. Figure 20.1 graphs the possible production levels. All possible solutions lie in the feasible (hatched) region. This area is called a *convex polygon* (the feasible points will always lie within a convex polygon). It is proved in linear programming texts that the optimum solution will always be at one of the corners of this polygon. If more than one corner is equally good, points on the line connecting the equally good points will also be optimal solutions.

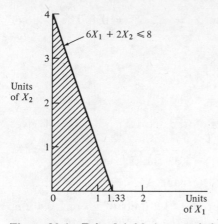

Figure 20.1   Primal (with 1 constraint).

While the origin ($X_1 = 0$, $X_2 = 0$) is a corner point (it is necessary that both X_1 and X_2 be nonnegative) and is therefore a feasible solution, it yields no profit. It is dominated by the point $X_1 = 1.33$, $X_2 = 0$, and by the point $X_1 = 0$, $X_2 = 4$. In Table 20.1 we evaluated two corner points as well as point $X_1 = 1$, $X_2 = 1$, and found that $X_1 = 0$, $X_2 = 4$, had the largest profit. The third corner point (0, 0) leads to a zero profit, and the point $X_1 = 0$, $X_2 = 4$ is the optimum solution.

Assume a second machine has the following constraint:

$$1X_1 + 2X_2 \le 2$$

This constraint further restricts the feasible solution region since machine 2 has only 2 hours of available time. Thus, we can make no more than 1 unit of

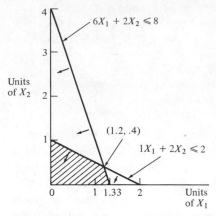

Figure 20.2   The primal (with 2 constraints).

product X_2 rather than the 4 we could make with only the single constraint. The new situation is graphed in Figure 20.2.

The two constraints intersect at the point $X_1 = 1.2$, $X_2 = 0.4$. The value of f at that point is

$$f = 4X_1 + 2X_2$$
$$= 4(1.2) + 2(0.4)$$
$$= 4.8 + 0.8 = \$5.60$$

The other two corner points result in profits of (the point $X_1 = 0$, $X_2 = 0$ gives zero profits):

$$f = 4(1.33) = 5.32 \qquad \text{at } X_1 = 1.33 \text{ and } X_2 = 0$$
$$= 2(1.0) = 2 \qquad \text{at } X_1 = 0 \text{ and } X_2 = 1$$

Thus, the optimum solution would be to produce 1.2 units of X_1 and 0.4 unit of X_2 per time period. The new constraint alters the optimal solution.

We can describe the situation (the objective function and the constraints) using the formulation below:

$$\text{Maximize:} f = 4X_1 + 2X_2$$
$$\text{Subject to:} 6X_1 + 2X_2 \le 8$$
$$1X_1 + 2X_2 \le 2 \tag{20.1}$$
$$X_1, X_2 \ge 0$$

X_1 and X_2 must be equal to or greater than zero, since they are physical quantities. Noninteger solutions are allowed, since fractions of product may be produced.

Figure 20.3 is identical to Figure 20.2 except that a series of (dashed) constant-profit lines have been drawn. The X_1 and X_2 axes measure units of profit as well

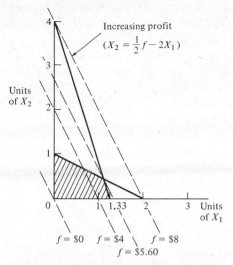

Figure 20.3 The primal with profit functions.

as units of product. Note that the lines are parallel. These constant-profit lines will help us to see why only corner points yield solutions of interest. We obtain a profit line by solving the objective function for X_2 and inserting specific values for f:

$$X_2 = \tfrac{1}{2}f - 2X_1 \qquad (20.2)$$

The profit line $f = \$5.60$ goes through the corner point $X_1 = 1.2$, $X_2 = 0.4$. While $f = \$8$ is a more desirable level of profit, it does not include any feasible-solution points. No level of production can be obtained that will result in $8 of profit. To reach that level of profit, one of the constraints would have to be relaxed.

The reader can see that profit is increased if we start with a profit line that goes through a feasible solution and move upward and to the right always touching at least one point in the feasible-solution area. (Move from $f = \$0$ to $f = \$4$, for example.) This process will always terminate at a feasible solution represented by a corner point (or perhaps by the line segment connecting two corner points). That is why the corner points of the feasible-solution area are of interest.

The simplex method of solution, to which we referred earlier, is a method of systematically moving from one corner-point solution to an adjacent one and testing to determine if a better solution has been found. When no better solution can be obtained by moving to an adjacent corner point, the method terminates: the optimal solution has been obtained.

If a third product (say X_3) is added, it would be more difficult to graph the solution process, but conceptually the same method of solution would be used. More constraints, however, can easily be incorporated. For example, if it is necessary that at least 1 unit of X_2 must be produced, the only feasible solution is to produce 1 unit of X_2 and zero units of X_1 (with a profit of \$2). This constraint is added to Figure 20.3 by drawing a horizontal line at $X_2 = 1$ and noting that all feasible solutions must be on or above this line.

It is important to note that the addition of a constraint can only have the effect of either leaving the solution unaffected or reducing the attainable profit. Adding a constraint then usually has a cost. This cost is the reduction in the attainable profit (the reduction in optimality) due to the added constraint.

Some of the above solutions involved noninteger values. If it is necessary that the solution be an integer (for example, the number of trips an airplane will make between London and New York) then a technique called integer programming (which is not discussed here) can be used.[2] The appropriate integer solutions are often not the same as would be obtained by simply rounding off a linear programming solution.

20.2 The Dual

The problem solved in Section 20.1 is called the *primal*. Every linear programming problem that is described as primal has a *dual*. If the primal is a maximization (minimization) problem, the dual is the opposite, a minimization (maximization) problem.

Continuing the above example, let

U_1 = cost per hour of using machine 1

U_2 = cost per hour of using machine 2

C = total cost per hour of using the machines

We know that machine 1 has 8 hours and machine 2 has 2 hours of available time; thus, we can express the total cost of using the machines in equation form as

$$C = 8U_1 + 2U_2$$

We want each unit of product to be produced up to the point where the total cost of production is at least equal to the net profit contribution (\$4 for X_1 and \$2 for X_2). Thus, we have[3]

$$6U_1 + 1U_2 \geq 4$$
$$2U_1 + 2U_2 \geq 2$$

The costs U_1 and U_2 are also nonnegative.

---

[2] If it is desired to shift from the assumptions of linearity, one must use nonlinear programming. Chance-constrained programming can be used to incorporate uncertain considerations. Where there is a sequence of decisions over time, the use of dynamic programming may be appropriate.

[3] There are routine methods for transforming primals into duals, but for our purposes it is important to understand the economic interpretation of the dual rather than simply have a method for obtaining it.

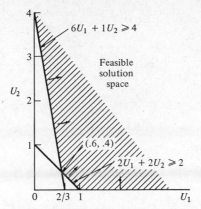

Figure 20.4   The dual.

The first equation reflects the fact that product X_1 takes 6 hours of time on machine 1 and 1 hour of time on machine 2. Thus the opportunity cost ($6U_1 + 1U_2$) is either going to be equal to $4 (in which case the product will be produced) or greater than $4 (in which case the product will not be produced). The same type of analysis applies to the second equation for product X_2 (which requires 2 hours of time on each machine). We wish to minimize total cost subject to the imposed constraints. This is in contrast to the primal, which was a maximization problem.

We can express this linear programming problem (the dual) as:

$$\text{Minimize: } C = 8U_1 + 2U_2$$
$$\text{Subject to: } 6U_1 + 1U_2 \geq 4$$
$$2U_1 + 2U_2 \geq 2$$
$$U_1, U_2 \geq 0$$

Figure 20.4 graphs the dual (minimization) problem. The feasible solutions are to the right and above the constraints. Again, only the corner points need to be examined.

Table 20.2 shows the costs associated with the three corner points. The table shows that values of $U_1 = 0.6$, $U_2 = 0.4$ minimize the total cost at a value of

Table 20–2   Machine Use Costs and Total Cost

U_1	U_2	$C = 8U_1 + 2U_2$
1	0	$8
0.6	0.4	$5.60
0	4	$8

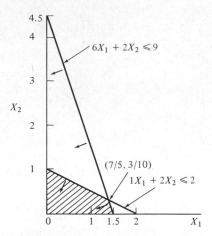

Figure 20.5   The primal: Adding one unit of machine time.

$5.60. Referring back to the solution of the primal, we find that the primal solution results in a profit of $5.60. The objective function of the primal and the objective function for the dual will be equal for the optimal solutions for each.

The solution of the dual indicates that the value of an hour of time on machine 1 is $0.60, and the value of an hour of time on machine 2 is $0.40. These results from the dual are called *shadow* or *accounting* prices and are the economic costs of using these factors of production.

Let us change the problem so that machine 1 has one more hour of time. We now have for the primal:

$$\text{Maximize: } f = 4X_1 + 2X_2$$
$$\text{Subject to: } 6X_1 + 2X_2 \leq 9$$
$$1X_1 + 2X_2 \leq 2$$
$$X_1, X_2 \geq 0$$

Figure 20.5 shows the new situation. In Table 20.3 we evaluate the three corner points and the profits for each.

Previously the maximum profit was $5.60; it is now $6.20, an increase of $0.60. This increase is equal to the value of U_1 that we computed as the value

**Table 20–3   Primal (with Two Constraints):
Extra Unit of Machine Time**

X_1	X_2	$f = 4X_1 + 2X_2$
1.5	0	$6
$\frac{7}{5}$	$\frac{3}{10}$	6.2
0	1	2

of an hour of machine 1 time. That is, we determined by means of the dual that the value of one more unit of time on machine 1 was worth $0.60, and when we added one unit of time on machine 1, the maximum profit increases by $0.60.[4]

Although we determined the dual from the basic facts of the situation, it can also be determined mechanically from the primal. For example:

1. The objective function changes. If the primal is to "maximize," the dual is to "minimize."
2. The sense of the constraints is reversed. If the primal is "$\leq$," the dual is "$\geq$."

In addition, there is a (matrix) transposing operation and an exchange of objective function and constraint constants. New variables must also be defined. Although a complete explanation of the process is beyond this text, placing the primal and dual side by side helps reveal what is taking place. Again, it is better to understand how the two problems are related economically than to simply memorize the mechanical transformation process.

Primal	*Dual*
Maximize: $f = 4X_1 + 2X_2$	Minimize: $C = 8U_1 + 2U_2$
Subject to: $6X_1 + 2X_2 \leq 8$	Subject to: $6U_1 + 1U_2 \geq 4$
$1X_1 + 2X_2 \leq 2$	$2U_1 + 2U_2 \geq 2$
$X_1, X_2 \geq 0$	$U_1, U_2 \geq 0$

20.3 Implications for Accounting

Let us consider the above primal problem a little further. The $4 represents the contribution of a unit of product of X_1 to profit (excess of revenues over incremental costs). In like manner the $2 in the objective function represents the contribution of a unit of X_2 to profit. This agrees with the basic marginal analysis of Chapter 2. The constraint equations bring in the fixed factors of production. Prior to linear programming, it was often suggested that fixed factors of production had no cost, the costs were sunk, but the accountant proceeded to allocate the original cost of the asset to the cost of the product being manufactured. The linear programming approach ignores the historical cost. It considers only the amount of the resources available and the incremental benefits that can be gained from them. The primal is solved without reference to the

---

[4] This statement assumes that a second constraint is not binding, which prevents the increase in production. For this reason, the value will only apply to a finite number of units since eventually another constraint will become binding. The range for which the dual variables hold can be determined by sensitivity analysis.

historical cost of the machines (or of other fixed factors) being used. Nowhere in the formulation of the primal is there reference to the actual cost of the machines used. But the real cost, the opportunity cost, of these factors is very much present in the analysis. The linear programming solution automatically considers these costs in arriving at the solution.

If it is desired to place a dollar value on the cost of using fixed factors, we can turn to the dual for a solution. The dual gives the shadow prices for each of the constraints that have been recognized. These shadow prices represent the real cost of utilizing the factor of production to produce the products being considered. They also represent the amount the firm could afford to pay to increase the amount of the factors of production so as to expand production (although one has to be careful, since these are marginal measures and they cannot be used without qualification in nonmarginal situations). The analysis focuses on the constraining factor in the problem, and this is as it should be.

The accountant's intuition through the years has been good. When it was said that the fixed-cost factors had zero cost, the accountant resisted since he knew that when the capacity was fully utilized, it meant that additional expenditures would be required to relieve the bottleneck. He allocated the actual costs that were incurred to product on the theory that it was not correct to say that only the variable costs were costs of product. The use of variable costs would lead to excessive expansion and lower selling prices than were justified by a full cost of production. The accountant of prior years had no way to estimate the opportunity costs of the many factors of production that were fixed in quantity and that serviced many different products. Now we have a better understanding of the relevant costs of the fixed factors. The dual to the linear programming problem enables us to calculate the shadow prices. They yield costs that are truly relevant for decision making.

20.4   Estimation of Variables

Linear programming solutions rely on estimates of contribution margins and of the technological coefficients (such as the number of hours required by product 1 on machine 1). These estimates are subject both to errors in estimation and to change. It is desirable to determine how the solution is affected by the use of different values. If the solution is not affected by large changes in these values, it would not be desirable to spend large sums refining the estimates. This could be done by solving the problem, again using different estimates.

Finally, it may be possible to introduce a new method of production. This would require a new linear programming formulation, and a solution to the new problem. The solution using the new data measures will indicate the improvements in the objective function. Against this improvement the manager would have to weigh the costs of changing the method of production.

20.5 Summary

This chapter has introduced the elements of linear programming, and how the solutions to the dual may be used to obtain estimators of costs of factors of production that are relevant for decision making. Although it is necessary to be aware of the limitations of any linear programming solution (for example, the linearity assumption may not hold), the concepts that have been suggested open the door for the accountant to arrive at a set of decision-oriented numbers rather than cost-based information from the past that is, strictly speaking, not relevant.

It is possible to disagree with the assumption of linearity, but if this assumption is accepted, the superiority of the shadow prices or dual variables of the linear programming solution over conventional cost measures must be accepted for purposes of marginal decision making.

Finally, we note that linear (and other) programming techniques have been adapted to several other managerial cost accounting problems with varying degrees of success. These include transfer pricing, cost allocation, joint product decisions, and the analysis of cost variances. Appendix 20A summarizes the results related to transfer pricing. The reader is referred to the Supplementary Readings for further examples.

APPENDIX 20A
TRANSFER PRICES AND MATHEMATICAL PROGRAMMING

Mathematical programming models can be used in transfer pricing problems.[5] As described in Chapter 19, setting the transfer price equal to marginal cost is not adequate to assure that the firm's optimal profit will be attained. First, there exist the cases where one division acts as a monopolist. Second, one division's activities may affect another's either by using up a scarce resource or by causing an upward shift in another division's cost function by bidding up the price of a scarce resource or causing the division to modify its technology. In either case the division causing the change tends to overproduce, since the costs to the other divisions do not enter its analysis. It is also possible for the activities of one division to create external economies, for example, by shifting to the right the demand schedule for the product of another division.

The task of the mathematical model is to induce a division to expand those activities that create external economies and contract those activities that create

[5] See W. J. Baumol and T. Fabian, "Decomposition, Pricing for Decentralization and External Economics," *Management Science*, September 1964, pp. 1–32. See also J. E. Hass, "Transfer Pricing in a Decentralized Firm," *Management Science*, February 1968, pp. 310–331, and A. Whinston, "Price Guides in Decentralized Organizations," in *New Perspectives in Organizational Research*, edited by W. W. Cooper, H. Leavitt, M. Shelly, New York: J. Wiley, 1962, pp. 409–417.

external diseconomies just enough to produce an optimum for the firm. The means by which this objective is obtained is through the addition to a division's earnings of a per unit subsidy for those activities creating external economies, and a per unit penalty to those activities involving external diseconomies.

In particular where linearity can be assumed, the overall problem can be decomposed.[6] In essence the divisions submit tentative proposed activity levels to central management based on the constraints attaching to their division and prices supplied by central management. Central management combines these tentative proposals in light of the interdivisional constraints to produce a revised set of scaled down activity levels and associated prices. The process continues in an iterative fashion until an optimum is reached.[7]

The method consists of six steps.

1. The company formulates the model (linear programming in this case) for the entire firm and breaks out the component parts for each division and the central office.
2. Each division submits to the central office an activity plan based upon the unit profit figures assigned to it by the central office.[8]
3. The central office then determines the effects of the divisional solutions on the other divisions and on the company as a whole. This the central office does by solving its own program.
4. The results of the central office solution yield temporary bonus and penalty figures that are used to create new contribution figures for the division's activities.
5. The divisions now resolve their problem using the new activity unit profit figures and resubmit the results.
6. The process is repeated until an optimal plan is determined, that is, until there is no need to modify the per unit profit figures used by the divisions.[9]

The solution technique involves solving the dual. The technique of solution is too complex to illustrate here.[10]

There is, unfortunately, a lack of complete independence in the process. Although the process starts with the actual costs and prices of a division, and

[6] The decomposition procedure is not restricted to the case where linearity is assumed. But see Hass, *op. cit.* The decomposition procedure is discussed in G. Dantzig and P. Wolfe, "Decomposition Principle for Linear Programs," *Operations Research*, 1960, pp. 101–111.

[7] The technique is not new having been advanced initially by A. C. Pigou, *Wealth and Welfare*, London: Macmillan, 1912, pp. 164–165. Recently it has been expounded by K. J. Arrow and L. Hurwicz, "Decentralization and Computation in Resource Allocation," *Essays in Economics and Econometrics*, edited by R. Pfouts, Chapel Hill, N.C.: University of North Carolina Press, 1960.

[8] At the first step these are based on market prices and the division's variable costs.

[9] Since only a finite number of plans are possible, the technique assures a solution after a finite number of steps. One application alluded to by Baumol and Fabian, *op. cit.*, p. 1, involves 30,000 constraints and several million variables.

[10] The reader is referred to Baumol and Fabian, *op. cit.*, for an extensive example.

one division need know only its own technology, subsequent solutions involve artificial contribution figures for each activity sent down by the central office. The final solution also involves a direct determination of the activity output levels by the central office despite the previous solutions transmitted by the division. The division managers must be told in the final analysis the resultant activity levels as they emerge from the central office solution. At this point the final decision is made in the central office and is merely communicated to the divisions. In a very real sense, this procedure represents only "quasi-decentralization," since the central office makes the final activity-level decisions.

When linearity no longer exists because of the nature of the interdependencies, the functional forms cannot be separated. Two results occur from this situation. First, a gaming problem arises as the interdependent divisions try to anticipate the levels of the variables that are selected by another division but affect their activities. Second, there is an increase in uncertainty resulting from the ambiguity arising because one division's decision variables are dependent in part on the decisions of another division in a way it cannot predict from price data alone.

Several solutions are possible. First, the interrelated divisions could be combined. Second, additional organizational constraints could be introduced into the programming model to mitigate the problem. A third possibility involves building the game problem into the mathematical solution.[11] The final decision in the latter case is essentially like that in which the final activity-level decisions are made by the central office.

QUESTIONS AND PROBLEMS

20–1 Graph the following problems and find the optimum mix of product.

$$\text{Maximize:} f = 2X_1 + 5X_2$$
$$\text{Subject to:} \quad X_1 + 3X_2 \le 16$$
$$4X_1 + X_2 \le 20$$
$$X_1 \quad \le 10$$
$$X_1, X_2 \ge 0$$

20–2 There are two products, X_1 and X_2:

Product	Hours of Machine Time per Unit	Incremental Profit per Unit
X_1	4	$2
X_2	2	4

The machine has 4 hours of free time.

a. Formulate the primal and dual linear programming equations.

[11] See Whinston, *op. cit.*, p. 439.

b. Graph the primal and the dual. What is the optimum mix?

c. Interpret the primal and the dual solution.

20–3 (Continue problem 20–2.) Repeat problem 20–2, parts a and b, assuming that the machine has 5 hours of free time.

20–4 Assume that two products, X_1 and X_2, are manufactured on two machines, 1 and 2. Product X_1 requires 4 hours on machine 1 and 2 hours on machine 2. There are 10 hours of excess capacity on machine 1 and 8 hours on machine 2. Each unit of X_1 produces a net increase in profit of $4 and each unit of X_2 an incremental profit of $3.

a. Formulate the linear programming problem. Determine the maximum profit and the product mix which results in that profit.

b. Determine the value of each hour of machine time by solving the dual.

20–5 (Continue problem 20–4.) Repeat problem 20–4, part a, assuming that machine 1 has 2 more hours of machine time.

20–6 The XYZ Company has the option of producing two products during periods of slack activity. For the next period, production has been scheduled so that the milling machine is free 10 hours and skilled labor will have 8 hours of time available:

Product	Machine Time per Unit	Skilled Labor per Unit	Profit Contribution per Unit
A	4	2	$5
B	2	2	3

a. Solve the primal problem (the number of units of A and B that should be produced).

b. Solve the dual problem (the cost of an hour of machine time and an hour of skilled labor).

20–7 The XYZ Company can produce two products on two machines. One product (X_1) sells for $4 and has variable costs of $3 per unit. A second product (X_2) sells for $4.60 and has variable costs of $4.10 per unit. Both products are made on a drill press (X_1 requires 3 hours and X_2 requires 2 hours of time per unit). Product X_1 also requires 5 hours of time on a grinding machine.

a. Using a graphical solution method, solve the primal and the dual. What is the profit for the optimum production mix?

b. Assume that 1 hour of additional drill time can be obtained for no charge. What is the new production mix? The new profit?

c. Assume that 1 hour of additional grinding time can be obtained for no charge. What is the new production mix? The new profit?

d. Compare your answers to parts b and c with the dual variables obtained in part a. How much would you pay for an additional hour of time on each machine?

20-8 A manufacturing firm produces two products, each of which must pass through two departments. Department 1 can process a maximum of 15 units of X_1 per day and a maximum of 20 units of X_2 per day. Department 2 can process a maximum of 25 units of X_1 per day and a maximum of 10 units of X_2 per day. Product X_1 sells for $100 and has variable costs of $65 per unit, and product X_2 sells for $110 and has variable costs of $70 per unit. The sales department of the firm notified the production foreman that no more than 10 units of X_1 can be sold per day regardless of how many are produced.
Using a graphical approach, find the optimal solution to this problem.

20-9 Delta Manufacturing Company manufactures two products, X_1 and X_2. The firm has enough excess capacity to produce at most 500 units in any combination.
The manufacturing process is such that the number of units of X_2 produced must be no more than twice as great as the number of X_1 produced. No more than 400 units of X_1 can be sold.
Graph the feasible region implied by the problem and find the solutions that exist at each corner of the convex polygon.

20-10 X_1 and X_2 are produced on two machines. Product X_1 requires 5 hours on machine 1 and 7 hours on machine 2. Product X_2 requires 6 hours on machine 1 and 3 hours on machine 2. Machine 1 has 30 hours of excess capacity available while machine 2 has 21. Product X_1 yields $7 of incremental profit per unit, and product X_2 yields $5 of incremental profit per unit.
a. Formulate the linear programming problem.
b. Solve the problem graphically.
c. Assuming that integer solutions are required, round the solution down (Why do we round down instead of up?) to the nearest whole unit for each product. Is this the optimal integer solution? If not find a better integer solution.

20-11 A manufacturing company produces two products X_1 and X_2 on two machines. The following facts apply to the two products.

	X_1	X_2
Per unit selling price	$10	$7.50
Per unit variable costs	6	2.50
Hours of machine 1 required per unit	5	2
Hours of machine 2 required per unit	5	8

Machine 1 has 30 hours of excess capacity available while machine 2 has 40 hours.
a. Formulate the linear programming problem.
b. Solve the problem graphically.

20-12 A manufacturing firm produces two grades of a product by blending different amounts of two ingredients. Grade A must be composed of at least 60%

ingredient 1 while grade B must be composed of not more than 70% of ingredient 2. Grade A sells for $20 per gallon while grade B sells for $10 per gallon. Ingredient 1 can be purchased for $10 per gallon but no more than 1,000 gallons per day are available. Ingredient 2 can be purchased for $3 per gallon but no more than 2,000 gallons can be purchased each day. Other variable costs associated with the production total $2 for each grade. The firm can sell as much as it can produce.

Formulate the problem of determining the optimal production schedule.

20–13 Two products, X_1 and X_2, are manufactured on three machines. Product X_1 requires 4 hours on machine 1, 2 hours on machine 2, and 5 hours on machine 3 for each unit produced. Product X_2 requires 1 hour on machine 1, 4 hours on machine 2, and 2.5 hours on machine 3 for each unit produced. Machine 1 has 20 hours of excess capacity available per day while machines 2 and 3 have 10 hours and 15 hours, respectively.

Each unit of X_1 produces a net increase in profits of $8, and each unit of X_2 produces an incremental profit of $5.

  a. Formulate the linear programming problem.

  b. Solve the problem graphically.

20–14 A manufacturing firm uses two machines for making 2 products, X_1 and X_2. Each machine has 24 hours of excess capacity available each day. The production foreman scheduled X_1 and X_2 such that only 4 units of each would be produced per day. The following facts apply to X_1 and X_2:

	X_1	X_2
Per unit selling price	$30	$42
Per unit variable costs	22	28
Hours of machine 1 required per unit	2	2
Hours of machine 2 required per unit	1	3

How much additional profit was foregone by the foreman's decision?

20–15 Two products, X_1 and X_2, are produced on two machines. The following information applies to each unit of the products:

	X_1	X_2
Selling Price	$30	$25
Materials	8	12
Direct Labor	10	5
Variable Overhead	2	1
Fixed Overhead (applied on the basis of machine 1 hours @ $0.50 per hour)	1.50	0.75

Machine 1 has 21 hours of excess capacity available per day and machine 2 has 15 hours available. Product X_1 requires 1 hour on machine 2 while product X_2 requires 3 hours on machine 2.

Formulate the linear programming problem, and determine the optimal production mix for the excess capacity.

20–16 A manufacturing firm has excess capacity that it is considering utilizing to make two products, X_1 and X_2. The selling price for X_1 is $25 and it would require $15 in variable costs for each unit produced. The selling price for X_2 is $22 and it would require $16 in variable costs for each unit produced. Storage space at the plant totals 10,000 cubic feet. Each unit of X_1 requires 10 cubic feet for storage, and each unit of X_2 would require 5 cubic feet for storage. The firm has 4,500 hours of excess capacity available on its machines. X_1 requires 3 hours for each unit and X_2 requires 4.5 hours for each unit. The sales department estimates that a maximum of 500 units of X_1 and 1,000 units of X_2 can be sold.

  a. Formulate the linear programming problem to maximize the increase in profits.
  b. Solve the problem graphically.

20–17 A manufacturer of small machinery produces three products which it ships from its plant in Cincinnati to its regional warehouse in Philadelphia. The shipping foreman knows that it costs the company $1 per pound to ship product X_1, $1.50 per pound to ship X_2, and $2 per pound to ship X_3. No more than two thirds and not less than one third the weight of each shipment can be composed of X_2; no more than 2 pounds of X_2 may be shipped, and the weight of X_3 in each shipment must be at least twice as great as the weight of model X_1. At least 4 pounds of X_1 must be in each shipment. The foreman would like to know the composition of each shipment in order to minimize the cost per pound.

  a. Formulate this problem as a linear program.
  b. Solve the problem graphically.

20–18 Few actual linear programming problems yield integer solutions even though many solutions, to be useful, must eventually be in integer form. Can you think of situations in which rounding a noninteger solution would yield the optimal or near-optimal integer solution? In what kinds of situations might rounding lead to bad solutions?

20–19 Ace Typewriter Manufacturers have studied the problem of determining the proper production mix for two of its most popular models. Model A sells for $150 and has variable costs of $90 per unit, and model B sells for $220 and has variable costs of $150 per unit. After considering all the constraints associated with the production mix, the company produced the following graph. All the constraints are "less than or equal" type constraints. Find the optimal solution to this product-mix problem.

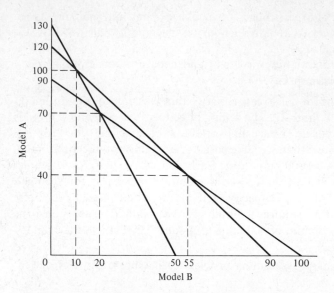

20-20 Four products, X_1, X_2, X_3, and X_4, can be produced by a company in any month. There are 1,000 machine hours available in any month, and any combination of products can be produced as long as the total machine hours is no more than 1,000. The following data applies to the four products.

Product	Hours of Machine Time per Unit	Incremental Profit per Unit
X_1	10	$10
X_2	5	20
X_3	6	18
X_4	8	32

  a. Formulate the production mix problem as a linear program.
  b. For each product, find the incremental profit per machine hour. The optimal solution is to produce as much as possible of the product with the highest incremental profit per machine hour. Find this solution.

SUPPLEMENTARY READING

BAUMOL, W., and T. FABIAN, "Decomposition Pricing for Decentralization and External Economics," *Management Science*, September 1964, pp. 1–32.

CALLAHAN, J., "An Introduction to Financial Planning Through Goal Programming," *Cost and Management*, January–February 1973, pp. 7–12.

CHARNES, A., W. W. COOPER, and Y. IJIRI, "Breakeven Budgeting and Programming to Goals," *Journal of Accounting Research*, Spring 1963, pp. 16–41.

DEMSKI, J., "An Accounting System Structured on a Linear Programming Model," *The Accounting Review*, October 1967, pp. 701–712.

DOPUCH, N., and D. DRAKE, "Accounting Implications of a Mathematical Programming Approach to the Transfer Price Problem," *Journal of Accounting Research*, Spring 1964, pp. 15–21.

———, J. BIRNBERG, and J. DEMSKI, *Cost Accounting*, New York: Harcourt Brace Jovanovich, Inc., 1974.

FRANK, W., and R. MANES, "A Standard Cost Application of Matrix Algebra," *The Accounting Review*, July 1967, pp. 516–525.

HARTLEY, R. V., "Decision Making when Joint Products Are Involved," *The Accounting Review*, October 1971, pp. 746–755.

HASS, J., "Transfer Pricing in a Decentralized Firm," *Management Science*, February 1968, pp. 310–331.

IJIRI, Y., F. LEVY, and R. LYON, "A Linear Programming Model for Budgeting and Financial Planning," *Journal of Accounting Research*, Autumn 1963, pp. 198–212.

JAEDICKE, R., "Improving Break-even Analysis by Linear Programming Techniques," *N.A.A. Bulletin*, March 1961, pp. 5–12.

KAPLAN, R., "Optimal Investigation Strategies with Imperfect Information," *Journal of Accounting Research*, Spring 1969, pp. 32–43.

———, and G. THOMPSON, "Overhead Allocation via Mathematical Programming Models," *The Accounting Review*, April 1971, pp. 352–364.

LIVINGSTONE, J., "Matrix Algebra and Cost Allocation," *The Accounting Review*, July 1968, pp. 503–508.

SAMUELS, J. M., "Opportunity Costing: An Application of Mathematical Programming," *Journal of Accounting Research*, Autumn 1965, pp. 182–191.

Chapter 21

Network Methods

Since they appeared in the late 1950s, network methods have achieved considerable application in planning, control, and performance measurement. To apply these methods, subactivities of a major project are specified and arrayed in order of their required completion. This requires the manager to determine those activities that must be completed in series and those that may be worked on in parallel. Probabilistic data concerning both time and cost can be integrated into the analysis for each subactivity. The procedure permits bottlenecks to be identified, the significance of deviations in expected completion times to be evaluated, and it helps in directing resources toward improving project performance. Further, time and cost data provide means of controlling total outlays, evaluating management performance, and predicting both additional costs and delays.

Several network methods are in wide use. This chapter concentrates on presenting the essentials of one of them, the Program Evaluation and Review Technique (PERT). There are more complex variations of PERT.

21.1 The PERT Method

For the PERT method to be applicable, several conditions must be satisfied.

1. There must be a well-defined set of activities (or jobs) that, when completed, indicate an end to the project.
2. It must be possible to specify the technological precedence conditions among activities, as well as the activities that can be started and stopped independently of one another.

3. Time estimates for each activity are required. These may be in the form of point estimates or probability distributions.

For an example, consider the project and the associated network diagram given in Table 21–1.

Table 21–1 Schedule for Project I

Activity Description	Predecessor Activity	Expected Completion Times (weeks)
a	None	8
b	None	7
c	a, b	10
d	None	7
e	c	6
f	d	4
g	f	7

The times will be treated as the means of individual probability distributions, one for each activity.[1] If desired, the entire distribution could be used and simulation methods applied to the solution. This project is diagrammed in Figure 21.1.

The circles in Figure 21.1 stand for the jobs or activities indicated by the letter inside; the arrows represent the completion of one task and the beginning of another. The numbers within the circles are the expected completion times. The earliest starting time for each activity, given the job-order dependencies, is indicated outside, above, and to the left of each activity. The earliest expected starting time of an activity is defined to be the earliest time that an activity can be expected to begin if all previous activities begin at their earliest expected starting times and finish using their expected times to complete.

The earliest expected finish time for an activity is given by the number outside, below, and to the right of each activity. It is defined as the time an activity is expected to be finished, assuming all predecessor activities begin at their earliest expected starting times and is equal to the earliest expected starting time for the activity plus its expected completion time. Thus, for example, activity c has an expected starting time of 8 weeks. Activity c cannot be started until the eighth week, since it cannot begin until activities a and b are both completed. Activity

[1] The managerial time estimates are usually considered to follow a beta distribution, and approximate estimates of the expected time are obtained using $E(t) = (t_o + 4t_m + t_p)/6$ where t_o, t_m, and t_p are managerial estimates of the optimistic, most likely, and pessimistic times, respectively. The time t_m is described here as the modal time, but it is often estimated using the median time, the time as likely to be exceeded as not. The times t_o and t_p must be defined precisely in application, since they can yield quite different results depending on definitions.

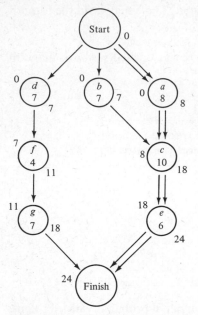

Figure 21.1   A program network diagram: Project I.

b requires an expected time of only 7 weeks, but the earliest expected starting time for activity c is 8 weeks, since activity a has an expected time of 8 weeks. The earliest expected finish time for activity c is the 8 weeks plus its expected completion time of 10 weeks, a total of $18 = 8 + 10$ weeks.[2] Where several activities feed into one activity—a and b feed into c, for example—the latest of the completion times of the preceding activities is defined as the earliest expected starting time for the next activity.

An examination of Figure 21.1 indicates that the project's expected completion date is 24 weeks. This is true despite the fact that activity g is expected to be completed by the end of the eighteenth week. There are three distinct paths from the starting activity to the finishing activity in this simple project. The longest path, start-a-c-e-finish, takes 24 weeks and is defined as the critical path. It is the bottleneck, and if the expected completion time of the total project is to be decreased, a reduction must be accomplished somewhere in the critical path. The critical path is marked by double arrows in Figure 21.1.

Suppose for the moment that the project in question did not need to be finished until the thirtieth week. Then with the computations as defined, there would

---

[2] It is not quite correct to call the figures outside the circles expected times (at least after the first activities on each path). Where paths are similar in length, ignoring one or more of them, which is what the method described does, tends to understate the earliest expected starting times of future activities. Thus, if the probability distributions were used and if the numbers used are expected times, the earliest expected starting time for activity c would exceed 8 weeks, since occasionally activity b would take longer than activity a.

exist an expected available safety factor of 6 weeks. The project could be delayed for 6 weeks and still be "expected" to be done on time. The term expected here is a probabilistic concept and implies a substantial probability that the total project time will exceed 24 weeks. It also ignores the probability that nonslack paths may delay the project.[3] This time of 6 weeks is defined as the total slack in the project.

The concept of total slack also applies to each activity. The total slack in an activity is the difference between the earliest expected starting time and the latest time it could be begun without delaying the expected completion date beyond the required date. For all activities on the critical path, the total slack of the activity is the same as that of the project, 6 weeks in this case. For activities not on the critical path, the total slack is the difference between the earliest expected starting time and the latest time that the activity could begin without delaying the required completion date. Thus, the project manager could expect to begin activity f as early as the seventh week. Further, he must begin it by the nineteenth week if the project is to be expected to be completed by the thirtieth week (activity f is expected to take 4 weeks and activity g 7 weeks). Therefore, the total slack in activity f is 12 weeks: $19 - 7$.

Another type of slack is the time an activity can be delayed without delaying the expected starting time of another activity. This is referred to as free slack. Some jobs will not have any free slack, since free slack requires parallel activities. Indeed, in the present example, only activity b has free slack. The free slack for activity b is one week.[4]

The importance of these slack measures is that they indicate the degree of impact a change in time efficiency has on the overall expected completion time. Furthermore, they suggest places where resources can be temporarily shifted to improve times on the critical path. The total slack measures show the project manager where he has or does not have elbow room in scheduling activities.

If the probability distributions for the times can be approximated with beta distributions (see footnote 1 for definition of terms), an estimate of the variance or activity i is given by $\sigma_i^2 = \frac{1}{36}(t_{pi} - t_{oi})^2$ where t_{pi} is the pessimistic time estimate for activity i and t_{oi} is the optimistic estimate. If there is a large number of independent activities on the critical path, the distribution of the total project time for the path can be assumed to be normal with variance:

$$\sigma^2 = \sum_i \frac{1}{36} (t_{pi} - t_{oi})^2 \tag{21.1}$$

The variance given by equation (21.1) does not reflect the effect of uncertainty in other paths which may also delay completion and thus has a built-in down-

[3] Assuming that the probability distribution for the total project completion time is normal, the probability of finishing in 24 weeks would be slightly less than 0.5.

[4] This concept is somewhat misleading since a delay of one day in starting activity b may delay the expected starting time for activity c, where the term expected is given a probabilistic interpretation.

ward bias. Despite this limitation it can be used to estimate the probability that a project would be finished by a given point in time. For example, if the expected time is 24, σ^2 is 36, and if the project deadline, t, is 30 weeks, the probability of finishing by the deadline date is given by the standard-normal distribution-function,

$$N_z(z) = N_z\left(\frac{t - t_e}{6}\right) = N_z\left(\frac{30 - 24}{6}\right) = N_z(1) = .08413$$

21.2   Resource Allocation in PERT Networks

Suppose now, however, that the required completion time is 17 weeks, a case of negative total slack. Sometimes nothing can be done about this situation, but often the input of more or better resources into the process permits a shortening of the expected times. For the example of this chapter, assume that the costs associated with different expected activity times are as shown in Table 21–2. Assume further that the cost estimates are independent. Under these assumptions, shortening one activity for a given cost has no effect on the costs

Table 21–2   Time-Cost Estimates by Activity

Activity	Expected Activity Time	Cost	Cost Increase per Unit of Time Decrease
a	8	$1,000	
	6	1,400	200
	5	1,900	500
b	7	800	
	5	2,000	600
c	10	1,500	
	7	1,800	100
	5	3,000	600
d	7	500	
	6	1,000	500
	3	1,900	300
e	6	1,100	
	5	1,300	200
	4	2,200	900
f	4	800	
	2	1,400	300
g	7	800	
	4	1,400	200
	1	5,000	1,200

of changing the times on other activities.[5] Finally, the assumption is made here that activities must be reduced in accordance with the discrete steps indicated in Table 21–2. (A continuous function could be used if appropriate.)

The total activity time without any change is expected to be 24 weeks, and adding up the costs for each activity yields a total cost of $6,500. This is illustrated in Table 21–3.

Table 21–3   Cost Project 1:
24-Week Completion

Activity	Cost (thousands)
a	$1,000
b	800
c	1,500
d	500
e	1,100
f	800
g	800
	$6,500

Since the total expected time is decreased by shortening the critical path, the next step is to search the critical path for the activity with the lowest cost increase per unit of time. The activity with this characteristic is c. Activity c is lowered by 3 weeks at a cost of $300 or $100 per week. With the incurring of this cost, the total cost is now $6,800, the expected time is 21 weeks, and the expected duration of the critical path is decreased by 3 weeks. Since the expected time still exceeds the required time of 17 weeks, the critical path is searched for the activity with the next lowest cost increase per unit of time decrease. In this project, activities a and e are identical. To break the tie, one simple rule that might be used is to pick one of the tied activities at random. Suppose that activity e is selected. Activity e is shortened by one week for a cost of $200. The total cost is now $7,000, the expected time is 20 weeks, and there is still no change in the critical path.

Continuing the procedure, activity a is now shortened by two weeks at a cost of $400 (the total cost becomes $7,400) and the expected time of the right-hand path is now 18 weeks. However, the expected time of the project is reduced by only one week, to 19 weeks, since a new critical path exists, namely, start-b-c-e-finish. Using the new critical path, activities b and c have identical cost increases per time period. Since activity c is relevant to more paths, it is reduced by two

[5] This may not be true in practice as, say, when marginal labor is hired or overtime is required. Where it is not true, allowance must be made for the dependencies, perhaps by using simulation methods.

weeks at a cost of $1,200. Total cost is now $8,600, but the expected total time is reduced only to 18 rather than to 17 weeks, since once again there is a new critical path, namely start-d-f-g-finish. The optimal choice is to decrease activity g by 3 weeks at a cost of $600. The total cost is now $9,200, the expected time 17 weeks, and the critical path is start-b-c-e-finish.

It may appear that the problem is finished. This is, however, not quite the case. The path start-d-f-g-finish now requires an expected time of 15 weeks. Suppose that activity g could be increased 3 weeks at a saving of $600, and instead of following the general procedure described above, suppose that activity d were decreased one week at a cost of $500. The expected completion time of 17 weeks would now also attach to this path and total costs would be reduced by $100 to $9,100. Adjustments of this type should be evaluated before the problem is considered resolved.

The steps used to shorten the total required time are:

1. Pick the activity on the critical path with the lowest-cost increase per unit of time. If there is a tie, pick one of the tied activities at random. (This tie-breaking procedure is an arbitrary rule.)
2. Decrease the expected activity time by the time saved, compute the expected total time, the total cost, and determine the critical path.
3. Repeat the process until either the expected total time is equal to or less than the required time, there are no more possible time savings, or the total cost exceeds available funds.

Since most project networks are quite complex, it is fortunate that these steps can be programmed for computers.

21.3 Some Problems in Application

The technique described in Sections 21.1 and 21.2 has been extensively employed for analyzing, planning, and scheduling large, complex projects. It is not without its problems, however.[6] Perhaps paramount among these is securing the data necessary to support the analysis. This includes the difficulties attendant in obtaining cost data that can be realistically applied to the scheduling problem. Too often the accounting department data are not relevant to that required by the problem.

A second substantial problem is the difficulty of obtaining useful probabilistic data. The activity-time distributions have traditionally been assumed to be adequately described by beta distributions. In fact, no empirical studies of activity-time distributions have been made.[7] The terms optimistic and pessimistic

---

[6] See K. R. MacCrimmon and C. A. Ryavec, "Analytical Study of the PERT Assumptions," *Operations Research*, January 1964, pp. 16–37.

[7] An appealing but equally unjustified alternative is the triangular distribution with $E(t) = (a + m + b)/3$ and $\mathrm{Var}\,(t) = [(b - a)^2 + (m - a)(m - b)]/18$, where a and b are the end points and m the most likely (modal) observation.

used, in part, to obtain the expected times may be too vague to produce valid estimates of the beta distribution parameters.

The use of probabilistic data in particular has implications for performance evaluation. If both cost and time data are subject to uncertainty, this uncertainty should be recalled when it is time to evaluate the managers who are responsible for a particular activity. Some attempt should be made to consider "normal variability" in his performance on individual tasks and to expect offsetting favorable and unfavorable performance over time and over several tasks. Unfortunately, the observations taken on several tasks may not be independent (for example, if they are worked on concurrently), and time and cost measures on the same activity (and perhaps even on several activities) are usually interrelated. These interdependencies must be considered where they exist. Also, changes in the resources available to the manager, the effects of learning, and favorable or unfavorable conditions (such as weather and strikes) must be considered in estimating the relevant probability distributions and evaluating results.

One possible performance measure that should not be overlooked is the marginal cost added to the project because a manager fails to complete his activity in time or requires the diversion of resources from other activities and hence alters their time or cost performance. Often if one activity is unnecessarily delayed, a new network analysis is required. Computers can and should be programmed to update the network on the basis of actual or estimated data on each activity. As part of this revision, the increase (or decrease) in costs created by an activity can be computed. These can be used, where estimated in time, to assist in optimal resource allocations. If they are computed after the fact, they can be used in measuring the performance of the manager responsible for the delay by charging them to his budget. It is also important that the effect of delays on the network be promptly relayed to the managers of other activities so they may adjust their plans. The effects of these delays should be considered if the results are used to evaluate performance.

There are several alternative time and cost-estimation procedures that could be used. Rough estimates of data could be used until the critical path is located, and effort could then be directed toward better estimate of times for the critical activities. Preconceived biases are common. One way to mitigate the bias problems is to estimate job times in random order. Responders may tend to add times mentally, and this in turn conditions their responses toward reaching a total time within the limit required by the project.

There are problems in establishing the network, including the possibility of omitting activities or misordering activities. Sometimes these problems can be reduced by having several groups produce independent networks and comparing the results. Often networks must be modified by the addition of interconnecting paths. Such additions may affect the expected completion time.

One of the more appealing extensions in PERT applications is the incorporation, using simulation, into the analysis of the entire probability distributions for the times and costs of each activity rather than just the mean and variance of those distributions.[8] Furthermore, it is possible to introduce dependencies between the time and cost data as well. Subjective probability distributions are obtained for the relevant variables and the project is simulated using Monte Carlo techniques. Each simulation run provides project time and cost data for the entire network. An evaluation of the suitability of the implied times and costs associated with the project may be attempted by examining the time and cost distributions. For example, if the time distribution associated with one set of decisions and costs is judged to be unsatisfactory, the simulation could be rerun for a different payment (or payments) to shift an activity's (or several activities') time distribution to the left. Decisions might then be made in terms of the trade-off of money for time saved and the probability of finishing on time. The trade-off may be difficult to evaluate, and hence it would be helpful if the benefits from an early finish and penalties for a late finish could be estimated.

Generally, there are benefits from finishing a project before the required time. These may include reduced financial charges and increased benefits from early completion. Similarly, there may be penalties, including lost contribution margins from a failure to finish by the required completion time. Given a project time distribution resulting from a Monte Carlo simulation, the expected net effect can be estimated by integrating the product of the function defining the benefits (penalties) with the probability density function for time, $f(t)$, over all values t. This is illustrated in Figure 21.2, when it can be assumed that the benefits from finishing early and the costs from finishing late are linearly related to time.[9]

While still in the planning phase, the manager may wish to consider the effect of the reallocation of resources or the use of additional resources to alter the project time distribution. This can be done by altering the activity distributions, presumably at some cost. As the project moves out of the planning and into the execution stage, such modifications may become more costly. The results of each reallocation policy could be evaluated by conducting a new simulation, evaluating equation (21.2) and comparing it to the cost of the additional resources committed to the project. This approach explicitly considers the costs involved

---

[8] See, for example, G. L. Thompson, "CPM and DCPM Under Risk," Reprint No. 384, Graduate School of Industrial Administration, Carnegie-Mellon University, 1968. Simulation methods using Monte Carlo techniques may be excessive. For an alternative, see W. H. Parks and K. D. Ramsing, "The Use of the Compound Poisson in PERT," *Management Science*, April 1969, pp. 397–402.

[9] The integration yields

$$b_u \int_0^{t_b} (t_b - t)f(t)\, dt - b_o \int_{t_b}^{t_c} (t - t_b)f(t)\, dt \tag{21.2}$$

where

b_u = unit dollar benefit from finishing early
b_o = unit dollar penalty from finishing late
t_b = required time
t_c = time such that $f(t) = 0$ for all $t > t_c$

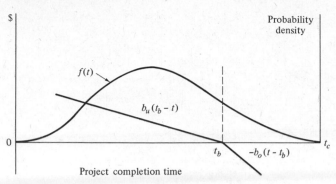

Figure 21.2 Diagram of one simulation.

in a failure to meet the project deadline, the likelihoods of the various completion times and costs, as well as the effects on expected profits of decreasing the completion times of one or more activities. The implicit assumption is made here that the net effect can be measured on the basis of the expected monetary values involved. It also implicitly assumes that the policy is found which optimally uses the additional resources. If the assumptions are met, additional resources should result in a shift to the left in the resultant project time distribution.

Presumably, the relationship between the additional resources committed and the net benefits realized will exhibit marginal decreasing returns. In computing these returns, the net gain obtained in the expectation of the project cost distribution from an early finish should be compared to the cost of obtaining it. The notion of opportunity cost should be used in evaluating the cost of alternative reallocation policies.

Consideration should also be given to the alternative of subcontracting, the use of slack time to shift resources, redesign of the system (for example, to convert series activities into parallel activities), and the use of a different technology.

The PERT technique has already been successfully used in construction, audits, computer installations, institution of control systems, competitive bidding, maintenance programs, new product development, and many other areas. With the advent of better techniques for handling some of the problems, it should find even more uses, as well as being used more effectively, in existing applications.

21.4 PERT-Cost and Control

The concept of PERT-Cost provides a useful approach to the control of projects already started.[10] Using this method, figures are kept on actual costs

---

[10] See H. W. Paige, "How PERT/Cost Helps the Manager," *The Harvard Business Review*, November–December 1963, pp. 87–95.

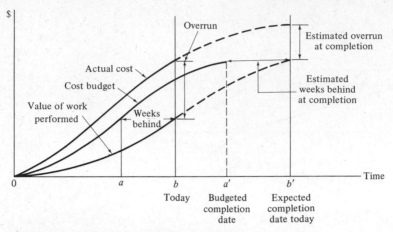

Figure 21.3 Operating schedule of performance.

incurred, budgeted costs (adjusted to reflect unforeseen changes, say in prices), and the time activities are completed. This information assists in determining the overexpenditure and time late to date and, thereby, an estimate of the overexpenditure and anticipated time late on the total project. Dividing a project into parts according to both the component activities and the responsible divisions of the firm permits the project manager to pinpoint trouble areas early and perhaps initiate corrective or ameliorating action. It also permits an evaluation of the statement so often made that: "Yes, I'm over the budget, but the work is substantially ahead of schedule." Figures 21.3, 21.4, and 21.5 suggest the essentials of this approach.

Figure 21.3 gives the overall picture of the project to date. The actual cost has been plotted up to the present time and projected to the expected completion date. The latter date is found by projecting the value-of-the-work-performed line until its height reaches the height of the cost-budget line at the original budgeted completion date. The value of the work performed is the budgeted value of those activities actually completed.

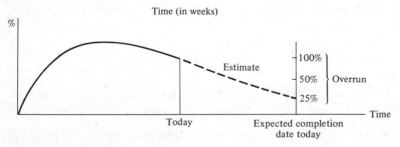

Figure 21.4 Expected overrun.

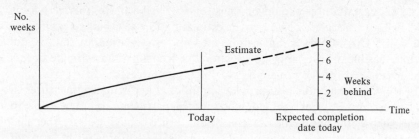

Figure 21.5   Expected time late.

When actual costs exceed the value of the work performed, the difference is an overrun. The overrun in the present example is quite large today but is expected to decrease by the time the project is completed. Actual cost less the value of the work performed as a ratio to the value of work performed gives the percentage overrun. This percentage is plotted and extrapolated to the expected completion data in Figure 21.4.

The cost-budget plot indicates just when work should be done as well as its cost. In this case it has taken $b - a$ weeks longer to complete the work done than was budgeted. The amount, $b - a$, then, indicates the time late. Figure 21.3 suggests that the project will be even further behind time when it is finished $b' - a'$. The weeks-late figure is also considered important enough to diagram separately. The fact that the weeks-late figure is predicted to become worse may have some relation to the expected decline in overrun, both in percentage and, somewhat less, in total. It would perhaps be surprising for the weeks-late figure to decline concurrently with a decline in the absolute value of the overrun.

The data on the entire project is perhaps most useful when broken down by tasks, departments, or both. Suppose, for example, that the following facts were available on a given activity at the twenty-second week:

Actual cost at week 22	$4.4 thousand
Budgeted value of work performed	$1.8 thousand
Budget time for value of work performed	11 weeks
Cost budget at week 22	$3.8 thousand
Estimated actual cost at completion	$5.4 thousand
Estimated time of completion (total)	36 weeks
Total budgeted value at completion	$4.0 thousand
Budgeted completion time	23 weeks

The above schedule of costs indicates that $2.2 thousand of budgeted value, $4 − $1.8, remains to be completed. However, it simultaneously predicts that it can accomplish the production task for $1 thousand, $5.4 − $4.4. This optimistic forecast of doing $2.2 thousand of budgeted activity on less than half that in actual expenditures should be questioned. Furthermore, this activity is 11 weeks behind schedule, $22 - 11$, while estimating 13 weeks behind at completion, $36 - 23$. This implies a much different level of performance than in the past. While feasible, it, too, appears questionable in light of an estimate of less costs than budgeted for the remaining work to be completed.

The PERT-Cost technique also provides additional performance measures in terms of overrun and weeks-behind schedule. In particular, it often leads to statements such as the one in the example about future behavior under specified conditions concerning resource availabilities that can be evaluated in terms of later performance.

21.5 Summary

The methods described in this chapter for programming and controlling large projects are appealing for several reasons. They are reasonably easy to understand and can be applied to a wide range of problems. They provide data for immediate and continuing control and reevaluation, and the graphical techniques provide additional means of communicating and interpreting results as well as pinpointing critical areas of concern.

New techniques, such as computer simulation, permit larger problems to be treated as well as a more accurate and complete treatment of existing applications. The underlying simplicity and the ability to focus attention on the critical issues involving important projects in a wide range of problem areas makes the technique important to the manager.

The PERT network requirement also requires the manager to think carefully through the logic of the project planning. This exercise can often point up trouble spots early and can suggest the need for redesign when such redesign can be most effectively implemented. Finally, it focuses additional attention on critical-activity time estimates and provides a basis for estimating and scheduling scarce resources.

QUESTIONS AND PROBLEMS

21–1 The chapter indicates that network methods are useful in planning, prediction, control of project cost and time, and performance measurement. Discuss the use of the PERT method in each of these dimensions.

21–2 What problems are created by using the terms "optimistic" and "pessimistic" to obtain managerial estimates of the relevant times?

21–3 What problems are created if an activity's completion is delayed?

21–4 Would you suspect that PERT techniques might be useful to builders of motels?

21–5 Can you think of some projects for which PERT would not be a desirable technique?

21–6 A project is diagrammed below. The numbers within the circles are the expected completion time in days.

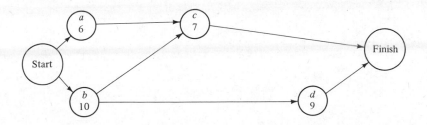

Required:
a. Compute the earliest expected starting time and the earliest expected finishing time for each activity.
b. If the project must be done within 21 days, what is the total slack or "safety factor"?
c. What is the critical path?
d. What is the total slack in activity d? In activity c?
e. What is the free slack in activity b? In activity a?

21–7 Assume that the following estimates apply to the project described in problem 21–6:

Activity	Optimistic	Pessimistic
a	2	10
b	6	12
c	5	9
d	7	11

Required:
a. Compute an estimate of the variance of the times of each activity.
b. Compute an estimate of the variance of the times of the activities on the critical path assuming that the activities on the path are independent.
c. Assuming that the probability distribution of times of the critical path is normally distributed, what is your estimate of the probability of exceeding

the 21 days that are allowed? Are there reasons to suspect that this estimate
is biased? If so, in which direction is the bias?

d. What is the probability that paths a, b, and c will exceed 21 days?

21–8 Consider the network shown in the figure:

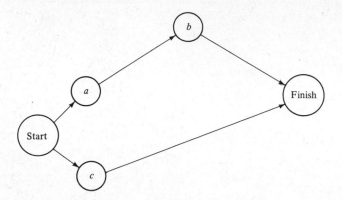

Assume that the probability that path a-b-finish will exceed the allowable time
is 0.6 and there is a 0.5 probability of path c-finish exceeding the allowable time.
The two paths are independent.

Required: What is the probability that the task will be done on time?

21–9 Assume that the probabilities of completing on time three different
(independent) paths are 0.8, 0.9, and 0.6. What is the probability of completing
the job on time?

21–10 Assume that the probability of completing three different (independent)
paths on time is 0.7 each. What is the probability of completing the job on time?

21–11 Assume that the probability of not completing three different (independent) paths on time is 0.3 for each path. What is the probability of not completing
the job on time?

21–12 A firm wants to be 97.5% certain of completing a job within a year. It
can organize independent task forces each with probability 0.6 of success. How
many task forces should be organized?

21–13 (This problem is quite a bit longer and more difficult than the others
given for this chapter.) Given the series of tasks and times for the tasks in the
following table, answer the questions relating to this specific network. Suppose
that you were given the network data in the accompanying table. It is not the
normal manner in which you receive data, but can you develop a network
diagram from these data similar to those in the chapter? For this purpose the
events represent the completion of one or more tasks and the start of new ones.
For example, event 5 occurs when the tasks requiring the expected times of
5.2 and 1.2 hours are completed and the task requiring an expected time of
17.0 hours is begun. Assume that work on the project is continuous.

Event (E)	Immediate Predecessor Event(s) (IPE)	Times from IPE to E (hours)			
		Optimistic Time	Most Likely Time	Pessimistic Time	Expected Time
15	14	2	3	4	3.0
	13	2	5	10	5.3
	12	1	2	4	2.2
	11	3	3	5	3.3
14	10	3	7	16	7.8
	9	4	6	10	6.3
	2	12	15	21	15.5
13	8	12	15	24	16.0
12	7	5	10	16	10.2
11	10	0	0	0	0
	6	2	2	5	2.5
10	5	12	16	26	17.0
9	4	1	1	2	1.2
8	3	3	4	6	4.2
7	3	2	4	5	3.8
6	3	10	14	20	14.3
5	3	3	5	8	5.2
	2	1	1	2	1.2
4	2	2	3	5	3.2
3	1	9	14	22	14.5
2	1	5	8	14	8.5
1 Start	None	0	0	0	0

Required:

a. Set up graphically an appropriate network diagram and indicate the critical path.

b. Explain how the *expected* time values were determined.

c. What are the earliest *expected* arrival times for events 5, 11, and 14?

d. What is the expected completion time for the entire project?

e. What is the most optimistic completion time for the entire project?

f. Suppose that the expected time required for the only job necessary to go from event 5 to event 10 were decreased to 5 hours.

   1. What effect would this have upon the earliest possible expected completion time?

   2. What effect would it have upon the earliest expected time of arrival at event 11?

g. If the expected time to go from event 5 to event 10 were cut by 7.5 hours, what would happen to the critical path?

h. How long can the single task between event 3 and event 6 be delayed without delaying the earliest expected time of arrival at event 11?

i. If the entire project must be completed in two days (48 hours), how much total slack exists in the network?

j. Explain how you would find the probability that the entire job will be completed by:
1. The most optimistic completion date?
2. The expected completion date determined by the critical path?
3. The target date of two days?

21–14 Consider the network problem shown (reflecting perhaps a machine setup) and the associated costs of reducing the most likely time. Assume that the given cost causes the entire distribution to shift to the left by the same amount.[11]

Activity	Immediate Predecessor Event(s)	Optimistic Time (days)	Pessimistic Time (days)	Most Likely Time (days)
A	—	2	5	2
B	—	2	5	4
C	A	3	5	4
D	B	6	12	8
E	C	5	10	7
F	D	3	5	4
G	E	4	10	6
H	A, F	1	2	1
I	G	3	6	5
J	H	4	9	7
K	I, J	2	5	3

Total Cost of Reduction of Mean Time by Days (dollars)

Activity	A	B	C	D	E	F	G	H	I	J	K
First day	10	14	15	20	20	*	20	20	30	30	30
Second day	30	30	40	40	35	*	35	60	65	65	100

* Cannot be reduced.

Required:

a. Determine the critical path and the expected completion time.

[11] Adapted from N. Dopuch and J. Birnberg, *Cost Accounting*, New York: Harcourt Brace Jovanovich, Inc., 1969.

b. Determine the total slack if the project must be completed in 25 days.

c. Estimate the probability that the job will be done in time.

d. What action should the company take to increase the probability of completion to 0.5?

e. If a probability of completion in time of say, 97% were desired, what estimate of the total days to be reduced from the expected time would you make? Would your answer be biased? If so, why?

21–15 Assume that the payoff functions for time early and time late in finishing a particular project are given by $100(24 - t)$ for early finish: $t < 24$, and $200(t - 24)$ for late finish: $t \geq 24$, where t is in days. The early finish function indicates a \$100 bonus paid on the contract for each day that the project is finished before the target date 24 days away. The penalty function indicates a \$200 penalty for each day that the project is late. Assume, given present cost and time estimates on the various activities that the finish date, t, has the following probability distribution:

$$f_T(t) = \begin{cases} \dfrac{1}{20}: & 16 \leq t \leq 36 \\ 0: & \text{otherwise} \end{cases}$$

Required: Compute the expected net bonus to be obtained. Are there any alternatives to accepting this result?

21–16 Suppose that in a given network system the engineering subsystem has the following reported facts for a job that is done uniformly over time in terms of cost incurrence as well as actual activity: cost incurred to date, \$6.6 million; cost of work completed (budget), \$3.7 million; original budget for engineering, \$6.0 million. The engineering department now estimates that it will cost a total (including past costs) of \$8.1 million to complete its subsystem. The project was expected to take 24 weeks. It is now the twenty-second week. Engineering now predicts completion in 10 more weeks.

Required:

a. What is the overrun percentage?

b. What is the value of the work left to be done in terms of the original cost budget?

c. How much more does the engineering department propose to spend to complete the task?

d. What is the predicted final overrun?

e. How far behind in weeks is the process now?

f. If engineering continued at its same rate, how many more weeks would you estimate until completion?

g. Comment on how realistic the engineering department's new predictions are?

21–17 What conclusions do you reach given the following project data?

Actual costs incurred to date	$80 thousand
Value of work performed	$60 thousand
Original budget time for work performed	12 weeks
Original cost budget today (week 10)	$50 thousand
Present estimated total costs at completion	$120 thousand
Present estimated total duration of project	16 weeks
Original estimated total budget at completion	$100 thousand
Original budget completion time	20 weeks

If they continued to work as they have to date, when would they finish and what would be the weeks-ahead figure?

21–18 The Jones Hangar Construction Company is building a new hangar for the Ithaca International Airport. The project's budget calls for a completion time of one year from its start on September 23, 1976, and a cost of $9 million. (The budget is based on the assumption of a uniform expenditure and completion of work over the year.) As of May 23, 1977, the company's industrial engineers estimate the budgeted value of the work completed to be $8 million although actual expenditures to date have reached $10 million.

Hap Hazard, the construction foreman, estimates he will be finished by July 23 and he estimates expenditures will run $2 million between now and then.

Required:

a. What is the overrun percentage 5/23/77? What is the value of the work remaining to be done 5/23/77?
b. How far behind schedule is the project now?
c. How much longer would you estimate the firm will take to complete the hangar if they continue to work as they have?
d. How much will they spend if they continue to work with the same efficiency as in the past?
e. What questions would you have for Mr. Hazard at this time, if any, concerning his estimates?

21–19 Discuss the cost control characteristics of PERT.

21–20 Suggest the types of activities that could be planned and controlled by PERT techniques. Also indicate those activities that would not be efficiently planned and controlled by PERT. In particular, what makes the technique useful to management?

SUPPLEMENTARY READING

BERMAN, E. B., "Resource Allocation in a PERT Network Under Continuous Activity Time-Cost Functions," *Management Science*, July 1964, pp. 734–745.
CROWSTON, W., and G. THOMPSON, "Decision CPM: A Method of Simultaneous Planning, Scheduling and Control of Projects," *Operations Research*, May–June 1967, pp. 407–426.

DeCoster, D. T., "The Budget Director and PERT," *Budgeting*, March 1964, pp. 13–17.

———, "PERT/COST—The Challenge," *Management Services*, May–June 1969, pp. 13–18.

Levy, F. K., G. L. Thompson, and J. D. Wiest, "The ABC's of the Critical Path Method," *The Harvard Business Review*, September–October 1963, pp. 98–108.

MacCrimmon, K. R., and C. A. Ryavec, "Analytical Study of the P.E.R.T Assumptions," *Operations Research*, January 1964, pp. 16–37.

Paige, H. W., "How PERT/COST Helps the Manager," *The Harvard Business Review*, November–December 1963, pp. 87–95.

Saitow, A. R., "CSPC: Reporting Project Progress to the Top," *The Harvard Business Review*, January–February 1969, pp. 88–97.

Swanson, L., and H. Pazer, "Implications of the Underlying Assumptions of PERT," *Decision Sciences*, October 1971, pp. 461–480.

Vazsonyi, A., "Automated Information Systems in Planning and Control," *Management Science*, February 1965, pp. 2–41.

Chapter 22

Cost Control and Statistical Techniques

Statistical methods are relevant and can be expected to find increased use in cost analysis and control procedures. This and the next chapter describe two particular applications. In this chapter statistical techniques are used to decide whether or not to investigate cost variances. In the next chapter regression techniques are used to estimate cost relationships.

Particular attention should be paid to the limitations and assumptions explicit and implicit to each technique. As with any quantitative technique, the assumptions must be understood before the applicability of the technique in a given situation can be determined.

22.1   Decision to Investigate Cost Variances

The conventional procedure in evaluating performance using budgeted or standard costs is to look at either the absolute size of the cost variance (the difference between actual and standard costs) or the percentage obtained by dividing the cost variance by the standard cost. Both of these measures rely upon the intuition of the manager, in deciding whether the variance should be investigated and whether the investigation should then lead to corrective action.

The analysis may be formalized by assuming that the expected value and standard deviation of the probability distribution for the cost variance are known when the process is in control. Next, the

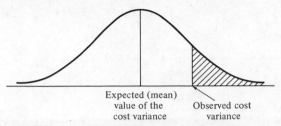

Figure 22.1 **Probability of an unfavorable cost variance as large as the variance observed.**

probability of an observation as unusual as the one observed is computed. This is illustrated in Figure 22.1. A normal probability distribution is used under the assumption that a number of independent factors influence the observed variance. The expected variance is not necessarily zero even if tight cost standards are being used.

Example

Suppose that the expected cost variance, based on relevant historical data, is $200 with a standard deviation of $10. Suppose also that a plot of the relevant historical data suggests that a normal probability distribution is a reasonable approximation.[1] A cost variance of $220 is observed. What is the conditional probability of a variance this large given that an unfavorable variance is observed?

The observed cost variance is two standard deviations from the mean[2]:

$$z = \frac{\text{observation} - \text{mean}}{\text{standard deviation}} = \frac{x - \mu}{\sigma} = \frac{220 - 200}{10} = 2$$

Using Table I, the probability of a positive deviation this large or larger is given by $N_z(-z) = N_z(-2) = 0.02275$. If this probability was calculated conditional on its being unfavorable (only 50%, the right half, of the curve is relevant if we know in advance that the variance is unfavorable), we must double the probability to obtain the probability of this variance given that the variance is unfavorable. We obtain about a 0.05 probability of such a large unfavorable variance.

If this probability is small, say less than 0.05 (depending on the importance the manager attaches to the cost in question), the particular cost variance is a candidate for investigation. This approach requires the manager to combine

[1] It is somewhat unusual for individual values to follow a normal probability law. Such behavior is not unusual for the means of large samples, but it is seldom the case for individual observations. If a normal distribution does not fit the data reasonably well, other logical choices might be tried, such as a rectangular or triangular probability distribution.

[2] We assume that the historical information provides a reasonable estimate of σ. An equally reasonable assumption would consider the data as only an estimate of σ and use a "t" rather than a normal distribution.

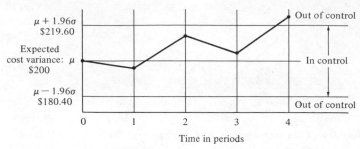

Figure 22.2   Cost variance control chart: 0.05 Probability.

intuitively the probability of a cost variance as large or larger than the one obtained with the dollar amounts involved and his feelings about the correctability of the situation, and then to compare the results with alternative uses of the available resources. Needless to say, it is a difficult task for the manager to juggle all these factors simultaneously.

To facilitate this process, control charts for cost variances are sometimes used. An example is shown in Figure 22.2. The plot of what the process has done is kept over time. If a point falls outside the control limits, $\mu \pm 1.96\sigma$ here (the value necessary to leave a 0.025 area in each normal-curve tail), an investigation is signaled. The point for period 4 provides an example. (The control limits do not need to be symmetrical but should, instead, reflect the costs and losses associated with the investigation decision.) The time plot provides the basis for both a visual analysis and for an examination of any trend in the data. This statistical control procedure has been commonly used by firms to control physical characteristics in production processes. This is simply an extension of that approach to cost control.

22.2   Decision-Theory Approach

We believe that the traditional procedures described in Section 22.1 are inadequate, because they fail to explicitly consider the costs and losses implicit to the decisions being made. The following section uses a decision-theory approach to deal explicitly with these issues.[3]

22.2.1 Setting Up the Problem

The cost-variance investigation decision involves a multistate process in which information about the states reaches the decision maker at discrete time periods.

[3] The discussion in this section is influenced by R. M. Duvall, "Rules for Investigating Cost Variances," *Management Science*, June 1967, pp. 631–641; and R. S. Kaplan, "Optimal Investigation Strategies with Imperfect Information," *Journal of Accounting Research*, Spring 1969, pp. 32–43.

This information concerns the state of the process over which the decision maker has some, but not complete, control. The decision maker is in turn faced with the question of whether to intervene in order to exercise that control. Exercising control here means first deciding whether or not to investigate the process prior to the next stage, and second, if investigation takes place, deciding whether or not to correct the process.

Through time, the process being reported on may change from being in control to being out of control, or vice versa. Thus, the process can be described as one in which the state variable is subject to transformation during each stage. These transformations (from control to out of control and vice versa) are only partially under the control of the decision maker through the manipulation of decision variables (which are assumed here to remain constant within each stage of the process). Furthermore, knowledge about the process in a given stage is probabilistic; that is, the information available about the process may or may not be indicative of the actual state of the process.

The description of the problem so far implies only a single process. In fact, at each stage the decision maker is monitoring several processes. The task is to select a subset of the processes for investigation given budget and other constraints and a desire to minimize costs. The constraints and cost minimization will usually prevent an investigation of all processes at each stage. Furthermore, the investigation action can be dichotomized in practice so that either an exploratory investigation at a substantially reduced cost or a complete investigation may be undertaken.

The probabilistic elements in the problem are several. First the process of transformation from an in-control to an out-of-control state (and vice versa) is in part probabilistic. The state of control shifts from stage to stage according to some random process as well as in response to the actions taken by the decision maker. Decisions to modify the process must be made on the basis of sample information which is also probabilistic. Finally, an investigation once initiated may fail to disclose a situation requiring adjustment when one exists; in addition, adjustment once undertaken may fail to restore the desired state.

Certain variables often included in a control system are not optimized in the present discussion but, rather, are treated as parameters (their levels are assumed fixed, although perhaps unknown). These parameters are the time interval between cost reports, the lag between measurement and control implementation, the cost of investigation and process of adjustment, and the accuracy of the information. Decisions are made concerning only the investigate decision and how information can be used to make this choice.

22.2.2 Simple Investigate-Decision Situation

Consider first a very basic problem in which monetary values are used to evaluate each state-action pair. The monetary values are assumed to reflect the consequences to the decision maker of each action under each state. Assume a two-state, two-action problem with states:

s_1: in control

s_2: out of control,

and possible actions

a_1: investigate

a_2: do not investigate

There are several implicit assumptions. One of these is that the incurred costs are reported on a periodic basis. Thus, a do-not-investigate action implies that the activity is continued at least until the next cost observation is available. An additional assumption made is that an investigation always reveals the cause of an out-of-control situation which can and will be immediately corrected.[4]

The cost of an investigation is assumed to be an amount C, the cost of correction is M, and the present value of the savings obtainable from an investigation when the activity is out of control is $L - M$, where $L - M > C$; if $L - M < C$, investigation would never be warranted. It is important to recognize that it is the value L rather than the specific cost variance under consideration (although the two may be related) that is important.

Reliable estimates of the investigation and correction costs, C and M, should be reasonably easy to obtain. On the other hand, the benefits from an investigation are more difficult to determine with precision. In the first place the benefits may be either of two forms. If the cost variance is caused by conditions that can be corrected, the benefit is the costs saved by the reduction or elimination of the cause of the variance. Alternatively, if the variance is caused by a permanent change in the process, the benefits in this case result from a change in the decision process that may enable the firm to avoid similar situations in the future. The value of L depends on the type of situation. For illustrative purposes, the discussion here will assume that the observed variance is of the correctable type.

It is assumed here that the relevant period over which the value of L is estimated is either the time from now until the process is expected to go out of control again or the time until the standards are expected to be revised. Under these conditions the present value of L depends on the future decisions that will be made. Hence, the present value of L depends upon following an optimal decision policy in the future. With these assumptions the problem becomes one amenable to discrete dynamic programming.[5] The difficulty in solving larger and more realistic problems involving many state values by this method suggests

[4] Another interesting question not examined here concerns the effect on the analysis of investigations that last longer than the time between successive cost observations. Also, the extension of this approach to a probabilistic detection and correction process is straightforward.

[5] See Kaplan, *op. cit.*, for an example of the discrete dynamic programming approach applied to this problem.

Table 22–1   General Cost Payoff Matrix (two-state form)

	States: s_j	
	s_1	s_2
Actions: a_i	In Control	Out of Control
a_1: Investigate	C	$C + M$
a_2: Do not investigate	0	L

that a somewhat different approach using estimates of the value of L may be valuable.

For purposes of this discussion, the value of L is estimated as the present value of the cost savings over the planning horizon. In the present example, assume that an out-of-control process causes a cost of $2,500 per period over a 14-period planning horizon. Using a time value of money of 0.14 per period yields a value of $15,000 for L. Assume further an investigation cost of $2,000, and if an out-of-control situation is uncovered, it costs $3,000 to correct it. If the process is out of control, it stays out of control.

Table 22–1 gives the general form of the cost payoff matrix associated with a two-state two-action problem. Typically, the values will be of a small-enough magnitude so that the decision maker is willing to act on the basis of the expected values.[6] If so, the action with lowest expected cost is best. Table 22–2 shows the costs for the present example.

The expected cost of each action is obtained by multiplying the payoffs by their probabilities and summing across states. If we let the probabilities of the two states be given by p_1 and p_2, respectively, these expected costs are:

$$\text{expected cost } a_1 = Cp_1 + (C + M)p_2 = C + Mp_2 \qquad (22.1)$$

$$\text{expected cost } a_2 = 0p_1 + Lp_2 = Lp_2 \qquad (22.2)$$

Table 22–2   Specific Cost Payoff Matrix (Two-state form)

	States: s_j	
	s_1	s_2
Actions: a_i	In Control	Out of Control
a_1: Investigate	$2,000	$ 5,000
a_2: Do not investigate	0	$15,000

[6] This is even more likely to be a reasonable approach if the firm as a whole is considered. However, from the individual's point of view, a utility analysis may be relevant, and this produces a control problem. This is particularly likely to be the case if the cost-control procedures in use reward the manager in an asymmetric way. Furthermore, individual utility functions may be related to the size of the amounts with which the manager, rather than the firm, conventionally deals.

Under these assumptions the investigate action should be taken if its expected cost is less than the expected cost of not investigating; that is, investigate if

$$\text{expected cost of action } a_1 < \text{expected cost of action } a_2 \qquad (22.3)$$

Substituting, investigate if $C + Mp_2 < Lp_2$, or if

$$C - (L - M)p_2 < 0 \qquad (22.4)$$

For the specific example in Tables 22.1 and 22.2, suppose that $p_1 = 0.82$ and $p_2 = 0.18$; then inequality (22.4) gives

$$\$2,000 - \$12,000(0.18) = \$-160 < 0$$

and investigation is the optimal action if the information and assumptions are accepted as presented.

It is assumed, further, that the decision maker can establish the prior subjective probabilities over the states.[7] These probabilities are required to use inequality (22.4).

22.2.3 Break-even Probability

To avoid making the expected-value calculations each time a cost value is observed, the break-even probability that equates the two actions can be obtained. Inequality (22.4) gives

$$C - (L - M)p_2 < 0 \qquad (22.4)$$

If this expectation is less than zero, the activity is a candidate for investigation; if it exceeds zero, the activity is not. Setting the expectation given by inequality (22.4) equal to zero and solving gives

$$p_2 = \frac{C}{L - M} \qquad (22.5)$$

or alternatively, using p_1,

$$p_1 = 1 - \frac{C}{L - M} \qquad (22.6)$$

for the break-even value. Hence, if $p_1 < 1 - C/(L - M)$, an investigation should be undertaken; if $p_1 > 1 - C/(L - M)$, no investigation is called for (at equality, the manager is indifferent). For the specific problem introduced earlier, the break-even probability is $p_1 = 1 - 2,000/12,000 = 5/6 = 0.83$. This implies that investigation is the preferred action even in cases for which the

---

[7] This is perhaps a feasible task for someone familiar with the activity, since only two states are involved. One merely needs to define the probability of the two states. Care is necessary, however, to provide for changes that may have taken place in the process. This implies that the prior probabilities should be based on relevant historical information adjusted for differences from past conditions by someone knowledgeable about the activity.

probability of being in control exceeds 0.5, as long as it is less than 0.83. If $p_1 < 1 - C/(L - M)$, an investigation is signaled; otherwise, it is not. As soon as the probability of being in control drops below $1 - C/(L - M)$, an investigation should be undertaken. The larger the cost savings and the smaller the costs of investigation and correction, the larger is the break-even value. The break-even value is independent of the stage at which we look at the process, and is therefore relevant to all time periods.

22.3 Revising the Probabilities of the States

In Section 22.1.2 we indicated that the manager must be able to estimate the probabilities of the states in order to use the methods of decision theory to make cost investigation decisions. The manager then observes a cost (or cost variance) and, using his prior knowledge and the new cost observation, he must estimate revised probabilities for the states.

We shall assume that the process may, at some point in time, be in either the control state or the out-of-control state. A change from the in-control state to the out-of-control state may occur during any time period. The process is assumed to begin in the control state and that at some future period it may change to the out-of-control state. It then remains in this state for the remainder of the planning horizon. For simplicity the change is assumed to occur at the start of the period. Furthermore, it is assumed that the transition occurs, if at all, prior to obtaining the cost observation. The following new symbols will be used:

$x =$ observed cost level

$q =$ probability of a transition from the in-control to the out-of-control state at the start of the period and before observing x

$1 - q =$ probability of no transition from the control state

$_0p_1 =$ prior probability of being in control after transition (before observing x)

$_0p_2 =$ prior probability of being out of control after transition (before observing x)

$_1p_1 =$ revised probability of being in control after transition (after observing x)

$_1p_2 =$ revised probability of being out of control after transition (after observing x)

The pre-subscripts were not needed before but are now useful in distinguishing the prior probabilities of the states after transition and the state probabilities revised on the basis of the observed cost level x. The initial probabilities of the states are given by p_1 and p_2 as before. We begin this analysis by examining the transition process.

22.3.1 Transition Process

The transition process is diagrammed in Figure 22.3. Note that if the process is already in the out-of-control state, it remains there with probability 1. The assumption is made that the transition probability q remains constant from period to period.[8] If an out-of-control process would always be discovered in the period during which the transition took place, then the parameter q could be estimated from the fact that the mean number of periods before the process goes out of control is given by $1/q$. Although we assume that the investigation of an out-of-control process will always disclose this result, the approach adopted does not assume that such an investigation will always take place. Thus, to use the mean number of periods when an out-of-control process is discovered tends to underestimate q.

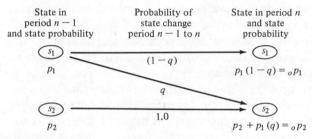

State in period $n - 1$ and state probability	Probability of state change period $n - 1$ to n	State in period n and state probability

Figure 22.3   The transition process.

If we assume for illustration that $q = 0.10$, and using $p_1 = 0.98$ and $p_2 = 0.02$, then

$$_0p_1 = 0.98(0.90) = 0.882$$

and there are two paths to being out of control

$$_0p_2 = 0.02 + 0.98(0.10) - 0.118$$

Since $_0p_1 > 0.83$, the critical probability, no revision is signaled yet.

22.3.2 Revision Process

We now turn to the actual revision process of the two prior probabilities, $_0p_1$ and $_0p_2$, based on the observed cost level, x. To do so we need to specify the form of the cost-observation distribution.

Assume that the cost-observation distributions in question are normal or

[8] The implications of a constant probability of transition to the out-of-control state is that the probability of moving to the out-of-control state n periods from the time the process starts is given by the geometric probability law to be

$$(1 - q)^{n-1}q$$

approximately normal with the probability *densities* $n(x \mid s_1)$ and $n(x \mid s_2)$.[9] The probability densities give the relative likelihoods of observing the given cost level x under the two possible states. In other words, they give the conditional probability of the cost observation dependent on the state. The symbol $E(x \mid s_j)$ represents the expected cost for the indicated state. This likelihood can be obtained from a table of the ordinates of the normal density function. This is illustrated in Figure 22.4. All the information needed to compute the revised probabilities is now available. The revised state probabilities can then be used to determine the expected cost from both actions (investigate and do not investigate) and thus provide a means for selecting between the two actions.

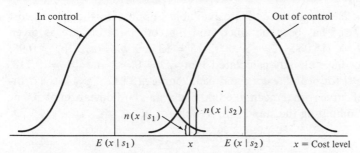

Figure 22.4 Normal cost observation distribution (two-state form).

In general terms, the process works as follows. First, the transition probabilities are applied to the estimated state probabilities from the last period, p_1 and p_2, to obtain the prior probabilities $_0p_1$ and $_0p_2$. Then a cost is observed and the prior probabilities are revised, by a method to be described shortly, to obtain $_1p_1$ and $_1p_2$. The revised value of $_1p_1$ is then used to make the investigation decision. If we investigate, the present analysis assumes that the cause of the variance is located and corrected and will not go out of control again over the planning horizon. If the investigation signal was in error, no cause will be detected, and $_1p_1$ becomes p_1 for the next period's transition and cost observation.

Suppose that a cost level, x, is observed that is more likely to occur when the process is out of control (see Figure 22.4). This observation decreases the probability of state s_1. If the probability attaching to state s_1 (being in control) is decreased enough, the expected cost from investigation is less than the expected cost from not investigating, and action a_1 is preferred.

The revision process is accomplished by using Bayes' Theorem. In the present context this theorem states that the revised probabilities of the two states are

$$_1p_1 = \frac{_0p_1[n(x \mid s_1)]}{_0p_1[n(x \mid s_1)] + _0p_2[n(x \mid s_2)]} \tag{22.7}$$

[9] If the observed cost is determined by a large set of independent additive factors, no one of which is dominant, these distributions may be approximately normal. When this is not the case, some attempt may be made to estimate the relevant distribution. The letter n in the notation $n(x \mid s_j)$ is used to indicate that the cost distributions are normal given state s_j.

and

$$_1p_2 = \frac{_0p_2[n(x \mid s_2)]}{_0p_1[n(x \mid s_1)] + _0p_2[n(x \mid s_2)]} \tag{22.8}$$

In order to use Bayes' Theorem, the conditional probability of the cost observation under each state is required. If the expectation and the variance of the cost observations are known for both the case in which the cost is in control and the case in which it is out of control, the data necessary to use Bayes' Theorem can be obtained.[10]

Example

Suppose that the facts in Table 22–3 are available. Suppose, further, that a cost observation of $7,125 has been obtained and that other factors are as given before. That is, $L =$ $15,000, $C =$ $2,000, $M =$ $3,000, $q =$ 0.10, $p_1 =$ 0.98, and $p_2 =$ 0.02. We have already calculated that $_0p_1 =$ 0.882 and $_0p_2 =$ 0.118. Now, using Table II for ordinates of the normal curve $n(\$7,125 \mid s_1)$ is the ordinate of the normal curve with a mean of 6,000 and a standard deviation of 500 at the point 7,125. Computing the standardized value, z, gives

$$z = \frac{7,125 - 6,000}{500} = 2.25$$

The ordinate at this point is 0.03174. Hence,

$$n(7,125 \mid s_1) = 0.03174$$

Similarly, given s_2 and $z = -.55$

$$n(7,125 \mid s_2) = 0.08628$$

Table 22–3 Cost Facts: Variance Analysis Problem

	General Situation		Specific Situation	
	s_1	s_2	s_1	s_2
Parameters	In Control	Out of Control	In Control	Out of Control
Expected cost observation	$E(x \mid s_1)$	$E(x \mid s_2)$	$6,000	$8,000
Standard deviation of cost observation	$\sigma(x \mid s_1)$	$\sigma(x \mid s_2)$	500*	500*

* Assumed to be independent of the state.

[10] It may be reasonable to assume that the variance remains unchanged whether the process is in control or not. This is assumed to be the case in this example.

Now revising, equation (21.7) yields

$$_1p_1 = \frac{0.882(0.03174)}{0.882(0.03174) + 0.118(0.08628)} = 0.73$$

and hence $_1p_2 = 0.27$.

Using the break-even probability of 0.83 calculated in Section 22.2.3, an investigation should be initiated since $_1p_1 = 0.73 < 0.83$. The conclusion depends on the priors, the observed cost, and the condition probability distributions.[11]

22.3.3 Relevance of Control Charts

Since a single observation may not trigger an investigation, and since successive observations may include observations that form a trend toward decreasing the revised probability of state s_1, it might be argued that it is reasonable to retain information about the sequence of information supplied by the cost observations. In other words, it could be maintained that a control-chart approach is relevant. Inspection of Figure 22.5 might suggest, for example, that even though the revised state probability has not yet dropped below the critical value, investigation may seem to be a reasonable action choice. This conclusion, however, is not valid from a Bayesian standpoint. The revision of probabilities using Bayes' Theorem gives the proper weight to the sample evidence and the prior probabilities if the conditional probabilities have been correctly estimated.

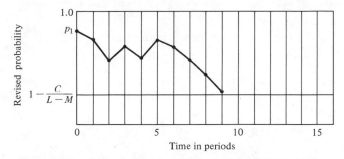

Figure 22.5 **Control chart for the revised probability of the state in control, s_1.**

22.4 Exploratory Investigations and the Value of Information

Suppose that a firm has a choice of conducting two levels of investigation. The first level of investigation might be essentially exploratory in nature.

---

[11] An easy complication is to introduce a probability that the process could also move from state s_2 to state s_1. However, realistic estimates of this number suggest that the complication is not worth the effort.

It would cost less than a full investigation, but it might not disclose the cause of an out-of-control situation. The exploratory investigation should be conducted if the expected benefits from this action exceed those from both waiting and those from a full investigation. The investigation decision will be discussed using the value of perfect information.

Suppose that perfect information were available concerning the actual state of the process at some (time) stage n. Then, if the state were s_1, no investigation would be undertaken with cost zero since it is known that the process is in control. This is expected to occur p_1 of the time. (Here p_1 is used as the probability of the state at the start of the period.) On the other hand, if the state were s_2, an investigation would be made with cost $C + M$ to find out the cause of being out of control and to lay the groundwork for correction. This occurs p_2 of the time. Thus, the expected cost with perfect information is given by

$$
\begin{aligned}
E &= 0(p_1) + (C + M)(p_2) \\
  &= (C + M)(p_2)
\end{aligned}
\tag{22.9}
$$

But without such information, the decision-maker's expected cost is the cost associated with the best action; this minimum cost is given by

$$
\text{Min} \begin{cases} C + M(p_2): & \text{investigate} \\ L(p_2): & \text{do not investigate} \end{cases}
\tag{22.10}
$$

Thus, the expected value of perfect information, call it E_p, and therefore the maximum value of processing additional information, is equal to the value obtained from equation (22.9) subtracted from the minimum of equation (22.10). This gives

$$
E_p = \begin{cases} C(1 - p_2) = C(p_1) & \text{if investigate is minimum} \\ (L - M - C)(p_2) & \text{if do-not-investigate is minimum} \end{cases}
\tag{22.11}
$$

For the specific problem introduced earlier and for period 1, assume that $C = \$2,000$, $L = \$15,000$, $M = \$3,000$, $p_1 = 0.73$, $p_2 = 0.27$, and $(L - M - C) = \$10,000$.

With perfect information the expected cost would be

$$
\begin{aligned}
E^* &= (C + M)(p_2) \\
    &= \$5,000 \times 0.27 = \$1,350
\end{aligned}
\tag{22.9}
$$

The expected cost without perfect information is

$$
\text{Min} \begin{cases} 2,000 + 3,000(0.27) = \$2,810: & \text{investigate} \\ 15,000(0.27) = \$4,050: & \text{do not investigate} \end{cases}
$$

The better decision is to investigate with an expected cost of $2,810. Since the investigate decision gives the minimum expected cost, the expected value of perfect information is

$$
E_p = C(p_1) = 2,000 \times 0.73 = \$1,460
$$

Table 22–4   **Expected Costs of Three Actions**

Case	Action	Expected Cost
a	Do not investigate	$L(p_2)$
b	Exploratory investigation	$C' + [L(1 - h) + hM](p_2)$
c	Full investigation	$C + M(p_2)$

or equivalently

$$E_p = \$2{,}810 - \$1{,}350 = \$1{,}460$$

Additional information is worth no more than the difference between the expected cost of the best action and the expected cost with perfect information. This difference is $1,460.

Assume now that the records required for an exploratory examination are being kept, that the cost of such an investigation is C', where $C' < C$, and the probability that the cause of an out-of-control situation will be discovered when it exists is h. The alternative of an exploratory investigation should be evaluated in terms of the expected cost associated with its use. The cost from the alternative of an exploratory investigation will amount to C' given state s_1, and $C' + Mh + L(1 - h)$ given state s_2 (where h is less than 1). The value h is the probability that an exploratory investigation will lead to the discovery (and thus correction) of an out-of-control situation when it exists. We note that such an investigation may be justified even if its cost exceeds the expected value of perfect information; that is, even if

$$C' > E_p \tag{22.12}$$

since perfect information still requires a cost C in the out-of-control state. In our example an h of 0.95 and a C' of $1,500 is sufficient to produce this result.

Three cases exist. The expected costs are given in Table 22.4. Setting case a equal to b and case b equal to c, two break-even probabilities, call them p_b and p_c can be determined. Typically, but not necessarily, p_b will exceed p_c. Using these break-even probabilities, the investigation decision can again be based on the probability p_1. The choices are illustrated in Figure 22.6.[12]

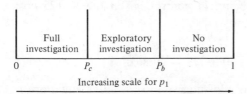

Figure 22.6   Investigation action choice using the revised probability of the in-control state.

[12] For the example here and assuming that $h = 0.4$ and $C' = \$200$, p_b is approximately 0.96 and p_c about 0.75.

Suppose that $p_c < p_1 < p_b$, so that an exploratory investigation is made. Assume that the investigation does not uncover any cause for the variance. The process may be either in or out of control at this point. However, before allowing the process to continue another period, the probabilities should be revised for any information provided by this investigation, and the full-investigation action should be compared to the action do not investigate. (This step need not be performed if the revision will increase p_1.)

These results bear directly on the extent of records to be maintained for control purposes. If $p_b < p_c$ for some process, a fact that may be ascertained in advance, an exploratory investigation will never be relevant and the necessary records to conduct one need not be kept. The likelihood of this situation increases as h decreases and as C' approaches C. The larger the difference $p_b - p_c$, the larger h and the lower C', the more value there will be to keeping the necessary records supporting an exploratory investigation.

22.5 Some Extensions

The next step would be to consider the cost-investigation problem when the state random variable is continuous rather than discrete. A second extension would examine multiple causes of cost variances, some, perhaps, uncontrollable. Further possibilities include relaxing the assumptions on the time interval between cost reports, introducing a lag between the investigation and the implementation of control, incorporating uncertainty into the cost estimates and the success of the control action, using dynamic programming as a solution technique, and developing techniques to estimate the transition probabilities. These tasks are considered by the authors to be important, but beyond the scope of this book.[13]

It is sometimes suggested that it may be necessary to make decisions on the basis of the sample information alone. The process of estimating the prior-state probabilities is felt to be too arbitrary and subjective. The procedure developed here can be used in this case where the probability of being in control is estimated by the relative likelihood of the cost observation under the two states. For example, the estimated probability of being in control, given the $7,125 cost observation, would be

$$_1p_1 = \frac{n(x \mid s_1)}{n(x \mid s_1) + n(x \mid s_2)} = \frac{0.03174}{0.03174 + 0.08628} = 0.27$$

The technique is equivalent (as the formula suggests) to assuming equal prior-state probabilities. The manager should realize this implicit assumption if he uses this approach.

---

[13] Many of these problems have not yet been resolved. For some insights on several, the reader should consult the Supplementary Reading for this chapter.

22.6 Summary

The problem of when to investigate a cost variance can be treated from a statistical decision-theory approach. This approach allows for the inclusion in the analysis of the costs from various actions and the subjective evaluations of the probabilities of the in-control and out-of-control states. The decision-theory approach can also be used to examine the value of information and hence the value of record keeping. The discussion extends to the value of exploratory investigations or other data-gathering systems.

A more complete solution, not attempted here, would consider the use of funds for control purposes together with other fund uses as part of the overall capital-budgeting cash-utilization problem. In such a formulation, the relevant planning period would probably differ from the cost-reporting period. The present solution also presumes an instantaneous adjustment by the firm.

A limited budget for investigation could be allocated by ordering those cost differences to be investigated in the order of the expected saving to be obtained from investigation. Since the cost of money is presumably incorporated into the computations as well as uncertainty, funds, ideally, should be made available to investigate any variance exceeding the critical ratio in equation (22.6). This is essentially part of the overall capital allocation problem of the firm for the period.

A major limitation of the analysis concerns the estimation of the relevant parameter values needed as inputs to the model. Of particular concern is the estimation of the savings, L, to be obtained from investigating an out-of-control situation. We have also simplified the analysis in several places, for example by assuming that a cost variance once investigated will lead to action that invariably places the process back in the control state, and it stays there. Extensions which allow for this assumption to be relaxed are contained in the Supplementary Reading to this chapter.

The attempt to examine the cost-variance investigation question from a decision-theory standpoint should lead to a more complete understanding of the more important variables (in terms of the sensitivity of the model to perturbations in the variables given their inherent variability) and their interactions even where the model's assumptions are not strictly met.

QUESTIONS AND PROBLEMS

22–1 Discuss the following questions. If a cost variance is investigated, will the cause of the variance be found? If the cause of the variance is found, will the situation be corrected? If the situation is corrected, is the firm better off because the investigation was conducted? If it is not investigated, will the variance continue in the future?

22-2 A process has an unfavorable variance reported of $7,600. It is estimated that these excess costs will continue if the process is allowed to continue without investigation and if the process is actually out of control. There is a 0.9 probability that the cause of the variance was a peculiarity of the one period and will not recur. This will be known at the end of the period if the variance does not recur. The cost of conducting an investigation is estimated to be $1,000, and the cost of correction is an additional $1,200. Assume that if there is something wrong, an investigation will reveal the problem and it will be corrected. If the variance is not corrected now, and if it recurs, it will be investigated next period.

Required: Should the investigation be conducted? Assume a zero time value of money.

22-3 The budgeted power cost is $20,000. The cost is budgeted at the expected amount when the process is in control. The expected cost when the process is out of control is $30,000. Management in charge of controlling the cost has indicated that there is equal likelihood of favorable and unfavorable variances and the standard deviation of the actual cost about the mean value is $6,000 for either state. Assume that the cost is normally distributed. The actual cost for January is $27,000 and the cost for February is $26,000.

Required:

a. Compute the number of standard deviations the January and February costs are from the mean amount for both the in-control and out-of-control cases.

b. Compute the probability of January's and February's costs being greater than $27,000 and $26,000, respectively, if the in-control state exists (if the cost fluctuations are caused by random factors).

c. Compute the probability density of each month's cost for both the case in which the process is in control and that in which it is not.

22-4 (Continuing problem 22-3.) Assume that the cost of investigation is estimated to be $4,000 and the cost of correcting is $1,000 for positive and negative variances. If the process stays out of control, the additional costs are estimated to be $7,000.

Required: If the manager initially believes it is equally likely the process is in or out of control:

a. Should the process be investigated at the end of January?

b. Should there be an investigation of the variance in February if the costs of no investigation and being out of control are again estimated to be $7,000?

c. Should there be an investigation in February if the costs of no investigation are estimated to be $6,500?

22-5 A process that is in control has an expected cost level of $100 with a standard deviation of $4. When the process is out of control, the expected cost level is $112 with a standard deviation also of $4. The manager estimates that the net present value of the future savings from investigating an out-of-control variance is equal to $43.25, a five-year annuity of $12 at 12%. The cost of investigation is $38.90 for each variance investigated. An investigation will always be successful and there is no correction cost.

Required:

a. Assuming equal initial subjective-state probabilities and normality, what cost level on any single observation should trigger an investigation? What assumption does this method implicitly make about the prior knowledge of the manager?

b. Suppose that equal probability is assigned to each state and assume that sample observations on the actual cost level can be obtained at a cost of .5 + 0.5n, where n is the number of observations. What is the maximum (not the optimal) number of observations that should be taken? Assume that no cost observations have been taken to date.

22–6 The classical statistical approach to problem 22–5, part a, would not specify the prior odds over the states. What problems does this raise? What prior knowledge about the states, if any, does it assume?

22–7 What can be done when the manager has very imprecise ideas about the prior-state probabilities?

22–8 Suppose that over time, the revised probability of the out-of-control state has consistently risen until it is nearly, but not quite, equal to the break-even value. Suppose that unless the next revision leads to either a decline in the value or an increase smaller than any previous increase, an investigation will be indicated. Need the decision maker wait for the next observation or would he be prudent to begin an investigation immediately?

22–9 Is anything gained or lost by accumulating several cost observations before revising the state probabilities?

22–10 Criticize the following statement: Simple decision models should not be relied upon since realistic situations are far too complex for such models to be useful.

22–11 Why is expected payoff a reasonable quantity to base decisions upon when magnitudes of all possible payoffs are relatively small?

22–12 How does a decision-theory approach to the problem of when to investigate cost variances improve upon the often-used control chart procedure?

22–13 What does it mean for a process to be in control?

22–14 The most recent cost report received by a manager of a toy company led him to estimate a 0.6 probability that the costs on a new line of preschool toys are out of control. From past experience with other preschool lines, the manager estimates that if the situation is as far out of control as the cost report suggests, the company could save the equivalent of about $1,000 per year for three years as a direct result of correcting the out-of-control situation. A full investigation to discover the source of the variance would cost $1,000, and it would take another $500 to correct the situation if the process is discovered to be out of control.

Required:

a. Assuming that the investigation cost would be incurred immediately and that the savings would occur at the end of each year, should an investigation be undertaken? Use a 0.10 rate of discount.

b. Find the out-of-control state probability such that the manager would be indifferent between investigating and not investigating.

22–15 The plant manager of How-Now Dairy Products noted a $1,500 unfavorable volume variance for the month of February. During January he had found and corrected a $1,000 unfavorable volume variance. Based upon past experience, the manager estimates that there is a 0.3 probability that the process will transit from in-control to out-of-control between two consecutive months.

Required:

a. Find the prior probabilities for the February control states.

b. Assuming that the reported variances from the in-control state are normally distributed with mean $500 and standard deviation $500 and that the observations from the out-of-control state are normally distributed with mean $2,000 and standard deviation $500, revise the state probabilities.

22–16 The cost of investigating a certain process is $1,000, and if it is out of control, the average correction cost is $500. The estimated present value of the savings associated with correcting a particular type of cost variance for this process is $5,000.

Required:

a. Graph the expected cost of each action as a function of $_1p_2$, the revised out-of-control state probability.

b. Find the break-even posterior probabilities.

c. Suppose that the actual $_1p_2$ for the period was 0.7 and that the probability of a transit from an in-control state to an out-of-control state is 0.25. Find the next period prior probabilities.

d. Do part c assuming that the actual $_1p_2$ was 0.2 instead of 0.7.

22–17 The revised probability that a process is in-control is 0.75.

Required:

a. If C is $100 and M is $50, how large must L be before an investigation is warranted?

b. If L is $2,000 and M is $500, what is the largest value of C for which an investigation is warranted?

c. If C is $500 and L is $5,000 how large can M be such that an investigation is still warranted?

d. Using the parameter values in part c with $M = \$2,000$, what is the maximum amount a firm should pay for additional information concerning the true state of the process?

e. Using the parameter values in part d, if h is 0.9 what is the maximum C' such that an exploratory investigation is justified?

22–18 A certain food processing firm regularly experiences unfavorable variance reports. Because of the nature of the business, many of the variances are owing to chance events and do not really indicate out-of-control situations. The plant manager feels that since a full investigation costs about $500, the firm could save a considerable amount of money by conducting exploratory investigations that would cost about $250. Past experience with one set of variances suggests that, on average, the cost of correction is $100 and the present value of the savings associated with correcting the situation is $1,000. Although an exploratory investigation is an attractive alternative, the manager knows that finding the causes of variances is a tricky job and that such an investigation would probably reveal the cause only half the time.

Required: Assume that the prior probability for the out-of-control state is 0.4 and that a variance of $800 is observed. What type of investigation should be undertaken if reported variances for the in-control state are normally distributed with mean 0 and standard deviation $500 and the out-of-control reported variances are normally distributed with mean $1,000 and the same standard deviation?

22–19 The following data apply to the past reports for a particular process:

Cost report—end of period 1	$300
Cost report—end of period 2	250
Cost report—end of period 3	400

Assume that if the process is in control, the reported cost is normally distributed with mean $200 and standard deviation $100. If the process is out of control, the reported cost is normally distributed with mean $500 and standard deviation $100. At the beginning of period 1 the process had just been corrected, and there is a 0.3 probability that a transition will be made from the in-control state to the out-of-control state between any two consecutive reports. The cost of conducting an investigation is $200 and the cost of correcting is $100. For this particular process, it is estimated that each out-of-control situation corrected results in a $500 saving at the present value.

Required: Construct a cost variance control chart with limits $\mu + 1.96\sigma$ and $\mu - 1.96\sigma$ for the 3 periods. Using this chart, what would have been the decisions for the three periods? Is this the same set of decisions that would have been made using a decision theory approach?

22–20 For a given process, the posterior probability of an out-of-control situation is $_1p_2$. The cost of a full investigation is $1,000 and the cost of correction is $200. The cost of an exploratory investigation, if undertaken, is $500 and there is a 0.8 probability it will determine that the process is out of control and at a cost of $200 eliminate the cause of the out-of-control situation. There is a 0.2 probability that the exploratory investigation will fail to determine that the process is out of control. The present value of the savings if the process is corrected is $2,000.

Required:

a. Graph the following functions of $_1p_2$ on the same axes and find the break-even probabilities:
  i. the expected cost of a full investigation,
  ii. the expected cost of an exploratory investigation,
  iii. the expected cost of not investigating.
b. Graph c' and E_p as functions of $_1p_2$.

SUPPLEMENTARY READING

BIERMAN, H., JR., L. E. FOURAKER, and R. K. JAEDICKE, "A Use of Probability and Statistics in Performance Evaluation," *The Accounting Review*, July 1961, pp. 409–417.

BIRNBERG, J. G., "Bayesian Statistics: A Review," *Journal of Accounting Research*, Spring 1964, pp. 108–116.

DEMSKI, J. S., "Optimizing the Search for Cost Deviation Sources," *Management Science*, April 1970, pp. 486–494.

DUNCAN, A., "The Economic Design of $\bar{x}$ Charts Used to Maintain Current Control of a Process," *Journal of the American Statistical Association*, June 1956, pp. 228–242.

———, "The Economic Design of $\bar{X}$-Charts When There Is a Multiplicity of Assignable Causes," *Journal of the American Statistical Association*, March 1971, pp. 107–121.

DUVALL, R. M., "Rules for Investigating Cost Variances," *Management Science*, June 1967, pp. 631–641.

DYCKMAN, T. R., "The Investigation of Cost Variances," *Journal of Accounting Research*, Fall 1969, pp. 215–244.

KAPLAN, R. S., "Optimal Investigation Strategies with Imperfect Information," *Journal of Accounting Research*, Spring 1969, pp. 32–43.

LEV, B., "An Information Theory Analysis of Budget Variances," *The Accounting Review*, October 1969, pp. 704–710.

LUH, F., "Controlled Cost: An Operational Concept and Statistical Approach to Standard Costing," *The Accounting Review*, January 1968, pp. 123–132.

MOCK, T., "Concepts of Information Value in Accounting," *The Accounting Review*, October 1971, pp. 765–778.

OZAN, T., and T. R. DYCKMAN, "A Normative Model for Investigation Decisions Involving Multi-Origin Cost Variances," *Journal of Accounting Research*, Spring 1971.

PRATT, J. W., H. RAIFFA, and R. SCHLAIFER, *Introduction to Statistical Decision Theory*, New York: McGraw-Hill Book Company, 1965.

RONAN, J., "Nonaggregation vs. Disaggregation of Variances," *The Accounting Review*, January 1974, pp. 50–60.

Chapter 23

Cost-Estimation Techniques

One of the more important elements in cost control is the determination of how costs change in relation to other measurable and controllable factors. The preparation of valid operating budgets, pricing decisions, establishing standard costs, developing performance reports, evaluating cost variances, and numerous other managerial activities often hinge on reliable cost estimates. The necessary estimates are frequently obtained through what might be called off-the-cuff or rule-of-thumb methods. These methods are at times somewhat formalized by the use of average data adjusted to reflect the plans of the organization and relevant economic or technological trends.

Lack of complete satisfaction with the results of such procedures, combined with the improvement in mathematical, engineering, and management methods, led to the development of several improved techniques for analyzing cost behavior. One of the more important techniques is represented by the application of industrial engineering methods, including efficiency, and time and motion studies, to the problem of estimating cost-behavior patterns. Such studies often involve an analysis of the underlying physical variables and conversion of the final results into cost estimates. The procedure works reasonably well for estimating the costs associated with direct materials, labor, and machine time. However, it is usually more difficult to estimate the costs of services, supervision, and the other indirect costs of operation. These cost factors may be common to several products or departments, and in addition there may be slack in one or more of the factors of production, allowing an increase in output without an increase in the factor's cost. Alternatively, a small increase in output may result in a large increase in costs. Further, because of indirect relationships with the activity levels of other departments, it may not be feasible to use the same engineering methods for estimating costs that are usually employed on direct or easily traceable costs.

In addition to engineering approaches, accountants also attempt to understand cost behavior through the analysis of historical and standard-cost data. The technique used concentrates on the fixed–variable cost distinction. Although this approach represents an improvement over *ad hoc* approaches, the fixed–variable approach makes several limiting assumptions that can substantially reduce the value of the subsequent analysis. First, the approach considers only one causal factor, typically an activity variable such as an output measure. Second, the technique assumes a linear relationship between output and cost at least over the relevant range. (Using the semivariable-cost concept, this limitation can be mitigated.) Third, cost predictions can be obtained, but the accuracy of these predictions is not known. Fourth, it tends to be insensitive to indirect cost allocations. Fifth, it relies heavily on the initial fixed–variable classification decision. Finally, even if the analysis is carried out for several periods, it is not clear whether the mean, the median, or some other summary cost statistic is the relevant measure.

One method in common use that illustrates these limitations is the *high–low method*.[1] Under this procedure two points are estimated. One of these represents estimated costs at the largest activity level anticipated; alternatively, it could be set at some percentage, say 20%, above the cost of a normal activity level. The other point represents a symmetrically placed point equally far below the normal level of activity. A straight line connecting the two points is then used to estimate costs for any activity level. The procedure is illustrated by the solid line in Figure 23.1. The method is quick and easily applied and may provide inexpensive and useful approximations in cases where costs are closely related to the variability

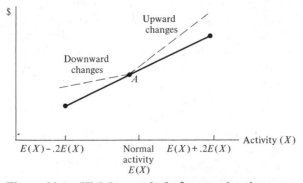

Figure 23.1   High-low method of cost estimation.

[1] The method was suggested to us by James Labick of Arthur Andersen & Co.

of a single activity measure. If costs exhibit sharper increases and smaller decreases as activity departs from the normal level at which the process is designed to operate, the dashed-line function in Figure 23.1 will give better estimates in the most likely region of operation, assuming that point A represents the present level of costs at the normal activity level. It is not unusual for costs to behave in this unsymmetrical pattern.

One technique that attempts to overcome some of the limitations inherent in the fixed–variable type of analysis involves the notions of multiple correlation and regression analysis. The statistical approach, it should be emphasized, is itself not free of limitations when applied in cost analysis and, for this reason, substantial attention is given to these limitations later in this chapter.[2]

In general, the dependent variable in the analysis is the cost of the activity being analyzed. Occasionally, a physical measure such as units of material or labor hours may be used if the costs are a known function of the physical measure. The independent variables may include output, batch size, number of employees, number of products or product variations, weather, and so on.

For example, suppose that the tasks performed in a service center consist of the repair and maintenance of several common business machines: typewriters, desk calculators, and adding machines.[3] The direct-labor costs of operating this department are considered by management to be a linear function of the time spent overhauling the various types of machines serviced during a given time period. Further, the overhaul time differs depending on the type of machine involved. In this example, labor hours rather than labor cost is the dependent variable. The independent variables are the number of machines of each type worked on in a week. Once a relationship has been established between the total hours worked and the hours required on each type of machine, total direct-labor costs may be estimated by multiplying each term by the associated labor rate.

Suppose that a linear relationship of the form

$$Y_i = b_0 + b_1 X_{1i} + b_2 X_{2i} + b_3 X_{3i} + U_i \qquad (23.1)$$

is assumed, where

Y_i = total direct labor hours in period i

b_0 = constant of regression (places height of plane)

b_1 = estimated overhaul time for a typewriter

X_{1i} = number of typewriters overhauled in period i

b_2 = estimated overhaul time for a desk calculator

---

[2] Some of the ideas in this section are developed further in G. J. Benston, "Multiple Regression Analysis of Cost Behavior," *The Accounting Review*, October 1966, pp. 657–672. See also J. Johnston, *Statistical Cost Control*, New York: McGraw-Hill Book Company, 1960; and R. Jensen, "Multiple Regression Models for Cost Control—Assumptions and Limitations," *The Accounting Review*, April 1967, pp. 265–272.

[3] This example may be found in P. R. McClenon, "Cost Finding Through Multiple Correlation Analysis," *The Accounting Review*, July 1963, pp. 540–547.

X_{2i} = number of desk calculators overhauled in period i

b_3 = estimated overhaul time for an adding machine

X_{3i} = number of adding machines overhauled in period i

U_i = disturbance term (incorporates the net effect of other factors) in period i

The weekly overhaul data in Table 23–1 are drawn at random from the last two years.[4,5] Before that time, this work was done by outsiders. Other conditions, including technical abilities, labor intensiveness, and so on, are assumed constant.

Table 23–1 Hours Worked by Week and Machine

Week	Typewriters Serviced	Calculators Serviced	Adding Machines Serviced	Total Hours
1	5	8	7	64
2	7	6	9	64
3	9	5	5	53
4	9	4	7	54
5	8	3	8	51
6	9	3	10	57
7	9	2	10	53
8	9	1	10	49
	65	32	66	445

The estimated regression based on these data is (see Appendix 23A for the general means of deriving a regression equation)

$$Y = 8 + 1.456X_1 + 4.016X_2 + 2.047X_3 \qquad (23.2)$$

The equation indicates that it takes 1.456 or about one and one-half hours on the average to overhaul a typewriter. This time differs substantially from that required for a calculator, and estimates of future costs should reflect the differences in repair activity to be undertaken by the service center. Care should also be taken to recognize the uncertainty in the estimates resulting from, for example, errors in measuring the dependent variable, hours.

Assuming that one wage rate applies to all employees, the direct-labor cost could be predicted by multiplying the estimated hours by the rate. If other variable costs in the department bear a constant relationship to the wage rate, total variable cost can be estimated using an estimate of total hours obtained

---

[4] Eight observations are used only to simplify the mathematics, in general much more of the available data would be used.

[5] The random selection may help reduce the serial correlation present, because the level of activity in a week is likely to be related to that in the previous and the following week.

from the equation. On the other hand, if wage rates differ and an average rate is not relevant, the direct-labor cost cannot be determined using equation (23.2). A new analysis that uses cost as the dependent variable may be required. Alternatively, a separate equation can be used for each type of labor.

The remainder of this chapter is subdivided into four sections. The first of these deals with the nature of the analysis and some of the fundamental data requirements needed to apply the mathematical correlation-regression model. The second major section examines the nonstatistical problems associated with implementing the analysis, and the third section discusses the inherent statistical difficulties. The fourth section discusses some issues in the use of statistical cost studies.

23.1   Nature of the Analysis

An early step in applying correlation-regression concepts to cost estimation is to think through the relationships between the variable to be predicted and the available independent variables. Typically, the dependent variable is related to the independent variables through some unit of association, such as output, input, or time. The concept of a unit of association is important because the validity of the regression equation and the numerical values emanating from the statistical analysis depend on the relevance and limitations that relate to the particular unit of association employed.

23.1.1   Unit of Association

Correlation-regression analysis may be adapted to either time series or cross-sectional data. Time-series data can be obtained from a single, stable process through time. Cross-sectional data are obtained from several homogeneous processes during a single time period. Because it is somewhat unusual for a firm to have a large enough number of homogeneous processes to provide sufficient cost data for cross-sectional analysis, time-series data will usually be more appropriate.[6,7] The example given in the previous section involves time-series data.

In time-series analysis the unit of association that connects the values of the dependent and independent variables is the time period. The time period is a convenient but not necessarily ideal unit of association from a theoretical point of view.[8] If, as may often be the case, decisions concerning the dependent

---

[6] The problems and procedures discussed in this chapter are relevant to time-series or cross-sectional data.

[7] Situations such as parallel production lines and associated service facilities may provide cases where cross-sectional analysis is appropriate. Care must be taken to assure that the range of observations is large enough to include the expected variation in future activity.

[8] The fact that accounting records are, almost without exception, kept on a time-period basis tends to lead to its use as the unit of association regardless of the underlying theoretical relationships.

variable (such as direct-labor cost) and the impact of the independent variables (such as direct-labor hours) are time-determined, then time is theoretically acceptable. On the other hand, the unit of association may, in fact, be output. In this case cost and labor hours are related because of output decisions, and using time as the unit of association could produce misleading results.

For example, the output of the period may be 100 units and the labor costs incurred during the period may be $500. But there may also be labor costs related to these same units incurred in other time periods. Correlating the labor costs with output on the basis of a common time period under these conditions would not provide a meaningful predictive relationship. A computation of equivalent units of work performed during the period might be helpful.

There is an implication here that is pervasive throughout all of applied statistical analysis. Knowledge about the process under investigation is indispensable to obtaining meaningful statistical results. Only when the manager and the statistician work jointly and understand and appreciate one another's expertise and relative contributions are useful results likely.

In the machine-overhaul example, a week's time period is the unit of association. This implicitly assumes that all costs associated with accomplishing repairs are incurred in the same time period as that used to tabulate the repairs. Alternatively, if the overhaul decision is related to previous machine usage or expected activity levels (and hence the need for repairs in the overhaul period), additional relationships can be developed that permit the value of the independent variables in equation (23.2) to be estimated with greater accuracy.

23.1.2 Length of the Time Period

The time period used to obtain measures of the dependent and independent variables must be long enough to permit the bookkeeping procedures to record accurately the associated costs, labor hours, and other factors needed in the analysis. For example, if cost data were recorded hourly, significant differences related to the time of day could occur. Leads and lags in recording can be particularly troublesome. For example, if a cost relevant to one period's activity (a bonus, for example) is recorded in a later period or if a cost relevant to several periods' activity is expensed in a single period (advertising is often treated this way), the resultant statistical relationships may turn out to be quite erroneous.

On the other hand, the time period must be short enough to avoid activity variations within the time period that tend to average out the very cost behavior that is of interest. One of the major uses of statistical analysis is prediction. To increase the opportunity for and accuracy of predictions, the data should cover as wide a range of activity as possible. This, too, suggests the value of short time periods, but what is a short time period depends on the activity under consideration and the environment in which the activity takes place.

The time period desired for predictive purposes can have an impact on the period used for recording purposes. The analysis of cost behavior should be one factor considered in the design of record-keeping procedures. Data lifted directly from cost records as normally maintained may lead to misleading results.[9] The manager must constantly examine the relevance of the data to his problem. Furthermore, to assure the relevance of the statistical techniques which rely on random-sampling techniques, the values of the unit of association should be selected randomly, as was done in the machine-overhead example.

23.1.3 Type of Analysis

Multiple correlation-regression analysis attempts to determine the constants involved in a functional relationship between a dependent variable and several independent variables. In general terms, such a relation can be written as

$$Y = f(X_1, X_2, X_3, \ldots, X_k)$$
$$= b_0 + b_1 X_1 + b_2 X_2 + \cdots + b_k X_k + U \tag{23.3}$$

Equation (23.1) is of this general form. The dependent variable, which may be cost, is written as a function of k factors, called independent variables. Rather than cost, the function could specify a relationship between output and several independent variables such as hours worked or machines used. This relationship formalized by equation (23.3) is called the regression equation. Determination of the regression coefficients, the b_j's, is the first task of the analysis. Sample observations are collected. Each sample includes a value for each of the independent variables and the dependent variable related by the unit of association. For the machine-overhaul example, the unit of association is the week, and each week provides one sample set of observations on each variable. The mathematical procedure by which the estimates of the b_j's are determined is called least-squares regression analysis and is described in Appendix 23A for the general case.[10] The resulting regression equation can be used to predict the values of the dependent variable, and hence cost, for given values of the independent variables.

A second task of correlation-regression analysis often involves estimating the reliability of the predictions. For this purpose several additional measures are required. These include estimates of the standard error of estimate, commonly written $S_{Y.12\cdots k}$, the standard errors of the regression coefficients, written S_j, and the estimated correlation coefficient, written R.

Rewriting equation (23.3), the more complete form of the mathematical expression for the example discussed earlier is given by

$$Y = 8 + 1.456X_1 + 4.016X_2 + 2.047X_3 \quad \text{(R)}$$
$$(S_1) \qquad (S_2) \qquad (S_3) \qquad (S_{Y.1,2,3}) \tag{23.4}$$

where the S_j are the standard errors of the regression coefficients, R is the

---

[9] The use of time periods as the unit of association can also lead to statistical difficulties which are discussed in Section 23.2.3.

[10] Other methods which minimize absolute rather than squared deviations also exist.

multiple correlation coefficient of the regression, and $S_{Y.1,2,3}$ is the standard error of estimate.

The use of a regression equation to predict values of the dependent variable and probabilistic statements concerning the error associated with any prediction depend on the validity of the assumptions of the model. In their strongest form, these assumptions are:

1. The expected value of the disturbance term, U_i is zero.
2. The dependent variable has constant variance regardless of the values of the independent variables.
3. The disturbance terms are not correlated.
4. The variation in the dependent variable results from the variation in the disturbance term (the independent variables are measured without error and hence only the dependent variable is a random variable).
5. The number of sample observations exceeds the number of parameters, b_j's, to be estimated.

The manager usually wishes to predict or estimate costs for specific values of the independent variables. He would prefer to construct the predictive relationship on the basis of observations of the dependent variable (say, cost or output) for specific values (say, of direct-labor hours and machine time) of the independent variable. Usually, however, he is unable to assign values to the independent variables and then observe the resultant cost. More often he will be using the available historical data. Moreover, he may not wish to discard past data merely because it does not represent the exact combinations of values for the independent variables that he expects to prevail in the future or that he would select to observe if conditions permitted. Relevant data are usually too scarce for this type of behavior.[11] When the independent variables and the dependent variable are the result of observation rather than predetermined, they are random variables and the assumptions of the analysis apply to the joint probability distributions of the dependent and independent variables rather than to just the conditional distribution of the independent variable.

Fortunately the same computations can be made under either set of assumptions. For example, the regression equation can be determined whether or not the independent variables are considered to be random variables. Furthermore (subject to certain limitations described later), predictions of the relevant cost levels can be made using the estimated relationship. When all variables are random variables, the correlation coefficient can be interpreted either as a measure of the strength of association or, in squared form, as the proportion of variation in the dependent variable explained by the independent variables used in the analysis. When only the dependent variable is random, the latter

---

[11] This does not mean that all historic data will be used. Unusual circumstances surrounding past data may lead to its rejection. For example, data from a period in which output was restricted due to a supplier's strike should be omitted.

interpretation applies. In the machine-overhaul example, values of the independent variables were not preselected; thus all variables are random variables.

If the second and third assumptions listed earlier hold, confidence intervals can be placed around the predicted value of the dependent variable.[12] This requires the value of the standard error. (Tests of the significance of the regression coefficients could also be conducted using their error measures, the S_j.) Thus, if the standard error of estimate $S_{Y.1,2,3}$ were 2.112, the manager could be 99% confident that in week 9, in which six typewriters, four calculators, and nine adding machines were overhauled, that the total number of hours, Y, would satisfy the relationship

$$43.223 - 2.58(2.112) \leq Y \leq 43.223 + 2.58(2.112)$$

or

$$37.774 \leq Y \leq 48.672$$

The value 43.223 is obtained first by solving equation (23.4) for $X_1 = 6$, $X_2 = 4$, and $X_3 = 9$. Then the intervals are obtained by adding and subtracting 2.58 standard deviation units. The value 2.58 is taken from Table I.

The correlation coefficient (assume it to be 0.9) indicates the closeness of the relation. One generally useful way to interpret it is to consider it in squared form. The coefficient of determination, as it is then called, indicates the percentage of the variability in total hours explained by the three independent variables used in the analysis. For the present case 81% of the variation in total hours is explained by the repair activity on three types of machines.

23.2 Problems in Applying Correlation-Regression Analysis

The problems in applying correlation-regression analysis can be examined under three headings:

1. Determining the relevant variables.
2. Specifying the form of the relationship.
3. Statistical difficulties.

23.2.1 Determining the Relevant Variables

The determination of the relevant cost-related factors is not an easy task. Variables may be overlooked because of a lack of recorded data on them. This

---

[12] The prediction can be considered as the average value of Y for the given X's or as a predicted individual value of it. The confidence interval depends upon which interpretation is relevant and is larger for individual estimates than for averages. The confidence interval given here and the one usually given applies (although it omits several terms usually quite small relative to the standard error) to an individual value.

fact makes it imperative that the accountant consult with those involved in the process before attempting to establish the relevant variables. Indeed, such discussion could lead to a decision to change the information processing system. An example of a variable that is often omitted from such studies is the external effect of an activity. For example, adequate maintenance and overhaul activity in one cost center may reduce repair costs of a second cost center because better-quality products produced by the first cost center cause less wear and tear on the equipment in the second cost center. Omission of a relevant variable can cause the regression equation to systematically over- or underpredict from period to period.

The relevant variables typically depend on the activities of a given cost center and may differ widely among cost centers. It is therefore important to properly associate cost with the relevant cost center. Failure to do so may not affect plant-wide relationships, but it can lead to poor decisions in the centers involved.

Determining the appropriate variables is a job for the manager, not the statistician alone. Only the manager can be expected to know, or seek out, the cause-and-effect relationships on which a convincing analysis can be based. Moreover, it is the joint responsibility of the manager and the statistician to assure that the variables are consistently defined over time and across reporting units.

Care must also be taken to ensure that basic changes in the environment, such as a substantial increase in the skills and abilities of the labor force, either did not occur over the period studied or are represented in some way in the relationship. The dummy-variable technique might be used for this purpose. This method uses an extra variable that takes on the value of 1 for an observation when the condition exists and zero otherwise. In the machine-overhaul example, a change in the type of calculator used could drastically alter the associated overhaul time. The change in calculator type could be represented by a dummy variable, by a separate independent variable for the new machine, or a different equation might be used.

Specification of the relevant variables must be accompanied by specification of the crucial variables. Invalid relations can result from the omission of a key variable, but it is usually both impossible and undesirable to attempt to incorporate all the cost-influencing factors into a single analysis.[13] Continuing relationships should be given particular attention, since it is easy to assume incorrectly that no substantive changes in the relevant variables have occurred, and thus the existing relationship is retained. Such may not be the case, however. For example, it may be that a previously near-constant factor, for example an input price, is now subject to substantial variation. If the cost of this factor were either omitted from the initial equation, or, alternatively, included as one of the independent variables in the relationship and if, for example, high input

---

[13] Relevant variables that show no significant correlation with the independent variable may be dropped. Either they lack sufficient variability or their effect is subsumed by other variables.

prices are associated with high activity, then the actual relationship between physical input activity and output cost would be obscured if the previous relation were continued. Changing the type of calculator used or the overhaul procedure could produce similar effects in the machine-overhaul example.

One possible means of allowing for changes of this kind would be to include a new variable to reflect the influence of the change in this factor. This alone would not be completely satisfactory for the price example because of the problems of multicollinearity created by the relationship between high input prices and high physical input activity as measured by another independent variable, that is, high activity might be generally accompanied by higher input prices. Multicollinearity makes it harder to estimate the effect attributable to the added variable. An alternative means of dealing with price factors is to use monetary measures for the variables involved and deflate them using a suitable price index. The interpretation of the results differs, however, depending on which approach is used. If, as is often the case, there is a desire to examine the effects of the price factor separately, or to use physical input measures, or unadjusted monetary measures, there is reason to adopt the first approach or a variant of it.

Since time is often the unit of association, attention should be given to influences that occur in various time periods. Perhaps the most common potentially cost-influencing factor associated with different calendar periods is the weather. This factor can be incorporated into the analysis using the dummy-variable method. Accomplishing this task may mean looking outside the firm's information system for relevant data, and this should be encouraged. Other examples of time-dependent variables involve seasonal factors such as holiday-season influences on production activity. Thus, overhaul activity may be high in periods of otherwise slack activity.

A sharp change in activity is one result that may accompany seasonal patterns but which is also a function of other factors, such as strikes and maintenance policy. It is often the case that cost behavior is asymmetric to large increases and decreases in activity (being sluggish on the downside), and this should be recognized, if costs are to be adequately estimated, again perhaps through the use of a dummy-variable or by a separate relationship for each type of period.

23.2.2 Specifying the Form of the Relationship

Cost relationships are not smooth, well-defined functions. Usually several functional forms fit the data equally well. Relationships are continuously undergoing change, and observations of these relationships are subject to multiple measurement errors. Relationships may also change over time either as a result of changes in economic conditions, technology, or learning (see Chapter 10). Such factors need to be considered in any attempt to forecast cost behavior. It is assumed in this chapter (perhaps unrealistically) that learning is not an important variable.

Under these conditions what is known about the underlying technological or economic basis of the relationship is critical. The manager (with expert assistance) is the one to provide this information, not the accountant or the statistician. Typically, the simplest relationship consistent with the theoretically determined cost-behavior pattern would be selected. In the final analysis, however, it is not whether the relationship selected perfectly represents the actual situation but whether it yields useful results, that is critical.

Relationships can often be transformed in order to make them easier to use. Logarithmic (the logarithms of the variable values are used) and square-root (the square roots of variable values are used) transformations represent just two of several possibilities. For example, a multiplicative cost relationship of the form $Y = b_0 X_1^{b_1} X_2^{b_2}$ which assumes that the effect of one independent variable depends on the level of the other, is transformed into the linear expression $\log Y = \log b_0 + b_1 \log X_1 + b_2 \log X_2$ by taking logs.[14]

The traditional regression equation, and the one discussed here, is obtained by finding the equation that minimizes the squared residuals. The implicit assumption is that the importance of the estimation error is a function of the squared prediction error. There is no implicit reason why it should necessarily be the case that doubling the prediction error quadruples the effect of that error. It is possible, for example, that the absolute errors better reflect the importance of the estimation error to the manager. If so, techniques that minimize absolute errors should be used. In some cases the fact that the necessary computer programs do not exist can prevent a more appropriate analysis. The manager must then hope the approximation achieved is adequate.

23.2.3 Statistical Problems

Any formal statistical analysis involves assumptions, and the impact of the failure of these assumptions to be fulfilled on any probabilistic statements made constitutes the subject matter of this subsection. The least-squares method of fitting an equation that is used to predict cost behavior can, however, be used to make predictions even though probabilistic statements may not be appropriate.

Several problem areas are explored here, including:

1. Measurement errors.
2. Correlations among the explanatory variables and between the disturbance term and the explanatory variables.
3. The distribution of nonspecified factors as they are reflected in the error term.

[14] Transformations are typically accompanied by implicit assumptions concerning the form of underlying probability laws and hence have important implications for any probabilistic statements made. For example, if a logarithmic transformation is made and, say, confidence-interval statements are to be made concerning predicted cost levels, the assumption must be made that the conditional probability laws (if regression analysis is relevant, or the joint probability laws if correlation analysis is called for) are log normal rather than normal in the untransformed values.

Measurement Errors

Errors in measurement can occur in either the dependent or independent variables. Errors in the latter are more critical when traditional least-squares techniques are used.

Independent measurement errors in the dependent variable only increase the disturbance term (assuming a linear relationship, at least after transformation). The increase in the error term means an increase in the standard error of estimate, and simultaneously a decrease in the correlation coefficients. The regression coefficients, the b_i, themselves are unbiased when measurement errors in the dependent variable exist. Measurement errors in the machine-overhaul example are most likely to be of this type.

Measurement errors in the independent variables are more serious. Such errors result in the disturbance term being correlated with the particular variable or variables to which the errors relate. Unfortunately, shorter time periods, which seem to be desirable for several reasons stated earlier, tend to increase the chance of this kind of measurement error. This may happen, for example, by recording an event or the measurement of the event in a period other than the one in which the related cost was recorded. Measurement errors in the independent variables are unlikely in the machine-overhaul example.

If the error is constant and a linear functional relationship holds, the effect is entirely on the constant term and is thus of minimal interest. Errors in the independent variable that cannot be considered in this or a similar fashion result in underestimates of the regression-slope coefficients involved. This is one reason that "activity" measures are often preferred to "cost" measures for the independent variables. Furthermore, the larger the relative measurement error, the larger the understatement and the bias does not disappear as the sample size increases. (The estimators are inconsistent.)

Least-squares predictions are, however, still appropriate because the statistical estimation process allows for the mistatements in the slope coefficients. Thus, measurement errors do not upset cost predictions, which is helpful, but they do prevent us from obtaining unbiased estimates of the effects of each independent variable as indicated by the slope coefficient. Johnston in his book on econometric methods (1972) discusses several methods of dealing with this problem.

Correlations Among the Explanatory Variables

The existence of correlations among the independent variables (or multicollinearity) makes it difficult to separate the effect of these variables. The production of two complementary products where the output of each is treated as an independent variable provides an example. Intercorrelation does not affect the validity of the predictions of the dependent variable provided that it is expected to continue in the future. However, the regression coefficients can no longer be used to estimate the marginal change in the dependent variable for a unit change in given independent variables holding the other independent variables constant. This is true because the lack of independence among the independent variables prevents the availability of sufficient information to determine the regression coefficients. Intercorrelation also causes an increase in the standard errors of the regression coefficients. This situation is especially likely to be a serious problem in cost-behavior studies, since several of the independent variables often move together; they exhibit near constant ratios.

In the machine-overhaul example, estimates of the regression coefficients are possible because the work was done in different ratios. Suppose, instead that there was a constant ratio (2-1-3) of the time required on the three types of machines. That is, if it took 6 hours in a given week to overhaul a typewriter, it would take 3 hours to overhaul a calculator and 9 hours for an adding machine.

The independent variables now move together. Activity on each is high at the same time and low at the same time. The independent variables are all perfectly correlated, and the estimated standard error, $S_{Y.12\cdots k}$, and the standard errors of the regression coefficients, the S_j, will be infinite, implying low reliability for the individual regression coefficients. Estimates can still be made of the total hours associated with overhauling combinations of two typewriters, one calculator, and three adding machines in a given time period if the intercorrelations are not perfect, but the estimates of the regression coefficients will have unnecessarily large standard errors.

This example is an extreme one, but it serves to suggest the problem whenever two or more of the independent variables are correlated. The situation is most common in cost centers with a relatively stable activity mix regardless of changes in total activity. Fortunately, most computer programs provide the correlations among the variables so that the problem can be recognized at that stage even if it is not expected on the basis of knowledge concerning the process.

Several means of dealing with this situation exist. Activities being examined that involve intercorrelation might be broken into subactivities that are analyzed separately. The accounting function can be of substantive assistance here. Another alternative is to find a common measure into which the intercorrelated variables can be converted. An example might be labor hours. Thus, the physical output of two or more difficult activities can in this way be converted to a single output measure. The resultant relationship measures the collective impact of a set of activities on cost.

The accountant can also be helpful in the process of cost allocation, and his subjective decisions are important. It is not whether judgment will be used but whether the judgments that must be made will increase or decrease the value of the output from the decision model.

Assumptions Concerning the Disturbance Term

When time is used as the unit of association, there is a danger that successive observations will be dependent. The cost (or time required) of some activity in period n is likely to be related to the cost (or time required) in period $n - 1$. This situation produces serial correlation among the disturbance terms. Serial correlation does not bias the regression coefficients, but it causes serious problems in using the standard error and the standard errors of the regression coefficients. Under the assumptions of the model, probability statements concerning deviations from the regression line should be independent of the unit of association, usually the time period for the particular observation, in cost studies. When serial correlation exists, this is not true. The problem can be handled using the generalized least-squares technique if we have some knowledge of how autocorrelation affects the disturbance term. A description of this technique is beyond the scope of this text.

The tendency for costs to be sticky when activity declines is one cause of serial correlation. Expanding activity often leads to increased employment of men and machines. When activity ceases to expand or declines, these factors of production are not easily reduced to reflect the new levels. A period's cost is heavily influenced by the level of cost in the previous period. Using a dummy variable to represent production changes (or regressing cost changes on output) could alleviate this problem.

A plot of the data may reveal serial correlation if the time of each observation is included with the point. The Durbin–Watson statistic can also be used to test for serial correlation. The value of this statistic is a common output to many regression computer programs. [See Durbin and Watson (1950–1951), Theil and Nagar (1961), or Johnston (1972) in the references.] Here, again, the manager should consider the activity and determine logically whether serial correlation is likely to be inherent to the data. If so, he should attempt either to avoid it or, at least, to recognize the limitations to the methodology caused by its presence. In terms of the machine-overhaul example, the presence of serial correlation prevents management from making valid probabilistic statements concerning estimated costs but it does not prevent predictions.

Resort is sometimes successfully made to first differences to avoid the problem of serial correlation. A problem is that measurement errors are magnified and hence the problems associated with these errors are more severe. A second problem arises if the disturbance term is not independent from one or more of the explanatory variables. Such situations are not uncommon in cost studies and typically arise from bookkeeping procedures. For example, if repairs are not considered as an independent variable and if they are typically made when the activity of one or more of the independent variables is low, then a negative correlation between these variables and the disturbance term will exist. Under this condition the regression coefficients are biased.

Another statistical limitation concerns the assumption of normality for the distribution of the disturbance term. The use of the normal probability law to make probabilistic statements is conditional on this assumption of normality. Perhaps it is more appropriate to state that the distribution of the disturbance term should be "close enough" to normal. If reasons exist for suspecting non-normality or statistical tests suggest that normality is doubtful, probability statements concerning the analysis should be made with caution. It is important to observe that transformations of the variables also affect the disturbance term and it is the distribution of the transformed variable that is relevant.

The estimation technique used in nearly all cases assumes further that the variance of the distribution of the disturbance term is constant over the range of values for the variables. In other words, the variance of the disturbance term is assumed to be independent of the dependent and of the independent variables. This situation is known as homoscedasticity (nonconstant variance is called heteroscedasticity). When this is not the case, that is, when heteroscedasticity exists, the standard errors of the regression coefficients are not correctly estimated. Furthermore, the standard error is a function of the level of the independent variables causing probability statements to be inaccurate.

Heteroscedasticity is difficult to test for, since a large number of observations is required. Again, resort may be made to a nonempirical analysis. For example, accounting data are likely to exhibit heteroscedasticity if the activity range is large, since at higher activity levels higher costs with inherently more room for variability are present. Numerically, if enough observations are available, heteroscedasticity may be indicated by plotting the squared differences between the estimated value from the regression line and the actual observation to determine if there is a relationship between the variability and the activity level. The existence of heteroscedasticity is usually countered by using logs of the data, square roots, or other transformations.

Most practical problems encounter several of the limitations discussed above. Unfortunately, although the impact of each separate problem can be inferred, it is not possible to infer the joint result of several violations of the simple regression model. The separate effects cannot be summed. Econometrics is presently struggling with the difficulties of simultaneous model violations.

23.3 Problems in the Use of Statistical Cost Studies

The early stages of cost-behavior studies are often characterized by a search for relationships using both what is presumed to be known about the situation and by working with the available historical data. Variables are plotted against one another, and possible forms for meaningful relationships are examined. From this work hypotheses emerge concerning the relevant variables and the functional form of the relationship. Such hypotheses should be confirmed using new data. But new data are generally not available. One way to circumvent this problem is to develop the hypotheses from a randomly selected subset of the available historical data. These hypotheses could be tested using the remaining data. Once the final relationships are established, all the relevant data should be used to estimate the statistical parameters. Anticipated changes in the environment must be considered in light of their impact on the relevant data to be used.

The interpretation of the results of the cost-behavior analysis are much the same as those for any other statistical analysis of this type. The slope coefficients, which measure the marginal impact on cost of a unit change in the independent variable, are useful only for recurring decisions in which the future can be assumed to be like the past (unless a means for incorporating additional information is appended). Furthermore, for predictive purposes an independent variable is useful only if it can be measured more easily than the dependent variable that it is supposedly being used to predict.

The slope coefficients in a cost-behavior study measure the change in the average cost for a unit change in the independent variable. If a correlation analysis is relevant, they also give the average change in cost per unit change in the independent variable.[15]

The functional relationship should be used for prediction with caution. Two types of predictions are important—those that extrapolate the relationship and those that interpolate from the relationship. Generally, predictions based on extrapolating the relationship outside the range of data points studied can be made only when the functional form of the relationship is well established by theory, and the general magnitude of the parameters can be verified from other studies. One of the problems, especially when several independent variables exist, is that the range of data is difficult to determine. Thus, a given prediction may involve values of two independent variables within the observed range of each taken alone, but not within their joint range of occurrence.

The problem of extrapolation extends immediately to the constant term. Unless the comments on the known form of the relationship are valid, the constant term should not be viewed as a measure of cost at a zero activity level, fixed cost. Typically, there are no data points for all variables at zero levels simultaneously.

Interpolation, which is more common, may also be questionable in given circumstances. First, there is the question of whether the joint values of the independent variables result in interpolation or extrapolation. Second, there is the question of the validity of the interpolation. For example, if a product is typically made in batches of say 1,000 and if the functional relationship is derived thereon, it may not lead to useful predictions involving odd-lot batches that require special handling of other processing costs.

Equation (23.3) is valid only for the range of data used to estimate the parameters in it. Thus, if the cost for overhauling nine typewriters, eight calculators, and ten adding machines in one week is desired, the relationship expressed by equation (23.3) may not be useful. Each of these activity levels has been experienced individually, but the three have not been experienced

---

[15] The importance of each independent variable depends on the regression coefficient and the variability of that variable. The beta coefficients can be used to establish the relative importance of the independent variables. The beta coefficient for a particular variable can be obtained by multiplying the regression coefficient for that variable by the ratio of the standard deviation for that variable to the standard deviation of the dependent variable.

concurrently. Thus, the suggested level of activity might require substantial over-time, or it might disrupt normal operating activity in some way. The point is that care should be taken in extrapolation and interpolation using such relationships.

In general, if it can be assumed that the relationships hold not only for the data points used to derive them but also for the new ones being examined, then predictions can be made. Probability statements, in turn, can be made if the statistical assumptions underlying the methodology and discussed above are also met. Nevertheless, sometimes predictions are required when one is not certain of the validity of the assumptions. In such cases it is often necessary to forge ahead. It is important to remember, however, the tenuous nature of these necessary decisions.

Multiple regression and correlation analysis is not generally used in cost-behavior studies. In part this also results from the general distrust of statistical methods not widely understood and often misused. For these and perhaps other reasons, it is difficult to get management to use the technique.

And yet the more meaningful data that this technique can yield coupled with the existence of ready-made computer programs to handle the input data quickly and relatively cheaply should provide strong arguments in its favor. Nevertheless, the marginal cost of obtaining the data and the predictions desired (including the opportunity costs of delay) must not exceed the marginal benefits from in-creased revenues or reduced costs achieved through improved decisions.

Finally, the accountant should be sure that he collects data relevant to implementing such procedures. The final form of the functional relation is only as good as the data used to derive it. The accountant's role in cost-behavior studies is a central and critical one to their success.

23.4 Exponential Smoothing

A simple technique for forecasting is called *exponential smoothing*. In this approach the forecast is based on two values: (1) the most recent value observed, and (2) the (exponentially smoothed) weighted average calculated in the prior period. The formula for the new weighted average is

$$A_i = \alpha X + (1 - \alpha)A_{i-1} \qquad (23.5)$$

where

X = most recent observation

A_i = (exponentially smoothed) weighted average in period i

$0 \leq \alpha \leq 1$ is the smoothing constant

Previous values of X are all included in the A_{i-1} term. Substitution will show that in period i, the $i - r$ value of X is multiplied by the factor $\alpha(1 - \alpha)^r$ where r is the measure of the time before i:

$$A_i = \alpha X + \alpha(1 - \alpha)X_{-1} + \alpha(1 - \alpha)^2 X_{-2} + \cdots \qquad (23.6)$$

The result of the technique is to give older observations less and less importance in determining the new average. The importance of the most recent observation to past observations in the average is determined by the value of the smoothing constant, α. The smaller this value is, the less weight the most recent observation carries in the determination of the new average.

Assume, for example, a set of values over the past of 100, 110, 125, 125, and 125 and a smoothing constant of 0.5. Then we find:

Period	X	A_{i-1}	A_i
1	100	—	100
2	110	100	105
3	125	105	115
4	125	115	120
5	125	120	122.5

As actual cost levels increase, so does the revised average, but it continually lags behind. The larger α, 0.5 here, the faster the series catches up but, also, the more sensitive it is to recent changes in the cost being estimated.

In most demand-prediction models, where exponential smoothing has received its major applications, α has been set below 0.1. In cost estimation this may or may not be appropriate. Equation (23.6) can be used with historical data to estimate α.

If there are no trend or seasonal factors to be considered, then our estimate for the next (or any future) period is given by A_i as determined from equation (23.5). But the method is also powerful enough to allow for adjustments when a trend is present or when a seasonal pattern is present or both.

When a trend is present in the data, the result obtained using equation (23.5) will lag too far behind. We need an exponentially smoothed estimate of the trend as a prediction base, since an exponentially smoothed estimate is appropriate to apply to exponentially smoothed data, the A_{i-i}. Such an estimate, call it b_i, is provided by

$$b_i = \alpha(A_i - A_{i-1}) + (1 - \alpha)b_{i-1} \tag{23.7}$$

Using b_i from equation (23.7) and some mathematics not reproduced here, the forecast for the next period is given by

$$A_i + \frac{1 - \alpha}{\alpha} b_i + b_i \tag{23.8}$$

or for any period s time periods ahead by

$$A_{i+s} = A_i + \frac{1 - \alpha}{\alpha} b_i + sb_i \tag{23.9}$$

Exponential smoothing is a relatively easy technique to use, and it is much less costly than regression analysis. However, it makes no attempt to get at the underlying causal relationships involved. Predictions can be made, but confidence intervals are not generally justified. Further, it is not possible to separate out the individual effects of the variables which underlie cost behavior. The method is most valuable in relatively less important problems, where quick and relatively cheap predictions are adequate.

23.5   Summary

Multiple correlation-regression analysis provides an important and powerful technique for estimating and predicting costs. If the proper assumptions are valid, probability statements can also be attached to predicted cost levels. Moreover, the sensitivity of the predictions to errors in estimation can be investigated.

The technique is subject to several limitations resulting from errors in the data and the techniques presently used by accountants to record cost information. The effects of these limitations on the estimating equation and the cost predictions should be borne in mind both in the design and in the use of cost-information systems. The more important cost predictions are, the more attention should be given to the length of the time period used to record costs, the establishment of cost centers, the assignment of costs to periods and centers, and so on.

The methods described are only as effective as the model and the data. For this reason it is imperative that the managers and the statisticians work with the accountant if they are to avoid applying highly sophisticated techniques to relatively naive data.

APPENDIX 23A
GENERAL LINEAR REGRESSION MODEL

The material in this appendix assumes that the reader knows matrix algebra.[16] If n observations are available on each of k variables, n equations can be written of the form

$$Y_i = b_0 + b_1 X_{1i} + b_2 X_{2i} + \cdots + b_k X_{ki} + U_i \qquad i = 1, 2, \ldots, n \qquad \text{(23A.1)}$$

where U_i represents a disturbance term to allow for the variables explicitly omitted from (23A.1). Using matrix notation,

$$Y = XB + U \qquad \text{(23A.2)}$$

where

$\quad Y = n$ by 1 column vector of the n observations on the dependent variable

$\quad X = n$ by k matrix of the n observations on each of k independent variables

$\quad B = k$ by 1 column vector of the unknown coefficients

$\quad U = n$ by 1 column vector of the disturbances

---

[16] For a discussion of the matrix algebra necessary to understand the development in this appendix, see J. Johnston, *Econometric Methods*, New York: McGraw-Hill Book Company, 1972.

What is desired are estimates of the b_j, $j = 1, 2, \ldots, k$. Assume that[17]

1. The expectation of the disturbance term is zero for all i, $E(U) = 0$.
2. The dependent variable has constant variance regardless of the associated set of values for the independent variables.
3. The disturbance terms are pairwise uncorrelated.
4. The source of variation in repeated observations results only from variation in the disturbance term (the independent variables are measured without error).
5. The number of observations exceeds the number of parameters to be estimated.

Then an estimate of Y is given by

$$\hat{Y} = X\hat{B} \tag{23A.3}$$

where $\hat{B}$ is a column vector of estimates of the b_j. The estimated errors are given by

$$Y - \hat{Y} = Y - X\hat{B} \tag{23A.4}$$

The least-squares technique minimizes the sum of the squared residuals. Since the residuals are given by equation (23A.4), the sum of the squared residuals is given by

$$(Y - X\hat{B})'(Y - X\hat{B}) \tag{23A.5}$$

where the prime indicates the transposed matrix. Multiplying out and taking the partial derivative with respect to $\hat{B}$ to minimize equation (23A.5) gives

$$-2X'Y + 2X'X\hat{B} \tag{23A.6}$$

Setting this result equal to zero and solving gives[18]

$$\hat{B} = (X'X)^{-1}X'Y \tag{23A.7}$$

where the exponent -1 indicates the inverse matrix. The values of the b_j appearing in equation (23.2) are derived using equation (23A.7), where the X matrix consists of the second, third, and fourth columns of Table 23–1, and the Y-column vector is the last column of Table 23–1.

QUESTIONS AND PROBLEMS

23–1 For what purpose might an organization want to know how costs react to changes in the level of activity?

---

[17] Under certain conditions, these assumptions may be relaxed in part without violence to the method.

[18] The computation of an inverse is illustrated in Johnston, *ibid*.

23–2 Suppose that the true unit of association between cost and labor input measured by direct-labor hours is the output level decision. Why might a misleading relationship result if time were used as the unit of association?

23–3 Cost and related data that might be used in a multiple correlation-regression analysis are available for given-length time periods. Usually these time periods are established for purposes other than cost analysis (tax purposes, for example). What problems can be encountered because of the failure to consider the analysis function in the design of the firm's information system?

23–4 The accompanying graphs illustrate three different cost–volume relationship. Assume that the diagonal lines represent the least-squares regression line

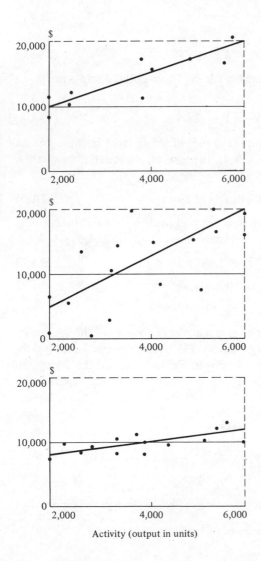

Activity (output in units)

determined mathematically from the underlying data in each case. Note that the data range from activity levels of from about 2,000 to 6,000 units.

    a. Using the top graph, what might the manager estimate fixed costs to be? Would you be satisfied with his estimate? Why?

    b. In which of the three cases does a change in activity have the greatest impact on cost?

    c. In which case does the relationship permit the smallest error in prediction? What does this suggest about the value of the analysis?

    d. In which case is cost most closely related to changes in output? Defend your choice.

23–5 Consider the inventory-control model, which leads to the following formula for the economic order quantity:

$$EOQ = \sqrt{\frac{2DP}{S}}$$

where

$$EOQ = \text{economic order quantity}$$

$$D = \text{annual quantity used in units}$$

$$P = \text{cost of placing an order}$$

$$S = \text{annual cost of storing one unit}$$

    What portion of the data necessary to estimate the relevant future values needed to use this model is available in the accounting records or in the firm's records in general? How is correlation-regression analysis relevant to the problem of determining the EOQ?

23–6 In the machine-overhaul example discussed in this chapter, suppose that during a week in July of a given past year one half of the calculators were replaced by a new and more complex type of machine. What should be done at the time of installation and now to assure a more meaningful cost analysis? Are there any special factors that might need consideration?

23–7 Supposing that a correlation-regression analysis in a service department uses two independent variables, namely, direct-labor hours and dollar value of materials. What effects on the estimates of future cost levels (the dependent variable) might be expected?

23–8 In a given cost analysis, data were gathered for each bimonthly period over the last four years. Plotting all the data available suggested a relationship between the activity and total employment that gave a very close estimate of total activity. On the basis of this preliminary investigation, the organization hypothesized that cost was a function of the total employment level and used that data for the previous four years to test the hypothesis. What conclusion concerning the hypothesis do you suppose they reached? What comments can you make concerning their methodology?

23–9 Three independent variables are used in a correlation-regression analysis. The ranges of observations on each are as follows:

$$X_1: 15 - 83 \qquad X_2: 25 - 52 \qquad X_3: 6 - 11$$

a. Assuming that each independent variable has the same regression coefficient, which one is most important in explaining changes in the dependent activity variable?
b. Would it be appropriate to use the regression equation to predict the activity level for values of $X_1 = 70$, $X_2 = 50$, and $X_3 = 10$?

23–10 If the regression equation for two independent variables and one dependent has the form

$$C = 20 + 4X_1 + 2X_2$$

where

$$C = \text{weekly cost for the activity}$$

$$X_1 = \text{direct-labor hours/week}$$

$$X_2 = \text{number of orders processed/week}$$

$$S_{c.12} = 5 \text{ (standard error of estimate)}$$

$$S_c = 6 \text{ (standard deviation of weekly costs)}$$

a. Explain the exact meaning of the numbers 20 and 4.
b. Explain the exact meaning of the value for $S_{c.12}$ and S_c.
c. Assuming normality, estimate the probability that the cost of the activity will lie between 46 and 50 if $X_1 = 4$ and $X_2 = 5$.
d. Assuming normality, estimate the probability that the cost will lie between 40 and 50 if $X_1 = 4$ and $X_2 = 5$.
e. Under what conditions would you be willing to use these estimates?

23–11 [19] The time spent adjusting and the setup cost required on a piece of machinery depends on the experience and training of the machine operator. For this reason a 10-week training program has been set up. After 10 weeks there will be a class of machinists in each week of the program. The manager of the department wishes to estimate the setup time (and cost) based on the number of weeks of training. Two machinists are selected at random from each of the 10 classes and the setup time on a typical job is measured. The results are shown in the table.

[19] Adapted from N. Dopuch and J. Birnberg, *Cost Accounting*, New York: Harcourt Brace Jovanovich, Inc., 1969.

| Weeks of Training W | $1/W$ X | Setup Times (minutes)* | |
		Machinist 1 T	Machinist 2 T
1	1.00	9.5	10.2
2	0.50	9.0	6.4
3	0.33	5.5	7.1
4	0.25	5.8	6.8
5	0.20	6.6	5.3
6	0.17	5.5	7.3
7	0.14	5.2	5.4
8	0.12	4.9	7.6
9	0.11	5.9	4.2
10	0.10	4.5	6.3

* A different pair of machinists are observed for each week.

Required:
a. The manager cannot decide whether model A or model B is more appropriate.

Model A: $T = b_0 + b_1 W + U_A$
Model B: $T = b_0 + b_1 X + U_B$

He is willing to assume that U_A or U_B is normally distributed with zero mean and constant variance. Using scatter diagrams (T vs. W and T vs. X) and whatever else you think is reasonable, choose between the models.
b. Suppose that the manager selects model B. Obtain estimates of b_0, b_1, and the standard error of estimate $S_{T.X}$. Use the following data and solve the 2 equation.

$$\sum X = 5.84 \qquad \sum T = 129 \qquad \sum X^2 = 3.0928$$

$$\sum TX = 44.439 \qquad \sum T^2 = 882.34 \qquad S^2_{T.X} = 0.9587$$

$$\sum T = nb_0 + b_1 \sum X \qquad \text{and} \qquad \sum TX = b_0 \sum X + b_1 \sum X^2$$

c. Suppose that the statistician asserts that model B is more reasonable than A because A implies that a machinist with no experience (or training) can set up the equipment in a finite expected time while a machinist with a great deal of time will be able to set up the equipment in a negative expected time. Model B, on the other hand, implies that a machinist with no experience cannot set up the equipment and that the machinist with a great deal of experience needs a finite time of at least b_0.
1. Do you agree? Why or why not?

    2. If you agree, would you be willing to use model B to estimate setup time for a machinist with 15 weeks of training?

    3. If you disagree, would you be willing to use model A for this estimate?

  d. Suppose that the study was made by observing the same two machinists in each of the 10 weeks. What problems are created? Do any problems result if two different men for each week are used at a point in time when the program is 10 weeks old?

  e. A machinist with five weeks of training set up the equipment in 3.8 minutes. Using the results of the study would you say:

    1. He was unusual? Why or why not?

    2. If so, what might explain this result?

  f. What interpretation can be given the correlation coefficient in this problem?

23–12 What does the least-squares criterion implicitly assume about the importance of the prediction error to the manager?

23–13 "If historically valid data on another variable is available, it should be included in the regression equation since predictions will be improved." Evaluate this statement.

23–14 Describe the effects on the results of a correlation-regression analysis caused by

  a. Serial correlation.

  b. Measurement errors in an independent variable.

  c. Intercorrelation between two independent variables.

23–15 A method regularly used to establish the fixed and variable fractions of a cost is the high–low method. The approach relies on the two extreme outputs to reflect the change in cost resulting from a change in activity. What limitations are present in this method?

23–16 A local firm is engaged in the process of applying a rust preventive coating to the underside of automobiles. It has data by months for five years on the amount of direct material and labor hours used as well as on the number of customers serviced and total costs.

A multiple linear regression equation is fitted to this data and yields:

$$T = 10 + 2M + 3L + C : S_{T.MLC} = 4$$

where

$$T = \text{total monthly cost in thousands}$$

$$M = \text{direct material costs in hundreds}$$

$$L = \text{labor cost in hours}$$

$$C = \text{customers serviced in hundreds}$$

A sentence or two at most is required.

Required:
a. Interpret the figure 10 in the equation in terms of what cost concept it represents. Is it a meaningful figure by itself? Why or why not?
b. Give the cost interpretation of the figure 3 in the equation. Why should one be careful of accepting this interpretation here?
c. Should the company expand the equation to consider a seasonal effect if one exists, say between summer or winter? Explain.
d. Would it be reasonable to use this equation to predict costs if the process remains stable? Explain.

23–17 Control procedures in many organizations require written explanations when actual results are worse than projections. These explanations usually require indications of corrective action to be taken as well as an explanation of present discrepancies. What effects do such procedures have on obtaining accurate forecasts? What can be done, if anything?

23–18 Costs that do not behave in a linear manner should not be treated as though they were linear. Comment.

23–19 Consider the cost of some activity. Suppose two independent variables are used, one in each of two simple single-variable regression equations to explain the cost variability. If the trend of points for the first independent variable is closer on the average to the regression line than for the second, is the degree of correlation greater for the first independent variable? If true would you use the first regression relation line and reject the second?

23–20 If the last observation is $1,250 and the smoothed average up to this point is $1,000, what is the prediction for the next period's cost level using a smoothing coefficient, α, of 0.2?

SUPPLEMENTARY READING

BENSTON, G. J., "Multiple Regression Analysis of Cost Behavior," *The Accounting Review*, October 1966, pp. 657–672.

BROWN, R., *Smoothing, Forecasting and Prediction of Discrete Time Series*, Englewood Cliffs, N.J.: Prentice-Hall, Inc., 1963.

DEAN, J., *Managerial Economics*, Englewood Cliffs, N.J.: Prentice-Hall, Inc., 1951, Chap. 5.

DURBIN, J., and G. WATSON, "Testing for Serial Correlation in Least Squares Regression," Pts. I and II, *Biometrica*, 1950, 1951.

JENSEN, R., "Multiple Regression Models for Cost Control—Assumptions and Limitations," *The Accounting Review*, April 1967, pp. 265–272.

JOHNSTON, J., *Econometric Methods*, New York: McGraw-Hill Book Company, 1972.

———, *Statistical Cost Control*, New York: McGraw-Hill Book Company, 1960.

McCLAIN, J., "Dynamics of Exponential Smoothing with Trend and Seasonal Terms," *Management Science* (forthcoming).

McCLENON, P., "Cost Finding Through Multiple Correlation Analysis," *The Accounting Review*, July 1963, pp. 540–547.

SPENCER, M. H., and L. SIEGELMAN, *Managerial Economics*, Homewood, Ill.: Richard D. Irwin, Inc., 1964, Chap. 5–9.

THEIL, H., and A. NAGAR, "Testing the Independence of Regression Disturbances," *Journal of the American Statistical Association*, 1961, pp. 793–806.

TROXEL, R. B., "Variable Budgets Through Correlation Analysis—A Simple Approach," *National Association of Accountant's Bulletin*, February 1965, pp. 48–55.

Tables

Table I. Normal Probability Distribution Function (Probabilities That Given Standard Normal Variables Will Not Be Exceeded—Left Tail)*
$N_z(-z)$. Also $N_z(z) = 1 - N_z(-z)$.

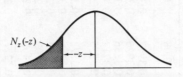

$-z$	0.00	0.01	0.02	0.03	0.04	0.05	0.06	0.07	0.08	0.09
.0	0.50000	0.49601	0.49202	0.48803	0.48405	0.48006	0.47608	0.47210	0.46812	0.46414
.1	0.46017	0.45620	0.45224	0.44828	0.44433	0.44038	0.43644	0.43251	0.42858	0.42465
.2	0.42074	0.41683	0.41294	0.40905	0.40517	0.40129	0.39743	0.39358	0.39874	0.38591
.3	0.38209	0.37828	0.37448	0.37070	0.36693	0.36317	0.35942	0.35569	0.35197	0.34827
.4	0.34458	0.34090	0.33724	0.33360	0.32997	0.32636	0.32276	0.31918	0.31561	0.31207
.5	0.30854	0.30503	0.30153	0.29806	0.29460	0.29116	0.28774	0.28434	0.28096	0.27760
.6	0.27425	0.27093	0.26763	0.26435	0.26109	0.25785	0.25463	0.25143	0.24825	0.24510
.7	0.24196	0.23885	0.23576	0.23270	0.22965	0.22663	0.22363	0.22065	0.21770	0.21476
.8	0.21186	0.20897	0.20611	0.20327	0.20045	0.19766	0.19489	0.19215	0.18943	0.18673
.9	0.18406	0.18141	0.17879	0.17619	0.17361	0.17106	0.16853	0.16602	0.16354	0.16109
1.0	0.15866	0.15625	0.15386	0.15151	0.14917	0.14686	0.14457	0.14231	0.14007	0.13786
1.1	0.13567	0.13350	0.13136	0.12924	0.12714	0.12507	0.12302	0.12100	0.11900	0.11702
1.2	0.11507	0.11314	0.11123	0.10935	0.10749	0.10565	0.10383	0.10204	0.10027	0.09853
1.3	0.09680	0.09510	0.09342	0.09176	0.09012	0.08851	0.08691	0.08534	0.08379	0.08226
1.4	0.08076	0.07927	0.07780	0.07636	0.07493	0.07353	0.07215	0.07078	0.06944	0.06811
1.5	0.06681	0.06552	0.06426	0.06301	0.06178	0.06057	0.05938	0.05821	0.05705	0.05592
1.6	0.05480	0.05370	0.05262	0.05155	0.05050	0.04947	0.04846	0.04746	0.04648	0.04551
1.7	0.04457	0.04363	0.04272	0.04182	0.04093	0.04006	0.03920	0.03836	0.03754	0.03673
1.8	0.03593	0.03515	0.03438	0.03362	0.03288	0.03216	0.03144	0.03074	0.03005	0.02938
1.9	0.02872	0.02807	0.02743	0.02680	0.02619	0.02559	0.02500	0.02442	0.02385	0.02330
2.0	0.02275	0.02216	0.02169	0.02118	0.02068	0.02018	0.01970	0.01923	0.01876	0.01831
2.1	0.01786	0.01743	0.01700	0.01659	0.01618	0.01578	0.01539	0.01500	0.01463	0.01426
2.2	0.01390	0.01355	0.01321	0.01287	0.01255	0.01222	0.01191	0.01160	0.01130	0.01101
2.3	0.01072	0.01044	0.01017	0.00990	0.00964	0.00939	0.00914	0.00889	0.00866	0.00842
2.4	0.00820	0.00798	0.00776	0.00755	0.00734	0.00714	0.00695	0.00676	0.00657	0.00639
2.5	0.00621	0.00604	0.00587	0.00570	0.00554	0.00539	0.00523	0.00508	0.00494	0.00480
2.6	0.00466	0.00453	0.00440	0.00427	0.00415	0.00402	0.00391	0.00379	0.00368	0.00357
2.7	0.00347	0.00336	0.00326	0.00317	0.00307	0.00298	0.00289	0.00280	0.00272	0.00264
2.8	0.00256	0.00248	0.00240	0.00233	0.00226	0.00219	0.00212	0.00205	0.00199	0.00193
2.9	0.00187	0.00181	0.00175	0.00169	0.00164	0.00159	0.00154	0.00149	0.00144	0.00139
3.0	0.00135	0.00131	0.00126	0.00122	0.00118	0.00114	0.00111	0.00107	0.00104	0.00100
3.1	0.00097	0.00094	0.00090	0.00087	0.00084	0.00082	0.00079	0.00076	0.00074	0.00071
3.2	0.00069	0.00066	0.00064	0.00062	0.00060	0.00058	0.00056	0.00054	0.00052	0.00050
3.3	0.00048	0.00047	0.00045	0.00043	0.00042	0.00040	0.00039	0.00038	0.00036	0.00035
3.4	0.00034	0.00032	0.00031	0.00030	0.00029	0.00028	0.00027	0.00026	0.00025	0.00024
3.5	0.00023	0.00022	0.00022	0.00021	0.00020	0.00019	0.00019	0.00018	0.00017	0.00017
3.6	0.00016	0.00015	0.00015	0.00014	0.00014	0.00013	0.00013	0.00012	0.00012	0.00011
3.7	0.00011	0.00010	0.00010	0.00010	0.00009	0.00009	0.00008	0.00008	0.00008	0.00008
3.8	0.00007	0.00007	0.00007	0.00006	0.00006	0.00006	0.00006	0.00005	0.00005	0.00005
3.9	0.00005	0.00005	0.00004	0.00004	0.00004	0.00004	0.00004	0.00004	0.00003	0.00003

* By symmetry this table also gives the area in the right tail for $+ z$.

Table II. Normal Probability Density Function: $n_z(z)$

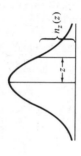

z	0	0.01	0.02	0.03	0.04	0.05	0.06	0.07	0.08	0.09
0.0	0.3989	0.3989	0.3989	0.3988	0.3986	0.3984	0.3982	0.3980	0.3977	0.3973
0.1	0.3970	0.3965	0.3961	0.3956	0.3951	0.3945	0.3939	0.3932	0.3925	0.3918
0.2	0.3910	0.3902	0.3894	0.3885	0.3876	0.3867	0.3857	0.3847	0.3836	0.3825
0.3	0.3814	0.3802	0.3790	0.3778	0.3765	0.3752	0.3739	0.3725	0.3712	0.3697
0.4	0.3683	0.3668	0.3653	0.3637	0.3621	0.3605	0.3589	0.3572	0.3555	0.3538
0.5	0.3521	0.3503	0.3485	0.3467	0.3448	0.3429	0.3410	0.3391	0.3372	0.3352
0.6	0.3332	0.3312	0.3292	0.3271	0.3251	0.3230	0.3209	0.3187	0.3166	0.3144
0.7	0.3123	0.3101	0.3079	0.3056	0.3034	0.3011	0.2989	0.2966	0.2943	0.2920
0.8	0.2897	0.2874	0.2850	0.2827	0.2803	0.2780	0.2756	0.2732	0.2709	0.2685
0.9	0.2661	0.2637	0.2613	0.2589	0.2565	0.2541	0.2516	0.2492	0.2468	0.2444
1.0	0.2420	0.2396	0.2371	0.2347	0.2323	0.2299	0.2275	0.2251	0.2227	0.2203
1.1	0.2179	0.2155	0.2131	0.2107	0.2083	0.2059	0.2036	0.2012	0.1989	0.1965
1.2	0.1942	0.1919	0.1895	0.1872	0.1849	0.1826	0.1804	0.1781	0.1758	0.1736
1.3	0.1714	0.1691	0.1669	0.1647	0.1626	0.1604	0.1582	0.1561	0.1539	0.1518
1.4	0.1497	0.1476	0.1456	0.1435	0.1415	0.1394	0.1374	0.1354	0.1334	0.1315
1.5	0.1295	0.1276	0.1257	0.1238	0.1219	0.1200	0.1182	0.1163	0.1145	0.1127
1.6	0.1109	0.1092	0.1074	0.1057	0.1040	0.1023	0.1006	0.09893	0.09728	0.09566
1.7	0.09405	0.09246	0.09089	0.08933	0.08780	0.08628	0.08478	0.08329	0.08183	0.08038
1.8	0.07895	0.07754	0.07614	0.07477	0.07341	0.07206	0.07074	0.06943	0.06814	0.06687
1.9	0.06562	0.06438	0.06316	0.06195	0.06077	0.05959	0.05844	0.05730	0.05618	0.05508

x	0	1	2	3	4	5	6	7	8	9
2.0	0.05399	0.05292	0.05186	0.05082	0.04980	0.04879	0.04780	0.04682	0.04586	0.04491
2.1	0.04398	0.04307	0.04217	0.04128	0.04041	0.03955	0.03871	0.03788	0.03706	0.03626
2.2	0.03547	0.03470	0.03394	0.03319	0.03246	0.03174	0.03103	0.03034	0.02965	0.02898
2.3	0.02833	0.02768	0.02705	0.02643	0.02582	0.02522	0.02463	0.02406	0.02349	0.02294
2.4	0.02239	0.02186	0.02134	0.02083	0.02033	0.01984	0.01936	0.01888	0.01842	0.01797
2.5	0.01753	0.01709	0.01667	0.01625	0.01585	0.01545	0.01506	0.01468	0.01431	0.01394
2.6	0.01358	0.01323	0.01289	0.01256	0.01223	0.01191	0.01160	0.01130	0.01100	0.01071
2.7	0.01042	0.01014	0.0^29871	0.0^29606	0.0^29347	0.0^29094	0.0^28846	0.0^28605	0.0^28370	0.0^28140
2.8	0.0^27915	0.0^27697	0.0^27483	0.0^27274	0.0^27071	0.0^26873	0.0^26679	0.0^26491	0.0^26307	0.0^26127
2.9	0.0^25953	0.0^25782	0.0^25616	0.0^25454	0.0^25296	0.0^25143	0.0^24993	0.0^24847	0.0^24705	0.0^24567
3.0	0.0^24432	0.0^24301	0.0^24173	0.0^24049	0.0^23928	0.0^23810	0.0^23695	0.0^23584	0.0^23475	0.0^23370
3.1	0.0^23267	0.0^23167	0.0^23070	0.0^22975	0.0^22884	0.0^22794	0.0^22707	0.0^22623	0.0^22541	0.0^22461
3.2	0.0^22384	0.0^22309	0.0^22236	0.0^22165	0.0^22096	0.0^22029	0.0^21964	0.0^21901	0.0^21840	0.0^21780
3.3	0.0^21723	0.0^21667	0.0^21612	0.0^21560	0.0^21508	0.0^21459	0.0^21411	0.0^21364	0.0^21319	0.0^21275
3.4	0.0^21232	0.0^21191	0.0^21151	0.0^21112	0.0^21075	0.0^21038	0.0^21003	0.0^39689	0.0^39358	0.0^39037
3.5	0.0^38727	0.0^38426	0.0^38135	0.0^37853	0.0^37581	0.0^37317	0.0^37061	0.0^36814	0.0^36575	0.0^36343
3.6	0.0^36119	0.0^35902	0.0^35693	0.0^35490	0.0^35294	0.0^35105	0.0^34921	0.0^34744	0.0^34573	0.0^34408
3.7	0.0^34248	0.0^34093	0.0^33944	0.0^33800	0.0^33661	0.0^33526	0.0^33396	0.0^33271	0.0^33149	0.0^33032
3.8	0.0^32919	0.0^32810	0.0^32705	0.0^32604	0.0^32506	0.0^32411	0.0^32320	0.0^32232	0.0^32147	0.0^32065
3.9	0.0^31987	0.0^31910	0.0^31837	0.0^31766	0.0^31698	0.0^31633	0.0^31569	0.0^31508	0.0^31449	0.0^31393
4.0	0.0^31338	0.0^31286	0.0^31235	0.0^31186	0.0^31140	0.0^31094	0.0^31051	0.0^31009	0.0^49687	0.0^49299
4.1	0.0^48926	0.0^48567	0.0^48222	0.0^47890	0.0^47570	0.0^47263	0.0^46967	0.0^46683	0.0^46410	0.0^46147
4.2	0.0^45894	0.0^45652	0.0^45418	0.0^45194	0.0^44979	0.0^44772	0.0^44573	0.0^44382	0.0^44199	0.0^44023
4.3	0.0^43854	0.0^43691	0.0^43535	0.0^43386	0.0^43242	0.0^43104	0.0^42972	0.0^42845	0.0^42723	0.0^42606
4.4	0.0^42494	0.0^42387	0.0^42284	0.0^42185	0.0^42090	0.0^41999	0.0^41912	0.0^41829	0.0^41749	0.0^41672
4.5	0.0^41598	0.0^41528	0.0^41461	0.0^41396	0.0^41334	0.0^41275	0.0^41218	0.0^41164	0.0^41112	0.0^41062
4.6	0.0^41014	0.0^59684	0.0^59248	0.0^58830	0.0^58430	0.0^58047	0.0^57681	0.0^57331	0.0^56996	0.0^56676
4.7	0.0^56370	0.0^56077	0.0^55797	0.0^55530	0.0^55274	0.0^55030	0.0^54796	0.0^54573	0.0^54360	0.0^54156
4.8	0.0^53961	0.0^53775	0.0^53598	0.0^53428	0.0^53267	0.0^53112	0.0^52965	0.0^52824	0.0^52690	0.0^52561
4.9	0.0^52439	0.0^52322	0.0^52211	0.0^52105	0.0^52003	0.0^51907	0.0^51814	0.0^51727	0.0^51643	0.0^51563

Example: $n_2(3.57) = n_2(-3.57) = 0.0^36814 = 0.0006814$.
Reproduced by permission from A. Hald, Statistical Tables and Formulas, New York: John Wiley, 1952.

Table III* Present Value of $1.00 $(1 + r)^{-n}$

n/r	1.0%	2.0%	3.0%	4.0%	5.0%	6%	7%	8%	9%	10%	11%	12%	13%	14%	15%
1	.9901	.9804	.9709	.9615	.9524	.9434	.9346	.9259	.9174	.9091	.9009	.8929	.8850	.8772	.8696
2	.9803	.9612	.9426	.9246	.9070	.8900	.8734	.8573	.8417	.8264	.8116	.7972	.7831	.7695	.7561
3	.9706	.9423	.9151	.8890	.8638	.8396	.8163	.7938	.7722	.7513	.7312	.7118	.6931	.6750	.6575
4	.9610	.9238	.8885	.8548	.8227	.7921	.7629	.7350	.7084	.6830	.6587	.6355	.6133	.5921	.5718
5	.9515	.9057	.8626	.8219	.7835	.7473	.7130	.6806	.6499	.6209	.5935	.5674	.5428	.5194	.4972
6	.9420	.8880	.8375	.7903	.7462	.7050	.6663	.6302	.5963	.5645	.5346	.5066	.4803	.4556	.4323
7	.9327	.8706	.8131	.7599	.7107	.6651	.6227	.5835	.5470	.5132	.4817	.4523	.4251	.3996	.3759
8	.9235	.8535	.7894	.7307	.6768	.6274	.5820	.5403	.5019	.4665	.4339	.4039	.3762	.3506	.3269
9	.9143	.8368	.7664	.7026	.6446	.5919	.5439	.5002	.4604	.4241	.3909	.3606	.3329	.3075	.2843
10	.9053	.8203	.7441	.6756	.6139	.5584	.5083	.4632	.4224	.3855	.3522	.3220	.2946	.2697	.2472
11	.8963	.8043	.7224	.6496	.5847	.5268	.4751	.4289	.3875	.3505	.3173	.2875	.2607	.2366	.2149
12	.8874	.7885	.7014	.6246	.5568	.4970	.4440	.3971	.3555	.3186	.2858	.2567	.2307	.2076	.1869
13	.8787	.7730	.6810	.6006	.5303	.4688	.4150	.3677	.3262	.2897	.2575	.2292	.2042	.1821	.1625
14	.8700	.7579	.6611	.5775	.5051	.4423	.3878	.3405	.2992	.2633	.2320	.2046	.1807	.1597	.1413
15	.8613	.7430	.6419	.5553	.4810	.4173	.3624	.3152	.2745	.2394	.2090	.1827	.1599	.1401	.1229
16	.8528	.7284	.6232	.5339	.4581	.3936	.3387	.2919	.2519	.2176	.1883	.1631	.1415	.1229	.1069
17	.8444	.7142	.6050	.5134	.4363	.3714	.3166	.2703	.2311	.1978	.1696	.1456	.1252	.1078	.0929
18	.8360	.7002	.5874	.4936	.4155	.3503	.2959	.2502	.2120	.1799	.1528	.1300	.1108	.0946	.0808
19	.8277	.6864	.5703	.4746	.3957	.3305	.2765	.2317	.1945	.1635	.1377	.1161	.0981	.0829	.0703
20	.8195	.6730	.5537	.4564	.3769	.3118	.2584	.2145	.1784	.1486	.1240	.1037	.0868	.0728	.0611
21	.8114	.6598	.5375	.4388	.3589	.2942	.2415	.1987	.1637	.1351	.1117	.0926	.0768	.0638	.0531
22	.8034	.6468	.5219	.4220	.3418	.2775	.2257	.1839	.1502	.1228	.1007	.0826	.0680	.0560	.0462
23	.7954	.6342	.5067	.4057	.3256	.2618	.2109	.1703	.1378	.1117	.0907	.0738	.0601	.0491	.0402
24	.7876	.6217	.4919	.3901	.3101	.2470	.1971	.1577	.1264	.1015	.0817	.0659	.0532	.0431	.0349
25	.7798	.6095	.4776	.3751	.2953	.2330	.1842	.1460	.1160	.0923	.0736	.0588	.0471	.0378	.0304
26	.7720	.5976	.4637	.3607	.2812	.2198	.1722	.1352	.1064	.0839	.0663	.0525	.0417	.0331	.0264
27	.7644	.5859	.4502	.3468	.2678	.2074	.1609	.1252	.0976	.0763	.0597	.0469	.0369	.0291	.0230
28	.7568	.5744	.4371	.3335	.2551	.1956	.1504	.1159	.0895	.0693	.0538	.0419	.0326	.0255	.0200
29	.7493	.5631	.4243	.3207	.2429	.1846	.1406	.1073	.0822	.0630	.0485	.0374	.0289	.0224	.0174
30	.7419	.5521	.4120	.3083	.2314	.1741	.1314	.0994	.0754	.0573	.0437	.0334	.0256	.0196	.0151
35	.7059	.5000	.3554	.2534	.1813	.1301	.0937	.0676	.0490	.0356	.0259	.0189	.0139	.0102	.0075
40	.6717	.4529	.3066	.2083	.1420	.0972	.0668	.0460	.0318	.0221	.0154	.0107	.0075	.0053	.0037
45	.6391	.410	.2644	.1713	.1112	.0727	.0476	.0313	.0207	.0137	.0091	.0061	.0041	.0027	.0019
50	.6080	.3715	.2281	.1407	.0872	.0543	.0339	.0213	.0134	.0085	.0054	.0035	.0022	.0014	.0009

* r is the rate of discount and n is the number of time periods.

n/r	16%	18%	20%	22%	24%	26%	28%	30%	32%	34%	36%	38%	40%	45%	50%
1	.8621	.8475	.8333	.8197	.8065	.7937	.7813	.7692	.7576	.7463	.7353	.7246	.7143	.6897	.6667
2	.7432	.7182	.6944	.6719	.6504	.6299	.6104	.5917	.5739	.5569	.5407	.5251	.5102	.4756	.4444
3	.6407	.6086	.5787	.5507	.5245	.4999	.4768	.4552	.4348	.4155	.3975	.3805	.3644	.3280	.2963
4	.5523	.5158	.4823	.4514	.4230	.3968	.3725	.3501	.3294	.3102	.2923	.2757	.2603	.2262	.1975
5	.4761	.4371	.4019	.3700	.3411	.3149	.2910	.2693	.2495	.2315	.2149	.1998	.1859	.1560	.1317
6	.4104	.3704	.3349	.3033	.2751	.2499	.2274	.2072	.1890	.1727	.1580	.1448	.1328	.1076	.0878
7	.3538	.3139	.2791	.2486	.2218	.1983	.1776	.1594	.1432	.1289	.1162	.1049	.0949	.0742	.0585
8	.3050	.2660	.2326	.2038	.1789	.1574	.1388	.1226	.1085	.0962	.0854	.0760	.0678	.0512	.0390
9	.2630	.2255	.1938	.1670	.1443	.1249	.1084	.0943	.0822	.0718	.0628	.0551	.0484	.0353	.0260
10	.2267	.1911	.1615	.1369	.1164	.0992	.0847	.0725	.0623	.0536	.0462	.0399	.0346	.0243	.0173
11	.1954	.1619	.1346	.1122	.0938	.0787	.0662	.0558	.0472	.0400	.0340	.0289	.0247	.0168	.0116
12	.1685	.1372	.1122	.0920	.0757	.0625	.0517	.0429	.0357	.0298	.0250	.0210	.0176	.0116	.0077
13	.1452	.1163	.0935	.0754	.0610	.0496	.0404	.0330	.0271	.0223	.0184	.0152	.0126	.0080	.0051
14	.1252	.0985	.0779	.0618	.0492	.0393	.0316	.0253	.0205	.0166	.0135	.0110	.0090	.0055	.0034
15	.1079	.0835	.0649	.0507	.0397	.0312	.0247	.0195	.0155	.0124	.0099	.0080	.0064	.0038	.0023
16	.0930	.0708	.0541	.0415	.0320	.0248	.0193	.0150	.0118	.0093	.0073	.0058	.0046	.0026	.0015
17	.0802	.0600	.0451	.0340	.0258	.0197	.0150	.0116	.0089	.0069	.0054	.0042	.0033	.0018	.0010
18	.0691	.0508	.0376	.0279	.0208	.0156	.0118	.0089	.0068	.0052	.0039	.0030	.0023	.0012	.0007
19	.0596	.0431	.0313	.0229	.0168	.0124	.0092	.0068	.0051	.0038	.0029	.0022	.0017	.0009	.0005
20	.0514	.0365	.0261	.0187	.0135	.0098	.0072	.0053	.0039	.0029	.0021	.0016	.0012	.0006	.0003
21	.0443	.0309	.0217	.0154	.0109	.0078	.0056	.0040	.0029	.0021	.0016	.0012	.0009	.0004	.0002
22	.0382	.0262	.0181	.0126	.0088	.0062	.0044	.0031	.0022	.0016	.0012	.0008	.0006	.0003	.0001
23	.0329	.0222	.0151	.0103	.0071	.0049	.0034	.0024	.0017	.0012	.0008	.0006	.0004	.0002	.0001
24	.0284	.0188	.0126	.0085	.0057	.0039	.0027	.0018	.0013	.0009	.0006	.0004	.0003	.0001	.0001
25	.0245	.0160	.0105	.0069	.0046	.0031	.0021	.0014	.0010	.0007	.0005	.0003	.0002	.0001	.0000
26	.0211	.0135	.0087	.0057	.0037	.0025	.0016	.0011	.0007	.0005	.0003	.0002	.0002	.0001	
27	.0182	.0115	.0073	.0047	.0030	.0019	.0013	.0008	.0006	.0004	.0002	.0001	.0001	.0000	
28	.0157	.0097	.0061	.0038	.0024	.0015	.0010	.0006	.0004	.0003	.0002	.0001	.0001		
29	.0135	.0082	.0051	.0031	.0020	.0012	.0008	.0005	.0003	.0002	.0001	.0001	.0001		
30	.0116	.0070	.0042	.0026	.0016	.0010	.0006	.0004	.0002	.0002	.0001	.0001	.0000		
35	.0055	.0030	.0017	.0009	.0005	.0003	.0002	.0001	.0001	.0000	.0000	.0000			
40	.0026	.0013	.0007	.0004	.0002	.0001	.0001	.0000	.0000						
45	.0013	.0006	.0003	.0001	.0001	.0000	.0000								
50	.0006	.0003	.0001	.0000	.0000										

Table IV   Present Value of \$1 Received per Period $\dfrac{1 - (1 + r)^{-n}}{r}$

n/r	1.0%	2.0%	3.0%	4.0%	5.0%	6%	7%	8%	9%	10%	11%	12%	13%	14%	15%
1	.9901	.9804	.9709	.9615	.9524	.9434	.9346	.9259	.9174	.9091	.9009	.8929	.8850	.8772	.8696
2	1.9704	1.9416	1.9135	1.8861	1.8594	1.8334	1.8080	1.7833	1.7591	1.7355	1.7125	1.6901	1.6681	1.6467	1.6257
3	2.9410	2.8839	2.8286	2.7751	2.7232	2.6730	2.6243	2.5771	2.5313	2.4869	2.4437	2.4018	2.3612	2.3216	2.2832
4	3.9020	3.8077	3.7171	3.6299	3.5459	3.4651	3.3872	3.3121	3.2397	3.1699	3.1024	3.0373	2.9745	2.9137	2.8550
5	4.8534	4.7135	4.5797	4.4518	4.3295	4.2124	4.1002	3.9927	3.8897	3.7908	3.6959	3.6048	3.5172	3.4331	3.3522
6	5.7955	5.6014	5.4172	5.2421	5.0757	4.9173	4.7665	4.6229	4.4859	4.3553	4.2305	4.1114	3.9975	3.8887	3.7845
7	6.7282	6.4720	6.2303	6.0020	5.7864	5.5824	5.3893	5.2064	5.0330	4.8684	4.7122	4.5638	4.4226	4.2883	4.1604
8	7.6517	7.3255	7.0197	6.7327	6.4632	6.2098	5.9713	5.7466	5.5348	5.3349	5.1461	4.9676	4.7988	4.6389	4.4873
9	8.5660	8.1622	7.7861	7.4353	7.1078	6.8017	6.5152	6.2469	5.9952	5.7590	5.5370	5.3282	5.1317	4.9464	4.7716
10	9.4713	8.9826	8.5302	8.1109	7.7217	7.3601	7.0236	6.7101	6.4177	6.1446	5.8892	5.6502	5.4262	5.2161	5.0188
11	10.3676	9.7868	9.2526	8.7605	8.3064	7.8869	7.4987	7.1390	6.8051	6.4951	6.2065	5.9377	5.6869	5.4527	5.2337
12	11.2551	10.5753	9.9540	9.3851	8.8632	8.3838	7.9427	7.5361	7.1607	6.8137	6.4924	6.1944	5.9176	5.6603	5.4206
13	12.1337	11.3484	10.6350	9.9856	9.3936	8.8527	8.3577	7.9038	7.4869	7.1034	6.7499	6.4235	6.1218	5.8424	5.5831
14	13.0037	12.1062	11.2961	10.5631	9.8986	9.2950	8.7455	8.2442	7.7862	7.3667	6.9819	6.6282	6.3025	6.0021	5.7245
15	13.8650	12.8493	11.9379	11.1184	10.3797	9.7122	9.1079	8.5595	8.0607	7.6061	7.1909	6.8109	6.4624	6.1422	5.8474
16	14.7179	13.5777	12.5611	11.6523	10.8378	10.1059	9.4466	8.8514	8.3126	7.8237	7.3792	6.9740	6.6039	6.2651	5.9542
17	15.5622	14.2919	13.1661	12.1657	11.2741	10.4773	9.7632	9.1216	8.5436	8.0216	7.5488	7.1196	6.7291	6.3729	6.0472
18	16.3983	14.9920	13.7535	12.6593	11.6896	10.8276	10.0591	9.3719	8.7556	8.2014	7.7016	7.2497	6.8399	6.4674	6.1280
19	17.2260	15.6785	14.3238	13.1339	12.0853	11.1581	10.3356	9.6036	8.9501	8.3649	7.8393	7.3658	6.9380	6.5504	6.1982
20	18.0455	16.3514	14.8775	13.5903	12.4622	11.4699	10.5940	9.8181	9.1285	8.5136	7.9633	7.4694	7.0248	6.6231	6.2593
21	18.8570	17.0112	15.4150	14.0292	12.8211	11.7641	10.8355	10.0168	9.2922	8.6487	8.0751	7.5620	7.1015	6.6870	6.3125
22	19.6604	17.6580	15.9369	14.4511	13.1630	12.0416	11.0612	10.2007	9.4424	8.7715	8.1757	7.6446	7.1695	6.7429	6.3587
23	20.4558	18.2922	16.4436	14.8568	13.4886	12.3034	11.2722	10.3711	9.5802	8.8832	8.2664	7.7184	7.2297	6.7921	6.3988
24	21.2434	18.9139	16.9355	15.2470	13.7986	12.5504	11.4693	10.5288	9.7066	8.9847	8.3481	7.7843	7.2829	6.8351	6.4338
25	22.0232	19.5235	17.4131	15.6221	14.0939	12.7834	11.6536	10.6748	9.8226	9.0770	8.4217	7.8431	7.3300	6.8729	6.4641
26	22.7952	20.1210	17.8768	15.9828	14.3752	13.0032	11.8258	10.8100	9.9290	9.1609	8.4881	7.8957	7.3717	6.9061	6.4906
27	23.5596	20.7069	18.3270	16.3296	14.6430	13.2105	11.9867	10.9352	10.0266	9.2372	8.5478	7.9426	7.4086	6.9352	6.5135
28	24.3164	21.2813	18.7641	16.6631	14.8981	13.4062	12.1371	11.0511	10.1161	9.3066	8.6016	7.9844	7.4412	6.9607	6.5335
29	25.0658	21.8444	19.1884	16.9837	15.1411	13.5907	12.2777	11.1584	10.1983	9.3696	8.6501	8.0218	7.4701	6.9830	6.5509
30	25.8077	22.3965	19.6004	17.2920	15.3724	13.7648	12.4090	11.2578	10.2737	9.4269	8.6938	8.0552	7.4957	7.0027	6.5660
31	26.5423	22.9377	20.0004	17.5885	15.5928	13.9291	12.5318	11.3498	10.3428	9.4790	8.7331	8.0850	7.5183	7.0199	6.5791
32	27.2696	23.4683	20.3888	17.8735	15.8027	14.0840	12.6466	11.4350	10.4062	9.5264	8.7686	8.1116	7.5383	7.0350	6.5905
33	27.9897	23.9886	20.7658	18.1476	16.0025	14.2302	12.7538	11.5139	10.4644	9.5694	8.8005	8.1354	7.5560	7.0482	6.6005
34	28.7027	24.4986	21.1318	18.4112	16.1929	14.3681	12.8540	11.5869	10.5178	9.6086	8.8293	8.1566	7.5717	7.0599	6.6091
35	29.4086	24.9986	21.4872	18.6646	16.3742	14.4982	12.9477	11.6546	10.5668	9.6442	8.8552	8.1755	7.5856	7.0700	6.6166
40	32.8347	27.3555	23.1148	19.7928	17.1591	15.0463	13.3317	11.9246	10.7574	9.7791	8.9511	8.2438	7.6344	7.1050	6.6418
45	36.0945	29.4902	24.5187	20.7200	17.7741	15.4558	13.6055	12.1084	10.8812	9.8628	9.0079	8.2825	7.6609	7.1232	6.6543
50	39.1961	31.4236	25.7298	21.4822	18.2559	15.7619	13.8007	12.2335	10.9617	9.9148	9.0417	8.3045	7.6752	7.1327	6.6605

n/r	16%	18%	20%	22%	24%	26%	28%	30%	32%	34%	36%	38%	40%	45%	50%
1	.8621	.8475	.8333	.8197	.8065	.7937	.7813	.7692	.7576	.7463	.7353	.7246	.7143	.6897	.6667
2	1.6052	1.5656	1.5278	1.4915	1.4568	1.4235	1.3916	1.3609	1.3315	1.3032	1.2760	1.2497	1.2245	1.1653	1.1111
3	2.2459	2.1743	2.1065	2.0422	1.9813	1.9234	1.8684	1.8161	1.7663	1.7188	1.6735	1.6302	1.5889	1.4933	1.4074
4	2.7982	2.6901	2.5887	2.4936	2.4043	2.3202	2.2410	2.1662	2.0957	2.0290	1.9658	1.9060	1.8492	1.7195	1.6049
5	3.2743	3.1272	2.9906	2.8636	2.7454	2.6351	2.5320	2.4356	2.3452	2.2604	2.1807	2.1058	2.0352	1.8755	1.7366
6	3.6847	3.4976	3.3255	3.1669	3.0205	2.8850	2.7594	2.6427	2.5342	2.4331	2.3388	2.2506	2.1680	1.9831	1.8244
7	4.0386	3.8115	3.6046	3.4155	3.2423	3.0833	2.9370	2.8021	2.6775	2.5620	2.4550	2.3555	2.2628	2.0573	1.8829
8	4.3436	4.0776	3.8372	3.6193	3.4212	3.2407	3.0758	2.9247	2.7860	2.6582	2.5404	2.4315	2.3306	2.1085	1.9220
9	4.6065	4.3030	4.0310	3.7863	3.5655	3.3657	3.1842	3.0190	2.8681	2.7300	2.6033	2.4866	2.3790	2.1438	1.9480
10	4.8332	4.4941	4.1925	3.9232	3.6819	3.4648	3.2689	3.0915	2.9304	2.7836	2.6495	2.5265	2.4136	2.1681	1.9053
11	5.0286	4.6560	4.3271	4.0354	3.7757	3.5435	3.3351	3.1473	2.9776	2.8236	2.6834	2.5555	2.4383	2.1849	1.9769
12	5.1971	4.7932	4.4392	4.1274	3.8514	3.6059	3.3868	3.1903	3.0133	2.8534	2.7084	2.5764	2.4559	2.1965	1.9845
13	5.3423	4.9095	4.5327	4.2028	3.9124	3.6555	3.4272	3.2233	3.0404	2.8757	2.7268	2.5916	2.4685	2.2045	1.9897
14	5.4675	5.0081	4.6106	4.2646	3.9616	3.6949	3.4587	3.2487	3.0609	2.8923	2.7403	2.6026	2.4775	2.2100	1.9931
15	5.5755	5.0916	4.6755	4.3152	4.0013	3.7261	3.4834	3.2682	3.0764	2.9047	2.7502	2.6106	2.4839	2.2138	1.9954
16	5.6685	5.1624	4.7296	4.3567	4.0333	3.7509	3.5026	3.2832	3.0882	2.9140	2.7575	2.6164	2.4885	2.2164	1.9970
17	5.7487	5.2223	4.7746	4.3908	4.0591	3.7705	3.5177	3.2948	3.0971	2.9209	2.7629	2.6206	2.4918	2.2182	1.9980
18	5.8178	5.2732	4.8122	4.4187	4.0799	3.7861	3.5294	3.3037	3.1039	2.9260	2.7668	2.6236	2.4941	2.2195	1.9986
19	5.8775	5.3162	4.8435	4.4415	4.0967	3.7985	3.5386	3.3105	3.1090	2.9299	2.7697	2.6258	2.4958	2.2203	1.9991
20	5.9288	5.3527	4.8696	4.4603	4.1103	3.8083	3.5458	3.3158	3.1129	2.9327	2.7718	2.6274	2.4970	2.2209	1.9994
21	5.9731	5.3837	4.8913	4.4756	4.1212	3.8161	3.5514	3.3198	3.1158	2.9349	2.7734	2.6285	2.4979	2.2213	1.9996
22	6.0113	5.4099	4.9094	4.4882	4.1300	3.8223	3.5558	3.3230	3.1180	2.9365	2.7746	2.6294	2.4985	2.2216	1.9997
23	6.0442	5.4321	4.9245	4.4985	4.1371	3.8273	3.5592	3.3253	3.1197	2.9377	2.7754	2.6300	2.4989	2.2218	1.9998
24	6.0726	5.4509	4.9371	4.5070	4.1428	3.8312	3.5619	3.3272	3.1210	2.9386	2.7760	2.6304	2.4992	2.2219	1.9999
25	6.0971	5.4669	4.9476	4.5139	4.1474	3.8342	3.5640	3.3286	3.1220	2.9392	2.7765	2.6307	2.4994	2.2220	1.9999
26	6.1182	5.4804	4.9563	4.5196	4.1511	3.8367	3.5656	3.3297	3.1227	2.9397	2.7768	2.6310	2.4996	2.2221	1.9999
27	6.1364	5.4919	4.9636	4.5243	4.1542	3.8387	3.5669	3.3305	3.1233	2.9401	2.7771	2.6311	2.4997	2.2221	2.0000
28	6.1520	5.5016	4.9697	4.5281	4.1566	3.8402	3.5679	3.3312	3.1237	2.9404	2.7773	2.6313	2.4998	2.2222	2.0000
29	6.1656	5.5098	4.9747	4.5312	4.1585	3.8414	3.5687	3.3316	3.1240	2.9406	2.7774	2.6313	2.4999	2.2222	2.0000
30	6.1772	5.5168	4.9789	4.5338	4.1601	3.8424	3.5693	3.3321	3.1242	2.9407	2.7775	2.6314	2.4999	2.2222	2.0000
31	6.1872	5.5227	4.9824	4.5359	4.1614	3.8432	3.5697	3.3324	3.1244	2.9408	2.7776	2.6315	2.4999	2.2222	2.0000
32	6.1959	5.5277	4.9854	4.5376	4.1624	3.8438	3.5701	3.3326	3.1246	2.9409	2.7776	2.6315	2.4999	2.2222	2.0000
33	6.2034	5.5320	4.9878	4.5390	4.1632	3.8443	3.5704	3.3328	3.1247	2.9410	2.7777	2.6315	2.5000	2.2222	2.0000
34	6.2098	5.5356	4.9898	4.5402	4.1639	3.8447	3.5706	3.3329	3.1248	2.9410	2.7777	2.6315	2.5000	2.2222	2.0000
35	6.2153	5.5386	4.9915	4.5411	4.1644	3.8450	3.5708	3.3330	3.1248	2.9411	2.7777	2.6315	2.5000	2.2222	2.0000
40	6.2335	5.5482	4.9966	4.5439	4.1659	3.8458	3.5712	3.3332	3.1250	2.9412	2.7778	2.6316	2.5000	2.2222	2.0000
45	6.2421	5.5523	4.9986	4.5449	4.1664	3.8460	3.5714	3.3333	3.1250	2.9412	2.7778	2.6316	2.5000	2.2222	2.0000
50	6.2463	5.5541	4.9995	4.5452	4.1666	3.8461	3.5714	3.3333	3.1250	2.9412	2.7778	2.6316	2.5000	2.2222	2.0000

Table V. Values of e^{-x}

x	0	.01	.02	.03	.04
0	1.000000	.990050	.980199	.970446	.960789
.10	.904837	.895834	.886920	.878095	.869358
.20	.818731	.810584	.802519	.794534	.786628
.30	.740818	.733447	.726149	.718924	.711770
.40	.670320	.663650	.657047	.650509	.644036
.50	.606531	.600496	.594521	.588605	.582748
.60	.548812	.543351	.537944	.532592	.527292
.70	.496585	.491644	.486752	.481909	.477114
.80	.449329	.444858	.440432	.436049	.431711
.90	.406570	.402524	.398519	.394554	.390628
1.00	.367879	.364219	.360595	.357007	.353455
1.10	.332871	.329559	.326280	.323033	.319819
1.20	.301194	.298197	.295230	.292293	.289384
1.30	.272532	.269820	.267135	.264477	.261846
1.40	.246597	.244143	.241714	.239309	.236928
1.50	.223130	.220910	.218712	.216536	.214381
1.60	.201897	.199888	.197899	.195930	.193980
1.70	.182684	.180866	.179066	.177284	.175520
1.80	.165299	.163654	.162026	.160414	.158817
1.90	.149569	.148080	.146607	.145148	.143704
2.00	.135335	.133989	.132655	.131336	.130029
2.10	.122456	.121238	.120032	.118837	.117655
2.20	.110803	.109701	.108609	.107528	.106459
2.30	.100259	.099261	.098274	.097296	.096328
2.40	.090718	.089815	.088922	.088037	.087161
2.50	.082085	.081268	.080460	.079659	.078866
2.60	.074274	.073535	.072803	.072078	.071361
2.70	.067206	.066537	.065875	.065219	.064570
2.80	.060810	.060205	.059606	.059013	.058426
2.90	.055023	.054476	.053934	.053397	.052866
3.00	.049787	.049292	.048801	.048316	.047835
3.10	.045049	.044601	.044157	.043718	.043283
3.20	.040762	.040357	.039955	.039557	.039164
3.30	.036883	.036516	.036153	.035793	.035437
3.40	.033373	.033041	.032712	.032387	.032065
3.50	.030197	.029897	.029599	.029305	.029013
3.60	.027324	.027052	.026783	.026516	.026252
3.70	.024724	.024478	.024234	.023993	.023754
3.80	.022371	.022148	.021928	.021710	.021494
3.90	.020242	.020041	.019841	.019644	.019448
4.00	.018316	.018133	.017953	.017774	.017597
4.10	.016573	.016408	.016245	.016083	.015923
4.20	.014996	.014846	.014699	.014552	.014408
4.30	.013569	.013434	.013300	.013168	.013037
4.40	.012277	.012155	.012034	.011914	.011796
4.50	.011109	.010998	.010889	.010781	.010673
4.60	.010052	.009952	.009853	.009755	.009658
4.70	.009095	.009005	.008915	.008826	.008739
4.80	.008230	.008148	.008067	.007987	.007907
4.90	.007447	.007372	.007299	.007227	.007155

x	.05	.06	.07	.08	.09
0	.951229	.941765	.932394	.923116	.913931
.10	.860708	.852144	.843665	.835270	.826959
.20	.778801	.771052	.763379	.755784	.748264
.30	.704688	.697676	.690734	.683861	.677057
.40	.637628	.631284	.625002	.618783	.612626
.50	.576950	.571209	.565525	.559898	.554327
.60	.522046	.516851	.511709	.506617	.501576
.70	.472367	.467666	.463013	.458406	.453845
.80	.427415	.423162	.418952	.414783	.410656
.90	.386741	.382893	.379083	.375311	.371577
1.00	.349938	.346456	.343009	.339596	.336216
1.10	.316637	.313486	.310367	.307279	.304221
1.20	.286505	.283654	.280832	.278037	.275271
1.30	.259240	.256661	.254107	.251579	.249075
1.40	.234570	.232236	.229925	.227638	.225373
1.50	.212248	.210136	.208045	.205975	.203926
1.60	.192050	.190139	.188247	.186374	.184520
1.70	.173774	.172045	.170333	.168638	.166960
1.80	.157237	.155673	.154124	.152590	.151072
1.90	.142274	.140858	.139457	.138069	.136695
2.00	.128735	.127454	.126186	.124930	.123687
2.10	.116484	.115325	.114178	.113042	.111917
2.20	.105399	.104350	.103312	.102284	.101266
2.30	.095369	.094420	.093481	.092551	.091630
2.40	.086294	.085435	.084585	.083743	.082910
2.50	.078082	.077305	.076536	.075774	.075020
2.60	.070651	.069948	.069252	.068563	.067881
2.70	.063928	.063292	.062662	.062039	.061421
2.80	.057844	.057269	.056699	.056135	.055576
2.90	.052340	.051819	.051303	.050793	.050287
3.00	.047359	.046888	.046421	.045959	.045502
3.10	.042852	.042426	.042004	.041586	.041172
3.20	.038774	.038388	.038006	.037628	.037254
3.30	.035084	.034735	.034390	.034047	.033709
3.40	.031746	.031430	.031117	.030807	.030501
3.50	.028725	.028439	.028156	.027876	.027598
3.60	.025991	.025733	.025476	.025223	.024972
3.70	.023518	.023284	.023052	.022823	.022596
3.80	.021280	.021068	.020858	.020651	.020445
3.90	.019255	.019063	.018873	.018686	.018500
4.00	.017422	.017249	.017077	.016907	.016739
4.10	.015764	.015608	.015452	.015299	.015146
4.20	.014264	.014122	.013982	.013843	.013705
4.30	.012907	.012778	.012651	.012525	.012401
4.40	.011679	.011562	.011447	.011333	.011221
4.50	.010567	.010462	.010358	.010255	.010153
4.60	.009562	.009466	.009372	.009279	.009187
4.70	.008652	.008566	.008480	.008396	.008312
4.80	.007828	.007750	.007673	.007597	.007521
4.90	.007083	.007013	.006943	.006874	.006806

Author Index

Subject Index